India and World Civilization

INDIA

AND

WORLD CIVILIZATION

by D. P. Singhal

Volume 1

MICHIGAN STATE UNIVERSITY PRESS

1969

★
★
★
★
★

For Devahuti

Contents

Since verbal science has no final end,
Since life is short, and obstacles impend,
Let central facts be picked and firmly fixed,
As swans extract the milk with water mixed.

The PANCATANTRA

India and World Civilization

Foreword

If the evolution of world-civilization could be reduced to a simple graphic illustration, the above symbol would perhaps be an accurate representation. The symbol's base is a solid figure, a pyramid, representing the community of those early cultures in which man sought to solve the problems of his environment. From the top of the pyramid spring divergent branches, bending first away from each other and then back again to form a new conjunction in modern times. These branches represent the diffusion of cultures and their later gradual reunification by new scientific and technological advances. Between these branches, even at their point of greatest dissociation, run slender criss-cross filaments linking them together, and representing the various ideas and skills which the civilizations of the world continued to borrow from one another throughout history. After the branches rejoin a cluster of divergent radians appear, representing the many unique developments which have resulted from the new cross-fertilisation of cultures, reaching out towards the future. The present study is an account of India's role in this cultural phenomenon.

Indian civilization is distinctive for its antiquity and continuity. Apart from its own vitality, the continuity of Indian civilization is largely due to its ability to adapt to alien ideas, harmonise contradictions and mould new thought patterns. Her constant contacts with the outside world also gave India the opportunity to contribute to other civilizations.

The earliest origins of the Indian civilization are traced to the period of the highly advanced urban Harappan cities. Since then, and even before, trade between India and the West had been an important contact which continued until the decline of the Roman Empire.

During the second millennium B.C. the Aryans came to India laying the foundation of Vedic Civilization. There are close resemblances between the language and mythology, religious traditions and social institutions of the Indians and Iranians on the one hand, and those of the Greeks, Romans, Celts, Germans and Slavs on the other. Contact between the Indians and the Greeks during the period of Persian ascendancy was close and constant, and became even closer after the military campaigns of Alexander. After Alexander's death his Empire dissolved, but for some two centuries Greek or semi-Greek principalities continued in the north-western regions of India.

By this time the Romans had become the dominant power in the West and Christianity had begun to spread. India and Rome maintained friendly relations—intermittent diplomatically but constant commercially. This brisk trade led to Indian settlements in Alexandria and to Roman and Egyptian settlements in India, and provided further opportunity for a cultural dialogue between Indian philosophy and science and the Hellenistic schools of Western Asia and Egypt. The accomplishments of this era of cultural syncretism have seldom been surpassed.

However, from the fall of the Roman Empire until the discovery of the direct sea-route between India and Europe in 1498 there was little direct contact between the two. This was a period of gradual social disintegration, political upheaval and intellectual stagnation in India. In Western Asia the Arabs were gaining power and it was they who transmitted Indian scientific thought and fables to Europe. At some stage during this period the Romanies began to move out of India towards the West carrying with them certain segments of Indian culture, especially music and dance.

The Europeans came to India in the last decade of the fifteenth century but their interests were mainly commercial. It was not until the last quarter of the eighteenth century that a real understanding of Indian learning began. The European intellectual world, Germany in particular, gradually became receptive to Indian religious thought and Sanskrit literature.

In recent times, in consequence of the frequent exchange of Indian and European scholars, and of improved technology, greater dissemination of Indian knowledge and thought took place. This includes Gandhi's ideas—especially his doctrine of non-violence and Satyagraha—which came to be known widely in the West.

Northwards, Indian cultural contacts extended through Central Asia to East Asia. Central Asia had been in the closest contact with India, and remained a thriving centre of Buddhist culture for nine or ten centuries. From Central Asia Buddhism travelled to East Asia and helped to build the philosophical and metaphysical framework of East Asian thought, and to mould the distinctive civilizations of China, Korea, Japan and Tibet.

Indians came into contact with the countries of Southeast Asia principally for commercial reasons. But wherever they settled they introduced their culture and civilization. In turn, they were influenced by the indigenous culture, laying thus the foundation of a new culture in the region. Indian cultural contact with Southeast Asia covers a period of more than thirteen hundred years, and segments of Indian culture even reached eastwards of this region, across the Pacific Ocean, the periphery of ancient America.

India was influenced by Iran, Greece and then Islam. The synthesis between Islamic and Indian cultures took several centuries to complete, and throughout India the pattern was an initial clash followed by fusion.

While India was in a state of political unrest and cultural stagnation, European powers and influences appeared in the country. The introduction of Western culture, English education and scientific techniques gave a jolt to India's traditional life. The long dormant intellectual impulse suddenly became active and a new Indian spirit was born, leading to the modernisation of India.

Whilst the transmission of ideas, goods and influences was mainly from India to the outside world in ancient times, in modern times it has been the other way round. If a broad generalisation is permitted, it would appear that there is hardly a major school of thought with which Indian thought has not entered into a dialogue at one time or the other, directly or indirectly.

The story has been told in bits and pieces in hundreds of works. This study seeks to put these pieces together in a co-ordinated whole to synthesize the original research of numerous authorities, including scientists, philosophers, historians, linguists, archaeologists and anthropologists. Most of the judgments are of specialists but have been woven together in a wider historical context. Often they appear in a new guise and give rise to new overall conclusions.

Transmission of ideas proceeded in a variety of ways. During the early phase it was mainly through the large-scale migrations of nomadic peoples. Later, as life became more settled, merchants, settlers and, to some extent, soldiers were the principal transmitters. With the expansion of intellectual life and organised religions, new classes of cultural couriers, such as scholars and missionaries, were added. Mediaeval military conquests, such as the Islamic, also transmitted ideas to and fro. In modern times, with scientific and technological advances, cultural exchange became prodigious.

The problems involved in the study of such a vast and varied subject are many and complex. When an encounter between two powerful civilizations takes place, its vibrations are felt at all levels and cultural synthesis proceeds in a variety of ways, some of which are not detected for a long time, and some never. During the long, evolutionary process of assimilation, the original character of an idea may be retained wholly, partly, or not at all. It is a kind of chain reaction giving rise to new ideas. All this, strictly speaking, is part of the impact of the new culture but, for an historian, it would be impossible to determine such influences with even rough accuracy.

Moreover, such impact generates both positive and negative response. Positive response would include direct borrowing, while endeavouring to bring out one's own inherent vitality of traditions and purity of beliefs. Negative response would include rigid defence of all traditional concepts and institutions which cements conservatism and leads to rigidity in society. Defence also often leads to irrational defiance, even to counter attacks. Reluctant to accept new ideas and yet unable to reject their validity, conservative resistance sometimes gives birth to further new ideas. Arnold Toynbee calls the three responses on the part of receiving civilizations "recoil," "adaptation" and "synthesis." No amount of human ingenuity can trace the full course of cultural interaction in all its ramifications through all these stages. At best the assessment of mutual influences must remain partial and even at times subject to divergent opinions.

Cultural interaction is not a wholesale transplantation of a culture. It assumes a certain degree of cultural development on the part of the participant groups. In assessing the degree of mutual influence, allowance must be made for the independent development of intellectual traditions in the various areas. For all ideas and concepts have a common beginning, however small and remote, in the primitive societies to which we trace our common ancestry; all human groups have, in their respective ways, wondered at the surrounding universe and have sought to see reality beyond it. The common nature of inquiry can lead to similar results, reached independently. Again, certain ideas of a fundamental nature, from which further theories have developed—some form of monism or dualism, for instance—have been common to all communities. Man's methods of reasoning are somewhat similar all over the world, as are human reactions. It is therefore to be expected that attitudes towards certain concepts would be common to all human groups. If, however, the cultural resemblances are too close in detail, too frequent in a given situation, or are accompanied by evidence of contact, mutual influence ought to be accepted.

The uncertainties of Indian chronology present a most difficult problem. Five thousand years or more of Indian history is generally classified into three periods: ancient, mediaeval and modern. There are differing views on both the nomenclature and dates covering each period. In fact, until some important dates were fixed with the help of Greek sources, there was an almost complete absence of dating in Indian history. Even now the dates of political events and the vast mass of literature which form the basis of cultural study are imperfectly known. Historical facts seem to dissolve in the hands of ancient Indians changing into epic poetry, sagas, mythology and legends. Time was unreal and of secondary importance. Consequently genetic analysis of philosophical ideas had little relevance to the value of ideas.

Considerable work, however, is being done in fixing Indian dates and a break-through may occur soon. Unless this happens the antiquity of a concept and consequently its nationality cannot be finalised. For instance, if an idea is known to have existed both in India and Greece at about the same time, by our present system of dating, it is not possible to know precisely whether it was of Indian or Greek origin.

There is, at present, a broad working outline of Indian history which has been compiled with the help of foreign sources. Naturally not all scholars accept its accuracy; Indian scholars generally suggest earlier dates for Indian works and events than do others. Until this dispute is resolved, the conservative dates, which are acceptable to those who assign later dates to Indian historical events, have been used in this study.

The vague usage by authorities of the terms Oriental, Western and Eastern in relation to cultural influences and concepts, without distinctly identifying the exact known or accepted area of their origin, presents no less a problem for the student of comparative culture. For instance, Iranian, Egyptian, Jewish, Chinese and Indian are often grouped under the term Oriental or Eastern and all Greek and Roman heritage as Western.

This work, I am aware, should have included many more illustrations than it does, but the consideration of cost and space imposed severe restrictions. Sometimes the difficulties of reproduction and copyright also narrowed the choice.

As no single system of transliteration of the non-English names is recognised as standard, and as my own linguistic equipment is too limited to opt for one or the other with conviction and finality, I have tried to use such versions of these names as are commonly used in modern standard writings, aiming at internal consistency and uniformity.

Because of the variety and technicality of the subject matter, the problem of detailed editing, despite the extreme care taken both by the author and the publishers, has presented numerous questions, some of which may not have been adequately resolved.

My debt of gratitude to numerous authorities, scholars, friends and colleagues is endless. Even if I tried I could not acknowledge by name my indebtedness to the authorities whose writings gave me inspiration, direction and support. Perhaps all historians face in some measure such a predicament. Without the contributions of many scholars upon whom I have drawn freely this work could never have been written. My friends and colleagues have been most generous in their help through discussion, encouragement and criticism. Again, it would be impossible to identify my debt to each of them individually. How does one trace the origins of ideas acquired consciously or unconsciously through reading, and discussions with colleagues or students?

I am particularly grateful to Professors K. A. Nilakanta Sastri and A. L. Basham who read through the whole manuscript with extreme care and patience and made numerous suggestions and criticisms without which the value of the work would have been considerably less. Whilst I have profitted a great deal by their most valuable comments, I alone am responsible for the opinions expressed.

I must also acknowledge my gratitude to Mrs. Mariel Tisdell (neé Eckermann) who helped me with research in a variety of ways and did many long and tedious translations from European languages, especially German. My thanks are due to Professor Namik Oğuztöreli, Dr. Paul Crook, Mr. John Harris, Mr. Clayton Bredt, Dr. Chris Penders, Dr. Sutjipto Wirjosuparto, Mr. Larry Sitsky, and Mr. Wei Ying Wan for reading various parts of the work and commenting upon them, to Mr. Barry Scott for helping me in compiling the bibliography, and to Mrs. Magda Sitsky, Miss Maria Chodzinski and Miss Mary Jane Emerson for typing the various drafts.

I would like to record my thanks to the University of Queensland for providing facilities for research and assistance with grants for travel and collection of material, and to the Social Science Research Council of Australia for assisting me with a grant to visit India on a study trip. Of all the University authorities, I am most appreciative of the help and encouragement generously given to me by Professor Gordon Greenwood. Finally, I would like to thank Miss Cheryl Malmborg for her industry and help in preparing the indexes.

Despite the wealth of scholarship available to me, this work suffers from various limitations because of my own incapacity to profit more by it.

D.P.S.

Chapter I

HARAPPA TO ATHENS

MAN IS much older than civilization. The written records forming the basis of history reveal only a fraction of our past, a fraction which is at best fragmentary and at worst chaotic. However, with the help of the relatively recent discipline of archaeology, the vista of history has been extended from about five thousand to almost a quarter of a million years, thus enabling the various pieces of the jig-saw puzzle of culture to fall into a somewhat more coherent pattern, even though many large sections of the puzzle remain missing. For thousands of years man lived as any other animal did. But, although one of the weakest of all animals, man alone was capable of adapting himself to his environment and of moulding it to suit his requirements. In many areas, including Europe, he merely adjusted his habits to natural conditions, in others he attacked nature. Consequently, by the seventh millennium B.C., man had begun to settle along areas watered by rainfall, rivers that did not freeze over, and inland lakes. He began cultivating the land and raising domestic animals whilst living in relative harmony with his kind.

The first signs of civilization emerged in the territories stretching westward from the Indus Valley to the Atlantic across western Asia, along the North African shore, and eastward to the Yangtze Valley.[1] In these areas well-organized village life soon developed. Improved agricultural techniques and growing stability led to a closer social organization in which each individual surrendered part of his freedom for the collective gain. As time passed large cities emerged with all the complexities of urban civilization. The earliest known civilizations were founded almost contemporaneously in India, Egypt, and Mesopotamia.

In spite of the paucity of evidence, there is enough to suggest that mankind has always pooled its knowledge and that even at the dawn of

1

civilization there was regular contact between societies and frequent exchange of ideas and artistic techniques. Indeed, the speed of cultural evolution has been so extraordinarily rapid, when compared with the organic evolution of man, that it "seems to be due to the distinctively human capacity of learning from one's neighbour; inventions and devices, created by one society as adjustments to its special environment, can be adopted by another to its rather different requirements."[2] It is, therefore, not surprising that Indian contact with other civilizations should be as old as history itself.

Whilst other ancient civilizations have long ceased to exist, Indian civilization has continued to grow despite revolutionary changes. The ancient cultures of Egypt, Mesopotamia, and Persia have not survived and their present cultures no longer form an unbroken chain linking past with present. Modern Egyptians, for example, are almost completely dissociated from the civilization which flourished on the Nile thousands of years ago. But in India today, Hindus seek inspiration from concepts similar to those originally advanced by their ancestors. Social institutions and relationships, language and literature, are far more continuous than even those of Greece and Italy. The antiquity of Indian civilization may in itself be a doubtful virtue, but the fact that it has survived would imply an extraordinary vitality and self-perpetuating quality surpassed nowhere and only approximately matched by Chinese civilization. Apart from this innate vitality, the continuity of Indian civilization has been largely due to its ability to adapt to alien virtues, to harmonize contradictions, and assimilate new ideas. No country was more frequently invaded and occupied by foreigners, yet, in ancient times, no civilization spread abroad more extensively than that of India.[3] And thus, occupying a central position in the cultures of the world, India has contributed enormously to human civilization.

Indian contacts with the Western world date back to prehistoric times. Trade relations, preceded by the migration of peoples, inevitably developed into cultural relations. This view is not only amply supported by both philological and archaeological evidence, but by a vast body of corroborative literary evidence as well: vedic literature and the Jatakas, Jewish chronicles, and the accounts of Greek historians all suggest contact between India and the West.

It is only during the past few decades that the prehistory of Asia has come to be studied seriously. The skeletal evidence of the archaeological excavations made thus far reveals that the earliest traces of farming communities in the Indian sub-continent are to be found in the area contiguous to Sind, on the western bank of the lower reaches of the Indus

River. The region is arid at present but there are indications—for example, stone-built dams erected to control floods—of greater rainfalls in the third millennium B.C. and of a jungle fauna including tigers, elephants, and rhinoceroses. Several distinct varieties of wheel-turned pottery—differing in colour and the character of painted designs—have been found in the region. Too little is known about these antecedent stages of human settlement in the Indus Valley from which emerged the earliest known civilization of India: the Harappan civilization which flourished around 2500 B.C. In this period great cities existed with well-planned houses (equipped with baths, chutes, sanitary arrangements), citadels, communal granaries, highly developed drainage systems and dockyards. There was an organized city government and a settled society. This advanced urban civilization represented an exceptional adjustment of human life to a specific environment.

Whilst the exact area and period of the Harappan or Indus civilization have yet to be firmly fixed, it is now accepted that it extended east and southward far beyond the Indus Valley and that it was certainly contemporary with the other earliest-known civilizations: Egypt and Mesopotamia where two non-Aryan races, the Sumerians and Semites, created amazing civilizations. Geographically, the Harappan civilization was probably twice the size of the old kingdom of Egypt and four times the size of Sumer and Akkad. The main settlements of Harappa, Mohenjo-daro, and Lothal are considerable distances from each other. Mohenjo-daro on the lower Indus River and Harappa on the Ravi River were separated by over three hundred and fifty miles. The smaller township trading centres and farming communities occupied a much more extensive area. Archaeological excavations of the last decade have resulted in a considerable extension of what were formerly believed to be the boundaries of the Harappan civilization to now include areas of Uttar Pradesh, north Rajasthan, and Gujarat. The Harappan civilization, therefore, occupied an area of approximately 840,000 square miles, stretching almost from Delhi to Bombay.[4]

Although these ancient civilizations were largely independent entities, the fact that direct contacts between them existed is supported by concrete evidence, mainly in the form of small objects of value. A number of seals of Indus Valley design and workmanship have been found at various sites in the Euphrates and Tigris areas. Close scrutiny of the seals found in Mesopotamia and a comparison with seals from various regions of western Asia positively indicate that they were either manufactured in the Indus cities or were close copies of Indus types.[5] The form of writing used in the Indus Valley, still to be deciphered,

3

resembles in many respects those used in Sumer and Egypt. This script is pictographic in character and, insofar as it has survived, is almost exclusively engraved on seals in the form of texts, some of which are accompanied by pictures of animals. The paucity of the known inscriptions, the absence of long texts in Indus characters, and the variety and multiplicity of the signs employed have made decipherment impossible so far, although several scholars claim to have discovered a clue to the Indus script. Hopefully more knowledge of the cultural and commercial intercourse between these civilizations will be available once these seals are adequately deciphered. However, it is not unlikely that the seals may be found to contain nothing of great importance.

Characters similar to those on the Indus seals have also been found on tablets excavated from Easter Island. This discovery has presented a difficult problem for the prehistorian. It is not known if the two belong to a common source, if one provided the model for the other, or if the similarity is purely accidental due to inaccuracies of drawing. If the Indus models travelled about thirteen thousand miles eastward, it seems strange that the characters should have remained unaltered, because figures generally do not remain identical during prolonged transmission. And, if the seals were actually made in the Indus Valley and taken to Easter Island, what is the explanation for the differences in arrangement between the two groups of seals? The Easter Island tablets have a boustrophedon arrangement—the alternate rows are upside down—which has not been discovered in the Indus seals so far. Furthermore, the Easter Island tablets are made of local or drift wood. Still, the parallel characters are close enough to suggest contact.

Evidence of Indian contact with the ancient civilizations to her west, however, is certain. Knobbed pottery vases came to Sumer from India and so did cotton. The historical origins of cotton are somewhat uncertain, but the antiquity of the Indian cotton trade is undoubted. In the Akkadian tongue, Indian cotton was expressed by ideographs meaning "vegetable cloth." Assurbanipal (668–626 B.C.) cultivated Indian plants including the "wool-bearing trees" of India. When the Greeks first saw Indians, the latter were dressed in "wool grown on trees." Herodotus mentions Indian cotton, and the first account of cotton grown outside the western boundaries of India was given in 350 B.C. by Theophrastus, who described the "wool-bearing trees" of Tylee (Bahrein), stating that cotton was cultivated in India as well.[6] When perennial cotton plants—originally native only to India—were first grown in western Asia is a matter of conjecture, but "since there is known to have been contact between Mohenjo-daro and contemporary civilizations in Babylonia, it seems likely that the cottons of the Indus Valley were distributed along the Persian coast and as far up the Persian Gulf as perennials could be successfully grown."[7]

Commercial intercourse between the Indus and the Tigris-Euphrates civilizations is also demonstrated by the Harappan manufactures found in Mesopotamia. Semi-precious stones, such as amazonite, came from Gujarat or even the Nilgiri Hills; food stuffs and metal from Rajasthan or Baluchistan; and shank shell from southern India. All these reached Mesopotamia during the last half of the third millennium B.C. Indeed, a colony of Indus merchants may well have settled in a Sumerian city. On the other hand, a white marble seal, an adze, pottery rings, and horned figures are some of the items imported from Sumer into the Indus region. Furthermore, some of the numerous naturalistic figurines of baked clay found in Indus cities depict persons of distinctly Mongolian features. Archaeological researchers have also brought to light Indus remains, belonging to 2000 B.C.–1000 B.C., in Southern Turkmenia in Soviet Central Asia.

In southern Afghanistan, French excavators have discovered remains of huge granaries, akin to those of Harappa, and a great mud-brick building belonging to the third millennium B.C., with a facade of half-columns suggestive of Mesopotamia. The full implications of these remains, insofar as they throw light on international contact, have yet to be properly assessed, but their discovery has led Sir Leonard Woolley to suggest, as an explanation of the similarities between the Indus and Sumerian civilizations, that the people of Sumer were newcomers from the East who had brought their arts and crafts with them, and that both peoples probably had a common origin.[8]

Indirect contact between ancient India and Egypt through Mesopotamia is generally admitted, but evidence of a direct relationship between the two is at best fragmentary and inconclusive. There are elements in the folk art, language, and rural culture of Bengal which have an affinity with their Egyptian counterparts and which have not been explained satisfactorily in terms of Aryan, Mongolian, or Dravidian influences. There are also similarities between place names in Bengal and Egypt,[9] and recently an Egyptian scholar, El Mansouri, has pointed out that in both Egypt and India the worship of cow, sun, snake, and river was common. These and other resemblances—such as a likeness between certain pottery ornaments of Mohenjo-daro and those of Egypt, between the Indus script and the Elamite script, between the caste system of India and a similar classification in ancient Egypt—are attributed to "ties of common Dravidian and Aryan blood." Furthermore, the Indian gods, Siva, Visnu, and Brahman, are likened to the solar gods of Egypt; as are Iswara to Osiris; Nandi to Apis; and Hanuman to Cynocephalus. Both in India and Egypt the lotus flower, too, was held sacred.

Of all the Egyptian objects and motifs indicating some contact between India and Egypt during the Indus Valley period, "the cord pattern occurring in a copper tablet in the Indus Valley and on three Egyptian seals is the most striking link between the two countries."[10] Indian products were certainly known since indigo, muslin and tamarind, for example, have been found in Egyptian tombs, and ebony, ivory, sandalwood, and cotton goods reached Egypt from India in the second millennium B.C.

Whether direct or through Mesopotamia, there is "concrete evidence of a network of trade linking up the whole area from the Tigris to the Indus and the Oxus and its extension west of the Euphrates as far as the Nile."[11] International trade on such a scale presupposes efficient organization and attractive profits. Trade was mainly overland, but the discovery of Indus-like seals in Bahrein in the Persian Gulf, the dockyard at Lothal in Gujarat, and a steatite seal at Lothal with two jumping gazelles flanking a two-headed dragon suggest that maritime trade existed as well. Flourishing commercial traffic naturally involved the movement of people. Skilled artisans travelled freely and settled wherever they found a demand for their skills. Agencies and depots must have been established for the collection and storage of freight and cargo. Trade always encourages the pooling of human experience and in the ancient world it was perhaps a more potent agency in the diffusion of culture than it is today. City life, cultivation of cereals, domestication of cattle and sheep, metallurgy, a textile industry, the manufacture of bricks and pots, and the drilling of hard stones for beads were some of the common features of these early civilizations. It cannot be stated with any certainty where these inventions originated, but their dissemination must have been due to mutual borrowing.

The Oriental Institute near Baghdad excavated at Tell Agrab a green steatite vase of typical Sumerian workmanship, portraying a humped bull in front of a manger. As the vase depicts a characteristic scene of an Indus cult, it is clear that by the middle of the third millennium B.C., an Indian cult was already being practiced in Mesopotamia. As in modern times, ancient foreigners demanded the comforts of their religion in a strange country, and this led to the transmission of cults and general religious dissemination. Since Indus manufactures were imported to Sumer and Akkad, and Indus cults were certainly known and possibly celebrated there, the Indus culture must have made contributions, however slight or obscure, to the traditions inherited by Europe from Sumer and Babylonia. Archaeology thus has shown that two thousand years before the earliest references in cuneiform texts to contact with India, she was sending her manufactures to the land where the roots of Western civilization lie. "In other words," as Gordon Childe puts it, "in the third millennium B.C. India was already in a position to contribute to the building up of the cultural tradition that constitutes our spiritual heritage as she notoriously has done since the time of Alexander."[12]

In both western Asia and the Indus Valley men wore a long beard, shaved their upper lip, and kept their hair very long. The swastika and cross were their religious and magical symbols. The demonolatry of Babylonia with its malignant serpents came to be known in India, and their Babylonian names are preserved in the *Atharva Veda*. The serpent Taimata against whom the *Atharva Veda* prescribes a charm, and who bears a non-Sanskrit name, appears to resemble closely the Assyrian dragon Tiamat. Both in India and Babylonia, physical and mental abnormalities were attributed to demons, and in both regions several powerful demons were believed to cause certain cosmic disturbances. Also fire was the messenger between gods and men in Babylonia as in India. Amongst the other striking similarities between the two cultures are the organization of society into cities; the use of picture signs for writing; and the continued but sparing use of stone, along with copper and bronze, for the manufacture of weapons, tools, and vessels.

Despite these similarities, the Egyptian, Mesopotamian, and Indus civilizations undeniably developed in their own independent ways and assumed distinct personalities. Their tools, weapons, and vessels have different forms, and the symbols of their scripts differ. The Indus civilization itself was thoroughly individual, deeply rooted in Indian soil, and was already forming the basis of modern Indian culture.[13]

The civilizations of Egypt and Mesopotamia were attacked, destroyed and were replaced from about 2000 B.C. by successive military empires which dominated western Asia. At about the same time the Indus civilization was also overrun by the Aryans. During the second millennium B.C. the continuous area of civilization extended from the alluvial valleys to cover most of western Asia and India, with an outpost as far distant as China. The political history of Mesopotamia, however, for the two thousand years before it came under Persian domination, is full of military conflict. Information concerning Indian contacts with the West during this, the later Indus, period is not precise, although documents from Babylonia and Asia Minor testify to some interchange. Recently, in the Babylonian texts of the kings of Akkad and in lexical texts, Leemans has identified two names, Magan or Makkan and Meluhha, with Makran in Baluchistan and with western India respectively.[14] The names of kings recorded in the Kassite documents (*ca.* 1760–1600 B.C.) recall Indo-Aryan deities. It was the Kassites who introduced into Babylonia the use of the horse for drawing chariots, and the late Babylonian name for a horse, *Susu,* seems to be derived from the Sanskrit *asva.*[15] The Kassites, who ruled for several centuries after 1800 B.C., and who were probably not entirely of Indo-European stock, appear to have borrowed some of their gods from the Aryans, for example *Surias* (Sanskrit *Surya,* sun god), *Maruttas* (Sanskrit *Marut,* wind god), *Bugas* (Sanskrit *Bhaga*), *Simalia* (Sanskrit *Himalaya*), *Dakas* (Sanskrit *Daksa,* a star god).

The kings of Mittani on the Upper Euphrates, of the fifteenth or sixteenth century B.C., frequently bore Aryan names, such as *Artatama,* *Sutarna,* and *Dusratta,* and they worshipped the vedic gods, *Mitra,* *Varuna* (u-ru-v-na), *Indra* (in-da-ra), and the twins *Nasatya* (na-sa-at-ti-i-ia), an alternative name for the *Asvins,* all of whose names are found in their cuneiform inscriptions. In 1907 Hugo Winckler startled the academic world by identifying four of the numerous gods mentioned in a treaty signed between the kings of Mittani and the Hittites in 1360 B.C. with those already known in vedic literature.

A fragmentary handbook on chariot racing found in the documents at Boghaz Koi, the Hittite capital in Asia Minor, further endorses the Indo-Europeans' common cultural heritage. Many of the technical terms used for so many circuits of the course are very close to Sanskrit. For example, *aikavartanna, teravartanna, panzavartanna, shattavartanna,* are used for one, three, five, and seven laps of the race. In Sanskrit *vartanam* means a turning. In discussing the Hittite deities, the Bull god and the Mother goddess, Garstang is most arrested by "the obvious parallelism with the symbolism and the ritual of the Indian god Siva, a result for which, however surprising, we are prepared by the inclusion of *Mitra, Varuna,* and *Indra* among the deities of Mittani."[16] The *Marianna* class of warriors among the Mittani is reminiscent of the vedic *Marya,* "the heroes." Numerals and other words of Aryan origin have also been identified in Mittanic texts. During the same period the Tell-el-Amarna tablets mention Aryan princes, such as Biridaswa of Yenoam and Suwardata of Keilah, in Syria and Palestine. The language of the Mittanis was not Indo-European, and although the Anatolian Hittites were mainly of Indo-European stock, having emigrated from the Araxes Valley sometime in the third millennium B.C., their subjects were non-Aryan Asians and it was the native language, the Babylonian script, and the local gods which the Hittites adopted. The numerals and divine and personal names referred to are actually the oldest specimens of any Aryan speech known to scholars and, significantly, they are in this form very nearly pure Indian, being much more akin to Sanskrit than to any Iranian dialects.[17]

The Phoenicians of the Levant, important in the ancient world as traders, explorers, and craftsmen, were also in contact with India.[18] The Phoenicians were immigrants to Syria from the Persian Gulf. They set up harbour towns and guarded them jealously throughout their history. The Phoenicians were possibly the most adventurous and skilled tradesmen of the ancient world, and their trade with India was profitable and lucrative. Although their territory was neither large nor fertile, their commerce made them rich and powerful. According to Jewish chronicles, as early as 975 B.C., Hiram, the King of Tyre, acting jointly with Solomon of Judah, demanded triennially a fleet to bring ivory, apes, peacocks, almug or algum trees, and precious stones from the port of Ophir. This may have been a port on the western Indian coast—there continues to be much speculation about its location—as the objects imported were unmistakably of Indian origin. Ophir was so famous for its gold that the expression "gold of Ophir" became proverbial in Hebrew.

The sources for ivory in ancient times were Syria, the Sudan, Somaliland, and India. The Phoenicians, who first seem to have imported it from Syria, found this source exhausted by the eighth century B.C. It was then that they turned their attention to India as a fresh source of supply and organized expeditions for that purpose.[19] Logs of Indian teak have been found in the Temple of the Moon at Mugheir built during the sixth century B.C. under the Chaldean Empire, and in the palace of Nebuchadnezzar (604–562 B.C.), who raised Babylonia to a new epoch of greatness. In addition to ivory, the Indians also exported at this time various kinds of birds and beasts (including the valuable Sind horses), cotton goods, gold, silver, and jewels. The Arab traders originally brought rice to Europe from the south Indian ports. Other Indian articles reaching the West from these ports at different times included cinnamon, ginger, pepper, and beryl.

Some of the articles of commerce mentioned in the Jewish annals bear names of Indian origin. For instance, *Kophu* (ape) in Hebrew, is *kapi* in Sanskrit; *eleph* (ivory) in Hebrew, is *ibha* in Sanskrit; and the Hebrew *almug* (sandalwood) is probably from the Sanskrit *valgu*.

In tracing similarities in literature, scholars, moreover, have noted the curious resemblance between the *Maha-Ummagga Jataka*[20] and the story of the judgement of Solomon.

During the reign of Solomon (973–933 B.C.) the position of Palestine, situated in easily accessible proximity to India, western Asia, and Africa, became much clearer than before. Solomon's father, David, during his campaigns, had occupied Ezion-Gaber on the Gulf of Akabah. Solomon retained this position because Ezion-Gaber, or the neighbouring port of Elath, was the point of embarkation for India and the Far East, and "he who possessed it and Palestine commanded the bridge which joined three continents."[21] After the death of Solomon, the Persian Gulf became the chief trade route between India and Asia Minor.

The recent finding in 1963 of a round stone-seal from Pandu Rajar Dhibi in Bengal and the identification of its script and pictographs with the Phaistos pictographs and "Linear A" scripts point to the possibility that the Indians of Bengal were in trading contact with the inhabitants of Crete during the second half of the second millennium B.C.[22]

There is considerable evidence to suggest that the ancient Indians were accomplished sailors and enterprising merchants. Allusions to Indian ships and seafaring activities in the vedic and Buddhist literatures are numerous and extensive. The *Baveru Jataka*[23] describes periodic voyages of Indian merchants to the kingdom of Baveru. Scholars equate this kingdom with Babylon, which had become a commercial metropolis after the overthrow of the Assyrian Empire in 606 B.C. The crowded marketplaces of Babylon were filled with merchants from distant lands—Phoenicians, Ionians, and Indians amongst them. References to ships holding seven hundred people are found in Jataka stories. These stories may exaggerate but there is no doubt that Indian seamen built ships larger than those usually employed, even at a much later date, in the Mediterranean.

Assyrian and Babylonian influence on India during the prehistoric and early historic periods must have been significant, although the nature and extent of this influence are very obscure. Bühler suggests that the Brahmi script used in Asokan inscriptions—the parent stock from which all Indian alphabets have been derived—was borrowed from Semitic sources, probably in the seventh century B.C. Other scholars, such as Rawlinson, find Bühler's arguments somewhat unsatisfactory. It has been generally held that the Brahmi script was derived from a foreign source, although there are wide disagreements as to the identity of that source. Since the discovery of the seals at Mohenjo-daro, however, scholars have begun speculating on the possibility that this alphabet may have developed from an earlier ideographic form of writing used in the Indus Valley itself. Therefore, judgement must be suspended until the writing is deciphered. Excavations in the Indus Valley have already led to a revision of the earlier view that Indian art had originated from a foreign source not much earlier than the third century B.C., and additional investigation may well lead to further reconsiderations. The influence, too, of Babylonian mythology on Indian literature, and of Chaldean astronomy on Indian scientific thought, has been suggested and disputed.[24]

The second stage of civilization in India began around 1500 B.C. with the coming of the Aryans who brought a civilization very different from that of the Indus. Still semi-nomadic, the Aryans were mainly occupied with war and cattle-raising and only secondarily with agriculture. The exact location of their origins has been a debatable point in history, sometimes vitiated by nationalistic feeling. Various theories, claiming north, central, or southeast European, or Asian origin, have been put forward. Some scholars even hold that not only did they originate in India but that the vedic civilization preceded the Indus civilization.[25] Most scholars, however, considering the evidence of philology and archaeology, maintain that the Aryans, or Indo-European peoples, originated somewhere in Central Asia or south Russia. It appears that around 2000 B.C. there existed at least a loose confederacy of tribes, stretching from south Russia to Turkistan, who shared certain elements of a common culture and who spoke closely related dialects within the Indo-European linguistic framework. Near the beginning of the second millennium B.C. these Indo-European peoples began to march out of their ancestral home in successive waves towards Europe and India. They reached India around 1500 B.C. Some historians believe they then destroyed the Indus Valley civilization, but evidence for this belief is inconclusive, and it appears to be a bold suggestion by Mortimer Wheeler.[26]

Thus began the period of the *Rig Veda,* one of the oldest and noblest books of mankind. Rabindranath Tagore has described the *Rig Veda* as "a poetic testament of a people's collective reaction to the wonder and awe of existence." In some ways a curious document, it is undoubtedly the earliest monument of Indo-European language, thought, and literature, and reveals a very high level of civilization, even though the Aryans were unfamiliar with the art of writing and possibly did not have a centralized and organized form of government. The *Rig Veda* represents the earliest developed phase of the evolution of religious consciousness and man's response to the immensity of the universe and the inexhaustible mystery of life.[27] The vedic culture, originally foreign to the country, gradually adapted itself to the Indian environment greatly changing its own religious, ethical, and economic content, and at the same time permeating deeply into Indian life, thought, and society. Indeed, it is this blending which forms the basis of Indian culture.

At about the time the Hittites emerged in Anatolia, the Aryans were spreading into northwest India. They probably proceeded in two directions in successive waves—westward and eastward. The Celts, the Greeks, and the Germans are the descendants of the former branch, whilst the Indians and the Iranians are descendants of the latter. There are close resemblances between the language, mythology, religious traditions, and social institutions of Indians and Iranians on the one hand, and those of the Greeks, Romans, Celts, Germans, and Slavs on the other. The theory that the Indo-Europeans were one people is mainly based on linguistic evidence, which has been successfully tested against archaeological studies in western Asia and eastern Europe. Even if they began as one people ethnologically, the complexity of the anthropological evidence suggests that many native groups mixed with them in the various lands where they settled and that they adopted many of the features of the local cultures, including the language.

The Indo-European group of languages—formerly known as the Aryan or Indo-Germanic group—includes most of the languages of Europe, North America, and India. Despite certain anomalies, the linguistic resemblances between the languages in this group can be presented in a convincingly systematized form which indicates a common source.[28] The grammatical forms and the basic words of the vocabulary, like father and mother and the numerals, are strikingly identical.[29]

The eastern branch of the Indo-European movement is often referred to as the Aryan movement, because the ancient peoples belonging to this group called themselves Aryas, a word which later acquired the meaning of "the noble ones."[30] The Aryans were further subdivided into the Iranians and the Indians. It is inevitable, therefore, that Indian contacts with Iran should be the oldest and the most prolonged. These contacts began in prehistoric times and continued into the Mughal and modern periods. Situated between the plains of the Euphrates and the Indus, Iran has occupied from the earliest times a position which made her one of the principal routes of commerce, conquest, and civilization. She has, through successive periods of history, influenced the culture of both her eastern and western neighbours, and has provided a bridge between India and the West. The Persian language, like French in Europe, became the language of cultured people over wide areas of Asia. Persian was the court language of mediaeval India and even today is one of the principal Indian classical languages. Its influence on modern Indian languages is enormous, and India has produced many excellent Persian scholars, both Hindu and Muslim.

The area lying between modern Iran and India, comprising parts of West Pakistan and Afghanistan, was culturally and, at times, politically a part of India. Until the rise of Islam this area was under the influence of Hinduism and Buddhism. Afghanistan was an integral part of the Mauryan kingdom (325–185 B.C.) and later of the Mughal Empire, and many Afghan rulers, including the Turki-Afghans, ruled over Indian territories. Consequently, there are many cultural similarities between the Indian and Afghani peoples. Furthermore, both in its vocabulary and grammatical structure, Afghani is very close to Sanskrit.

Even during pre-Aryan days, contact existed between India and Iran. This is indicated by such evidence as the parallels between the pottery motifs of the two countries and finds of identical objects in both countries. But close resemblances between Indian and Iranian culture date from the days of their common Indo-Aryan origin. It seems most likely that the Indians and the Iranians lived together for some time, perhaps on the Iranian Plateau, before the Indian group moved into India. It is, however, surprising that the cultural link between pre-Aryan India and Iran should have been severed, rather than strengthened, as a result of the migrations of the Aryans into India through Iran.[31]

Although evidence of continued contact between the vedic Indians and the Iranians is not explicit, there is no doubt that the vedic religion has much in common with Zoroastrianism, and that vedic Sanskrit closely resembles the language of the *Avesta*. The Iranian god Mithra, who centuries later found his way into the Roman world and became a popular sun god of the Roman troops, and the vedic Mitra were undoubtedly originally identical. He is invoked as god of light in both religions together with the god of heaven, who is called Varuna in the Vedas and Ahura in the *Avesta*. The beginnings of Zoroastrianism, however, mark a dividing line between the vedic and Iranian Aryans. In the *Avesta* many of the vedic deities became devils,[32] whilst on the other hand, Ahura, asura, came to mean "demon" in the Vedas. By changing the relative statures of the gods, Zoroaster endeavoured to convert the old polytheism into a spiritual monotheism. Varuna was raised to a position of supremacy, having been invested with the sublime majesty of the guardian of the cosmic order (Old Persian *Asa* or Sanskrit *Rta*) and Indra was relegated to the armies of evil against whom the righteous man must fight on the side of Ahura Mazda.[33] Zoroastrianism was almost contemporary with Buddhism, and it is significant that both religions were a protest against the archaic practices of the old Aryan religions.

India was closely allied to Iran in commerce, and indeed through Iran to the areas further west. This commercial contact between India and the West was an important feature of the ancient period and continued unbroken until the decline of the Roman Empire. Merchandise, although it travelled from India to Europe, changed hands at various prominent emporia and was bartered many times in transit. Trade was brisk, and was conducted over both land and sea routes.

The existing overland trade route to the West, largely unheard of before the time of Darius, probably because of the dangers of the journey, lay through northwestern India to the Khyber Pass and thence across the Hindu-Kush to Balkh which stood on the silk route, the main highway linking East and West. Through this route India had connections with Iran, Greece, Rome, Central Asia, and China. Several routes ran from Balkh to Central Asia and China, as well as two routes to the West. One western route crossed the Oxus River (Amu Darya) to the Caspian Sea and then to the Euxine (the Black Sea); the other, entirely by land, lay above the border of the Karmanian Desert to the north, passed through the Caspian Gates and reached Antioch (now Antakya in Turkey) by way of Hecatompylos. Another important route, probably the oldest and easiest, was through the Persian Gulf, from the mouth of the Indus River along the coast to the mouth of the Euphrates River. The ships then proceeded up the Euphrates and joined the overland route at Seleucia which connected Antioch and the Levantine ports.[34] Another sea route, somewhat circuitous, followed the Persian and Arabian coasts to Aden and then to Suez through the Red Sea. From Suez the goods were carried overland either to Egypt or to Mediterranean ports, such as Tyre and Sidon.

Although a very strong probability of constant communication by land and sea between India and western Asia is clearly indicated, real evidence of political and cultural intercourse emerges only with the rise of the Achaemenians in the sixth century B.C. after the overthrow of Babylon, the last of the great Semitic empires of western Asia, by Cyrus (559–530 B.C.) who laid the foundations of a vast Persian Empire. This event marked a major advance in the history of Iran, and in fact in the history of the world, for the Achaemenians conceived Iran as a state and made it a reality. An extensive Persian empire emerged through a series of conquests stretching from the Indus to the Aegean. It included the ancient kingdom of Egypt, Sind and Western Punjab in India, and some Greek city states in Ionia. Darius (521–486 B.C.) reorganized the Empire, throughout the length and breadth of which ran good roads punctuated by imperial military posts.[35]

This great and powerful Empire lasted until it was demolished by Alexander in 331 B.C. It is not known exactly how far Persian power extended, but it is said that the Indian province was the twentieth and the richest *satrapy* added to the Persian Empire. Herodotus tells us of the wealth and density of the population of India, and that it paid 360 talents of gold dust to Persia per year as tribute, an amount which was almost one-third of the revenue of Darius' whole Empire.[36] There is no doubt that Darius, who according to Herodotus was called a merchant by his subjects, and his successors were not satisfied with the existing trade and sought its extension. They wished for oceanic trade, with direct contact between India and Egypt, and a direct sea route around Arabia to Africa, through the Red Sea, and thence by some sort of a canal to the Mediterranean.

During the early period of the Mauryan administration, palace organization, court etiquette and deportment were still greatly influenced by Persian ideas and models. Even the Mauryan idea of empire was perhaps inspired by the Iranian example. The imperialism of the Maurya monarchy, especially of Asoka, was a synthesis of Indian, Achaemenian, and Hellenistic ideas.[37] The Maurya Empire was conterminous with the Seleucid Empire of Syria and Iran, because it included within its boundaries parts of modern Afghanistan and Baluchistan which belonged physically to the Iranian Plateau.

The Indian national emblem which contains four lions and a wheel borrowed from the Sarnath pillar of Asoka, is faintly reminiscent of Assyro-Persian prototypes, although clearly modified by Indian sentiment; the *dharmachakra* (the wheel of the law) is, however, also a symbol of the Buddhist faith. As examples of ancient animal sculpture, Asoka's pillars, combining realistic modelling with idealistic dignity and finished in every detail with perfect accuracy, are hardly surpassed in any country or, indeed, in later Indian art.[38]

The use of stone for columns and statues during the Mauryan period instead of ivory, wood, or clay, is also attributed to Graeco-Persian influence. Some scholars have noticed Iranian influence on Chandragupta's system of communications and in Asoka's practice of inscribing rocks and columns, although Asoka's use of such inscriptions to promulgate edicts was profoundly original. Through these edicts he spread the simple and human teaching of the Buddha and preached that true conquest was the conquest of self and the conquest of men's hearts through dharma.[39]

Indian punch-marked silver coinage was on a Persian standard, and the Kharoshthi script was derived from Aramaic, used by the Achaemenians in their official documents.[40] This Kharoshthi script remained in use in the northwestern region of India until the fourth century. The origin of Mauryan court art, however, is a subject of keen controversy, although general opinion appears to favour some Iranian inspiration. Havell, for instance, pointing out that symbolism in Indian art is thoroughly characteristic of Indo-Aryan thought, attributes the resemblances between early Indian and Iranian art to these peoples' common racial origin and imaginative heritage.[41] Certainly, differences of form and type separate the Mauryan columns from those of Achaemenian Iran.[42]

The modern term Hindu, by which the majority of the Indians are now known, is of Persian origin. Indians were known to Persians as the inhabitants of the land of Sindhu, the Indus River. The Persians softened the initial S to H, thus making it Hindu, a name which has survived and come to be applied in a much wider and more complex sense. The Ionian Greeks, who came to know of India through the Persians, transformed the word into Indus (Ἰνδός), and the land of Indus came to be known as India.[43]

Iranian political contact affected India in another important way during this period. India's relationship with the Western world from this time on became increasingly political as Persia provided a common meeting-ground for Greek and Indian merchants, warriors, scholars, and travellers. Perhaps at no other period in early history was communication by land more open, or conditions more favourable for the interchange of ideas between India and the West.

It was during this period (ca. 510 B.C.) that the first Greek, Scylax of Caryanda, is known to have visited India.[44] A mercenary sea captain, he was sent by Darius to explore India beyond the Indus, to trace the river down to its mouth, and then to sail back to Persia examining the coastline. After an eventful journey of over two years, he reached Arsinoe, modern Suez. He is thus not only the first Greek known to have visited India but also the first known to have made the Red Sea voyage.[45] It was probably Scylax's account of his adventures, now lost, which formed the basis of Herodotus' narrative of India. Herodotus' account, however, is full of inaccuracies and is hardly more than a medley of travellers' tales. Hecataeus of Miletus, a contemporary of Scylax and the father of Greek geography, was the first Greek to mention India, having also gathered his information most probably from Scylax's account. Hecataeus' work, too, is unfortunately lost.

Another Greek account of India, *Indika,* was partially preserved in the Library of Photius (ninth century). Ctesias (*ca.* 400 B.C.), the author, lived at the Persian court for seventeen years as a royal physician, but in spite of his excellent opportunities for acquiring knowledge about India, he packed his narrative with deliberate lies.[46] The unreliability of Ctesias' information has seldom been disputed. In a recent study, A. R. Burn reaffirms this opinion of Ctesias, describing him "as reckless of truth and concerned only to make an impression; and even when he does tell us a detail which might be true, it is always well to remember the Martichora."[47]

Indian soldiers, clad in cotton garments and equipped with bows and arrows of cane, formed part of the Persian army which fought heroically against the Greeks under Xerxes (468–465 B.C.). India also supplied Persia with chariots and horses, and an Indian contingent formed a part of Darius III's forces which fought Alexander at the historical Gaugamela battle in 331 B.C. These are the earliest known instances of Greeks and Indians facing each other in large numbers.

Although parts of India and Greece were joined in the same state, being the two ends of the Persian Empire, there is a great scarcity of historical materials which might determine with any degree of certainty the nature and volume of the cultural intercourse involved, especially before the campaigns of Alexander. This was the time of the rise of philosophical reflection in Greece and the revolt against the traditional Homeric religion. In India, as well, it was the time of the Buddha and Mahavira who had protested against the finds of the Vedas. Both India and Greece produced civilizations during this period which were to determine for generations the habits of thought and ways of life not only of their own peoples but of many races far beyond their frontiers. The fact that both India and Greece were going through a phase of spiritual unrest and intellectual agitation must have increased not only the ease but the frequency and volume of the exchange of ideas.

In fact, all over the world an unprecedented intellectual revolution was taking place which was to have a lasting influence on human thought. Prophets emerged proclaiming revelations from God, and philosophers appealed to the inherent reason in man. In the Middle East, a succession of outspoken Jewish religious and social reformers appeared, commonly known as "the prophets"—Amos, Hosea, Isaiah, and

17

others. In China, Confucius taught rational morality and in Iran, Zarathustra (Zoroaster) endeavoured to purify the prevalent religion of polytheism, ritualism, and magic.[48] It is noteworthy that this widespread intellectual revolution in the ancient world, which was probably the first of its kind in history, should have been preceded by the rise in India of the Upanishads, whose authors were also urged on in their quest for reality by their dissatisfaction with the existing forms of vedic teachings and practices.

During such a period of intense intellectual activity, free contact between India and Greece may reasonably be assumed to account for some of the parallels between Indian thought and Greek philosophy. Ardent classicists dispute the existence of Indian influence as vigorously as any other influence, because according to some, such as Sir Henry Maine, no progress at all would have been possible for the Romans, the Germans, or the English without the Greek heritage.[49] But there has been too much inclination among Western writers to idealize the Greeks and their civilization, and they have tended to discover too much of the contemporary world in the Greek past. Greek patrimony was claimed not only in the realm of thought, but in handicrafts, the techniques of mining, the essentials of engineering, the processes of finance and trade, political systems, trial by jury, civil liberties, schools and universities, gymnasia and stadia, games and sports, art and literature, and Christian theology and practice. In fact almost everything was traced to ancient Greece. In all that concerned intellectual activity and even faith, modern civilization was considered to be an overgrown colony of Hellas. The obvious Greek failings, their shortcomings and the unhealthy features of their civilization, were rationalized and romanticized.[50]

Modern research, however, has marred this comforting image and is helping to put Greek culture into its proper historical perspective showing that, like any other culture, it inherited something from preceding civilizations, profited from the progress of neighbouring cultures and, in turn, bequeathed much to later generations. The Greeks are now regarded as simple, natural, and reasonable people, responding healthily to their environment. A people of mixed descent, like the rest, the classical Greeks were not pure Hellenes by blood; they were not even a nation. It was during the Persian wars that the tribes in the various regions around the Aegean Sea first achieved a kind of national identity against what they called the "barbaroi." Driven mainly by the fear of foreigners and the need to organize a common defence, the various tribes banded together, and, in this respect, Greek nationalism could be termed a Persian contribution. Though abundantly patriotic, the Hellenes never desired a Greek nation common to all. Their patriotism seems to have been mainly confined to the narrow limits of a particular glen or district, and this is well illustrated by their regional hatreds. Athenian Greeks disliked Ionian Greeks, and fought Sparta in disastrous wars; Boeotia hated Attica, and Attica despised Boeotia as much as it did the Scythians.

It is significant that, although the Indians and the Greeks had come from the same Indo-European stock, they met as strangers in the sixth century B.C. Persian Empire. Soon, however, the cousins became associates in a common cultural enterprise. Similarities in language, accompanied by similarities in religious beliefs, indicate that these two peoples must have either been in close contact at some early period or have had a common origin, even though neither had any recollection of those times. For example, the gods of heaven (Varuna—Ouranos; Dyaus—Zeus) and the dawn (Ushas—Aurora) were common to the Greeks and Indians. The most prominent characteristic of the gods of both races was their power of regulating the order of nature and banishing evil. The Olympian religion of the Greeks and vedic beliefs had a common background. The Greek concept of *logos* was very close to the vedic *Vac*, which corresponds to the Latin term *Vox*. In a passage of the *Rig Veda*, Vac is praised as a divine being. Vac is omnipotent, moves amongst divine beings, and carries the great gods, Mitra, Varuna, Indra, and Agni, within itself.[51] The doctrine of Vac teaches that "all gods live from Vac, also all demi-gods, animals and people. Vac is the eternal being, it is the first-born of the eternal law, mother of the Vedas and navel of immortality." Vedic Aryans attached such great importance to the spoken word that one who could not correctly pronounce Sanskrit was called *barbar* (meaning stammering). The Greek *barbaroi* had the same meaning. There is also a striking similarity between the social life described in the Homeric poems—the *Iliad* and the *Odyssey*—and that found in the Vedas.[52] Homeric gods, like the heroes who believed in them, often rode in horsedrawn chariots. Horse-chariotry was a feature of the life of the Indo-European people, and appeared in western Asia sometime after 2000 B.C. The Homeric idea of a language of the gods is also found in Sanskrit, Greek, old Norse, and Hittite literatures.[53] Some scholars, like Fiske, have even asserted that elements of the Trojan war story are to be found in the war between the bright deities and the night demons as described in the *Rig Veda*.[54] On the other hand, the Indian epics, the *Ramayana* and the *Mahabharata,* also works of great literary merit and deep cultural significance, have been said by some scholars, like Weber, to have been inspired by the Homeric poems. Few, however, hold this view now, and most authorities agree with Winternitz that the Indian epics have an indigenous tradition of their own. Whilst the artistic quality and superficial resemblances between these Greek and Indian works are undoubted, the characters they describe are in every instance remote, having only a superficial basis in actuality, and the historicity of the narratives must remain open to doubt.[55]

Although the ancient Greeks did not possess any real knowledge of India, from Homer it is clear that even then they used articles of Indian merchandise which were known by names of Indian origin, such as Kassiteros (Sanskrit, *Kastira*), elephas (Sanskrit, *ibha*), and ivory.[56]

The earliest beginnings of Greek philosophy lie in the Milesian or Ionian school of the sixth century B.C. Thales of Miletus, regarded as the father of Greek philosophy, was a merchant of whom little is known. He was, however, the first philosopher to express his ideas in logical terms.[57] He predicted the correct time of an eclipse which occurred in 585 B.C.—the first fixed date in Greek philosophy and generally regarded as its starting point.[58] The Ionian philosophers were mainly regarded by later generations as "men of science." Extremely curious about the nature of the external world, a *cosmos* as they called it, the pre-Socratic Greek thinkers, Thales, Anaximander, and other Milesians did not exclude the possibility of a divine agency, but their conception of such an agency differed from the contemporary Greek polytheism. The Ionian philosophers paid no attention at all to the Olympian gods and ignored the Greek *theologia,* the stories or legends of the gods. Yet they had religious ideas and principles, such as the conceptions of *Moira* and *Dike* —of purity and impurity—and the concept of the universe as an ordered cosmos and therefore one.[59] Whilst the idea of cosmic law and order appears in simple form in Anaximander, Xenophanes clearly sets forth the concept of a divine intelligence pervading and regulating the world, and Anaxagoras advances the idea of a world-arranging Mind. The Milesians also reflected on the question of the one and the many, and held that all things emanate from a single living substance. They believed that the world arose out of a primal unity, and that this one substance was still the permanent base of all its being, although now appearing in different forms and manifestations.[60] Before the end of the century, however, philosophical speculation in Greece underwent a change of spirit under Pythagoras (532 B.C.) and Greek thought became essentially mystical.[61]

By contrast, philosophical thought in India in the sixth century B.C. had become quite mature. It had reached a stage which could have been arrived at only after long and arduous philosophical quest. Jainism and Buddhism, the latter enormously influential in Indian and neighbouring cultures, had emerged by this time. But even before their advent, the philosophical reflections of the early Upanishads (900–600 B.C.) had set forth the fundamental concepts of Hindu thought which have continued to dominate the Indian mind.

It is perhaps necessary to point out that there has often been a wide divergence between Indian and Western interpretations of Indian thought. Coomaraswamy once even declared that a true account of Hinduism may be given in a categorical denial of most of the interpretations that have been made by Westerners or Western-trained Indians.[62] For example, whilst Western scholars have generally suggested that monotheism arose late in Indian thought, growing out of an earlier polytheism, Indian scholars have pointed out that there was more polytheism in the later vedic hymns than in those of the earlier period. Distorted analyses of Indian thought are, however, rapidly declining both in influence and frequency and an accepted and more accurate interpretation has begun to emerge. Certainly, the divergence of opinion has never proceeded completely along nationalistic lines. In fact, many Western scholars, such as Guenon, are apt to be too generous and too ready to admit that "the position of the West in relation to the East is that of a branch growing out of the trunk,"[63] or like Evans-Wentz, who declares: "Today as it did in the days of Pythagoras, of Plato, of Plotinus, of Appolonius of Tyana, and of other truth-seekers who have been the shapers of the culture and faiths of the occident, 'From the Orient cometh the Light.' "[64]

The tradition of Indian philosophic thought is as complex as it is long, but because of the Indian indifference to chronology, it is impossible to present the detailed development of this thought in its proper historical perspective. Similarly, little is known about the individual thinkers of Indian philosophy, although our knowledge of its various systems is relatively rich. Ancient Indians, it appears, concentrated almost exclusively on philosophies and disregarded philosophers. The complexities of Indian philosophy have arisen through centuries of deep reflection on the many aspects of human experience, and, in the search for some reality behind the external world, various methods have been resorted to ranging from the experimental to the purely speculative. In consequence there developed six basic systems of Hinduism, four main schools of Buddhism, two schools of Jainism, as well as the materialist thought of Carvaka.[65] In spite of this diversity, Indian philosophy in general is distinguished by a concentration upon the spiritual; a belief in the intimate relationship of philosophy and life; an introspective approach to reality, which does not, however, neglect the study of the physical world; a tendency towards monistic idealism, which has not been oblivious to the claims of materialism; and an extensive use of intuitive reasoning for the realization of the ultimate.

Probably the oldest philosophical tradition in the world is to be traced in the ancient Vedas, although there are some prominent pre-vedic elements even in this tradition such as: the influence of forests in the life of the people; temple worship accompanied by the contemplation of the divine in a more concrete form; the elevation of animals, birds, and trees to a position of importance in the scheme of the universe; and the exaltation of the female aspect of the divine.[66]

Although the religious and philosophical spirit of India emerges distinctly in the *Rig Veda*, the Upanishads are its most brilliant exposition, for the vedic civilization was naturalistic and utilitarian, although it did not exclude cosmological and religious speculation. Man offered sacrifice to God as if bound in a contract with Him to obtain material prosperity. One of the most significant concepts of vedic India was that of *rta*, the idea of the true order of the world, a concept that may be considered the forerunner of *dharma* of ancient and even modern times.[67] In the Vedas a unique march of the human mind from the worship of half-personified powers of nature, such as fire, wind, and rain, to the conception of the Absolute, the One, is clearly seen. In the beginning there was no clear distinction between one deity and another as all were phenomena of nature. The same name was employed to signify more than one deity, and the same power was attributed to a number of gods. This led to the belief that they were all one in reality. Later, there arose a series of deities, Prajapati, Aditi, Prana, and Kala. But gradually the vedic thinkers, discarding all anthropomorphism, arrived at a single primordial reality, the underlying unity. They call him "many who is really One." It was this tendency towards monism which was later systematically developed in the Upanishads.

Older than Plato or Confucius, the Upanishads are the most ancient of philosophical works and contain the mature wisdom of India's intellectual and spiritual attainment.[68] They have inspired not only the orthodox systems of Indian thought but also the so-called heterodox schools such as Buddhism. In profundity of thought and beauty of style, they have rarely been surpassed not only in Indian thought but in the Western and Chinese philosophical traditions as well. The Upanishads have greatly influenced Indian culture throughout history and have also found enthusiastic admirers abroad. Schopenhauer was almost lyrical about them and Max Müller said: "The *Upanishads* are the . . . sources of . . . the Vedanta philosophy, a system in which human speculation seems to me to have reached its very acme." The Upanishads are saturated with the spirit of inquiry, intellectual analysis, and a passion for seeking the truth. Being works of a host of sages and scholars, speaking out of the fullness of their illumined experience over a period of centuries, they contain, naturally, many ambiguities and contradictions. The spirit of all upanishadic inquiry, however, was that the final essence or truth was the *Atman*—the spark of divinity within all beings—and that a search for this was man's highest duty. Although a logical and coherent system of metaphysics may be lacking in the Upanishads, it does not matter in comparison with their outburst of the joy and emotion of intuitive experience. The general and overriding tendency found in these texts is toward absolute monism, contained in the recognition of unity between Atman, the individual principle, and *Brahman,* the cosmic principle or essence of the universe, with the emphasis on self-realization. "The Universe is Brahman but the *Brahman* is the Atman." The Upanishads do not argue against the existence of many different gods, but argue that there is one Being of whom all the gods are manifestations, and the real, which is at the heart of the universe, is in the infinite depths of the self. Brahman is Atman and the Truth is within us. Brahman is the universal spirit approached from the objective side; Atman, the self, is the same universal spirit approached from the subjective side. Atman is imprisoned in man's body, mind, and understanding, all of which foster in him a congenital ignorance of his own infinitude and of his oneness with all beings. The true goal of human life is liberation, *moksha,* from this captivity. During the period of the Upanishads, moksha became the end and transcendent knowledge, *jnana,* the means. The gods and sacrifices were dethroned from their position of supremacy, religious formalism and ritualism were discarded, and even the knowledge of the Vedas was considered inadequate. Knowledge is exalted above works as the means of realizing truth, and the highest wisdom is to know the self (*atmanam viddhi*) which is the primal spirit, or pure awareness, distinct from bodily states and mental happenings. "I am *Brahman*" and "Thou art That" are the two key teachings of the Upanishads.[69]

The Upanishads form a principal source for the Indian schools of philosophy. In fact, whilst the Upanishads were being compiled or arranged, the Indian philosophical systems began to be formulated into recognizable traditions. It is difficult to tell how these systems were formulated, but they are generally classified into two major divisions:

the *nastika* and the *astika*. The former includes those schools of thought, such as the Buddhist, Jain, and the Carvaka, which neither regard the Vedas as infallible nor attempt to impose their own validity on vedic authority. These schools deny the Atman doctrine of the Upanishads. The latter division, astika, comprises the six main orthodox schools of thought, Samkhya, Yoga, Vedanta, Mimansa, Nyaya, and Vaisesika, which accept the upanishadic teaching.

Indian philosophical thought, in contrast to the Western tradition, has remained more stable and more clearly continuous. In spite of its metaphysical nature and religious overtones, Indian philosophy is essentially practical, aiming at realizing spiritually what is known intellectually. Knowledge without vision is meaningless. Hence, Indians call their philosophy *darshana*, vision. One progresses from knowledge gained through study, *sravana*, through contemplative meditation and ethical discipline, *nididhyasana* and *manana*, to the final vision, *saksatkara*. Philosophy and religion in India are intertwined, because religion for the Hindu is experience or an attitude of mind, a transformation of one's being, a consciousness of the ultimate reality, not a theory about God. Whatever view of God the Hindu may adopt, he believes that the divine is in man. The supreme being, which is both absolute and God, is conceived as the object of philosophical inquiry, or jnana, and as an object of religious devotion, *upasana*. In religious experience the conception of ultimate reality and that of a personal god are reconciled, although in religious thought the reconciliation is not easy to effect. Philosophy, as religion, is seen in India as a means to an end, not as an end in itself. Hence, there is no room for dogma or intolerance in Indian tradition because the roads to truth are more than one. The infinite reality cannot be comprehended by the finite human mind.

Indian philosophy developed over a period of many centuries in various widely separated regions, yet the philosophers traversed more or less the same path and in many aspects closely anticipated the same philosophical concepts which emerged later in the West. The Indian conception of the bearing of philosophy on life is uniformly the same in almost all systems of Indian philosophy and has inspired all philosophical and religious teachings. That philosophy should not remain just an academic theory but should transform the whole life and lead men to the path of self-realization, ultimately bringing them back to the level of other men, making them share the common duties of social life in a perfected form, and binding them with ties of love together in one humanity, is the final wisdom of Indian thought.[70]

As the principal systems of Indian philosophy originated in times for which there is little chronological data available, their beginnings cannot be traced with any exactitude. There is some disagreement amongst scholars as to the period and order of emergence of the six systems, darshanas, of Indian philosophy, but it is generally agreed that the foundations of these schools had been laid before the time of the Buddha, although further developments may have taken place later. Some of these schools, such as the Samkhya, were probably well established by the time of the Buddha's birth.[71]

Thus, perhaps, India is the home of philosophy. Certainly India is a country where philosophy has always been very popular and influential. An American scholar has stated that teachers of philosophy in India were as numerous as merchants in Babylonia.[72] The sages have always been heroes of the Indians, and some of their festive celebrations were marked by relentless debates between the chief exponents of rival schools of thought. If philosophy did emerge in India earlier than in Greece, and if the two countries were in close contact soon after this emergence, it is not unlikely that Indian thought had some influence on Greek philosophy, especially on those aspects which appear somewhat alien to the Greek tradition and resemble the Indian. Theoretically, it is quite feasible, however, that the Greeks had reached their conclusions independently or that they were influenced, as has often been postulated, by the older civilizations of the Nile and the Euphrates.

The similarity between the theory of Thales, that water is the material cause of all things, and the vedic idea of primeval waters as the origin of the universe, was first pointed out by Richard Garbe. The resemblances, too, between the teachings of Pythagoras (*ca.* 582–506 B.C.) and Indian philosophical beliefs are striking. Whereas the Milesians, or Ionians, in eastern Greece had sought the first principle of all things in matter and were absorbed in a scientific explanation of the universe, Pythagoras in western Greece sought it in form. The answers given by Pythagoras and his followers to questions about man represent a more developed stage in abstract thinking and constitute a distinct stream in Greek thought, which had the greatest influence on later developments of Greek philosophy and was notably influential on the thinking of Plato. Pythagoras was an exceptionally outstanding thinker, a founder both of Greek mathematical science and of philosophical cosmology. He was the first to give the name cosmos—an untranslatable word combining notions of order, fitness, and beauty—to the world and to call his own pursuit of knowledge *philosophia* (the love of wisdom) rather than *sophia* (wisdom) which he thought pretentious. He was also the first Greek to teach the doctrine of metempsychosis in the Hellenic world. Pythagoras drew inspiration from the legendary Thracian poet and bard, Orpheus, whose cult included several features absent in the Homeric religion, such as the belief in the immortality of the soul, in its transmigration from body to body, in the existence of an individual and a universal soul, and in the purification of the soul.[73] Connected with the belief in the transmigration of the soul is the most important of the Pythagorean taboos, the abstention from taking animal life. The beast or bird that one eats may be inhabited by the soul of one's ancestor. Initiation into the Pythagorean society required, in addition to the purification of the body by abstinence and self-control, a purification of the mind by scientific study. If the transmigration of souls is possible and usual, then all life is akin. In common with the early thinkers of the Upanishads, Pythagoras believed that "all souls are similar in class and the apparent distinctions between human and other kinds of beings are not ultimate."[74] As in Indian thought, the purpose of life in the Pythagorean system is to gain release from reincarnation through virtue. Pythagoras' cosmic dualism of matter and form—on one side the world of nature and the elements, on the other the spirits, both being combined in organic nature—is also vaguely reminiscent of the *dvaita* (dualistic) philosophy of the *Samkhya*, which recognizes two ultimate realities, *prakriti* (nature) and *purusha* (spirit).

Pythagoras, being a mathematician, expressed his cosmology in mathematical terms. The world in his philosophy is a mixture of light and darkness, good and evil, the formless and the form. The imposition of limit (*peras*) on the unlimited (*apeiron*) created the limited (*peperasmenon*). In the Indian scheme, prakriti is the ultimate cosmic energy—primal matter which exists externally—and is the basis of all objective existence, physical and psychical. Purusha, the conscious principle of creation, coexists eternally with prakriti. The evolution of unconscious prakriti can take place only through the presence of conscious purusha. Both are eternal, devoid of characteristics, and formless. Prakriti in its transformations becomes a perceivable object, whilst purusha, the self, remains the perceiving subject. Pythagoras' doctrine that nothing can arise which has not existed before, and that nothing existing can be annihilated is exactly parallel to the Samkhya doctrine about eternity and the indestructibility of matter. The Samkhya system is so termed because it observes a precision of reckoning in the enumeration of its principles; Samkhya being understood to signify "numeral." Hence its analogy to the Pythagorean philosophy has been presumed.

It was Sir William Jones, the founder of comparative philology, who first pointed out the similarities between Indian and Pythagorean beliefs. Later, other scholars such as Colebrooke, Garbe, and Winternitz also testified to the Indian inspiration of Pythagoras.

The history of Pythagoreanism is a particularly controversial subject in Greek philosophy. Early evidence is lamentably scanty, and it is almost impossible to recover the earlier forms of Pythagorean speculation. An insight into Pythagoras' thought during its formative stages might well have led historians to the source of his inspiration. Herodotus, like Plato and others who attributed all wisdom to Egyptian sources, suggested that Pythagoras obtained the doctrine of rebirth from Egypt. This was natural as the Greeks were deeply impressed by the antiquity of Egyptian civilization.[75] However, it is now quite evident that the Egyptians did not believe in the transmigration of souls at all.[76] In discussing the sources of influences on Pythagoras, Gomperz points out, "There is a far closer agreement between Pythagorism and the Indian doctrine not merely in their general features, but even in certain details, such as vegetarianism, and it may be added that the formulae which summarize the whole creed of the 'cycle and wheel' of births are likewise the same in both. It is almost impossible for us to refer this identity to mere chance."[77] It does appear more logical to believe that Pythagoras accepted the most popular Indian theories of the time, which he could well have been aware of, than to speculate that he invented a theory alien to Greek tradition yet firmly held in neighbouring regions. Almost all the doctrines ascribed to him, religious, philosophical, and mathematical, were known in India in the sixth century B.C. The coincidences are so numerous that their cumulative force becomes considerable. The transmigration theory, the assumption of five elements, the Pythagorean theory in geometry, the prohibition on eating beans, the religio-philosophical character of the Pythagorean fraternity, and the mystical speculations of the Pythagorean school all have their close parallels in ancient India. Every one of the Pythagorean doctrines "which we know formed the 'gospel' of Pythagoras and the Pythagorean brotherhood at Crotona, was an almost exact reproduction of the cardinal doctrines of the Indian Vidya and the Indian Yoga—so much so that Indian Vedantins today do not hesitate to claim Pythagoras as one of themselves, one of their great expounders. . . ."[78]

Pythagoras' doctrine of metempsychosis appears without any connection or explanatory background, and it was regarded by the Greeks as foreign in origin. Where did Pythagoras gain access to Indian doctrines? Did he travel to India? Although he was a great traveller, it seems impossible that Pythagoras should have made his way to India at so early a date, but he could quite well have met Indians in Persia.[79] Such a possibility seems more likely when it is recalled that Pythagoras was still living in his Ionian home when Ionia came under the Persians, and that it was an age of intellectual ferment. It is also not unlikely that the early immigrants who peopled Greece had come from the East and brought with them some ideas of Indian origin.[80]

Pythagoras also created an organized celibate brotherhood, somewhat like the Buddhists, but for political, economic, and religious purposes, which exercised a very wide influence. In fact, the influence of the Pythagorean order grew to such an extent that it incurred the wrath of the tyrant Cylon. Pythagoras himself is said to have met his death by assassination, and after his death many of his followers were burned at the stake in mass executions. After these massacres Pythagoreanism came to an end as a political force, although it continued to survive as a religious cult.

In contrast to Pythagorean dualism, there developed at about the same time in southern Italy, an offshoot of Milesian thought of monistic character, known as the Eleatic school, which incorporated the foundations of Greek metaphysics.[81] In 545 B.C. Ionia had become a Persian province, which led Xenophanes (ca. 570–475 B.C.) to move to a new home in Elea. Xenophanes, Parmenides, and Zeno of Elea sought for the one reality underlying material phenomena in very much the same spirit as some of the later vedic hymns and the Upanishads. They tried to prove, unlike Heraclitus, that neither multiplicity nor movement could exist, and they concluded in favour of a stricter notion of unity and the existence of an absolute being. They taught "of a single god who worked by intellection alone, and posited an essential connection between divinity, eternity, reality, and spherical shape."[82] This Eleatic philosophy of a basic unity in all things, the whole of reality consisting of a single, motionless and unchanging substance, is similar to the upanishadic doctrine of the All-one.

Born about 515 B.C., Parmenides was the founder of the Eleatic school and furthered the Greeks on the path of abstract thought, setting the mind working without reference to external facts. He "dealt a death blow to material monism of the Ionian type."[83] His philosophy of the one absolute existence which is being and thought (*sat* and *cit*) at the same time, his recognition of not-being (*maya*) as conceptually antithetical to the idea of being and as essentially non-existent, his explanation of the plurality of the world which is only apparent, his distinction of the phenomenal and the noumenal (the *vyavaharika* and *para-*

marthika) are akin to the upanishadic teachings as interpreted by Samkaracharya.[84] Gomperz finds an exact parallel to the blissful primary being of Melissus, with its total lack of initiative and influence, in the lore of the vedantic philosophy in which the world is similarly represented as a mere delusive appearance with a central being whose sole attributes are essence, thought, and bliss (*sat, cit,* and *ananda*).[85]

Eleatic criticism of the Ionian philosophy gave rise to a school of pluralist thinkers who saw truth on both sides and attempted to reconcile the two lines of reasoning. This school included Empedocles (*ca.* 495–435 B.C.) who sided with the Eleatics in his denial of becoming but assumed the reality of motion, Anaxagoras, and the founders of Atomism, Leucippus and Democritus. Although the Atomic theory would appear to be the natural outcome of the mathematical knowledge of the Greeks, F. Schlegel has suggested its inspiration in the atomistic notions existing in India at the time. Both Leucippus and Democritus had travelled widely in the East and possibly met Indians in Persia.

Early Greek philosophy was principally metaphysical and only with the emergence of the sophists did it become predominantly humanistic. Born in Thrace about 485 B.C., Protagoras was the first to call himself a sophist. He taught neither science nor scholarship, but conduct. His famous saying, the Protagorean dictum, that man was the measure of all things, became a philosophical doctrine. The sophists were highly expensive travelling professors in the art of success. Little is known about them, and they were not very serious thinkers. They were generally uninterested in absolute religious or moral values, having accepted the widespread notion that morality was a relative concept and a matter of the conventions of particular societies. Socrates (*ca.* 470–399 B.C.) disagreed with this sort of moral relativism, and this eventually led to his conflict with Athenian society. Ironically, sophistic humanism found perfection in Socrates, who regarded the sophists of his day with a certain derision.

With Socrates, as with Plato later, the central preoccupation came to be man, and it was through an understanding of man's nature and behaviour that philosophical thought reverted to questions relating to God and the universe. Socrates preached that the most important thing in life was for man to know what he was and what he was for, and to care for his soul, and he believed that "virtue is knowledge." Socrates wrote nothing and claimed to know nothing, except that whilst he knew that he knew nothing, others did not. Socrates' most lasting contribution was the inspiration he gave to his pupil, Plato.

Historically, Socrates marks a decisive point in ancient Greek thought; whilst restraining the excesses of dogmatism, he did not relinquish the possibility of a knowledge suited to human faculties. Socrates did not precisely formulate a doctrine and is therefore hardly assigned a place in philosophy. He devised the process of induction and founded the study of ethics in its own right, having detached it from religion. Yet he was a deeply religious man and often talked of his inner voice. During the course of his trial, he said that this voice first came to him when he was a child and that it always forbade but never commanded him to do anything which he did not want to do. Unlike most thinkers, Socrates never claimed that he had seen the truth himself, and, in fact, he delighted in confessing his ignorance. Yet he had some convictions of truth which he called inspirations. He *knew* that reality is good and nothing but good, and that this reality could be found, if the search were earnest enough. He arduously sought to find the secret of life and that knowledge which serves the soul. He sought for the truth which reveals God, for the reality which makes goodness real, makes virtue unshakeable, and *realizes* the perfection of the soul's relations to all existing things. It was his faith, which he did not attempt to prove, that reality, goodness, and God are all one. He could not think of a real cause which was not good, nor a good which was not nous (wisdom), nor a universe which was not basically both nous and good. In fact, all his questions were but variations of a single question. What are knowledge and ignorance? What is the one? What are the many? What is right? What is the ideal state? Each and all of these were different aspects of his supreme quest: "How shall we find God and be like Him?" It was in this respect that he, and later Plato, turned philosophy into religion and fused metaphysics, ethics, politics, and all other disciplines into an indissoluble unity, just as the Indian thinkers had done in relating all their thought to the one reality.[86]

The view that Socrates could have been aware of Indian philosophy receives added support from the fact that Indian scholars visited Athens during his time. Aristoxenus (*ca.* 330 B.C.), the author of the *Harmonies* and a pupil of Aristotle, is reported by Eusebius (*ca.* 264–364 A.D.) to have mentioned that certain Indian scholars visited Athens and that one of them asked Socrates his views on the scope of philosophy. "An inquiry into human phenomena," replied Socrates. "How can we inquire into human phenomena," the Indian exclaimed, "when we are ignorant of divine ones."[87]

The whole history of Greek and Indian philosophy seems to be a continual dialogue between rational thought and analysis on one side, and religious mysticism on the other, although in India religious mysticism, not in the sense of ecstatic exaltation of the soul but the realization of God within the soul, or "integrated thought" or creative insight, has a more central place. These lines of development have progressed separately and simultaneously and have crossed and recrossed frequently. Intellectualism and mysticism sometimes ran separate courses, and at other times combined to form new ideas.[88] Finally, rational thought was exhausted and philosophy was transformed into mysticism in the form of Neoplatonism. Indian influence upon mysticism is more easily admitted, for instance in the mystery cults of Orphics and of Eleusis.[89] Orphic beliefs common with Indian doctrine were those of rebirth, the immortality and godlike character of the soul, the bondage of the soul in the body, and the possibility of its release by purification. It was a simple concept of union with the divine and of an immortality consequent upon that union. The Orphic was an ascetic who believed that the source of evil lay in the body with its appetites and passions and these had to be subdued before any progress could be made.

The mystic tradition found in these movements, as well as in the doctrines of Plato and Pythagoras, is certainly un-Hellenic.[90] The Greeks generally regarded the corporeal man as the real man and the soul merely as a sort of image. But in the Orphic philosophy the soul is eternal and indestructible whilst the body is transient, unclean, and contemptible. The Greeks also generally enjoyed life on earth, but the Orphics regarded it as a sort of imprisonment. An Orphic phrase, "the wheel of birth," may be a literal translation of the Sanskrit *janma-chakra*. Zeller, who upholds the independent tradition of Greek philosophy, concedes that the central idea of the Orphic cult of the liberation of the soul from the body is wholly foreign to Greek nature, and is of Indian origin, acquired by the Greeks through Persia.[91]

The Orphic movement began in the sixth century B.C. and lasted well into the Christian era, and, although it comprised only a small minority of religious devotees, it exercised a profound influence on Greek and Christian religious thought. A concept of sin and conscience, a dualistic view of the body as evil and of the soul as divine, entered into Greek thought; and the subjection of the flesh as a condition of release for the soul became one of the main purposes of religion.[92] Pythagoras probably got some of his concepts from them. The pantheism and asceticism of stoicism and the mysticism of the Neoplatonists can also be traced in part to Orphism, as can Plato's diametrically opposed body and soul. "Plato was not only the greatest original genius of Greek religious thought," writes Guthrie, "but also the one to whom the Orphic cycle of beliefs made the strongest appeal."[93]

31

The Eleusinian cult does not differ from the Orphic cult in theoretical background except that it places greater emphasis on the correctness of ritual. Although it offers supernatural hopes, it makes salvation dependent upon ritual purification rather than upon nobility of life. This cult also wielded extensive and enduring influence both on later Greek thought and Christianity. The great Greek poets, such as Sophocles (*ca.* 495–406 B.C.) and Euripides (*ca.* 480–408 B.C.), often referred to both cults in their writings.[94]

The mystic tradition finds its fullest expression in Plato (427–347 B.C.), a great admirer of the Pythagorean school. It is significant that Pythagoras is the only great Greek thinker whom Plato never criticizes. In fact, he speaks of him with the utmost reverence, and resembles him in spirit and aim as well as in substance.

Plato lived in a period when the great classical age was coming to an end in Greece. The fratricidal strife of the Peloponnesian War (431–404 B.C.) had weakened the Greek city states, and Plato wrote in a period of transition. He participated in politics for a while during his early life and wrote mostly on this subject. Behind his writing, however, there lay a profound philosophy and his thought has had an extensive, deep, and lasting influence on the European intellectual tradition.[95] Indeed, the influence of Platonic philosophy on world history can hardly be overestimated. At first it was disseminated through the Academy Plato had founded and later through a variety of philosophical systems, such as the Aristotelean, Jewish-Hellenistic, Neoplatonist, and Christian.

In Plato's philosophy the central issues concern man and his social, political, and religious conduct. But for his solutions he looks beyond appearance to reality. The material world is made up of "appearances," or phenomena, which are only shadows of reality. These phenomena may be perceived by the senses but are unreliable as sources of truth. The truth or truly real is something unchanging, eternal, and divine. It is the world of forms or ideas with its ultimate principle, the good. Plato's idea of the good is very close to the supreme God of the Upanishads. The prayer of the oldest Upanishad

> From the unreal lead me to the Real
> From Darkness to the Light
> From Death to Immortality[96]

is frequently reflected in Plato's *Dialogues*. The dominating thought in Plato is that ordinary man is not truly awake but is walking about like a sleep-walker in pursuit of phantoms. The things which we see are our shadows, and the realm of truth and reality lies beyond. The well-known analogy of the cave[97] in which he illustrates the position of those who are unaware of the truth, reminds us of the Hindu doctrine of maya, the "illusion of the senses." Plato likens the human race to men assembled in a cave, bound, with their backs to a burning fire, and seeing the shadows projected on the wall before them of the people passing behind them, they mistake them for real objects. He made a clear distinction between appearance and reality, as well as between the worlds of thought and sense.

Plato considered the soul to be indissoluble and immortal and the body a fetter to which men were chained "as an oyster to his shell." The body is a tomb of the soul, the source of evil from which the soul longs to be purified.[98] After death the soul passes into other organisms, higher or lower depending on the extent to which the knowledge of good and evil has been pursued by the soul in its previous incarnation. The soul ascends to the vision of divine reality, which Plato calls "The Good" and which is the highest of the ideas or forms, or God himself. To perceive this good is the loftiest goal of knowledge, and the pursuit of wisdom is to loosen the soul from being fastened or glued to the body. For Plato asceticism is one of the most effective ways of liberating the soul from its physical encumbrance, because each emotion of pleasure and pain is a nail riveting the soul to the body. This concept is somewhat alien to the Greek spirit.

To the ordinary Greeks the body counted for a good deal. They made physical education an important part of their training by placing considerable emphasis on games. The essential unity of human soul and divine spirit, the immortality of the human soul, its escape from the restless journey of reincarnation, contempt for the body and the phenomenality of the material world, are all ideas that clash headlong with Greek popular beliefs. Until the fifth century B.C. the word "soul" (psyche) did not have any flavour of puritanism or metaphysical status for a Greek, nor was the soul regarded as the reluctant prisoner of the body; it was the life or spirit of the body and was perfectly at home there. The lasting contribution of the new religious ideas was the suggestion of the divine origin of the soul which was continually at odds with the body. It was this innovation which Rohde has called "a drop of alien blood in the veins of the Greeks."[99] Where did this drop come from? Scholars have given a variety of answers, but most suggest Eastern origins in Asia Minor or beyond in India.

The essence of mysticism, that reality cannot be perceived by sense but can only be reached by inner experience, is present in some form or other in Greek thought from Pythagoras to Plato. In an analysis of Indian and Western religious thought, Radhakrishnan observes:

> The divine origin of the soul, its pre-existence, its fall into corporeality, its judgment after death, its expiatory wanderings through the bodies of animals or men according to its character, its final redemption from the cycle of rebirth and return to God, are common to the mystery cults of Plato and Empedocles. This tradition is something which Hellenic thought, untouched by alien speculation, was perhaps not very likely to have developed, and we have it in a striking form in Indian religion.[100]

Oriental influence on Plato, especially Persian, has been acknowledged by a host of European scholars, such as Jaegar, Reitzenstein, Bidez, and Cumont.[101] If Plato's thought could be influenced by outside ideas such as the Orphic-Pythagorean doctrines, it could be so influenced again. Indeed, there is good reason to believe that he had learned something of Persian religion from a Chaldaean pupil at his Academy and from his friend, Eudoxus, the astronomer, and an admirer of Zoroastrianism. There are also a significant number of scholars, such as Colebrooke, Royle, Pococke, William Jones, and Enfield, who support the theory of Indian influence on Plato's thought.[102]

In a relatively modern and comprehensive study, E. J. Urwick has analyzed Plato's thought and pointed out striking parallels, both in fundamental concepts and in details, between Plato's teachings and those of the vedantic philosophy in India. Urwick is not so much concerned with tracing the degree of Indian influence on Plato as in claiming that platonic doctrines are not easily understood without reference to Indian teaching. He does not claim that all of Plato's writings must be interpreted from a transcendental standpoint and are beyond ordinary rational criticism. But he does maintain that behind his works as a whole there is a background of faith which does not conform to any intellectual philosophy. It is in this sense that Plato's metaphysics, ethics, politics, and science are fundamentally religious rather than rational.

Urwick concentrates his attention on the *Republic*, which he regards as the comprehensive epitome of Plato's thinking, and suggests that Plato and the Indian sages were "occupied with the self-same search, inspired by the same faith, and drawn upwards by the same vision."[103] Urwick has argued at length with great detachment and a remarkable understanding of both the Indian and the Greek traditions of thought.

Impossible as it is to represent his view with justice without writing at some length, it must be observed that he illustrates parallelism not only in Indian and Greek thought, but in the words used to express them as well. He finds that Plato's

conceptions, arguments, and conclusions are in most cases identical with those of the Hindu Scriptures; the language in which he clothes them is often extraordinarily similar; several of his metaphors are repetitious of metaphors found in the older writings; and the psychological and ethical terms to which he gives a semi-technical use might serve excellently as translations of the corresponding technical terms in the Sanskrit.[104]

The three Indian *gunas* (qualities or elements—or the constituents of prakriti), *tamas, rajas,* and *sattva,* have exact equivalents in Plato's *epithumia, thumos,* and *logistikon,* which both constitute and explain the nature of the soul and the state. Epithumia, like tamas, represents blind desire with its character of ignorance; thumos, like rajas, is the element of power and passion; and logistikon, like sattva, is the rational quality which harmonizes the soul and illumines it. The Indian triad, however, is more ethical in its connotation than Plato's terminology.

Just as Manu described the Hindu *Varna* system as having been based upon the three principles in the individual soul, so did Plato divide his state into three classes—guardians, auxiliaries, and craftsmen —representing the three psychical elements.[105] Furthermore, the old Ionian society in Attica was divided into four tribes, associated in tradition with Ion and his four sons, and thus this system is said to have been of Asian origin, presumably Aryan. Aristotle mentions this system as the first and the earliest.[106] Both in Ionia and India, certainly there once existed a social state which was adapted to the fourfold way of life. But in the former the priests were put after the agriculturists. Plato, however, was inclined to place the priests first, as had been done in India.

Plato's conversion of the soul is identical with the *vairaga* of the Vedas; his contrast between ordinary knowledge and true wisdom corresponds to the contrast between *vidya* in the sense of knowledge and *adhyatmavidya* or direct perception of the spiritual universe; his *nous,* the higher arc of soul divine and immortal, is the *atman* or the spiritual consciousness of the vedantic doctrine; his *dikaiosune* or righteousness is the dharma of Indian philosophy, which appears as the crown and glory of each path, but with a very different meaning in each case. His doctrine of *Anamnesis* or recollection is identical with the doctrine of the origin of all true knowledge proclaimed by Vedantins, and his correlative theory of eternal ideas, designated as his greatest contribution to Western metaphysics, has an astonishingly close counterpart in the vedanta doctrine.[107]

The doctrine of reincarnation has been a common belief in numerous religions from the Hindus to the Druids, and the Greeks could have acquired it from any one of them.[108] But when it appears side by side with many other essential elements of Hindu teaching, as it does in the philosophies of Pythagoras and Plato, it is fair to assume that it was derived most directly from India.

It seems, however, somewhat surprising that in spite of such close parallelism there should be no specific acknowledgment of the awareness of Indian thought in Plato's writing. It is also strange that such detailed information should have been transmitted to Plato without the aid of any written works; for which, once again, there is no historical evidence, although Plato had hinted as early as the *Phaedo* at his willingness to learn from barbarians as well as Greeks. Whether he meant by the term barbarians, Indians, or only Persians, or both, cannot be deduced by such a vague reference. It is true that Plato was not habitually used to making acknowledgments, but he does acknowledge, even if vaguely, his Greek theological sources. Would he not have done the same for the Persian or the Indian sources, if he had really relied on them? Lack of reliance, however, does not indicate the absence of awareness. Indeed, awareness does not even imply acceptance. Even the rejection of an alien thought must leave behind some legacy of intellectual stimulation. If Plato were aware of Indian thought—and there is enough evidence to reason that he could have been providing his friend Eudoxus was—it would be abusing his intellectual integrity to suggest that he had not reflected upon it, and that he had rejected Indian ideas, banishing them from his mind, just because they were alien. Ancient scholars were much more intellectually receptive than they are generally credited with being. Greek and Indian thinkers were amongst the least prejudiced of them all. Their intellectual arrogance never followed the lines of national distinction. Their contempt was directed, if at all, not at the men of different nations or cultures, but at those who possessed no culture at all. An untutored Greek surely would have been held in much less regard by Plato than a barbaric scholar or a Vedantin from India. Could not the absence of definite acknowledgment of Indian thought on the part of Plato be explained, therefore, by the fact that his knowledge of it was indirect, fragmentary, and, at best, uncertain? Few scholars, even today when it is so fashionable to litter one's writing with prodigious footnotes, would specifically acknowledge their debt unless they were sure of their source and accuracy of understanding. Yet it is equally, or even more, difficult to accept the theory of a completely independent intellectual growth in the face of such striking similarities both in fundamental ideas and in details, particularly in view of the evidence of political and commercial contacts between the two peoples.

One enormous difficulty in appreciating commentaries on Plato and in resolving divergent opinions stems from the very nature of his writings and personality. Both are rich and complex, and an ingenious scholar can easily dig out extracts from Plato's *Dialogues* to suit his objective. In fact, many students have done so, and Plato has been revealed at various times "as a complete sceptic and as a complete mystic, as a pupil of Aquinas, as a Cambridge Platonist and as one of Nature's Balliol men, as an early Christian and as a very early Nazi."[109]

Whether Plato was influenced by Indian doctrines or not, his philosophy, as that of Greece in general, has its own distinctive personality. Whilst the sages of the Upanishads were principally concerned with moksha, release from the cycle of births, Plato mainly preached about the formation of an ideal state. He raised the concept of dualistic mysticism from a religious belief to scientific theory and made it a dominant principle of Western philosophy by transforming it into a philosophic system embracing the whole cosmos.[110] Again, there are many things in Plato's *Dialogues* which are alien to the Indian mind.

Just as Plato departed from his teacher, Socrates, so did his greatest pupil, Aristotle, depart from him, although Aristotle later kept a good deal more Platonism in his thinking than is often admitted. He shared Plato's concern for the goodness of personal and social life, and his ideal of certain and unchanging knowledge. But, although he did not completely reject transcendent realities, he did think that "the objects of philosophic knowledge must be found in and through the world our senses show us, and not in an altogether transcendent world of eternal realities knowable only by the disembodied reason."[111] Less attractive ideologically than Plato, although more orderly, Aristotle refused to believe that the world was anything but real. Yet he had accepted as a young pupil the whole of Plato's philosophy, including the doctrine of ideas, and the immortality and transmigration of the soul. If he later felt compelled to depart from it, he could not make a clear break. Plato's legacy never fully left him and his metaphysics fundamentally remained the same. "For all his reaction towards the standpoint of common sense and empirical fact," observes Cornford, "Aristotle could never cease to be a Platonist."[112] His idealism, however, takes a definite shape in his humanistic works, the *Ethics* and the *Politics,* and his best known contribution thus lies in the sphere of moral philosophy.

Although no one has suggested any contact or mutual influence between Aristotle and the famous Indian political thinker, Kautilya, Saletore, an Indian historian, has noted in a recent study sufficient parallels and contrasts between the systems of these two philosophers to suggest the value of a close comparative study of their ideas. Kautilya was a contemporary of Alexander, though younger in years than Aristotle. It was, in fact, only two years after the death of Aristotle in 322 B.C. that Kautilya became the prime minister of Chandragupta Maurya (320–296 B.C.).[113] Saletore suggests that in spite of divergences, there is a fundamental similarity between their views concerning the nature and functions of the state. For instance, both regard justice as the basis of the state, and self-sufficiency in matters of food, armed forces, and so on as its general function. Both share the view that the state must be concerned with virtue, and both stress the idea of happiness in relation to the state. Amongst the contrasts, Saletore points out that whilst Aristotle's state is to be happy in isolation, well administered with good laws and without conquests, Kautilya could not conceive of a happy state unless it had conquered its neighbouring states.[114]

During the period when Aristotle flourished, contact between India and Greece became much closer, almost direct. His prince-pupil, Alexander, had established Greek paramountcy in the northwestern part of India. And, if the premature death of Alexander in 323 B.C. had not been followed by that of Aristotle himself a year later, it is not unlikely that Aristotle would have visited India, meeting the scholars he so much wanted to, or else, would have received Indian scholars in Greece. Whatever may have been the political consequences of Alexander's death and the disintegration of the Macedonian Empire, the Indo-Greek cultural partnership did not receive as much impetus for expansion as it might otherwise have.

Amongst the factors that contributed to cultural intercourse between India and Greece, a major one must have been the affinity between Indian and Greek attitudes. Both were inquisitive peoples, firmly believing in reason. In India, one often finds the *guru* (teacher) asking the *sisya* (pupil) to be sceptical and always questioning; *sanka* (doubt) is the stepping-stone to spiritual knowledge. Never considered to be in conflict with the right kind of faith, honest doubt, in fact, was considered a corrective to the excesses of the latter. The divine value of an honest doubt is not to be denied. Whilst the guru is the guide in the quest and he alone can dispel the darkness of ignorance, the sisya must draw the guru out by his intellectual scepticism, exercised with the utmost respect for the guru. An Indian disciple is a blend of intellectual independence and extreme devotion for his teacher, attributing all of his accomplishments to the latter. Plato, in this respect, was a true Indian sisya, for he gave Socrates all the credit for his own wisdom. The Jnana Yoga of the *Bhagavad Gita* literally means the path of union through the knowledge and perception of God achieved by intellectual realization. The importance attached to reason in the *Gita* is very great. Krishna asks Arjuna to seek salvation in the wisdom of reason.[115]

The teachings of both the ancient Greeks and the Indians are often in a dialogue form, either between the "knowing guru" and the "doubting sisya" or between two equally matched intellectuals holding divergent views. Already in the early Upanishads, the dialectic method was used to explain empirical and transcendental truths. Knowledge about Brahman was imparted through a system of *samvada* (discussion)—distinct from *vivada* (dispute)—and the discussion progressed gradually from the empirical to the transcendental interpretation. The dialectic method of the Buddha's argument, in which he starts by putting himself in the mental position of the questioner gradually leading his opponents up to his conclusions, is the same as that of the Socratic dialogue.[116] The Greeks, like the Indians, were constantly seeking a religion and philosophy of life which would affect all their activities and produce equilibrium and a sense of harmony.

Geographically and climatically India is very different from Greece. Comprising as it does the land and islands scattered around the Aegean Sea, Greece has, unlike India, no real rivers that are navigable and suitable for ports, and no forests, although in ancient times it is said to have been more wooded than now. But in spite of these differences it is noteworthy that both nations chose mountains as the abode of their gods: the Greeks chose Olympus and the Indians the Himalayas.[117] By and large, neither the Greek Olympian gods, nor the Indian Himalayan deities are credited with having created the world. In fact, Zeus is "one of the very few gods with recognizable and undoubted Indo-Germanic names, Djeus, the well-attested sky and rain-god of the Aryan race."[118] Divinity in Greece, as in India, was cheap; in fact, in India, all beings are supposed to have the divine spark within them. There was a god for everything. Both in India and Greece, gods, such as Indra and Zeus, occasionally came down and practiced deceit, disguising themselves in order to obtain the affections of mortal women. Both races addressed their gods on equal terms. Unlike the Indian gods, however, the Greek gods were malicious, twisting human beings they did not like. And there was no higher god, as there was in India, to check their arbitrariness.

Both Indians and Greeks were fascinated by mathematics and metaphysics. Mathematics excited the Greeks most; Plato was an ardent student and over the door of his Academy was inscribed "a credit in Mathematics is required." Fond of geometry, the Greeks instinctively looked for unity and order in the universe.

Most Greeks were neither pleasure-seekers nor ascetics and accepted life as it came. In ancient India, although there were ascetics, the great majority of people led a healthy life of comfort and, in fact, revelled in physical pleasures without regarding them as evil or immoral. The common conception of ancient India as a country of forest retreats, hermitages, and saint-philosophers is grossly incorrect. Life in ancient India was divided between a highly organized and sophisticated temporal life on the one hand, and the simple and austere life of religious faith and spiritual advancement on the other. It was a materially advanced, socially enlightened, and psychologically uninhibited society in which the pleasures of the flesh received healthy attention.

Although at times saints may seem to be more than abundant in India, she has had her share of sceptics and heretics. Even the beliefs of Hinduism prescribed the fourfold goal of human life: *dharma, artha, kama,* and *moksa.* These are not easily translatable terms, but they generally mean righteousness, prosperity, enjoyment, and liberation. Hindu piety which aimed at moksa (integration of the individual with the universal resulting in the cessation of transmigration) through *jnana yoga* (meditation), *karma yoga* (selfless action), and *bhakti yoga* (devotion), allowed all three avenues to run through the four *ashramas,* or stages of ideal life of equal duration. The young aspirant began as a *brahmachari* pledged to a life of abstinence and study, at the end of which he entered the life of a *grihastha* (householder), raising a family and discharging his duties to society. Pursuit of wealth and pleasure was permitted within the bounds of moral law. After the expiry of the period of active life, the grihastha with his wife retired to a forest retreat to meditate on things of the spirit in quietude and live the life of a *vanaprastha.* Free from social bondage, and enriched by knowledge as well as experience, he could reflect more profitably on the problems of life and reality. It was only after this, a kind of refresher course, that the recluse could qualify to become a *sannayasin,* renouncing all worldly possessions, pleasures, and ties of family, nation, and community. A sannayasin had no caste, no religion, and no home. He led the life of a wandering preacher, feeling at home everywhere and exclusively devoted to the service of God. This was the peak of the ideal life and had enormous prestige with Hindus. The fact of its great prestige alone suggests that it was seldom attained. In fact, more often than not the whole scheme of life was not practiced as prescribed.

Whilst the Greek civilization, brilliant for its splendid achievements, was unhappily short-lived, the ancient Indian civilization has continued to grow and, in spite of its various vicissitudes, has retained its original spirit. This spirit is best described as the tendency, whilst finding joy and harmony in the present, to reflect, as the Greeks did, on the supremacy of an inner life.[119] Although ancient Greece is supposed to be the fountainhead of European civilization, it is India, because of her organic continuity in cultural development, which is perhaps closer in spirit and outlook to ancient Greece than the nations of present-day Europe. Without questioning the immense legacy of Greece to Western civilization, it must be observed that the modern Europeans are in many ways different from the ancient Greeks.

The most typical feature of the ancient Greek mind was a sense of the wholeness of things. For example, a typical Greek was several things at once, just as Solon was political and economic reformer, man of business, and poet. The *polis* itself was not a machine for governing, but something which touched almost the whole of life. In contrast, the modern mind divides, specializes, thinks in categories. This difference is reflected in the contrast between Greek and, for example, Gothic arts; between Greek tragedy and English classical drama. In contrast to the Greek heritage, Gothic architecture delights in a multiplicity of parts and Elizabethan tragedy in the whole complexity and richness of life. One could cut a scene from Shakespeare—and he has often been abridged—but not from a Greek play. The Greek hero was an attempt to combine the virtues which the later Western world divided between the knight and the churchman. The sharp distinction which is normally drawn between the physical and the spiritual world, the body and the soul, was foreign to the Greeks at least until the time of Socrates and Plato.[120] The Greeks had a sense of beauty, particularly in connection with the human form and its surroundings, which led to perfect order and balance, even an aesthetic mysticism, in their art and literature.

Yet it was this Greek insistence on the wholeness of things, on reason as much as form, on seeking boldly to explain all nature in nature's terms, that laid the foundations of science and of Western civilization. With all their love of philosophy, the Greeks examined nature not only affectionately but critically. For centuries they combined philosophy and science in one adventurous quest, and set out to explain the world in all its aspects. Although they were hardly scientists in the modern sense, for they lacked the methodical, accurate, and detailed power of observation and of relating observed facts to theory, it was their philosophy which gave birth to science. They considered wisdom not as a "mere theoretical explanation of the world but also a definite practical attitude towards life. In this respect Greek thought shows a striking similarity with the main trend of the Indian philosophical system."[121]

Amongst the Western peoples, the Greeks were the first to attempt to devise an articulate system of concepts concerning the universe and the unknown. They invented the word "philosophy," and their observations and reflections on such problems as the origin and nature of matter, of mind, of goodness, of truth, of reality, and on a vast variety of other themes, all constituted part of their philosophy. But they distinguished philosophy from mythology and also from the pursuit of knowledge for utilitarian ends. A philosopher was a disinterested seeker of knowledge, wanting to know for the sake of knowing.[122]

The origins of the cultural greatness of ancient Greece lie, significantly, in Asia Minor. Ancient Greece, it may be recalled, comprised two parts, European and Asian, divided or joined by the Aegean Sea. The Asian part of Greece, Ionia, was colonized, according to early tradition, by refugees from the European side of Greece or the Greek mainland, who were escaping from the Dorians and other tribes, and the general similarity between Ionians and Greeks was fostered and increased by the frequent and growing intercourse between them. Although they sprang from the same stock, they were not the same people. The European Greeks were a mixed race as were the Ionians; the intermixing elements in European Greece came from the north, and in Ionia they came from Asia. Later, a large Ionian immigration into Europe formed an important section of European Greece. Indeed, between these two peoples there had always existed bitter rivalry. It was these Ionians, the Graeco-Asians, who not only ushered in an era of intellectual revolution in Greece, but constituted its most progressive and enterprising section. Greek thought, rationalistic as well as empiricist, owes its inception to the Ionian school of philosophy comprising Thales, Anaximander, Anaximenes, Anaxagoras, Heraclitus, Pythagoras, and others. Herodotus, the father of history, and Hippocrates, the founder of scientific medicine, although both Dorians, wrote in Ionic. Homer, too, most likely came from Smyrna (Izmir), located in the northern part of the Asian west coast. Aesop, the Greek author of the *Fables,* came from Asia Minor. Even the humble origins of the classical drama, a real literary achievement on the part of Attica, are sought in Asia Minor and the Ionic element of the Athenian population. Delivering the Gifford lectures half a century ago, Sir William Ramsay observed: "The general tendency in modern estimates of Greek thought is to regard Athens as the 'Eye of Greece, Mother of Arts, and Eloquence,' whereas the true source of almost every branch of literature and science, and the earliest great names in almost every department, belong to the cities and colonies of the Old-Ionians."[123]

In tracing the origins of abstract ideas in remote antiquity, it must be admitted that one can hardly be certain or expect unanimity amongst scholars. Whilst scholars during the last century were generally receptive to the theory of Eastern influence on Greek thought, the modern tendency has been to deny or diminish it. Typical of this attitude is Nilsson who denies the origin of Greek dualism in the doctrine of Zoroaster concerning the contest between good and evil in the world but traces it in "Plato's doctrine of the antithesis between the perishable and changeful world of phenomena and the eternal and higher world of the Forms."[124] This may be an overstretched interpretation of Platonic thought but the theory of substantial Eastern influence, too, can be an exaggerated estimate. The communication of philosophy is in general exceedingly difficult; at best, only fragments of thought can be transmitted through layers of peoples, periods, or religions. No record has been found to suggest that the Greeks possessed any written Indian works or vice versa. Furthermore, even if they had had access to some, it is doubtful if they could have read them or had them translated. Whatever scholarly communication there was between the two peoples was oral.

There is no documentary evidence to prove Indian influence on Greek thought. The evidence which has survived is largely circumstantial and is far from being conclusive. In fact, it consists of deductive reasoning, not of certain proof; however, it is strongly suggestive and renders the theory of Indian influence on Greek thought well within the realm of probability. First, there is considerable evidence of close contact between India and Greece. Second, according to Greek tradition, Thales, Empedocles, and others travelled to Oriental countries to study philosophy.[125] Third, the mystical resemblances and parallels at times are too close and too frequent to be purely coincidental. Fourth, features which are attributed to an Indian origin are much in character with Indian thought and alien to Greek attitudes. Finally, these concepts and

43

ideas were definitely known to have existed in India long before they emerged in Greece. This is quite an impressive array of evidence, even if it is not conclusive. Hence, one may be inclined to agree with E. R. Dodds, who suggests an "Oriental background against which Greek culture arose, and from which it was never completely isolated save in the minds of classical scholars."[126] In any case it can hardly be denied, as Macdonnell puts it, that "there is at least the historical possibility of the Greeks having been influenced by Indian thought through Persia."[127]

Much of the uncertainty about the influence of India upon Greece is because most of the contemporary literature on the Greek side has been lost, and on the Indian side it was perhaps never preserved. The Indian lack of an historical sense is proverbial and may well be attributed to the attitude reflected generally in Indian philosophy that time is of secondary importance and that the historical context of philosophical ideas can have little relevance to their quality. The Indians possibly concentrated more on absorbing and reflecting upon foreign influences and ideas in order to fit them into their own mould and reproduce them in modified forms. They were not concerned with names or origins; only the content mattered.

Chapter II

CONTACT BY CONQUEST

UNTIL THE Greek cities of Ionia were captured by Cyrus in 546 B.C., the Greeks lived undisturbed by neighbouring powers. At first the Greek cities offered little resistance and Persian domination was mild. The Greeks were left to develop their own culture and institutions, except for what they voluntarily adopted from the Persians, whose king was looked upon by the distant Greeks as the supreme embodiment of earthly power and glory. Later, however, the conflict became more serious. A Persian punitive expedition against Athens and Eretria was defeated in 490 B.C. Athens became the champion of Greece, and fear of Persian power compelled the Greeks to organize into a nation. They were unable to achieve political unity, but, a cultural unity, with local divergences, was developed. Thus began the great classical age of Greece. It was the period of Socrates, Plato and Aristotle, Pericles, Herodotus, Sophocles and Euripides, the Athenian democracy, and unparalleled prosperity.

During the fourth century B.C., however, internal strife and conflict set in followed by chaos. Between 354 and 338 B.C. Philip of Macedonia completed his conquest of Greece and united it under his rule. After his death two years later, he was succeeded by his son, Alexander, who rose to become one of the most famous conquerors of history. Once Greece was stabilized and reorganized, it was inevitable that they should proceed against their traditional enemy, Persia. In 333 B.C. Alexander soundly defeated the Persian army led by the king himself. Two years later he finally demolished Persian power by defeating their army (which included Indian contingents under the command of the Bactrian and Arachosian satraps) at Gaugamela. Alexander's victory was an exceptional feat, for few empires in history have been as powerful as that of

Darius, and Alexander emerged as the unchallenged ruler of a vast empire stretching from Greece well into Iran. The meteoric rise of Alexander marked a new epoch in world history and introduced an era of Graeco-Macedonian ascendancy which, though short-lived, left an indelible mark on Western civilization. Few periods of European history have seen greater political changes than the century and a half that followed the emergence of Alexander's power.[1]

Determined to conquer the eastern part of the Persian Empire and India, Alexander with a Graeco-Persian army crossed the Hindu Kush, invaded the Punjab in 326 B.C. and defeated, at heavy cost to himself, its ruler Paurava (Porus). Alexander wanted to press eastward toward the Ganges Valley and Magadha, but his troops refused to advance, for they were too tired to face the powerful monarch of Magadha. They had heard rumours of a vast nation Prasioi (Sanskrit Prachya, eastern) ruled by a king named Xandrames with a mighty army. Alexander himself was anxious to keep going till he reached the sea which he believed, as did Aristotle, encircled the earth and communicated with the Caspian and the Persian Gulf. He was also anxious to see the Ganges and the area through which it flowed, because he had been told that the Ganges was much more impressive than the Indus, the sheer magnitude of which had already filled him with surprise, despite already having seen the Nile, the Euphrates, and the Tigris: "No country he had hitherto visited was so populous and well cultivated, or abounded in so many valuable productions of nature and of art, as that part of India through which he had led his army."[2] And when he was informed of the even greater riches and beauty of the country ahead, he was naturally eager to continue on.

The enforced withdrawal from India was a shock to Alexander from which he never recovered. He suffered a further serious blow when his most trusted commander drank himself to death. In the midsummer of 323 B.C. at the age of thirty-two, he fell ill; heavy drinking aggravated his illness and resulted in his death.[3] Although extreme alcoholism was rare in Greece, Alexander was much addicted to drinking and, according to Polycleitus of Larisa, was always accompanied to camp by flute players, both male and female, who drank with him until daybreak.

The military and political greatness of Alexander is beyond question, and even before his early death he had become a legendary figure. Had he lived longer, there is no telling what influences he might have brought to bear on world history.[4] He had become increasingly ambitious and dreamed of conquering the world. He considered himself a divine hero and employed his power ruthlessly to gain success and obedience. In a state of anger and drunkenness, he murdered his friend Clitus with his own hands, and his best general, Parmenion, was dispatched by hired assassins. In the pursuit of power he had lost personal peace.[5] If Alexander was vainglorious, and at times cruel and vengeful, it was probably the legacy of his superstitious, scheming, and hate-ridden mother, Olympias. Although only half-Greek himself, Alexander was full of the Greek spirit of inquiry, having been tutored by Aristotle. In spite of the fact that the Macedonians regarded themselves as Hellenes, the Greeks refused to treat them as a part of the Greek nation and, indeed, called them barbaroi. Aristotle himself was not, strictly speaking, a Greek, but came from Stagirus in Chalcidiee, east of Macedonia.

Alexander was frustrated in his plans to advance further east, to build great roads, and to set up sea communications, but he did succeed in establishing a Graeco-Asian empire. Although this empire did not survive his death, it left behind a bridge connecting the principal centres of ancient civilizations. Across this bridge began a traffic in ideas and culture, thus enriching the course of human history. His expedition to India, in terms of cultural intercourse between East and West, can only be compared to the discovery of a direct sea route to India by Vasco da Gama. Like da Gama, Alexander did not discover a new country, nor did he open up a forbidden land, but he did inaugurate a new process of cultural fusion, and greatly increased and enhanced the existing cultural relationships.[6]

Alexander founded about seventy new cities with the aim of creating a mixed Greek and Asian empire; of these Alexandria in Egypt was the greatest, later becoming an important centre of commerce and culture for the Hellenic and Roman worlds.[7] Aiming by marriage to bring the Asians and Greeks together in common military service and thus create a joint commonwealth, he took two Asian brides—Roxane, daughter of Oxyartes of Bactria, and Statira, daughter of Darius from Iran—and more than ten thousand of his troops including eighty of his principal associates, such as Hephaestion and Seleucus, married Asian women. Naturally, these Asian brides transmitted some of their culture to Greek families.[8]

On his Indian expedition Alexander was accompanied by a number of scholars whose purpose was to acquire knowledge about ideas and religions. His staff also surveyed the roads in the Asian areas, which led to increasing traffic both in commerce and culture. Many of Alexander's companions and officers were men of high attainments in literature and science. Some of them wrote their memoirs recording their impressions of India. Whilst some wildly exaggerated tales received currency due to inaccurate observation and imprecise writing, the Greeks learned much about Indian thought and lore. Aristotle, having retired to Athens, could not accompany Alexander but had sent in his stead his nephew Callisthenes of Othlynthus, a philosopher and historian.[9] Anaxarchus, a Democritean, and his pupil Pyrrhon (275 B.C.) who formed the Pyrrhonian school of sceptic thought before the time of the Stoics and Epicureans, are also said to have accompanied Alexander on his eastern campaign. Alexander's first halt beyond the Indus was at the great seat of Indian learning, Takshashila, a large and prosperous city from which he sent his ultimatum to Porus.

Anxious to acquaint himself with Indian thought, Alexander made contact with Indian sages and scholars. According to Arrian, he had very much wanted one of the Indian ascetics to join him, "since he so much admired their endurance." The Indian ascetics, however, rejected Alexander's overtures pointing out that his conquests meant nothing to them and that they had no need of anything he had. An old Indian sage, Dandamis, dismissed both offers of wealth and threats of death with equal contempt. After this invitation had been rejected, Alexander finally persuaded another Indian, Calanus, to accompany him.[10] So keen was Alexander to have Indian sages with him, that, having failed to persuade more than one to join him, he began capturing many of them charging that they had helped the enemies of the Macedonians.

Alexander's expedition appears to have made little impact on the contemporary Indian mind, for no mention of the event occurs in the literature of the period. It seems that India did not view the appearance of Greeks on her soil with undue worry or fascination. The Greeks were known to Indians under the Persian form of their name *Yavana* (also *Yona* and *Yonaka*) which was the Sanskrit form of the Persian *Yauna*, which in turn was a derivative of *Ionian*. The Indians did not even learn that the Greeks called themselves Hellenes, and India received nothing of the culture of their country from them.[11] Indeed, Alexander's expedition to India has been described by scholars, such as E. B. Havell, as nothing more than a mere raid, making little difference to India and leaving behind no impression on Indian civilization. For the conditions "which made Greek culture an inspiration for her Roman conquerors had no counterpart in India. The Indo-Aryans, unlike the Romans, had their classic literature, their epics and philosophy, before Athens was built . . . and at the closest contact of Hellenic and Indo-Aryan culture the latter had by far the greater vitality and creative power."[12] Havell points out, as does Coomaraswamy, that no Greek inscriptions have yet been discovered in India. Yet there are scholars, such as

Weber, Windisch, and Niese, who have claimed that Indian civilization was a by-product of the Macedonian civilization. Whilst it is understandable that there should have been a tendency in the West to exaggerate the influence of Greece on India, it is fantastic to assert that ". . . we can say that Greek culture in western Asia, caused by Alexander, led to the growth there of the idea of spiritual unity, as pointed out by Christianity, and that by inspiring Chandragupta to form the Maurya Empire Alexander caused the spread of Buddhism and perhaps the union of China under the first Han Dynasty."[13] In one statement all considerations of historical evidence, context, and chronology have been subordinated to wishful thinking.

The only permanent effect of Alexander's raid seems to have been the establishment of a number of Yavana settlements in the Uttarapatha.[14] Even the short-lived administration Alexander tried to establish was copied from the Achaemenian model not unfamiliar to India. Furthermore, negotiations between the Indians and Greeks were channelled through Persian interpreters. An indirect political result of Alexander's incursion, however, was the destruction of the petty states of the northwestern parts of India, thus paving the way for the rise of the Maurya Empire. Although on the whole the country was left undisturbed, one cannot deny that Hellenism had been brought to the very doorstep of India and that the centuries-old indirect and sporadic contact between Indians and Greeks was thereafter made direct, extensive, and close, leading to an intensification of the processes of cultural interaction. These processes were in no small measure sustained and advanced by the subsequent emergence of the Indo-Greek kingdoms in northwest India.

The death of Alexander in 323 B.C. precipitated the Greek world into an emergency for which no provision had been made, and serious repercussions followed. Alexander, who even in his own short life span had come to be known as the Great, was in fact a restless person who preferred conquest to the consolidation of power, and, possibly, even war for its own sake. He gave, in any case, less attention to the organization and administration of the territories he conquered than "to purely military problems and matters affecting the basis of his own personal power."[15] He gathered a vast empire stretching from the Aegean Sea to the Indus, but, if he had lived longer, it is said that he would not have known what to do with it, except conquer more. Disregard of organization, coupled with Alexander's extreme concentration of power in his own hands and the ruthless execution of his expansionist designs, left behind no powerful body to effectively fill the vacuum created by his death. Disaffection, dissensions, and distrust had already exacerbated relations between his commanders in his own lifetime. In the latter years of his life, Alexander had become far more despotic and tyrannical, even more so than he had been in the early days when he had destroyed the ancient city of Thebes to warn the Greeks not to repeat their efforts to throw off the Macedonian yoke. Having styled himself a god, he had come to lean heavily on the Persian aristocracy. Old friends were considered more dangerous than adversaries, and they were promptly eliminated on the slightest suspicion. His progress "through Asia was marked by court intrigues, political trials, and the liquidation of subversive elements. His last two years saw a reign of terror among his high officers and provincial governors, and his death may have anticipated a major rebellion in Greece."[16] The absence of a legal heir, or a recognized successor, or an outstanding soldier provided the opportunity for Alexander's generals to eliminate the remaining members of his family, including his posthumously born son, and to fight it out for power amongst themselves. Personal ambition dominated their devotion to the dynasty. It was fortunate for them that at this time no foreign power was strong enough or aggressive enough to take advantage of their conflict. A prolonged struggle for domination inevitably followed (ca. 322 to 281 B.C.), and Alexander's loosely knit empire split into a number of component parts, each ruled by a Macedonian dynast with all the pomp of monarchy. Of these, three kingdoms were most important: Syria including the eastern part of Alexander's kingdom, Egypt, and Macedonia. The largest and the richest was Syria, where Seleucus established his dynasty with his capital in the great city of Antioch; the Ptolemies, descendants of Ptolemy Lagus, ruled Egypt with Alexandria as their capital, and controlled the sea; and Macedonia, of which Greece was still a dependency, after much bloodshed and strife passed on to the descendants of Antigonus. Seleucus tried to expand into India in 306 B.C. but had to retreat before the forces of the powerful empire of Chandragupta Maurya. The Mauryan king probably married a Greek princess, acquired large parts of the former Greek-Asian kingdom, and received at his court a Greek envoy, Magasthenes, who has left behind invaluable information on the India of his day.

The founders of these dynasties were soldiers who were principally concerned with retaining their power and who were "generally expected to marry their sisters to keep the stock pure."[17] Macedonia was the original national monarchy, and the other two were in a way usurpers. Each of them, especially at the beginning of their rise to power, had ambitions of gaining absolute supremacy over the others and restoring

Alexander's empire. Consequently, these kingdoms fought themselves to exhaustion before the Romans, who had begun to emerge as a dominant international power during this period, established their sovereignty over them. Macedonia was the first to fall to Rome in 167 B.C., and it was followed by Egypt in 30 B.C. The Syrian kingdom, plagued by rebellions and succession troubles, pursued a precarious existence in varying degrees of independence between the Romans on the one side and the Parthians, the inheritors of the Achaemenian Empire, and the Mauryans on the other, until the rise of the Arab power in the seventh century. But for all practical purposes, the Syrian kingdom ceased to be important after about 160. B.C.

These powers are commonly called "Hellenistic," a term originally applied to non-Greeks who admired and copied Greek civilization, and the period of their independent existence (323 to 30 B.C.) is similarly designated.

Whatever the political consequences of these conflicts and strifes may have been, they certainly caused large-scale movements of peoples, as distinct from armies and hordes of nomads, from one area to the other. Thus, people living in distant regions came into closer contact with each other and accelerated the processes of cultural intercourse. Asia became a land of opportunity for Greeks. Greek soldiers were soon followed by Greek traders and settlers in large numbers to Egypt and the far corners of the former Persian Empire. Inevitably their Asian counterparts responded in a similar manner. Consequently, the following Hellenistic Age saw the development of thought, both scientific and philosophical, in which a variety of national traditions were freely mixed.

The Mauryan kings, especially the first three, maintained close diplomatic relations with the Hellenistic kingdoms. Syria, which was the home province of Seleucus and his successors, was in close diplomatic contact with the Mauryan Empire of India. Megasthenes lived at the court of Chandragupta, and Deimachos came on an ambassadorial mission to King Bindusara.[18] The Thirteenth Rock Edict of Asoka refers to five Greek rulers—Antiochus, Ptolemy, Antigonas, Magas, and Alexander—and there are indications that Asoka's missionary activities had reached Greek states. A. S. Altekar suggests that "Asoka's Buddhist missions were operating in western Asia, Egypt and Macedonia and the rise of the Essene sect, to which Jesus belonged, has been attributed to the influence of the Buddhist missions."[19] Asoka's Greek-Armenic inscription recently excavated at Kandahar would further strengthen the view that there was close contact between Mauryan India and the Hellenistic world, and that there must have been a well-established colony of Greek settlers or Greek-speaking people to justify inscriptions in Greek. Megasthenes tells us that there was a separate department at Pataliputra to look after foreigners, which would indicate the usual presence of a number of foreigners, such as envoys, tourists, and traders in the Mauryan Empire.

After the decline of the Mauryan Empire, Indo-Greek principalities emerged in the northwestern region of India, providing yet another bridge between India and the Hellenistic world. Alexander's Indian expedition, followed as it was by the rise of the Seleucid kingdom in western Asia, created settlements of Greeks—Indo-Greeks or Yavana— in the northwestern regions of India, although there is considerable evidence, both literary and numismatic, that even before Alexander's advent, Indo-Greek colonies had existed in this area. Whilst the Mauryans were powerful, the Indo-Greeks remained subdued. They were far removed from the centre of Mauryan power, and the influence of the Seleucids had always been at best precarious. The decline of the Mauryan power on the one hand, and the rise of the Parthians challenging the Seleucid supremacy on the other, made it possible for these Indo-Greeks to set up their own independent or semi-independent states. By about 250 B.C. they had disavowed the Seleucid Empire which at that time covered Persia and Syria, and forty years later their independence was recognized by Antiochus. In about 190 B.C. Demetrius I had established his authority in the Indus region and for the rest of the century the area remained under Indo-Greek rule. By this time, these peoples had become essentially Indian in religion and thought. Buddhism had been prevalent in India for well over two centuries, and its exponents had developed an exceptionally dynamic character, a highly sophisticated creed, and, under Asoka's inspiration, an unprecedented zeal for missionary work. The greatest of the Indo-Greek kings was Menander (Milinda) (*ca.* 180–160 B.C.), and he was converted to Buddhism by Nagasena.[20] The Mauryan domination of the Indo-Greeks for a long period possibly expedited their adaptation to Indian ways. Indeed, to describe the Indo-Greeks as Greek at all is somewhat misleading; they were even less Greek than modern Australians are English.

These Indo-Greek principalities which survived for some two centuries played a very significant role in both Hellenistic and Indian history. During this period many Greeks settled in India and gradually became integrated into Indian society. Trade between India and the Hellenistic world increased considerably, and was regarded as enormously important to Seleucia. The outburst of prosperity in that city between the years 175 and 150 B.C., and the heavy increase in the out-put of its mint, almost exactly coincides with the great period of Indo-Greek rule in India, from Demetrius to Menander. Enormous quantities of ivory and spices from India were exhibited by Antiochus IV in his triumph at Daphne in 166 B.C.[21] The Indo-Greek trade was so brisk that Parthia, through which the land trade passed, also grew wealthy.[22] The Greek word *drachma* passed into Indian languages through Prakrit *dramma* to *dam*.

Although no trace of Greek architecture has ever been found in either India or in the borderlands, India is indebted to Greece for improve-ments in coinage, astronomy, and sculpture.[23] Greek sculpture appealed to the Indian imagination, and the Gandhara school of sculpture, which flourished in the northwestern parts of India and Central Asia, is a fine example of this assimilation. The sculpture is usually described by the name of the ancient territory where it primarily flourished, Gandhara, the capital of which was Purusapura (modern Peshawar), although other finds of this art form in Khotan and in the vicinity of Kabul render this title somewhat misleading. Gandhara sculpture is also de-scribed as Graeco-Buddhist after the statues of the Buddha cast in Graeco-Roman style, although this sculpture really developed only after the Greek domination of this part of India was in the historical past, and its principal patrons were the Sakas and the Kushans who came from Central Asia.

The precise chronology of Gandhara sculpture is uncertain and the questions posed by its different styles are an art historian's delight. The school began to emerge in the middle of the first century B.C. after the decline of Greek power and before the rise of the Kushans. It reached its peak roughly between 50 and 200 A.D., coinciding with the reign of the great Kushan kings. None of the sculptures found is later than 400. The best period of Gandhara art was contemporaneous with the Flavian and Antonine periods in western Asia and Europe, and with the reliefs at Amaravati in South India, as well as with many sculptures at Mathura. The Gandhara school, however, stands apart from the main current of the evolution of Indian art. The technique used is, no doubt, basically Hellenic, but it is modified by Iranian, Scythian, and Indian traditions and trends, for the period during which Gandhara art evolved witnessed the advent not only of the Greeks, but of other foreigners who ruled these territories. About the beginning of the first century B.C., the Indo-Greeks had been overpowered by the Parthians and Sakas, a warlike people of Scythian extraction. They ruled over the northwestern parts of India until the end of the first century A.D. The new invaders, called Yueh-chih by the Chinese and Kushans by the Indians, first settled briefly in Bactria and in the valley of the Oxus; they then penetrated into the Indus territory. Their empire, which attained its peak under Kaniska, was on the crossroads of the Hellenistic, Persian, Chinese, and Indian cultures, and in terms of cultural intercourse it was one of the most productive periods in ancient history.[24]

The themes depicted by the Gandhara school are purely Indian and almost exclusively Buddhist, and the image of the Buddha in numerous guises dominates the compositions. A major explanation of this appears to be that in the area concerned Indian cultural and religious influences had been at work for a long time, and Gandhara art, devoted to Indian culture but employing an eclectic technique, really represents a stage in the process of assimilation of the Greeks in this region.[25] Once Indianization had commenced, the Greeks placed their artistic skill at the service of a foreign religion, an act unparalleled in Hellenistic history, and helped create for it a new art form. Whether the Greeks were Buddhist or not, they worked for the Buddhist world. "Nothing can be more eloquent of the Indianisation which was taking place and of the attitude of Greeks generally to Buddhism; it has been well said that the art of Gandhara was born of Buddhist piety utilising *Yavana* technique."[26] Coomaraswamy, however, does not view Gandhara art very kindly. He regards it as a phase of Roman provincial art mixed with Indian elements, which gives the impression of profound insincerity and only faintly expresses the spiritual energy of Buddhist thought.[27]

The Gandhara artist's portrayal of the Buddha in human form was in itself an innovation, probably Greek, and to render him in terms of the Graeco-Roman divine figures with their typical features, such as robed in a Roman toga with wavy hair, was wholly foreign to Indian notions. The Gandhara artist turned the Buddha into an Apollo, but the image bore all the iconographic marks and traits of the Indian tradition, all the canonical symbols traditionally belonging to him, and the reliefs depicting scenes from the Jatakas remained unchanged even in the minutest details. The Gandhara image of the Bodhisattva starving himself to death is perhaps "the most incongruous example of the mixture of India and Greece. Here a thoroughly un-Greek theme has been rendered in an equally un-Indian style."[28]

Whilst the influence of the Gandhara style did not penetrate India proper, it did continue to influence the art of Central Asia until the destruction of the Buddhist monasteries in the second half of the fifth century by the Ephthalites or White Huns, who, having overpowered Persia, advanced towards India. But, in its way, it deeply impressed

Indian and Asian cultures. The iconographical, rather than the aesthetic, representation of the Buddhas, Bodhisattvas, and scenes from the Buddha legend gripped the Indian imagination and thereafter it travelled with Buddhism to Indonesia, Burma, Cambodia, Thailand, Ceylon, and other Buddhist settlements. Through Central Asia it penetrated to China, Japan, and Tibet. Consequently, countless statues of the Buddha and the Bodhisattvas are found in the Buddhist world, many of which are excellent examples of the exquisite local artistic traditions.

Vedic religion did not provide for idol-worship and there were no temples in vedic India. In vedic times, conception of a personal deity, which is the indispensable psychological basis of iconographic representation, did not exist. Although Visnu, of whom many iconographical representations are found, is a vedic deity and his personality is vividly described in a few hymns, the earliest iconographical representations of him (dated 401) are two four-armed figures standing one on either side of the door guarding the Chandragupta cave at Udayagiri.[29] The teachers of the upanishadic period were only interested in liberation from the realm of name and form, and they did not ask artists to represent sages or saviours. They were so disinterested in external appearances that their strict monism was not conducive to iconographical reproduction. Early Buddhism was strongly opposed to the Buddha being represented by statues. In Indian art the Buddha's presence was indicated by the Bo-tree, or the wheel of law, or some other symbol. For centuries Indian Buddhists felt a repugnance to depicting the Buddha in human form. Even the great royal patron of Buddhism, Asoka, who experimented with various styles of representational art and pioneered the growth of lithic art in India, felt neither the need nor the compulsion to cast a single image of the Buddha or his disciples.[30] But Greek influence in Bactria was strong and statues of Apollo—like statues of the Bodhisattvas—began to appear, and these were soon followed by images of the Buddha himself. This, in turn, gave tremendous impetus to image-worship amongst the Hindus, which has come to form such a dominant feature of popular Hinduism that images are to Hindu worshippers what diagrams are to geometricians.

Opinion, however, is divided as to whether image-worship was practiced by the Indians before Alexander's campaign or not. It should be noted that in the popular religions of the early Indians a strong anthropomorphic undercurrent was present. It remained subdued under the dominance of the vedic religion, but later it received impetus under the theistic devotional cults. There is epigraphic data revealing Vaisnava shrines in the various parts of India during the pre-Christian and early Christian periods, and it may be that very early images, of which there is definite evidence, have been lost because of their perishable materials. Finally, this innate anthropomorphism and iconolatry asserted itself with vigour and found expression in images of the divinities or saviours, especially the Buddha, during the period of Mathura art, which, although contemporary with if not anterior to the Gandhara school, had its own independent and unbroken sequence of development. And it has been argued that the Gandhara Buddhas had little or no influence, and that all the later Buddha statues were derived from the purely Indian art of Mathura.

The isolation of India has never been absolute, and Mathura, being the converging point of ancient routes from all directions, was one of the principal areas visited by travellers. Whilst Mathura art has a long and glorious tradition of continuous and autonomous evolution occupying a very important place in the history of Indian art, no one has dated the Mathura Buddhas before the Christian era, and they are usually assigned to the second century. Thus, in chronological order the Gandhara Buddha is older than the Mathura Buddha. When this order of priority is considered together with the knowledge that the Mathura artists were aware of the contemporary Gandhara tradition, the possibility of Mathura having borrowed the idea of Buddha statues from Gandhara becomes very strong. Features alien to the Indian tradition and in conformity with that of Gandhara, such as drapery hanging in curved folds from the figures of the Buddha and certain motifs such as the woman and the acanthus, appeared on some of the Mathura figures of the later period.[31] It appears that Mathura art developed its own tradition of iconographical representation, but the Gandhara influence accelerated this process and gave it a new dimension by introducing the expression of the divine image in human form. Between them, these two schools introduced the figures of the Buddha and Bodhisattvas into Buddhist art. In this enterprise the Gandhara school may well have been the dominant partner, for it is extremely unlikely that without its inspiration, direction, and competition the Mathura school could have, on its own, given rise to mass worship of images. Although this cult had existed in some parts of India before the advent of the Greeks, it remained on the whole insignificant and fragmentary until the Greeks gave it impetus.

The Greek influence on Indian coins and gems is undoubted. The datable history of Indian coinage begins in 600 B.C. with silver and copper punch-marked coins.[32] These coins were primitive in conception, irregular in shape, and crude in execution, and whilst important to historians, their aesthetic value is negligible. With the penetration of Hellenistic, Roman, and Parthian influences through the Indo-Greeks, the form and character of Indian coins changed radically. Artistically interesting, the chaste and elegant workmanship of the early coins from the second century B.C. to the first century A.D. clearly reveals the Hellenistic tradition. With the passage of time, the Hellenistic influence weakened and Indian characteristics began to assert themselves. However, the Indians learned from the Greeks the art of embossing both sides of their coins.

A large number and variety of engraved gems have been found all over northwest India, and these are undoubtedly Hellenistic in conception and workmanship. The motifs and themes employed are Greek and the gems often bear legends in Greek and early Brahmi or Kharoshthi scripts. In the first and second centuries the Greek inspiration gave way to the Roman.

Yavana bodyguards, engineers, and girls were in demand in India. Even in the extreme southern Tamil country, the Greeks were sought after. In the very early Tamil literature of the Sangam period (first three centuries), clear references are found to Yavana traders, soldiers, palace guards, night-watchmen of the streets, and lamps of Yavana workmanship. Kalidasa (fifth century) in one of his plays represents the king as being accompanied by a body of Yavana women. These girls had already appeared much earlier in the plays of Bhasa. This is confirmed by other evidence, including Greek. Amongst the articles which Indian kings would buy, as listed in the *Periplus,* occurs "good looking virgins for concubines" and it appears to have been a standing order. Poseidonius also testifies to this traffic in girls.

Greek influence on the Indian theatre has also been suggested, for the first curtain is called *Yavanika* (the Greek curtain). It is also claimed that the Indians borrowed from Greek drama their ideas of the screen, the parasite, and the clown, but there is little evidence to support the assertion that the Greek tragedies and Homer's works were known in early India, and Yavanika could not have been borrowed from the Greek stage for there the curtain was not used. Although Greek dramas were not acted against a curtain, Roman, and possibly Greek, mimes were, and Yavanika may suggest the influence of Greek mime on Indian drama. A more likely origin of this word would appear in a Prakrit modification of the Sanskrit word *Yamanika* from the root yam, meaning "to bind," "to fix," used for a curtain with ropes to fix it.[33]

By the time Greek influence had emerged in India, Hindu drama had already assumed a distinctive personality with a highly evolved form. Indeed, the art of the drama seems to have been well established in India from the earliest times. Apart from the tradition of the divine origin of Sanskrit drama, there is in the *Rig Veda* a remarkable series of dialogue-hymns with a dramatic element, such as the famous "Pururavas and Urvasi" hymn.[34] The grammarian Panini refers to acting in the fifth century B.C., and in the fourth, Kautilya describes theatrical companies. In the art of puppet plays, which certainly appears to have developed a couple of centuries before Christ and possibly even earlier, a point of culmination can be seen in the development of drama, as well as an impetus for it. At the Sitabenga and Jogimara Caves in the Ramgarh Hills in Bihar, inscriptions can be found dating from the third century B.C. which suggest the existence of a developed dramatic art, and at Sitabenga Cave, even a sort of crude stage has been excavated in the rock. The earliest available specimens of literary drama are found, however, in the fragments of some Buddhist dramas of Asvaghosa, the court poet of Kaniska, and the earliest available dramatic works are the thirteen plays ascribed to Bhasa (*ca.* 200–300).

Basic differences in approach and style between Indian and Greek drama are also revealed upon close scrutiny. It was during the fifth century B.C. that drama emerged in Greece as a highly developed art form. Furthermore, whilst the Hindu theatre was intimate and restricted to a limited audience of scarcely four hundred spectators, the Greek amphitheatre could seat twenty thousand. Greek drama was not divided into acts, but the Sanskrit *natakas* (plays) had definite divisions ranging from four to ten acts. The unities so rigidly adhered to by the Greeks were unknown to Sanskrit dramatists either in theory or practice. For example, the unities of classical drama were not strictly observed by Sanskrit dramatists, although each act was usually limited to "one course of the sun" and each play to one year, but unity of place was not regarded as a necessity, and subsidiary plots entwined the main trunk of Sanskrit plays. A Hindu play was composed expressly to mark a certain occasion, such as a coronation, triumphal procession, religious festival, or marriage, and was generally not revived after the occasion had passed. The Greek concepts of tragedy and early Attic comedy, as in Aristophanes, were totally alien to the spirit of Indian drama. The latter in general is more romantic, mythological, and metaphysical than the Greek. However, Indians must have had opportunities to watch Greek plays, as a scene from *Antigone* appears on a fragment of a locally manufactured vase found near Peshawar.

A few common Greek words, such as the words for pen, ink, book, and camel, found their way into Sanskrit, and a few Sanskrit words reached the West, but on the whole there was surprisingly little exchange of language.

It is also somewhat surprising that India, who had borrowed freely from Persia and had never been averse to foreign ideas because of the all-inclusive nature of her thought, should have refrained from profiting by Greek art. A possible explanation may be found in the different concepts of art and beauty held by the Greeks and Indians. The Greeks loved beauty for its own sake and found not only joy but truth in it, whereas the ancient Indians, whilst loving beauty, sought some deeper significance in their work, some vision of the inner truth as they saw it. Whilst the Greeks had a passion for form, the Indians were obsessed by the formless. Indian art was much too firmly embedded in Indian religious thought and its metaphysical basis to find an affinity with Greek art. Another reason for India's failure to profit from Greek art may have been the inability of the Indo-Greeks to transmit Greek influence to India, for they were only remotely in contact with Hellenic culture and, in fact, became Indianized themselves during the period of Mauryan domination. Furthermore, the Greeks came to India not with the zeal of missionaries but on military campaigns and remained to carry on commerce.

Discussing in some detail this interaction between Greek and Indian civilizations during the Indo-Greek period, W. W. Tarn, a great admirer of Greek civilization and of its intrinsic vitality, observes that although two peoples living side by side for a long time on good terms must be mutually influenced, India adopted little of Greek culture. And whatever little she did adopt, did not last. In explanation he suggests that "Indian civilization was strong enough to hold its own against Greek civilization, but, except in the religious sphere, was seemingly not strong enough to influence it as Babylonia did; nevertheless we may find reason for thinking that in certain respects India was the dominant partner."[35] Indians living in Greek principalities as Greek citizens did not even take Greek names, as was common enough amongst Asian people at the time. They kept their own customs and culture. Greek rule was eventually overthrown everywhere and by the middle of the first century nothing of them was left. Tarn says that ". . . except for Buddha-statues, the history of India would in all essentials have been precisely what it has been had Greeks never existed."[36]

As the era of classical antiquity and Greek exclusiveness declined, an enervated Greek culture was accorded rejuvenating influences by Eastern cultures. The limited world of the city-state was transformed into large-scale government, the Greek polis was replaced by the world-state, and a new conception of world power was born. The old distinctions between the Greeks and the barbarians were replaced by world culture, and Hellenism, under the impact of Asian culture, became elastic and cosmopolitan. The repercussions of this change were almost all-embracing. Social and economic life had to be remodelled, political institutions and religious beliefs had to be recast, and experiments had to be made with new ideas. Concepts of a universal state, universal monarchy, universal law, and universal religions and philosophies began to spread. During this period there developed the conception of an emperor's divinity and absolute monarchy which played an outstanding part in European thought and political life. It enshrined Julius Caesar in a state cult as "Divus Julius"; it inspired Augustus (the assumption of this name, which has strong associations with divinity, by Octavian is in itself significant); it helped the Papacy and the Holy Roman Empire during the early mediaeval period; and it later led to the extravagant claims of the Tudor and Stuart kings in England, the Bourbons in France, and the Czars in Russia. The theory originated in an age in which religion, theology, and politics were inextricably mixed, and it came to be articulated in mediaeval times during the conflict between Pope and Emperor to assert the claims of sovereignty of the latter, and to find a positive theoretical support for the rejection of papal claims to spiritual, as well as temporal, overlordship.

It is commonly suggested that Persia provided Alexander with the inspiration for this theory of the divine right of kings, for after his remarkable military successes he pronounced himself a god. It is impossible, however, to obtain unanimity on a question which cuts deeply into national pride, but the dispute can be narrowed. The widespread cult of the divine rulers, which progressively developed into a dominant force in Europe, was entirely an internal growth evolved in a Western environment. Alexander had realized it, if at all, only briefly and almost in passing, in western Asia and the Levant. Taylor's contention that the monarchy which Alexander established was itself a combination of Greek and Macedonian traditions and the Persian conception of the king as an absolute power, the ideal representative of his people in every secular and religious office, is historically invalid.[37] Tarn, for example, strongly disputed Taylor's assertion that the Persians worshipped their kings and that their practice had influenced Alexander in his claim to divinity.[38] Consequently, Taylor partly revised his earlier opinion but maintained that the Persians had a form of ruler-worship, which must be considered in discussing the Hellenistic ruler cult, thus presumably conceding that the evidence of direct Persian influence on Alexander's deification is negligible.

The Achaemenian kings were not gods and did not claim divine rights. In Egypt there existed a cult according the king a divine status and authority. But the influence of Egypt on later Greek king-worship, and in the transformation of the Macedonian monarchy into a Ptolemaic god-kingship, seems to have been comparatively unimportant.[39] If the Persians prostrated themselves before their king, it was a perfectly respectable form of court etiquette which in no way implied worship, and which has parallels in many other countries, such as kowtowing in China. Kings, modern or ancient, have always demanded and received from their subjects devoted respect far above that which is normally given to an elected head of state. King-worship is in reality nothing more than a form of flattery. Before, during, and after the Hellenistic age, and even in modern times, king-worship has always been at best deference, and ordinarily hypocritical and insincere—a political gimmick. Seldom have people anywhere seriously believed in the divinity of kings, although they may have acknowledged it in helpless dependence on his power, from fear of punishment, in the expectation of reward, or simply as a trivial irrelevancy, immaterial one way or the other. It is also doubtful whether even the kings, who never tired of claiming it, seriously believed in it beyond its efficacy as a political device to command blind obedience. Hence, to regard the Persian custom of prostration as indicative of king-worship is erroneous. It is also true that Macedonians and Greeks found this custom repugnant. In fact, Callisthenes, who had done more than anyone else to spread Alexander's fame through his writings, who had even extravagantly invented the story that the oracle of Apollo at Dityma had broken its long silence to endorse the oracle of Ammon that Alexander was the son of Zeus, and who had supported Alexander in his claims to divinity, refused to submit himself to this Persian custom even at the risk of Alexander's displeasure, thus courting certain execution which followed soon after on a charge of alleged conspiracy.

If in Persia and Egypt there was some evidence that men had come to believe in a single universal society under the authority of a powerful king who could receive undivided obedience from his subjects, it could hardly be taken as constituting indisputable proof of prevalent king-worship. In return the king received devotion, loyalty, and gratitude. To receive adoration is not to be a divine incarnation. In Greece too, long before Alexander, some Greek rulers had claimed divinity and had been worshipped during their lifetimes, although this may have been a political measure rather than an official cult.[40] The Hellenistic historian, Duris of Samos, tells us that the Spartan leader Lysander, the first man to gain widespread power in the Hellenic world, was also the first man to be worshipped, and that he would very likely be a man "to whom Alexander might naturally look back as a forerunner of his power in the Greek world."[41] The tyrant Heraclea (363–352 B.C.), intoxicated with power and wealth, called himself the son of Zeus and thought of himself as Zeus in person. He used his divine pretensions deliberately to strengthen his tyrannical rule.

Of course, in contrast to the Semites, who markedly distinguished between God and man, the Greeks conceived gods in human form and elevated men to the rank of gods. It was common practice in Greece to promote founders of cities to the rank of hero and to offer them "hero-worship" after their death, although in later times the term "hero" came to be used for men whom death had removed from the envy and rivalry of their companions. But there were some men—such as Dion, given heroic honours in 356 B.C. by the Syracusans—who were accorded this status in their lifetime. Homer, certainly, uses the Greek word *heros* freely for his heroes while they were still alive.[42] Hero-worship— for example the cult of Hercules and of Ammon—was quite common in Greece, and the distance between hero-worship and king-worship surely must be a short one.

It is true, however, that the worship of kings by Greek cities was somewhat different from the official cults instituted by the kings themselves. In Persia too there was no such official cult at the time. The oracle of Ammon, which had pronounced Alexander to be the son of Zeus, was well known in the Greek world for its incorruptibility, and Alexander, like all Greeks, believed in it and insisted on its validity. Lysander sought its aid unsuccessfully in his efforts to give himself divinity. Alexander's father, Philip, was deified by some of his followers, and Plato was similarly honoured by his scholars. Aristotle, Alexander's tutor, argued in a famous passage of the *Politics*, presumably with Alexander in mind, that there might exist in a state an individual so pre-eminent in political insight and virtue that he should be followed as "a god among men" and for whom there was no law, because it would be wrong to treat a person, so unequalled in virtue and political capacity, as an equal. He should not be a member of the state at all; he should be above it. So Alexander's deification, even if it had received any impetus from the Egyptian or Persian examples, had deeper roots in Greek concept and practice. Sir Ernest Barker put it clearly that "However foreign it may seem to the Greek idea of the state as a free association of citizens, the conception of the deified ruler was none the less rooted in Greek habits of thought; and the actual deification of Alexander may be traced among the Ionian Greeks in the beginning of his campaign, before he touched the soil of Egypt or of Persia."[43] In addition to Egypt, Greece also began and perpetuated the deification of rulers. For a full half-century after Alexander's death no ruler claimed divinity for himself, but, during this interval, "many Greek communities voted of their own accord divine honours (temples, images, altars, priests, processions, games, sacrifices) to their rulers."[44] There was nothing oriental in this king-worship, it was a purely Greek political phenomenon. To the common man the power of a king was self-evident whilst that of a god had to be accepted on trust.

In a recent reassessment of Alexander, E. Badian has attempted to explain Alexander's claims to divinity in terms of his growing insanity. He suggests that the severe psychological impact on him caused by his failures in India led Alexander to discover the insecurity of power, which all his scheming could not overcome, and this in turn drove him to seek refuge in the greater exercise of power, and finally to seek and believe in his own divinity. His success in his purges and in the Susa marriages and his dealings with the mutineers only increased the resulting instability and led him to ask for absolute authority, like that of a god dispensing the fate of mortals.

He had always liked and encouraged the story that he was the son of the god Ammon (a Libyan god whom the Greeks identified with Zeus and whose oracle he had visited). The myth had been useful to inspire loyalty, particularly in Greeks, whose religion had a place for such things. But he now actually began to believe in his own divinity. About the middle of 324, he sent envoys to Greece demanding that he should be worshipped as a god. There are many anecdotes about the reluctance with which the Greeks complied. . . . Nor had he anything to gain by deification of this enforced sort: divine status would give him no significant political rights in a Greek city state, and men's opinion of him would not change for the better. There is no escape from the conclusion that he wanted deification purely for its own sake, for psychological and not for political reasons. As for the Greeks, they had to obey.[45]

Considering that stories were afloat even during his own lifetime which cast doubt on his paternity—that Alexander was not the son of Philip but the begotten son of a god—it would seem logical that Alexander should have been anxious to establish his divinity and establish his kinship with Zeus-Ammon. Tarn, however, who took a view of Alexander that was somewhat romantically coloured, says that Alexander never called himself son of Ammon, resented being called so, and that he similarly never called himself son of Zeus, although he allowed others to call him so. He became god of his empire for entirely political reasons.[46] Whether he was being vainglorious or Machiavellian would make little difference to the main argument that Alexander introduced the element of divinity into kingship.

An historical reason, which has not often been emphasized, for the currency of the cult of king-worship may have been that of the three kingdoms which acceded to Alexander's heritage only Macedonia had a legal right to this heritage. The Seleucids and Ptolemies were illegal intruders or usurpers. They naturally desired some basis for their power other than force, and this they found in making themselves divine rulers. The Seleucids became gods after death—although later divine status was bestowed upon living Seleucids as it was upon the Roman Emperors—but the Ptolemies, following the practice of the Pharaohs, became gods during their lifetime.

Besides the new concepts of kingship and kingdoms, the Hellenistic age saw the development of the universal philosophies of Stoicism and Epicureanism, the two most profound systems of antiquity to emerge after Aristotle's death. The popularity of mystery cults, such as the Eleusinian and the Orphic, also increased. The chief feature of this period was that as philosophy and science parted ways, philosophy and religion united. The Hellenistic age, especially the period between the foundation of the Lyceum about 325 B.C. and the end of the third century, saw the transformation of Greek science from an untidy heap of scattered observations into systematic disciplines. In some branches, such as mathematics and astronomy, it reached a level that was not attained again until the sixteenth century. Giving expression to the newly emerged world consciousness in Greece, the two chief philosophical systems of the period—the Stoic and the Epicurean—revived the old principles of Ionian monotheism.

As an inevitable consequence of Alexander's conquest, much of Greek thought was rendered obsolete and useless, especially those theories of morals and of social organization which were the most typically classical and which taught that happiness in the highest sense was possible for members of limited and self-governing societies. Now the very structure and nature of society underwent change; the sovereign city-state ceased to exist. With the expanding state, the horizons of the mind also widened. For the first time in Greek history, Greek institutions stood exposed to rational criticism and traditional ways of life were subjected to the pressures of cosmopolitan culture. Also for the first time in Greek history, "it mattered little where a man had been born or what his ancestry was: of the men who dominated Athenian intellectual life in this age, Aristotle and Theophrastus, Zeno, Cleanthes, and Chrysippus were all of them foreigners; only Epicurus was of Athenian stock, though by birth a colonial."[47]

For a time Greek philosophy kept its concern for the ordering of human life in accordance with the earlier concept, but it became increasingly interested in the individual rather than the community. The process of change was initiated by the nihilistic pronouncements of Pyrrhon (ca. 360–270 B.C.) who, together with Anaxarchus, had accompanied Alexander to India. He questioned the validity of existing presuppositions; for him the only certainty was that of no certainty at all. He declared that definite knowledge of any subject was impossible and that the principal aim of man was to lead a virtuous life. He wrote no works, except a poem addressed to Alexander, but his philosophical system was recorded by his pupil, Timon of Philius. Although his school did not expand greatly, the Pyrrhonian scepticism may be regarded as a forerunner of the Stoic and Epicurean schools. Only a short time later the Stoic philosophy was introduced into Athens by Zeno of Citium (335–263 B.C.), who established a complete system of philosophy encompassing logic, epistemology, physics, and ethics. Stoicism, which taught a natural unity of men amongst themselves, a moral and spiritual community with all peoples and gods, and that happiness was the result of freedom from physical appetites and of obedience to the will of the gods, was the most inspiring of Hellenistic philosophies and by far the most dominant. Its teachings exerted a greater influence on the lives of men and the development of states than either the Academy or the Lyceum.[48]

Zeno came to Athens from Cyprus but he was a Phoenician. The population of his native city, where a number of Asian relics have been excavated, included settlers from Phoenicia and his mother tongue was Phoenician. In the beginning his followers were known as Zenonians but they later came to be known as Stoics because he used to discourse promenading up and down the colonnade or porch (stoa) of Peisianax. Not only was he a Phoenician but three of his immediate successors— Heraclides, Antipater, and Zeno of Tarsus—also came from Phoenicia, having been born at Tarsus, on the coast of Cilicia, which had become a kind of outpost of Stoicism. Considering that all of them came from the west Asian territory, which at the time was a principal meeting-ground between Asia and Greece, it is not unreasonable to assume that some sections of Zeno's philosophy, particularly those which sharply depart from classical Greek thought and resemble Indian doctrines, may have been influenced by the latter. Some scholars, however, in an effort to show historical and natural continuity have suggested that Stoicism was an attempt to simplify Aristotle's views on metaphysics, psychology, and ethics. It is unnecessary to stretch one's imagination in accepting the view which suggests historical continuity, because alien ideas are seldom imported wholesale and seldom supplant existing systems of thought in a well-developed society. Alien ideas certainly cannot alter the thinking processes of those philosophers who have received most of their training in native traditions and who continue to work in their native land. But to deny an Asian impetus to Zeno's philosophy altogether would be untenable. Whilst he carried over from Aristotle an interest in the physical world, it cannot be denied that Zeno introduced a new moral tone and religious earnestness into his philosophy. Thus, the whole system was transformed, and it is difficult to justify assertions that the end product is a natural continuation of Aristotelean thought.

It must be recalled that during this period, the post-classical age, the individual came to use tradition, instead of being used by it. Indeed, "it is in this age that the Greek pride in human reason attains its most confident expression."[49] Although this process began with Aristotle, it was first sharply defined by Zeno. He and the early Stoics came from Asia and "though they might inherit Greek physics and metaphysics, they were free from the prepossessions and prejudices of Greek political thought."[50] A possible channel of contact the Stoics had with Indian thought lay in the Cynic school. The Cynic philosophy of Hellenistic times sought virtue and moral freedom in liberation from desire and rejected worldly goods. It may very well have been influenced by Buddhism, since Buddhism at this time was a vigorous proselytizing religion, and Asoka had sent embassies, possibly including some missionaries, to Ptolemy of Egypt, Antiochus of Syria, and others, just before 250 B.C. "with healing herbs and yet more healing doctrines." Stoics were certainly influenced by the Cynic doctrines, and it is therefore quite likely that the *Koinos nomos* of the Stoics was influenced by the Buddhist universal "law" of karma.

The Stoics were not concerned with the idea of community in a limited, self-governing city-state but visualized a universal society, a brotherhood of man. Thus, they introduced into Western thought an ethic of universal brotherhood based on a direct altruistic relationship between man and man, overlooking the differences of race or colour.

In Stoic philosophy the whole universe is conceived of as only one substance, one *Physis*, in various states, and that one substance is reason, which is, in turn, God. Reason, God, nature, Zeus, fate, world-soul, and providence are all simply different names for the same reality. Everything is a derivative of God and therefore is God. God is reason, pure and whole, and man has a fragment of divine reason in him. This fragment is the ruling principle which determines his way of life. Absolute conformity and submission to the divine reason, which permeates the universe, is virtue, and virtue is the only thing that matters. The law of the universe is also the law of our own nature, and we can only realize ourselves truly by conforming to the purpose of God, whose service is perfect freedom. This links man with God and with his fellow man. From this general philosophical principle flowed all the Stoic concepts: a world-state, the brotherhood and equality of human beings, and an all-pervading natural law based on the reason and instinct of man in harmony with the logos, the spirit of universe, a concept which strongly influenced the Roman legal system.[51] The power of this belief comes out clearly in the prayer of the Stoic Emperor of Rome, Marcus Aurelius, to the divine universe:

Everything suits me that suits you well, O Universe: nothing in your good time is too early or too late for me: everything is fruit for me which your seasons bring, O Nature: from you all things, in you are all things, to you are all things. The poet says 'Dear city of Cecrops': will you not say 'Dear city of God'?[52]

The founders of Roman or later Stoicism were possibly Panaitios and his pupil, Posidonius of Apamea in Syria (*ca.* 135–51 B.C.).[53] The latter, after travelling a good deal, settled at Rhodes where in 78 B.C. Cicero, amongst others, studied under him and reproduced many of the ideas of his teacher in his Latin philosophical treatises. Virgil also drew from his ideas. Posidonius, a man of immense learning, was not an original thinker but a brilliant exponent of a blend of Stoicism and Platonism, and of the religious doctrines of the East. He epitomized the Hellenistic culture and his writings represented with unique completeness the general mind of the Greek world at the dawn of the Christian era.[54] The main object of his philosophy was "to make men at home in the Universe," which was one great city of gods and men alike, with fiery ether above and the world of men below, in which the human soul sought to rejoin its own element by soaring upwards after death. In this system room could be found for the deification of rulers which was shown to have been common in the Hellenistic world. For if the dead moved upwards or went home to God, it was natural to think of them as being deified. Following this, even the great living might be regarded as sent by "Providence" or "the eternal and immortal Nature of the Universe," to be saviours of the community of the human race.[55]

It was during the latter period of the Roman Republic that Stoicism developed as a powerful force, and it has often been said that it gave a soul to the young emerging Roman Empire. It was certainly the greatest system of organized thought in the Roman world, and its influence on Roman jurisprudence was considerable. It influenced, amongst others, Seneca, the tutor of Nero; Epictetus; Marcus Aurelius; and Aratus of Soli, who amply compensated for his somewhat mediocre poetry by revealing the hand of Providence behind the movement of the stars.[56] Stoic ideas, in fact, provided an almost perennial source of inspiration to later thinkers, such as Erasmus, Montaigne, and Grotius.

The rival system to Stoicism was Epicureanism, so called after its founder Epicurus (341–270 B.C.), who was a native of Samos off the coast of Asia Minor. He came to Athens and founded his school in 306 B.C. The two schools were continually engaged in controversy, but although they were essentially very different, there were many points of agreement between them. Based on an entirely naturalistic interpretation of the universe, Epicureanism taught that pleasure and the absence of pain were the principal aims of life. Pleasure came from virtue, reason, justice, and knowledge of nature. It did not specifically deny the existence of gods but it did not admit their control of human affairs. The Epicureans shared Stoic monism but they did not find a moral pattern behind society and rejected the idea of a natural law, excluding all divine interference in the course of the world. The gods, if they existed, did not interfere with human life. By keeping the gods out of worldly affairs, the Epicureans hoped to secure the peace of mind to contemplate the true nature of the gods. Their aim was to liberate mankind from superstition and the fear of death by insisting upon pleasure as the prerequisite of a wise and righteous existence. Epicurus discovered very early in life that men torture themselves with unnecessary fears of evil stemming either from their fellow men or God. Man had to rid himself of this fear, and depend on his own resources to reach inner peace by living in accordance with truth without fear or desire. Death was like sleep, an unconscious state and not to be feared: "God is nothing to be afraid of: death is nothing to worry about: good is easy to get: evil is easy to bear." The Epicureans were not sensualists or godless scientists as they have often been described. The aim of life was happiness, which could not be achieved as long as men were ridden with passions, and a sensible moderation and self-control alone could achieve serenity.[57] They had much in common with the Taoists who advocated a similar withdrawal and contemplation and "they were influenced by Indian philosophies, with their negative but benevolent attitude to life."[58] Epicureans are chiefly noted for their strong sense of reality, which found its expression in physics as materialism, and in ethics they focused interest on the present life with a special insistence on its corporeal side.

Both Stoicism and Epicureanism appear to be a response to Alexander's dream of human brotherhood in which Macedonians and Persians, Greeks and barbarians, were all alike. Both, in transcending the city-state, conceived of a universal life process. Both discerned a pattern behind life and institutions. Both regarded death as a release, the Epicureans from everything and the Stoics from the corruption of the body. Both emphasized individualism—the solitary, self-centered individual. Both aimed not at the discovery of truth but at the satisfaction of practical needs. Both stressed happiness as the aim of life and preached detachment from passions and emotions, because unfulfilled desire brought unhappiness; indeed, happiness was to be achieved in Epicureanism by holding no opinion at all. Both schools made the same arrogant claim that without philosophy there can be no goodness—a claim which neither Aristotle nor Plato ever made.[59] But Stoics went a good deal farther, striving not only for happiness, but aiming at an ideal of selfless duty. In this burdensome life the noble deed was its own reward. The Stoic philosophy was in this sense more constructive, and more greatly influenced the Romans and later Christianity, and, through its influence on men in positions of power, it contributed to the efficiency of government.[60]

Emphasis upon selfless action, the conception of the world-soul with man containing a spark of the divine fire, and the renunciation of sensual pleasures are doctrines which have an upanishadic ring, although their development from early Greek thought is also possible. The idea, however, that an individual can be self-sufficient and have no business with the world, remarks John Bowle, "is profoundly alien to earlier Greek thought. It is more akin to the political abnegation of the East; it destroys the assumption, so attractive in the writings of Plato and Aristotle, that the moral interest of the State and the individual naturally coincide."[61] Both Hinduism and Buddhism stress that complete detachment from the world of fear and desire is the supreme goal of wisdom. In this respect, "The *Bhagavad Gita* and the Buddhist scriptures present strange harmonies of language with the Stoic teachings. . . ."[62]

The fact that during this period the Eleusian and Orphic mystic cults reappeared and increased in popularity further supports the view that Indian ideas were current in the Hellenistic age and were gaining converts. The reappearance of mystery cults in its turn was influenced, as were other schools of thought, by the changed nature of the Greek world. The establishment of Greek kingdoms further east encouraged increasing numbers of Greeks to travel to Asian lands in the performance of varied civil, military, and commercial services. Many of them stayed for prolonged periods and often married into Asian families. It was, therefore, only natural that together with other ideas and experiences, Asian mystery gods and cults should have travelled back with the Greeks to the West, and provided stimulus to those cults which, although somewhat dormant at this time, had existed there for several centuries.

Chapter III

THE AGE OF SYNCRETISM

WHILST AN intellectual transformation was taking place in the Hellenistic world, India was emerging as a dynamic and powerful state under the Mauryas. China, hitherto unrecognized, almost unknown, and politically divided, was assuming the forceful and unified national personality she was to maintain from the time of the Chin and Han Dynasties onward. The Greek kingdoms were gradually declining but long before Greek power collapsed in Asia by the middle of the first century, a new dominant power, the Roman, had begun to emerge in the West.

According to tradition Rome was founded in 753 B.C. and her early history is mostly shrouded in legend. The real Roman rise to world power appears to have begun in the middle of the third century B.C. when Rome rapidly extended her authority over an enormous variety of people outside Italy. Carthage, a powerful enemy, was defeated and destroyed by the Romans in the three Punic wars (264–241, 218–201, and 149–146 B.C.).

In about 212 B.C. the Romans began to interfere with the affairs of the Hellenistic world. In 205 B.C. they made Egypt their protectorate, finally annexing it to their empire in 30 B.C. after the defeat of Anthony and Cleopatra by the forces of Octavian. Africa was Rome's fifth province, and it was through Africa and the countries ringing the Mediterranean that Rome felt Indian influence. From about 200 B.C. until A.D. 300, Indian religion and thought played a considerable part in these Mediterranean countries. Whole Indian creeds and philosophies certainly were not transplanted into Roman soil, but enough fragments, combinations, and variations of Indian beliefs reached the Roman world to interact effectively on the prevalent local doctrines. Indian

71

thought reached Rome mainly through Iran, Babylonia, and Egypt; however, whilst one can detect many remarkable resemblances between Indian thought and the philosophies of the Graeco-Roman age, there is no record of borrowing. But records can disappear, and their absence in itself is not evidence against mutual influence. For example, Indian influence on ancient Southeast Asia is indisputable, even though it cannot be stated with certainty how or when Indians arrived there. The state of the Seleucids, although it continued to rule areas of Southwest Asia from Syrian Antioch, had been eliminated from the peninsula of Asia Minor. Macedonia was captured in 167 B.C. and finally annexed by Rome in 149 B.C. Greece followed two years later.

The annexation of Egypt brought the Roman frontiers of culture and commerce closer to India. This proximity became even greater when Rome gained her sixth and richest possession on the farthest coast of the Aegean Sea in 133 B.C. where the Attalid dynasty of Pergamum had broken away from the Seleucids. The last king of Pergamum had bequeathed to Rome his state, which comprised the most heavily populated part of Asia Minor, full of famous and highly developed cities and rich in agricultural resources, textiles, and other industry. This heritage brought Rome "a source of fabulous profit for its officials and financiers, and of potent influences upon its culture, religion and racial composition."[1]

From the beginning the Roman Empire was divided into two distinct parts—the Hellenized East and the Roman West. The former was an amalgam of Eastern and Greek cultures, in which Hellenic speech and culture was sometimes a veneer and sometimes a genuine influence. Beginning as Greek states, the kingdoms in Asia Minor and Egypt gradually absorbed local concepts and customs, and Eastern thoughts and habits. Alexandria, founded by Alexander in about 332 B.C. and situated on the western edge of the Nile delta, was the capital of the Ptolemies in Egypt,[2] and as the glory of Athens wilted away, Alexandria gradually became the cultural capital of the new scientific, literary, and philosophical studies, and the commercial emporium of the East and West. It was second only to Rome in importance. Alexander could not have foreseen that one day, because of its connection with India, Africa, and Rome, his city would become so cosmopolitan, with a fine library and museum, and attracting philosophers, artists, scientists, and others from the Mediterranean and Indian areas. The greatness of Alexandria began when the body of Alexander was enshrined there in a magnificent mausoleum, the Sema, after Ptolemy had diverted the funeral cortège to Egypt, whilst it was proceeding from Syria to Macedonia, on the pretext that Alexander had expressed the wish to be buried in the oasis of the god Ammon.

At the same time Ptolemy transferred his capital from Memphis to Alexandria. New influences began to pour in and the city grew in stature and importance. It became a busy harbour, a thriving centre of international trade with its splendid commercial facilities, and above all the repository of a cosmopolitan culture.[3] It had the biggest lighthouse of antiquity, 480 feet high, and a zoo for which rare animals were imported from all over the known world.[4] The museum, technically a temple of the Muses, the goddesses of arts and sciences, became a centre of literature and learning. Under the guidance of the first two Ptolemies it became an academy of letters and science, whose members, at times numbering about one hundred, received generous financial assistance. The library attached to the museum was liberally endowed by the Ptolemies and became the greatest library in the Hellenistic world with collections of rare and original works. At the time it was burnt when Julius Caesar, during his Egyptian campaign, set fire to the ships in the harbour, it is said to have contained about a million volumes.

A fresh beginning was made and another library was built at the Serapium, a considerable distance from the harbour. This library also was destroyed, presumably by the Emperor Theodosius of Constantinople, who, being a devout Christian, did not approve of old Greek books which contained, according to him, pagan knowledge and philosophies. The contribution of Alexandria to knowledge in the realms of literature, philosophy, art, and science, is enormous, and, if its library had not twice been destroyed, our debt, no doubt, would have been incalculably greater.

Antioch, the capital of the Seleucids, was the next most important city in the Hellenistic world, and it also played a formative part in the culture of the Roman Empire for a long time. The Seleucids had founded cities throughout their dominions to help in the expansion of Hellenism. Their success appears to have been somewhat limited, however, for Greek cities in Syria, Mesopotamia, and Babylonia were like Greek islands in a sea of Asian population untouched by Hellenism. "Posidonius, himself a Syrian Greek, held no high opinion as to the purity of Hellenism among his compatriots. And this diluted Hellenism of the cities was not likely to penetrate very deeply into the thousands of villages with their Semitic population."[5]

A modern form of Greek was spoken in the Hellenistic world, including Alexandria, and Hellenistic culture was a combination of cosmopolitan and older Greek cultures. Unity of currency, new roads, improved harbours and lighthouses, and larger ships facilitated intercourse and trade. The tremendous work done by the Achaemenian rulers of Persia in opening up the lands of western Asia and linking them by means of a network of roads, including the famous "Royal Road" connecting Ephesus and Susa, and a postal system extending to Bactria and India, was continued by the Hellenistic states, and still later by the Romans after their annexation of the kingdom of Pergamum.[6]

It was from this world that the Romans acquainted themselves with the cultural and intellectual heritage of the past. Culture flourished in Egypt under the Ptolemies, and because of well-developed commerce with the outside world, Egypt became increasingly prosperous. She already had brisk trade relations with India. In fact, Indian contacts with Egypt were anterior to the emergence of Greek power in Alexandria. The tale of Egyptian explorations by land and sea from the earliest times to reach the Land of Punt (India) is a fascinating and a romantic narrative.[7] But it was at the end of the fourth century B.C., when the Ptolemies came to the throne of Egypt, that Indo-Egyptian commerce received a great impetus, especially under Ptolemy II, who also paid great attention to the African coast, where he founded colonies as far as the island of Socotra. The importance of East Africa was considerable, for here the Hellenistic armies obtained ivory, tortoise shell, slaves, and elephants.[8] The Greeks had learned from India the use of elephants in war when Chandragupta gave five hundred elephants to Seleucus.

Indian trade with Egypt, however, was by overland routes through western Asia. If there had existed an earlier sea route, it was forgotten by the time of the Ptolemies. But the anarchy reigning in Syria following Alexander's death, together with the rise of the hostile kingdom of Parthia and its defeat of the Roman legions in 53 B.C. at Carrhae, rendered the overland routes uncertain and increased the importance of the hitherto unpopular sea route.[9] During this period the Romans and the Ptolemies witnessed the development of a profitable commerce between the two great civilized regions of the time, the Mediterranean countries and India. Egypt, furthermore, unlike other parts of the Hellenistic world, could be directly reached by sea from India, and this encouraged maritime intercourse.

The perilous desert journey, however, between the Nile and the Red Sea was something of a deterrent. Attempts were made from time to time to build a canal between the waterways, but these invariably proved unsuccessful. Darius the Great tried it, and so did Ptolemy Philadelphus (285–246 B.C.), but both failed. Consequently, the latter revived the old idea of a port on the Egyptian coast of the Red Sea, connected with the Nile by a desert road furnished with convenient and comfortable resting points. The road, roughly about two hundred fifty miles long, linking Coptos on the bend of the river Nile, and the port Berenice on the Red Sea coast, was punctuated by eight watering places and the journey took eleven or twelve days under favourable conditions. In 274 B.C., Ptolemy Philadelphus built the port of Myos Hormos, one hundred eighty miles north of Berenice, thus cutting the desert journey by five days. Inevitably Myos Hormos soon became the ideal port for eastern trade and eclipsed all competitors.[10]

Almost two centuries later Strabo the geographer, who lived in the reign of Augustus, visited the port of Myos Hormos and found that it was still the greatest centre for east Indian trade, and that about one hundred twenty ships sailed from that port to India, probably in a single season. A few bold sailors even reached the mouth of the Ganges.[11]

Brisk trade led to Indian settlement in Egypt and Egyptian colonies in India. That contact between India and Egypt had become closer during this period is confirmed by Athenaeus, who says that Indian women, hunting dogs, cows, and spices carried on camels figured in the processions of Ptolemy. The saloon of Ptolemy Philopator's (221 B.C.) yacht was lined with Indian stone. Indian figures found at Memphis may indicate the existence of an Indian settlement, and a Ptolemaic grave stone has been excavated bearing signs of the wheel and trident. The infant deity Horus is represented in Indian postures seated on a lotus. In papyrus fragments an account exists of some Greek mariners who were shipwrecked on the Malabar coast and hospitably entertained by a local king. Again, there has been discovered in the temple of Redesiya, on the desert route to the Red Sea, "a dedication by an Indian to Pan, pointing to a real and direct intercourse between the two people."[12] Hultzsch mentions finding a solitary silver coin belonging to the period of Ptolemy Soter in a Bangalore bazaar.

From this monopoly of the sea commerce between India and Europe Ptolemaic Egypt gained the extraordinary wealth and power for which she was famous. It was fortunate for Egypt that there was no serious competition from other powers, especially Syria who could have considerably intensified her own trade with India through the Persian Gulf. Possibly the internal situation in Syria was too chaotic to encourage international trade.

A striking piece of evidence of the Egyptian-Indian trade is provided by Rostovtzeff, who points out that the financal and economic organization of Ptolemaic Egypt was very similar to that of Chandragupta

75

Maurya and his successors as set forth in Kautilya's *Arthasastra*. For instance, the three state monopolies, oil, salt, and mines, and their organization, as well as a far-reaching state socialism under the rule of "enlightened monarchs," were common to both India and Ptolemaic Egypt.[13]

The date of the *Arthasastra*, which is unique for its compression, carefully compiled detail, and political realism, is somewhat controversial—and probably will always remain so—but most scholars accept it as a work of the early Mauryan period. The volume of polemical writing surrounding the dating of this work is much too large to lend itself to brief review.[14] Of those scholars who place the date of this treatise much later, Keith, whose writings include such divergent subjects as the history of Sanskrit literature and the history of the British Empire, was the chief exponent: "That the work was a product of c. 300 (A.D.) written by an official attached to some court, is at least plausible, if it cannot be proved."[15] Keith's view is surprisingly infirm and indeed appears to fluctuate. Elsewhere he "assigned it to the first century B.C. while the matter very probably is older by a good deal than that."[16] A number of scholars have disputed this somewhat indecisive opinion and, whilst admitting to some later interpolations in the work possibly to bring it up-to-date, have endorsed the opinion originally advanced by Shamasastry that it is a Mauryan document based upon the knowledge and experience of the pre-Mauryan administrative practice and theory of state craft. Even if parts of the *Arthasastra* reflect Mauryan or pre-Mauryan conditions, Indian influence on Egyptian administration or vice versa may be significantly indicative of a much closer exchange of ideas between India and ancient Egypt than has hitherto been believed.

During the unsettled period when the strong rule of the early Ptolemies was declining and the Romans were not yet firmly in command of Egypt, the eastern trade suffered a brief set-back. Once Rome had established its authority, however, it took positive measures to continue, and in fact to vigourously encourage, the Ptolemies' policy of trading with India directly through sea or land routes which, although still in use, lay through hostile Parthia. In 25 B.C. Augustus, whose cold-blooded cruelty during the Roman civil war aroused repulsion but did help to restore order and prosperity in Rome, sent an expedition to secure command of the sea route to India, having perceived it to be in the interests of Rome to encourage the lucrative trade of Arabia and India. To secure this trade the Romans attempted to make the highways safer, improve the existing facilities, and acquire new areas for better routes. Military expeditions were also organized to cope with piracy and raiders. The road across the desert from Coptos to Myos Hormos was carefully marked into stages, depots were made for storage, water reservoirs were built, and armed guards provided protection for traders and travellers. A fleet was stationed in the Red Sea at the time and there are some accounts of merchants' ships having been armed for defence against raids. Later Hadrian (117–138) built an entirely new road to the Red Sea through level country and furnished it with halting stations.

A few decades later, in 45, the epoch-making discovery of the monsoon winds (attributed to Hippalus during the reign of Claudius) drastically altered the whole aspect of sea-borne trade between India and Rome. Strabo mentions that by a strange though eventually happy mischance an Indian sailor mistook his course and reached Egypt half dead. The Greeks in Egypt nourished him back to health and the Indian, in gratitude, piloted Hippalus back to India along the monsoon routes. Whilst knowledge of these winds was probably new to the Greeks, the Indians and the Arabians had known and made use of them for centuries.[17]

The monsoon winds blow over the Indian Ocean from the northeast in winter and from the southwest in summer. Once their currents were known it became possible to sail far more speedily and directly from Indian to Egyptian ports. Alexandria could now be reached within two months or even less, as against the thirty months taken by Scylax, the pioneer Greek sailor, to sail from India to Suez. A trader could now leave Egypt in July and reach the Indian ports by the end of September. There he could dispose of his merchandise and acquire a cargo of the luxuries so much in demand in Rome and begin his return journey by the end of November. Helped by the northeast monsoons he would sail to Aden and then, via the Red Sea, reach Alexandria about February, thus easily completing the entire trip well within a year. In fact the journey from Rome to India could be completed in less than sixteen weeks. It took about two weeks from Rome to Alexandria, about three and a half weeks from Alexandria to Berenice, a month for descending the Red Sea, and forty days from Ocelis (Cella), a port on the Red Sea coast of Arabia, to the nearest port in India.[18] Also, the ships could now sail on the high seas away from the pirate-infested coast. Furthermore, the trade monopoly of the Arab towns was broken up and, although they attempted to create difficulties, they were firmly suppressed. The West was determined to trade with India without any intermediary. The voyage could be undertaken either from the Egyptian or Nabataean side, although the former was more usual. There were three Egyptian ports: Arsince at the Gulf of Suez; halfway down the coast was Myos Hormos; and finally the distant Berenice. Traffic in goods and people now increased enormously, and whereas about twenty ships a year made the journey before the discovery of the monsoon winds, a ship now left Egypt for India almost every day.

Rome, enriched by the spoils and tributes from so many foreign lands, had acquired a taste for luxuries of every kind. The capital of the greatest empire ever established in Europe was filled with people who had inherited great wealth and whose sole occupation was the enjoyment of these riches. The returning generals found their villas dull, rustic, and old-fashioned, made all the more unbearable because they had brought back with them masses of coinage, bullion, and slaves. They had developed expensive tastes whilst in other continents, and now they had the means to indulge those tastes at home. They did so with feverish haste and great display. Oysters were brought all the way from Spain or Brittany, and wild beasts were imported from the farthest corners of Egypt to be featured in games. Common men, always keen to emulate the fashion determined by the elite, soon followed, and before long even the country surrounding Rome was involved. One may gain some conception of the vast wealth of the generals from the inheritance of the Emperor Augustus who, despite his claims to divinity and pursuit of sexual debauchery, had amassed nearly forty million pounds in twenty years. In modern values this would be many times more. Senators owned property in every province, had incomes of over a hundred thousand pounds per annum, and kept thousands of slaves. Seneca himself owned several hundred citronwood tables imported from Mauritania. The senators would spend forty thousand pounds on a single carpet for their homes. Pliny relegated to second rank those whose annual income was less than sixty thousand pounds. Even men of infamous character were rich. As for the emperors and their favourites, "they strove to astound the world by their fantastic follies. Luxury in food, in attire and in furniture surpassed every example of sumptuous idiocy which our own epoch can show."[19] Gaius (Caligula) (37–41), whose chief obsessions were cruelty and sexuality, wore cloaks adorned with emeralds and robes woven of pure silk—an extremely expensive article in Rome at the time, especially purple silk. He drank precious stones dissolved in vinegar and served his guests with gilded bread and meat. At Lucullus' triumphal feast about three million litres of wine were consumed. Roman banquets were remarkable by any standards for the enormous quantities of food and drink consumed, but they were crude, and at times repulsive, affairs, totally lacking in the elegance of the Greeks. It was, for example, considered an accomplishment to be able to vomit at will in order to resume eating. Roman sexual life was equally uncontrolled, sadistic, and full of crude perversions. The youth of the country, clad in garments laden with gold and pearls, poured out their wealth at the feet of fashionable courtesans and would squander a fortune in a matter of hours. Greek sexual life was also extravagant, but it was remarkably immune from inelegance and perversions, if homosexuality is not included in this category. Roman pursuit of pleasure was spectacular but repulsive, lacking dignity, restraint, and an understanding of the very nature of pleasure. Even the greatest of the Mughals or the Sungs would have envied the extravagance, although not the crudity, of the Roman Emperors. Whilst the rich led a life of unparalleled laxity, kept armies of servants and slaves, and gave interminable feasts, millions of hungry men were wandering through the streets of Rome and the surrounding countryside.

Of all the goods in particular favour with the luxury-loving Romans, Indian products were the most popular. To meet the demand, new and greater efforts were made to increase trade with India and this was accomplished to a degree which would appear astonishing even today. The Romans demanded Asian luxuries on an unprecedented scale. Chinese silk, Indian pearls, jewels, fine muslin, drugs, spices, condiments, incense, ghee, ivory, dyes, cosmetics, oils, and perfumes, all fetched high prices.[20] It appears that toward the end of the first century the greatly prized Chinese silk (Sericum or Seric silk) as well as furs were being shipped from Indian ports to the western countries, because the land routes were blocked by Parthia and the sea route had gained such popularity. Cinnamon was also one of the most important exports and its price in Rome was high—about 1500 denarii per Roman pound for the best quality cinnamon and fifty denarii for the cheapest *cassia*. One of the most sought after Indian products was cotton muslin, which was so fine that the Romans called it *nebula*. Pepper, which remained one of the most highly prized luxuries of the West until modern times, was very expensive—about fifteen denarii a pound—and yet greatly in demand.[21] It was consumed in such large quantities that, as a concession to the people, no import duty was placed on it in Rome.

In return, Western merchants carried tin and lead to India, minerals which India herself did not possess, as well as wine, coral, and glass—a widely exported Roman product, especially coloured glass—brightly coloured girdles, and gold and silver coins. Special presents were carried for kings, including maidens for harems. However the principal means of exchange with India was gold. Pliny bewailed the enormous drain on Rome's resources created by the demand for eastern luxuries. There was not a year in which India did not take at least 550 million sesterces from Rome,[22] an equal amount going to Arabia and China. The gold which came from taxation and pillage in Spain and Dacia, stayed in Rome only briefly before transit to Asia. Great quantities of Roman coins found in South India where jewels and spices were sold bear Pliny out. He also tells us that Indian wares cost a hundred times more in Roman markets than in Indian markets.[23] Later, Vespasian's policy in 69–79 of cutting down extravagant expenditure may have made some difference in the import of luxury goods from India but there is no concrete evidence that it did. At the same time commerce in cotton and other industrial goods continued steadily. This is supported by the fact that Roman coins belonging to the period after the reign of Nero (54–68) are more often found in those parts of India where cotton was grown. There are considerably fewer Roman coins of the third century to be found in India, which may indicate a decline in commerce.

Trade between Europe and Asia was so brisk that, despite the hostility of Parthia towards Rome and their periodic clashes, and despite the increasing popularity of the Red Sea route, the Persian Gulf route nevertheless carried a flourishing trade and land-borne trade also grew considerably. This trade led to the rise of great cities along the routes, and of new ports on the coasts. Petra, the town of Nabataeans, and Palmyra, which commanded the caravan routes to Asia, served as terminal points for the maritime trade of the Red Sea and the Indian Ocean. Gerra, Ommana, the Charax Spasini, were all large mercantile towns to which Indian vessels regularly brought cargoes of timber, black-wood, and ebony, whilst Arabia sent the frankincense and spices of Cana. In return for these goods the region exported pearls, which, however, were not as valuable as the famous Indian ones. From Charax a route ran up to the Euphrates joining the well-known over-land route near Seleucia.[24]

Both Ptolemy in his *Geography* and the unknown author of the *Periplus Maris Erythraei* testify to the number of merchants engaged in Indian trade, and thus to its volume. Ptolemy draws his information from men who had been to India, many of whom had lived there for a long time. The *Periplus*, which is a kind of practical handbook for merchants presumably written by an Egyptian Greek merchant from Berenice, contains a detailed account of its author's coasting voyage to India. The *Periplus* amongst other things mentions the import of Greek girls for Indian harems and various references are found to Indian residents in Alexandria. The Jatakas are full of references to Buddhist merchants and their adventures on voyages to distant countries, and to the overland caravans that took days and nights travelling east and west across deserts.

Trade inevitably led to some tourism and especially to Roman and Indian settlements in their respective areas of influence. There was a Yavana colony at the mouth of the Kaveri River and foreign populations were known to have existed in the Madura district. Mercenary Roman soldiers attending Indian princes are mentioned in Tamil literature. The Tamil area was one with which the Romans had considerable commercial relations, for it had cloth, dyes, and pearls to offer. Hence, it is not surprising that Tamil poems sing of Yavana ships bringing wine and other wares to their ports.[25] A late map shows a temple of Augustus at Musiris on the west coast of India (Cronganore in Kerala), which would indicate that there must have been a large enough Roman settlement to erect a temple honouring their deified Emperor. Sir Mortimer Wheeler, however, boldly declares that the "Temple of Augustus" at Musiris indicates an "official arm" long enough to reach the Malabar Coast.[26] No trace of this temple has yet been found, but the probability of its existence cannot be excluded. To regard it as evidence of a kind of imperial outpost, however, rather than a normal structure built by a colony of foreigners, is beyond understandable historical speculation.

Dion Chrysostom, the Greek rhetorician and sophist, who lived in the reign of Trajan (98–117) mentions that the population of cosmopolitan Alexandria included many Indians who had come there to trade.[27] Pausanias refers to the merchants of India and to the marvellous creatures they brought, including parrots.[28]

Of the several branches of natural science that flourished in the Hellenistic and Roman world, the revival of geography was one. Several works on Indian geography appeared describing the country with varying degrees of accuracy. Some well-known works in this area are Strabo's *Geography*, regarded as the most important geographic work of antiquity; Arrian's *Indika;* the Elder Pliny's *Natural History;* and Ptolemy's *Guide to Geography*.[29] The unknown author of *Periplus Maris Erythraei* travelled through India and left an eye-witness account of the Red Sea and of the Arabian and Indian coasts.[30]

Trade between India and Rome continued to thrive steadily during the second and third centuries A.D. With the rise of the great Gupta power the heart of the Indian Empire moved inland toward central India, and a splendid cultural renaissance set in with a distinctive Indian character. This, however, interrupted the maritime trade between Rome and India. The emergence of the Sassanian Empire in 227 also checked direct communication between the two nations. But contact continued through Alexandria, to which Indians flocked in increasing numbers, until the fall of the Roman Empire in the fifth century and the consequent decline of Alexandria.

Indian trade with Rome had an extremely important influence on Indian contacts with the countries of Southeast Asia. Rome's appetite for luxuries was so great that India could not satisfy it. Indian supplies of precious stones, ivory, and spices had begun to run out. Consequently, Indian traders began searching eastward for fresh sources of supply. They imported goods from the countries of Southeast Asia and then exported them to the Roman world. This Indian commercial contact with Southeast Asia gradually bloomed into an exceptionally fruitful cultural intercourse. With the decline of the Roman Empire, the Roman demand ceased and the entrepôt trade of India collapsed.[31]

Roman emperors took an increasing interest in Indian affairs and, in marked contrast to their commonly arrogant attitude toward foreign ambassadors, accorded dignified and courteous receptions to Indian envoys. The political importance of the Indian states as allies against the Parthians and later Sassanians was a major reason for Rome to cultivate the Indian kings, especially those who occupied the northwestern and Indus Valley regions. Drawn more and more eastward by the problems of internal political turbulence and expanding eastern frontiers, the Roman emperors succumbed with fascination to Asian institutions and religions.

Although India had had diplomatic relations with Syria, Egypt, and other countries, she had not dispatched a mission to Rome before the time of Augustus. An Indian embassy was sent to the Roman Emperor, when he was on the island of Samos in 21–20 B.C. by the Indo-Parthian King Azes II.[32] It was mainly Augustus' realization of the value of Indian trade and, possibily the value of a political alliance against hostile powers in western Asia, which was responsible for an era of Indo-Roman diplomatic contact that was to last for the next three centuries.[33] With Kushan power replacing that of the Indo-Greeks in India, this diplomatic contact became much more regular. The vast Kushan Empire, which included Afghanistan, Bactria and much of Central Asia, comprised a variety of nationalities—Indo-Greeks, Parthians, Scythians, Iranians, Chinese, and others. The role of the Kushans in providing a meeting ground for the great civilizations of the time, and in disseminating Buddhism to Central Asia and beyond, has been extremely important.

It is true that contact between India and other civilizations was anterior to the rise of the Kushans but at no time was it greater. The cosmopolitan nature of the Kushan Empire is aptly illustrated by their coins, many of which carry a Persian title for the king in Greek letters and the effigy of the king in Turkish dress. The Kushan kings were in close contact with Roman authority in western Asia. The political ambition of the Romans to expand into India also brought them nearer to the Kushan frontiers. The Kushans, it is suggested, also imported a large number of Greek sculptors from Asia Minor, who settled in the Punjab and were associated with the Gandhara school of art.

Roman historians, discussing Indian missions in Rome, make specific references to the Indian embassies that visited Trajan (98–117), Hadrian (117–138), Antoninus Pius (138–161), Marcus Aurelius (161–180), Heliogabalus (218–222), Aurelian (270–275), Constantine (323–353), and Julian (361–363).[34] Two Indian embassies were probably sent to Justinian (527–565). The ancient Romans, who had dealt with a variety of foreign emissaries from both within and without their vast empire, had usually disregarded all diplomatic etiquette and theory. In contrast, India, who never acquired territorial possessions outside her own national frontiers, had a highly developed and clearly prescribed theory of the art of diplomacy. The Persians were also noted for their cultured diplomatic behaviour. The Roman rulers did not provide for a distinct foreign affairs department, and they appear to have cared even less for diplomatic negotiations. It was mainly the Greeks who acted as intermediaries between the foreign powers and the Roman emperors. Gibbon has described graphically the treatment Aurelian accorded the ambassadors of the Alemanni, who were required to prostrate themselves on the ground in front of the king, before they were commanded to rise and permitted to speak. Aurelian treated them with contempt, reproached them, and finally dismissed them.[35] "A crude haughtiness," says Saletore, "marked the dealings of the Romans with the foreign monarch which had something of the Macedonian insolence in it. Their entire diplomacy was directed towards one end—the display of their military might."[36]

Indeed, despite their many brilliant achievements in political and military organization, jurisprudence, communications, and architecture, the Romans were on the whole a very unimaginative people. In marked contrast to the small city of Athens, they contributed very little which was original to human heritage during the long centuries of their domination. Culturally, they were a destitute relative of the Hellenes. Even their accomplishments were drawn, at least partially, from the experience of Greeks, Egyptians, and Persians. The Persian system of satrapies presents many parallels to the Roman provincial system, and Darius possessed many of the qualities for which Augustus is so admired. The Roman system of internal communications, including the network of roads and the postal system, is reminiscent of Iran. In fact, only in recent years has the Roman debt to Persia been fully realized.

The Romans added little to what had been devised by Greek philosophers in about 300 B.C., although some of them expressed Greek thought better than the Greeks had done. For example, Lucretius stated the doctrines of Epicurus with a much greater intensity.[37] The only Greek school of thought which found firm roots in Rome was Stoicism. Although the Romans borrowed much from the Greeks, felt a passionate admiration for Greek culture, and suffered from a sense of inferiority to the Greeks, they disliked the contemporary Greeks and denounced them as unscrupulous. At times, even Greek philosophy suffered in popularity.

In architecture, the Romans were technical innovators and, although they inherited much from the Etruscans and the East, it was they who invented concrete and devised the dome.[38] Their sculpture, also an important contribution, was very significant in Byzantine art where Eastern influences were also active.

The ordinary Roman was generally ignorant of the history of mankind and of foreign peoples, and he had no knowledge of economic laws or of social possibilities. In some ways, the Romans were even primordial. In the third century B.C., whilst Asoka had renounced war and was preaching non-violence and compassion for all other beings, the Romans were indulging in human sacrifice, and "much that we learn of the religion of republican Rome carries us far back beyond the days of decent gods, to the age of Shamanism and magic."[39] Their slavery practices were infamous for their savagery. The gladiatorial combats, which the Romans introduced in 264 B.C., are illustrative of a morbid mentality and the extremes of cruelty—even by Roman standards. It was not until the first century A.D. that Seneca expressed the protest of the human conscience against such barbarism.

Gilbert Murray, whilst pointing out that of the three most important strains—Greek, Hebrew, and Roman—in the Western inheritance, the Roman influence is by far the most striking and visible, further comments that behind almost everything Roman the real moving spirit is Greek, including the Latin alphabet, Roman law and political ideas, scientific knowledge, architecture, and literature.[40] The Romans, however, were able rulers; they had courage and a sense of justice, but were otherwise ruthlessly practical men. They were a receptive people, willing to copy and imitate whatever they regarded worthwhile, and were tolerant of the ideas and institutions of others. They drew upon Greek and Asian cultures whose moral excellence they admitted. The Roman role in spreading Greek philosophy and in helping it to survive the gradual decay of Greek culture would alone render our debt to them great. In addition, Rome, gave a practical, revitalizing turn to philosophical thought.

But in spite of their superiority in armed strength and political organization, the Romans were often haunted by the fear of an Eastern empire. The influx of the Eastern peoples into Rome was so great that some historians have characterized the history of the Empire during the first three centuries as "a 'peaceful infiltration' of the Orient into the Occident."[41] An important factor which contributed to the mounting influx of Asians and Africans into Rome was the Roman lack of racial or colour prejudices. It is said that Romans were more friendly with Afro-Asians than with the Jewish people. Then too, a great many of Nero's senators and knights were of slave or foreign descent.[42]

In such an atmosphere of flowing diplomatic and commercial contacts it was natural that Indian thought should have reached the Romans. The existence of such contact is supported by the recent discovery of a third century work attributed to St. Hippolytus,[43] and entitled *Kata Pason Aireseon Elenchos* (Refutation of all Heresies) also known as *Philosophoumena*, which contains a brief exposition of the Brahmanas of Tagabena (Tungabhadra) in South India. A detailed study of the text made by Jean Filliozat has shown that Hippolytus, in championing the cause of Christian orthodoxy, was attacking the doctrine of the Upanishads. That such an attack on the Indian scriptures was made would suggest that Roman intellectuals had become greatly interested in the doctrines which came from India during the third century.[44] No wonder Plotinus, who wrote approximately a decade after the *Elenchos*, developed such a keen desire to know more of Indian thought that he joined the military expedition of Gordian in order to travel in the East. It was perhaps the rise of Christianity that put an end to the influx of Indian doctrines into Rome.

Indian commerce and culture possibly travelled even farther west than Rome to Scandinavia. This possibility is suggested by the second century inscriptions found at Junnar in western India which refer to the benefactions of two Yavanas, Irila and Cita, who have been interpreted as the amber merchants of Scandinavia. Kushan coins have been discovered in Gaul and Scandinavia, further suggesting commercial relations between India and Scandinavia. The excavations carried out in the mid-nineteen fifties on a small island called Lillion, or Helgo, in Lake Malaren, about twenty miles west of Stockholm, uncovered many foreign objects, including an exquisite bronze statue of the Buddha seated on a lotus throne with crossed legs. According to Wilhelm Holmqvist, who conducted the archaeological investigation, the Buddha is of Indian or Central Asian origin. This is an amazing discovery, which may lead to even more surprising knowledge about the cultural contacts between ancient India and the West.[45]

It was at this time, when the commercial, diplomatic, and intellectual contact between India and the West was at its height, that Buddhism began to spread in the regions of Central and Western Asia.

The missionary zeal of the Buddhist *Sangha* was responsible for the expansion of Buddhism abroad. Buddhism was the world's first proselytizing religion. It is said that after attaining enlightenment the Buddha was at first reluctant to preach his doctrine, because he feared that people would be unable to understand it, but later he decided to spread his teaching for the benefit of those who could grasp something of its meaning. Consequently, he organized the Buddhist Sangha, which was to consist of men, who, having learned the doctrine themselves, would wander from place to place preaching the doctrine to laymen and disputating it with followers of other faiths. The Sangha was to be run on democratic lines in which the individual monks were subordinated to the collective authority of the monastery. An important instruction to the *bhikshus,* or monks, was: "Let no two of you go in the same direction," the implication of which was that a new area of activity should be selected by each individual monk. Not only were the members of the Sangha thus compelled to look for distinct spheres for themselves, but in due course they also acquired the will to do so. Whilst the Sangha initiated the process and encouraged monks to go out and preach, it did not direct, superintend, control, or co-ordinate their activities, thus allowing unfettered scope for individual initiative to adjust itself to a new environment. This, perhaps, may explain the successful, enthusiastic, and many-sided missionary activities of the individual Buddhist monks.

The Sangha has a two-sided meaning in Buddhism. It is a fraternity of the entire body of monks, and at the same time a bond of association amongst monks. In the former sense the word refers to a "body of persons" and in the latter to the "confederation which makes them one body." Both concepts of the Sangha, concrete and abstract, appear in usage. In its abstract aspect Sangha is a spiritual unity, and in its concrete aspect it is an institution of Buddhism. In the beginning the abstract aspect was more important, and each individual monk was a Sangha in spiritual communion with other monks. Later as Buddhism spread the concrete aspect became uppermost from the historian's viewpoint. The unitary Sangha became plural and the wandering monks came together in monk communities. Each community came to be called a Sangha, and Sangha continued to multiply, finally assuming the form of monastic establishments, functioning as centres of learning and culture, and thus playing a remarkable and dynamic role in the history of Buddhism. Buddhist monasticism was a source of authority and intellectual advancement, and a stabilizing influence in society. Wherever Buddhism spread, monks came, settled, and built monasteries. Buddhist monk communities and monasteries, unlike their counterparts in the Christian world, were never isolated from society.[46] The monk-and-laymen intercourse remained an essential feature of Buddhist monastic life, enabling the monks to influence the life and culture of the people, and in return be influenced by them.

However, it was not until the reign of Asoka, the first great royal patron of Buddhism, that missionary efforts to preach the gospel of the Buddha abroad were set into motion. Before Asoka dispatched his emissaries abroad, however, he insisted that his own people, as is indicated by his pillar edicts, practice the observance of truth, restraint, kindness, charity, purity, respect for elders and teachers; and to control evil thoughts, such as anger, ferocity, conceit, envy, and misguided self-will. He advocated complete religious tolerance and respect for all pious men, irrespective of their denomination, including even the materialists, and called upon all religious denominations to refrain from self-praise and denunciation of others. Deeply influenced by the Buddhist ideas of compassion and *ahimsa*, nonviolence for all living beings, he sought to bring all people closer to the gods in virtue. To help his people understand and follow his lead, he appointed religious officers in different regions and had his edicts carved on rocks and stone pillars. He himself undertook tours, contacting scholars and ascetics to enrich his knowledge, and performed numerous acts of charity and piety.[47]

It was during Asoka's time that the third Buddhist Sangili Council was held at Pataliputra in 247 B.C. to discuss religious affairs and to determine the true nature of the Buddhist faith, *dhamma*.[48] A major consequence of this Council appears to have been the decision to send religious missions to various regions of India and to other countries. Buddhist literary sources reveal that such missions were sent to the country of the Yavanas (Ionian Greeks); to Gandhara, Kashmir, and the Himalayan regions in the north; to the western part of India,

Aparantaka; the southern parts, Vanavasi and Mysore, and farther south to countries as far as Ceylon and the Malay Archipelago. The celebrated thirteenth rock edict of Asoka (probably belonging to 256 B.C.) refers to his religious missions to such far off kingdoms as those of Antiochus (Antiyoka) II, King of Syria; of Ptolemy (Turamaya) of Egypt; Antigonos (Antakini) of Macedonia; Alexander (Alikasundara) of Epirus, an ancient district of northern Greece; and Magas of Cyrenia, in North Africa. Asoka compares his missionary triumphs to the military conquests of other monarchs. Whether or not Asoka's endeavours to spread the dhamma, both at home and abroad, were of the dimensions suggested by the evidence of Buddhist texts, there is no doubt that his efforts were mainly responsible for the popularization of the teachings of the Buddha both in and out of India. Once the process was initiated, however, the inherent quality of the creed, backed by the zeal of its monks, began to gain converts and adherents with increasing speed.

By the time Buddhism began travelling abroad, it was already centuries old and had become a well-organized, articulate doctrine, with a powerful and widespread base in India, well poised to infiltrate into other lands. During Asoka's period the bulk of the Theravada Buddhist Canonical works was in existence. The Pali Canon was settled during his reign and committed to writing later in 88–76 B.C. Being a proselytizing religion by nature, in the second century B.C. Buddhist ascetics (*Samanas*) were found in western Persia and in Bactria in the first century B.C. Later, nascent Christianity met full-grown Buddhism in the academies and markets of Asia and Egypt.[49] Following Asoka's missions, Indian sects gained a firm foothold in Egypt during the Ptolemaic period. Traces of an Indian settlement at Memphis have been found in the form of Indian figures and a Ptolemaic grave stone bearing the signs of the wheel and trident. References to a flourishing Buddhist convent, with a Greek chief, Mahadhammarakkhita, who went to Ceylon with other monks to attend a religious ceremony in the second century B.C., are found in the Buddhist *Mahavamsa,* as well as other works.[50] Photius refers to the presence of Brahmana in Alexandria.

Buddhism was founded in the sixth century B.C. by Siddhartha Gautama who, having renounced the life of royal luxury and worldly pleasures, set forth on a spiritual quest for a remedy for man's ills. Four experiences were the immediate causes of his "Great Renunciation": the sight of an old man, a sick man, a dead man, and a wandering *Sadhu*. The first three represented the misery of existence, and the fourth suggested a possible way out. Through a long period of spiritual ordeals and experimentation, physical suffering, ascetic practices, and meditation, he finally gained the supreme Enlightenment, becoming the Buddha. He did not claim revelation or divinity; indeed, he preached a religion of intense self-effort in which there was no need for God or the supernatural. His teaching was empirical, scientific, and therapeutic, and one which was free from tradition and clerical authority. Developing over a period of twenty-five centuries and gaining a vast following in numerous countries, Buddhism today is a highly sophisticated and complex religion, but its whole doctrine revolves around *Ariyasaccani,* the four Ariyan truths: that there is *dukkha,* suffering; that it has a *samudaya,* cause; that there can be *nirodha,* suppression of it; and there is a *magga,* path, known as the Middle Way in principle and the Noble Eightfold Path in practice, to accomplish this. Thus *nirvana* or *nibbana* can be achieved.[51]

In its early phase Buddhism in India was not very different from other ascetic movements, but during the period of Mauryan ascendancy it emerged as a distinct religion. In the following Sunga-Kanva period, despite the loss of royal patronage, Buddhism retained its hold on the Indian mind. A number of famous Buddhist establishments like the Bharhut stupa, the Karle caves, and the Sanchi stupa belonging to this period, testify to the great prosperity enjoyed by Buddhism. It had developed from a monastic religion into a popular one, and had become theistic with the Buddha and his relics as objects of worship.

It was during this early phase that Buddhism began to be adopted by some of the Greek populace settled in the northwestern regions of India; others, as shown by the Besnagar Column, became Hindus. The Greek King Milinda (Menander) was a great champion of Buddhism. In the Pali text *Milinda-panha* ("Questions of Milinda"), Menander figures as one of the characters and is described as Yonakanam raja Milinda, the king of the Yonakas.[52] Subsequently many Greeks in India adopted Buddhism and generously donated to Buddhist establishments. If Buddhism had not established itself in this region as firmly as it did, its further expansion into Western and Central Asia would have been very difficult, if not impossible.

After the period of Asoka, the reign of Kaniska (first century A.D.) marks the next prominent landmark in the annals of Buddhism. Tradition represents Kaniska as a great patron of Buddhism, and associates him with Buddhist scholars who shaped it in later times. Kaniska's reign marked a turning point, not only in the history of Buddhism, but also in Buddhist art and literature. It witnessed the rise of Mahayana Buddhism, which later developed into one of the chief schools of

89

Buddhist doctrine, and the magnificent literary activity begun by Parsva, Asvaghosa, Vasumitra, and others. Pali was replaced by Sanskrit. The celebrated Gandhara school of art reached its peak and sculptures of the Buddha and Bodhisattvas began to appear. It was also largely through Kaniska's efforts that Buddhism was carried into Central and eastern Asia. There was ceaseless missionary activity throughout his empire which reached from central India to Central Asia. His reign may be characterized as the starting point of Asian culture.

Once Buddhism had reached Central Asia there would seem to have been every reason to aim primarily at those areas west of Asia with whom India had been in commercial and cultural contact for centuries. However, traces of Buddhist impact that far west are very few and inconclusive. Possibly this is because the West had been an almost endless scene of wars or it may be that Buddhism was too formidably opposed by various other organized religions, particularly Zoroastrianism, Islam, and Christianity.

References to the Asian countries west of India are found in Buddhist literature, for instance in the *Baveru Jataka* (No. 339) and possibly in *Sussondi Jataka* (No. 360). Indeed, it would appear that Asoka had focused his attention more on the West than on the East. After all, Indian contact with Persia had been close and dated from the Achaemenian period. Although Persian interest in Buddhism really developed after its establishment in Tokharestan under the Kushans, it is not unlikely that some fragments of Buddhism had filtered through to western Asia during Asoka's period. The *Mahavamsa*, which contains the traditional account of the early Buddhist proselytizing efforts, mentions the country of the Yavanas where the Buddhist monk Maharakkhita preached the *Kalakarama Suttanta* to large audiences and is said to have converted one hundred seventy thousand Greeks, ten thousand of whom entered the Sangha. Further accounts of Buddhist activity among the Yavanas are inevitably garbled, but there is some historical support for the prevalence of Buddhism there. Whilst the figures quoted are evidently a gross exaggeration, the suggestion that the country of the Yavanas should be identified with some district in the Kabul valley and not further westward is contradicted by the thirteenth Rock Edict of Asoka, which refers to the distant realms of the Yavana kings. The Pali texts even represent the Greeks as taking part in missionary work. For example, the third Buddhist Council held at Pataliputra not only decided to send Buddhist missionaries to the distant Yona countries, but also called upon a Greek *bhikshu*, Yona

Dhammarakkhita, to go to the Aparantaka country, the western region of India, and preach the dhamma there.[53] This would suggest that the teachings of the Buddha had begun to appeal to Greeks even before the time of Menander, and that they had begun to produce monks of such ability and accomplishment that they could preach Indian doctrines to Indians.

Writing centuries later, the famous Arab scholar Al Biruni also acknowledged the existence of Buddhism in western Asia, although his sequence of historical narrative is obviously confused and disorderly. According to him, Khurasan, Persia, Iraq, Mosul, and the country stretching up to Syria, had at one time been Buddhist. Later, Buddhism was replaced by the doctrine of Zarathustra (Zoroaster), who went from Adharbaijan and preached Magism in Balkh. King Gushtasp and his son Isfendiyad patronized this religion and spread the new faith by both force and treaties. They founded fire-temples throughout their empire, from the frontiers of China to the Greek Empire. The succeeding kings made Zoroastrianism the state religion of Persia and Iraq; as a result, the Buddhists were banished and forced to emigrate to the countries east of Balkh. Then came Islam. Whilst Al Biruni's account of Buddhism's prevalence in western Asia before Zoroastrianism is obviously inaccurate, it would be erroneous to disregard the whole statement. It is possible for a chronicler or a historian to confuse dates of events which occurred centuries ago, but it is extremely unlikely that he would confuse facts. That Buddhism was practiced in this area during the ancient period and first suppressed by Zoroastrianism, and later by Islam, must be accepted as substantially true, particularly when viewed in the light of other similar literary references. The hostility between Buddhism and Zoroastrianism is hinted at in the *Bhuridatta Jataka* (No. 543), and Zoroastrian texts mention disputes with Buddhists.[54]

Hsüan-tsang, the Chinese scholar, wrote in the seventh century that Lang-kie (ka) Lo, a country having a separate government for each of its valleys under the sovereignty of Persia, contained more than a hundred monasteries with over six thousand Buddhist monks, and that there were several hundred Hindu temples, many of which belonged to the Sáiva Pasupata sect. In the capital, Su-tu-le-ssu-fa-lo, there was a large and very handsome Mahesvara statue, highly revered by the Pasupatas. As in India, both Hinduism and Buddhism, orthodoxy and heterodoxy, were accepted beliefs.[55] Hsüan-tsang, who possibly did not visit Persia (Po-la-sse) personally, says it contained many Deva-temples and that there were two or three Sangharamas, with several hundred priests who principally studied the Hinayana teaching according to the Sarvastivadin school. The *patra* of the Buddha was in the palace of the Persian King. The fact that it was the Hinayana school which was prevalent in Persia would suggest that Buddhism had been established there very early.

Archaeological evidence also supports the presence of Buddhism in western Asia. Aurel Stein discovered a Buddhist monastery in the area around the Helmund River in the Sistan region on the Afghan-Persian border. In Turkistan at a place called Dandan-Viliq, a picture of a four-armed Bodhisattva in the guise of a Persian with black beard and whiskers and holding a *vajra* (thunderbolt) in his left hand, has been found. This suggests not only the existence of Buddhism in Persia, but also that it had assumed a distinctive character in its new environment, a phenomenon which generally comes after a long period of localization.

Mani, the founder of Manichaeanism, who preached his doctrine during the third century, speaks of the Buddha as a messenger of God in his work *Shaburqan* (Shapurakhan). That Manichaeanism was influenced by Buddhism is further supported by the fact that a Manichaean treatise written in the style of a Buddhist sutra, speaks of Mani as the Tathagata, an attribute of the Buddha and Bodhisattvas. There are close resemblances between certain Manichaean works and the Buddhist *Suttas* and the *Patimokkha,* and, according to Cyril of Jerusalem, the Manichaean scriptures were written by one Scythianus and revised by his disciple Terebinthus who changed his name to Buddas.[56]

Although there are no remains of old Parthian translations of Buddhist texts, it is known from Chinese accounts that a number of Persian Buddhist scholars, after studying at the Buddhist centres of Tokharestan, went to China in the second and third centuries and collaborated in the translation of Buddhist texts into Chinese. The names of Parthian Buddhist monks in Chinese are distinguished by the prefix An (Ngan) from the old Chinese name of Parthia An-she (Arsak). Indeed, it was a Parthian prince, known to Chinese history as Ngan-she-kao or Lokottama, who made the first organized effort to translate the Buddhist canon into Chinese. He lived at the monastery of Pa-ma-ssee (the White Horse Monastery) during the second century, and founded a school of translators known because of its excellence as "unrivalled" in the systematic interpretation of Buddhism. He himself translated more than a hundred Buddhist texts into Chinese, of which fifty-five are available. It was at this school that the first Chinese monk, Yen-Fo-t'iao or Buddhadeva, learned Sanskrit.

The reasons for the decline of Buddhism in western Asia, in marked contrast to its brilliant successes in other areas of Asia, are somewhat obscure. But some explanation may lie first in the inhospitable attitude of the powerful Sassanin Empire (226–651) with its intense Iranian nationalism towards religious and cultural proselytization, and later in the phenomenal spread of Islam, which not only cut off the West from Buddhist spiritual influences, but actually dislodged it from Central Asia.

Hinduism, although not a proselytizing religion, had also reached western Asia. A Hindu settlement was established in Armenia in the Canton of Taron in the second century B.C. under the patronage of King Valarasaces of the Arsacidae dynasty. These Hindus built fine cities and temples, but the temples were destroyed early in the fourth century by St. Gregory the Illuminator.[57]

Of the various intellectual and religious movements that developed in the Graeco-Roman world during this period, the three most important were Christianity, Gnosticism, and Neoplatonism. All three were, either directly or indirectly, influenced by Indian concepts.

The historical origins of Christianity are inexactly known and the traditional story reverentially accepted by the faithful is a subject of dispute amongst historians. The problems—textual, literary, and historical—presented by the New Testament are being consciously scrutinized in a scientific manner by scholars, many of whom are devout Christians. Albert Schweitzer, who is regarded almost as a modern Christian saint, declined to accept the historicity of the traditional view of Jesus. In a similar vein Mahatma Gandhi said in an address on Christmas Day, 1931: "I must say that I have never been interested in an historical Jesus. I should not care if it was proved by someone that the man called Jesus never lived, and that what was narrated in the Gospels was a figment of the writer's imagination. For the Sermon on the Mount would still be true for me."[58] It seems natural enough to assume that the teachings of Jesus, as in any religious belief, would be the core of the Christian faith rather than the evidence of his historical existence.[59] Yet, it has frequently been asserted by Christian theologians, such as Reinhold Niebuhr, that Christianity is the only fully historical religion and it stands or falls on the truth of certain events which took place nearly two thousand years ago. On the other hand, a body of Christian thinkers is developing which does not believe that the abandonment of Christianity's claim to historicity would injure the ends of the faith.

Irrespective of the historical character of Jesus and of an intimate

93

connection between the activity of God and the course of human history, Christianity is basically an historical religion in the sense that it was not a sudden or miraculous transformation but an amalgam of slow, tedious, and laborious growth to which both the accidents of history and the deliberate decisions of eminent theologians have contributed their full measure.

Although the exact time and year of his birth are uncertain, it was during the reign of Augustus Caesar that Jesus of Nazareth was born, probably in 4 B.C., in Judaea, and it was in 29 that he was crucified whilst Tiberius was the Roman emperor. Reverent disciples trace his ancestry to the royal dynasty of David and his birth is ascribed to immaculate conception, an act of God, and they, as distinct from historians, believe him to be an incarnation of God, whom the Jews were the first to recognize.

Little is known of his childhood—beyond the dramatic stories of his birth—and little of his manner of life before he began to preach his divine message at about the age of thirty. Very shortly afterward, possibly between eighteen months and three years, he was accused by his countrymen of trying to set up an independent kingdom of Judaea and found guilty.[60] Consequently, he was crucified along with two thieves by the Roman authorities. Having died as Messiah and Redeemer, Jesus Christ, it is believed by his followers, arose from the dead and founded the Christian Church which gradually spread throughout the world, beginning with the work of the apostles. The believer admits that Jesus was a Jew who inherited Judaic tradition, but he disregards the continuity between Christianity and earlier doctrines, and the fact that Jesus lived in Galilee, the northern part of Palestine, which was closely connected with Syria by highways, and where there was a far greater mixture of races and ideas than in Jerusalem. Ignoring these things, he assumes the originality of the Christian faith. Jesus knew classical Hebrew and some Greek, but his mother tongue was Aramaic, which was spoken all over the Syrian world. He was a popular teacher attracting audiences from various sections of the populace.

The traditional account of Christian origins concentrates almost exclusively on the incidents connected with the rise of Christianity, giving the impression that nothing else was happening at that time in the area. Actually the situation was vastly different. It was a period of intense political activity and diverse religious practices, and it would hardly be an overstatement to suggest that in every city and village in the Roman Empire there were activities, customs, and rituals that eventually played a part in the moulding of Christianity. Everywhere there were signs of religious restlessness. The vacuum created by the decline of authority of the official religions of the city-states was filled by the cults of salvation. The stars were worshipped, and the legions of demons were regarded as having infested both earth and sky. A wide variety of beliefs and disbeliefs from all corners of the Hellenistic world and its neighbouring areas intermingled to produce a miscegenous brook of faiths and fears. The world of the first century was indeed one of transition, and there were great forces at work which paved the way for Christianity. A major contributing factor to this spiritual restlessness may well have been the very nature of Roman society, which, like the Greek, was based on slavery and by modern standards was callous and sensual. The unfortunate were despised and the fortunate were insecure. Despotism and tyranny were the order of the day as well as indiscriminate displays of pride without honour. Life revolved around violent sports in which men and beasts were tormented and killed, giving morbid pleasure to spectators. The uneasiness of men's hearts expressed itself in profound religious unrest.[61]

Some kind of religion has always existed in human society, although, until the rise of universalized religions, it was extremely local and personal. Early religions may appear crude or illogical to the modern mind but their adherents were next to none in the intensity of their conviction and faith in their deities. Yet they were most tolerant of each other's gods and beliefs. Religious intolerance appears to be one of the consequences of the quest for a universal religion, and a phenomenon previously almost unknown. The later introduction of organization into religious orders increased the scope and depth of religious strife and persecution. In antiquity, once the armed conflict was resolved, both the conqueror and the conquered consciously or unconsciously allowed the fusion of their gods, a process called theocrasia. A good example of such a fusion can be seen in the assimilation of Aryan and Dravidian gods in India. The process of assimilation, grouping, or rationalization of the new and old gods, however, varied with local conditions. The history of early theology is full of compromises and mutual adaptations.

When Roman rule extended to include the Hellenistic world, the existing local cults could not serve the needs of an expanding state comprised of distinct and distant nations. Greek philosophy itself was in a transitional stage, seeking new expression to fit the new world through Scepticism, Stoicism, and other schools. Along with this a tide of mysticism was developing, encouraging people to seek satisfaction through personal mystical experience. A common and new religion was needed, and the Romans, although generally disinterested in religious speculations, had to attend to it. They experimented with *Dea Roma,* the Goddess of Rome, as the supreme deity presiding over all the other local deities, but it did not succeed, possibly because of its obvious artificiality.[62] An exceedingly practical and hardy people, the Romans were singularly ill-equipped to work out a synthesis of philosophy and religion, or a common form of worship, or to produce doctrines dealing with unseen reality. They sought the satisfaction of their most personal religious emotions in exotic cults, for state religion rather inspired patriotism than stimulated spiritual life. Their hard-headed political attitude subordinated the religious urge. The glamorous potency of Jupiter, the sky god, of Juno and Minerva in their capitoline temple, and of the household gods (penates), Vesta the hearth-goddess, Janus the guardian deity of gates, and many others, as well as the careful measures taken to maintain their rites and sacred buildings with great pomp and show, and their insistence on superstition, must have held them in awe of their gods. It was left to history to answer the needs of the time.

The syncretic nature of Christianity is well known, although its historical evolution has been a complex phenomenon in which theological disputes and religious strife have frequently been interlinked with political conflicts. Founded in Judaism, which in its turn was a development of Hebrew religion, it soon came into close contact with a variety of Greek and Eastern religions and philosophies prevalent in the Hellenistic world and with Roman paganism which in itself was equally complex: "Not only did it preserve the heritage of Greek culture; it was also enlivened and enriched by the influx of religions from the Near East."[63]

Christianity has been described as a Graeco-Roman phenomenon in a Jewish mask. Enslin expresses the same opinion somewhat more forcefully, stating that the claim for Christianity as the "faith once and for all delivered to the saints" is, to an historian, utterly untenable. For Christianity was the child of Judaism, which, within a score of years, became a Gentile cult, adopted new concepts, and borrowed from all with which it came into contact.[64] It was a product of its times, combining the Graeco-Judaic heritage of exclusiveness with the newly emerging trend for universalism in a growing world of mixed peoples living in distant lands. Universalism gave Christianity its proselytyzing zeal and its exclusive claim to complete monopoly of the approaches to God.

Indeed, Jesus furthered the prophetic teachings of Judaism. He employed the old phraseology and imagery but gave them new meaning. He used the traditional material, gave it his own emphasis, and moulded it into a distinct doctrine. The core and strength of his teaching was the doctrine of the kingdom of Heaven, in which the sovereignty of God was supreme and absolute, and the nature of God was fatherly, loving, and forgiving. Jesus was not greatly concerned with speculative questions about God, or with abstract theories of his relationship to the soul and to the world. His fatherly love, his transcendent righteousness, his mercy, his goodness, were the facts of immediate experience. The certainty of God lay in the reality of consciousness and not in deductions by formal logic.[65] The love of one's fellow men and the renunciation of worldly possessions were the important ethical tenets of Jesus' teachings.

Jesus called himself the Son of God and also the Son of Man, but he made little distinction between the two; in fact, he did not even stress very much who or what he was. He emphasized his teachings. Furthermore, in the Hellenistic world the title "Son of God" did not have the same connotation as the faithful give it today. It was in fact fairly common. Greek gods had sons, and famous men were often regarded as sons of particular gods; for instance, Plato and Augustus as sons of Apollo, Alexander of Zeus-Ammon. The Gnostics, too, were more or less treated as divine. The title that occurs most often in the Gospels is "Son of Man," as used by Jesus himself. The implications of these terms have been long disputed, but it appears that Jesus was reluctant to assume the title "Son of God."[66] However, the New Testament refers to Jesus throughout as the Messiah. The title "Son of God" was frequently used for Jesus Christ when Christianity spread into the Mediterranean world. It was borrowed from the Old Testament where it was applied to David and other leaders. As the Jews were expecting the arrival of a Messiah, it was perhaps convenient to describe Jesus in Jewish terms. The title "Lord and Saviour" was also used for Messiah and was more comprehensible and agreeable to the Greeks.

Christian indebtedness to the Jewish scriptures is more than amply demonstrated by the fact that the Christians regard the Jewish Bible as the Old Testament or Covenant of God with the ancient Israelites, and their own Bible as the New Testament or Covenant made by God through Jesus Christ. It has long been said that the New Testament lies hidden in the Old Testament, and that the Old is made explicit in the New.

If the evidence of the recently discovered Dead Sea Scrolls is considered, Christianity would appear all the more to owe its existence not to divine intervention but to the processes of social and political evolution. It was by sheer accident that in early 1947 some Bedouin

Arabs, whilst replenishing their freshwater supply at a spring on the northwestern shore of the Dead Sea, seven miles south of modern Jericho, found these scrolls in the caves of Qumran. Some six hundred manuscripts have emerged from these caves but only a dozen are complete. News of the first discovery was greeted with great excitement on all sides, and amongst the seven scrolls then recovered from the tall jars in the shepherd's cave were copies of the biblical book Isaiah a thousand years older than any Hebrew Old Testament then known. Whereas the translators of the Scriptures had had to rely on mediaeval copies no older than the ninth or tenth centuries, texts were now available which the palaeographers dated as belonging to a century or so before Christ.[67] Within a year the scrolls were widely known amongst scholars and the intense debate, the so-called "Battle of the Scrolls," began concerning their exact date.

These scrolls contain accounts of the puritanical and covenanting Jewish sect, the Essenes, about whom a good deal was already known from the ancient historians, particularly from Josephus of the first century. The accounts bear such close resemblances to the New Testament, particularly to St. John's Gospel, that, if they are anterior to the beginnings of Christianity, Jesus would appear, according to scholars such as Dupont-Sommer of the Sorbonne and the more popular Edmund Wilson, an astonishing reincarnation of the earlier Essene teachers, and their ideas and beliefs would have anticipated Christianity. The Essenes were conspicuous for their quietism, extreme piety, asceticism, abstinence from sensuous pleasures, adherence to the Mosaic Law, communism, and secretiveness about their sectarian teachings. They lived in a communal settlement, a sort of monastery, by the shores of the Dead Sea. They were also known for their faculty of beauty and clairvoyance. The oldest manuscript recovered so far is a small papyrus palimpsest whose pre-Exilic Hebrew script has been dated to the sixth or seventh century B.C. Other documents inscribed on parchment, papyrus, potsherds, and even slats of wood, range in date from the third century B.C. to mediaeval times. The buildings at Qumran were destroyed by Vespasian in 68 during the First Jewish Revolt.

Opinion amongst theologians and scholars is sharply divided and the volume of their interpretations is continually mounting. The Christian scholars, however, point out that similarities between the priestly Essene Teacher and Jesus Christ were slight and irrelevant compared to the differences. The former, a leader of an extremist, exclusive sect living a puritanical life, may well appear quite contrary to Christ, who freely mixed with people and claimed to be the prophet of God. Even if the

Essene Teacher was crucified, the Christian apologists argue that his death was not held as an atoning martyrdom as was Jesus' crucifixion. Whatever the final verdict, if agreement is finally reached at all, the new evidence has certainly caused a close re-examination of primitive Christianity, which may well revolutionize the approach of traditional Christian beliefs to Judaism.[68]

When conscious adaptation is viewed along with the indirect and imperceptible influence of other religions prevalent at the time and in the regions where Christianity first emerged, the syncretic nature of early Christianity becomes markedly visible. Syncretism, adaptation, and resemblances between religious faiths, however, must be qualified by the consideration that all religions are fundamentally the same and that their missions are not competitive but complementary.

Of the mystery cults—including those of Demeter, Dionysos, Isis and Serapis, the religion of the Great Mother (Magna Mater), Cybele and Attis, Jehovah and Baal—which were prevalent in the Roman world, the Persian cult of Mithraism, named after the faithful saviour who gave his life in sacrifice for his people, was the most widespread, the most moral, and commanded the highest devotion. At one time, especially in the second and third centuries, it appeared that Mithraism would fill the widespread religious need. In Rome alone there were at one time or another more than a hundred temples dedicated to Mithra. Considering the immense popularity of the Egyptian goddess Isis throughout the Roman Empire, the emergence of Mithraism as the dominant faith clearly testifies to its power and prestige.

Mithraism was a formidable competitor of early Christianity. Renan's observation has often been quoted that if Christianity had failed, the whole of Europe would have been Mithraist. Before Mithraism, which no longer survives as a form of worship, could be suppressed and its temples in Rome demolished by Christians, Christianity adopted many of its doctrines and ceremonies. The Mithraic traditions and doctrines are collected in the *Avesta,* and a *yasht,* a special hymn of praise, is dedicated to Mithra. Mithra is the Persian name of the vedic Mitra, the deity of light and truth, warring against the powers of darkness in association with Varuna. In India he was, in fact, regarded as the sun. In vedic texts, the connection between Mithra and the bull, which later became the focal point of Mithraism, is perhaps more clearly found than in the *Avesta.* But the cult of Mithraism appears to have come to the Roman Empire from Iran, having been introduced to Rome by Cilician seamen in about 68 B.C. In Zoroastrianism, Mithra held a subordinate place amongst the gods with a status of a *Yazata,* but his worship, fostered by the Persian kings and modified by Semitic influence, took deep root in western Asia under the successors of Alexander, from where it expanded further westward. Mithra was conceived as the intermediary between man and the Supreme God and the redeemer of the human race. Mithraism, in contrast to other mystery religions, contained a long and detailed account of the life of Mithra from his miraculous creation from a rock by the good power of Ahuramazda, to his ascension in the chariot of the sun into heaven. He was the invincible warrior who attended upon the Lord of Life, Ahuramazda, in eternal opposition to the evil god of Death, Angra Mainyu.

Mithraism was enormously popular in the Roman army, especially amongst the officers, for Mithra was the unconquerable hero and a symbol of bravery and skill against the toughest possible enemy. Therefore, the chief instrument of the faith's dissemination was the army, which included large numbers of Asian soldiers. Thus, Mithraism was gradually carried to the remotest corners of the empire. In the garrison areas on the Rhine, the Danube, and the British frontier, numerous shrines dedicated to Mithra have been found. Over twenty Asian regiments of auxiliaries are known to have been stationed in various parts of Europe, the ranks of which were regularly refilled from the same areas. During the third and fourth centuries there were frequent shiftings of forces between the eastern and the western parts of the Roman Empire. But despite these opportunities for spreading the cult and its own great popularity, circumstances conspired against Mithraism and "the ultimate success, permanent and undoubted, fell to the combination of Jewish and Greek worship called Christianity."[69]

There are, however, many similarities between Christianity and Mithraism. Besides sharing faith in a divine mediator and the hope of resurrection, both taught the efficacy of prayer, sacramental union with God, and his providential presence in all events of daily life. Baptism, Confirmation, and the Eucharist of the Christians are analogous to certain rites of Mithraism. It is not unlikely that Mithraic usages may have passed into the practice of the Christian Church, and the influence of Mithraic architecture on its Christian counterpart is undoubted. But the redeemer, Mithra, unlike Christ, had no historical personality.[70] Both faiths borrowed from each other, although Christianity appears to have done so more extensively.

The early Christians were also profoundly impressed by the personality and legends of Orpheus. This is attested to, for example, by his presence in the art of the Roman catacombs. The much discussed haematite seal-cylinder, or amulet, of possibly the third century, now preserved in Berlin, shows a crucified man with the name "Orpheus" inscribed around it in Greek letters. This is regarded as evidence of the syncretism of Orphic and Christian ideas. It is also suggested that the crucifixion of Orpheus was an old tradition, and that Christian representations of the crucifixion in art do not go back beyond the fifth or sixth century.[71] Both the Orphic Dionysos and Jesus Christ were the sons of God; both suffered, died, and were resurrected. In fact, in the Hellenistic world other gods, such as Osiris and Adonis, were associated with similar legends. It is suggested, therefore, that if Christianity borrowed, it did so from the general religious trend of the period rather than from Orphism alone. Some Christian eschatological dogmas are traced to Orphic beliefs. The idea of purgatory has its origin in the Orphic notion of an intermediate state of life on earth after death and the final bliss of the deified soul.[72] However, the most characteristic parts of Orphic eschatology, reincarnation and the wheel of birth, find no place in orthodox Christianity.

By this time the Jews had dispersed throughout the Mediterranean world, building their synagogues, and retaining their distinct identity. Rome recognized Judaism as a permitted (licit) religion. The gospel had to be preached to the mixed audiences of the Hellenistic world in intelligible terms. These audiences, in turn, interpreted the teachings in a way that suited their own spiritual needs. Hellenistic Christianity thus came to vary from the original Palestinian version. "Hellenistic Christianity was no unitary phenomenon, but mainly a remarkable product of syncretism. It was full of tendencies and contradictions, some of which were to be condemned later on by orthodox Christianity as heretical, and which also explain the struggles between the various tendencies, of which the Pauline Epistles give such a vivid impression."[73] Examples of such contradictions and alterations are innumerable. The person of Jesus is sometimes defined in terms of Jewish and apocalyptic categories, sometimes as the "Lord" of the cultus, as a mystery deity, yet sometimes as the Gnostic redeemer, the pre-existent being from the heavenly world, whose earthly body is only an out-worldly garb. The Christian community is sometimes described in Jewish terms as the people of God and in Gnostic terms as the "body of Christ," into which individuals are incorporated by means of the sacraments of Baptism and the Lord's Supper.[74]

These contradictions were inevitable for Christianity was in its formative stages struggling to gain converts in a highly complex and mixed community. It not only profited by the concepts and experiences of others but sometimes made concessions to them to gain their accep-

101

tance. For example, the view of Jesus as a redeemer of mankind was not a Judaic concept, nor was it held by the first Christians in Palestine. The Messiah the Jews and the Christians expected was not the Son of God, but a messenger of God. But Mithra was a redeemer of mankind and so were Tammuz, Adonis, and Osiris. It was when Christianity spread into the pagan world that the idea of Jesus as a saviour God emerged, emulating already existing concepts. It may be recalled that during the early days little was said of Jesus the teacher; it was Christ the Saviour who was the Christian Lord. Whether it had been Jesus or Mithra, it would have made little difference in the redemptionist doctrines, sacraments, and observances. It was only in 324, several centuries later, that the Church at the Council of Nicaea, called by Emperor Constantine, formally accepted by a majority vote Jesus Christ as the Saviour God.[75] It was the birthday of Mithra, 25 December (the winter solstice), that was taken by the early Christians as the birthday of Jesus. The need and urgency for early Christianity to compromise with existing traditions are further illustrated by the fact that even the Sabbath, the Jewish seventh day, Saturday, appointed a day of rest by God in the Mosaic Law and hallowed by his own resting on this day after the work of Creation, was abandoned in favour of the Mithraic first day, the Day of the Conquering Sun, Sunday. The worshippers of Mithra were called "Soldiers of Mithra" which is probably the origin of the term "Soldiers of Christ" and of the exhortations to Christians to "put on the armour of light," Mithra being the God of Light. The most frequent theme of Christ as the Good Shepherd is reminiscent of a similar identification of Mithra, who was often called the Good Shepherd. And it is interesting to note that since Mithra was addressed as *Dominus,* Sunday must have been "the Lord's Day" long before Christian times. Concepts such as "the blood of the Lamb" or "Taurus the Bull" were similarly borrowed from Mithraism. The Last Supper (the Eucharist) was taken from Mithraism to combine with the sacred meal of Palestinian Christianity. The ceremony of eating an incarnate god's body and drinking his blood is of remote antiquity, with its origin in cannibalistic practices, and there could have been several sources for the Christian rite, but its connection with the Mithraic Eucharist is most apparent.[76] The Mithraic Eucharist is the commemoration of Mithra's Last Supper in a cave with Sol Helios before ascending to heaven. Some scholars believe the Resurrection of Christ derived from the Vigil of Mithra, who after his death reappeared to watch continuously over the faithful. The extent of the indebtedness of Christianity to pagan religion is so great that, "provided there was a Judaic-Christian nucleus at all, very little indeed need have been supplied by the Palestinian Christians."[77]

No country affected the development of the Christian religion more profoundly than Egypt; indeed, no city affected the development of the Christian religion more profoundly than Alexandria. In Horus, who was at once the son of Osiris and identical with Osiris, the Christians found an illuminating analogue. And, like Isis, the mother of Horus, Mary was elevated to a rank of quasi-divinity. Christianity also adopted the forms and symbols of popular cults. For instance, its priests copied the characteristic garments of the Egyptian priests. One accretion followed another and the original revolutionary teaching was buried under acquired customs.

In monasticism alone Egypt laid an indelible mark on Christianity. The formation and development of monasticism did not take place in the Greek-speaking capital Alexandria, but amongst the native Coptic-speaking Christians of Egypt. The influence on the Church of early ascetics produced by Coptic Christianity proved to be considerable. "Although monasticism spread quickly thence to Syria, it is admitted that the first Christian hermits and monasteries were Egyptian and there is some evidence for the existence there of pagan hermits. Egypt was a most religious country, but it does not appear that asceticism, celibacy or meditation formed part of its older religious life, and their appearance in Hellenistic times may be due to a wave of Asian influence starting originally from India."[78]

The most outstanding legacy of Egypt, which deeply influenced all later history of the Church, "has been the scientific Platonizing theology, which the Catechetical school of Alexandria was beginning to fashion at the close of the second century and which the comprehensive genius of Origen carried to a successful issue in the first half of the third century."[79] Pantaenus, the founder of this famous Christian college at Alexandria, who played a significant role in the spread of Christianity in Egypt, was one of the earliest Christian missionaries on record to visit India in the third century. It was he who found that there was a Christian church in India reputed to have been founded by St. Bartholomew. Clement of Alexandria, whose knowledge of India was remarkably accurate for the time, was Pantaenus' pupil and occupied the chair vacated by his teacher for the last twenty years of the second century. A pupil of Pantaenus and Clement, as well as of the Neoplatonist, Ammonius Lacoas, Origen became the head of the Catechetical school in 203. Origen was a man of enormous learning and greatly influenced Christian thought. His belief in metempsychosis, described as heretical, was possibly determined by Indian doctrine. Pointing out that mankind has two different ideals, detachment and love, Bevan comments that the Christian doctrine has also preached detachment in much the same way as did ancient Greece and India.[80]

A number of scholars, including those who accept the intrinsic superiority of Christianity, have maintained that Christianity's rise in the Roman world was largely due to its syncretic nature. Christianity acquired greater strength in its struggle against existing faiths by voluntarily adopting their better elements. People, regardless of their colour or nationality, travelled freely in the Empire and Eastern peoples visited Rome in increasing numbers. Their religious beliefs won large numbers of converts in Roman society, thus narrowing "the gap between the old religions and Christianity, and in such a way as to make the triumph of Christianity an evolution, not a revolution."[81]

Religions spread generally through immigration, conversion, and conquest. The expansion of Islam was largely a matter of conquest, which did not figure at all in the spread of Buddhism. Christianity, however, spread in all three of these ways, although during the early centuries it was mainly carried across national frontiers by missionary zeal and the movement of people. In spite of the inadequacy of reliable information on the subject, there is considerable evidence to suggest that there was a great deal of racial intermixture in Rome. By the time of Nero, a great many of Rome's senators and knights were descendants of slaves, many of Eastern stock, and the native population had dwindled to a surprisingly small proportion of the whole; by far the largest part of the populace—perhaps ninety percent—had Oriental blood in their veins. When Paul reached Rome as a prisoner, the city itself had an Eastern population of above half a million. The immense popularity of the Eastern mystery cults in Rome, as testified to by the frequent street processions of devotees celebrating exotic rites, songs, and dances, and by widespread discussions about purification from sin, immorality, and the imminence of God in the soul, would indicate not only the increasing number of non-Roman peoples but also the growing influence of imported doctrines. Authorities, such as Cumont and Dobschutz, hold the view that a great religious conquest can be explained in moral terms alone. In other words, these Eastern cults offered something of greater moral value and stronger human appeal than the old Roman religion,[82] whilst the socially altered character of Rome and the diffusion and popularity of these new religions had prepared the Roman people for the reception of Christianity.[83]

India had been in close contact with the areas in which the accounts of the Gospels originated and the Jewish faith flourished, and it is more than likely that Indian religious ideas and legends were well known there. Indians possessed a greater missionary zeal for spreading ideas, rather than making converts, than they are generally credited with. Some Indian influences on the developing ideas of early Christianity were felt directly, whilst others were transmitted through other prevalent religions and intellectual movements. Even to understand the Jewish religion, which formed the immediate background of Christianity, non-semitic influences on Palestine and Syria must be considered.

Numerous authorities, such as Hilgenfeld and Renan, maintain that there was Buddhist influence on the Essene doctrines. And it was through this Jewish sect that Buddhist influences reached Palestine and later filtered through to Christianity. On the authority of Philo (25 B.C.–A.D. 40), Josephus, and Pliny, the Essenes were a peace-loving people who despised riches and lived in villages because the cities were rife with evil. Extremely charitable, they practiced love of God, virtue, and man. They thought of pleasure as evil, objected to animal sacrifice, abstained from temple-worship, ate no meat, and drank no wine. They abjured marriage but adopted other peoples' children. They were known for their simple piety, sense of justice, powers of endurance, and brotherly love. Admission into their sect was difficult, requiring years of probation, oaths of rigorous discipline, good conduct, and secrecy. They regarded the body as corruptible, but the soul as immortal, entombed for a time in the flesh, from which, when released, it rejoices and mounts upward. They accepted the doctrine of the pre-existence of the soul. The life led by the Essenes was "just as might have been evolved by seekers after truth who were trying to put into practice in another country the religious ideals of India. There are differences: for instance these communities laboured with their hands and observed the seventh day, but their main ideas, retirement from the world and suppression of the passions, are those of Indian monks and foreign to Egyptian and Jewish thought."[84]

Although few in number—about four thousand—their influence was totally out of proportion to their numbers. John the Baptist was possibly an Essene who had spent his period of preparation in the vicinity of the Dead Sea. The evidence of the Dead Sea Scrolls clearly suggests that the community of Qumran near the Dead Sea represented a type of Judaism which was "particularly subject to external influences."[85] Moffatt remarks, "Buddhistic tendencies helped to shape some of the Essenic characteristics."[86] Jesus himself was greatly influenced by the tenets of the Essenes, even if he did not actually belong to this sect or live with them at Qumran during the time preceding his ministry. His teachings of non-resistance to evil and salvation by the forgiveness of sins, like those of John the Baptist whom Jesus regarded as his master and forerunner, have been attributed to the Essenes. It is significant that the Essenes, who, through the discovery of the Dead Sea Scrolls, have come to claim a share in the development of Christian doctrine, were in 1867 described by a German scholar, Hilgenfeld, as Buddhist.[87]

The Book of Enoch, a remarkable Hebrew work which was written before the rise of Christianity in about 80 B.C., is believed to be the source of some Christian beliefs. Although full of non-Jewish speculations, the book was written for the Jews and deals with their final deliverance, the blessed lot of the righteous, and the damnation of the wicked. The older of the two forms of the book never mentions the speculations about the Son of Man, the later one does. Enoch, the saint of hoary antiquity who was transported alive to heaven, preaches of the coming world judgment. His sermons lack the charm and elegance of the parables of Jesus, but Jesus' maxims are related to and dependent on this literature in style and construction, and "the contents of many sayings of Jesus are related to those of Enoch and some may almost appear as quotations."[88] The four titles attributed to Jesus in the New Testament—the Christ, the Righteous One, the Elect One, and the Son of Man—are all to be found in the Book of Enoch. But the idea of a Son of God who was also a Son of Man, as Rudolf Otto points out, certainly did not originate in Israel but has its roots in Aryan antiquity. Although what ancient figure was once the starting point of this concept is unknown, there is no doubt that "the phrase, 'this Son of Man' points back in some way to influences of the Aryan past."[89] Radhakrishnan carries the argument a little further and concludes: "When Jesus manifests His spiritual insight by His suffering unto death He inherits the Kingdom. He is the Son of Man and the Son of God. It is the ancient Hindu tradition which Enoch illustrates and Jesus continues."[90]

In a detailed analysis of non-Jewish influences on early Christianity, Otto has traced the Indian influence on a number of the ideas set forth by Enoch. The process of spiritual ascent, unclothing and reclothing, described in the Book of Enoch, has a clear analogy in the Indo-Aryan East. Altered and abridged but unchanged in essence, the process is found in India in the *Kaushitaki-Upanishad*. Composed long before the birth of Christianity, this text details the ascent of the soul and its journey through the higher spheres: the sphere of the moon as entrance to the lower celestial region, the sphere of fire, the ever higher spheres, and finally the Brahman sphere where the soul enters the world above and meets Brahman itself.[91] The predicates which are attributed to Enoch's God are also found in the Upanishads.[92] Eschatological systems put forth in the apocalyptic Book of Enoch, on which the Christian eschatology was modelled, had a more remote origin in ancient Aryan sources. The concept of the Kingdom of God, although its interpretation is a controversial topic in Christian theology, is one of the most fundamental of the beliefs which are generally held to have been appropriated from Judaism.[93] "The ultimate source of the idea of the Kingdom," observes Otto, "lies still farther back in the prehistoric period of Aryan religion, viz. in Asura religion. The latter arose before the separation of Iranians and Indians, whose oldest sacred documents exist interspersed in the Veda of India."[94] By the time of the *Rig Veda,* however, this concept of Kingdom had become a definite term, *Kshatra Varshishta,* the most glorious Kingdom. It is described as spiritual, truthful, and purposeful. And the prayer is offered:

> O, that we
> In your far extended Kingdom
> Which protects many, may be made one.[95]

The Hindus, the Buddhists, and the Zoroastrians, like the Christians, have maintained that the Kingdom of God is not of this world, and is not to be identified with a paradise on earth. The universalism and pacifism of Jesus conflicts with the Jewish exclusiveness and militarism. His Kingdom was open to all alike, irrespective of race and nationality. His preachings of a life of self-control tantamount to asceticism and otherworldliness, forsaking parents and possessions, are not in accordance with Jewish tradition, which has little in it of an ascetic character and has accepted the uninterrupted continuance of the present world order. But self-control and asceticism were emphasized centuries ago both by the Upanishads and the Buddha. "It is not too much to say," wrote Rhys Davids, "that almost the whole of the moral teaching of the Gospels as distinct from the dogmatic teaching, will be found in Buddhist writings, several centuries older than the Gospels; that for instance, of all the moral doctrines collected together in the so-called Sermon on the Mount, all those which can be separated from the theistic dogmas there maintained are found again in the Pitakas."[96] The Christian view of future life, again, was not determined by Jewish nor by prevalent Hellenistic conceptions. The Jews were satisfied with the conception of Sheol, because the jurisdiction of Yahweh, a god of the living, did not extend to it, and they stressed the importance of life on earth. Excepting the mystery cults of Plato and Pythagoras, Greek eschatology was primitive and singularly unattractive whilst Roman belief in immortality was feeble. Christian ideas of eschatology, such as the consciousness of sin, the need of healing and redemption, or rewards and punishments, which were so different from those of the Old Testament and yet so well-developed, may well have been formulated in the atmosphere where Eastern mystical experience and intellectual speculation had reacted on Western concepts.

Jesus, no doubt, principally enlarged and transformed the Jewish conceptions but he did so in the light of personal experiences in a cosmopolitan area where a variety of cultures, including that of India, had intermingled to produce a distinct religious environment. "In his teaching of the Kingdom of God, life eternal, ascetic emphasis, and even future life, Jesus Christ breaks away from the Jewish tradition and approximates to Hindu and Buddhist thought. Though his teaching is historically continuous with Judaism, it did not develop from it in its essentials."[97] Whilst Judaism was not a proselytizing religion, Christianity and Buddhism were.

Jesus has been described in a variety of ways, ranging from a nationalist leader to a messenger of God, and even God Himself. This diversity of opinion arises mainly because knowledge of his brief and stormy career is at best fragmentary and, more significantly, owes its existence to the early Church. The four Gospels which preserve the memory of facts were based on a living tradition and written long after the crucifixion of Christ at various dates from 65 to around 100. These Gospels agree in most essentials but differ in minor details. The New Testament comprises these four Gospels, a Church history, twenty-one epistles, and an apocalypse. Most of these were originally written in Greek—although perhaps some Gospels were based on prototypes composed in Aramaic. The Gospels are attributed to four saints, Mark, Matthew, Luke, and John in this chronological order; and the Church history, or the Acts of the Apostles, to Luke.[98] Of the thirteen epistles attributed to St. Paul six are of major significance. The Apocalypse, or the Revelation of St. John The Divine, is attributed to the apostle John but is almost certainly the work of some unidentified Ephesian mystic. It is addressed, in epistolary form, to the seven churches in Asia. Most of the canonical books of the New Testament, especially the epistles of St. Paul and St. John, do not belong to the Palestinian tradition. And the Greek influence on them is keenly debated.[99]

Scholars have been profoundly struck and at times perplexed by the remarkable similarities between the Gospel story and the life and teaching of the Buddha, as told in the *Lalitavistara,* and between the Buddhist and Christian parables and miracles. Both the Buddha and Christ were miraculously conceived and wondrously born and angels rejoiced at both births,[100] although there is no story of a virgin birth in Buddhism, the paternity of Suddhodhana never being questioned.[101] It is also not claimed that the Buddha was the Enlightened One from birth. The annunciation of the child to Mary is, however, paralleled—although remotely—by the dream of Maya at the commencement of her conception. Again, Christ was born in the royal tribe of Judah and not the priestly tribe of Levi; the Buddha was born in a royal household of the *Kshatriya* (warrior), and not the Brahman (priestly) caste.[102] An identity in the names of the mothers, Maya and Mary, through Maia, the mother of the Greek Hermes and Roman Mercury, the messenger of the gods to man, has been suggested.[103] Mary is luminous before the birth of Christ and the child is born without pain or impurity. Just as the aged Simeon sang worshipping the infant Christ, "Lord, now lettest Thou Thy servant depart in peace, for mine eyes have seen my salvation," so the old hermit Asita, who visited the infant Buddha, paid homage and lamented that he would not live to see the Great Enlightenment which he prophesied. Whether the Evangelists appropriated the Buddhist tale and grafted it into their own conceptual tradition or not, there is no doubt of the antiquity and originality of the Buddhist legend. Both Jesus and Siddhartha revealed their unusual wisdom at about the same age, twelve: Jesus through learned discourses, Siddhartha through meditation.

Nothing is known of Jesus' life during the next seventeen years and there have developed a variety of legends and literature suggesting that he travelled in India, or Egypt, or lived with the Essenes at Qumran. The Gospels, however, refute these suggestions by implication. Whether Jesus travelled abroad or not, that he chose to remain unknown after having revealed himself and his wisdom causes some surprise. As Jesus is claimed to be God, it could not have been a period of preparation. In contrast, more is known of the Buddha's life, his childhood, youth, marriage, increasing discontent with the world, renunciation, quest of Enlightenment, and finally his attainment of the Buddahood, followed by a long period of missionary activity until he died. Whilst Jesus was born as the Christ, Siddhartha became the Buddha.[104]

Christianity, like Buddhism, is based on the teachings of a divine founder, in contrast to the two semitic religions, Islam and Judaism.

In the Quran, the prophet Muhammad is categorically asserted to be a man like any other, and Judaism has no single founder. "Christ" is the Greek rendering of the Hebrew "Messiah," the "Anointed" who had long been awaited, whilst the Buddha is "the incarnation of *buddhi,* the Sanskrit word for divine, intuitional intellect, the intermediary between Absolute Truth and man's mind, and therefore fundamentally the same as the Word or Logos which descends from God to man, from Absolute Being to limited and reflected being."[105] If Christ was betrayed by Judas, the Buddha was harassed by Devadatta. The parallel of the beloved disciple John can be found in Ananda, yet neither of these two was chosen to step into the shoes of the Master after his death. Both the Buddha and Christ were miraculous healers, although miracles play a smaller part in Buddhism. There is a sense of expectancy in both religions; the Christians await the second coming of Christ and the Buddhists the Maitreya Buddha.[106] Both the Buddha and Christ command their disciples to collect a treasure which neither moth nor rust would corrupt, nor thieves steal. Indeed, the similarities even in detail are many and close. For instance, in *Illisa Jataka* (No. 78) the Buddha miraculously feeds five hundred "Brethren" with a single cake, just as Christ fed a multitude of four thousand with a few loaves of bread. In the *Silanisamsa-Jataka* (No. 190) an eager disciple of the Buddha, who finds no boat to take him across the river and who was deeply absorbed in thoughts of his Master, walks on the water which solidified under his feet. In the middle the waves rise and he loses his faith and begins to sink. When a renewed mental effort fortifies his faith in the Buddha, he goes safely to the other side. Max Müller remarks that mere walking on water is not an uncommon story, but walking by faith and sinking for want of it can only be accounted for by some historical contact or transference, "and in this case we must remember that the date of the Buddhist parable is chronologically anterior (some centuries) to the date of the Gospel of St. Luke."[107] Winternitz suggests that a number of Buddhist legends in the Apocryphal gospels are so clearly Indian in character that their Egyptian or Palestinian origins can hardly be sustained. Images prostrate themselves before the young Christ in a temple in Egypt just as they do before the young Buddha in the temple of Kapilavastu. The similarity between the temptations of the Buddha and Christ and their transfiguration is too close for them to be wholly independent of each other. Both the Buddha and Christ, as was Zoroaster, were tempted by the Evil One at about the same time in their careers. All the accounts of the transfiguration of the two teachers agree not only in describing the shining body but in including a reference to impending death. Even in the most Judaic of the epistles in the New Testament the phrase "the wheel of birth" occurs, which Schopenhauer ascribed to Indian influence. The ethical system of Buddhism is substantially reproduced in Christianity. "To love one's enemies, to bless them that curse, to do good to them that hate, to turn the other cheek, to leave the cloak with him who takes the coat, to give all to him who asks, which are the teachings of Jesus," observes Radhakrishnan, "are precepts not only taught but practiced in their extreme vigour by the Buddha in his many lives, according to Jatakas."[108] Both Christ and the Buddha, as did the Upanishads before them, demanded the sacrifice of natural existence as the condition of a new richer life. Possibly some of the stories and incidents are common tales of a widespread folklore. Yet, not all similarities between the two religions can be traced to natural evolution.

Many similarities between Christian and Buddhist monastic systems, vestments and rituals, the worship of saints, images, and conceptions of heaven and hell are remarkably close. All religions have sacrifice, priests, incense, and an idea of faith, but when these universal similarities are accounted for and when all allowance is made for similar causes and coincidences, it is hard to believe that a collection of practices such a clerical celibacy, confession, the veneration of relics, and the use of rosary and bell, could have originated independently in both religions.[109] Celibacy, relics, and confession have no counterparts in Jewish, Syrian, or Egyptian antiquity, whereas they are known to be old Buddhist institutions. In 1842 two French missionary travellers to Tibet, Huc and Gabet, were shocked at the close resemblances between Catholic and Lamaistic ritual.[110] Indeed, Lamaistic Buddhism, which did not follow the serene metaphysical teaching of the Buddha closely, represented demons and torments of hell as lurid as those of mediaeval Christianity. The similarities between the Tibetan religion and Christianity are so close that the former has often been designated as a corrupted form of Christianity.

In spite of these many parallels and similarities, the two religions are greatly different in temperament. Whilst Buddhism is rationalistic, non-dualistic, and even agnostic, Christianity is completely devotional and dualistic. The Buddha did not teach of God and His relation with this world, but Christ's main thesis was that God created this world which He loves deeply. The Buddha preached that nirvana was unobtainable by pleasure or rites but only through an unselfish life of renunciation. Christ taught neither asceticism nor metempsychosis. Unlike the Buddha, Christ ate flesh, allowed himself to be anointed, and drank wine—indeed is credited with miraculously producing it when wine-cellars ran out—and prescribed it for religious purposes. He praised poverty and the poor. Keyserling, however, noticed a great affinity of spirit between Mahayana Buddhism and Christianity; and although he considered Mahayanism to be far superior to Christianity philosophically, he felt that it could not be compared with Christianity in efficaciousness. In a recent study, Osborne discusses the two doctrines in some detail and suggests that in spite of their diversities, the same fundamental doctrines do exist in both religions. Apart from the many other similarities, he has endeavoured to show that "the Christian doctrine of original sin and redemption corresponds to the Four Noble Truths that form the doctrinal basis of Buddhism; that there is suffering, that there is a cause for suffering, that there is a cure for suffering, and that there is a path to this cure."[111]

Broadly speaking, both religions were missionary, zealous to bring other men into their fold, and were universal in outlook postulating that all men share a common human nature, feel a common need for salvation, and have a capacity to avail themselves of that salvation. A number of scholars from different countries, such as Rudolf Seydel, A. J. Edmonds, and Richard Garbe, have insisted on the Christian indebtedness to Buddhism. Others, apart from those who instinctively find it uncomfortable to acknowledge Christian obligation to non-Christian sources and insist on its originality and divine revelation, deny such an indebtedness and attribute all similarities to parallel development. There is no documentary proof of borrowing or of the suggestion that Jesus had travelled in the East. However, in the nineteenth century, Nicholas Notovitch published a study, *The Unknown Life of Christ,* asserting that during his long period of obscurity Jesus had stayed with Brahman and Buddhist monks, who had initiated him into Indian religions. The book was first published in French and was edited, abridged, and translated into English by Violet Crispe in 1895. This study was based on the materials Notovitch had collected during his travels in India and Tibet, particularly on the records of Saint Issa discovered by him at the convent Himis. Inevitably the book excited fierce controversy and reproach from some theologians. Max Müller disputed Notovitch's assertions and questioned the authenticity of the latter's evidence. Despite this, Notovitch reaffirmed his views when the English version was published.

Equally unknown is how Christianity arrived in India during the first century. The Syrian Christians of Malabar believe that their form of Christianity is apostolic, derived directly from the Apostle Thomas.[112]

The Apostle is said to have landed at Malankora near Cronganore, then a thriving port on India's west coast, in 52 and to have founded a number of churches in southern India. He then crossed over to the east coast where he died in 68. Over the place he was buried at Mylapore, then called Calamina in Madras, there still exists the magnificent Tomb of St. Thomas which is, however, now empty, the Portuguese having removed the remains to Lisbon in 1523.[113] The evidence certainly does indicate that India and Christianity were in close contact during the period of the latter's formative stages. If Christianity could reach India during the first century and find a sanctuary so firm that it has survived all these hundreds of years, why could not Indian religions, especially Buddhism which was equally proselytizing, reach western Asia and the Graeco-Roman world and find a footing there? The road surely must have been open both ways.

Once Christianity was introduced into India, it was inevitable that it should have had some influence on Indian religious thought. In fact, it is surprising that it did not have more influence, fertilizing Indian thought in much the same way as Buddhism did in China. For, whilst retaining an identity of its own, Buddhism also gave rise to a new syncretic philosophical school, Neoconfucianism. In contrast, Christianity retained its separate identity and inspired no new schools of philosophy. However, in the last century Albrecht Weber and other scholars suggested that the cult of Krishna with it emphasis on *bhakti,* love or devotion, was a corrupt form of Christianity. Weber's theory aroused lively literary debate, and many Indologists opposed his view. Bhandarkar pointed out the positive existence of the Krishna cult in India prior to the advent of Christianity; Krishna is mentioned in Panini's *Vasudeva Sutra* and in the works of Patanjali. Supported by this evidence, Garbe exploded Weber's assertion finally by pointing out that the cult of Krishna was already of some importance in the first century B.C. The priority of the cult of Krishna, however, cannot rule out the possibility that it later adopted some legends or features from Christianity.

Whilst Christianity was forming, other religious movements were afoot. Some neglected the Old Testament altogether and relied on the prevalent and peculiarly Hellenistic fusion of concepts of philosophy and science. Amongst the better known religious movements of Alexandria are Jewish Platonism, Gnosticism, and Neoplatonism. Despite their distinct personalities and varied inspirations, they all shared certain beliefs, such as an abstract concept of God as the transcendent absolute unity, the notion of an intermediary power to bridge the chasm between God and the world, the connection of matter with the principle of evil, and an emphasis on the ability of asceticism to realize absolute truths. Mysticism was particularly stressed and the dominant belief was in the immortality of the soul, imprisoned in a mortal body, which expressed itself in the Greek words, *soma sema*, the body a tomb. Belief in the Ptolemaic system of astronomy and in the auxiliary systems it created was also popular. These concepts which were widely held in the Graeco-Roman world during the first two centuries were neither Jewish nor Christian in origin. It is extremely significant that it was against this background, and indeed during the period of ascendancy of non-Jewish and non-Christian doctrines, that these syncretistic religious movements developed. These movements were so alien to Greek traditions that M. Vacherot asserts that the philosophy of the Alexandrians derived nothing from Greek philosophy except its language and its methods; the essentials were all Eastern.[114]

With Philo (*ca.* 25 B.C.–A.D. 40), Jewish philosophy reached full maturity. He interpreted Jewish scriptures freshly and systematically. Not much is known of his life, but his pious and generous character clearly emerges from his many works expounding Judaism to the Hellenistic world. Deeply impressed by Greek philosophy, he aimed to reconcile Jewish thought and customs with Greek ideas, particularly Plato's. The biblical concept of God emphasized both the transcendence and the immanence of the Supreme Being, which did not quite agree with either the Platonic notion of God as the idea of the good which was the measure of all things, or the Stoic concept of Logos as an all-pervading divine principle. Plato's God was wholly transcendent, and the Stoic one wholly immanent. In working out a reconciliation between the biblical and the Greek concepts, Philo treated the Universe as a graded hierarchy of beings from stones to plants, animals, men, demons, and gods. Philo's God is the essential being of the world, eternal, indescribable, and omnipresent. Yet, he saw matter also as distinct, eternal, and increate, although it has no life, motion, or form until infused with divine force. To create the world by giving form to matter and to establish a link with man, God employed a variety of intermediary beings, designated as angels by Jews, *diamones* by Greeks, and ideas by Plato. The world, which was a stage in the ascent of the soul to God, is God's only beloved Son produced by the union of God with his knowledge. The distinction which Philo made between a transcendent God and wisdom or knowledge departs from the Hebrew doctrine of creation, because it admits the pre-existence of wisdom, although this distinction between God and wisdom is also made by an earlier

Jewish text, *The Book of Wisdom*. In spite of his devotion to Jewish thought, Philo was very appreciative of the contemplative monks of Egypt, the Therapeutae, and also of the Essenes in whose precepts the influence of Hindu and Buddhist thought has already been noted.[115] There is a distinct mystic element in Philo's thought. The way to a vision of God lay through a detachment from the world and an embracing of the contemplative life, which must be preceded by "excising desires, pleasures, griefs, fears, follies, injustices." The body is the source of evil and man must free himself from its chains. Divine vision can be gained only when he is "lifted above and out of himself." Philo's insistence on monotheism, his contempt for idolatry, and his claim that the Jews had in the Mosaic revelation the highest religious knowledge were, no doubt, Judaic, but other elements in his mysticism which are paralleled in Hindu thought could have been influenced by Indian mysticism. For there is no doubt that genuine Indian mysticism had found a firm foothold in western Egypt, and its first fusion appears to have been with the Egyptian Judaism of Alexandria.[116]

Another important school of thought in the first century was Neopythagoreanism. Very little is known of but two of its members, Apollonius of Tyana (born in 4 B.C.), and Moderatus of Gades.[117] Apollonius of Tyana came to study at Taxila in India about 50. The knowledge of this visit comes from his biography written by Philostratus about 217, although the authenticity and reliability of this work has frequently been questioned. Apollonius, a Gnostic, preached and practiced strict asceticism. He renounced wine, meat, and other physical pleasures. He was opposed to blood sacrifices and insisted on prayer and contemplation. Freedom from wealth, possessions, and desires was the only worthwhile goal of life. He acquired so great a reputation as a saint and wandering prophet that he came to be worshipped as a god. Temples and shrines were erected in his honour in Asia Minor and he was held to be a rival to Jesus Christ by the opponents of Christianity. Others accused him of sorcery and called him the prince of impostors, but, according to his disciples, he "taught the purest of religions, and in India especially, a country which long before Egypt and in different fashion had enjoyed the favour of divine wisdom, had found the evidence and inspiration to support his faith."[118]

Neopythagoreanism was the first product of an age in which abstract philosophy had begun to lose prestige, and it attempted to introduce a religious element into pagan philosophy in place of what had come to be regarded as an arid formalism. Many Neopythagoreans, like many

Neoplatonists, made conscious efforts to arrest the growth of Christianity by converting philosophy to a non-Christian religion. The founders of this school sought to invest their doctrines with the halo of tradition by ascribing them to Pythagoras and Plato. They identified the good with the one and emphasized the fundamental distinction between the soul and the body. God was to be worshipped and the soul freed from the body, and, in the interest of the spiritual purity of the soul, sensuous pleasure was to be abandoned. It is said that Neopythagoreanism provided a link between the doctrines of Plato and Neoplatonism. Certainly, the similarities between Essene thought and Neopythagoreanism are close and striking. In any case there are elements in this philosophy not only of Pythagoras' and Plato's systems but also of Indian philosophy.

Jewish philosophy as interpreted by Philo may or may not have been influenced by Indian thought, but the speculations of its rivals, the Gnostics, including Valentinus and Basilides, definitely were, for Gnosticism was a deliberate attempt to fuse Christian, Platonic, and Indian ideas. Most Gnostics were strongly anti-Jewish, professedly Christian, and regarded the God of the Old Testment as an inferior being. The nature and significance of Gnosticism, however, has been a matter of controversy since its inception. A very significant product of the Hellenistic age, it is sometimes stretched to cover all varieties of Hellenistic mysticism, including the doctrines of Plotinus in spite of his criticism of the Gnostics. It is common practice nowadays to include the Mandaean and Manichaean religions, as well as part of the Hermetic literature, as "gnostic." In antiquity the followers of the gnostic systems did not usually describe themselves as "Gnostics," and the Christian preachers spoke of them as members of various sects often named after their founders. Apart from the reason that different interpretations were given to the term "gnostic," which is held to be the distinctive feature of the movement, a major reason contributing to this confusion must be the religion's very syncretistic nature, for it was a movement which covered many sects and widely differing tenets prevailing in the Graeco-Roman world during and prior to the early days of Christianity when it was gradually crystallizing into the ancient Catholic Church.[119]

The gnostic movement came into prominence at the beginning of the second century and reached its height in the latter half of that century. By the middle of the third century it had begun to wane, although it continued in other forms for a century or two, and many of its ideas survived in later mysticisms. Its last, and perhaps greatest, manifestion was in the composite religion of Mani. It was revived in mediaeval Europe and is reputed to be connected with the downfall of the Templars. In modern times much of the symbolism of the Freemasons is held to be unmistakably Gnostic in origin.[120]

Gnosticism, as an intellectual activity, was chiefly concerned with attempting to work out a reconciliation between philosophy and theology, although, during its heyday, it had support from men of both philosophy and science. Its fundamental concept, gnosis, or the knowledge of God, is similar to the *Jnanakanda* of the Hindus, but many of its adherents interpreted "gnosis" not as "knowledge" or "understanding," but as "revelation." It was deeply mystical, and like other mystical religions, subscribed to the ultimate object of individual salvation, seeking a secure and comfortable habitat for the soul after death, and worshipping a redeemer or deity. Gnosticism also emphasized the special value of sacraments, rituals, acts of initiation and consecration, and symbols and formulae.

Only a few of the Gnostic texts, which were extraordinarily numerous, survived destruction by their Christian opponents. Consequently, our knowledge about the Gnostics is derived almost exclusively from the extracts and fragments found in the writings of those Christians who attacked and sought to discredit Gnostic doctrines. Broadly speaking, Gnosticism is regarded as having descended from Indian mysticism, heterodox Judaism, heterodox Christianity, or Hellenism. All these views are widely held. The controversy, however, appears to be futile because Gnosticism, being a deliberate syncretism, contains certain elements from all these blended into its own mould. It was regarded for a long time as an "acute Hellenization of Christianity" and as a movement within Christianity, but further research has now established that it was "really a religious movement of pre-Christian origin, invading the West, from the Orient as a competitor of Christianity."[121] Kennedy has described it as "Orientalism in a Hellenic mask" and to a careful student the close similarity amongst the teachings of the Upanishads and early Buddhism and Gnostic theories is obvious.

Although Gnosticism began as a synthetic phenomenon, it soon assumed a distinctive and integrated personality of its own. It had a definite attitude toward life and a clear interpretation of human existence. The various Gnostic sects differed in detail and emphasis, but in basic beliefs they shared a similar philosophy. They all believed that the world was bad, being controlled by evil or ignorance, and could not be redeemed. But the divine spark imprisoned in men could attain salvation by divine grace. A cardinal feature of Gnostic thought is the dualism of God and world, of man and world, and of man within himself. The Gnostic God is transcendent and alien in nature to the universe, which He neither created nor governs. There are two worlds: the spiritual (good and light) and the material (evil and dark). The highest goal of the soul, or, in the language of Gnosticism, man's true inner self which originated in the world of light, is to shake off its imprisonment in the body, give up its fallen and alien life on earth, and find its way back to the world of light ascending through lower worlds and the spheres of heaven—the seats of archons (rulers). The soul is a part or spark of the Primal or Heavenly Man, who existed before the world began. Ignorance is the essence of mundane existence, hence the need for divine revelation. The soul, entombed in the body, is assisted in its efforts for freedom by the Supreme Deity, who in his pity for the captive sparks of light sends down his Son, the heavenly figure of light, to redeem them. In Christian systems this saviour figure is identified with Christ. Hence, Gnosticism was a "redemptive religion based on dualism," which gave it an affinity with Christianity. Whilst the idea of the *demiurge* (artificer), the leader of the archons, who created the world and rules it, is related to the Hindu idea of Isvara, no distinction is recognized in Gnosticism between the creator of the world and the Supreme Deity, although in Indian thought it is. The Indian emphasis on dualism may have been inspired by Persia.

Even though some of the gnostic ideas found a place in Christian thought, Christianity gradually came to look upon it as a heretical perversion and bitterly resisted its ideas. W. R. Inge has called the Gnostics representatives of "barbarised Platonism."[122] Yet, it was Gnosticism which in the initial stages gave an enormous impetus to many of the sacramental and mystical ideas in Christianity. The Christian emphasis on salvation in religion and the consolidation of its Church are the result of Gnostic influences.[123] Gnosticism had, in fact, an even wider impact on the religious and philosophical literature of the Hellenistic period. It is found in the Jewish philosopher Philo and in Neoplatonism, despite Plotinus' polemic against it.

There is no doubt that the Gnostic dualism is somewhat weak and ambiguous. There are two opposed principles at the root of all things— the kingdoms of light and darkness in perpetual conflict, but there is one God over all. Matter is a force of blind desire opposed to the force of light, but light will triumph and matter will be dissolved. The identity of the Gnostic tenets with Buddhistic views, such as the quality of the divine emanations, asceticism, penances, self-collection, and absorption into the godhead, is obvious.[124] The Gnostic aphorism "split the stick, and there is Jesus" is parallel to the Indian "Brahman sleeps in the stone."

Indeed, many of the Gnostic sects believed in pre-existence and the rebirth of human souls. The great Gnostic teacher Basilides, who taught at Alexandria about 120-130 and was a contemporary of Valentinus, produced an independent system which did not attract as many followers as did Valentinus' system, but which did make a deep impression. Basilides certainly borrowed his philosophy from the East, which he ingeniously interwove into the framework of Christianity. He conceived of 365 heavens, each superior to the other and each less concrete, less material, than the one below it. The only way to escape reincarnation was to rise to a superior sphere of peace. Through *Karma* action souls came to the world tainted with the guilt of evil deeds done in another existence. He firmly believed in the transmigration of the soul, and his pessimism and theory of personality have strong Buddhist affinities. The redemption through the ascent of the self, a kind of rebirth; belief in the unity of the human race, for all men are fundamentally endowed with divine spark; and the belief in ascetic practices to purify and strengthen the self bring to mind Indian thought. He described God as devoid of all attributes—like the Hindu concept of the *Nirguna* God.

Basilides was an Egyptian who embraced Christianity. Before his conversion he had followed the doctrines of the Eastern gnosis. Judging by the account left by his contemporary Clemens, Basilides appears to have never been a Christian—Tertullian calls him a Platonist—but rather to have joined the new notions of Buddhism, which is regarded by King as the true source of many of the primary Gnostic ideas, to the esoteric doctrines of the Egyptian priesthood. Indeed, "the introduction of Buddhism into Egypt and Palestine affords the only true solution of innumerable difficulties in the history of religion."[125]

The Gnostic doctrine of the plurality of heavens is essentially Indian; its "three qualities" resemble the "three *gunas*" of the Samkhya system. The resemblances between Gnostic doctrines and Mahayana Buddhism are well known, particularly between the *Pistis Sophia* and the *Saddharma Pundarika*. The Pistis Sophia refers to the methods by which ecstatic experiences are obtained, and it is indicated that salvation can be achieved by a knowledge of the mysteries and by renouncing the world. It is said to have been derived from the philosophical formulations of Valentinus—probably the most famous of all the Gnostics whose activity may be dated from about 130 to 150. In his "System of Emanations" all proceed from the First Cause in pairs, male and female—a feature which pre-eminently stamps his scheme as borrowed from Indian theosophy, in which every principle is divided into a male and female energy, each exactly like the other, "the same distinguished by their sex alone."[126]

Epiphanius in his *Life of Manes* details the circumstances which introduced Buddhistic theories into Gnostic teaching. Manes or Mani (215–276), before beginning his Gnostic mission, had been the slave and later the sole heir to a wealthy widow, who had herself inherited all the belongings of a certain Terbinthus, surnamed in Assyrian, Budda. Terbinthus, in his turn, had been the servant of a wealthy merchant Scythicus, who had a knowledge of Indian religions through his frequent trade-trips to India. Later he began to preach new doctrines, and there can be little doubt that these were not original but had been learned in India. His tradition was carried on by his slave and sole disciple, Terbinthus, and finally manifested itself in the mission of Manes.[127]

Bardesanes (Bardiasan, 155–233), the highly esteemed Gnostic teacher whose treatise on Indian Gymosophists is frequently quoted by later writers, such as Porphyry, evidently had learned much about India from an Indian embassy to Syria (218–222). He describes in accurate detail life in a Buddhist monastery, a visit to a cave temple in India, and the discipline and mode of life of the Brahmans and Buddhists.

Radhakrishnan takes the discussion of Indian influence on Gnosticism further. He finds the Gnostic dualism ambiguous and illustrates a number of parallels between Gnosticism and the Upanishads. According to his reading of Gnostic teaching, the perfect Gnostic is the man who is free from the world and master of himself, and who, having broken off from the outward symbols of religion, has realized the truth. Furthermore, he agrees with Bousset that the basic Gnostic tenets were well developed before Christianity. Gnosticism was not the child of Christianity but in fact a parent of its philosophy. It was a serious attempt to identify Christianity as a religion with Eastern speculations on the origin and end of things. This correlation of religion and philosophy is typically characteristic of Hindu thought. During the first century the Gnostics supplied Christianity with the philosophy it was seeking. "Gnosticism is by no means a mere attempt to reject the Old Testament and hellenize the Gospels. What it did was to introduce into Christianity not the pure spirit of Greek philosophy but conceptions of Eastern religions which by the first century had taken their place everywhere in the Roman Empire."[128]

The Hermetic tradition of Egypt, which flourished during the first three centuries, is somewhat Gnostic in character and a most interesting variety of Hellenistic mysticism. It is considered to be "the development of religious thought in Egypt under Persian and Indian influence which formed a basis of later Jewish and Greek developments."[129] Although it originated in Egypt, the authors of this movement were Egyptian Greeks. The Hermetic texts, intended to guide men to mystical experience, do not contain any suggestions of ceremonies, sacraments, or of a hierarchy. Nor does God need gifts, except those of praise and adoration, for He is all things that exist. For the Hermetics God is ineffable—and He is the Supreme Reality transcending all pre-eminence and excelling all praise. He is the Creator and Father of the Cosmos, which is in His image. Man is of a divine nature, and he who knows himself passes into God. The Hermetic mystic sees unity in all things, and the purgation and illumination of the soul brings him the consciousness of a universal fellowship. The Hermetics were possibly an esoteric brotherhood, consisting of small groups with a teacher who, like a Hindu guru, guided them in their quest for truth.

Gnosticism found new life in the third century in the rise of the Manichaean religion in Sassanian Persia. Its founder, Mani, a native of Ecbatana, had travelled to India and aimed to establish a universal religion which was a fusion of Zoroastrianism, Buddhism, and the Gnostic doctrines. Many Manichaean books have been discovered in Central Asia, but in most other places the followers of Mani were persecuted and their books destroyed. A Manichaean treatise, found at Tun-huang in China, is in the form of a Buddhist sutra. It speaks of Mani as the Tathagata, a synonym for the Buddha, and refers to the Buddhas of Transformation (Hua-fo) and the Boddhisattva Ti-tsang. A confessional formula, *Khuastuanift*, found in the same area, is akin to the Buddhist *Patimokkha*. It advocated asceticism, metempsychosis, and celibacy, and emphasized the contrast between the principles of light and darkness. Until recently Mani's teaching was regarded as clearly dualistic in the metaphysical sense; it is now accepted that his outlook was substantially the same as that of the Gnostics.[130] During the fourth century Manichaeanism spread widely both in the East and the West. Because it forbade the worship of images and animal sacrifices, it incurred the wrath of the Roman emperors. It also entered into a prolonged struggle against Christianity throughout the fourth century. Augustine was a Manichaean for nine years from 373–382.

Gnosticism was one of the most powerful movements affecting Christian doctrine and thought, and, although it had passed its peak by the latter part of the third century, it continued to be influential until the decline of the Roman Empire in the fifth century. At the height of its power, it influenced two of the chief exponents of Alexandrian Christianity, Clement and Origen. Clement was deeply influenced by Basilides and thus by Buddhist thought. A person of great learning, he worked to achieve a consistent theology. He wrote his *Stromata* nearly sixty years after the death of Basilides, and used Greek philosophy to interpret the Christian tradition liberally—not merely as a missionary expedient but in order to weave it into the texture of Christian theology. He refers to the universality of suffering; pain and fear are as inherent in human nature as rust in iron, and, quoting Basilides on rebirth, he suggests that every human act is fruitful and that if its consequence is not apparent in this life, it will be in a future one.[131] It was, however, in his brilliant successor, Origen—born about 185 and the first important theologian to appear after Paul and John—that the Church had someone who could firmly blend the two streams of Greek thought and Christian tradition. A pupil of the founder of Neoplatonism, Ammonius Saccas, Origen's Supreme Being is the Neoplatonic One. He spoke of Christ as God-Man. The Father is the origin of all being and is purely spiritual, whilst the Son of Logos, begotten by the Father, is essentially God, though subordinate to Him. The doctrine of the incarnation of the Logos gave the Christian faith a medium for interpreting itself to Greek-thinking people. Origen admits pre-existence and the future rebirth of souls. For him Christ, who possessed a soul like any other, was more a teacher than a redeemer. He advocated prayer in the name of Jesus but refused to address it to Him. He distinguished between a mystery religion for the educated and a mythical one for others and justified this by the examples of "the Persians and the Indians."[132] Origen preached asceticism and taught that at the end of the present world dispensation many men would follow reversing the cycle of destruction and restoration. His thought sometimes reveals striking parallels with that of his great contemporary, Plotinus, perhaps due to their common master Ammonius Saccas. Origen's chief doctrines were given up by the Christian Church but the tradition of Clement and Origen was continued by the three Cappadocians, Basil of Caesarca, and the two Gregories.

Meanwhile, there emerged a somewhat alien movement, Neoplatonism, which marked the last phase of Hellenistic thought, and which, following tradition, was a distinctive blend of old ideas, especially Platonic, and new ideas drawn from various schools. It developed essentially in an age of transition.[133] After a long period of preparation Neoplatonism reached its culmination in the work of Plotinus (205–*ca.* 270), one of the greatest thinkers of the ancient world.[134] The teachings of Plotinus and his school in Rome set forth doctrines which were essentially Hellenistic and syncretic. In its later forms, characterized by the Syrian school led by Iamblichus and the Athenian school of Proclus, it was transformed into a well-developed scholasticism of dynamic polytheism—a designation often given to Indian theology, which regards God in Himself as Nirguna and yet the source of all power behind the universe. Neoplatonism then underwent a further change, passing into a theurgical mystery cult. It is, however, its first phase which is of greater historical importance. In any case it continued to be the dominant philosophy of the ancient world within which the Christian culture in both its forms, Byzantine and Western, was taking shape. Many of the eminent Christian thinkers of this period, which has been designated as the most formative period of Christian theology, were greatly influenced by Neoplatonic thought.

The relationship between Neoplatonism and Christianity was somewhat precarious and fluctuating in the beginning. A period of compatability was followed by antagonism, but finally various Neoplatonic principles were absorbed by Christian thinkers.

In his own writings Plotinus tells us little about himself so that any personal information comes from the biography his disciple and editor, Porphyry, wrote as an introduction to the *Enneads*. It is curious that Plotinus, whose ideas and teaching have deeply influenced the intellectual history of the world, did little to perpetuate his thought.[135] A native of Egypt, probably of Locopolis in Upper Egypt, the modern Assiut, he spent his formative years at Alexandria. Having studied under several philosophers there, he became a disciple of the Platonic teacher Ammonius Saccas (175–242) who had abandoned Christianity. Plotinus came to study at Alexandria at the somewhat advanced age of twenty-seven and attended Saccas' lectures for ten years. Besides Plotinus, Saccas had other pupils including Erennius and Origen.[136] In 243 at the age of thirty-nine, Plotinus was greatly attracted by Eastern thought, and, in the hope of learning Indian and Persian philosophy at first hand, he accompanied the military expedition of Emperor Gordian against the King of Persia. The expedition, however, ended in the assassination of the Emperor, and Plotinus, having escaped with some difficulty to Antioch, returned to Rome in 244, where he lived and taught for the rest of his life. It is not known if he succeeded in contacting any Indian philosophers on his somewhat abortive trip.

Plotinus believed that there is a transcendent First Principle behind everything, which he calls the One or the Good, and which is beyond the reach of human thought or language. It is a positive and dynamic reality and is the source of all defined and limited realities. From the One proceeds, by a timeless generation, the first of the derived realities, named by Plotinus *Nous*, which is the Divine Mind and also the world of forms and ideas. From Nous proceeds soul which is universal and is the intermediary between the "intelligible" world of Nous and the phenomenal world of sense. The individual souls are like parts of the Universal Soul. The highest ideal of the good and wise man, and the supreme goal of human endeavour, is contemplation of and gradual union with the Good, the Absolute.

Plotinus intellectualized religion. He saw the world indivisible as a realm of values, highest of which was the Deity of Logos. He proceeded from the idea of God and concluded with the demand for union with God—God is the ultimate source and the final goal of all being. He is without limit, form, or definition. "The One is the One and nothing else, and even to assert that it 'is' or that it is 'one' is false, since it is beyond being or essence. No 'name,' can apply to it; it eludes all definition, all knowledge, it can neither be perceived nor thought. It is not in movement, nor is it at rest. It is infinite, without limits, and since it has no parts, it is without structure and without form."[137] Everything flows from God, but what is derived is an image and reflection of the original essence. The first emanation of the Being is Nous, thought, which is at the same time the highest Being; Nous engenders soul, which is the creator of the universe in time and space. There is thus an eternal process of emanation and continuous interpenetration of being. The universe is the soul, soul is contained in Nous. Nous is contained in the One and the One contains all.

Plotinus' conception of the One has undeniable affinity with the Hindu doctrine of Spirit, "the seed of all seeds," and his conception of soul corresponds with the Hindu teaching of the Atman. His idea of God as the One, "the good, the pure thought, the pure actuality," reminds one of *Sachchidananda* of the Upanishads. The absorption of the individual soul into the world-soul as described by Plotinus shows Indian influence: "Souls which are pure and have lost their attraction to the Corporeal will cease to be dependent on the body. So detached they will pass into the world of Being and Reality." Plotinus' theory of distinction between emanation and creation is similar to that of *Advaita Vedanta* between *Vivarta*, or appearance, and *parinama*, or modification.[138]

The Neoplatonist strives to free his soul from his body through modification and to attain union with the Supreme, in the same way as the Yoga doctrine of Patanjali. Whilst Pythagoras taught rebirth (remembrance) and abstention from the flesh, he said nothing about the end—*moksha,* or liberation—which the Neoplatonist sought and which is the cardinal Hindu doctrine.

Plotinus believed in rebirth, transmigration of soul, and the law of *karma.* Until highest wisdom is attained and the individual soul is absorbed in the Universal Soul, successive births occur which are like one dream after another. A man's destiny is conditioned by his search for truth, beauty, and goodness, and failure involves reversion to a lower life-form—which is an Indian doctrine.[139] Plotinus, somewhat like the Upanishads which placed more stress on jnana than on *karma,* regarded action as a feeble result of contemplation. He taught that nothing possessing real value can perish. In India this "knowledge of God" is known as "Brahma-Vidya," which claims an insight into the divine nature superior to science, and holds that through the development of higher faculties an individual can obtain divine revelation. Nous is both individual and universal, like Atman and *Paramatman.* The true way of life for Plotinus is the way which leads the soul to itself in its unity with Nous and so to the One. The soul must be inwardly detached from the activity of the senses and the bondage of matter. Matter is evil, although Plotinus did not approve the Stoic practice of gaining freedom from matter by suicide. He sums up his doctrine of mystical purification in the command: "cut away everything." Renunciation of this world and detachment from all activity for the sake of a better world, however, did not imply condemnation of this world. This detachment from external being is reminiscent of Hindu teaching in which the soul must be freed from the subjection of the body to attain union with the Supreme through meditation. Like the Upanishads, Plotinus also said that since the One is "within, at the innermost depth" we must turn our gaze within, ignoring the external world, to seek the divine vision or the Supreme Light. The term "vision" is in itself insufficient, since it implies the duality of seen and seer, which does not exist. The light by which we see the One is the radiance of the One. The vision of the One or the attainment of direct contact with reality is the transformation of our being, reaching our goal, and is to become divine ourselves. Self-realization through wisdom, jnana, and meditation is an old teaching of the Upanishads.[140] Plotinus practiced meditation and concentration intensely. "Four times while Porphyry was staying with him, the wise heirophant 'went beyond the choir of virtues as a man leaves behind him the statues of the gods to enter the sanctuary' and reached ecstasy or communion and identification with the

Infinite."[141] Although his philosophy is highly religious, he was indifferent to public worship. To find God, Plotinus had no need to enter a temple or bow before an image. Our destiny is entirely in the life within us; the soul has only to turn again towards the lost communion. Prayer is the silent yearning of the soul for affinity with the Supreme One. Plotinus refused to regard the soul as a prisoner in a satanic jail with no hope of salvation except by the supernatural intervention of a redeemer. For him the soul could force itself to rise to ecstatic union with the One. Mainly interested in contemplative and spiritual life, Plotinus devoted little attention to the questions of social morality and wrote no treatise on ethics.

Plotinus himself led a simple life, disregarding the body and practicing vegetarianism. The abstention from sacrifices and animal food of Neoplatonism is, of course, in agreement with Buddhism. Actually Buddhism appears to have been so popular at Alexandria that Clement of Alexandria (150–218) declared that "the Greeks stole their philosophy from the barbarians." Indeed, he was the first Greek to mention the Buddha by name.[142]

Christian scholars, such as F. C. Burkitt and W. W. Inge, although admitting Plotinus' interest in Indian thought and even his journey to the East in quest of further knowledge, insist that there are no traces of Indian influence in his work, and that Neoplatonism is a true child of Hellenism.[143] In sharp contrast to these views there are a number of scholars, including some pro-Hellenes, who accept the theory of Eastern influence. Considering that Plotinus had studied in Alexandria where Eastern religious thought was prevalent, and that his journey to the East, at some risk to himself, would not have been undertaken unless he had not only a keen interest in the East but had actually acquired a competent knowledge of Indian thought, it seems likely that Plotinus was influenced by Indian ideas. He was, it is true, not primarily interpreting Indian philosophy, but rather clarifying and elaborating Plato's teaching with his knowledge of Greek tradition and Indian concepts. Numenius, whose influence on Plotinus was considerable, had himself sought confirmation of the fusion of the doctrines of Pythagoras and Plato in the religions of India, Persia, and Egypt.[144] Some classical authorities, such as Zeller, who maintain the independence of Greek thought would not consider Neoplatonism to be a part of the Greek philosophical tradition because it is contaminated by Eastern features. Similarly, Bacherot and Brehier are also convinced of Indian influence on Neoplatonism. Indeed, most scholars, including those who reject the theory of indebtedness to India, such as Keith, readily admit Indian influence on Neoplatonism.[145] One may conclude then that Neoplatonism was certainly influenced by Indian philosophy, although it is not always possible to distinguish what was taken from Pythagoreanism or Buddhism. It would be wrong to claim that the movement or its character was predominantly Indian, but to disclaim all Indian influence is untenable. It does draw heavily upon Plato's "Good," Aristotle's "Spirit," Stoicism, and Philo but the similarities between Neoplatonism and the Vedants and Yoga systems are likewise obvious.

Plotinus had many points of agreement with Gnosticism. For example, he agreed that the Supreme Being is beyond existence, and that the soul has a divine spark but has lost its way and must return to its original home. Yet, he criticizes the Gnostic doctrine of total depravity, holding that vice is always mixed with some good and no human being is completely bad. He also disputed the Gnostic view of the creation of the world in time. Some of his disagreement with the Gnostics may have arisen from the fact that whilst Gnostics looked upon themselves as Christians, Plotinus did not consider himself as such.

Plotinus' pupils were not of the same intellectual stature as their master. Malchus, a Phoenician better known by the Greek form of his name Porphyry (232–304), was a man of great learning but not of striking originality. Other Neoplatonists who commanded respect were Iamblichus and Proclus.

Prophyry collected, arranged, and edited the writings of Plotinus in the famous work entitled *The Enneads*. Porphyry, before he became a pupil of Plotinus, had written a treatise, *Philosophy from the Oracles*, showing his deep interest in Eastern religious thought. Differing from his teacher, Porphyry advocated image worship and strict asceticism. For him, the source of evil was not so much in the body as in the desires of the soul. Porphyry is famous for his work *Against the Christians* in which he criticized Christian doctrines, and although he was filled with the lofty philosophy of Plotinus, "the need of revelation, redemption, asceticism and immortality inspires him with a faith like that of his opponents."[146]

Porphyry's pupil Iamblichus more than anyone else was responsible for the conversion of Neoplatonism into a theurgic spiritualism, as found in the schools of Athens and Pergamum. By the beginning of the fifth century the academy founded by Plato had become Neoplatonist and it was here that Neoplatonism reigned for two centuries under the Christian Empire. It was also taught at Alexandria by Hypatia. Proclus (416–435) was not a creative thinker but a systematizer who "carried to its utmost limits the ideal of the one comprehensive philosophy that should embrace all the garnered wisdom of the ancient world."[147] In an ordered exposition of the system, Proclus methodically defended Neoplatonism and gave it a somewhat devotional orientation. His influence upon early mediaeval thought was considerable, although somewhat accidental. The school at Athens was closed by Justinian in 529, and the murder of Hypatia put an end to the Alexandrian school. But by this time Christian theology had accepted and absorbed the spirit of Neoplatonism, which became a potent factor in the growth of Christian mysticism. It was a striking end for a movement which had been opposed by Christianity, and whose works had been condemned to be burned by a decree of the Council of Ephesus in 431 and later in 448 by a law of Theodosius II.

St. Augustine, who was born in 353 in Thagaste in modern Algeria, was successively a pagan, a Manichaean, and a Neoplatonist before his conversion to Christianity. He was violent tempered and his sexual morality was loose. Later, tormented by conscience, he developed a remarkable degree of intuitional insight into the processes of his own mind. It was through his reading of Plotinus that he came to Christianity and he naturally tried to introduce the central principles of Neoplatonism into Christianity. Augustine admits his great indebtedness to the works of Plotinus and Porphyry in his *Confessions*. So deep was the influence of Neoplatonism on Augustine's spiritual evolution that he has been described as a "Christian Plotinus," and it was mainly through his writings that the tenets of Plotinus were transmitted to the Middle Ages in the West.

Augustine's mysticism was intellectual, and his vision of God was on a far higher level than that of the mystics who followed him. His views on God and matter, freedom and evil, and the relation of God with the world were adopted from Neoplatonism. It was he who conceived the idea of a universal church. Where Neoplatonism and the Christian faith came into conflict, Augustine subordinated the latter to the former. In his peculiar fusion of the two different doctrines, Neoplatonic mysticism had precedence. For the goal of all prayer was the return to the infinite One, the essential unity with the highest good.[148]

Neoplatonic ideas also came into Christian theological tradition through that most successful of pseudonymous writers, "Dionysius the Areopagite" (*ca.* 500), who expounded Christian mystical theology in Proclus' terms and whose writing had an exceptionally great influence both in Europe and Asia.[149] Dionysius the Areopagite was a Syrian and is traditionally the founder of Christian mysticism. He claimed to have enjoyed ecstatic union and preached quietism as a preparation; to

speak without words and understand without knowledge: "seek therefore silently and mystically, that perfect and primitive union with the
Archgood." Dionysius' system is described by Inge as "the ancient religion of the Brahmins masquerading in the clothes of Gnostics, Manichaeans, Neoplatonists and others."[150]

It was perhaps this influence of a diluted and diffused Neoplatonism
on Christian theology which was the most historically important part of
the Neoplatonic contribution to European thought and culture. Indeed,
Neoplatonic influence can be detected in many places, not only in
theology, in metaphysics, in logic, and in moral philosophy but also
in the early history of European science and mediaeval and Renaissance
art. From the twelfth century on it was reinforced in the West by the
mediaeval Latin translations of Proclus and of the great Arabic philosophers who owed much to Neoplatonism. In the sixteenth century the
Greek texts of the Neoplatonist philosophers themselves became available in the West again. Even in modern times, despite criticism, its
influence has been significant, and without an understanding of Neoplatonic thought it is not possible to properly appreciate European
culture.

However, Christianity, despite frequent doctrinal menaces from other
contemporary syncretistic philosophies, continued to spread throughout
the Roman Empire, weaving an increasing number of converts into a
new communty of ideas and religious order. The attitudes of the rulers
varied between uncompromising hostility and toleration. The Roman
emperors were generally intolerant to religions, including Christianity
which they regarded as a Jewish sect. The Christians refused to pay
homage to the Emperor's image and challenged the divinity of Caesar,
thus incurring charges of treason. At the end of the third and the beginning of the fourth centuries, Christianity clashed openly with the
Roman Empire. After years of persecution under the Emperor Diocletian, the associated Emperor Galerius issued an edict of toleration in
317. In 324, Constantine, who was well disposed toward Christianity and
who had been an associated emperor, became the sole ruler of the Roman
Empire. He embraced Christianity on his death bed in 337, having
earlier abandoned all pretentions to divinity and having put Christian
monograms on the army banners and shields. Thus, Christianity became
the official religion of the Roman Empire.

Whilst Christianity as a united front was engaged in its struggle
against the Roman Empire, it also was engaged in violent internal disputes, many of which were about the divinity of Jesus. Ignoring the
teachings of charity, service, and brotherhood, the Christians became

involved in torturous, agitated, and elusive argument, calling each other heretics and persecuting, excommunicating, and executing each other. The chief disputants were the Arians, who taught that Christ was less than God; the Sabellians, who taught that he was a mode or aspect of God; and the Trinitarians, who taught that the Father, the Son, and the Holy Ghost were three distinct persons, but one God. Spite, dogmatism, and rivalry over theological refinements threatened to destroy Christianity. It was at the Council of Nicaea, convened by Constantine in 323, that the view of the Trinitarians was upheld. Christ, the Son, was declared to be consubstantial with God the Father and coeternal.[151] Although these controversies and persecutions against the spirit of Jesus produced a succession of unhappy and cruel disputes which injured Christianity as a whole in the fourth and fifth centuries, they also generated a zeal, often base and malicious, amongst Christian to propagate their faith.

Chapter IV

PAX ARABICA,
THE CHANNEL-BED OF CULTURE

FOLLOWING THE death of Marcus Aurelius in 180, the Roman Empire began to decay because of corruption and indiscipline, and declined in power because of internal strife and mounting outside pressure. Toward the end of the third century the Empire nearly disintegrated under attacks from Germans and Persians. But it was saved and reformed into a new empire by Diocletian (284–305), and later reorganized and further restored by Constantine (288–337). The efforts of these two Emperors, however, only succeeded in prolonging the process of dislocation. Whether the rise of Christianity with its train of bitter religious conflicts and persecutions was a contributing cause of the Roman decline or not, the two certainly coincided. During the following hundred years, Roman authority gradually weakened, Roman armies suffered defeats, and Rome was sacked. By the end of the fifth century there was nothing left of the Roman Empire in the West. Europe lapsed into the Dark Ages for centuries. Total and devoted acceptance of the authority of the new faith, as interpreted by its priests or guardians on earth, inculcated amongst the people an attitude of surrender and they handed over the right and responsibility of thinking to others. Passive submissions suppressed scientific inquiry and academic integrity, the main characteristics of the preceding age of Alexandrian syncretism. Intellectual stagnation, religious intolerance, and racial and regional exclusiveness characterized Europe for the next thousand years.

Meanwhile, Constantine had founded Constantinople (Nova Roma), present-day Istanbul, in 330 as the capital of the eastern branch of the Roman Empire. Later, when the West fell, the eastern branch, as the Byzantine Empire, maintained the Graeco-Roman tradition against and alongside the rising power of Islam until it collapsed before the Ottoman Turks in 1453.

Whilst the Roman Empire was declining, in India the Gupta Empire, noted for its exceptional cultural advancement and dissemination, had emerged early in the fourth century. Not since the days of the Mauryas had India been united under one political power. By the end of the fifth century, however, Gupta power had declined. It was revived somewhat in the seventh to the tenth centuries under Harsha, the Palas, and the Gurjara-Pratiharas but the forces of decline had set in and the great ancient period came to an end. In India, too, thought lacked creativity and social institutions had lost their vigour and freshness. Except for an occasional spark, intellectual curiosity had given way to religious superstitions.

During the seventh century (when Harsha Siladitya was in power in India, the West had retired into seclusion, the great Persian and Byzantine powers had exhausted each other in a series of wars, and China had begun to re-emerge into greatness under the T'angs) there arose in Arabia a unique combination of the forces of a new religion and a new political power. The Islamic religion and Arab power changed the course of history decisively and created one of the world's most brilliant civilizations. The power of faith gave the Arabs, a Semitic people separated from their main stock, national consciousness and a vast empire, and it gave the world a religion and a culture. It is a unique historical episode that the Arabs, who were traders and travellers, lived in a desert country and had no high degree of civilization, should have been so suddenly transformed by Islam as to reach great heights in cultural and political advancement. In its triple role—faith, state, and culture—Islam dominated the Middle Ages and continues to be one of the most significant forces in human society. During the period of Arab hegemony Islam assimilated in its creed people of different nationalities or races more successfully than did the Greeks, the Romans, or the Anglo-Saxons, and inspired in them a strong feeling of brotherhood and a measure of harmony. There is nothing comparable until the nineteenth-century expansion of Christianity, and that too is said to have been much less successful in inculcating a sense of brotherhood. Despite their frequent cruelty and ruthlessness, civilization is deeply indebted to the mediaeval Arabs for the development, preservation, and dissemination of both the Western and Eastern cultural heritages. They founded universities at Baghdad, Cairo, and Cordova, and for several centuries made more contributions in science and philosophy than any of their contemporaries.

Although most Muslims today are neither Arab nor speak Arabic, their culture is the product of Arab inspiration and enterprise. The Arabs at the peak of their power and creative effort, in Damascus and Baghdad, in Toledo and Cordova, either by original contributions or by what they learned and transmitted from ancient Greece, Persia, and India, played a vital role in human progress.

Information on pre-Islamic Arabia is scanty, but in the seventh century, Mecca, like Petra and Palmyra before it, had come to be known as a financial and commercial centre in the Arab world.[1] Mecca's rise as a mercantile city may be due to the conflict between the Persian Empire and Byzantium, because the wars between them resulted in the closing of the more northern trade routes between East and West. Indeed, the dismembering of the Greek Empire after the death of Alexander had led to the growing importance of Arabian routes in international trade. During the Hellenistic period the monarchs of both Syria and Egypt had attempted to monopolize these trade routes, but neither Alexander nor his successors could conquer Arabia. However, in spite of its increasing importance in trade, Mecca still remained politically and socially very much a city organized to conform to a nomadic way of life. There was practically no centrally organized and uniform system of government, and the city was ruled by a group of clans. Lawlessness and violence were common and moral life was lax, centring around dancing girls, slavery, and harems.

The religion of the pre-Islamic Arabs was inarticulate and polytheistic. Ridden with superstition, they worshipped a multiplicity of deities and sacred stones, and gave little thought to the question of a life after death. A legion of *jinn* (genii), good or evil, were subordinate to a rich pantheon of deities. The centre of stone worship was the temple of Mecca, known as the *Kaaba,* which attracted pilgrims from all over Arabia. There were a number of idols in the temple, representing various gods, one of whom was called Allah (Al Ilah). Allah was probably the tribal god of the Quraish, amongst whom Muhammad was born. Muhammad preached that Allah was the only God. He transformed the existing emblems into Islamic objects. He purged the Kaaba of its images and, having first prescribed prayer towards Jerusalem, later altered the direction toward the Kaaba. Thus, the relentlessly iconoclastic Muslims revere as immeasurably holy a temple which was once a flourishing seat of idol worship. A significant feature of Arabic life around the year 600 was a number of wandering hermits and ascetics with a monotheistic tendency and a craving for solitude.

Considering that from the earliest times the Arabs had always been enterprising in international trade and commerce, and that Arabia was so close to the spheres of earlier civilizations and of later religions,

Christianity and Judaism, it is indeed a puzzle that it should have remained almost unaffected by any of them. Islam, like Christianity, is based on God having revealed himself, although the means and nature of that revelation differ in the two religions. However, Islamic theology is simple. The term Islam in its Arabic form means surrender, a submission to the will of God, and, in its Hebrew origin, it means peace. Founded by Muhammad (*ca.* 570–8 June 632), who combined religious genius with political finesse, the Islamic religion is detailed in the Quran; the word "Quran" literally means a discourse. The Muslim holy book, like the Jewish-Christian Bible, is a compilation and the orthodox followers assert that every word in it was inspired by Allah.[2] It is, however, unlike the Bible, principally the word of one person. At different times over a period of about twenty-two years, Muhammad dictated his revelation in fragments of unequal length which were written down by scribes on parchment, leather, or palm leaves and stored without any consideration of order and care. By order of the Caliph Abu Bakr in 633, after the death of the Prophet, the remaining fragments were collected and arranged according to length—with the longest first and the shortest last—in complete disregard of logical or chronological order. The task was carried out by Zaid ibn Thabit, who had been Muhammad's secretary. From Zaid's manuscript several versions of the text gained currency and, as there were no vowels in the script of the time, people read and interpreted the text differently. In 651, therefore, Caliph Othman appointed a commission of three Quraish scholars to scrutinize and standardize the work. The revised version was widely circulated and since then the text, consisting of 114 chapters or suras, has been preserved with exceptional purity.[3] Muslims hold the Quran as the word of God and inimitable in style, and it has thus exercised a unique influence on the Arabic language and literature. The need to keep the holy book uncorrupted, unfold its deeper meaning, and elucidate its obscurities caused Muslims to devise a science of grammar and lexicography, and to compile and interpret the pre-Islamic literature, verses, and traditions.

Muhammad's central message is uncompromising monotheism and the perdition of idolaters. He preached the existence, the unity, and the perfection of Allah—of whom Moses, Jesus, and others were the earlier prophets, and Muhammad the last. He taught kindness, honesty, and Islamic brotherhood. He respected both the Law (*Torah*) and the Gospel as true revelations, the word of God to Jews and Christians. He did not claim any divinity for himself, or perform any miracles—other than transmitting the revelation of the Quran. He sought nothing beyond the acknowledgment that he was Allah's apostle. It is not, however, enough for a Muslim to believe in the message given by Muhammad but also in Muhammad as the Seal of the Prophets: *"Lailaha illa-l-lah, Muhammadun rasulu-l-lah."* (I testify that there is no god but God, Allah, and that Muhammad is the Messenger of God.) Allah is the source of creation and knowledge and the object of worship, and to believe in his messenger requires a perfect belief in the angels, the scriptures, the messengers, the day of resurrection, and the principles on which the code of laws is based.

In style the Quran follows the model of the Hebrew prophets, and is largely an adaptation of Judaic doctrines, tales, and themes. Its monotheism, prophecy, faith, repentance, the last judgement, heaven and hell, appear to be Jewish in form and origin. It departed from Judaism mainly in asserting that the Messiah had come. The separation of the divine and the human is emphasized in the Quran even more than in Judaism. Quranic teaching is less indebted to Christianity than to Judaism, although its earnest preaching of repentance in fear of the coming judgement perhaps has a Christian ring. The Quran, however, has great reverence for other Prophets, including Jesus, whom it calls "Son of Mary," Messiah, Prophet, Word, and acknowledges his miracles. But it does not call Jesus the Son of God, denies the Trinity, and deplores the divisions within Christianity. Although the teachings of Islam are rooted in the Judaeo-Christian tradition, they are shaped into a distinctive doctrine by the original thinking of Muhammad and by the assumptions and preconceptions natural to Arabs.

In 610, Muhammad began to preach publicly the divine knowledge he had received. Whilst he secured some converts, the majority of the Meccans adopted a hostile attitude. Consequently, in 622 Muhammad was forced to migrate with a small band of followers to Medina (Yathrib) over two hundred miles north. In Medina he found greater support and, through his sagacity, statesmanship, and military genius, he soon built up his prestige and power, both temporal and spiritual. From then on his cause prospered. Within ten years he became the undisputed ruler of Medina, Mecca, and the neighbouring areas. Many other tribes throughout Arabia also acknowledged his suzerainty and subscribed to the new faith.

The system of political organization which Muhammad devised, weaving the nomadic tribes into a new community which demanded surrender of personal independence and of ancestral tradition, was alien to the Arabs. Yet, with remarkable ingenuity he succeeded in subduing tribal rivalries and prejudices. Thus, the emergence of Islam as a state or political entity began with Muhammad's military conquests and pacification of the hitherto unruly Arabs, mostly Bedouins. After his death both Islamic religion and polity developed and flourished under the Caliphate.

Muhammad appointed no successor and after some conflict and rivalry Abu Bakr, a faithful friend of the Prophet, was elected the first Caliph or Khalifa of Islam; Khalifa literally means "deputy" or "representative." Despite dissensions and underlying disunion, which gave birth to permanent schisms in the body politic of Islam, the new régime was extraordinarily successful. The Arabs were now firmly welded together into a theocratic community, *Umma*, under the command of "Allah and his Prophet" and soon they were joined by countless people of non-Arab origin in Islamic brotherhood.

At the beginning of the seventh century western Asia was divided between the two rival powers of Byzantium and Persia. The former was Greek in culture, Christian in religion, and mainly Roman in administration, and was in a state of disarray because of internal quarrels. The Persian Empire was ruled by the Sassanians, was Zoroastrian in religion, Persian in culture, and weakened by external wars. The two powers were unable to successfully confront the Arab advance which suddenly burst upon them. In 642 Alexandria, protected by walls and towers and guarded by the Byzantine fleet, fell to the Arabs. The hub of intellectual and cultural life for about a thousand years and the proud possessor of some of the best monuments of antiquity, Alexandria lay in ruins before the arms of the Arab commander Amr ibn al-As.[4] According to a well-known story, the manuscripts from the famous library supplied fuel for the public baths for six months. The story also relates the oft-quoted remark allegedly made by Caliph Omar ibn al-Khattab (*ca.* 634–44) when he consented to the destruction of the library: "If these writings of the Greeks agree with the book of God, they are useless and need not be preserved; if they disagree, they are pernicious and ought to be destroyed." The story, however, is no more than a fable. It makes its first appearance in the solitary report of a stranger, Abul Faraj, who wrote five hundred years later.[5] The reported sentence of the Caliph is alien to the traditional precept of the Muslim casuists who had expressly commanded the preservation of captured religious texts of the Jews and Christians, and had declared that the works of profane scientists and philosophers could be lawfully applied to the believer.

Seldom in history has there been a parallel for transcribing a falsehood with such persistence, conviction, and indignation, in spite of contrary evidence. Gibbon, like many other scholars, denied both the fact and the consequences. In fact, the Arabs were far too fond of books and knowledge to behave in this manner. They built a number of famous libraries in their empire, and their librarians were often men of high learning. But many other Asian conquerors, such as Mahmud of Ghazni, Holagu, and Genghis Khan, destroyed libraries. European in- vaders from Palestine and Syria burned the magnificent library at Tripolis during the First Crusade. Many early and mediaeval Christian enthusiasts burned libraries, archives, and works of art in North Africa, pre-Columbian America, Rome, and Asia. It is likely that Emperor Theodosius of Constantinople destroyed all or part of the library of Alexandria because, as a devout Christian, he did not approve of pagan books—Greek or Asian.

During the reign of Walid (705–715), Arabs landed in Spain in 709 and soon conquered the Iberian peninsula. The Arab expansion in the West was only checked in 732 by the Franks under Charles Martel on the plains of Tours. By this time Persia, and Western and Central Asia were under their domination.[6] The vast empire, which the Arabs had conquered for Islam and its Caliphs between northern Spain and Transoxiana, was twice as large as the Roman Empire had ever been.

The staggering rapidity with which the Arabs expanded westward may have been partly due to the internal conflicts within the Christian world and the Western persecution of the Eastern Christians, who con- sequently were alienated from their Western co-religionists. Also, it appears that Arab expansion was an unintentional extension of internecine wars; civil wars imperceptibly developed into wars of conquest. Whether or not the spectacular conquests were initially an expansion of the Islamic religion or of the Arabian nation is much debated. Whilst the role of religion as an inspiring force in the Arab conquest must be admitted, it would be wrong to underestimate the part played by Arabism. In fact, in the early phase of its expansion Islam was identified with Arabism, as is suggested by the attitude of the Arabs who held the non-Arab Muslims to be somewhat inferior. The newcomers could only enter the faith by becoming *malawi* (clients) of one or the other Arab tribes. There is no doubt that first in Arabia, then in the neighbouring areas of western Asia, and finally in successive waves of conquests the Arabs organized their own lives and those of the conquered according to the ordained way of Islam and the evolving patterns of cultural interaction between their own and local traditions.

Arab penetration of India began in 712 under Muhammad bin Kassim through the defeat of Dahar, the ruler of Sind. This action was not followed up and Arab rule in India remained confined to the small desert principality in Sind for the next five hundred years, during which time Arab relations with the neighbouring Indian states were cordial.

The Arab conquest of a variety of peoples under one hegemony gave fresh impetus to cultural exchange and a cultural dimension to Islam. But, despite their brilliant military victories, the Arabs failed to suppress factionalism and dissension within their own body politic. The rivalries over the Caliphate led to frequent armed conflicts, to a change in the capital of the Islamic Empire, and to fragmentation of the Caliphate into splinter groups. It is often said that the rule of the first four Caliphs (632–660) was the only period when the Muslim state was run according to the Islamic concept. These Caliphs are therefore called *al-Khulafa al-Rashidun,* rightly guided Caliphs. Under their rule Islam was firmly established in Arabia and spread far beyond its borders. Yet, dissensions were so deep that the last three of these Caliphs were murdered. In 656 when the fourth Caliph Ali was engaged in fighting a combination of his adversaries, the seat of the Caliphate was transferred from Medina to Kufa. Five years later, following the murder of Ali, Muawiya, the ruler of Syria and an enemy of Ali, became Caliph and founded the Umayyad Caliphate with Damascus as the new capital of the Muslim world.[7] By the eleventh century the Arab Empire had begun to disintegrate. In the thirteenth century the Mongol attacks, under Genghis Khan and his grandson Hulagu, dealt Arab power a shattering blow. Their successors reigned in Persia until the second wave of invaders from Central Asia under Timur (1380–1405) spread devastation throughout western Asia. The unity of Islam was, in a political sense, destroyed. The defeated Abbasids, who had succeeded the Umayyads, established their line of the Caliphate in Cairo. This lasted until 1517 when it was overthrown by the Ottoman Turks who retained the Caliphate until it was abolished by Kemal Ataturk in 1924.

The replacement of the Umayyads by the Abbasids in 750 was a landmark in Islamic history. Arab nationalism and Islam were no longer identified as one and Arab dominance of the Islamic world was supplemented by Persian ascendancy. Thus, the Arab kingdom became increasingly cosmopolitan, although the centre of Islamic power moved from the Mediterranean province of Syria to Persia, a country intersected by many trade routes and with a long, rich history.

The Abbasid Caliphate was stronger than the Umayyads, although no less despotic. The Caliph, accorded new dignity and titles plus the pomp and ceremony of an elaborate and hierarchic court, came to be regarded as the deputy of God himself rather than the deputy of the Prophet of God. Although the seat of Islamic power was now located in Persia, Arab aristocracy retained its supremacy. Yet the Abassids were not quite as "Arab" as the Umayyads were. The Caliph himself belonged to a great Arab family although the mothers of the Abbasid Caliphs for generations were Persians. Persian nobles filled the court and Persian soldiers the army. For a time Arabs and Persians forgot their national differences under their obedience to Islam but this position could not last indefinitely; political rivalries and dormant ambitions were bound to come to the surface eventually.

In 762 the capital of the new Caliphate was moved from Damascus to Baghdad, which, occupying a commanding position on the overland route between India and the West, assumed the role of Alexandria and kept the torch of learning alive when Europe was plunged into barbarism. Baghdad remained the centre of intellectual life until about the end of the tenth century when this function was transferred to Cordova in Spain. Both capitals were focal points of Arab culture. The cultural atmosphere of Baghdad was so magnificent that it became a true *Dar al-ulum*, or House of Learning, and during this period scholarship reigned supreme. The nation of warriors rapidly became both the patrons and cultivators of intellectual pursuits. Piety was no longer its own reward, and learning was accorded munificent patronage. This was Islam's age of glory which reached its peak under the most eminent of the Abbasid Caliphs, Harun Al Rashid (786–809). The famous *Arabian Nights* have made his name almost a household word. He defeated the Byzantine Emperor Nicephorus and occupied Constantinople in 782. Although the solidarity of the Islamic power was broken up into splinter Caliphates—Spain in 756, Morocco in 788, and Tunisia in 800 became virtually independent under local dynasties, and Egypt fell out in 868—one of the most momentous periods in the history of thought and culture began.

Always great travellers and world traders, the Arabs, taking advantage of their political supremacy, became the chief navigators and merchants of the early Middle Ages. It was, in fact, an Arab pilot who took Vasco da Gama across the Indian Ocean in 1498. Arab ships sailed the length of the Mediterranean and there was great activity between the ports of the Persian Gulf, such as Siraf, Basra, and Ubulla, and India and beyond. The rivers of Iraq linked the Gulf with Baghdad, and the direct Red Sea route between the Indian coast and the Egyptian ports, too, continued to be dominated by the Arabs. Thus, East-West contact during the period of Arab ascendancy became still closer. Within a few years of their occupation of the Syrian and Egyptian coastlines, the Arabs built and manned great war fleets which were able to defeat the powerful and experienced Byzantine navy and to control the Mediterranean, so vital for the security and expansion of their empire.

It is said that the ascent of Arab greatness was due to their commercial enterprise. In addition to the sea routes, the overland routes connecting Arabia, western Asia, India, and China were extremely busy. The merchants of Baghdad imported Chinese silks and Indian spices, as well as tigers, panthers, elephants, panther skins, rubies, white sandalwood, ebony, and coconuts. Cotton was originally imported from India, but later it was cultivated in eastern Persia and spread westward as far as Spain. From Baghdad the merchandise was dispatched to Spain and thus to Europe. Land routes also linked Baghdad with Africa and Russia. The number of Arab coins dating from the late seventh to the early eleventh centuries, found not only in the Volga basin but also in Scandinavia, especially Sweden, and some even in Britain, would indicate how widespread Arab commercial influence was in the early Middle Ages.

The extensive and prosperous commercial life of the Arab world was inevitably reflected in its thought and literature. Merchants, soldiers, and scholars travelled the Islamic Empire from Spain to India in search of knowledge, glory, and profit, thus accelerating cultural intercourse. The Islamic civilization which resulted did not possess a well-defined personality, having acquired regional variations over its long period of historical development. Fluidity and diversity were the principal characteristics of classical Islamic civilization. But, although the Islamic culture is highly syncretic, it is founded in Arab culture, initiative, and endeavour.

In turn, however, Arab culture itself was rooted in an amazing synthesis of the intellectual achievements of older civilizations. The Arabs had little indigenous culture, and much that was not very attractive. They mainly borrowed from Indian, Greek, and Persian sources. The preservation and the integration of these various streams of thought was the principal Arab contribution to world civilization. The syncretic nature of Arab culture is well illustrated by the fact that three of their most important gifts to the West—Aristotle, Arabic numerals, and paper—came from Greece, India, and China respectively.

Arab culture developed in western Asia where the scientific heritage of the Greeks, enriched by contributions from Persia and India, was translated and publicized in Syrian, Hebrew, Aramaic, and Pahlavi. In the neighbourhood of Baghdad the Nestorians founded a school at

140

Jundishapur which was primarily concerned with the study of Greek philosophy and science. At the same time Indian philosophical and scientific works were also studied and translated. Al Kindi, commonly regarded as the greatest philosopher of the Arabs, wrote in the Preface of his *Metaphysics:* "It is fitting then for us not to be ashamed to acknowledge truth and to assimilate it from whatever source it comes to us, even if it is brought to us by former generations and foreign peoples. For him who seeks the truth there is nothing of higher value than truth itself; it never cheapens nor abases him who searches for it, but ennobles and honours him."

The Arabic translations of Greek and other philosophical texts began in early Abbasid times under the patronage of the Caliphs, Al Mansur and Al Rashid. But with the reign of Al Mamun (813–33) a brisk, new phase of development in Arabic literature began. The Caliph was an extraordinary man and he used his authority to enforce a liberal stand-ard of orthodoxy. He wholeheartedly supported the pursuit of knowledge and he himself participated enthusiastically in academic discussions. The *Bayt al hikma* (the House of Wisdom, a kind of a library and museum reminiscent of the Alexandrian Library), founded at Baghdad in 830, with its impressive library and observatory, attracted scholars and encouraged intellectual pursuits, and in the *divans* of the Caliphs the most renowned scientists, poets, and scholars assembled to debate their views. The most illustrious name in this circle was that of Al Khwarizmi, who wrote on mathematics, astronomy, and geography.

Whilst Harun Al Rashid was fond of literature and philosophy, Al Mamun was interested in the sciences, especially biology. Thus, in order to enable Arab culture to assimilate the neighbouring cultures, Al Mamun encouraged exchange with India. Arab scholarship, in direct contact with Indian, Greek, and Persian systems of thought, now bloomed into its most brilliant period of development. Hitherto Muslim learning had been influenced only indirectly by the older centres of culture. The impact of the foreign systems of thought on Arab learning was so great that it has been compared to the reintroduction of Greek literature into Europe at the Renaissance.

Al Mamun's immediate successors followed his example enabling foreign influences to find fullest expression throughout the empire. Thus, the period of rich new developments in Arab learning which began with the reign of Harun Al Rashid reached its zenith during the reign of Al Mamun and his successors. However, from 850 to 950, whilst Baghdad remained the chief cultural centre, various other centres sprang up challenging Baghdad's supremacy. Cordova in Spain became quite famous, and Ghazna, Samarkand, Merv, Herat, Tus, Nishapur, Ray, Isfahan, Shiraz, Musul, Damascus, Jerusalem, Cairo, Qairawan, Fas, Marrakush, Toledo, Seville, and Granada also played significant roles in the spread of learning. It was from Toledo, for instance, that Europe first learned that scholarship had no national frontiers but belonged to the whole of mankind. At Toledo Arabs, Jews, Greeks, Christians, Spaniards, Frenchmen, Germans, and others worked together.

Scholars and translators counted amongst themselves persons of pure and mixed Arab descent, converts to Islam, and Christians, some of whom belonged to the Greek Orthodox Church although the majority were Nestorians or Jacobites. Even many of the mediaeval Arab philosophers were not of Arab descent. For example, Al Farabi was a Turk, and Al Razi (Rhazes) and Ibn Sina (Avicenna) were Persians. This led the Arab historian Ibn Khaldun to comment that it was strange that most of the learned Muslims were, with rare exceptions, *Ajam* (non-Arabs); and even those savants who claimed Arab descent spoke a foreign language, had grown up in foreign lands, and had studied under foreign masters. The peoples of Islam were bound together by religion and language but included peoples of varied nationalities. More important, they were in close contact with a variety of non-Muslims, such as Chinese, Indians, Mongols, Malays, Greeks, Copts, Syrians, Magians, Berbers, Sicilians, Spaniards, Franks, and Jews. Consequently, many important scholars who published their work under Islamic patronage were not Muslims. For example, the great chemist, Jabir ibn Hayyan, was probably a Sabian; the physicians, Hunayn ibn Ishaq, Ibn Butlan, and Ibn Jazla were Christians.

In different groups and schools the activity of translators continued in degrees of varying intensity until the eleventh century. Whilst during this period a number of original Arab works were also written, translation work was not regarded as merely mechanical or inferior. Although there were some Greek manuscripts available in the cities of western Asia at the time, these were mainly Syriac translations of the Greek originals. Many of the translators were not accomplished philosophers, but without their painstaking work the development of Western thought would have been seriously impaired, and its link with the Greek past would never have been forged. Even Arab philosophy would have hardly come into existence, as these translations laid the foundation of an Arab style and built a complex framework of Arab philosophical terminology. The translations also made it possible for the Greek and Islamic systems of thought to pass on to mediaeval Jewry, giving Jewish philosophy a much needed intellectual stimulus.

The Arabs of the day were enthusiastic, accurate, and prolific translators, and they would often undertake long journeys in search of manuscripts. It is not commonly realized that, in addition to a number of Greek works, they also translated many Indian and Persian studies, with the help of Persian and Indian translators. In fact, the translation movement began when a Persian Muslim master of the Arabic language and style, Abu Muhammad ibn al-Muqaffa (*ca.* 760), rendered the *Pancatantra* into Pahlavi, and several works on medicine and logic, into Arabic. Ibn al-Muqaffa served under Isa ibn Ali, uncle of the first Abbasid Caliph, Al Suffah (750–54). His Arabic version, *Kalila wa Dimna*, of the splendid Indian tales led to translations into some forty European and Asian languages.

The Arabs had studied Indian and Persian works long before becoming interested in Greek thought. By that time, at least one thousand years had intervened between the Hellenic and Arab cultures and whatever Hellenic heritage had reached the Arabs came to them through Syria and Alexandria and was already influenced by Eastern ideas. The classical period of Greek philosophy was long over, and its original flavour had been highly spiced by later schools, such as Neoplatonism. Plato and Aristotle were read through their later exponents' interpretations, and these in the Syriac versions. From the fourth century Greek philosophy and its Neoplatonic commentaries, and Greek science were studied in the schools and monasteries of Syria and Mesopotamia. In fact, some Greek philosophical texts, lost through Byzantine neglect or deliberate destruction, are preserved only in Arabic translations. For example, the lost treatises of Galen, Greek commentaries on Aristotle, and sections of a paraphrase of Plotinus are found only in the Arabic version. The value of Arab translations of the works of Aristotle and his exponents is appreciably great. Whilst Neoplatonism gave rise to acute controversies involving the relationship between pantheism and the unrelenting monotheism of the Quran, a number of scholars were engaged in making Greek science and philosophy accessible to the Arabic-speaking world. The history of this literary activity is somewhat uncertain. The earliest known translator was Qustah ibn Luqa of Baalbak, who lived about 835 and who not only translated Aristotle and other writers but wrote profusely himself on scientific subjects. Later, Arabic learning was enriched by even more prominent and prolific writers, such as Humayan ibn Ishaq (d. 873); Al Kindi (d. 850), called the philosopher of the Arabs because he was of pure Arab descent and who is credited with no fewer than 265 treatises on a wide range of subjects from music to medicine; Al Khwarizmi, who studied not only the Greek works on mathematics and astronomy but also the Indian systems, and who by the use of Indian numerals revolutionized mathematical calculations; and Al Farabi (870–950).

Arabic literature reached across the Islamic world with exceptional rapidity, and the intellectual stimulation it provided to the regions between China and Spain laid the foundation of a new age. The Arabs not only preserved old knowledge, but, by providing a bridge between cultures, rejuvenated Western civilization.[8]

The Arabs transmitted Hellenic and Eastern knowledge to the West at a time when the latter needed it most, and they also gave the West an extremely rare gift, the spirit of scientific inquiry, observation, and experimentation. European science owes its existence to the Arabs. They elevated science from metaphysical speculation and put it on the path of experimentation and operation. Their concern with identification and verification, and thus with observation, accurate description, and measurement helped to develop an objective scientific attitude. The Arabs had, of course, acquired this disciplined approach to scientific observation from Alexandria where it had existed for some time. It must also have partially originated in the East because, although the Greeks systematized, generalized, and theorized, they did not practice sustained observation, collection of data and positive knowledge, minute methods of science, and investigation and experimentation. They were inquisitive and curious, but curiosity alone is not enough for science.

Contact between India and the Arab world goes back to the beginnings of recorded history. The long-established trade between the Persian Gulf and India resulted in several notable Arabic works, such as the *Chain of Histories* and *Marvels of India,* in addition to manuals of navigation in prose and verse. With the rise of Islam these ties were intensified, and the transfer of the capital of the Arab Empire from Damascus to Baghdad in 762 established closer links with the sea routes to India and China. Merchandise was carried from Baghdad to Basra, and thence to Siraf, the main Arabian port of embarkation situated in the Persian Gulf. From Siraf goods were transported to India, Southeast Asia, and China. The proximity of the new capital to the Persian Gulf gave a fresh impetus to trade with southern India. The Arabs exchanged goods with Gujarat, Kathiawar, Konkan, Malabar, the Coromandal coast, Bengal, the Andaman and Nicobar Islands, western Sumatra, Malaya, Indochina, and China. Close cultural and commercial contacts between the Arabs and southern India continued until the arrival of the Portuguese in India at the end of the fifteenth century.

The Arabs appear to have had a high regard for India. *Saif-i-Hindi* (the Indian sword) was their favourite weapon. There is some evidence to suggest that at the time of Prophet Muhammad, Indian tribes resembling the Jats were settled in Arabia and Iraq. When Ayasha, the favourite wife of the Prophet, fell ill she was reported to have been treated by an Indian physician from the Jat tribe. Arab interest in India is also well attested to by the record of the numerous Arab travellers to India, such as Sulaiman the merchant, Abu Zaid Sirafi, Dulaf bin Muhalhil, Buzurg bin Shahryar, Masudi, Istakhri, Ibn Haukal, Muqaddisi, Al Biruni, and Ibn Battuta, who has been called "The Traveller of the Arabs" because of his extensive journeys. Arab historians were generous in their appreciation of India. Said Al-Andalusi in his *Tabaqat al-Ulam* called India "a mine of wisdom, a source of law and politics," and Indian scientists were acknowledged to be masters of the science of numbers (*ilm al-adad*), of geometry and astronomy, and to have surpassed all other peoples in their knowledge of medicine. Yaqubi characterized the Indians as men unsurpassed in science, especially astronomy. The period between 500 and 800 was indeed a remarkable period of scientific activity in India, especially in astronomy and mathematics. Abu Mashan described India as a noble country and said that all ancient peoples acknowledged the excellence of her peoples' wisdom, knowledge, and sense of justice. The Abbasid Caliphs, Al Mansur, Harun Al Rashid, and Al Mamun, even recruited Indian or Indian-trained ministers during their administrations. These ministers were known as Barmaks (a derivative from Pramukha), Barmakites, or Barmecides who were originally Buddhists and Heads (Pramukha) of the Nava Vihara at Balkh.[9] This temple later came to be known as the great Magian fire temple, and its high priest bore the title of Barmak. Upon the foundation of the Abbasid Caliphate, Khalid was the first Barmak to hold the important office of state under Saffah and Mansur (754–775) and his son Yahya was the tutor of Harun Al Rashid, who upon his accession to the Caliphate appointed Yahya as his grand vizier (prime minister).[10] Under the patronage and tactful administration of the Barmaks, Baghdad became a centre of Indian learning.

From this time on Arab and Muslim historians, geographers, and travellers began to visit India increasingly. Ahmad bin Yaqub bin Jafar, who came to India in the tenth century, compiled a list of Indian works translated into Arabic. Muhammad bin Ishaq ibn al-Nadim in his encyclopaedic *Kitab al-Fihrist* mentions repeatedly a wide range of works on Indian thought.

The two most eminent scholars and greatest minds of the Arab world,

Al Biruni (973–1048) and Al Khwarizmi (d. *ca.* 850), whose works profoundly influenced the growth of scientific thought in Europe, were well versed in Indian thought and languages. Al Biruni had travelled widely in India and had painstakingly learned Sanskrit in order to translate Indian scientific writing into Arabic. It was only after visiting India that he wrote his monumental work on mathematics, physics, geography, and astronomy. He translated some works of Indian philosophy, such as *Kitab Patanjal* and Kapila's *Sanka*. He wrote *Kitab al-Bayan*, a work on the principles of Indian rhetoric, and even a history of India, *Tarikh al-Hind*, in which he pointed out that the Hindus were too arrogant about their science and country. His work on the comparative chronology of nations, *Al-Athar al-Baqiyah an al-Quran al-Khaliyah*, is well known and often quoted by European writers.

In physics Al Biruni used the displacement method to calculate the specific weight or gravity of eighteen different precious and semi-precious stones. He also experimented with great accuracy on some minerals. In mathematics he finalized Arab knowledge and the use of Hindu numerals, solving many intricate problems relating to angles, conics, and cubic equations. He also made outstanding contributions "to the principles of hydrostatics, which he investigated in the artesian wells of India."[11] His work on India, a product of some thirteen years of labour, in content and scientific method is outstanding in Arabic literature. He translated many Indian books into Arabic and, more curiously, several Arabic translations from the Greek into Sanskrit. He represented that "happy and fertile blend of Arabic and Indian literatures which is one of the best fruits of Muslim civilization."[12]

By the time the Arabs arrived the Indians had mastered many astronomical concepts, amongst them were the solar system; the lunar mansions; the *nakshatras*; the precession of the equinoxes and the determination of its rate; the establishment of the lunisolar year; the spherical shape of the sun, moon, earth, and the other planets; the calculation of mean distances of the planets based on the theory of equal linear motion; the rotation of the earth on its axis; the revolution of the earth around the sun; and the assumption of interplanetary attraction as an explanation of equilibrium.

Astronomy requires sophisticated mathematics, and the use of the trigonometric sine was introduced as a contribution to the mathematical representation of astral positions. It is in the *Surya Siddhanta*, a work of the fourth century, that the trigonometric sine is first mentioned. The most renowned of all the Arab astronomers, Muhammad ibn Jabir al-Battani (877–918) whose astronomical tables superseded Greek knowledge and were widely diffused throughout mediaeval Europe, introduced into Arab science the use of ratios, sine, and tangent, which were contained in Aryabhata's geometry. When Copernicus (1473–1543) replaced the hitherto prevalent concept of the closed and hierarchical cosmos, which had survived since antiquity, with that of the homogeneous and infinite universe of modern science, he extensively used the contributions to trigonometry made by Abul-Wafa (940–998) who continued the work of Al Battani. In fact, trigonometry was first studied by the Arabs as a branch of astronomy, and only later studied independently.

The Indian decimal notation and the concept of zero were similarly passed on to Europe through Arab scholarship when Al Fazari translated Brahmagupta's *Siddhanta* in 771 under the title *Sindhind,* although it was not until in the nineteenth century that Colebrooke first noticed the connection between the two. This treatise was brought to Baghdad by an Indian astronomer, who had come on a political mission from Sind to the court of the Caliph Al Mansur. Ibn al-Adami, confirmed by Al Biruni, has recorded in detail the manner in which Indian astronomy was introduced at Baghdad. Later, Yaqub ibn Tariq incorporated in his *Tarkib al-Aflak* principles of Indian astronomy. The *Khanda-Khadyaka* of Brahmagupta, called by the Arabs Al Arkand, and Aryabhata's and Varahamihira's works on astronomy were also studied. Al Biruni translated *Surya Siddhanta* of Varahamihira.

Al Khwarizmi, who laid the foundation of Arab astronomy and higher mathematics, and to whom the world is indebted for its present knowledge of algebra, was greatly indebted to Indian scholarship. In his work on algebra entitled *Book of Calculation of Restoration and Reduction,* Al Khwarizmi used Indian as well as Greek and Babylonian sources. His arithmetic was based on the Indian decimal notation and numerals and had tremendous influence on mathematics in Europe through its translation into Latin in the twelfth century. During the latter half of the eighth century an Indian brought to Baghdad two important scientific treatises on astronomy and mathematics. Al Khwarizmi abridged the astronomical work, *Siddhanta,* into Arabic about 820 and used its tables in revising Ptolemy's and constructing his own. The trigonometric tables of Al Khwarizmi were translated into Latin by Adelard of Bath in 1126. Through the replacement of Ptolemy's calculus of chords by the calculus of sines or trigonometry, astronomical knowledge made great advances. Other contemporary writers such as Fazl bin Hatim Naziri and Hassen bin Misba also made use of the Indian system. In the ninth century Al Kindi wrote a tract on Indian computation, *Hisabul Hindi*. It was through the Arabs that Indian astronomy, despite the complete isolation of India from Europe during the Middle Ages, exercised an indirect influence on modern Western astronomy. The Indian system with its theory of the "trepidation," or pendulum movement, of the fixed stars found wide acceptance amongst the Arab astronomers of Spain, but since it conflicted with the Ptolemaic system of the continuous precession of the equinoxes, it gave rise to a considerable body of polemical and critical writing. This reached its peak in the thirteenth century and influenced Christian circles in Europe. One positive aspect of the Crusades was that they, unintentionally although unavoidably, provided an opportunity for cultural intercourse between Europe and Asia during the mediaeval period.

Long before the Arabs began translating Indian scientific works, the Persians had begun the process of synthesizing Indian knowledge with Persian, which had reached its zenith during the reign of Anushirwan (Kushro I, 531–579). Syrian astronomers, such as Severus Sebokht, also knew of Indian achievements and in 662 he wrote of Hindu numerals—the first known mention of them outside India—and of Hindu computation which excelled the spoken word and was done with nine symbols. Hence, the possibility of Indian ideas having reached the Arabs through Persian texts cannot be ruled out.

Whilst the development of Arab science, especially astronomy and mathematics, was largely inspired by the various prevalent Alexandrian traditions and sustained by the qualities of Arab scholarship, the first major impulse came from India. But the Arabs' own tradition of astronomy—in their long desert journeys they depended on the stars for the direction—had received considerable encouragement through the establishment of several observatories under the Umayyad and Abbasid Caliphates. The Muslims looked upon astronomy as the noblest and most exalted of sciences, for the study of stars was an indispensable aid to religious observances, determining for instance the month of *Ramadhan* and the hours of prayers. The observatory at Jundishapur in Iran, a centre of learning especially in medical science, was particularly suited as a focal point for Western and Indian contact. Even after the decline of the Abbasid Caliphate, interest in astronomy continued. In the thirteenth century the Mongol conqueror Hulagu Khan, who had deposed the Caliphate of Baghdad, and who was led by his superstitious belief in astrology, founded the great Margha observatory at Azerbaijan. This observatory was well known for its monumental instruments, and India was always in close contact with it. Here Arab, Persian, Greek, Chinese, and Indian learning interacted on one another.

About a century and a half later in the fifteenth century, Ulug Begh, grandson of the Turkish conqueror Tamurlane, built an observatory in Samarkand and it was here that new planetary tables and a new star catalogue were prepared, the first since Ptolemy's. It is quite possible that the renewed inspiration for erecting observatories at Jaipur, Delhi, and elsewhere in the seventeenth and eighteenth centuries, with their wonderfully accurate instruments, came from Central Asia. They almost certainly had their ancient counterparts although no material evidence is now available. In the seventeenth century, despite traditional objections, certain Indian astronomers began to introduce Arab and Western ideas. For example Kamalakara borrowed generously from the Arabs when he wrote his *Siddhantaviveka* in 1658.

When the Arabs assumed the position of political ascendancy in the world, medical science in India was already mature. It was inevitable, therefore, that the Arabs should have been attracted by Indian developments in this field. Even at the time of Alexander, says Garrison, "Hindu physicians and surgeons enjoyed a well-deserved reputation for superior knowledge and skill," and some scholars have suggested the influence on Aristotle of Indian medical ideas.[13] Barzouhyeh, who prepared a Pahlavi version of the *Pancatantra* during the reign of Anushirvan (531–579), visited India to acquire proficiency in Indian medicine and other sciences. Ibn al-Nadim relates that when Caliph Harum Al Rashid suffered from a serious disease which baffled his physicians at Baghdad he called for an Indian physician, Manka (Manikya), who cured him. The Caliph rewarded him richly and Manka settled at Baghdad and was attached to the hospital of the Barmaks. Having acquired a thorough knowledge of Islamic religion and languages, he translated several books from Sanskrit into Persian or Arabic. There are records of many other Indian physicians who practiced medicine amongst the Arabs; two of them were Ibn Dhan and Salih, reputed to be the descendants of Dhanapati and Bhela respectively. Ibn Dhan was appointed the director of his hospital by the Barmak Yahya, and he is credited with having translated books from Sanskrit into Arabic and Persian. Indian physicians were superintendents of the hospitals at Baghdad. Indian medical works were rendered into Pahlavi and Arabic during the Abbasid Caliphate; amongst them were Caraka, Susruta, the *Ashtangahrdaya,* the *Nidana,* the *Siddhayoga,* and other works on diseases of women and their treatment, poisons and their antidotes, on drugs, medicaments, intoxicants, nervous diseases, etc. Susruta's manual was translated by Manka and entitled *Sasru;* Ibn Dhan translated two other Sanskrit works, describing them as *Sindhstan* and *Istsangir.* Greek medical

149

works were also translated and the Arabs were quite familiar with them as well.[14]

Ali bin Rabban's pupil, Abu Bakr Muhammad ibn Zakariya al-Razi (865–925), began the golden age of Arab medicine. He anticipated Pasteur by more than one thousand years, for when ordered by the Caliph to build a new hospital, he hung up pieces of fresh meat in various parts of Baghdad and chose the site where the meat putrefied most slowly, because, as Pasteur was to demonstrate, the atmosphere was purer and bacteria less active. Al Razi was a Persian who knew Greek, Persian, and Indian medicine. He was one of history's great doctors and one of the two greatest Muslim physicians and chemists; the other being Abu Ali Ibn Sina (Avicenna). He was a prolific writer who produced about two hundred books, half of them on medicine. His greatest work on general clinical medicine, *Al Hawi,* was translated into Latin by Gerard of Cremona and remained a standard text in European medical colleges until the seventeenth century. It draws heavily on Graeco-Arabic and Indian sources.[15]

Al Razi and Al Ashau propounded the Arabic system of atomism. That this system was founded by someone very familiar with Indian sciences would explain the Arab adoption, almost wholly, of the Indian atomic theories, as enunciated by the Nyaya-Vaisesika and the Jain and Ajivika schools of thought, in marked preference to the Greek atomic theory founded by Leucippus and Democritus.[16]

As Arab medicine developed, it spread through North Africa and reached its highest expression in the University of Cordova in Spain. In addition, other streams of thought converged on the College of Salerno near Naples, the first medical school in the Christian world. The Church played no part in its foundation, for it was reputedly started by four masters—Elinus the Jew, Pontus the Greek, Adale the Arab, and Salernus the Latin—in the tenth century, perhaps even earlier. It was certainly much older than the Universities of Paris and of Bologna, which are regarded as the two archetypes of the European university.

Arab toxicology, which marked the advance from alchemy to rational medicine, was, as reflected in the works of Ibn Wahshiya, Jabir, Maimonides, and others, greatly influenced by Indian concepts, and especially the *Book of Shanab. Shanab* may well have been the Arabic version of *Caraka* for the work is based on the *Carakasamhita,* particularly in its identification of poisonous substances and distinctions between "mobile" and "immobile" poisons.[17]

Arab and, indirectly, European indebtedness to Indian science is indeed great. Mediaeval Europe miserably lacked any scientific culture until Eastern knowledge reached them through Arabic translations. The Romans, being a practical people, were uninterested in speculative or pure scientific thought, and in consequence they completely disregarded the progress made in scientific fields in the schools of Alexandria and elsewhere: "Not a single Roman left his mark on mathematics, mechanics, or technology."[18] Without the Arabian contribution it is unthinkable that the West could have absorbed the scientific knowledge of India, Persia, Greece, and Alexandria as it did, thus laying the foundation of its own superb progress.

It was in Spain that the Arabs achieved their greatest conquest in Europe and it was through Spain that they made their most enduring contributions to European civilization. On the eve of Arab conquest Spain was in a weak and deplorable state. The Arab rule was tolerant, liberal, and a welcome change. The Arabs introduced scientific irrigation and a number of new crops, such as cotton, rice, sugar cane, and citrus fruits, the first three having originated in India.[19] The changes they brought about in the system of land tenure paved the way for Spanish prosperity. Industries such as textiles, wool, pottery, paper, silk, and sugar-refining were developed and important gold, silver, and other mines opened up. In architecture there developed the new Hispano-Moorish style, which produced such world-famous buildings as the Alcazar in Seville and the Alhambra in Granada.

There are Spanish historians who attempt to minimize the Arab heritage of Spain, and some even conclude that Arab domination retarded Spanish life, but there is considerable evidence pointing to the deep indebtedness of Spain to the Arabs. The Amirs of Arab Spain were enthusiastic patrons of scholarship, and Arab Spain was a citadel of cultural heritage and progress. Whilst most of Europe was in a decadent decline, both materially and spiritually, the Spanish Muslims created a splendid civilization and an organized economic life. During the reign of Abdurrahman (912–961) Spain rose to the foremost place in European civilization. The Umayyad ruler, with his capital in Cordova, was exceptionally talented, a valiant soldier, and a wise ruler with many intellectual interests.[20]

The great variety of races in Muslim Spain probably hindered the immediate integration of societies and cultures. But once momentum gathered, development was impressive. Arab science and philosophy dominated Spanish thought and life from the beginning of the ninth to the end of the thirteenth century. In practical life, including legal and military organization, Arab influence was so great that some Christian writers, such as Alvaro of Cordova, lamented the situation. The official language of Muslim Spain was classical Arabic; the Arabs were the backbone of the Spanish army, and they married freely into Spanish families. The study of Muslim law and theology introduced Arab books giving a fresh impetus to Arab learning. Scholars, students, and book-sellers flocked to Cordova and it soon became the intellectual capital of the Western world. The royal library was one of the best in Spain, and there were, in addition, a number of celebrated private libraries in Cordova. The impact of Arab culture on Spain eliminated the local distrust of philosophy and astronomy and cleared the way for their study and growth, first in Spain, and later throughout Europe. Spanish scholars, attracted by this movement, travelled in the East, read the works of Greek and other philosophers, and, upon their return, served as another channel of communication with the rest of Europe. "Muslim Spain played a decisive part in the development of art, science, philosophy, and poetry, and its influence reached even to the highest peaks of the Christian thought of the thirteenth century, to Thomas Aquinas and Dante. Then, if ever, Spain was 'the torch of Europe.' "[21]

With the destruction of Cordova at the beginning of the eleventh century by the Berbers, Toledo became the centre of Muslim learning in Spain, and it retained this position after the Christian conquest in 1085.[22] Toledo attracted scholars from all parts of Europe, including Britain. The Italian Gerard of Cremona, who is credited with having carried more of Arabic science into Europe than any other single scholar, Alfred the Englishman, Michael the Scot, Hermann the German, Herman Dalmata the Slav, all worked in Spain during the twelfth and thirteenth centuries. The greatest name in English science before Robert Grossetete and Roger Bacon, Adelard of Bath, was a student of Arab science and philosophy in the twelfth century. He learned Arabic, as did the other scientists of the day, and by the end of the thirteenth century, Arab science had been transmitted to western Europe and absorbed, and Spain's work as an intermediary was done.

A major reason why the Arabs left a vast heritage of scientific conceptual synthesis and not of speculative thought, may be because religiously and philosophically their implicit faith in Islamic thought did not allow them sufficient receptivity to other influences. But, in science and commerce they were not so inhibited and thus absorbed freely from whatever quarters they could.

Chapter V

NATURALISM AND SCIENCE
IN ANCIENT INDIA

SCIENCE AND philosophy were both highly developed disciplines in ancient India. However, because Indian philosophic thought was considerably more mature and found particular favour amongst intellectuals, the tradition persists that any early scientific contributions came solely from the West, Greece in particular. Because of this erroneous belief, which is perpetuated by a wide variety of scholars, it seems desirable to examine briefly the history of Indian scientific thought.

The history of science in general is a comparatively new field and a comprehensive account of Indian science and technology has yet to be written. Despite the fact that a vast literature in Sanskrit is no longer available, there are many documents waiting to be investigated.[1] Beginning with the earliest known Indian civilization, the Indus Valley, with its pottery wheel, cotton textiles, Indus script, and two wheeled carts, there is a good deal of material and texts to work from. By the beginning of the third millennium B.C. in India, as in China, Egypt, and Mesopotamia, scientific development was well advanced. Excavations carried on at the sites of the Indus civilization have revealed remnants of an ancient civilization unsurpassed in civil engineering accomplishments, particularly baths and drainage. Whilst much is known of the hygienic measures of the period, little is known of the scientific knowledge upon which they were based.

In ancient India, as in Greece, there was much speculative thought about astronomy, mathematics, physics, and biology. But mathematics and mysticism are inextricably mixed in early Greek thought, and Greek belief in magic, divination and oracles was perhaps more pronounced than its counterpart in India. It is therefore untrue to assert, as recent European writers particularly have done, that Greece was the

153

home of pure science. Equally untenable is the claim of those Indian historians who overemphasize India's contribution to scientific thought. Both India and Greece, whilst having their own traditions, had direct and indirect effects on each other in science as they did in philosophy. In fact, long before the Greeks, the Indians had learned to employ the dialectic method to grasp empirical and transcendental truths, although in India, more perhaps than in ancient Greece or the modern West, reason and truth, logic and mysticism, the visible and invisible, have always been regarded as inseparable.

The practical application of science to human affairs was as poor in India as in any other ancient society. In fact, this was not achieved until the eighteenth century; until then science and technology developed separately. In the seventeenth century, called "the cradle of modern science," Francis Bacon (1561–1626) through his *Novum Organum* established a new methodology in the experimental interpretation of nature. Although he failed to appreciate that the new science must be based on mathematics, he wrote as a philosopher exposing the inadequacy of old theories. He believed that mind, liberated from prejudice and generalization, could by knowledge attain sovereignty over nature. With little aptitude for practical science he yet understood the enormous importance of a new way of investigating nature. He considered that "the purpose of science was not to make up new theories about the nature and principles of things, but to lay firmer foundations of human power and greatness. So Science was to minister to the Arts —to medicine, navigation, industry of all kinds."[2] At about the same time René Descartes (1596–1650), the founder of analytical geometry in France, also insisted on a new methodology basing his concept more on deduction than experience. He commenced by subjecting everything to the test of doubt, including doubt itself. He insisted upon proof by experiment, thus laying the foundation of modern scientific research, and advocated the practical application of scientific conclusions. The Italian astronomer and experimental philosopher, Galileo Galilei (1564–1643), was the first, however, to employ the modern scientific method in its fullness. He was an enthusiastic and versatile man, skilful with his hands, a fine writer, and a competent mathematician. He founded the science of mechanics in physics. However, his brilliant researches and remarkable work incurred the wrath of the Church and he was incarcerated by the Inquisition at the advanced age of seventy. (There is hardly a parallel in India where a difference in interpretation either in metaphysical or scientific thought was so unkindly suppressed.) In view of the work of Galileo and other Italian scientists, it is suggested that modern science, like modern art, sprang from Italy. It was then that scientific thought emerged from the realm of natural philosophy and formed the basis of modern technology. It is this scientifically based technology upon which contemporary civilization is built. Whilst science makes technology possible, technology, in turn, widens scientific horizons.

The spirit of scientific enquiry and a rigorous correlation of cause and effect in explaining natural phenomena were particularly evident in ancient India. The connection between Indian philosophy and medicine, mathematics, astronomy, and technology is, strangely enough, seldom realized much less recognized. Indian thought contained a strong element of philosophical naturalism or realism from which stemmed scientific ideas. These, however, did not always come to fruition with the same consistency and speed as in Italy or Europe during the modern period. Yet, "concrete ideas on the ultimate structure of matter, the evolution of elements and their combination to form diverse substances of the earth, the classification of the compounds, etc., clothed in speculative language peculiar to them, appear to have been put forward first by the Indians."[3] Ancient Indians "measured the land, divided the year, mapped out the heavens, traced the course of the sun and the planets through the zodiacal belt, analyzed the constitution of matter, and studied the nature of birds and beasts, plants and seeds."[4]

Whilst in Western civilizations the interest has been increasingly focused on single sciences, in the Indian world the ontological viewpoint has been generally preferred, and it would thus appear that "in India, through all periods, the special sciences are rooted in and developed on the underlying unifying cosmic concepts and presuppositions of which the single scientific result is only a special case and phenomenon, a demonstration and a facet, as it were, of the universal cosmic law. This universal vision in India has never been lost."[5]

The beginnings of Indian scientific thought are traced to the same source as those of Indian metaphysics and religion, the *Rig Veda*. The Vedas, being essentially works of poetic imagination, cannot be expected to contain much spirit of scientific inqury, yet there are remarkable flashes of intuitive conjecture and reason. In some of the hymns, especially in Book X, strong naturalistic trends are found, whilst many of them make the gods appear only slightly removed from the natural phenomena which they represent. They express a kind of simple nature worship in which man, who is regarded as "king of animals" and "first of beasts," is wonder-struck at the mighty forces of the universe. Indeed, in one of the most remarkable of the vedic hymns—the "Song of Creation"—a searching inquiry as to the origin of the world is made; it is certainly the earliest known record of philosophic doubt.

> Then was not non-existent nor existent;
> There was no realm of air, no sky
> beyond it.
> What covered in, and where? and what
> gave shelter?
> Was water there, unfathomed depth
> of water?

The hymn goes on to say that in the beginning there was neither death nor immortality, nor day nor night. All that existed was void and formless. Then arose desire, the primal seed and germ of spirit. But,

> Who verily knows and
> who can declare it,
> Whence it was born and
> whence comes this creation?
>
> The gods are later than this
> world's production
> Who knows, then, whence it
> first came into being?[6]

In this hymn, which contains the essence of monism, can be seen a representation of the most advanced theory of creation. Reality is not named here; it is not identified with any of the gods. Indeed, the gods come after the world's creation. The vedic cosmos was self-sufficient and self-perpetuating, unlike the Greek cosmos which implied pre-established harmony and a stabilized order brought within the phenomena from outside. Order is immanent in the Indian cosmos, not an externally determined law.

The vedic civilization was naturalistic and utilitarian although it did not exclude cosmological, religious, and mythical speculations. The Vedas also allude to many scientific notions, some of which are also found in ancient Iranian texts. In addition to detailed information about diseases, drugs, and stars, some rather remarkable ideas relating to the order of the world were common to both the Vedic and Iranian documents. The world was conceived as governed by a cyclical law, *rita* (the world-balance or world-course), meaning both normal and true. Rita, of which Varuna was the custodian, was the law of nature and its normal course was illustrated by the revolution of the planets and the rhythm of the seasons. A balance was conceived of between the universe and the human and animal kingdoms. Unlike its Greek equivalent, in which a planned order was introduced by an all-powerful creator, vedic rita was the functional balance of an already existent single phenomenon in which each part functioned according to its own law of activity, and all of them together balanced each other in the general rhythm of the universe. In the ancient Iranian *Avesta,* this law was called *asha* and in Achaemenian texts *arta.* One of the Achaemenian inscriptions even refers to an *arta brazmaniya,* (Brahmanic order). The notion of rita "is very important, since, referring as it does not only to the natural but also to the moral order, it represents an overall determinism. It differs from strict scientific determinism in that it rejects all apparent irregularities out of hand, simply because they are irregular. It is less concerned with physical laws than with norms, less with order, as such, than with 'good' order."[7] The idea of Brahman was associated with that of *vak* ("the word") which made the sacred rites effective, and regulated the movement of the world. Cosmophysiology and astronomy were the two fundamentals of vedic science based on the observation and understanding of real phenomena, although an irrational magic element flourished side by side with them.

It was in the later vedic period, however, that scientific thought or the philosophy of naturalism became articulate. There is some evidence to suggest, despite the destruction by priests and others of materials pertaining to materialist ascendancy, that at times it even dominated the Indian scene. The authority of the vedic hymns declined and intuition gave way to inquiry, religion to philosophy. It was an age keenly alive with intellectual interest and inevitably one of many-sided, even divergent, development. Whilst there were many anomalies, contradictions, and complexities in Indian thought, in which sorcery and science, scepticism and faith, and licence and asceticism co-existed, the emphasis was on intellectual fervour and inquiry and on acceptance of the independent and objective world. Formalized Indian logic was empirical. Indeed, the two trends in Indian thought, trancendentalism and naturalism, have always been neatly bound together without any obvious contradictions. The germs of free speculation and scepticism were already present in the *Rig Veda.* The Upanishads developed this spirit of inquiry, and traces of naturalistic and scientific thought in them are quite significant. Consequently, the worship of imaginary gods, the vested interests in religion and theology, and speculation about things that could not be perceived or subjected to sense experience were clearly denounced. In upanishadic cosmology, Brahman is not like the conception of God, a demiurge, seated outside the world which he created and controlled. There was no extraneous matter from which God created the universe. The direction of the world was caused by the world itself and natural phenomena were not concerned with human values; moral rules were humanistic conventions made by men living in society. Truth was seen through direct perception, *darshana. Lokayata,* or materialism, literally the philosophy or worldliness of the people, was the only Sastra for which perceptual evidence was the authority. Matter became the only reality which alone was cognizable by the senses. The ultimate principles were the four elements—earth, water, fire, and air—which were eternal. Akasa (space) was believed to be a substance from which nature derived its whole structure, and from which were evolved the other four elements: "From that Self (Brahman) sprang ether (Akasa, that through which we hear); from ether air (that through which we hear and feel); from air fire (that through which we hear, feel and see); from fire water (that through which we hear, feel, see, talk, and smell)."[8] (It is very interesting that early Indians seemed to know that sound was transmitted through the air and not through a vacuum.) Thought was a function of matter, and nature operated without any interference from the gods.

The Upanishads were the key to the mysterious relationships of the things of this world. Their main purpose was to look at the world objectively. In attempting to explain the multiplicity and diversity of phenomena by simple natural laws, they did sometimes confuse the superficial with the fundamental. They declined to submit, however, to the inevitable destiny, which indicated their desire to comprehend nature in terms of reason. In the early Upanishads, Uddalaka, possibly a fictitious character, is portrayed as representing a naturalistic point of view in marked contrast to Yajnavalkya, who represents the idealistic view. Uddalaka's hylozoistic view of the world was quite distinct from the vedic cosmological and theogonic tradition, and is anterior in Indian literature to that of the Ajivikas, or of Carvaka or Lokayata, usually called the first materialistic school. Indeed, it was a period in which man rejected the principle of authority and insisted on the validity of reason. The Indians propounded natural philosophy through various systems—the Samkhya-Yoga, the Nyaya-Vaisesika, and the theories of Carvaka and Uddalaka are clearly naturalistic.

According to the Carvakas there was no world beyond the present one, and knowledge could be acquired only through sensory perception; what could not be perceived did not exist. Their metaphysics was an unqualified materialistic monism, claiming that the world was made up of the four elements and consciousness was a material and transitory modification of these elements; their ethics were hedonistic. Virtue and vice were not absolute values; they were merely social conventions. Life was to be lived joyously. The end of man was unrestrained enjoyment. God, religion, and immortality were illusions. Their system assumed various forms of philosophical scepticism, logical fatalism, and religious indifference. Its origins are traced as far back as the *Rig Veda,* but the main work *Brhaspati Sutra (ca.* 600 B.C.) is not available. Fragments of information found in other texts reconstruct their materialist doctrine. They played a role in Indian thought somewhat similar to that of the atomists and sophists in Greece. In fact, the philosophies of Buddhism, Jainism, and the Ajivikas are strongly rationalistic. The Buddha has often been called atheist, because of his indifference to God. According to Buddhism, man must depend upon himself for salvation, not upon divine intervention. Buddhism is not incompatible with scientific research, and it fostered scientific speculation in India and elsewhere: "The Buddha's purpose was primarily philosophical, ethical, but his thought was distinctly of a scientific nature."[9]

Jainism also contains outstanding naturalistic elements. The world (loka) consists of matter, of atomic particles, whilst man controls his own moral life without supernatural assistance.

The Samkhya system, which has been described as the ruling philosophy of pre-Buddhist India and an orthodox system having its roots in the Upanishads, is essentially rational, anti-theistic, and intellectual. The major concern of Samkhya is to explain the workings of nature through perceptual knowledge. It contradicts the tenets of supernatural religion by substituting evolution for creation. The world is not a creation of God but the product of the interaction between the infinite number of spirits and the ever active *prakriti* or the potentiality of nature. According to Richard Garbe, it was in Samkhya doctrine that complete independence and freedom of the human mind was exhibited for the first time in history.[10] Samkhya, probably the oldest Indian philosophical system, furnished the background for the Yoga system, and the early Buddhist biography *Lalitavistara* includes both Samkhya and Yoga in the curriculum of study for the young Buddha.[11] Samkhya is generally ascribed to Kapila and Yoga to Patanjali. The general metaphysical position of these two systems with regard to soul, nature, cosmology, and ultimate goal is almost the same except that Yoga acknowledges a god (Isvara) and stresses yogic practices for the liberation of the atman, while Samkhya denies Isvara and suggests that sincere philosophic thought is sufficient to reveal truth and thus bring about liberation. Samkhya looks upon the individual as a dynamic complex of material processes arranged around an immaterial, fundamental principle of consciousness, and this distinction between *purusha* and prakriti and their conjoint functioning is the principal doctrine of this system. Prakriti is the sum-total of material processes, but without the light of consciousness, purusha, it is blind and ineffective. On the other hand, light without means of action is in the same position. Purusha, as the unchanging principle of intelligence, reflected in prakriti creates the visible universe. This heterogeneous universe (*srishti*) is a development out of homogeneous prakriti, and to prakriti it returns. There has been no creation nor will there be a destruction. The present world is but one of a series which have existed and are yet to be.[12]

Whilst the Samkhya-Yoga system confined itself to the principles of cosmic evolution, the Nyaya-Vaisesika dwelt on the method of science, elaborating the concepts of mechanics, physics, and chemistry. Nyaya-Vaisesika combined two systems embodied in the sutras attributed to Gotama and Uluka respectively. Both are realistic systems based on independent reasoning, opposing earlier phenomenalism and idealism. Nyaya stresses logic and epistemology; Vaisesika, physics and metaphysics. Both, however, have the liberation of self as their goal and agree in essential principles, such as the nature of self and the atomic theory of the universe. The Nyaya-Vaisesikas regard existence as the most obvious characteristic of things. Atoms and souls, space and time, are mere sounds and symbols having no meaning apart from experience. They dismissed Samkhya cosmology but accepted the atomic doctrine of the four elements. Thus, in spite of the strong current of idealistic thought which finally eclipsed naturalism in India, science figured prominently in Indian intellectual life.

Ancient Indian work on grammar was not only more objective, systematic, and brilliant than that done in Greece or Rome but is illustrative of their scientific methods of analysis. Although the date of Panini's grammar, the *Ashtadhyayi*, which comprises about four thousand sutras or aphoristic rules, is uncertain, it is the earliest extant scientific grammar in the world, having been written no later than the fourth century B.C. But prior grammatical analysis is clearly evidenced by the fact that Panini himself mentions over sixty predecessors in the field. For example, the sounds represented by the letters of the alphabet had been properly arranged, vowels and diphthongs separated from mutes, semivowels, and sibilants, and the sounds had been grouped into gutturals, palatals, cerebrals, dentals, and labials. Panini and other grammarians, especially Katyayana and Patanjali, carried the work much further, and by the middle of the second century B.C. Sanskrit had attained a stereotyped form which remained unaltered for centuries. Whilst Greek grammar tended to be logical, philosophical and syntactical, Indian grammar was the result of an empirical investigation of language done with the objectivity of an anatomist dissecting a body. It was the discovery of Sanskrit by the West and the study of Indian methods of analysis that revolutionized Western studies of language and laid the foundation of comparative philology.

Science is essentially a series of experiments requiring various external aids. Lacking the finer and more precise instruments for experimentation, the ancient Indians used a careful analysis of observation. B. N. Seal, analyzing this method of scientific research, pointed out that the processes of perception, observation, experiment, fallacies of observation, inference, and hypothesis were very accurately defined and strictly followed.[13]

Hindu research in exact science, before the beginnings of modern science in Europe, covers the period from the *Rig Veda* to the middle of the fourteenth century represented by Madhavacharya's *The Sixteen Systems of Philosophy* (1331) and Gunratna's work on logic, the *Rasaratna-Samuchchaya* (1350). This period may be divided into four somewhat overlapping phases. The first phase is that of the vedic literature lasting until about 800 B.C. The second, represented by the *Vedanga Jyotisa*, the *Srauta, Grhya* and *Dharmasutras*, Manu and Yajnavalkya, Garga and the Jain works, came to an end about the third century A.D. The third, the period of the Siddhantas, which gave rise to the important works of Aryabhata (born 476), of Varahmihira (*ca.* 475–550), and of Brahmagupta (born 598), lasted until the rise of Islam. The fourth covered the mediaeval period of Indian history.

There is a divergence of opinion as to the scientific importance of the vedic texts. According to J. Filliozat and other recent scholars, these texts were the first attempts to systematize and codify scientific thought in astronomy and physiology.[14] In contrast, early Indologists, such as Macdonell and his pupil Keith, looked upon them as somewhat vague cosmological fancies and found extremely little sign of astronomical study in the vedic period. Nevertheless, it is certain that the vedic Indians knew something of astronomy and that it had a high utilitarian value for them, as it did for all peoples of antiquity who possessed some elementary knowledge about the celestial bodies and meteorological phenomena. The priest-astronomer, for example, could give information of utmost value to a people who were largely agricultural. The vedic priests had to make careful calculations of time for their rituals and sacrifices, and also the headman of the tribe, as in other ancient societies, had to determine the time of sowing and harvest. Moreover, astronomical periods played an important role in vedic thought, for they were considered to be successive parts of the ever returning cosmic cycle. The temporal aspect of that cycle was only one facet of the creative cosmic power, of the "word" of Prajapati, the world spirit whose wisdom was expressed in the Vedas. The year was the Prajapati's unit of time and the *Satapatha Brahmana* states that the Veda contains as many metrical divisions (10,800), as there are "moments" in the year of the world spirit.[15]

The *Rig Veda* lists a number of stars and mentions twelve divisions of the sun's yearly path (rashis) and also 360 divisions of the circle. Thus, the year of 360 days is divided into twelve months. The sun's annual course was described as a wheel with twelve spokes, which correspond to the twelve signs of the zodiac. In the *Vedanga Jyotisa*, a brief treatise of which there were two recensions, one with forty-three verses and the other thirty-six concerned exclusively with chronological calculations, the vedic Indians determined the equinoctial and solstitial points and associated them with Agni and Indra, and Mitra and Varuna. Composed at the close of the vedic period, the *Vedanga Jyotisa* contains the most important of the short texts on the principles of the calendar. Its main purpose was to fix the dates of ceremonies so that they could coincide with the given moments in the cosmic cycle thus ensuring its regularity. The principles listed are, however, too condensed to give direct information about the prevalent astronomical concepts. The calendar was arranged on the basis of a five year cycle of 1830 days, with a 366-day year divided into three equal seasons. The cycle equalled approximately sixty-seven sidereal months and contained sixty-two syndocal months. To keep each year to the traditional twelve months, two months—the thirty-first and the sixty-second—were omitted in each cycle. Thus, lunar and solar reckoning coincided at the beginning and middle of a cycle. Asoka is known to have used these figures in calculating the precise duration of his intended Buddhist pilgrimage.

In the *Yajur Veda* are listed twenty-seven or, if *abhijit* is added, twenty-eight constellations called nakshatras, unquestionably the most important astronomical item in the vedic texts. For a long time the nakshatras were regarded as lunar mansions or divisions in the path of the moon. It was also thought that lunar reckoning was used to calculate months, and a period of five years with sixty-two lunar months, called *yuga,* was established to make it correspond with the solar year. In reality, the nakshatras were used to follow the motions of the sun, as well as those of the moon and the planets. The calendars of the vedic and later periods were never either purely lunar or purely solar but lunisolar, for Indian astrologers have always looked upon astronomical phenomena as indivisible.[16]

As this list of nakshatras is virtually identical with the Chinese *sieu* or *hsui,* J. B. Biot, in the middle of the last century, and de Saussure, at the beginning of this, mistakenly suggested that India borrowed it from China. But since Biot formulated his opinion, it is now accepted as certain that the first complete list of *sieu* is later than the Indian nakshatras.[17] It would now seem that China probably borrowed from India. With Buddhism a good deal of Indian scientific knowledge travelled to China. Hindu astronomical instruments were introduced into China, and there were Hindu astronomers on the astronomical board of the Chinese government. However, at present there is no proof of contact between India and China at the time of the *Yajur Veda,* and it is possible that China developed her system independently. It has been somewhat hesitatingly asserted by J. Needham, well-known for his generous view of Chinese science, that both systems, Indian and Chinese lunar mansions, were probably originally Babylonian.[18] This is clearly untenable because, although astronomy was studied in Mesopotamia, there is no trace of such a system having existed there. If it had existed, it would have survived as an alternative to the zodiac, a much less precise system for calculating the position of the sun by the heliacal rising and setting of the stars. The nakshatra system, associated with the vedic religion of sacrifices, not only continued to grow in India uninfluenced by the Greek zodiac when Alexandrian astrology was introduced, but it spread to other countries. The Sassanid Persians, the Arabs, and the Copts in Egypt all marked the moon's course of approximately twenty-eight days by that number of asterisms, regarded as "lunar houses." Even before the Arabs, this idea is found in a Hermetic Greek text. Since no equivalent of the nakshatras has been discovered in ancient Iran, or any other western country, it must be assumed that the Arabs had taken it from Indian astronomy.[19]

The Indian theory of the great cycles of the universe and the ages of the world is of older origin than either Greek or Babylonian speculations about the "great year," the period within which all the stars make a round number of complete revolutions. But there is remarkably close numerical concordance in these theories.[20] The Indian concept of the great year *(mahayuga)* developed from the idea of a lunisolar period of five years, combined with the four ages of the world (yugas) which were thought to be of unequal perfection and duration, succeeding one another and lasting in the ratio of 4:3:2:1. The last, the *kaliyuga*, was one-tenth of the mahayuga or 432,000 years. This figure was calculated not only from rough estimates of planetary and stellar cycles, but also from the 10,800 stanzas of the *Rig Veda*, consisting of 432,000 syllables. The classical astronomers calculated the great period as one of 4,320,000 years, the basic element of which was a number of sidereal solar years, 1,080,000, a multiple of 10,800. According to Berossus, the Babylonian great year was a period of 432,000 years, comprising 120 "saroi" of 3,600 years apiece.[21]

Although the Vedas have survived the onslaughts of time and climate, it is common knowledge that many other works dealing with Indian culture, including science and astronomy, have been lost. After the vedic literature, the next existing scientific works belong to the early Christian era—a gap of more than a thousand years. During this period there appears to have been a great upsurge in astronomical studies. By the early Christian era, India had had a long period of contact with Greece, Persia, and western Asia. Consequently, it was at this time that the *Siddhanta* astronomy, filled with notions of Greek astrology, first made its appearance. The five astronomical systems, the Siddhantas—*Surya, Paitamaha, Romaka, Paulisa,* and *Vasistha*—are summarized by Varahamihira, the sixth century astronomer, in his *Panchasiddhantas.* The *Romaka* and the *Paulisa* may well have been influenced by Rome and Paul of Alexandria, although some scholars maintain the theory of their independent growth. The *Paulisa,* however, seems to have been a purely astronomical, not astrological, work, and, if it was influenced by some unknown Greek work, the influence cannot be defined accurately. The *Romaka* is the more likely text of the two to have come under Greek influence, but it is quite likely that the *Romaka* was composed by a Greek who had settled in India and who was familiar with Indian as well as Alexandrian astronomy. None of these systems, however, stood the test of time, each being dislodged by a new one. Of the Siddhantas only the *Surya Siddhanta* is extant. It has been described as "a pocket-book for accomplished scholars rather than a textbook for students." Although the Indian astronomers had noticed very early, because of their fairly accurate determinations of the sun's position through their nakshatra system, that the equinoctial and solstitial points do not remain stationary, it was centuries later before reference was made to this fact in the *Surya Siddhanta,* which speaks of a libratory motion rather than a rotatory precession. It has therefore been suggested that this concept was a Greek contribution to Indian astronomy. There are, however, many divergences between the numerical elements of Ptolemy and of the *Surya Siddhanta*. Hence, if there were some Greek influence on this work, it must have been before the Ptolemaic period.

The Indian astronomer, Aryabhata, lived during the period in which the *Surya Siddhanta* was composed. He was born in 476 and reputedly completed his famous work, *Aryabhatiya,* at the age of twenty-three. A concise and brilliant work of astronomy and mathematics, containing the customary four sections and 121 couplets written in terse style, the *Aryabhatiya* must have followed a long tradition of scientific thought to have attained the maturity it did. The *Aryabhatiya*, whilst mainly in agreement with the *Surya Siddhanta,* introduced certain concepts of its own. Aryabhata's new epicyclic theory, the sphericity of the earth, its rotation on its axis and revolution around the sun, the true explanation of eclipses and methods of forecasting them with accuracy, and the correct length of the year were his outstanding contributions. The Arabs preserved the theory of the sphericity of earth, and Pierre d'Ailly employed it in 1410 in his map, which was used by Columbus. Aryabhata was one of the most original and brilliant Indian scientific thinkers, yet his work did not exert much influence on Indian thought inside or outside the country. His theory of the earth's rotation remained isolated and no later works alluded to it. It was the *Surya Siddhanta* that exercised the greatest influence on those countries neighbouring India.

Varahamihira, who wrote the *Panchasiddhantas* summarizing the astronomy of the five Siddhantas, flourished in the middle of the sixth century. In his work the *Brhatsamhita* (the Great Compendium), which describes the motions and conjunctions of celestial bodies and their ominous significance, he shows a mastery of wide fields of knowledge and is thoroughly skilled in language and metre. In his two books on purely horoscopic astrology, *Brhakjataka* and *Laghujataka,* the earliest works of Indian astrology, he used many Greek astrological terms, beginning with the *hora.* It was Varahamihira who asserted that although the Yavanas were Mlecchas and their astronomy inferior to Indian, they must be honoured like rishis or seers for having originated the science of astrology. He does not pay the Greeks any similar compliment for their accomplishments in astronomy or mathematics. Speaking of the Siddhantas, he observes that the *Paulisa* and the *Romaka,* which were inspired by European treatises, were accurate, but the Hindu standard work, the *Surya Siddhanta,* was more accurate. Indeed, the credit for developing astrology as an extension of astronomy must go to the

Greeks. Even though it is a popular pastime of the Indian priesthood, no astrological considerations are found in any vedic, Buddhist, or Jain texts before the Christian era. During the period immediately prior to the Christian era, however, it appears, some Indians were named after stars, for instance Brihaspatimitra, friend of Brihaspati (Jupiter). But it was much later, under the influence of the Greeks, that horoscopic astrology gained immense popularity in India.

The classical period of ancient Indian astronomy is considered to have ended with Brahmagupta, who was born in 598 and worked in Ujjain. He wrote his Brahma *Siddhanta* in 628, and the *Khandakhadyaka,* a practical treatise on astronomical calculations, in 664. He rejected Aryabhata's doctrine of the earth's rotation saying: "If the earth move a minute in a *prana,* then whence and by what route does it proceed? If it revolve, why do not lofty objects fall?" Al Biruni, whilst criticizing him for his unjust attack on Aryabhata, calls him the most accomplished of Indian astronomers. He was, like his predecessor an excellent mathematician.

By this time, Indian contributions to astronomy included the solar system in which the earth and the planets move around the sun; the lunar mansions or the nakshatras; the precession of the equinoxes and the determination of its rate; the establishment of the lunisolar year; the names of the week days; the calculation of the mean rates of motion of the planets (bhaganas) based on continued observations; the construction of an astronomical calendar on a scientific basis; the spherical shape of the sun, moon, earth, and the other planets; the calculation of the mean distances of the planets based on the theory of equal linear motion; the rotation of the earth about its axis; the assumption of interplanetary attraction in order to explain equilibrium; and the measurement of the position of the sun, the latitude of the place of observation, and time, etc. with the help of the shadow of the gnomon.[22]

Several other eminent astronomers are known to have flourished, such as Lalla and Bhoja. But it was not until 1150 that the *Siddhantaasiromani* of Bhaskaracarya (Bhaskara) appeared, and after Bhaskara no appreciable progress in Indian astronomy is recorded, although some popular works were written. Changadeva founded a school in 1205 to carry on the work of his grandfather, Bhaskara, but it was short lived. It appears that Indian scholars devoted most of their energies to expounding the ancient traditions, and, in marked contrast to their ancient counterparts, were uninfluenced by Persian influences.

According to Burgess, there was "very little astronomical borrowing between the Hindus and the Greeks . . . since in no case do the numeri-

cal data and results in the system of the two peoples exactly correspond."[23] Moreover, the Hindus possessed an important body of
astronomical knowledge no less significant than that of the Hellenistic
astronomers long before they came into contact with Greece itself or
with Alexandrian science. But it would be unnatural not to expect intellectual stimulation on both sides and exchange of ideas during a period
of close contact between India and the Western world. Whilst the
tradition of astronomy in India was ancient and independent, it certainly received impetus from Alexandrian science. There are, furthermore, some technical terms in both Greek and Indian astronomy which
were borrowed from each other. For instance, *aux* of European astronomy is from the Sanskrit *ucca*, borrowed through the Arabs; Greek
pepton has become *lipta* in Sanskrit; *dekanos, drkana; trignos, trikona.*

It is practically impossible to separate mathematics from astronomy
during the period of Arab ascendancy, for almost every mathematician
was also an astronomer or an astrologer or both. In India, mathematics
was also pursued in close connection with astronomy; hence, the astronomical works of Aryabhata, Brahmagupta, and Bhaskara also carry
important sections on arithmetic and algebra.

Recent research has led to a greater acceptance of the theory of Indian
contribution to mathematics, a science far more advanced in India than
in any other nation of antiquity. Both ancient Indians and Greeks were
extremely fond of mathematics and both made important discoveries,
but their outlooks were somewhat different.[24] The Greeks devoted their
attention to geometry, subordinating arithmetic, algebra, and astronomy
and looked upon magnitude not as number but as length, whilst the
Indians based their mathematics on numbers. They had a clear conception of abstract number, as distinct from the numerical quantity
of objects or spatial extension, which enabled them to develop algebra
and to make more complicated calculations than could the Greeks.

Whilst rigorous logic and systematic treatment are the outstanding
features of Greek geometry, boldness of conception, abstraction, symbolism, and ingenuity are the main features of Indian mathematics.[25]
In India, as in Greece, science and philosophy interacted on each other.
For example, the Greeks being fond of geometry saw a symmetry in the
universe, and in India, the conception of *sunya*, void or nothingness in
Hindu and Buddhist philosophies, suggested to Indian mathematicians
the power and utility of symbols. The philosophy of the void or *sunya-
vada* urged that the world was neither real nor unreal, nor both nor
neither. Bringing this metaphysical notion into the realm of science

and giving this conception a form, a shape, and a symbol must be regarded as one of the greatest events in the history of human thought and progress, indeed the basis of all scientific calculations. The concept of sunya or zero is not just a mathematical and scientific discovery, but is deeply rooted in all branches of Indian thought, especially metaphysics and cosmology. Zero is the transition point between opposites, it symbolizes the real balance between divergent tendencies. It transcends all empirical data, and yet it is the basis of all empirical data. It is simultaneously the All and the None. It was originally conceived of as a symbol of Brahman or Nirvana, expressing the sum of all distinct forms. In the third century B.C., the eminent mathematician Bhaskara wrote a treatise dealing in great detail with the concept of Nirvana. The term sunya occurs in vedic literature and is used in Sanskrit literature in the sense of blank (*abhava*), insignificant or negligible (*tuccha*), incomplete (*a-sampurana*), and less (*una*). Most of the ancient Indian mathematicians defined zero as the sum of two equal and opposite quantities.[26]

For a long time it was believed in Europe that the symbol of zero and the decimal system of notation were of Arab origin, but it is now universally acknowledged that these passed from India through the Arabs to Europe.[27] The numerals first appeared in Arabia in 830 and were written in Arabic from right to left and, according to their position, counting from the right, they represented units, tens, hundreds, thousands, etc. Whenever the number to be expressed lacked units, tens, or hundreds, a point was placed in the appropriate place of the "word," which was the forerunner of the modern zero.

The mathematical implications of zero and infinity were never more than vaguely realized by the Greeks. Until the appearance of the Indian system, the nations of antiquity did their fundamental arithmetical operations by using symbols for writing numbers. They did not use the zero symbol, and their task was thus extremely tedious and limited. In the Indian notation, unlike that of any other ancient people, any number no matter how large could be easily expressed. Instead of assigning a distinct symbol to each number, Indian mathematicians introduced a place-value notation, which made it simple to produce numbers of indefinite length. The introduction of the Indian system led to remarkable scientific progress first in mathematics and then in the broad sphere of the exact sciences. Most of the great discoveries and inventions of the West would have been impossible without a developed system of mathematics, and this, in turn, would have been impossible if European science had remained saddled with the unwieldy system of

Roman numerals. "The unknown man who devised the new system was from the world's point of view, after the Buddha, the most important son of India. His achievement, though easily taken for granted, was the work of an analytical mind of the first order, and he deserves much more honour than he has so far received."[28] Praise for the unknown scholar must be unreserved, but would it have been possible for anyone, however ingenious, to achieve such heights of analytical scholarship without a sound tradition and a well-developed school of mathematical learning? Even if there is only scattered and fragmentary evidence, it must be clear that to not only give rise to such theories but to sustain and transmit them to other cultures required a highly intelligent school of mathematical thought. Little is known of the development of Hindu mathematics, but the few manuscripts that are available bear ample testimony to the sophistication it had achieved by whatever route.

Some scholars definitely date the origins of zero (sunya), and possibly of place-value notation, to as early as *ca.* 200 B.C. because reference to sunya is found in the *Pingala-Chandah-Sutra* composed at about that time. There is general agreement that this system of zero and place-value notation was in use in India in the fifth century A.D., and that the Syrians and the Indochinese had come to know of it by the end of the sixth century. The old system of numeration was still widely used in Europe even as late as the fourteenth century; however, no work on arithmetic using the old system has been found in India. The *Bakshali Manuscript,* alleged to belong to the fourth century A.D., uses the new system, giving general solutions of numerous mathematical problems on which other texts are silent.[29] The precise date, however, of this manuscript is uncertain, and, unless the date of the Bakshali Manuscript is definitely settled, any argument concerning the antiquity of zero must remain tentative. However, Aryabhata, who wrote *Aryabhatiya* in 499, and who had extracted square and cube roots by the method in use today, must have either used a decimal notation with nine figures plus a zero, or an abacus, where empty spaces represented the zero symbol.[30]

J. Filliozat, however, believes that the zero was either borrowed by the Indians through Babylonian officials, or more likely, "was reinvented during the earliest centuries of the Christian era by the Indian scholars." However, he does not question that it was from India that the zero spread during the Middle Ages to Asia and through the Arabs to Europe.[31] It appears that the principle of local value was used in the sexagesimal system found on Babylonian tablets dating from about 1600 B.C. Babylonian records from the centuries immediately preceding the Christian era contain a symbol for zero, which, however, was not used in computation. But India was the first country to use the complete decimal system of place-notation. What suggested the form for the zero is, of course, a matter of conjecture; the actual form of the zero symbol varied from region to region.

It was probably in the twelfth century that Europeans learned this Indian system through the Arabs. Leonardo of Pisa, also called Fibonacci, an Italian merchant, who published his *Liber Abbaci* in 1202, laying the foundation of modern mathematics in Europe, was educated in Barbary where he became acquainted with the so-called Arabic numerals. Of all the methods of calculation, he found this to be the best.

In algebra, too, the Indians made outstanding and lasting contributions. It is now commonly accepted that the Arabs were not the discoverers, but merely the transmitters of algebra. Indians were the first to recognize the existence of absolutely negative quantities. They differentiated between positive and negative quantities by attaching to the one the idea of "possession," and to the other the idea of "debts." The conception of opposite directions on a line, as an interpretation of plus and minus quantities, was familiar to them. Being a science dealing with unknowns, algebra could make definite progress only when a proper symbolism was devised. The Indians, accustomed to abstract thinking, evolved the appropriate symbolism by using the letters of the alphabet to denote unknowns together with arithmetical signs and suitable rules for calculations. Once this symbolism was devised, advance was rapid. In the fifth century, for example, Aryabhata could express large numbers by means of syllables, for Indian phoneticians had devised a phonetic alphabet including fifteen vowels, twenty-five stopped consonants, and eight other letters. Indians evolved a sound system of extracting square and cube roots, wrote numerical co-efficients and algebraic equations, evolved the rules of transportation of terms, classified equations according to degrees, and solved quadratic and indeterminate equations. Indian contributions in the field of the theory of indeterminate equations has been hailed as one of their greatest contributions to algebra.[32] The Greeks, hampered by their emphasis on geometry and the lack of proper symbolism, tackled indeterminate equations but with much less success. In the seventh century, Brahmagupta (598–660) was the first to discover the complete solution of the quadratic equation. His work was furthered by Mahavira in the ninth century. In the twelfth century, Bhaskara framed rules for finding permutations and combinations, and invented the fraction form. The Arabs and later the Europeans made great advances in algebra, but up to the end of the eighteenth century this progress was along Indian lines. Although modified, the present day algebraic symbolism remains Indian in all essentials. According to Hankel, algebra was really invented by the Indians, if algebra is defined as the application of arithmetical operations to both rational and irrational numbers of magnitudes. "Both the form and the spirit of arithmetic and algebra of modern times are essentially Indian."[33]

Diophantus of Alexandria (third century), the first Greek algebraist and the father of algebra in Europe, may have gotten his inspiration from India. Whilst there is no definite proof of this, it is significant that his work *Arithmetica* appeared quite suddenly, ran counter to all previous mathematical trends, and was a far cry from pure Greek geometry.[34] Without him, it has been said that there would have been no Greek science of algebra. He introduced the idea of an algebraic equation expressed in algebraic symbols and his treatment is purely analytical and completely divorced from geometrical methods. In addition to introducing various algebraic symbols, he also discovered new properties of numbers and solved many kinds of determinate and indeterminate equations. His system is very similar to that of Indian algebra. Struik points out that the first general solution of indeterminate equations of the first degree, $ax+by=c$ (a, b, c integers), is found in Brahmagupta. It is therefore incorrect to call linear indeterminate equations Diophantine equations. Furthermore, while Diophantus still accepted fractional solutions, the Hindus insisted on integer solutions. They also advanced beyond Diophantus in admitting negative roots of equations.[35] That communication of thought from India to Alexandria did take place is evident from the fact that certain philosophical and theological doctrines—for example, those of the Manichaeans, Neoplatonists, and Gnostics—show unmistakable resemblances to Indian teaching, and it is difficult not to suspect Indian inspiration behind Diophantus' work.[36]

Whilst Indians made their mark primarily in algebra and arithmetic, the beginnings of their mathematics strangely enough are found in geometry, the field in which they were least proficient. The knowledge of geometry began in the vedic age, and the earliest examples are found in the Sulvasutras (the rules of the chord which form part of the vedic Kalpasutras). This was largely a practical and empirical geometry, dealing with the exigencies of religious life and rituals.

Vedic altars and sacrificial places were constructed according to strict geometrical principles. The *Vedi* (altar) had to be stacked in a geometrical form with sides in fixed proportions, and brick altars had to combine fixed dimensions with a fixed number of bricks. Again, the surface areas were so designed that altars could be increased in size

without change of shape, which required considerable geometrical ingenuity. Geometrical rules found in the *Sulvasutras*, therefore, relate
to the construction of squares and rectangles, the relation of the diagonal
to the sides, equivalent rectangles and squares, equivalent circles and
squares, conversion of oblongs into squares and vice versa, and the
construction of squares equal to the sum or difference of two squares.[37]
In such relations a prior knowledge of the Pythagorean theorem, that
the square of the hypotenuse of a right-angled triangle is equal to the
sum of squares of the other two sides, is disclosed. In these treatises are
also found a few interesting approximations in terms of unit fractions.
The fractions used are all unit fractions and the expression yields a result
correct to five decimal places. The vedic Indians knew the mensuration
of the triangle, the parallelogram, the rectangle, and the rectangular
parallelepiped. The constant ratio between the circumference and the
diameter of a circle was known to the Indians later. They also studied
the mensuration of the circle, the cone, the sphere, and the pyramids.

It is curious, however, that these geometrical constructions which
were remarkable for their age do not occur in later Hindu works, which
appear to have disregarded completely the mathematical results of the
Sulvasutras. If the continuity of tradition had been maintained and
developed as in Egypt and Mesopotamia, the story of Indian geometry
might be different. Jainism, however, did encourage mathematical
studies, and in its sacred books the value $\pi = \sqrt{10}$ is found.

Indian attainments in geometry fall short of those of the Greeks;
Indians were mainly interested in mensuration and practically ignored
giving definitions, postulates, axioms, or steps of logical reasoning. The
possibility, however, of the Greek mathematician Hero of Alexandria,
who flourished at about the beginning of the first century B.C., having
been influenced by the *Sulvasutras* cannot be ruled out. It is also possible
that the Indian mathematician, Brahmagupta, was familiar with Hero's
work. Whilst distinguishing between approximate and exact areas,
he gives Hero's formula for the area of a triangle as a function of the
sides, $\sqrt{p(p-a)\ (p-b)\ (p-c)}$. Brahmagupta and later Mahavira, however,
made a remarkable extension of Hero's formula by giving
$\sqrt{(p-a)\ (p-b)\ (p-c)\ (p-d)}$ as the area of a quadrilateral whose sides
were a, b, c, d, and whose semiperimeter was p. In spite of the Greek
superiority in geometry, it was Aryabhata who gave the usual modern
approximate value of π. The Greeks put it as $\pi = 22/7$ whereas the
Indian mathematician expressed it in the form of a fraction $\pi = \dfrac{62,832}{20,000} = 3.1416$. Later mathematicians improved this value, already

far more accurate than that of the Greeks, to nine places of decimals. The correct value of π was not known in Europe before Peurbach (1423–61).

Considerable work was done in trigonometry, and Indians were familiar with some formulae not even known to the Greeks. In Varahamihira's *Panchasiddhantas* are found notations for unit radius $\pi = \sqrt{10}$, sin 30 = ½, sin 60 = $\sqrt{1 - \frac{1}{4}}$, $\sin^2 Y = (\sin 2Y)\, 2/4 + [1 - \sin\,(90° - 2Y)]\, 2/4$, and a table of twenty-four sines. The Greeks calculated in terms of chords and used the ratio of the chord of the circle to its diameter. Ptolemy's chords were reckoned on a diameter of 120. By using the half-chord and a radius of 120, the Indians obtained a table of sines directly. Every Indian treatise on astronomy contained a table of sines, and functions of the trigonometric sine were clearly known and applied. The following formula given in the *Surya Siddhanta* (*ca.* 400)

$$\sin\,(n + 1)\,\theta - \sin\,n\,\theta =$$
$$\sin\,n\,\theta - \sin\,(n - 1)\,\theta - \frac{\sin\,n\,\theta}{225}$$

used for calculating the tables of sines was not known either to the Greeks or the Arabs.[38] The Sanskrit term *jya* or *jiva*, a derivative from *ardhajya* or *ardhajiva*, half-chord or bow-string, became first *jiba* and then *jaib* in Arabic and finally sinus in mediaeval Latin.

Nothing like a true system of natural philosophy existed amongst the ancient peoples of Greece and India, although in their writings many brilliant conceptions are seen. Hindu physicists, however, made some comprehensive and co-ordinated efforts to advance hypotheses about nature, matter, and energy, although they were closely linked with religion and philosophy. The greatest weakness of Indian science, as that of Greece, was its vision of physics as philosophy and not as mechanics. Yet, it was an attitude which was not entirely unfruitful. Natural philosophy as propounded by the Indians conformed mainly to three systems: (a) the Nyaya-Vaisesika, dealing principally with the method of science and elaborating the concepts of mechanics, physics, and chemistry; (b) the Samkhya-Yoga, which confined itself to the principles of cosmic evolution; and (c) Vedanta and other systems, which contributed little directly to the development of the physical sciences. As early as the time of the Buddha, possibly even before him, the universe was classified by the elements, and most schools of thought believed that the elements, other than ether, were atomic. The Nyaya-Vaisesika school of physicists especially propounded the atomic theory and "believed the single atom to be a mere point in space completely without magnitude." They also analyzed the general properties of matter, such as elasticity, cohesion, impenetrability, viscosity, fluidity, porosity, etc. They asserted that atoms cannot exist in an uncombined state, and they could not believe matter to be infinitely divisible. The Jains regarded the atoms not only as infinitesimal, but also as eternal and ultimate. Umasvati analyzed in 50 the mutual attraction or repulsion of atoms in the formation of molecules.

The Samkhya system, in attempting to explain the process of cosmic evolution on a scientific basis in relation to energy as the principle, may have foreshadowed Darwin in some ways, although its ideas, embodied as they are in metaphysical language, are not easy to correlate with the modern scientific terminology of evolution. Almost every school conceived motion, both atomic and molecular, as underlying the physical phenomena of sound, light, and heat. Motion was defined somewhat as it is today, as the change of position of a particle. Not only molar and molecular motions were postulated but also the subtle motions inside the atoms themselves. Both matter and energy were known to be indestructible; and although constant, they were subject to changes in collocation, with this transformation going on continually. Brahmagupta foreshadowed Newton by declaring that "all things fall to the earth by a law of nature, for it is the nature of the earth to attract and keep things." But the law of gravitation itself was not anticipated.

Great progress was made in India in mineralogy and metallurgy. The mining and extensive use of gold, silver, and copper was undertaken in the Indus Valley in the third century B.C. In the vedic period extensive use was made of copper, bronze, and brass for household utensils, weapons, and images for worship. Patanjali, writing in the second century B.C. in his *Lohasastra,* gives elaborate directions for many metallurgic and chemical processes, especially the preparation of metallic salts, alloys, and amalgams, and the extraction, purification, and assaying of metals. The discovery of aqua regia (a mixture of nitric and hydrochloric acid to dissolve gold and platinum) is ascribed to him. Numerous specimens of weapons made of iron have been excavated, probably belonging to the fourth century B.C. Iron clamps and the iron stag found at the Bodhgaya temple point to the knowledge of the process of manufacturing iron as early as the third century B.C. The famous iron pillar in Delhi belonging to the fourth–fifth century A.D. is a metallurgical wonder. This huge wrought iron pillar, 24 feet in height, 16.4 inches in diameter at the bottom, and $6\frac{1}{2}$ tons in weight has stood exposed to tropical sun and rain for fifteen hundred years, but does not show the least sign of rusting or corrosion.

The *Periplus* mentions that in the first century A.D. Indian iron and steel were being exported to Africa and Ethiopia. Indian metallurgists were well known for their ability to extract metal from ore and their cast products were highly valued by the Romans, Egyptians, and Arabs. Their skill in tempering steel, the secret of manufacturing the so-called "Damascus blades," was well known.[39] Although no definite judgement can be reached until rigorous metallurgical analysis has been made of the "damascened" swords found throughout Eurasia, Edouard Salin, an authority on the metallurgy of early mediaeval longswords, suggests that "the marvellously skilful twisting and fagoting of thin rods of steel and iron of different qualities that produced the laminated Merovingian blades was inspired by Indian Wootz steel, which achieved similar results by crystallization."[40] Persians considered Indian swords to be the best, and the phrase, *Jawabi hind,* literally meaning "Indian answer," meant "a cut with the sword made of Indian steel." That the art of metallurgy was highly developed in ancient India is further reaffirmed by the fact that the Gypsies, who originated in India, are highly skilled craftsmen, and it has been suggested that the art of the forge may have been transmitted to Europe through Gypsies. Steel was manufactured in ancient India, and it was being exported to China at least by the fifth century A.D. That the Arabs also imported steel from India is testified to by Al Kindi, who wrote in the ninth century.[41]

Corresponding progress was made in the allied branches of science, for example botany, plant pathology, and zoology. Indian achievements in chemistry had some influence on the Arabs and the Chinese, although in India, as elsewhere, chemistry did not begin as a branch of science in its own right. In the beginning, perhaps, it was pure alchemy, concerning itself with the transmutation of baser metals into gold. But it soon became allied with medicine, metallurgy and the industrial arts. The earliest evidence of chemical knowledge in India is in painted pottery traced to the Indus Valley period. Chemical knowledge later became an adherent of the Tantric cult. Herbs and plants with active healing properties were deified. The juice of the *soma* plant, for instance, was supposed to confer immortality; even in the *Rig Veda* it is described as *amrita* (Greek ambrosia), giving immortality to gods and health to sick men. In *Somarasa* the dawn of Hindu alchemy is traced. But it was during the Tantric period that the practice of alchemy reached its highest development in India.[42] Nagarjuna, the reputed author of the renowned Tantric treatise *Rasaratnakara,* stands pre-eminent among the Indian alchemists.[43] He is also said to have written a treatise on metallurgy.

During the post-vedic period, when the medical system of India was rationalized, Indian chemists devoted their attention to making medicines and drugs. By the sixth century they had succeeded in producing many important alkalis (*kshara*), both for internal and external use, acids, and metallic salts by processes of calcination, distillation, sublimation, steaming, and fixing, described in *Rasaratna-Samuccaya*, a valuable medico-chemical work. Medicines were classified into two types: one promoting longevity, health, and strength, and the other curing disease.

Even in technology Indian contributions to world civilization were significant. The spinning wheel is an Indian invention, and, apart from its economic significance in reducing the cost of textiles, is one of the first examples of the belt-transmission of power. The stirrup, certainly the big-toe stirrup, is of second century B.C. Indian origin. The ancient blow-gun (*nalika*), which shot small arrows or iron pellets, may well have been a forerunner of the air-gun which is supposed to have been invented by the Europeans in the sixteenth century.

More important, however, is the fact that India supplied the concept of perpetual motion to European thinking about mechanical power. The origin of this concept has been traced to Bhaskara, and it was taken to Europe by the Arabs where it not only helped European engineers to generalize their concept of mechanical power, but also provoked a process of thinking by analogy that profoundly influenced Western scientific views.[44] The Indian idea of perpetual motion is in accordance with the Hindu belief in the cyclical and self-renewing nature of all things.

The ancient Indians were very interested in preserving life and caring for the body. Consequently medical science, including surgery, developed in India as early as the Indus Valley period and was widely studied and practiced. Indian medicine was called *Ayur Veda* and is practiced even today; in fact, in recent years it has been growing in popularity and is being harmonized with modern medical knowledge and techniques.[45] Whilst some scientists disregard Ayurvedic medicine as a relic of an antiquated past, others defend it with an overemphasized patriotic fervour as a fully mature system of medicine. Both are partisan views with only partial validity at best. At its height, however, Indian medicine was exceptionally advanced and gave evidence of a rational, scientific spirit unparalleled by other civilizations. Indeed, of all the natural sciences of ancient India, medicine was the most important. It was closely connected with the Samkhya and Vaisesika physics and was probably the basis of the logical speculations subsequently codified in the *Nyayasutras*.[46]

The beginnings of medical science in India have been traced to the proficiency of the Indus Valley people in town-planning, sanitation, and hygiene. Representing the oldest surviving examples of town-planning, the Indus cities had baths, lavatories, drains, fresh water tanks, and interior courtyards. The main drains were cleared by lifting large, specially made brick manhole covers, and the whole conception indicates a remarkable concern for public health. In the vedic hymns, especially in the *Atharva Veda,* we find the healing art along with the belief in demons of disease and magical rituals and remedial incantations to entice evil spirits away from the patients.[47] In these texts, however, references to anatomy, embryology, and hygiene are found as well as references to a great many diseases and plants with medicinal properties. Vedic medicine, in common with that of other ancient peoples, was primarily magico-religious. In Europe, as in various other areas, even as late as the fifteenth and sixteenth centuries, disease was looked upon as a punishment from God, and the cure was sought through priests rather than professional medicine.

Vedic Indians classified diseases by their major symptoms, such as pain, emaciation, and fever, without seriously examining the possible relationships between associated symptoms. They seldom investigated the pathogenic causes of the diseases. Remedies were generally based on plants, incantations, and practices of mimetic magic. Whilst there is no marked difference between diseases and demons in vedic medicine, and no sense of diagnosis in the accepted sense of the term, there are frequent indications of empirico-rational elements. Thus, magical attributes and practical knowledge were intermixed. The vedic Indians closely studied the human body and its structure as is evidenced by the richness of anatomical terminology in vedic Sanskrit.

During the period of the rise of Buddhism in India, great progress was made in medicine. Jivaka, a contemporary of the Buddha, is credited with numerous and wonderful cures, especially for children. Indian kings founded hospitals and appointed physicians for both men and animals. The canonical works of the Buddhists contain a number of medical statements, and Patanjali's reference to *vaidyaka* speaks for the development of medical science in the centuries preceding the Christian era. The famous Buddhist university at Nalanda during the seventh century comfortably accommodated ten thousand students in philosophy and medicine. The principal doctrines of the Vedas later formed the general basis of Indian classical medicine. *Ayur Veda* is the principle source for texts commonly used during the first centuries of the Christian era, but only a few works of this period have survived.[48]

The four principal ancient authorities are Charaka (first-second centuries A.D.), Susruta (sixth century B.C. to fourth century A.D.), Vagbhata (*ca.* 600 A.D.), and Atreya (sixth century B.C.). These dates are controversial and these are conservative estimates. None of the texts (principally the Samhitas) produced during this period represents an initial effort at systematic description of medical science; indeed, all clearly point to an existing tradition and confine their attention to collecting the known facts and disseminating the knowledge gained. They are edited manuals rather than works of individual scholars. George Sarton accepts A. F. Rudolf Hoernle's dating of Susruta and Atreya, as the sixth century B.C.[49] Filliozat, having analyzed the evidence in some detail, suggests that *Susruta Samhita* is a work of the last centuries before the Christian era, and that *Charaka Samhita* could be slightly anterior to the Christian era.[50] The medical works of Vagbhata, of which the *Ashtangahrdaya Samhita* is best known, also probably appeared in the late classical period.

Atreya, a physician, taught at the Kasi (Benares) University, and his younger contemporary Susruta, a surgeon, at Taksasila (Taxila) University. Charaka was a physician living at the court of Kanishka, and was looked upon as the spokesman for and editor of Agnivesa, a disciple of Atreya. Filliozat is of the opinion, therefore, that the famous system of medicine known after Charaka really belongs to Atreya, a contemporary of the Buddha. Susruta transmitted the doctrine attributed to Divodasa, King of Banaras and incarnation of Dhanvantari, the mythical holder of amrita, the liquid of immortality. Like *Charaka Samhita, Susruta Samhita* is based on ancient traditions and sources. These Samhitas are didactic texts in prose and verse of varied metres, and "are the products of a fully evolved system which resembles those of Hippocrates and Galen in some respects, and in others had developed beyond them."[51] The creative period of ancient Indian medicine closed with the Samhitas of Caraka and Susruta, and they have remained the standard works of Indian medicine and surgery respectively. Later medical writers either imitated or elaborated on them. The most important texts which augmented the Samhitas were the *Yogasataka* and the *Amrtahridaya*. The former is a medical compendium and was very popular and used widely at the time, having been translated into other Asian languages. It is consulted in Ceylon even to this day. Indian tradition assigns this work to the Buddhist patriarch Nagarjuna, but this is doubtful. The *Amrtahridaya* is a lengthy medical treatise in four sections and it has survived only in its Tibetan translation. Indian medicine, it would appear, progressed rapidly during the vedic and Buddhist periods, and, after a period of systematization, rationalization, and cautious advance, came almost to a standstill in the Middle Ages.

Although based on experience and observation, the doctrines of *Ayur Veda* are not empirical. A peculiar reflection of the general theory of the Samkhya in its medical conceptions can be seen as well as an enumeration of the elements (*pancabhutas*) which constitute the material content of the universe. The human body, the seat of consciousness (*cetana*), is also composed of these elements. Of these five, space and earth—which correspond to organic cavities and firm tissue—are inert, and the remaining three are active substances. Wind, fire, and water act in the body in the form of breath (*vayu*) located below the navel; bile (*pitta*) located between the navel and the heart; and mucus or phlegm (*kapha* or *sleshman*) located above the heart. These three elements are counted both as constituents (*dhatus*) and as morbid elements (*dosas*), and the doctrine is known, therefore, as either *tridhatu* or *tridosha*. It is the basis of Ayurvedic diagnosis and therapeutics. Health consists of a normal quantitative relationship between these primary constituents, and if there is an imbalance, disease, or *dhatu-vaisamya*, results.[52]

Nosology was highly developed and diseases were classified in three ways: according to the main organic element responsible for them, according to their anatomical situation, and according to the nature of the major symptoms. Susruta paid a good deal of attention to observing the symptoms of diseases.

Anatomy was also studied in this period in India. The vedic hymns refer not only to the heart, lungs, stomach, intestines, and kidneys but also to imaginary constituents of the human body, for example, *ojas* (energy) and *rasa* (vital fluid). In the evolution of Indian anatomy, facts and data concerning the human body were accumulated and rationalized into various schools of anatomical thought, chief of which were the schools of Caraka and Susruta. In their Samhitas they deal with embryology and histology in addition to anatomy proper. The total number of muscles in the body is 513, and the ancient Hindus described 500 muscles—400 in the extremities, 66 in the trunk, and 34 in the area above the collarbone—and they were familiar with ligaments, sutures, lymphatics, nerve plexuses, fascia, adipose tissues, vascular tissue, and the mucous membrane of the digestive canal. Hindu anatomy included some fanciful numerations of the parts of the body, such as 360 bones, 800 ligaments, 300 veins, 500 muscles, and 7 layers of skin. It must, however, be pointed out that the Hindus calculated these figures by including as separate bones the teeth, nails, cartilages, and prominent parts of bones now known as "processes" or "protuberances." Whilst there were major gaps and errors in their knowledge of anatomy, it was surprisingly accurate for the age.

The formation and development of the embryo was a subject of considerable speculation and controversy in the various schools of medicine. The question of prenatal influence, which is being given increasingly serious consideration by Western physicians, was intensively studied by Hindu doctors. They prescribed detailed rules for the care of expectant mothers, who were to be given a pleasant environment, kept away from excitement, and given appetizing food in moderate quantities.

As early as the vedic period, Indians possessed considerable knowledge of physiology. The vedic term *rasa* has been likened to the "humours" of ancient Greek medicine. Physiological processes were regarded as having counterparts in nature at large, such as bile acting in the human body much as fire acts on water. The prime mover of life was the breath (*prana*) which was only a manifestation of the wind, the moving force of the universe. Vedic physiology was a highly developed pneumatic doctrine, based on the belief that multiple breaths circulate inside the organism through a system of internal canals. These breaths were given distinct names, and this vedic concept became fundamental in Indian classical medicine. However, the pathological doctrine of the tridosha, which included the notion of breath, did not appear as such in the vedic Samhitas. Breath not only governed respiration but all the other physiological processes as well. "Ancient India was familiar with a pneumatistic theory by which all human activities, both bodily and mental, and all natural activities as well, were attributed to the play of puffs of air originating in the wind, the universal driving power."[53] Although this doctrine was not codified and expounded until later, all its essential elements were present in vedic texts, even to the assigning of technical names. These and other Indian texts belonging to the period between 1000 and 500 B.C. refer to the concept that bile is of an igneous nature and to the theory concerning the part played by the pituitary gland which represents the aqueous element. The basic doctrine, upon which subsequent Indian medical science was based, held that the breath, the bile, and the pituitary gland became the three associated factors. Some scholars suggest that Indian physiology was more comprehensive, and it is a mistake to believe that it consisted only of the tridhatu or vital fluids of the body. It is to this mistaken belief that the neglect of the study of Indian medicine is mainly attributed.[54] The theory, however, was far more profound, and also more ancient, than that of the Greeks. Filliozat points out that the breath of life circulating in other parts of the body was a common notion in ancient times but nowhere else were its technical details so precisely listed and systematized.[55]

There are striking parallels between the ancient Greek and Indian systems of medicine, and because of this many Western writers have suggested that the Greeks influenced Indian medicine. The possibility of mutual influence cannot be ruled out, but it should be remembered that whilst Hindu writers acknowledged their debt to Greek astronomy, they made no reference to foreign influences in medicine. Nor do Hindu medical classics, as pointed out by William Jones, contain a single technical term which points to a foreign origin. On the contrary, Hippocratic doctrines such as the emphasis on prognosis, on direction to physicians, and on diet and regimen in preference to medicines, the doctrine of the four humours and conception of the influence of seasons on their fluctuations and on dietetics, the quotidian, tertian, and quarton fever, and several others, bear too close a similarity to anterior Indian practices to be coincidental.[56] Hippocrates (ca. 460 B.C.), who dissociated medicine from superstition, systematized the empirical knowledge then available, and founded inductive and positive medicine, was certainly familiar with Indian drugs such as pepper, ginger, and cardamom. Whilst Hippocrates was laying the foundations of Greek medicine, Indian medicine was already a well-developed system, with an extensive pharmacopoeia and intricate surgical operations. Hippocrates' treatise *On Breaths* refers to diseases as processes in nature in almost the same way as did the school of Atreya and the vedic texts on winds and organic breaths. Whilst the general agreement between these doctrines of Hippocrates and those of Indian pneumatism is unmistaken, and whilst there are recognizable similarities in details of pathogenic representations, differences do occur. For instance, whilst *On Breaths* explains epidemics through spots introduced in the body by inhaled air, the Indian texts contain nothing similar. If there was any borrowing from India, "it has been in the shape of general ideas and it has been of an entire part of the Greek medical text rather than that of the author of the manual *On Breaths* acting alone."[57] In explaining the similarity between the Greek and Hindu traditions, Sarton admits the possibility of mutual influence but does not exclude independent thought on facts of common experience.[58]

Similar analogies are also noted between Indian pathology and Plato's theory, as developed in the *Timaeus*, which is practically identical with the Indian doctrine of the tridosha, and cites the same three elements—air, fire, and water, or breath, bile and mucus. Whilst Plato's exposition is extremely rudimentary, his classification of diseases into three groups—those caused by the disequilibrium of the elements, and those due to phlegm and bile—is much in accord with the classical Indian doctrine. Whilst elements of the doctrine of the *Timaeus* may be found scattered in various texts, no Greek medical text has been found which grouped them in the same manner as Plato did. In contrast, "only in Indian doctrine is found in the form of a received doctrine a pathogeny similar to that of Plato."[59] Plato's theory of phlegm is quite similar to that of the sleshman of Indian medical men. Plato's conception of bile, its "hot and liquid" nature, agrees fully with the old vedic idea of the igneous nature of bile. Even such notions as haemorrhagic diseases caused by an eruption of the bile into the blood are common to Plato and the *Ayur Veda*. The intermittent fevers enumerated by Plato were also known to the authors of the *Atharva Veda*, although their causes were explained differently.

Despite these differences, the case for Indian influence on Plato's doctrine is somewhat strengthened when it is recalled that Plato's belief in metempsychosis and his theory of ideas are also closely parallel to Indian philosophical doctrines. As the Indian doctrines preceded Plato, Greek influence on India must be ruled out. Moreover, although Plato does not mention his sources, his doctrine is closer to the Indian than any contemporary Greek school.

That the Greeks were aware of and esteemed Indian medicine is supported by contemporary Greek writings. Arrian, in describing Alexander's Indian expedition, points out that Greek physicians had no cure for snakebite but the Indians had. Consequently, Alexander gathered a body of skilful Indian physicians to attend him and his men. Another Greek, Nearchos, also bears testimony to the skill of Hindu physicians in toxicology. It is certain that at the time of Alexander Hindu physicians and surgeons were considered superior to those of the Greeks, even by the Greeks themselves.[60] Citing Megasthenes, Strabo says that "there is a class of physicians among the Indians, who rely most on diet and regimen and next on internal application, having a great distrust of the effects of more powerful modes of treatment."[61]

Indian medical knowledge, although considerable, was in many respects imperfect. Indians realized the importance of the spinal cord and knew of the nervous system but did not understand them fully. Even though they understood the functions of the heart, their ideas about its structure were rudimentary. Like Aristotle, Indian doctors held the mistaken conception that the heart was the seat of intelligence and the organ of consciousness, although some scholars dispute this on the grounds of the distinction between *mana* and *hrdaya*, two words translated as heart but having different connotations in Sanskrit. The Indians, however, knew that the heart receives impure blood, sends it to the liver, where it is purified and then returned to the heart. The sensory and motor nerves were believed to ascend to and descend from the heart. Later, however, this misconception was corrected. Like Galen, the Greek scientist of the second century, the Tantrists and Yogists in India came to know the real importance of the brain and the spinal cord; in fact, the Tantric mystical text *Shiva Samhita* describes the nervous system more accurately than medical treatises. Indian scientists made valuable observations on the senses and sense-perception but their knowledge of brain functions was limited. They knew the digestive system and its fluids well and described its processes clearly.

Diagnoses were made from symptoms and calculations of the vital elements involved. Diagnostic methods were highly advanced, and Susruta divided 1120 diseases into "natural" and "super-natural," taught palpation and auscultation of the heart, lungs, and womb, and advocated the inspection and use of the special senses.[62] He also gives a very recognizable description of malarial fever, which is attributed to mosquitoes. A favourite method of diagnosis was urinalysis. Feeling the pulse was studied with scrupulous care and thoroughness, and Hindu physicians achieved exceptional competence in the use of palpation long before Prayagoras of Cos, who is credited in the West as the first physician to teach the value of the pulse in diagnosis.

Whilst notions of hygiene were mainly based on physiological theories, treatment was based on observation. Proper diet and regimen were carefully detailed and the use of drugs was subordinated to diets, baths, enemata, emetics, inhalations, gargles, urethral and vaginal injections, and blood-letting by leeches or cups. Some scholars such as Garrison have interpreted a passage in Dhanvantari's *Sacteya* as indicative of Hindu knowledge of vaccination as early as 550; this was not known in Europe until the eighteenth century.[63] Essential diabetes mellitus was recognized as madhumeha (or "honey-urine") and its usual symptoms of thirst, foul breath, and languor were known.

Indian surgery (*salya*), was well advanced for the times. It is frequently mentioned in the *Mahabharata* that surgeons regularly accompanied the army. By the second century, surgery had become a well-developed art and was regarded as the most important branch of medicine. The methods of dissection, however, were too imperfect to give any accurate knowledge of the internal organs and of the vascular system of the body. Knowledge of the human body remained primitive in ancient India, as in other contemporary civilizations, where anatomy and physiology lagged behind clinical practice. Priestly influence confused this and "the concepts of anatomy were weird and wonderful."[64] The Indian surgeons endeavoured to make up for their lack of precise knowledge of anatomy by the concept of *marma* (a marma is a junction or meeting place of five organic structures—ligaments, blood vessels, muscles, bones, and joints). There were 107 marmas in all divided into five groups on the basis of the seriousness of injury.

This concept made possible efficient study of regional anatomy. As early as the third century B.C. there were hospitals in India and the numerous rock inscriptions of Asoka testify to the popularization of medical treatment of men and animals. Surgery flourished in these hospitals several centuries prior to the Christian era. Indian surgeons had attained considerable expertise in extracting the dead foetus, recovering foreign bodies from body tissues, and treating different kinds of inflammation. Their cataract operations attracted wide attention and their mode of couching cataracts has survived to the present day. The art of cutting and setting bones had reached a high degree of skill, as had plastic surgery. They treated fractures and dislocations with a special splint made of withes of bamboo, which was subsequently adopted in the British army as the "patent rattan cane splint."[65] Indian surgeons were expert at the repair of noses, ears, and lips; and it was from them that the army surgeons of the East India Company learned the art of rhinoplasty (which means turning down a flap of the skin of the forehead to repair unsightly nose defects).

Susruta describes a surgical technique of dissecting organs, after they have begun to disintegrate in water, which makes him a forerunner of Lacanchie, who introduced hydrotomy in the nineteenth century. Susruta, marred somewhat by excessive scholasticism and classifications, describes many surgical operations—hernia, cataract, lithotomy, caesarian section—and about 121 surgical instruments—scalpels, lancets, saws, scissors, needles, hooks, probes, detectors, forceps, and syringes—all of which belong to modern surgical practice. These instruments were properly handled and carefully prepared according to elaborate rules. The sterilization of the wound by fumigation is one of the earliest known examples of antiseptic surgery. Three surgical methods were prescribed: instruments, caustic, and cautery (*agni karman*), but as a rule the Indians believed in helping nature to effect a cure, rather than in resorting to more violent methods.

In certain cases they employed anesthetics, even at a very early date.[66] Insensibility to pain was produced by the use of medical liquors, drugs like belladonna, and Indian hemp (*cannabis indica*). The one operative process the Hindus did not know was ligaturing—the method of tying the end of a blood vessel. Whilst skilfully amputating limbs, they checked haemorrhage by cauterization, boiling oil, or pressure. More than a thousand years prior to Oliver Wendell Holmes' "wandering friar" they "cut for stone." The Indians even introduced a special method of tying intestinal wounds. Since normal sutures caused the intestines to become constricted, they joined the lips of the wound and had them bitten by large ants. Later the body of the ant was cut off, leaving behind the mandibles as clamps which were acceptable to the human system. The abdominal wall was closed by ordinary sutures. The Arabs later adopted this system and passed it on to the West. It survives to this day, especially on the Somali coast.[67]

The Indians were particularly adept in teaching surgery. Having realized the value of rapid, dexterous incision in operations without anesthesia, they required the students to begin by practicing on plants. The hollow stalks of water-lilies, or the veins of large leaves, or the blood vessels of dead animals, were punctured and lanced. Soft fruits or leather bags filled with water were incised or tapped as training for operations on hydrocele or any other disorder of a hollow cavity. Fresh hides of animals or dead bodies were used in the demonstration of scarification and bleeding. Flexible models of the human body were used for practice in bandaging. The use of the probe was practiced on hollow bamboos. In training students in this way the Indians were the pioneers of many recent teaching techniques in experimental surgery.[68]

The ancient Indians undoubtedly excelled all other nations of their time in operative surgery. Their concern for physical health and their achievements in medicine must confuse the image of India as a land of pure metaphysics and otherworldliness. Yet, it may well have been this very Hindu attitude towards life, their very theory of nature, which led to their success in medicine. They did not look upon the universe as a mere fortuitous concourse of atoms, or as a puzzling labyrinth of purposeless activities and inactivities, but as a cosmos capable of consistent explanation, an ordered sequence of cause and effect, a mighty whole of which human beings were just one part. For the Hindus, philosophy, science, and religion were inseparable, being different aspects of real knowledge. This belief led them to study medicine, not as an isolated art, but as a branch of their pursuit of reality. In classical Greece too, a similar belief in the systems of nature—philosophy regarding the human being as part of the whole of nature—had governed the art of medicine. A number of the alleged treatises of Hippocrates reflect this attitude. The philosophy of nature influenced medicine and began to transform it. It was only later that an adverse reaction set in and medicine became more of an empiric art.[69]

Not only human beings and animals, but plants are also part of the cosmic immanent life-force, and all are interrelated. This concept significantly conditioned the Indian attitude and had a bearing on their accomplishments in pharmacology. The nourishment received from the plant's vitality transformed itself naturally into the strength of the animal and human body. Western intellectuals have often been surprised by the discoveries in plant pathology and crystallogeny of the Indian scientists trained in their own traditional way.[70] A modern Indian scientist, Sir J. C. Bose (1850–1937), was able to demonstrate the pulsating life-force in plants and their biological changes in his laboratories at Calcutta and Darjeeling, with the help of accurate modern Western instruments. He demonstrated the effects of air, sleep, food, drugs, etc., on plants and established a complete parallel between the responses of plant and animal tissues.[71]

The Indian pharmacopoeia, consisting mainly of vegetable substances and herbs, was particularly rich and remarkable for its range and value. Susruta listed 760 medicinal plants, many of which came into the *materia medica* of the West and are still there. Special emphasis was given to aphrodisiacs and poisons along with antidotes for snake and animal bites. Garlic was praised in a hymn in the Bower manuscript found in 1890, and is now accepted as possessing the ability to check gastric ulcers. The soporific effects of *hyoscyamus* and cannabis indica were known, and so was the purgative effect of honey in the newborn infant. Mercury was used as an internal remedy from a very early date. Even more significant was the drug *rauwolfia serpentina*, extracted from the leaves of a plant in the Himalayan foothills, which was in use from antiquity as a tranquilizer. Present day medicine, having extracted its active principle *reserpine*, now uses it in cases of hypertension and as a treatment for mental cases. Amongst other Indian drugs adopted for use in modern pharmacopoeia are *ishabgol* and *triphala*. Turmeric (*haridra*) is used in Indian curry as an antiseptic ingredient. Triphala, like other Indian drugs, was perhaps known to later Greek authors such as Actuarius and Myrepsus through the Arabs. What Actuarius calls *trypala* or *tryphera parva* was Indian *triphala*, both in name and the constituents of the compound, and was recommended for use as in India.[72]

Apart from using plants for dietetic purposes, Indian physicians also used them as electuaries, infusions, powders, ointments, and enemas, as well as errhines, which were not commonly prescribed by Western physicians. Indian physicians were not content with merely growing, gathering, and compounding the various medicinal herbs, but they even studied the effect of the seasons upon plants.

The Indians gave careful and thorough attention to hygiene and diet. They studied climatic influences on various diseases and examined hydropathy. Hindu medical texts recommend rinsing the mouth with warm or cold water before and after meals, as well as at other times. The use of oil as unguent for massage, for dropping into the ears, and for rubbing into the soles was suggested for general physical fitness, as was regular exercise. The anointing of the whole body before taking a bath was suggested for its invigorating effect. Rules pertaining to diet were elaborate in relation to various ailments and governed even the daily intake of food for a healthy person. Generally, half the stomach was to be filled with food, a quarter with water, and the rest left empty.[73] Cleansing the teeth was particularly advocated, and massage was a favourite remedy for both physical and mental ailments. Regular sleep and early rising, and the drinking of a certain quantity of water daily at sunrise were believed to be an aid to good health and long life. Indians even today follow many of these recommendations.

The ancient Indian medical system is being scientifically studied and restored in India today, and many of its early drugs and medicines are finding their way into modern medicine. The physician (vaidya) was a respected member of society and was expected to maintain the very high standard of professional and ethical conduct prescribed in medical texts. Hypnotism as therapy, according to Garrison, appears to have originated with the Indians who often took their sick to temples to be cured by hypnotic suggestion. The Englishmen responsible for this technique in England—Braid, Esdaile, and Elliotson—certainly got their ideas from their contact with India. In India hypnotism had been practiced as a cure in certain diseases, because Indian physicians devoted their attention to the psychic as well as the physical side of life. In the *Mahabharata* there is mention of the two classes of diseases, physical and mental, which were interlinked and interdependent.[74]

Since animals were regarded as a part of the same cosmos as humans, it is not surprising that animal life was keenly protected and veterinary medicine was a distinct branch of science with its own hospitals and scholars. Numerous texts, especially of the postclassical period, *Visnudharmottara Mahapurana* for example, mention veterinary medicine. Megasthenes refers to the kind of treatment which was later to be incorporated in Palakapyamuni's *Hastya yur Veda* and similar treatises. Salihotra was the most eminent authority on horse breeding and hippiatry, and Jadudatta gives a detailed account of the medical treatment of cows in his *Asva-Vaidyaka*.

Indian ability to make surgical instruments, astronomical instruments, and other scientific apparatus, as well as their meteorological accomplishments would imply a certain competence in mechanical devices and technological proficiency. Although not conclusive, there are ample references in Indian literature to mechanical devices beginning with the *Rig Veda*, the epics, and the Puranas, to the *Meghaduta*, the *Rajatarangini*, and the various *Yantras*. How far applied science was developed in India cannot be stated with any certainty, but the *Samarangana-sutradhara* ascribed to Bhoja includes a brief narrative of Indian technology and technonomy which makes it appear to be both ancient and accomplished.

Whilst science developed in the West during the Renaissance, changing the whole character of society and attaining unbelievable successes, India entered a mediaeval period and science declined. The reasons for this decline are complex and still largely speculative, because investigation is seriously handicapped by the pathetic lack of information. Various explanations are given, none of which is wholly convincing. Even in China where the scientific tradition was continuous and productive, it declined during the mediaeval period. What is more surprising is that in China, with all her emphasis on things material and concrete, and her progress in the application of science to human affairs, medical progress remained almost stationary until the present day, although the Chinese knowledge of anatomy and anthropometric measurements was exceptional. A possible explanation for the decline in Indian science may be that it proceeded in the wrong direction by pursuing alchemy and occultism. But the major reason must lie in the general stagnation of thought and learning during this period in India and the disappearance of the tradition of university and secular education. Despite its loss of creative activity, however, Indian science continued to have some influence over other regions such as Central Asia and the Indonesian Archipelago.

Chapter VI

MYTHS, FABLES, MUSIC AND GAMES

IT HAS BEEN claimed that India is the original home of literary fiction and intellectual games. Whatever be the merits of this assertion, there is no doubt that stories of Indian origin have long been told in distant lands of Asia and Europe in a variety of forms, giving delight to countless people, often without reference to or awareness of their sources. Centuries before Kalidasa's *Sakuntala* captured the fascination of Western intellectuals at the end of the eighteenth century, Indian myths and tales were widely known, and the influence of Visnusarman, the mythical author of the *Pancatantra,* the most famous collection of Indian fables, was widely felt.

Once again it was mainly the Arabs, and the Iranians before them, who transmitted Indian fables and folklore to Europe, either through Turkey or Spain. From Constantinople Indian stories were transmitted to Venice and Naples through trade contacts and thence they found their way into the works of Boccaccio, Chaucer, Cervantes, Shakespeare, Le Sage, La Fontaine, Voltaire, and other famous Western writers. With each story-teller the story assumed a new look, eventually reaching a stage at which it often bore only a feeble resemblance to the original. It was not until Western scholars discovered Sanskrit language and literature in the latter part of the eighteenth century that the Indian contribution to the world's fiction came to be appreciated, although its full extent is yet to be systematically assessed. This discovery of Sanskrit led to the beginnings of comparative philology, the study of comparative religions and philosophies, knowledge of Indo-European antiquities, and to the recognition of parallels between Indian and Western literatures, especially in fables and fairy tales.

The story of how Indian fables reached the remote corners of Europe,

Asia, and even Africa is a fascinating study; for it is not merely a case of single or isolated stories reaching other countries by way of merchants and travellers from India, but of entire Indian books becoming the common heritage of mankind through the medium of translations.

There are, of course, various kinds of folklore and folktales, and scholars have devoted much effort to give them exact descriptions. At present we are chiefly concerned with fables and myths. Although these are somewhat interrelated and difficult to separate into their respective traditions, it is generally accepted that the story which is embedded in rituals, morals, and cults and which endeavours to explain some natural phenomena or religious problem is a myth, whilst the story which is intended to amuse, to instruct, and to point out a moral is a fable. Myths generally deal with the deeds of gods or heroes and man's primitive beliefs and intellectual attempts to explain nature. Myth is now commonly associated with the incredible or the wholly imaginary. But this was not the original sense in which the ancient Greeks, who coined the term, used it. Many ancient myths even describe the creation and organization of the universe, the evolution of mankind, and the emergence of civilization.

Despite the resemblances between the mythologies of the ancient peoples, myths differ widely in plots, motifs, and treatment, reflecting the characteristics of the respective environments in which they were produced, and scholars hold divergent views about their scope and importance. About a century ago mythology was regarded as a study of ancient peoples, mainly those of Greece and Rome. Modern scholars, despite their recognition of a close association between myth and religion, take a wider and more accurate view of the subject. Some scholars, however, look upon myths as hardly more than superstitious fairy tales of little intellectual importance and historical significance. Yet, others see in myths a remarkable expression of human insight and spirit. Whatever be its actual nature, scope, and significance, the value of mythology in understanding the mental processes of early man, his beliefs and feelings as expressed in writing and visual art, can hardly be denied. Goethe maintained that the early peoples had their ideas in intuitions of fancy, whereas modern men articulate them into notions.

Originally a fable was just a tale, a simple expression of man's desire to amuse himself, but over a period of time it was provided with a "moral," and became a vehicle for teaching a lesson in morality or wisdom in an entertaining style. It has, therefore, acquired a twin objective, to amuse and to instruct. With the surprising exception of the pre-Buddhist Chinese, all peoples in all societies have incorporated in their literature entertaining yet instructive stories.[1] Most fables are beast fables because they describe imaginary adventures of animals who act and feel like human beings. An explanation for this characteristic may well be the close proximity primitive man had with wild and domestic animals, and his dependence on them.

This distinction between myth and fable, although somewhat valid by virtue of common concurrence, is not quite applicable to Indian tradition. For whilst the ancient civilizations of Greece, Iran, Egypt, and other countries have disappeared and their mythologies have been displaced by well-defined and well-organized religious beliefs, such as Christianity and Zoroastrianism, thus allowing their folklore to develop distinctly, the Indian civilization and religion has been a continuous organic growth which did not displace mythology. Again, the amorphous nature of India's religious beliefs, and the fact that her religion and philosophy are inseparable from her literature, make it difficult to distinguish Indian myth from fable. For example, stories found in vedic literature, such as that of Pururavas and Urvasi, can be both myths and fables.[2] The Jataka tales, dealing with the birth stories of the Buddha, and the stories in the *Mahabharata,* although rooted in religious culture, are considered to be fables.

Sanskrit achieved excellence in most forms of literature. Sanskrit works on religion and philosophy are unsurpassed, and Sanskrit poetry, as contained in lyrical and dramatic works, compares favourably with the most beautiful European works. Although the qualities of Sanskrit literature are not well known in the West outside a limited circle of specialists, it is outstanding in its imagination and perception, especially in gnomic poetry. The Sanskrit aphorism and didactic style of verse, best illustrated in Indian fables and folklore, are most valuable contributions of Indian literature.[3]

Ancient Indian fiction is especially notable for its diversity of theme, setting, situation, and characterization. Whilst some stories are filled with a spirit of piety and religious devotion, others advocate a secular and even naturalistic attitude towards life. There are realistic images of noble sages, profound thinkers, detached men of wisdom, distraught poets, restless wanderers, voluble astrologers, credulous peasants, greedy priests, flattering courtiers, arrogant scholars, cunning traders, and a wide variety of people, many of whom are recognizable today in Indian society. Whilst some stories are pure flights of fancy, others provide a necessary corrective to the excesses of imagination through their realism; and whilst some are profound and substantial, others are simply interesting and amusing.

191

India has often been characterized as the most religious country in the world in somewhat the same way as China is described as pre-eminent in porcelain, Japan in drawing, and the West in technology. Porcelain is made throughout the world, but it is in China that the art has reached perfection. So in India has "man gone to the farthest limit of his religious faculty."[4] Consequently, mythology is one of India's richest traditions. It is also one of the oldest, and, because of the common origins of the Indo-European peoples, it is connected with the mythologies of Greece, Iran, and Italy. Such similarities of religions and mythical ideas, however, are only limited: partly because the Greeks, having left the Indo-European peoples, entered regions where more complex societies already flourished, and partly because it appears that the themes of Indo-European mythology were relatively simple.[5] Reflections of the ancestral links in mythologies can be seen in the tales of Hercules, Thor, and Indra. Whilst Hercules was a son of Zeus by Alcmene, and was later deified, Indra is described in the vedic hymns as a national god of the Aryans and the patron of the military nobility with the thunderbolt as his principal weapon. He is, however, a wholly anthropormorphic deity, and his passion for *soma* borders on intemperance. Like a simple mortal, however, he is formidable and bellicose to his enemies, but good and generous to his followers, helping them in war. His struggles against the Dasyus may be somewhat reminiscent of Hercules' heroic exploits and there is some resemblance between Indra and Zeus. Both were principal gods, and both had salaciously succumbed to the charms of pious mortal women and impersonated their husbands to seduce them.

Kern has suggested a comparison between the ape king, who in a Jataka tale makes himself a bridge over the Ganges for his following, and a similar episode involving the Irish King Bran, and further suggests that the function of the Roman pontifex may be pertinent.[6] In fact, similar features of the Irish and Greek mythologies can be explained only by their common Aryan mythological heritage. Whilst little is known of the mythology of the continental Celts, and Irish mythology is fragmentary in form and distorted by its transmission through the centuries, mythical conceptions and visions in Ireland are more archaic, even if recorded much later, than those of Greece and India. The Celts were known in the ancient world for their positive beliefs concerning the survival of the soul, and their conception of a "happy otherworld" was similar to that of the early Greeks. Of all the Indo-European peoples, the Greeks and the Irish alone have fully preserved the early version

192

of this conception. Similarly, the myth of Oedipus, essentially Greek in its mature construction, reflects an Indo-Aryan influence.

The myth of the "world-egg," which was designed to describe the origins of the universe, and which relates that heaven was formed from the upper shell of the egg laid by Nyx and earth from the lower, cannot be purely Greek in origin as alleged. It is also found amongst the Persians, the Indians, and other peoples in varying versions. In fact, the vedic *Brahmanda* is much older. The Greeks, no doubt, placed their own construction on an original Indo-European tale, whilst the vedic hymns preserved the myths in their primitive forms. Max Müller observes: "Nowhere is the wide distance which separates the ancient poems of India from the most ancient literature of Greece more clearly felt than when we compare the growing myths of the *Vedas* with the full grown and decayed myths on which the poetry of Homer is founded. The Veda is the real Theogony of the Aryan races, while that of Hesiod is a distorted caricature of the original image."[7] However, in the early Vedas the story material is limited, and, despite the fact that the vedic hymns are voluminous in comparison with Homeric hymns, the latter on the whole narrate a story more consistently. The fact that certain chief gods were common to all of them would lend weight to the view that the earliest hymns of the Aryans may have constituted the nucleus for many Greek, Celtic, and Persian myths. The Sanskrit *deva* (god) is the Latin *deus*, Greek *theos*, Lithuanian *dewas*, Irish *dia*. The greatest of the heavenly beings, who was heaven himself, was *Div*. He is addressed as *Dyaus Pita* in vedic hymns, he is *Zeus Pater* in Greek, *Jupiter* in Latin, *Tius* in German. The Greeks appear to have regarded him as the supreme god, the giver of all things, and in some contexts, as just God. Vedic *ushas* (dawn) is Greek *eos; haritas*, another name of *surya* (sun), is Greek *charites*. The "Sons of Zeus," the two Dioscuri, are compared to the twin Asvins of Indian mythology. Some Greek gods, such as Earth (*Gaea*), Dawn (*Eos*), Sun (*Helios*), and Moon (*Selene*), are also common nouns, which may suggest that some vague divinity was attached to them from Indo-European times. Therefore, one often notices similarities amongst the names of the peoples, and sometimes the exploits of gods or heroes, in the legends of the Indo-European peoples. Many of the outstanding tales and motifs in several European mythologies bear so strong a likeness to each other that they can only have originated from a common prototype, and these similar features are in common with the myths of India. Beyond the proof of common origin, the Greeks and the Indians developed their own independent and complex tradition in mythology.

The spread of Indo-European myths and legends, dating from a common ethnic past, and the similarities amongst the mythologies of Indo-European peoples are a distinct branch of study, which has little to do with the migration of fables in strictly historical times from India to Arabia, to Greece, and to the West, either orally or, more importantly, by translations or adaptations. The two migrations—that of the Indo-Europeans and their myths and the migration of the fables of their descendants—were separated by about two thousand years. It is, therefore, not surprising that when the history of fables and their journeys is examined, the emerging picture is somewhat more definite, as there is relatively more material available from which to draw conclusions.

It is possible to follow the passage of certain fables from one country to another; however, it must be pointed out that the art of story-telling is far older than history. As a popular tale is copied and recopied from one collection to another over a period of centuries and across continents, it seldom remains intact, often undergoing even changes of plot and characterization. Hence, to trace the history of a story, which, for example, may have been transmitted from India to Persia and western Asia, thence to Italy, France, and finally to Britain, must remain an exceedingly complex investigation. Yet, sometimes resemblances between various tales are so close, and their interrelation so inextricable, that the hypothesis of common origin becomes inevitable.

Scholars have now been engaged in the study of folklore for more than a century, and there is much material setting out divergent views on the questions of the origin, dissemination, meaning, and nature of folktales. Serious consideration of these questions appeared for the first time in the second edition of the Grimms' *Kinder und Hausmärchen* (folk tales for children and the home, more usually known as *Grimm's Fairy Tales*) in 1819. The Grimm brothers, Jacob and Wilhelm, had given little thought to the problem of the origin of folktales when they issued their first edition, but between the first and second editions similar tales from other countries had been published, especially from Serbia, raising the need to explain the similarities and identical plots. Also, the discovery of Sanskrit had opened up new vistas in comparative literature. More than a quarter of a century later, in 1856, Wilhelm Grimm suggested that the resemblances found not only amongst the stories of nations widely separated by time and distance, but also amongst those which are neighbours, consisted partly in the basic plot and the delineation of characters, and partly in the weaving together or disentangling of incidents. There are, however, certain situations which are so commonplace and natural that they occur anywhere, in the same way as some thoughts seem to emerge simultaneously. Hence, it is possible that the same or very similar stories arose in different countries quite independently of each other. To Grimm the fairy tale was an inheritance from the remains of Indo-European mythical poetry. He was, however, talking of the folktale in a broad sense, but he did distinguish between two types of tales: one, which showed close resemblances to others in the Indo-European language family, was doubtless inherited from a common Indo-European antiquity; the other, which contained dissected or broken-down myths, could be understood only by a proper interpretation of its parent-myths. Perhaps an example of this is the Anglo-Saxon epic *Beowulf*, comprising more than six thousand verses or half-verses, which was composed before 750. Certain of its features which resemble those of Asian mythology can be more easily explained by the common Indo-European past than by suggesting the migration of ideas so far westward at that time, although the possibility cannot be altogether ruled out.

With the awareness of the importance of Sanskrit at the beginning of the nineteenth century, many eminent European scholars and linguists, especially German, took an exceptionally keen interest in the problem of reconstructing the parent speech from which most of the languages of India and Europe descended. Although many details remained unsolved, the overall framework with its various subdivisions had become clear by the middle of the nineteenth century. The general approach to the subject was well illustrated in the works that followed, such as those of Max Müller, Angelo de Gubernatis, John Fiske, and Sir George Cox, who all stressed that the parallels in folklore and myths from Ireland to India were principally an inheritance from a common Indo-European past, and traced their origins to the *Rig Veda*. For instance, the trick of dragging stolen cattle backwards into their place of hiding without leaving behind their footprints to escape detection appears again and again in the mythology of different Indo-European peoples.[8]

Whilst some scholars were exploring the *Rig Veda* and its influence on the folktale, others were also finding India the origin of folktale tradition from another point of view. As early as 1838, Loiseleur Deslongchamps suggested that European folktales could probably be traced to India, but it was Theodor Benfey who took up this suggestion and carried it to its logical conclusion. Although he had already advanced this view in some of his previous studies, it was expressed with clarity and authority in the Introduction to his edition of the

Pancatantra in 1859. Whilst Benfey believed that most of the animal fables originated in the West and were, more or less, transformations of the so-called *Aesop's Fables,* he believed folktales had originally come from India. He found fairy tales which had been included in Indian works such as the *Pancatantra,* the *Sukasaptati,* and the *Vetalapancavimsati,* in later Indian languages referred to as *Baital Pachisi.*[9] He pointed out, however, that some animal fables give the impression of having an Indian origin, for many considerations indicated that the Indians, well before their acquaintance with the animal fables of Aesop, had invented a good many stories of a similar kind. The difference between Indian fables and Aesop's is that whilst Aesop's animals act in conformity with their own nature and characteristics, the Indian fables treat the animals as if they were men masked in animal form. When the essentially didactic nature of the animal fable, which is exclusively an Indian characteristic, and the Hindu belief in the transmigration of souls are taken into consideration, the theory of Indian origin of fables is further reinforced.

Benfey's arguments were very convincing. To each story from the *Pancatantra* he appended exhaustive notes elaborating and illustrating his opinion with scrupulous and profound scholarship. Jacob Grimm agreed with him and the students of folklore in the nineteenth century generally accepted the position, although there was some criticism. For example, it was claimed that too much reliance was placed on literary sources and that insufficient attention was paid to the actual movement of fairy tales from one nation to another.

Another important scholar in the field was Reinhold Köhler (1830–1892), who published annotations of the main collections of European tales, and thus helped to clarify the mutual relationship of the various tales and motifs. He was, however, mainly an editor and commentator and was little concerned with theories of historical origins. A strong supporter of Benfey's basic ideas was Emmanuel Cosquin (1841–1921), who published an extremely valuable series of monographs. His *Contes populaires de Lorraine* (1887) is regarded as the French equivalent of *Grimm's Fairy Tales.* He studied numerous motifs and tales, always emphasizing their relationships with Indian parallels which he was convinced represented the originals. His studies paved the way for more definitive work by other scholars. Cosquin, however, was also impressed by the antiquity of Egyptian folklore, and he felt that even though all tales may not have originated in India, India had certainly served as the great reservoir for tales of varied nationalities which, in turn, flowed out all over the world.

The Finnish school, distinct in its method of investigation whereby a fairy tale was analyzed according to its events and motifs, worked through all available sources item by item and tried to find the original parts of each fairy tale. They emphasized the fact that folktales may be composed by any people, and that the possibility cannot be ruled out that a variety of tales may have spread from various centres. But whilst it was theoretically possible for folktales to originate in any country, they attributed most of them to India. It was suggested that there were "streams of fairy tales" and "waves" in which everybody participated because every listener became a narrator afterwards.

In the 1870's, however, a reaction against the theory of folklore diffusion set in. Reinforced by the Darwinian concept of organic evolution, the British school of anthropology gave rise to the anthropological theory. E. B. Tylor claimed in his book *Primitive Culture* (1871) that a number of customs, ideas, and religious convictions could be traced in like form in all primitive and civilized people, so that similar intellectual prerequisites producing similar forms of fairy tales must be assumed.

Andrew Lang insisted that folklore was close to the surface of civilized life, being the remains of ideas as old as the stone elf-shots and older than the cult of bronze. He detected in proverbs, riddles, nursery tales, and superstitions, the relics of a stage of thought which was dying out.[10] In support of his view that folklore beliefs were not peculiar to any one race he cited the story *The Mystery of the Pezazi*, which was current in a very similar form in Ceylon and Mexico. The curious coincidence of the "midnight axe" described in both versions was held by him as the expression of a common state of superstitious fancy, not an indication of common origin. If Lang had known there was considerable evidence of cultural diffusion between southern Asia and ancient America, he would not have found this parallelism so striking.

Andrew Lang's anthropological theory asserted that the fairy tale had been common to all primitive peoples, and thus had the tradition of parallel development. He used the discovery of Egyptian folktales along with the stories mentioned in Herodotus and Homer in his sometimes satirical opposition to the theory of Indian primacy in folklore. He also pointed out many primitive ideas in modern folktales and suggested that these tales had survived from a very ancient time. Lang's position of parallel development of culture everywhere is untenable for it would manifest itself in analogous tales. Without undermining the considerable value of Lang's reasoning and conclusions, his interest in the contributions of primitive man may have been somewhat over-pronounced because of the remarkable work with the concept of organic evolution done by British anthropologists during the second half of the nineteenth century.

Besides Lang, other scholars had come to take an interest in the beliefs and practices of primitive peoples and begun to collect and compare data, pointing out various parallels in development. They attempted to show that all mythological stories said the same things in different ways. The most famous example is Sir James George Frazer's *Golden Bough* originally published in twelve volumes. A remarkable collection of logically arranged data on primitive beliefs and practices, Frazer's work attempted to show that story motifs, practices, and beliefs were almost identical amongst the American Indians, the natives of Australia, and those of South Africa. The assumption was that all peoples had gone through the same stages of culture in a direct line of evolution and that in each stage they reacted to the world and expressed themselves in the same way. In higher stages there may be survivals of the earlier stages. This theory of the direct and parallel evolution of cultures and of survivals in culture, as illustrated by Lang and Frazer, and later by J. A. MacCulloch in *The Childhood of Fiction,* is undoubtedly of great interest, but it neglects to consider that culture is a matter of historical development for each people who are subjected to a wide variety of internal and external influences. Except in the vaguest and most general sense, therefore, parallelism between different peoples, especially if they are far removed, must remain an uncertain and untenable inference. At best, it could be only a rare coincidence. This theory also underestimates the role which the diffusion of the elements of tribal life has played, and pays little attention to the great community of interest amongst peoples within particular "cultural areas." Noting similarities in the tales of distant lands without adequate consideration of the possibility of their being connected in human tradition, could hardly sustain the theory of independent and parallel growth. The value of the work done by Frazer and other scholars, however, is considerable because it notes a vast number of interesting similarities in narrative patterns and poses important questions.

There were three principal theories about the origins of folktales: the mythological school, mainly German, subscribed to the view of common Indo-European ancestry and inheritance; the anthropological school, mainly British, advocated the parallel development of culture all over the world; the Indianist school traced every tale to India. All of these theories were partially correct and incorrect. In spite of divergent theories, however, the doctrine of integration prevailed, and the migration of folktales has been like the rings formed when a stone is thrown into a pool, spreading equally in all directions. The mythological school, like the anthropological school, was not primarily interested in how tradition was diffused from one place to another, or from people to people.

Modern anthropological research has led to revisions in the generalizations about primitive man, and the realization that many of the resemblances in the cultures of primitive peoples are not real identities, either from the psychological or historical viewpoint. In fact, systematic examination of the geographical and historical factors clearly reveals a particular culture being continually influenced by its neighbours. The problem of the dissemination of cultural traits, including the folktale, is admittedly a complex one. Examination of the folktale involves the reconstruction of the original story form by unwrapping the layers imposed by time and locality and then tracing its passage through history. Moreover, the fact that the Benfey school and the Finnish school maintain their "Indian theory"; the fact that the question as to the relationship between the fairy tale collection of *Alf Laila Wa Laila* (literally, *The Thousand Nights and One Night,* or the *Arabian Nights*) and older European collections has not yet been answered; the fact that the anthropological theory becomes problematic in light of Peuckert's theory that the origin of all fairy tales dealing with magic must be connected with the observation and use of herbs and plants; and finally, the fact that De Vries' theory of archetypes has not been effectively dealt with must suggest, amongst other things, the complex nature of the problem.

The earliest Indian fables are found in the vedic literature, the *Mahabharata,* the Jatakas, and the famous collections known as the *Pancatantra* and the *Hitopadesa.* These collections fall broadly into two categories: those compiled for the purpose of religious preaching, such as the Jatakas and the other storybooks of the Buddhists and Jains written in Prakrit; and those intended to inculcate political doctrines and worldly wisdom, and to entertain, written in Sanskrit, such as the *Pancatantra.* The oldest beast fables known in India occur in the *Chandogya Upanishad,*[11] in which animals are introduced as actors and speakers. There are other stories dealing with the metamorphosis theme representing the gods in the forms of animals associating with men. Indeed, there are even earlier illustrations of this form of story: for instance, the story of Manu and the fish, that of Indra's metamorphosis into a bird, and the Rig Vedic simile of the sun as a vulture or falcon hovering in the air.[12] The theory of the transmigration of souls, applied equally to both man and animal, must have favoured the development of this form of tale. Indeed, the Buddha himself—during the period of his previous incarnations—appears in the guise of various animals in the old Jatakas.

The great variety of anecdotes with animal heroes throughout world literature is quite impressive. For the tellers of folktales everywhere and in every age, the human and animal worlds are never too distinct. The idea of a hunter disguising himself in the skin of an animal is quite common. This ambiguity extends even to mythologies, and as a consequence many deities appear one day in human guise and the next in the image of a beast. Folk tradition is generally very careful in its choice of animals, selecting only those that can make their actions appear as nearly human as is possible, and, of course, keep their character constant. Thus, the jackal is crafty, the hare is swift and wily, the cat is a hypocrite, and the lion is strong but gullible.

Whilst Indian fables and tales date from remote antiquity, they were, perhaps, not used for a definite purpose and not reduced to a literary form until a much later period. The ancestor of the popular tale may have been such vedic *akhyanas* as are preserved, for instance, in the Rig Vedic dialogue-hymn of Pururavas and Urvasi, or in such early legends as that of Sunahsepa. But it is going too far to seek the origin of the beast fable in the Rig Vedic hymn[13] in which the chanting Brahmans are compared to croaking frogs who are portrayed as more magical than didactic, or in the upanishadic parable of the dogs searching out a leader to howl for food for them, which may have been a satire or an allegory. It may also be somewhat questionable to clearly identify in the *Mahabharata* fables a distinct literary form although the motifs of the clever jackal, the naughty cat, and the greedy vulture are employed for moral instruction. All these, as well as the Jataka technique of illustrating the virtues of Buddhism by means of beast stories, may have been the basis for the well-developed beast fable in the *Pancatantra*. In its mature form, it departed from the simple parable or beast tale by bringing out the latent didactic motive clearly and deliberately and setting it artistically in a framework of connected stories in which the thoughts and deeds of men were attributed to animals.

It is not possible to neatly separate the Indian fable from the tale. The *Pancatantra*, although mainly composed of beast fables, also includes folktales and stories of human adventure, whereas the tale, as represented by the *Brihatkatha*, sometimes contains elements of the fable and a didactic motive.[14] However, the beast fable diverged considerably as an independent literary creation from the popular tale, which was not didactic and in which the stories of human life and popular ideas in myth and magic found expression.

The Jatakas are a collection of over five hundred stories, arranged in twenty-two *nipatas* (sections). They reflect an aspect of the literary, as well as popular, taste of the land. Each story gives an account of an incident in the previous existences of the Buddha as a Bodhisattva. These stories are held by the believer to be true, but they are really an assorted collection of popular folklore and historical tradition in the form of fables, fairy tales, riddles, puzzles, legends, humorous superstitions, and accounts of the social life of ancient India. At some period in antiquity, certainly well before 300B.C., it had become customary to identify the principal hero of each of these popular stories with the Buddha himself in a previous birth, and this identification was not entirely imaginary. Indeed, it is solely due to the growth of this idea that there is preserved "the most complete, the most authentic, and the most ancient collection of folklore in the world—a collection entirely unadulterated, as modern folklore stories so often are, by the inevitable process of passing through a Western mind."[15] In each story, the Buddha narrates, although not in first person, an experience of a past life to explain a present incident showing its moral implications. Because these tales bear upon the previous lives of the Buddha, scholars fix their origin in a period after his death. Yet, they have not explained how the tales can be attributed to men of later times if the Buddha were the actual narrator of each story. In fact, this mode of telling tales was an old one; it was not difficult to replace a sage or a wise man with a Bodhisattva. Any story, however secular or frivolous, could easily be transformed into a Buddhist tale by having its principal character identified with the Bodhisattva. There were several diverse types of Jatakas and in the early forms there was no place for Bodhisattvas. They were largely folk literature in which beast fables and fragments of historical tradition, as well as tales of wisdom, had been collected for instructive or didactic purposes.

The Jataka tales, however, have a definite religious significance. The only secular surviving collection of beast fables in Sanskrit is the *Pancatantra,* which exists in various versions and has, perhaps, a more interesting history than any work in world literature. Over two hundred different versions of the work are known to exist in more than fifty languages, and about three-quarters of these languages are not Indian.[16] Its range has stretched from Java to Iceland. As early as the eleventh century the *Pancatantra* had reached Europe, and by the end

201

of the sixteenth it had been translated into almost all the major languages of Europe. Few books in history have been translated into so many languages and it is doubtful if any secular book has had a wider readership.

All the versions emanate from a single original text which has not been preserved. Its earliest recensions have been classified into four main groups, each representing a diversity of tradition. The first is the lost Pahlavi version from which the old Syriac and Arabic versions were derived, and it was through this source that the *Pancatantra,* in a somewhat modified form, was introduced into the fable literature of Europe. The second is a lost northwestern recension from which the text was incorporated into the two Kashmirian Sanskrit versions of Gunadhya's *Brihatkatha,* made respectively by Ksemendra and Somadeva (eleventh century). The third is the common lost source of the Kashmirian version, entitled *Tantrakhyayika,* and of the two Jain versions, the Simplicitor Text, well known from the Bühler and Kielhorn edition, and the Ornatior Text of Purnabhadra (1190), called *Pancakhyana.* The fourth is also the source of the southern *Pancatantra,* the Nepalese version, and the Bengali *Hitopadesa.* Of these, the *Tantrakhyayika* best represents the original. The nature and extent of the transformation to which the work was subjected in course of time make the problem of reconstruction extremely complicated, but the close examination of the various existing versions made by Hertel and Edgerton succeeded to a great extent in recreating the original *Pancatantra.*

From the very beginning the *Pancatantra* had a deliberate literary form, being the instruction in the art of statecraft given by a learned scholar, Visnusarman, to three unintelligent but impressionable young princes. Its theme is not morality but practical wisdom in the affairs of life. It passed as a text book of *artha* (worldy wisdom) or *niti* (polity), which is one of three objects of human desires for the Hindus—the other two being dharma and kama. It repeatedly quotes verbatim from the celebrated Indian text on polity, the *Arthasastra:* "Like that work, it is designed especially to advise rulers in the arts of government. It is then, a 'Mirror for Magistrates' or 'Fiirstenspiegel.' "[17] It teaches the art of being an accomplished, successful, and happy social being; it does not concern itself with the possibility of living as a saint or an ascetic. Whilst insisting on the misery of poverty—"twas better to be dead than poor"—the *Pancatantra* does not glorify the acquisition of wealth. Money is a means to an end, to be able to live—"a Man to thrive must keep alive." Once security and freedom from worry are obtained, real joy comes from resolute and wise action, from contact with friends, and especially from the worthy exercise of the intelligence. Niti is the integrated development of the powers of man, in which security, prosperity, resolution, friendship, and learning are harmoniously blended to produce the utmost joy of life. The *Pancatantra* is therefore closely related to the *Nitisastra* and *Arthasastra,* although not directly opposed to the *Dharmasastra.* This is important, because even if the beast fable stresses the practical art of diplomacy in human affairs, rather than the strict code of uprightness, it does not teach the politics of profit at the expense of morality. Its five parts—*mitrabheda, mitraprapti, samdhivigraha, labdhanasa,* and *apariksitakaritana*—from which it derives its title, deal respectively with how friends and allies are lost; how they are won; the principles of war and peace; how gains are lost; and the dangers of hasty action. Each part is a narrative complete in itself, and together they constitute a perfect whole.[18] The stories are recounted in a simple and graceful prose narrative without attempting to creat elaborate stylistic effects or sentimental digressions. Its technique of inserting a number of stories within the framework of a single narrative is distinctive, although this feature of combining a number of fables is also used in the popular tale. In bringing together unconnected stories, considerable ingenuity has been employed to achieve unity and completeness of effect. The numerous general gnomic stanzas which punctuate the narrative are dictated by the didactive motive of the fable.

Originally intended as a work for imparting political wisdom to princes, the *Pancatantra* is now principally a storybook in which the story-teller and the political teacher are unified in one personality. At times the charm of story-telling is subordinated to the professed practical objective, and the tedious exposition of polity prevails over simple and vivid narrative. Such instances, however, are not numerous. Discrepancies doubtless appear in the different versions, but most of the stories are well and amusingly told, showing the author as a master of narrative, as well as a perfect man of the world, who never departs from an attitude of objective observation and whose considerable fund of wit and humour is often disguised behind his pedagogic seriousness. Because of its beauty and its wisdom the *Pancatantra* is one of the best storybooks ever composed.

In the absence of the original text it is impossible to determine the age of the *Pancatantra* with accuracy. The original version could have been composed any time between 100 B.C. and 500 A.D. However, it is certain that by the middle of the sixth century A.D. it had acquired wide fame even outside India. Its popularity within India is well illustrated by the various abridged versions of it available from Nepal to South India.

The Pahlavi translation was made by Barzuyeh (or Burzoe), the physician of the Sassanian King Khusru Anushirvan (537–79), by royal command.[19] This translation was obviously made from a Sanskrit version. Soon after, in 570, it was rendered from Pahlavi into Old Syriac by Bud, and his version, although imperfectly preserved, is still extant. It was thus virtually contemporary with the lost Pahlavi version. The Bud translation has been edited and translated twice into German by modern scholars. Almost two centuries later, about 760, the Pahlavi version was translated into Arabic by Abadallah ibn al-Muqaffa under the title *Kalila wa Dimna*. The title appears to have been taken from the names of the two jackals, Karataka and Damanaka, who play prominent parts in the original Sanskrit version of the *Pancatantra*. The diffusion of translations from then on was much wider still, and the Arabic version became the source of numerous versions in several continents.

Comparatively few Indian fables reached the West before the tenth century. Apart from those contained in the translations of the *Pancatantra*, there were stories handed down by oral tradition. In the tenth century, India became better known to the Islamic world, and from then on literary sources became more important than the oral tradition. Indian scientific and literary works were now translated into Persian and Arabic, were diffused all over the Islamic world in Asia, Africa, and Europe, and, because of the frequent conflicts between the Muslims and the Christians, also throughout the Christian West, particularly the Byzantine Empire, Italy, and Spain.

Hindu and Buddhist classical works had spread earlier to those countries and regions in the vicinity of India, primarily because of Buddhist missionary expansion. With this literature, from about the first century on, tales and fables penetrated without interruption into China and further east. They also reached Tibet and from there travelled with Buddhism to the Mongols, who adapted them to their own language with many changes and modifications. In addition to the *Vetalapancavimsati* and the *Vikramacaritra*, it is certain that the Mongols were also familiar with a third collection of stories, the *Sukasaptati*. Considering that the Mongols were in power in Europe for almost two hundred years, it seems more than plausible that many of these stories reached Europe through them. In the introduction to his translation of the *Vetalapancavimsati*, Heinrich Uhle points out that there is a Mongolian version of many of the Vetala stories in the language of the Kalmucks—a Mongolian race living on the Caspian Sea—called *Siddhi-Kur*. This Mongolian version became known in 1804 through Benjamin Bergmann's book *Nomadic Wanderings in the Region of the Kalmucks* but was not identified until 1857 by Benfey as being borrowed from India.[20] A Mongolian translation of the Arabic version of the *Pancatantra, Kalila wa Dimna,* is ascribed to Malik Said Iftikhar uddin Mohammad bin Abu Nasr, who died in 1280.

Another Syriac translation was made from this Arabic version in the tenth or eleventh century, and in about 1080, a Jew, Simeon Seth, translated it into Greek entitling it *Stephanites kai Ichnelades,* and stating in the Preface that the book originally had come from India. This, in turn, led to an Italian version by Giulio Nuti in 1583, two Latin versions, one German, and various translations in the Slavonic languages. At the beginning of the twelfth century, a Hebrew version was made by Rabbi Joel; this was translated into Latin by an Italian, John of Capua, between 1263 and 1278, was called *Liber Kalilae et Dimnae, Directorium vitae humanae,* and attained great popularity in the later Middle Ages. In 1480 two printed versions of this book appeared, and it has been reprinted in modern times. In 1483 a German translation appeared by Antonius von Pforr called *Das Buch der Beispiele der alten Weisen,* which is the best and most famous mediaeval version of the *Pancatantra.* It was repeatedly printed and, besides influencing German literature, was rendered into Danish, Icelandic, and Dutch.[21] The fact that four dated editions appeared at Ulm within four years of its first publication in German, followed by thirteen more during the course of the next hundred years, shows the importance of the *Pancatantra* at the time. A Spanish version appeared in 1493 and from it two Italian renderings by Firenzuola and Doni were made in 1548 and in 1552 respectively. In 1556 a French translation was made from Firenzuola's version. From Doni's version Sir Thomas North, the translator of Plutarch, made an English rendering under the title *The Morall Philosophie of Doni* in 1570, almost exactly one thousand years after the Syriac translation. No less than six renderings had intervened between the original Sanskrit and the English version. North's translation was reprinted in 1601, the year after the East India Company had been given a royal charter to trade with India and further east.

After the Islamic conquest of Spain, numerous works were translated from Arabic into Latin or Spanish, including a Spanish translation of *Kalila wa Dimna* in 1289, entitled *Calila e Dymna.* This, or another translation from Arabic, was rendered into Latin verse by Raimond de Beziers in 1313, but it was not published. In the thirteenth century, another translation from Arabic straight into Latin verse was made by Baldo under the title *Aesopus alter*. These renderings of the Indian fables were extremely popular, and indeed were read more widely in Europe, according to Max Müller, than the Bible or any other book.[22] Not only were complete translations read but individual stories were incorporated into sermons, homilies, and works on morality. Inevitably they were modified, improved, and localized to the extent that the original forms were forgotten. The speed and ease with which such tales spread testifies to the pleasure and joy with which they were heard and repeated. Because of their appeal, the tales from India seem to have been quickly assimilated, and their specifically Indian features could not be preserved in the rapid transit from one people to another.

Another Indian work, the *Sukasaptati* (seventy stories of a parrot), similar to the *Pancatantra*, also travelled westward through translation. During the fourteenth century it was translated into Persian under the title *Tutinameh*, and later rendered into Turkish. From the Persian account many tales passed to Europe through western Asia, and one of these was made famous by Gottfried V. Strassburg's *Tristan and Isolde*.

In 1026 a work on Indian history, originally translated from the "Indian language" into Arabic by Abu Salih bin Su'ayb bin Jami', was rendered into Persian. This version, by Abu-l-Hasan 'Ali, was quoted or summarized in a later Persian work of unknown date known as the *Mujmil al-Tawarikh*. It was actually a version of the *Mahabharata* story translated from a late Prakrit version.[23]

Another mediator of Indian tales was the famous *Arabian Nights*. Muslim fundamentalists consider this collection noxious, because they believe that pleasant stories stimulate sinful desires as much as wine, music, or sculpture. This work, however, has been instrumental in fashioning Western man's image of romantic love. Many of its approximately two hundred stories (264 in the Arabic version) are from Indian storybooks, and all the main elements of its framework are derived from Indian ideas. The prologue is very similar to that of the *Pancatantra* as is the idea that the stories are recounted to save someone's life. The *Samugga Jataka* (No. 436) tells the story of the *asura* (demon) who unsuccessfully put his beautiful wife in a box to guard her from going astray. The tale in all its essentials recurs in the *Arabian Nights*. Numerous animal fables contained in the *Arabian Nights* are traceable to Indian sources: for example, "The Barber's Fifth Brother" (6ee), "The Merchant's Wife and the Parrot" (134b), "The King's Son and the Afrit's Mistress" (134w), "The Fakir and His Pot of Butter"

(161b), "The Hedgehog and the Pigeons" (17). The world-famous story of Sindbad is a tale of Indian origin. The Arab historian Al Masudi expressly said that the *Kitab el Sindbad* was derived from India. This work is identical with the Persian *Sindibad-namah,* the Syriac *Sindban,* an Arabic version contained in the *Arabian Nights,* the Hebrew *Sandabar,* the Greek *Syntipas,* and a number of other books in European languages. The Greek *Syntipas* contains numerous passages that can be undertood properly only by recognizing that they are merely variations of a Sanskrit original, and everything supports the conclusion that here is yet another case of an Arabic work rendered from a Pahlavi translation of a Sanskrit text.

Most probably Jewish writings were also responsible for the dissemination of Indian tales in Europe, especially in the Slavonic countries. The influence of the *Haggadah,* a Jewish collection of tales and parables, on mediaeval and modern European fiction has been very great. From literature these stories were passed on to the people, and after being modified went again into literature, to the people, and so on, assuming in this process of alternation between literature and folklore the character of national truth and individual unity which gives many of them their great poetic quality. The very fact that a work can sustain the interest of a wide variety of peoples living in distant lands for more than a thousand years indicates its great intrinsic merit.

It was, however, in 1859 that the first direct translation of the Sanskrit *Pancatantra* was made in a European language by the German scholar Benfey. In 1952 the *Pancatantra* was newly translated into German by Alsdorf. Although available in English in several editions for centuries, it was not directly translated from the Sanskrit into English until 1924 by Stanley Rice who entitled his work *Ancient Fables and Stories.* A year later, Arthur W. Ryder also translated the *Pancatantra.*

The most important of all the later adaptations of the *Pancatantra* is the *Hitopadesa* (Salutary Advice) which, owing to its excellent literary merit, is one of the most popular and best known Sanskrit works in Europe. Containing twenty-five of the *Pancatantra's* stories, it is in fact a new work. Its authorship is uncertain as well as the date of its compilation. Probably composed in Bengal somewhere between 1000 and 1300, it contains seventeen stories which are not found in any of the recensions of the *Pancatantra.*[24] Besides Indian languages it has been repeatedly translated into European languages. It was in 1861 that Sir Edwin Arnold, the celebrated poet of *The Light of Asia,* translated the *Hitopadesa* from Sanskrit to English.

Apart from these literary channels, individual Indian tales must have reached Europe through Arab merchants, travellers, and Gypsies. Somewhat similar to the story-tellers in rural communities of India, Gypsy story-tellers all over the world take their recitals very seriously, and firmly adhere to a certain form, consisting of definite openings, links, and tags as common and stereotyped as in India. However, story-telling in most societies tends to conform to a set pattern.

One of the most remarkable examples of the migration of Indian tales is the acceptance of the Buddha as a Christian saint. During the eighth century, a Christian, St. John of Damascus, was living at the court of Caliph Al Mansur, during whose reign the Arabic version of the *Pancatantra* was prepared. John wrote a story of *Barlaam and Josaphat* in Greek as an exposition of Christian doctrines and theology, enlivening it by fables and parables. The Christian clergy did not like it because it was a religious novel. Nevertheless, it became immensely popular and was translated into numerous languages. As early as 1204 it was even translated into Icelandic. The major theme is accompanied by a body of fables and parables mostly of Indian origin. Although the Barlaam story is not a direct translation of any Indian original, it is, in fact, the story of the Great Renunciation of the Buddha. Recent researches suggest that the Greek version of St. John had originated from *Balavariani*, a Georgian version of the Buddha story. *Balavariani*, in its turn, was a derivation from an Arabic version.[25] In the sixteenth century Josaphat was made a saint both in the Greek Orthodox and Roman Catholic Churches. That the founder of an "atheistic" Asian religion should have been transformed into a Christian saint is, indeed, an amazing episode in religious history. In spite of striking similarities between the careers of the Buddha and Josaphat, it was only in the last century that the Buddhist origin of this Christian cult was realized.

Throughout mediaeval Christendom, *Barlaam and Josaphat* was accepted as an exposition of the ideals of Christian monasticism and asceticism. The churches celebrated the festival days associated with the Indian hermit Barlaam and his royal pupil Prince Josaphat with appropriate solemnity, and "their relics were invested with exceptional healing power." In the literary world too, the influence of the Barlaam story was deep and lasting. It inspired outstanding writers such as Guy de Cambrai, Rudolf Von Ems, Lope de Vega, Leo Tolstoy, and Shakespeare, who borrowed from it the story of the Caskets.[26]

The introduction of delightful Indian tales into mediaeval Europe at a time when asceticism was strong there is of considerable significance. The worldliness and sensuality of the Indian fables must have helped to bring European literature back to its natural course. Hence, almost immediately after their arrival in Europe, Indian fables appeared in Giovanni Boccaccio's (1313–1375) *Decameron* and Don Juan Manuel's *Conde Lucanor,* unrivalled examples of mediaeval prose. The *Decameron* is an extraordinary work of literary art, containing witty and amusing tales of adventure and the love of people of every class and character. Its influence on European literature has been incalculable, especially on Italian fiction. Whether Boccaccio was aware of it or not, many of his tales, which he either heard in Naples or collected from other works such as the *Gesta Romanorum,* were of Indian origin.

Other popular European storybooks such as the fourteenth century *Gesta Romanorum,* whose authorship is uncertain; Chaucer's (*ca.* 1340–1400) *Canterbury Tales;* La Fontaine's *Fables;* St. Rapola's *Märchen;* and Grimm's *Tales* include fables of Indian origin. For instance, "The Passion of St. Eustace and his Companions" included in the *Gesta Romanorum* (Tale CX) has its origin in the Jataka tale *Mahasutasoma* (No. 537). The Indian fables became known in Europe as the *Fables of Bidpai* (Pilpay), because in the translation one of the wicked kings is reclaimed to virtue by a Brahman sage, Bidpai. La Fontaine in the second edition of *Fables,* published in 1678, expressly confessed his indebtedness to Indian tradition. In the Preface he says: "It is not necessary that I should say whence I have taken the subjects of these new fables. I shall only say, from a sense of gratitude that I owe the largest portion of them to Pilpay the Indian sage."[27] The story of the ebony horse in Chaucer's "Squires' Tale" came from India via Persia, Egypt, and Spain to France *(Le Cheval de Fust)* and thence to Chaucer's ears. The theme of the three caskets and of the pound of flesh in the *Merchant of Venice* are of Buddhist origin, and stories derived from the *Pancatantra*—the "Gullible Husband" and the "Butler and the Blinded Brahman"—were adapted by Boccaccio. Many of the immensely popular tales found in Hans Christian Andersen's fairy tales, such as the "Magic Mirror," the "Seven-leagued Boots," "Jack and the Beanstalk," and the "Purse of Fortunatus," have been traced to Indian sources. Chaucer's "Pardoner's Tale" is an adaptation of a story in the *Vedabbha Jataka* (No. 48) or of the ploughshares eaten by mice in the *Kuta Vanija Jataka* (No. 218). The story "The Three Fastidious Brahmans" found its way to Siberia and Lapland through Central Asia, and from there to Jutland, where Hans Christian Andersen wrote his "Princess on the Pea." The *Jungle Books* of Kipling are a revival of the beast fables. "The Transposed Heads" from the *Brihat Kathasarit-*

sagara inspired Thomas Mann to write a delighful story *Die Vertausch-
ten Kopfe.*

One of the most popular fairy tales in Europe is the romantic story
of "Beauty and the Beast." It is found in its numerous variations in
practically every country of the world. For centuries children have
sympathized with its amiable heroine. It first appeared in Europe in
1740 in Madame de Villeneuve's *Contes Marines.* Ralston has examined
in detail its numerous variants, compared their similarities, and has
demonstrated it to be of Indian origin.[28] According to Max Müller, the
"Story of the Master Thief," the complex legend of *Rhampsinitos* as
reproduced in *Gesta Romanorum,* appears to be an adaptation of a story
in *Hitopadesa.* The Sanskrit tale is that of a Brahman who, upon being
told by three thieves in succession that the goat he was carrying was in
fact a dog, throws away his load for the thieves to pick. The essence
of the story is that a man will believe almost anything if three people,
seemingly unconnected with each other, repeat the same thing. The
story of the "Judgement of Solomon" may be one of the earliest examples of Indian fable migration and is based on a story in the *Maha
Ummagga Jataka* (No. 546). In the Indian story, the real mother lets
the child go at once when he cries upon being pulled apart by the two
claimant mothers. The story of the "Dog and the Sparrow" in Grimm's
collection is remarkably close in details to the story of "The Nautch-
Girl and the Parrot," in the *Baital Pachisi.* In both, a bird vows to
bring about the ruin of a human being; in both, the bird helps avenge
unjust injury; and in both, the guilty come to grief in consequence of
their own voluntary acts. Such a series of events is not likely to have
been imagined independently by different tale-tellers in almost identical
forms, and one is inclined to accept the chronological influence of the
stories. Numerous Jatakas, such as *Virocana Jataka* (No. 143), *Jambu
Khadaka Jataka* (No. 294), *Dipi Jataka* (No. 426), have parallels in
such well-known fables as "The Ass in the Lion's Skin," "The Fox and
the Crow," and "The Wolf and the Lamb." The Russian popular story
"The Friend," like other stories about evil spirits, has been traced to
Indian sources. Marusia's demon lover is akin to the Arabian ghoul or
the Rakshasa of Indian mythology, as described in the Arabic story
of Sidi Noman and the Indian story of Asokadatta and Vijayadatta in
the fifth book of the *Kathasaritsagara.* Another Russian story, the
"Fox-Wailer," which is a variant of "Jack and the Beanstalk" in which
a fox is described as wailing, is said to be of Indian origin. For de
Gubernatis points out that such "howling" is more in keeping with the
nature of the Eastern jackal than with that of its Western counter-

part, the fox.[29] The Russian story of Norka corresponds to an Indian one. Again, the story *Schastie and Neschastie* (Luck and Bad-luck) is a variant of the story of Vira-Vara found in the *Hitopadesa* and of a similar one in the *Pancatantra*.

How stories undergo change during the course of migration is illus-stated by Max Müller with *La Laitiere et le Pot au Lait* from La Fontaine's *Fables*.[30] Few stories have travelled through so many transla-tions. A milkmaid, Perrette, carrying a pail of milk on her head to market, indulges in daydreams. From the proceeds of the sale of the milk she will buy eggs, and then from the profits made on the eggs will buy chickens, and so on. At the prospect of her approaching wealth she suddenly gives a jump of joy, thereby dropping her pail of milk. Her milk is spilt and her riches are gone. In the original from the *Pancatantra*,[31] Svabhava Kripana (a born miser), a Brahman, having filled his bowl with rice hangs it near his bed and dreams of the profits he will make in time of famine from his hoarded rice, buying goats and cows, marrying a rich girl, and living in luxury. Imitating the ways of the rich, he dreams himself attempting to assert authority over his family, and he kicks the bowl over. The moral of this Indian story, that "he who makes foolish plans for the future will be white all over," became transformed through La Fontaine's adaptation of it, into what is a popular proverb in English—"don't count your chickens before they are hatched."

Again, the well-known Welsh story of Llewellyn's dog Gelert, as told in William R. Spencer's ballad, "Bedd Gellert," is the Welsh transforma-tion of the *Pancatantra* story[32] of the Brahman who, having left a mongoose to guard his child in a cradle during his absence, returns and finds the mongoose with its mouth covered with blood. Assuming that the mongoose had bitten the child, he kills it at once. Later he discovers a dead cobra near the child and is filled with great remorse. In the Welsh version, the mongoose and the snake are altered to a dog and a wolf. The idea of killing hastily a faithful animal under such circum-stances has occurred independently to different peoples in distant lands, but in this case, scholars have been able to trace back the successive stages of transformation of the story from the *Pancatantra* version to the Welsh version.[33]

The story of the fox who succeeds in stealing the young magpies originated in the *Pancatantra*, and was later incorporated in the Reynard cycle and in the work of Hans Sachs. Along with this artistic tale, and undoubtedly influenced by it, there developed a folktale, well known in northern and eastern Europe, in which the fox threatens to push down the tree in which the magpie has its young. The crow gives good advice to the magpies and saves them. The fox avenges himself by playing dead and catching the crow. The action in the latter part of the tale is the opposite of that in the literary fable.

Another tale which appeared first in the Jatakas and then spread widely is the story of the tar baby, the essential point of which is that the trickster, generally a rabbit, is caught by a tar baby, some kind of sticky image. Often the rabbit's enemies dwell upon how he could be punished. Very ingeniously, the rabbit pretends to agree to various kinds of punishment suggested, begging not to be thrown into the brier patch. His enemies, misled into thinking that it would do him most injury, throw him into the briers and the rabbit escapes. This tale of the tar baby was studied very thoroughly by A. M. Espinosa in more than one hundred and fifty versions. Later he supplemented the original number by an additional one hundred and fifteen. It seems this story reached the Negroes and Indians of America through several routes. It came from India to Africa, where it is very popular and where it underwent some characteristic modifications before being carried, presumably by slaves, to America. Another route lay through Europe to Spain and then to American colonies. Yet, it could have travelled across the Pacific many centuries earlier.

Before any overall assessment of the Indian inspiration of European beast fables is made, it should be pointed out that the literary fable collections from India are only one of four principal sources upon which Western tradition appears to have drawn. The other three are Aesop's fables, the mediaeval literary animal tales brought together in the cycle of Reynard the Fox, and the purely oral tradition, a very important part of which was developed in Russia and the countries of east Europe. The interrelation of all these influences is extremely complicated, and the writing of the history of a particular animal tale extraordinarily difficult.

India's influence on the mediaeval fables is not seriously questioned and fable migration during the Middle Ages can be traced through the translations of Indian tales. But when parallels and identities are noted in the ancient tales, and where there is no concrete evidence of borrowing other than through human contact, analysis of the historicity of oral tradition has to rely to some extent on conjecture, which no matter how valid is frequently disputed.[34]

Parallels and similarities between Greek and Indian fables are quite obvious, and a number of scholars have carefully analyzed both their historical roots and internal structure. Since the beginning of scholarly interest in fable migration in the middle of the nineteenth century, arguments have been sharply divided on the question of the historical relationship between the so-called Greek *Aesop's Fables* and Indian fables. Although the debate is somewhat subdued at present, opinion is no less divided. As far as the antiquity of the fable itself is concerned, the case for India is unassailable. The dispute is over the priority of the beast fable.

The argument favouring the Greek origin of the beast fable is based almost entirely on chronology, and the main confusion arises because Indian chronology is not firmly fixed. Disputes concerning the dates of major Indian works, although considerably narrowed, remain unresolved. Max Müller held the opinion that in almost every case of parallelism, the borrowing was done by the Greeks. Amongst the many scholars who shared this view were Otto Keller and Johannes Hertel. Against them, Theodor Benfey, who regarded India as the home of all folktales, held the view that India had borrowed animal fables from the Greeks, although he also stressed the existence of an independent Indian tradition in this respect. Another Sanskrit scholar, A. Weber, first subscribed to the theory of Indian origin but later reversed his opinion. A. Wagener *(Essai Sur La rapports qui existent entre les apologues de l'Inde et apologues de la Grece)* shared Weber's former view that in almost every case the Greeks were the borrowers. Weber's latter view was vigorously opposed by Keller in his work *The History of the Greek Fable* (1862). He fully believed in the Indian origin of the fables and that they were transmitted to Greece through an ancient Assyrian connective link.

The Greek fables belonging to different dates were collected in *Aesop's Fables* in the third century by Valerius Babrius, a Hellenized Roman who, in his Preface, refers to two sources for his material: Aesop for the Hellenic fable and Kybises for the Lybian fable. This is the oldest non-Indian collection of fables available, although Demetrius reputedly made a collection in Athens in 300 B.C. Three-quarters of the fables are about animals, and the rest deal with planets, natural elements, such as the sea, rivers, and the sun, and a few with gods and men. The work was soon translated from its original Greek and Latin versions into a variety of European languages. It is said that a French collection appeared in the tenth century, followed by many others and culminating in the seventeenth century in La Fontaine's *Fables*. Evidently, not all of the stories are of Greek origin—although some certainly must be. The collection comprises the *Life of Aesop;* four books derived from the *Romulus,* a collection of the mediaeval prose renderings of Phaedrus, a Greek freedman of Augustus in the first century; a selection of the *Fables* of Avian; and some fables from other sources. The bulk of the stories are the renderings of Phaedrus, who refers not only to Aesop but also to Anacharsis the Scythian, a possible source of Indian influence.[35]

Jacobs has suggested that Babrius' collection, which ran to about one hundred fables, was derived directly or indirectly from a Sinhalese embassy which came to Rome in 52. It is suggested that the *Life of Aesop* itself was modelled on the Persian or Babylonian "Story of Ahiqar," which Benfey has "identified with a well-known Indian type."[36] Indeed, the historicity of Aesop is doubtful, although Herodotus mentions him as a maker of stories who lived in the sixth century B.C. and who was the slave of a Samian citizen called Iadmon. Considering Herodotus' undeveloped sense of history, his uncritical reliance on oral tradition, and his gift of imagination, his testimony must be accepted with caution. Later writers also refer to Aesop but there are inconsistencies in their accounts.

However, Aesop's historical existence is immaterial; his name was certainly common in fifth century B.C. Greece as the author of fables, whilst the earliest Indian fables on record date back to the upanishadic period—the *Chandogya Upanishad*—and the tradition may have been much older.

Those who assert the priority of the Greek fable maintain that the Indian fable cannot be older than the fourth or fifth century B.C. This date is based on the assumption that Indian folktales and the *Pancatantra* are of Buddhist origin, and that the Buddhist Jatakas, another source of Indian fables, were composed after the Buddha. There are several flaws in this argument and its assumptions. The Buddha, accepting the conservative estimate, was born about a century before Herodotus who was supposedly born between 490 and 480 B.C. Hence, it is not unlikely that the tradition of Buddhist birth stories had become quite powerful in India before the time Aesop began his compositions. Jataka legends occur even in the canonical *Pitakas* and it is now generally accepted that the *Sutta* and *Vinaya Pitakas* containing Jataka tales are at least older than the Council of Vaisali (*ca.* 380 B.C.). This conclusion is confirmed by the bas-reliefs depicting scenes from the Jatakas in the Stupas of Sanchi, Amaravati, and especially of Bharhut, where the titles of several Jatakas are clearly inscribed. If there were a collection in existence in the fourth century B.C., the oral tradition upon which it was inevitably based must have been considerably older.

Most of the tales in the Jatakas open with "once upon a time when Brahmadatta was reigning in Banaras"; the previous incarnation of the Buddha was in the reign of Brahmadatta's son Kashyapa. "It is therefore possible, that a separate collection of beast-fables existed, connected with this Kashyapa, which was incorporated in the *Jatakas* assuming him to be a pre-incarnation of the Buddha."[37]

More important, however, are the flaws in the assumption that the tradition of folklore in India is of Buddhist origin. Fables, as mentioned above, had been found in vedic literature which by even the most conservative chronological standards predates Aesop by at least five centuries. The most dominant form in Aesop, that of the beast fable, is recorded in the Upanishads, definitely pre-Buddhist and pre-Homeric.

The fact that the Jataka tales are Buddhist does not by itself prove that the folklore tradition behind them is also Buddhist. Moreover, there is definite evidence that the Jatakas are related to pre-Buddhist Indian works. R. P. Mehta wrote an account of pre-Buddhist India in 1939 mainly from the Jatakas. He has also shown the pre-Buddhist ancestry of the Jatakas, which, without the idea of the Bodhisattva, originally consisted of a verse or verses and a prose narration embodying a folktale, and were generally intended to impart a moral.[38] That the Jatakas have a non-Buddhist Indian ancestry has been suggested by other scholars too, such as Franke, who points to the parallels between the *Mahabharata* and the Jatakas and suggests that the common tales in these two works are not the outcome of direct borrowing but are connected through some other common source.[39] If the Buddhist tales themselves are of pre-Buddhist origin, then the argument that the stories collected in the *Pancatantra* were originally Buddhist tales and as such belong to a later period is invalid. Yet, it may be observed that although Buddhism certainly influenced many tales in the *Pancatantra*, and that this fact led Benfey to conclude that the Indian fables were of Buddhist origin, it is now certain that the work originated from Hindu sources and later was revised by Buddhist and Jain editors. Hertel proved quite effectively that in its earlier form the *Pancatantra* was purely a Hindu work. Macdonnel endorsed Hertel's opinion that there could be no doubt that, in the style of the *Tantrakhyayika*, it was one of the earliest products of the artificial literature of India. "The general atmosphere is that of Brahmanism, while no relation to Buddhism can be found in the book. The view once rather widely held that the *Pancatantra* was of Buddhist origin must therefore be rejected."[40] Hertel's work did not quite solve the problem of the comparative antiquity of the Indian and the Greek fable, although he maintained that the *Pancatantra* was written down in the second century B.C. but that the actual stories were probably much older. Furthermore, he insisted that the Indian fables were original, because the use of fables to give instruction in politics was essentially Indian.

Indeed, apart from the historical evidence, the literary evidence also leans to the Indian side. The fables have had too luxuriant a growth in Indian literature to admit the theory of borrowed origins without more substantial evidence. No other literature can vie with Sanskrit in the richness of fables and stories when we consider the Jatakas, Buddhaghosa's *Dhammapada Commentary*, the *Pancatantra*, and the *Hitopadesa*. In Greek literature before Aesop only eight complete fables are known, with a dozen others merely referred to, including "The Ass's Heart," "The Countryman and the Snake," "The Dog and the Shadow" —all of which can be traced to India. When one remembers also that many of the stories in the *Arabian Nights* are of Hindu origin, it is not easy to accept the view that the Indian tales could have a Greek source. The Indian mentality was particularly favourable to the growth of fables, animal stories, and fairy tales, because of the Indian belief in transmigration, which effaces the difference between the human and the animal worlds. Indians are extremely kind to animals for they believe in their independent existence, and without such sympathetic treatment it seems unlikely that the beast fable could have been written.

In supporting the theory of Indian origin, Keller pointed out that the relation existing between the fox and the lion has no real basis in the nature of the two animals, whereas the jackal does relate to the lion as portrayed in Indian fable. Weber, who later advanced the theory of a Semitic origin for the Greek fable, contended that the jackal existed in the land of the Semites, and that the Greeks changed the jackal to a fox, and when the Indians took over the story they changed the fox back to a jackal.[41] This is a plausible explanation, but in the context of all the evidence its efficacy is much reduced. That the migration of fables was originally from East to West, and not vice versa, is clearly illustrated by the fact that the animals and birds who play the leading parts—the lion, the jackal, the elephant, the peacock, the tiger, the monkey, and the crocodile—abound in Indian jungles and rivers, but not in Greece. It is not possible to read Indian literature without being constantly impressed by the sense of the forest.

Evidence in the Talmudic-midrashic literature and the parallels between Indian, Jewish, and Greek fables and parables also lend weight to the theory of the early westward migration of the fable from

India to Greece. The parable of the blind and the lame, for instance, which is so popular in Jewish literature, and which is most likely of Indian origin, was known to the Greeks of the fourth century B.C. It is possible that the Palestinian writers got it directly from India, but it is more likely that it came from the Greeks or Hellenistic Jews in the second century A.D. Again, the legend about David's harpstrings has a parallel not only in Indian folklore in the *Pancatantra,* but also in the Greek legend of Aeslus' harp. The description of the world as a wheel frequently found in rabbinic writings could have been borrowed from India through the Greeks; although in rabbinic literature it is used as a metaphor, whilst in India it is associated with the dominant philosophical concept—transmigration. In *Midrash Rabba,* a commentary on the Pentateuch *(Five Rolls),* Indian fables are found and appear to have been taken directly from India, because they have Indian features but not Greek. For example, the Jewish story of the bird who has built a nest on the sea shore only to find it threatened by the waves and who tries to bail out the water with its beak, but is rebuked by another bird, has no parallel in Aesop, but is similar to the *Kaka Jataka* (No. 146). It is also possible that the *Pancatantra* fable in which the mouse, transformed into a girl by Yajnavalkya, declines in succession to marry the sun, the clouds, the wind, and the mountain could have formed the basis of the famous Abraham legend in which Abraham observes that one element subdues another: fire is extinguished by water, and clouds are dispersed by wind.

The *Pancatantra* is distinguished from the Greek *Fables* of Babrius by its purpose. In the guise of witty fables, the *Pancatantra* teaches the lessons embodied in such famous works of polity as Kautilya's *Arthasastra.* The technique of moralizing the various stories in pointed memorial passages, not general maxims but special labels to distinguish the points of individual fables, is novel and interesting, and the essential nature of the stanzas is gnomic or recapitulatory rather than dramatic or interlocutory. A great deal of floating gnomic literature in Sanskrit must have existed prior to this, paving the way for these passages of didactic wisdom. The fact that the *Pancatantra* is a *Nitisastra,* the book of niti, and that the Greeks had no equivalent term, plus the fact that the purpose of political instruction was essentially Indian and not Greek, would further endorse the originality of the *Pancatantra.* Wherever the introduction of the fable is traced, it is almost invariably associated with political applications. Rabbi Joshua ben Hananiah applied the fable of "The Wolf and the Crane" to prevent a revolution of the Jews against Romans. Krylor and his followers in Russia made use of the fable to reflect upon the bureaucracy; and when Aesop was first translated into Chinese, the officials soon suppressed the edition because they considered the fables to be directed against them.[42]

Whilst the relation between the mass of *Aesop's Fables* and the *Pancatantra* stories cannot be demonstrated, in some cases there is plausible evidence of borrowing. Edgerton has recently analyzed two tales which seem certainly to have been borrowed from India: "Ass in Panther's Skin" and "Ass Without Heart and Ears" of *Pancatantra* Book III and Book IV respectively.[43] However, even if the priority of the Indian fable is conceded, it does not explain the existence of a vast number of Greek fables which have no parallel in Indian literature. No one could seriously suggest that all Greek fables have been borrowed from India. Clearly, both countries had an independent tradition of fables and it is likely that the fable as a type did not arise exclusively in either India or Greece, but that some migration of fables occurred when communication between the two countries arose.

Sangita, the Indian tradition of music, is as old as Indian contacts with the Western world, and it has graduated through various strata of evolution: primitive, prehistoric, vedic, classical, mediaeval, and modern. It has travelled from temples and courts to modern festivals and concert halls, imbibing the spirit of Indian culture, and retaining a clearly recognizable continuity of tradition. Whilst the words of songs have varied and altered from time to time, many of the musical themes are essentially ancient.

Sangita, which originally meant drama, music and dance, was closely associated with religion and philosophy. At first it was inextricably interwoven with the ritualistic and devotional side of religious life. The recital and chant of mantras has been an essential element of vedic ritual throughout the centuries. According to Indian philosophy, the ultimate goal of human existence is moksha, liberation of the atman from the life-cycle, or spiritual enlightment; and *nadopasana* (literally, the worship of sound) is taught as an important means for reaching this goal. The highest musical experience is ananda, the "divine bliss." This devotional approach to music is a significant feature of Indian culture.

The origin of Indian music is enshrined in beautiful tales and legends. It is a common Hindu practice to attribute the beginning of a branch of learning to a divine origin through the agency of a rishi. Siva, also called Nataraja, is supposed to be the creator of Sangita, and his mystic dance symbolizes the rhythmic motion of the universe.[44] He transmitted his knowledge of cosmic dance to the rishi Bharata, through one of his *ganas,* Tandu. The dance was called *tandava* and Bharata thus became the first teacher of music to men, and even to *apsaras,* the heavenly dancers. Similarly, the rishi Narada, who is depicted as endlessly moving about the universe playing on his *vina* (lute) and singing, is believed to be another primeval teacher of music.

The Indian musical tradition can be traced to pre-vedic times in the Indus Valley civilization. From the excavations at Mohenjo-daro and Harappa, musical instruments such as crude flutes, vinas with seven strings, drums, and a bronze statue of a dancing girl, have been found. During the vedic period a wide variety of musical instruments—wind, string, and percussion—were in use. The goddess of music, Sarasvati, who is also the goddess of learning, is portrayed as seated on a white lotus playing the vina.

The ancient Hindus were familiar with the theory of sound (*Gandharva Veda*), and its metaphysics and physics. The hymns of the *Rig Veda* contain the earliest examples of words set to music, and by the time of the *Sama Veda* a complicated system of chanting had been developed. By the time of the *Yajur Veda,* a variety of professional musicians had appeared, such as lute players, drummers, flute players, and conch blowers. Buddhist texts also testify to the prevalence of Sangita, both religious and secular, in early India. Music in India, however, reached its zenith during the Gupta period, the classical age of Indian art and literature.

Indian music is based upon a system of *ragas* and is improvised or composed at the moment of performance. The notes which are to convey certain definite emotions or ideas are selected with extreme care from the twenty-five intervals of the *sruti* scale and then grouped to form a raga, a mode or a melodic structure of a tune. It is upon this basic structure that a musician or singer improvises according to his feeling at the time. Structural melody is the most fundamental characteristic of Indian music.

Every classical Indian tune must be in a particular raga or *ragini;* the latter term, the feminine of raga, implies an abridged or modified raga. The word raga is derived from a Sanskrit root, *ranj* or *raj,* literally meaning to colour but figuratively meaning to tinge with emotion. The essential feature of a raga is its power to evoke emotion. The term has no equivalent in Western music, although the Arabic *maqam iqa* corresponds to it. Oversimplified, the concept of raga is to connect musical ideas in such a way as to form a continuous whole based on emotional impact. There are, however, mixed ragas combined in a continuous whole of contrasting moods. Technically, a raga is defined as "essentially a scale with a tonic and two axial notes," although it has additional characteristics.

The word raga appears in Bharata's *Natyasastra,* and a similar concept did exist at the time, but it was Matanga (fifth–seventh century) who first defined raga in a technical sense as "that kind of sound composition, consisting of melodic movements, which has the effect of colouring the hearts of men." This definition remains valid today. Before the evolution of the raga concept in Bharata's time, *jati* tunes with their fixed, narrow musical outlines constituted the mainstay of Indian music. These were only simple melodic patterns without any scope for further elaboration. It was out of these jati tunes that a more comprehensive and imaginative form was evolved by separating their musical contents and freeing them from words and metres.

Indeed, a raga is basically a feeling, the expression of which has come to be associated with certain notes and twists of melody. A musician may compose in the same raga an indefinite number of times, and the music can be considerably different each time. Although a raga is inexhaustible, it can be recognized in the first few notes, because the feelings produced by the musician's execution of these notes are intensely strong. The effect of Indian music is cumulative rather than dramatic. As the musician develops his discourse in his raga, it eventually colours all the thoughts and feelings of the listeners. Clearly, the longer a musician can dwell on and extend the theme with artistic intensity the greater the impact on the audience.

Unlike Western music, which from the mid-eighteenth century constantly changes and contrasts its moods, Indian music, as well as Arabic and Iranian, always centres in developing and exalting one particular emotion. The musician, if he is sufficiently skilled, can "lead his audience through the magic of sound to a depth and intensity of feeling undreamt of in other musical systems."[45] Indian music is essentially impersonal, reflecting "an emotion and an experience which are deeper and wider and older than the emotion or wisdom of any single individual. Its sorrow is without tears, its joy without exultation and it is passionate without any loss of serenity. It is in the deepest sense of the word all-human."[46] It is an art nearest to life; in fact, W. B. Yeats called Indian music "not an art, but life itself," although its theory is elaborate and technique difficult.

The possible number of ragas is very large, but the majority of musical systems recognize seventy-two (thirty-six *janaka* or fundamental, thirty-six *janya* or secondary). New ragas, however, are being invented constantly, as they have always been, and a few of them will live to join the classical series. Many of the established ragas change slowly, since they embody the modes of feeling meaningful at a particular time. It is for this reason that it is impossible to say in advance what an Indian musician will play, because the selection of raga is contingent upon his feelings at the precise moment of performance.

Indian music recognizes seven main and two secondary notes or *svaras*. Representing definite intervals, they form the basic or *suddha* scale. They can be raised or lowered to form other scales, known in their altered form as *vikrita*. The chanting of the *Sama Veda* employed three to four musical intervals, the earliest example of the Indian tetrachord, which eventually developed into a full musical scale. From vaguely defined musical intervals to a definite tetrachord and then to a full octave of seven suddha and five vikrita was a long, continuous, and scientific process. For instance, Bharata's *Natyasastra*, the earliest surviving work on Indian aesthetics variously dated between the second century B.C. and the fourth century A.D., in its detailed exposition of Indian musical theory, refers to only two vikrita notes, *antara* and *kakali*. But in the *Sangita Ratnakara*, an encyclopaedia of Indian music attributed to Sarngadeva (1210–1247), the number of vikritas is not less than nineteen; *shadja* and *panchama* also have acquired vikritas.[47] It was during the mediaeval period that Ramamatya in the south, and Lochana-kavi in the north in his *Ragatarangini* referred to shadja and panchama as constant notes. Indian music thus came to acquire a full fledged gamut of *mandra, madhya,* and *tar saptak*.

The scale as it exists today has great possibilities for musical formations, and it has a very extensive range included in the microtonal variations. The microtones, the twenty-two srutis, are useful for determining the correct intonation of the notes, their bases, and therefore their scales (gramas). The Indian scale allows the musician to embellish his notes, which he always endeavours to do, because grace plays the part in Indian music that harmony does in European music.

Whilst Indian music represents the most highly evolved and the most complete form of modal music, the musical system adopted by more than one-third of mankind is Western music based on a highly developed system of harmony, implying a combination of simultaneously produced tones. Western music is music without microtones and Indian music is music without harmony. The strongly developed harmonic system of Western music is diametrically opposed in conception and pattern to the melodic Indian system. Harmony is so indispensable a part of Western music today that Europeans find it difficult to conceive of a music based on melody alone. Indians, on the other hand, have been for centuries so steeped in purely melodic traditions that whilst listening to Western music they cannot help looking for a melodic thread underlying the harmonic structures.

The fundamental and most important difference between the European and Indian systems of rhythm is respectively one of multiplication and addition of the numbers two and three. The highly developed *tala*, or rhythmic system with its avoidance of strict metre and its development by the use of an accumulating combination of beat subdivisions, has no parallel in Western music. On the other hand, the Indian system has no exact counterpart to the tone of the tempered system, except for the keynote, of Western music. Consequently, just and tempered intonations are variously conceived which eliminate the possibility of combining the melodic interval theory of the sruti system with the Western modulating, harmonic, arbitrarily tempered theory of intervals. With its tempered basis, larger intervals, and metred rhythms, Western music is more easily comprehended than Indian music, which seems to require a certain musical aptitude and ability to understand its use of microtones, the diversification of the unmetred tala, and the subtle and minutely graded inflection.[48]

Considering the divergence between these two systems, it would be difficult to imagine that one is indebted to the other, even in a small measure, or that there could have been any points of contact between the two. But Western music, as it appears today, is a relatively modern development.

In early times melody was the sole component of Western music, as is revealed by the Gregorian chants, which may well be the archetype of Western classical music. One or more male voices used to sing these single threads of notes without accompaniment. Pope Gregory, in the seventh century, revised them into their present form. During the long period between Pythagoras and Bach, who successfully incorporated the Pythagorean comma in *The Well-tempered Clavichord*, Western music, like Indian music, was not modulating and largely free in improvization and ornamentation. Because of Western music's assimilative character and genius for compromise, however, notes in the harmonic series gradually began to dominate it. This made it, on the one hand, increasingly sophisticated and complex, and, on the other, reduced progressively its freedom of elaboration and improvization, subordinating it firmly to the direction of the conductor. And, whilst it has been much poorer modally, melodically, and rhythmically than Indian classical music, it is perhaps that very restriction and constriction that provided the essential compression necessary before polyphonic counter-point, and finally harmony, offered new and promising avenues for development and expansion.[49]

The real indebtedness of European music is to Greece and Arabia. When, after the fall of Rome, music began to be fashionable again, it was the understanding of the Greek theory and of Byzantine practice, imperfect as it was, which led to the systematization of music in Europe. Later, some Arab influence percolated through the Romance countries. But Arabia, Persia, and the countries of the Greek and Roman world were in contact with India, and it is not unlikely that some Indian influence in this sphere had reached Europe well before the advent of the Gypsies.

The ancient Western world was aware of the existence of a highly developed system of Indian music. According to Curt Sachs, it was the South Indian drum *tambattam* that was known in Babylonia under the name of *timbutu*, and the South Indian *kinnari* shared its name with King David's *kinnor*. Strabo referred to it, pointing out that the Greeks believed that their music, from the triple point of view of melody, rhythm, and instruments, came to them originally from Thrace and Asia.[50] Arrian, the biographer of Alexander, also mentions that the Indians were great lovers of music and dance from earliest times. The Greek writers, who made the whole of Asia, including India, the sacred territory of Dionysos, claimed that the greater part of music was derived from Asia. Thus, one of them, speaking of the lyre, would say that he caused the strings of the Asian cithara to vibrate. Aristotle describes a type of lyre in which strings were fastened to the top and bottom, which is reminiscent of the Indian type of single-stringed *ektantri vina*.

The vina is really neither a lute nor a harp, although it is commonly translated into English as lute. Generally known in its construction as bow-harp, the vina must have originally been developed from the hunting bow, a type of a musical bow, *pinaka,* on which a tightly drawn string was twanged by the finger or struck with a short stick. To increase the resonance a boat-shaped sound box was attached, consisting of a small half-gourd of coconut with a skin table or cover, through which a bamboo stick was passed longitudinally, bearing a string of twisted hair resting on a little wooden bridge placed on the skin table. This was the *ekatari,* or one-stringed lute of India, which soon produced its close relative, the *dvitari* or two-stringed lute. Later, additional strings were inevitably added. Whilst it is possible to trace the passage of the slender form of the fingerboard instrument, *pandoura,* from Egypt to Greece, it was not until they came into contact with the Persians that the Greeks became acquainted with the bow, a fact which may reinforce the view of the Indian origin of the Greek lute.

Although many varieties of the vina have been evolved, it existed in its original form, now extinct, in the vedic and pre-vedic times. This is known from the excavations at Mohenjo-daro and Harappa. There is sufficient evidence that some of these musical instruments were constructed according to the heptatonic, *sampurna,* scale with seven notes. However, in the other contemporary civilizations of Egypt and Mesopotamia, similar instruments have also been found. The vina is often shown in the hands of the musicians on the early Buddhist sculptures at Bhaja, Bharhut, and Sanchi and is still in use in Burma and Assam. In Africa it is used by many Nilotic tribes. A bow-harp, known as an angle-harp, closely resembling the Indian vina can be seen in the mural-paintings at Pompeii.

The two earliest Greek scales, the Mixolydic and the Doric, have an affinity to early Indian scales. Some recent British writers, for example the editors of *The New Oxford History of Music,* have attempted to exclude Indian influence by making the somewhat strange suggestion that the term "India" meant countries much nearer. Whilst the evidence pointing to the direct influence of India on Greek music is slight, there is enough of it to suggest serious Greek interest in Indian art. In addition, there are parallels between the two systems, which may or may not be connected. It is certainly true that the seven note scale with three octaves was known in India long before the Greeks were familiar with it. Pythagoras' scheme of cycle of the fifth and cycle of the fourth in his system of music is exactly the same as the *sadja-pancama* and *sadja-madhyama bhavas* of Bharata. Since Bharata lived several centuries after Pythagoras, it has been suggested that he borrowed the scheme from Pythagoras. At the same time it has been pointed out that Indian music, dating as it does from the early vedic period, is much anterior to Greek music, and that it is not unlikely that Pythagoras may have been indebted to Indian ideas. In almost all other fields of scholarship in which he was interested, a close identity between his and the older Indian theories has already been noted.

Whilst no title of any Sanskrit work on music translated at Baghdad is available, there is no doubt that Indian music influenced Arab music. The well-known Arab writer Jahiz, recording the popularity of Indian music at the Abbasid Court, mentions an Indian instrument known as *kankalah,* which was played with a string stretched on a pumpkin. This instrument would appear to be the *kingar,* which is made with two gourds. Knowledge of Indian music in the Arab world is evidenced by an Arab author from Spain, who refers to a book on Indian tunes and melodies. Many technical terms for Arab music were borrowed from Persia and India. Indian music, too, was influenced in return, incorporating certain Persio-Arab airs, such as *Yeman* and *Hiji* from Hijaz. At the beginning of their rise to power, the Arabs themselves had hardly any musical system worth noting and mainly practiced the existing systems in the light of Greek theory. Since Indian contact with western Asia had been close and constant, it would appear likely that the Arabic maqam iqa is the Persian version of the Indian melodic rhythmic system, traga tala, which had existed for more than a thousand years before maqam iqa was known.

Yehudi Menuhin is convinced that

we would find all, or most, strands beginning in India; for only in India have all possible modes been investigated, tabulated, and each assigned a particular place and purpose. Of these many hundreds, some found their way to Greece; others were adopted by nomadic tribes such as the Gypsies; others became the mainstay of Arabic music. However, none of these styles has developed counterpoint and harmony, except the Western-most offshoot (and this is truly our title to greatness and originality), with its incredible emotional impact corresponding so perfectly with the infinite and unpredictable nuances, from the fleeting shadow to the limits of exaltation or despair, or subjective experience. Again, its ability to paint the phenomena of existence, from terror to jubilation, from the waves of the sea to the steel and concrete canyons of a modern metropolis, has never been equalled.[51]

It was during the fifteenth and sixteenth centuries, after the discovery of the direct sea route, that India came to be directly known in Europe. It also happened to be the period of the Renaissance, the advent of the Gypsies in Europe, and of the first flood of progress in Western music. Indian music came to be better known in the West during the eighteenth and nineteenth centuries but a wide appreciation of Indian music in western Europe has yet to articulate and mature.

Western interest in Indian music during the past century has proceeded along two distinct lines: first, a purely academic interest by scholars in the nature of Indian music especially in France, Germany, and Britain; and second, adoption by Western composers of Indian themes. This interest in Indian music was, in fact, a part of a wider interest in Indian culture which had fascinated some European intellectuals after their discovery of Sanskrit's rich heritage.[52]

In 1863 Albrecht Weber published in Berlin a critical study of some of the earliest texts on Indian scales. Later in 1888, Hermann Oldenberg published a book about the hymns of the *Rig Veda,* which included a lengthy chapter dealing with vedic metres. About the same time, Martin Haug's work on the *Sama Veda* appeared giving the particulars of accents and notations. At the turn of the century, Ludwig Reimann, in a book about various instruments located in European museums, gave a detailed description of several Indian instruments. Richard Simon published with notations a critical edition of the compositions of Somanatha. He attempted an interpretation of the system of grace notes adopted in the *Ragavibodha.* The French scholars have included J. Grosset and Victor Charles Mahillon, and more recently, Alain Danielou.[53] Amongst the English writers, the best known are C. R. Day, who in 1891 published a book on *The Music and the Musical Instruments of Southern India;* Anne Wilson, who wrote a short book on Indian music; Alexander Ellis; Charles Myers; and E. Clements who published his *Study of Indian Music* in 1913. A year later, A. H. Fox-Strangway's famous and profound book *Music of Hindustan* was published, and in 1921 Herbert A. Popley brought out his work *The Music of India.*

With the advance of learning and national consciousness in India, it was inevitable that Indian scholars should write in English on Indian music, aiming their interpretations at Western or Westernized readers. By far the most effective and brilliant exponent of Indian art, including music, was Ananda K. Coomaraswamy, whose writings are as remarkable for their depth of investigation and reflection as for their masterly exposition.

Excluding works which have mainly employed Asian themes in a purely Western idiom to provide for novelty or colour, such as *Lakme* by the French composer Delibes or *Madame Butterfly* by Puccini, there have been a number of Western composers, such as Gustav Holst, Albert Roussel, Oliver Messiaen, Paul Dukas, Vincent d'Indy, and Florent Schmitt, whose interest in Indian music has been serious and artistic. Richard Wagner (1813–1883) was indebted to Indian music, especially for his theory of the "leading motive," *leitmotiv.*[54] He had been influenced by Indian thought, especially Buddhism, and probably was familiar with Asian music through Latin translations and conversations with the German philosopher Schopenhauer on the subject.

Maurice Delage and Albert Roussel consciously embodied the result of Indian inspiration in their work with great skill and success. Albert Roussel (1869–1937) was a French composer who visited India as a young man and spent some time at Bombay, Ellora, Jaipur, and Varanasi. The influence of this visit can be seen in two of his major works, *Evocations* and *Padmavati.* The first is a work in three movements and is inspired by his recollections of the Ellora Caves, Jaipur (or Udaipur?); and Varanasi and the River Ganga. The second work is an opera-ballet in two acts which deals with the story of the legendary Queen of Chittor. The general treatment of the work is in the romantic heroic model of Western opera, but there are many instances, such as rhythms in 5/4 and 7/4, which testify to Roussel's deep interest in the melodic and rhythmic devices of Indian music. One of the songs, sung by Nakamati, is supposed to be based on an Indian melody. Various other melodic passages—modal in character—and their harmonic treatment have also been affected by Indian rhythmic devices. Maurice Delage, known for his study of and admiration for Indian music, incorporated his Indian inspiration in *Quatre Poems Hindous* and *Raga Mallika*. Gustav Holst, who studied Sanskrit seriously, dealt with Indian themes in his fine settings of the *Hymns from the Rig Veda,* the settings of several songs from Kalidasa, and two operas *Sita* and *Savitri,* based on a well-known Indian legend.

Indian music has apparently come to fill a need in Western art, and provide inspiration to Western composers who are looking beyond the Western heritage for fresh stimulus. Not unnaturally they find the highly developed, sophisticated, and complex Indian melodies very attractive. Amongst such composers are Oliver Messiaen, Henry Cowell, Colin McPhee, Alan Hovhannes, and Peggy Glanville-Hicks. Henry Cowell, amongst other works, has written a *Madras Symphony* dedicated to the Music Academy of Madras. Peggy Glanville-Hicks' opera, *The Transposed Heads,* based on a story by Thomas Mann which, in turn, was based on an Indian tale, stimulated an exciting controversy on the validity of its form when it was produced in New York. The composer had reversed the traditional basis of composition, and instead of using melody and harmony as structural assets, with minimal rhythm, she used melody and rhythm as the basic structural elements underscoring the harmony, thus to some extent following the Indian system.

A modern Indian scholar of Western music, Kaikhosru Sorabji, points out that although there has been little understanding of Indian classical music, the rhythm of which is far too subtle and complex "to be transcribed so as to be within the technical and musical capacities of suburban drawing rooms," the attraction and awe of Asian culture, religion, and philosophy is so great for Westerners that Asian themes are accepted with alacrity by many of them. It is, therefore, not so much in the adoption of these themes and in superficial extremes that the influence of Indian music is felt, but rather "in rhythmic intricacy, in richness and efflorescence of elaborate detail, in abundant, intricate arabesque, in melodic lines which, without imitating, suggest by their contours relationship with melodies of Oriental types."[55] There are a number of European musicians who accept Eastern inspiration without making a point of acknowledging it. For example, Claude Debussy did not consciously acknowledge his extra-European inspiration, but it is quite clear that without it certain very typical aspects of his art would have remained either undeveloped or underdeveloped, and he could not have produced such masterpieces as *L'Enfant Prodigue, L'Après-Midi, La Mer, L'Île Joyeuse,* and *Les Parfums de la Nuit:* "In all these there is a suppleness of rhythm, a richness and delicacy of colouring, and a flexibility of melodic line that shows very plainly their Asiatic affinities and sympathies."[56] Strauss' music-drama *Salome* also clearly shows marks of Asian inspiration.

In recent years, Indian music, like other forms of Indian art, has had a great revival both in India and abroad. Yehudi Menuhin has been mainly responsible for introducing Indian music to contemporary Western audiences. He went to India in 1952 on a concert tour and was immediately captivated by the music. From this time on he has taken every opportunity to write and speak of Indian music. In 1958 after Indian musicians had begun to visit Britain, Lord Harewood travelled widely in India listening to the music. In 1963 he sponsored a large-scale Indian participation at the Edinburgh Festival, and Indian music has now become one of the chief features of this annual festival.

For several years a number of leading Indian musicians have visited Western, as well as Asian, countries. Their performances have gained increasing popularity. Commenting upon the growing popularity of Indian music in the West during the Edinburgh Festival of 1963, the music correspondent of *The Times* said: "The impact of Indian music is immediate, although like any subtle art it needs a lot of understanding fully to appreciate it. I was once asked to arrange for a famous Indian musician to play at a British university, but the professor of music warned me that the performance should not be long, since the audience was not used to Indian music. After the concert, which was shorter than it need have been, the professor came up with beaming face and said 'But why didn't you tell me it would be so enjoyable?' "[57]

The advent of Indian music in the West has inspired promising young composers to weave the two musics—Indian and Western—into a new syncretic composition. For example, Mr. Peter Feuchtwanger, whose works have recently been gaining increasing recognition in the United States and Europe, has been commissioned by Yehudi Menuhin to compose a work for violin, sitar, tabla, and tambura. Menuhin himself has made a best selling record, "East meets West," in which he plays raga with Ravi Shankar. And strangely enough the emergence of pop music in Europe has led to an increase in the popularity of Indian music in the West. The Beatles, Rolling Stones, Yardbirds, and other groups have created a mounting enthusiasm for Indian music amongst young people by using the sitar in their recordings.

Inspired by Western interest in their music, Asian countries have also begun to organize international musical gatherings. In 1961 there was a major conference in Tokyo which brought together artists from both East and West. Nicholas Nabokov inspired the Tokyo conference and one of the major outcomes of it was the establishment of the International Institute for Comparative Music Studies at Berlin. Two years later, in 1963, the conference was repeated in Israel, although on a somewhat less ambitious scale. Later, Delhi became the venue of an International Festival and the first Commonwealth Arts Festival in 1965. This expanding mutual interest amongst musicians and musicologists of Europe and Asia will no doubt have wide repercussions on both sides.

Although Western interest in Indian music has been serious and continuous, recordings of Indian music are rarely found in Western homes and markets. In contrast, Indians play Western music more frequently and widely, but have made hardly any sustained study of it. Whilst European research on Indian music is meagre, there is hardly any Indian scholarship on Western music; the works of Sorabji are a rare exception. Yehudi Menuhin believes that Western music has reached a point where there is very little room left for the personal expression of the performer, and it is at this moment particularly ripe for Indian influence, which might be most helpful in

the flexibility of the tone-row, melodic freedom and invention, including ornamentation; the peculiar technique of uniting melody and pulse of Indian music; the ability to improvise with requisite training and the release of creative energies in the performers; the quality of serenity, a type of unique, exalted and personal expression of union with the infinite; and study of the incredibly complex rhythmic organisation of Indian music. The rhythmic patterns in Indian music are as determined and precise as the patterns of ornamentation, again leaving no margin for the minute ebb and flow of the individual pulse. This is a prime example of unbounded intellectual complexity holding the emotional surge in check.[58]

For a long time the invention of chess was ascribed to various peoples ranging from the Egyptians to the Welsh, and ever since the Arabs transmitted it to Europe more than a thousand years ago, it has been held in great esteem there. It commands an authority which no other board game has ever attained, and has been described as "a philosophy, a contest of mental athletics to which the very young bring an instinctive genius, and the old the distillation of their experience." The complexities of tactics and the almost unending possibilities of manoeuvre have made chess the pastime of the intellectual élite. It began as a war game to be fought between the contesting maharajas, and it was regarded in mediaeval Europe as one of seven knightly accomplishments—a release and pleasant diversion from the monotony and tedium of aristocratic life. Today, its enthusiasts belong to a common fraternity in which all class distinctions are subordinated to the supremacy of the skilled.

At first the Church frowned upon chess, but later St. Thomas Aquinas discovered in it a useful allegory of life, death, and the social structure. The black squares on the chessboard symbolized vice, the white ones virtue, and the game ended in all the pieces being swept off the board into the democracy of death. This imposed spiritual analogy possibly added to the mysterious power of the game, but, as time went on, this alien and mystical character which inhibited chess during the Middle Ages gradually vanished, and once again it assumed the role of a pleasant pastime.

It was after the discovery of Sanskrit by European scholars that the Indian ancestry of chess was realized and acknowledged, although Thomas Hyde, the first writer to deal with non-European games, suggested the Indian theory in 1694 in his *De Ludis Orientalibus*. Towards the end of the eighteenth century, Sir William Jones wrote that chess had been known to Indians in antiquity as *caturanga*, meaning the four wings of the army, which are described in the *Amarakosa* as elephants, horses, chariots, and infantry. One of the early Sanskrit texts, the *Bhavishya Purana*, contains a tale of a prince who lost all his possessions in a game of chess played with dice. Chess must indeed go deep into early Indian history, because it was associated with astronomical symbolism throughout its growth. According to H. J. R. Murray, who published his monumental study *A History of Chess* in 1913, chess descended from an earlier Indian game called *astapada*, played on a board containing 8 x 8 cells.[59] Whilst it is certain that games have travelled from one country to another, gaps in information and changes in names and rules often blur the course of diffusion.

Chaturanga was taken to Persia in the sixth century during the reign of Anushirvan (531–579) where it came to be known as *chatrang*, which according to the Arabic phonetic system became *shatranj*. The earliest reference to chess in Persia is found in the *Karnamak-i-Artakh Shatr-i-Papakan*, written about 600. In the tenth century, the poet Firdusi related a traditional story in his epic poem *Shahnama* of how chess came to Persia through an envoy of the King of Hind. Subsequently, it became known to the Arabs and also to the Byzantine court through the marriage of Khusru Parviz, the grandson of Anushirvan, to the daughter of the Byzantine Emperor Maurice. There are numerous Arabic references to chess. For example, Al Masudi, writing about 950, mentions that chess had existed possibly as long as a thousand years before his generation.

The earlier theory of the Persian origin of chess has now been discarded, because the evidence supporting the Indian theory is overwhelming. The Arabic word shatranj is not only an exact derivation of the Sanskrit chaturanga but is regarded as a foreign word by the Persians and Arabs. Furthermore, *al-fil*, the Arabic name for the bishop, means the elephant, otherwise *alephhind*, the Indian ox. From Persia the Arabs took it to Spain, and from there it spread to the court of Charlemagne about 760. It is also possible the game may have reached France from the Byzantine court for the monarchs of the two courts exchanged diplomatic missions and courtesies, and amongst the presents from the aged Empress Irene to Charlemagne was a chess set in which the two prime ministers (vazirs) had been replaced by two powerful queens. Another theory holds that chess was introduced to Europe during the period of the Crusades, but there is evidence to suggest that chess was known in Italy before the First Crusade.

From India, chaturanga travelled to China and then to Japan. The earliest reference to chess in China is found in Niu Seng-Ju's *Yu Kuai Lu* (Book of Marvels) written at the end of the eighth century. The countries of Southeast Asia learned chess both directly from India and, as in the case of Siam, indirectly through China. Modern Japanese chess is very different from its immediate parent in China, and both differ from Euorpean chess, although all share a common ancestry.

Indeed, the earliest recognizable diffusion of games from India is to China, and this is possibly a result of the spread of Buddhism from India to China. During the first millennium A.D., Indian racing games began to reach China. Karl Himly, an authority on the history of Chinese games, on the strength of a passage from the *Hun tsun su*, a work of the Sung period (960–1279), suggests that the Chinese game *k'shu-pu* was invented in western India and spread to China in the time of the Wei Dynasty (220–265). Again, according to *Wei-shu*, k'shu-pu was brought to China in ancient times from Hu country, which at the time meant a country somewhere in the vicinity of India. K'shu-pu is, in fact, the Chinese adaptation of the Indian *chatush pada* (in modern Indian language, *chaupur*). The game apparently had four other successive names in China, *wu-sho* (spear-seizing), *thshan-han* (long row), *po-lo-sai-hi,* and *shwan-liu* (double sixes). The last of these names, however, may belong to *nard,* a different game related to the Greek *table,* and which, according to a Persian tradition, was introduced into northern India towards the end of the sixth century by a Persian minister of Anushirvan. Nard is mentioned in the mediaeval Iranian romance, *Chatrang-namak* (probably written between 650 and 850), which also speaks of the introduction of chess into Iran.

However, the ninth century Arab writer, Al Yaqubi, and other early sources refer to nard as an Indian invention to illustrate man's dependence on chance and destiny. The board stands for the year; it has twenty-four points representing the hours of a day. It is divided into two halves of twelve points each, signifying the months in a year. The thirty men (*kilab*) stand for the days in a month. The two dice are day and night, and the sum of opposite faces of the dice is seven for the days of the week.[60] As this symbolism was also known to Byzantine Greeks, it is not conclusive evidence of the Indian origin of nard. But as far as China is concerned, shwan-liu was introduced from India in the seventh century, whilst wei-ki, the oldest and best of the native Chinese games, originated around 1000.[61] Cubical dice (*chhu-phu* or *yu-phy*), although found in ancient Egypt as well as in India, are generally thought to have reached China from India, possibly quite early. The prominence of the number six in the *Book of Changes* is said to have been derived from the six sides of a cubical die.

The Japanese game *sunoroku* (or *sugoroku,* backgammon), which was played at the royal court of the Nara rulers, and which is still a popular game in Japan, may well have originated in India, for it is derived from the Chinese game k'shu-pu, which as stated earlier is known in its original Indian form as *chatush-pada.*

What is perhaps more significant is that the dice used in Japan today —cubes, each six-faced, numbered one to six—have exactly the same form as the dice found amongst the relics of the Indus Valley civilization.[62] The significance of this point becomes greater when it is noted that dice are marked similarly throughout the world from ancient times. But the Indus dice, cubical or tabular and made of pottery, were marked, except in one example from Harappa, not so that the sum of two opposite sides is seven as they are today, but rather, with one opposite two, three opposite four, and five opposite six.

Indian games appear to have reached as far west as ancient Mexico. Writing in 1881, Edward Tylor, the first important exponent of parallelism in cultural development, pointed out that the ancient and popular Mexican game of *patolli* was very similar to the Indian *pachisi,* and concluded that it must have come from Asia. Pachisi is a very popular game in India with almost all classes of people. Mogul emperors, especially the great Akbar, were very fond of the game and played it with all the regal trimmings on courts made of inlaid marble, the remains of which can still be seen at Agra and elsewhere. Patolli also was popular with the Mexican aristocracy as well as the peasantry. Mexican gamesters would walk about with their patolliztli mat and markers, and the Emperor Montezuma reputedly watched his nobles playing at court. Addicted to gambling, the Mexicans were also passionately fond of another dice game, *tlachtli.*

About seventeen years after Tylor, Stewart Culin showed that even the cosmic meaning of the Mexican game, its relation to the four quarters of the world and to the colours ascribed to them, was essentially the same as in pachisi, particularly in its Burmese variation. Kroeber, who did not find much evidence of contact between India and ancient America, conceded that the mathematical probability of the two games being invented separately, agreeing by chance in so many specific features, was very low. Also, the close correspondence between the rules of the two games does indicate a firm connection.

Pachisi, in fact, is played all over the world, and, as expected, it has acquired certain local characteristics and is called by different names in different countries. However, its Indian ancestry is easily proved. In Burma it is known as *pasit,* in Somaliland *bakkis,* in Persia *pachis,* in Arabia *barjis,* and in Spain *parchis.* In Britain it is popularly known as Ludo, a modified version of the Indian pachisi, having been patented and introduced in 1896.[63]

Chapter VII

ROMANIES:

LORDS OF THE OPEN COUNTRY

ROMANIES, or Gypsies as they are popularly known, had their origin in India. They are the descendants of tribes who left the banks of the Indus, traversed a number of intervening countries over a period of centuries, and arrived in Europe more than five hundred years ago. For a long time they were mistakenly believed to have come from Egypt and the word "gypsy"—a misnomer—is a derivative of Egyptian. Today there are six million or more Gypsies scattered throughout Europe and North and South America.[1] They are found throughout Asia and Africa and there are even isolated bands in Australia and New Zealand. Their love of nature and liberty is unrivalled in history. These gay, colourful, unique, and somewhat mysterious people wander about the world in small groups never demonstrating a definite pattern of movement. Romanticized for their music, dancing, and folklore, they are a people with identity but no nationality, political rights or freedoms, written history, art or science, or any international organization, agency, or movement to plead for them.[2]

Despite their significant contributions to European cultural life over a period of centuries, Europe on the whole has not accepted them with kindness. They have been frequently persecuted throughout the period of their known history. The Nazis alone killed about half a million Gypsies in concentration camps for the sole crime of possessing an irrepressible urge for freedom and an attitude of defiance against any kind of regimentation.[3] The very presence of such a group in their midst made the Nazis uneasy. Other European countries also have a sordid record of Gypsy-persecution. Whatever their faults, the Gypsies did not come into Europe as bandits or as tramps. They have always been skilled in metal work and music and dancing. At worst, Gypsies have been guilty of trivial crimes, such as theft without violence, generally involving items of food and clothing—much less serious crimes than are common occurrences amongst most advanced and modernized communities.

Soon after their arrival in Europe they were characterized as a people who spoke a strange language and practiced sorcery. The peasants were alarmed and the state officials in towns disturbed by their presence. In 1427 the Bishop of Paris excommunicated them and they were driven out of the city. They were blamed elsewhere, as they are even today, for thefts, exactions, and black magic, but above all for being foreigners. The Parliament of Paris ordered their expulsion in 1539. In 1560 the Estates General of Orleans called upon "all those imposters known by the name of Bohemians or Egyptians to leave the Kingdom under penalty of the galleys."[4] The decree was applied with extreme severity, and penalties, ranging from cutting off ears to hanging and "breaking on the wheel," were carried out indiscriminately and expeditiously. There are many other early accounts which refer to similar repressive laws and punishments. No matter how hard it is for us to imagine the dark depths of superstition and fear that prevailed in Europe at the time, the ruthless persecution of Gypsies must invite severe comment.

The period when the Gypsies first appeared in Germany was fraught with extraordinary events: the coming of the Black Death, the quarrels of the three Popes, the burning alive of John Huss, and the Battle of Agincourt. These tragedies, epidemics, and scourges of nature were attributed to Gypsies. The Reichstag held at Speyer in 1489, regarding them as "traitors to Christian countries," ordered their banishment from the Rhineland and the Palatinate. The Prince Elector of Mainz even congratulated himself for having put to death all the male Gypsies in his region, and for flogging and branding their women and children.[5] In the sixteenth century in Bavaria alone, hundreds of peaceable Gypsies, including children, were put to death by torture and fire on charges of witchcraft and communion with spirits. In 1724 in Beyreuth, fifteen Gypsy women, aged from fifteen to ninety-eight, were hanged in a single day. Two years later, Charles VI ordered the death of all male Gypsies in Austria. In the early eighteenth century, Gypsies were arrested on sight, flogged and branded, and if found again put to death without mercy.

In Spain their persecution was equally harsh. They were banished by royal edict under threat of terrible penalties as early as 1499. Later in Toledo in 1523, and in Madrid in 1528 and 1534, edicts revived this order and threatened the *Gitanos* with the galleys. But many hid in caves and avoided the merciless persecution of Ferdinand, Charles V, and Philip II. The Spanish kings made many laws for what they regarded as the protection of their subjects from pernicious people. "Perhaps there is no country in which more laws have been framed," wrote George Borrow, "having in view the extinction and suppression of the Gypsy name, race, and manner of life, than Spain."[6] It was during their successive banishments from Spain that many Gypsies temporarily overcame their fear of the sea, sailed for South America, and penetrated into Brazil, Peru, and Chile. Later a somewhat more liberal policy was introduced—they were to be called neo-Castilian—and Gypsies in Spain multiplied with surprising rapidity. They were, however, not permitted to use their own language, Romani, or to wander about the country. This prohibition is still in force and, discriminatory as it appears, it did force many of them to settle down. Since 1873 they have been allowed to do more or less what they please in Spain.

Poland, Sweden, Norway, and Denmark also tried to expel Gypsies from their territories. In Romania they were enslaved and forced to work under inhuman conditions without any wage except a small meal of maize porridge. In addition, they were flogged naked, for little or no reason, and iron hooks were fixed in their necks as a punishment and to prevent them from sleeping. There were slave markets where Gypsies were sold by public auction in groups or whole families. It was only in 1852 that slavery ended and their situation improved somewhat.

In Hungary and in Transylvania also, Gypsies were forced into slavery. Under the pretext that the Gypsies had committed heinous crimes, charges never supported by evidence, the authorities imposed unspeakable penalties on them. In 1782 the Hungarians hanged, beheaded, or broke on the wheel forty-one Gypsy men and women. Others were driven by soldiers into dangerous swamps to die by drowning.[7] Yet, in Hungary Gypsies enjoyed, in the midst of slavery, more freedom than anywhere else.

Gypsies were also severely persecuted in Britain, and it was infinitely more difficult for them to escape detection there, because England has little wilderness to offer as means of escape or protection. They arrived there some time in the middle of the fifteenth century and quickly dispersed throughout the British Isles. (How, with their fear of water, they crossed the North Sea or the English Channel is somewhat of a puzzle.) For a while the Gypsies remained unmolested, but during the reign of Henry VIII severe measures were taken against them. In 1537 Lord Thomas Cromwell, the keeper of the Privy Seal, advocated the wholesale banishment or execution of Gypsies, and a dreadful campaign of persecution was begun. Merely being a Gypsy was esteemed a crime worthy of death, and "the gibbets of England groaned and creaked beneath the weight of Gypsy carcasses, and the miserable survivors were literally obliged to creep into the earth in order to preserve their lives."[8] During the reign of Elizabeth I (1558–1603), who accused the Gypsies, amongst other misdeeds, of hiding priests and emissaries of Rome, even more extreme measures were introduced. In 1563 they were ordered to leave the country within three months under penalty of death. As late as 1882, by an Act of Parliament, all persons purporting to be Gypsies, telling fortunes, wandering abroad, or lodging under tents or carts were to be treated as rogues and vagabonds. Legal discrimination against the Gypsies continued in Britain in varying degrees until the beginning of this century. In 1908 the laws were relaxed and they were given relative freedom and accommodation to settle down to their traditional life and culture. However, a strong prejudice still exists in parts of Britain, and "No Gypsies Served" is a sign openly displayed in the windows of many English village inns today.

In Scotland, after a brief period in the sixteenth century during which they were in favour with the kings, Gypsies were condemned in 1573 as murderers, thieves, and sorcerers, and their execution was sought. The Privy Council of Scotland promulgated a decree giving Gypsies the choice between sedentary work and expulsion. In 1597 an Act of Parliament was passed, which was reaffirmed in 1600, authorizing the government to punish Gypsies along with vagabonds and beggars with penal servitude for life. In 1627 all Gypsies were ordered to be forcibly recruited into the army, and in 1665 they were to be banished to the West Indies, Jamaica, and Barbados. In 1715 nine Scottish Gypsies were transported to Virginia, and they appear to be the first British Gypsies in America, the forerunners of the many thousands now living there. France deported Gypsies to America; Portugal and Spain sent them to Africa and South America. Britain also banished Gypsies to Australia. In fact, deportation appears to have been a common practice, and at one time or another almost every European country deported Gypsies to distant lands.

In Russia, however, Gypsies did not encounter any serious hostility, although life for them must have been harsh in the wintry vastness. They are mentioned as being in Russia since 1500, and there are no records of oppression or persecution under either the Tsarist or Soviet régime. On the contrary, there seems to have been a bond of friendliness between Russians and the Gypsies. Local governments in Russia are known to have made sincere efforts to integrate them into a settled life, although they were not completely successful. Gypsies continued to wander about the country unmolested for some time, although since 1956 they have been prohibited by law from leading a nomadic life. In Russia, Gypsy music and dance have always enjoyed popular, as well as aristocratic, appreciation, and today in Moscow there is a Gypsy theatre, "Romen," and the study of their culture is encouraged.

During the nineteenth century, although generally less persecuted in Europe than before, Gypsies were automatically regarded as criminals. They were accused of kidnapping children, suspected of sorcery, and invariably treated with scant justice. Even today they are looked upon with extreme suspicion, apprehension, and contempt. A stereotyped image of the Gypsies dominates the thinking about them. No people in history have been made to suffer what they have. Suffering is so much a part of their life that a Gypsy proverb designates it as "a badge of honour."9

Existing knowledge about Gypsies is hopelessly inadequate and this ignorance has resulted in either unreasonable fear, prejudice, and antagonism, or in the myth of the noble savage. Articles, newspaper reports, or television programs seldom attempt a true representation of their life and history. They are, perhaps, victims of their determined refusal to lead a settled life, believing that those who are prejudiced against them have no understanding or appreciation of their adherence to true liberty. No wonder the Spanish novelist, Miguel de Cervantes, who was familiar with Gypsy life and culture, acclaimed the Gypsies in his *La Gitanilla* as "the Lords of the Universe, of fields, fruits, crops, forests, mountains, of rivers and springs, of the stars and all the elements."

In spite of persecution, hostility, and apathy, the Gypsies could not be exterminated or even subdued for any length of time. They have survived all over the world; have remained the happiest, gayest, and the most light-hearted of people; have achieved a gigantic migration without losing their identity; and represent an exceptional example of a well-defined cultural group. It is almost incredible that the group of over a hundred which first appeared in Germany in 1417 should have not only survived but grown into the millions spread throughout the world today.

If settled peoples hold them in contempt, the Gypsies reciprocate the attitude in equal measure, but they most dislike those amongst themselves who desert the realm of open space. Their stock of abusive epithets, mainly reserved for the semi-settled Gypsies, is quite rich, and they have derogatorily designated non-Gypsies as *gadjo* or *gaujo* (peasant, yokel, bumpkin, or clodhopper). English Gypsies call half-breeds *posh-rat*, and less than half-blood Gypsies and vagrants *didakyai*. Muslim Gypsies of the Balkans call Christian Gypsies *das* (Sanskrit *dasa*, infidel, non-Aryan). Whilst they themselves infiltrate everywhere, they allow little penetration from the outside. They consider themselves superior to all other peoples, unequalled in purity, health, and wisdom, and zealously guard the purity of their Romany blood. A Gypsy marrying a non-Gypsy is excluded from the Romany community for all time, and children of mixed marriages cannot even call themselves Roms.

A Gypsy on the road knows the taste of real liberty and he regards modern man as little more than a mere cog in a gigantic machine tied to money, convention, and a timetable. Throughout the centuries Gypsies have fought, lied, cheated, and suffered numerous humiliations and penalties to retain their own individuality, language, and cultural identity.

Attempts have been made in the past, and are still being made, to turn Gypsies into useful citizens, to show them the advantages of education and fixed employment, to integrate them in settled societies, and to rehabilitate them. Maria Theresa, the Empress of Austria, initiated a movement to integrate Gypsies into European society in 1761. She called them New Hungarians, but her efforts were largely unsuccessful. Later nineteenth-century efforts were somewhat more successful: Archduke Joseph of Prussia set up Gypsy settlements, and Catherine II of Russia gave them crown lands. In Britain Gypsy societies were founded for their reform and education. In central Europe today they receive special encouragement, scholarships for education, and consideration in employment. In a ceremonious procession in Delhi, Nehru led these "followers of Rana Pratap," a liberty loving king of Rajasthan who suffered a homeless existence in preference to submission and a life of comfort and riches, to free allotments of land on the outskirts of the city. But their love for open spaces has been far too deep to be easily uprooted. Or perhaps it is their pride in being different from the rest of mankind and their unwillingness to make concessions that have enabled them to survive both repressive measures and encouragements to incorporate themselves in a community. Their persistent refusal to align themselves with non-Gypsies baffles European sociology just as it humbles non-Gypsy pride. Even today the majority of Gypsies are relentless nomads, although there are some, especially in Britain and eastern and central Europe, who live a partially settled life in villages or suburbs. But they too hasten to take to the road during fine weather.[10]

The genealogy of the Gypsies is highly complex, but they are divided into three principal tribal groups—the *Kalderash*, the *Gitanos*, and the *Manush* (also called the *Sinti*). Outside these major groups there are other Gypsies, as distinct from non-Gypsy nomads, as for example those in Britain who appear to resemble all three in part but none wholly. Charles Duff places the British Gypsies into a fourth category of their own. All these groups are authentic Romanies, and are generally of dark appearance with black hair, white teeth, brown eyes, and supple gait, except the Kalderash, many of whom have fair skin and some even blue eyes and fair hair. The Kalderash, who came westward from eastern Europe and now live mainly in northern and northwestern Europe, and the Manush, who wander about generally in Germany, France, and Italy, consider themselves the oldest and the best; the former even look upon themselves as the only "true" Romanies. The Gitanos, called *Gitanes* in France, are mainly concentrated in Spain and France, with an offshoot called *Ciganos* in Portugal. This differentiation is of Gypsy origin, and each group seeks to project an inflated image of themselves. They speak diverse dialects and rarely intermarry. In spite of the dispersion of their groups and lack of uniformity in many of their customs, all Gypsies regard themselves as one people and are very proud of their race:

> I wouldn't be a noble
> My birth is no disgrace
> I'd rather be a Gypsy,
> The same as all my race.[11]

The basic language of all Gypsies is Romani, although each group inevitably grafted on the foreign idiom, vocabularies, and pronunciation through centuries of living in various countries.[12] Although Gypsies have never had a written language and have retained the tradition of their language by word of mouth over generations, they have kept it relatively pure. The social customs and manners, taboos and superstitions, laws and religious beliefs, and their *patrin* (or *patteran*), although varying from group to group, are fundamentally the same.

Few scholars today doubt that the original home of the Gypsies was India. Whilst the case for their Indian origin is overwhelming, it is not definitely known when they first began to leave India and under what circumstances and on what scale they did, or were compelled to do so.

240

Nor has it been settled exactly where in India they originated, just as it is uncertain that Gypsies were originally a nomadic people. Jan Kochanowski, a Gypsy scholar, has recently suggested that they were not nomads in the beginning.[13] Should this be accepted as historically valid, it will substantially affect prevalent ideas of Gypsy history and sociology. Indian history is very indifferent on the subject, and the paucity of relevant material is disconcerting.[14] The Indian aspects of Gypsy history must be extremely fascinating and instructive, but they remain obscure and complex.

Considering that there are many Greek words in the Gypsy language, and that all Gypsies still count in Greek, Verovici is of the opinion that the first exodus of the Gypsies from India happened at the time of Alexander's invasion. On the other hand, Grellmann believed that the Gypsies had been driven out of India by Timur and his savage hordes at the end of the fourteeth century. This view appears to rely partly on a reference to Gypsies made by Arab Shah in a chapter of his biography of Timur, which is a classic in Arabic literature. But this reference describes not only some curious details of Gypsy life in Samarkand, but also their extermination by Timur because the Gypsies were constantly rising in rebellion against him. Since Timur had annihilated the Gypsy population of Samarkand before he invaded Indian territory, the theory that his invasion caused the wandering of the Gypsies must be abandoned. Moreover, this theory is contradicted by the evidence of the existence of Gypsies in Europe before this date.

According to Jan Kochanowski, Gypsies were the original survivors of the army of the famous Chauhan Rajput ruler of Delhi, Prithvi Raj, after its disastrous defeat by the forces of Muhammad Ghori in 1192. They carried out guerilla campaigns against the Ghorid rulers for some time from their mountain resorts and jungle hideouts, but were not victorious and lost most of their men. The remaining few split into three groups, one of which left India through Afghanistan to Europe, founding the modern group of Gypsies, whilst the other two remained in India and mingled with the peasants and artisans.

Another theory holds that the Gypsies came to Europe from India through Persia. The Persian poet, Firdusi, mentions in his *Shah Namad* that about the year 420 the Sassanian King of Persia, Bahram Gur, requested Shankhala, the Maharaja of India, to send him people capable of entertaining his poor subjects whose lives were miserable without music and amusements. Soon Bahram Gur had collected twelve thousand Indian musicians, men and women alike, to amuse his people. The Indians were assigned land and given facilities to cultivate it. But the musicians neglected agriculture, consumed the corn seed, and incurred the wrath of the Persian King, who seized their musical instruments and commanded them to roam the country earning their living by singing.

The accuracy of Firdusi's narrative may be coloured with some literary imagination, but his account is supported by the Arab historian, Hamza of Isfahan, who wrote in 940, about half a century earlier than Firdusi. Both writers called these musicians by terms which later came to mean Gypsies. Firdusi uses the ordinary Persian word *Luri*, and Hamza the word *Zott*, which is merely the common Arabic pronunciation of the Indian word *Jat*, and which is also one of the modern Syrian words for Gypsies. It is possible that Firdusi borrowed the episode from Hamza. His account, nevertheless, testifies to the presence of Indian musicians in western Asia from early times. The Arab conquest of Sind in the eighth century may have provided further impetus to Indian artists and entertainers to travel westward.

Charles Leland, who identifies the Gypsies with the Jats of northern India, suggests that they were taken away in large numbers as slaves by Mahmud of Ghazni during his Indian invasions. Mahmud, having later acquired fairer slaves from Persia, released many of his Indian captives, who then wandered westward. This theory, however, does not explain why the prisoners chose to wander westward upon their release rather than return home. An explanation, if the story is true, may perhaps be sought in the caste structure of Hindu society. The released slaves, who by the rigid code of caste may have performed prohibited deeds, would have had little hope of rehabilitating themselves in Hindu society. Disinclined to return, and detached from their natural habitat, they may have opted for the life of freedom without losing their identity.

In Arab chronicles there are frequently references to wandering tribes called Zotts. Evidence is also found of a tribe of roaming cattle breeders, who lived long ago at the mouth of the Indus, and who raised their tents wherever their black water buffaloes could graze. The Arabs tried several times to conquer them, but were driven back each time.

Under Walid (705–715), during whose reign the Arabs landed in Spain, the Zotts agreed to terms of peace but Walid later realized that their loyalty could not be relied upon. In 710 he took a great many of them prisoner and led them to the borders of the Tigris in Kurdistan. Six years later, under Yazid II, still more prisoners were transported to Antioch with their cattle and tents. About a century later, in 820, the Zotts had become so powerful that they defied the Arab power and for fourteen years waged a continuous war against the Arab armies, inflicting heavy losses and capturing a great quantity of booty. It was only after long and costly warfare that the Zotts were subdued by the Arabs under Al Motasim in 834. The Arab commander took about twenty-seven thousand prisoners—men, women, and children—with him to Baghdad and then deported them, first to Khanikin, northeast of Baghdad, and then to Ainzarba and to other places on the northern frontier of Syria.

In 856 the Byzantians, called the "Rums," captured Ainzarba from the Arabs and took the Zotts prisoner. The year 856 is the approximate date of the first appearance of Gypsies in Byzantine territory. That the Byzantians were called Rums and that the Gypsies later called themselves Roms may be significant, or pure coincidence. But the whole episode is too well authenticated and well knit to be lightly dismissed. This evidence indicates that the migration of the Gypsies from India occurred during or before the eighth century, and that in the ninth century Gypsies were living in Lower Mesopotamia. This is supported by Byzantine records, which speak of a people closely resembling Gypsies, called *Athinganoi* (or *Azingahoi*), who are characterized as magicians, and who were living in Constantinople about 810. About two hundred years later a Georgian monk noted the arrival at Mount Athos of a group of people, *Atisincani,* who were forthwith styled as "sorcerers and thieves."

John Sampson seems to have come to the conclusion that the Gypsies were in Persia before 900.[15] He believed that in Persia they divided into two bands: the one, called *Ben* Gypsies, travelled southward into Syria and became the ancestors of the present Gypsies of Syria, Palestine, Egypt, Persia, and Transcaucasia; and the other, the *Phen* Gypsies, first settled in Armenia and then migrated westward through Byzantine Greece.

Other philologists, such as Miklosich, believe, however, that Gypsies could not have left India before 1000 because the evolution of the modern Indian languages, with which Romani is associated, did not take place until that date. Whilst serious consideration must be given to such opinions, it cannot be overlooked, as Sampson argued, that the huge gap between the break up of the Prakrits and our first knowledge of the modern languages does not allow any positive statement to be made in this respect. In fact, Miklosich himself did not altogether reject the possibility of an earlier Gypsy exodus from India. At a time when modern Indian dialects were taking definite shape, the Gypsies may have taken with them the germ of corruption and developed an analytic form of language similar to that of the other Indian idioms. A contemporary scholar, Brian Vesey-Fitzgerald, whilst claiming no expertise in philology and not denying the Indian origin of Gypsies, does not quite accept the accuracy of the dates advanced by the experts. For philologists "are at work on something, an indefinite something at that, which happened at least eight hundred years ago, before the earliest of them set to work. Can they be definite to a century or two or three?"[16] The bulk of opinion, however, accepts the view that their dispersion began somewhere about the tenth century.

Whilst the date and manner of the Gypsy exodus from India remain somewhat uncertain, there is relatively better evidence available regarding the times of their recorded appearances in the various countries of the West. These records, however, cannot exclude the possibility that the Gypsies may have been in Europe long before official mention was made of them.

For some time the generally accepted date for the first appearance of the Gypsies in Europe was 1417 when a small band of men and women were discovered in Germany at Luneburg, bearing letters of safe conduct from various princes, such as Emperor Sigismund, and the King of Hungary. In that year Gypsies were also noticed in other parts of Europe, in Moldavia, Hungary, and Switzerland. But there is a good deal of evidence that they had been in Europe for quite a while before this date.[17] Their leaders bore Christian names, such as Andrew, Michael, and Thomas, which suggests a long stay amongst Christian peoples and nations. Gypsies may have reached Spain or Bohemia, part of present-day Czechoslovakia, before the fourteenth century, or the lower Balkans as early as the eleventh century.[18] They were certainly on the Greek island of Corfu early in the fourteenth century, which would mean that the Italians had come into contact with them quite early, for the island belonged to Venice from 1401 to 1797.[19] Indeed, it is known from a Venetian Viceroy, Otkaviano Buono, that there were Gypsies in Peloponnesus even before the end of the fourteenth century, for some time about 1395 he confirmed the privileges granted to the *Acingani* of Nauplion by his predecessors. At about the same time there is evidence of the presence of Gypsies in Moldavia and Wallachia. In 1387 Mircen I, Prince of Wallachia, renewed a grant that had been made by his uncle Vladislav to the monastery of St. Anthony at Voditza of forty *salaschi* (tents or families) of Atsegane.

Bataillard, who held the opinion that the Gypsies had reached Europe in prehistoric times and that it was they who had brought the knowledge of metallurgy to Europe, sought to prove that the alien people known as *Bemische*, living in the bishopric of Wurzburg before 1400, were Gypsies. Also, in 1348 Gypsies were present in Serbia. The records and town accounts of the fifteenth century contain notices of payments made to Gypsies in Central Europe.[20] There were Gypsy settlements at Hildesheim in 1407, at Basle in 1414, and at Meissen in 1416. From that time on, there is no scarcity of records.

By 1438 thousands of Gypsies had begun to pour into Europe over-running Germany, Italy, and France. They were highly disciplined and well led, and they travelled with astonishing speed. They reached France in 1419, arriving in Paris in 1427, in Britain about 1430, in Spain by 1447, and in Russia in 1500.[21] And within a few years of their arrival, measures were being taken in every country for their suppression and banishment.

Inevitably these people, who suddenly descended at about the same time, were called by different names in different countries, although they were most commonly known as Gypsies, Bohemians, and at one time Saracens. They were called Assyrians or Ethiopians in England, Ismaelites in Hungary and Romania, *Tatern* (Tartars) in Germany, *Taltera* in Sweden—remarkably close to the name of a tribe of smiths in northern India called *Tathera*—Pagans in Bavaria and the Low Countries, Wanderers in Arab countries, Philistines in Poland, *Luri* in Iraq, *Karaki* and *Zangi* in Persia, *Caraque* and *Romanichel* in France, *Cinghames* or *Tchinganes* in Turkey and Syria, and *Katsiveloi, Tsiganos, Atsincanoi,* or *Athinganoi* in Greece.[22] Most of these epithets were employed to point them out as foreigners and heretics.

There are some obvious and close resemblances between the Jewish *diaspora* and the Gypsy dispersion. No other human migration in history can be compared with these two. Both peoples were reputedly compelled under a curse to wander about indefinitely. Both have been persecuted throughout history and both have, in spite of it, stoutly managed to preserve their distinctive identity. In a way the Gypsy diaspora has been far more widespread even than that of the Jews. Inspired by such superficial similarities, a relationship between the two has been suggested, but this theory has never left the sphere of hypothesis or found any valid support. Apart from a variety of differences of language and culture, the Jews have never shunned sedentary civilization and have integrated themselves into the national cultures of the lands of their adoption.

For several centuries after their first appearance in Europe, no systematic study was made of the Romanies, and the history and culture of these people remained heavily overlaid by a variety of myths, legends, and fantastic hypotheses. It seems incredible that a people should have lived so long in Europe, suffering general contempt and state persecution, and yet not have attracted academic curiosity and attention. But then Europe itself was in a state of transition and intellectual rejuvenation, and was not well equipped, until the rise of comparative philology, to seriously examine the Gypsy problem.

Some scholars of the Bible regarded Gypsies as the cursed descendants of Cain, whereas others claimed Egyptian origin for them. But in either of these views there is little evidence of a non-legendary nature. A major reason for attributing Egyptian origin to the Gypsies may well have been the inexplicable mediaeval European custom of dubbing all travelling showmen and mountebanks as "Egyptians." With the passage of time, it is not unlikely that the real usage of the term Egyptian was forgotten, making it possible for its literal meaning to give rise to an erroneous belief. A few of the Gypsy legends speak of their Egyptian origins, but it is doubtful if these legends were invented by the Gypsies themselves. A people who had lost all definite recollection of their past during their wanderings might easily incorporate the commonly held belief of their origin in some of their stories. In any case, such legends are few and not very definite. If early generations of Gypsies knew their exact origins, they did not transmit the knowledge to their descendants. When they first appeared in Germany, however, they claimed to have come from Lower Egypt, doing penance, by a seven years' wandering, for the sin of their forefathers, who had refused hospitality to the Virgin and Child.

Other legends pointing to their origin in the regions of Mesopotamia and ancient Asia also do not withstand serious scrutiny.[23] In contrast, however, Gypsy legends identifying India as the country of their origin are far more numerous and carefuly preserved. In Gypsy lore India is commonly referred to as the *Baro Than* (the Great Land). One of their legends, told with slight regional variations, claims their antiquity in India as far back as the invasion of Alexander. They had to leave India under the curse of a sorcerer, who condemned them to wander over the face of the earth forever, never to sleep twice in the same place, never to drink water twice from the same well, and never to cross the same river twice in one year. There are also some old Persian legends which tell of a people called *Mutes* coming from India before the time of Alexander.

Of all the evidence linking the Gypsies with India, the linguistic one is the most important. Andrew Borde, an eccentric physician who lived during the reign of Henry VIII, was the first person to make a vocabulary of the Gypsy language in 1542 under the mistaken belief that it was the current language of Egypt. In 1597 Bonaventura Valcanius, in his curious book *De Literis et Lingua Getarum*, also gave specimens of Romani as Nubian. But it was in the eighteenth century that the increasing contact with India led scholars to notice linguistic similarities between the Romani and Indian languages; to investigate deeper into the origins, manners, and customs of Gypsies; and finally to fix India as their original home. It was a fortunate accident of history that a Calvinist cleric at Almas in Hungary, Stefan Valyi, met three Indian students from Malabar whilst he was studying at the University of Leiden and noticed the close resemblances between their language and that of the Romanies of his country. He drew up a vocabulary of one thousand Indian words, put it before some Gypsies at Raab, and found that they understood most of it. The publication of his unexpected, although very important, discovery in 1763 gave rise to further investigation which shattered the theory of the Romanies' Egyptian origin, although it did not remove the possibility that they might have come to Europe by way of Egypt. J. C. Rüdiger published his discoveries regarding the Indian origin of Romanies in a book entitled *Neuester Zuwachs der Sprachkunde* in 1782. He was followed a year later by H. M. G. Grellmann, whose much more copious work firmly established the Indian origin of Gypsies. It was translated into English at the beginning of this century and has passed through three editions.

According to John Sampson, however, it was an English scholar, Jacob Bryant—and not Rüdiger—who was the earliest to discover the Indian origin of the Romanies.[24] It was not until 1844–45, however, when the German philologist, August Friedrich Pott, who strangely enough had never come into contact with Gypsies, published his famous work, *Die Zijeuner in Europa und Asien,* that the foundations for really scientific, especially linguistic, research into the Gypsy question were laid. In consequence, the theory of the Indian origin of the Gypsies came to be systematically investigated and increasingly accepted. The study of the Gypsy language was greatly helped by the development of comparative philology, which came into vogue after the discovery of Sanskrit in the early nineteenth century. Later, Alexandros Georgios Paspates (usually called Paspati), Max Müller, Weislocki, von Sowa, Kopernicki, Franz Miklosich, A. C. Woolner, and a host of other scholars who were primarily philologists, agreed in assigning the birthplace of the Romani language to India.

A major study was made by Paspati and published in 1870. He was a Greek doctor of medicine but had devoted much of his life to the study of the Gypsies, the *Tshinghanes,* of the Ottoman Empire. He believed that the true history of Gypsies, especially in the absence of written history and definite oral traditions, was to be found in their language. The language of the Gypsies in Turkey was a kind of half-way house in the path of evolution of the Romani language from India to the West. Hence, Paspati's able study proved to be of great value to the students of Romani. Between 1872 and 1881, the Austrian philologist, Franz Miklosich, published his monumental studies on Gypsies, specializing in Romani dialects.

Meanwhile, George Borrow, in his novels *Lavengro* and *The Romany Rye,* published about 1845, and in *The Gypsies in Spain,* had told the public for the first time much about this subject, and his influence was great both in England and on the European mainland in awakening an interest in Gypsy history and culture.

John Sampson (1862–1931) was an eminent comparative philologist and a sound classical scholar who devised an excellent phonetic alphabet for writing spoken Welsh Romani. He devoted a lifetime of study to the Gypsy language, and it took him thirty-two years of painstaking effort before he could publish his work on Welsh Romani in 1926, *The Dialect of the Gypsies of Wales.* This was a major landmark in the study of the subject, because the Gypsies of Wales preserved the purity of their traditions most loyally, so much so that "they are almost the only ones in the world to use Romani language in a state of purity, including grammar and syntax." Thus, philologists after careful research spread over a century established a definite identity between the various dialects of the Romani.[25] They also established a certain relationship amongst Romani, Sanskrit, and the modern Indian languages. The resemblances are so close and so numerous that even a non-specialist can detect them. More than half of the fundamental vocabulary of Romani is related to languages spoken today in northern India. Romani grammar and vocabulary cannot be explained except by Sanskrit.

However, there is no general agreement on the exact locality of the origin of Romani in India. Miklosich, in his *Beitrage Zur Kenntniss der Zigeunermundarten* in 1878, argued that Romani had some kinship with the Dard and Kafir dialects. His view was followed by Pischel and later by J. Block in the brilliant introduction to his *Formation de la Langue Marathe.* Sampson, however, opposed this connection of Romani with the Dard group. A. C. Woolner connected Romani with languages spoken farther into India and drew some striking parallels with Western Indian Pahari. In Grellmann's opinion, the original home of these people was the same as that of the Jats. Pott, Bataillard, Trumpp, and Burton also concluded that the relation between Romani and the dialect of the modern Jats was so close that there could be no doubt that the roots of Romani lay in the north of India. De Goeje, relying on Arab chronicles, believed that the Jats, Zotts, and Doms were related to Gypsies. John Beames, an Indian civil servant who was a reputed scholar of Sanskrit, considered the language more closely related to Sindi. The localities suggested ranged from the Hindu Kush Mountains area to the Indus region. A present-day authority on the Indo-European languages, Sir Ralph Turner, however, has argued that Romani originally belonged to a central Indian group of dialects and subsequently migrated to the northwestern group.[26] The problem remains unresolved mainly because knowledge of the Indian dialects of the period when the Gypsies left India is unavailable. But the fact that Romani appears to be related to several dialects may suggest that the Gypsies were already a nomadic people at the time of their departure from India.

Although the Gypsies have no system of writing, they do possess a comprehensive list of conventional signs which they use to communicate with each other. This secret code is called *patrin* and consists of items chosen from nature, such as cocks' feathers, pieces of trimmed wood, etc. These are made into signs which can be carved or drawn on trees, gates, and wood. Patrin in Romani means a leaf, and is related to Sanskrit *patra* which is variously used for designating letter and leaf. By arranging these signs in a certain way, one tribe can easily communicate with other tribes along its route of travel.

Romani is related to Sanskrit in the same way as the Romance languages are to Latin.

The following list of cardinal numbers illustrates the point:

Romani	*Hindi*	*English*
yek	ek	one
dui	do	two
trin	tin	three
star or chtar	car	four
pansh	panc	five
sho	che	six
eft (haft in Persian)	sat	seven
okht-octo	ath	eight
nu	nau	nine
dash	das	ten

The following are a few examples of Romani words with their Hindi and English equivalents:

Romani	Hindi	English
yakh	ankh	eye
yag	ag	fire
kalo	kala	black
ker	kar	to do, make
kan	kan	ear
devata	devata	deity
nak	nak	nose
bal	bal	hair
rat	rakt	blood
tud	dudh	milk
marva	marna	to die
amaro	hamara	ours
gra	ghora	horse
dant	dant	teeth
lon	lun	salt
kameva	kam	love
than	sthan	land
mas	mans	meat
tu	tum, tu	you
chib	jibh	tongue
manush	manush	man
puro	burha	old
salo	sala	brother-in-law
phen	bahin, Ghen	sister
phral	bhrata, bhai	brother
dzamutro	jamatar	son-in-law
sasro	sasur	father-in-law
sasuy	sas	mother-in-law
kak	kaka	uncle

The sentence is generally constructed in the same way in Romani and Hindi. For example:

Romani: Ja, kik kon chalavelo o vurdo.
Hindi: Ja, dekh kaun chalaaya dvar ko.
English: Go and see who has come to the door.

Romani: Main hun kalo.
Hindi: Main hun kala.
English: I am dark.

Romani: Mero sero dukkers.
Hindi: Mero sir dukhe.
English: My head aches.

Conjugations of verbs and declensions of nouns, etc., follow the Hindi pattern. The feminine ending *i* is found in both. Romani has two genders: *o* represents the masculine and *i* the feminine. For instance *boro rye,* a great man, and *bori rani,* a great lady. In Romani the feminine of *kalo* is *kali,* as in Hindi the feminine of *kala* is *kali;* in both the adjective means "black."

As in Hindi, the Gypsies use the same word (*kaliko*) for tomorrow and yesterday, which again is very close to Hindi *kal* (or *kalko*). Similarly, Gypsy *shoshoi* signifies both hare and rabbit as does Sanskrit *sasa.* The Gypsy habit of coining new words by compounding two or more words is also reminiscent of the Sanskrit *Sandhi Samasa* system. However, the Romani vocabulary is very limited, and it has few verbs.

It is inevitable that the Romani vocabulary should include a number of words from the languages of those countries through which the Gypsies wandered. There are, consequently, many words in Romani of Iranian, Greek, and Armenian origin. Furthermore, the Gypsies from the time of their arrival in Europe readily assimilated many words from Russian, German, Polish, Hungarian, and other languages. In fact, the careful scrutiny of these borrowings has been the chief means of establishing their routes of dispersion. For example, as the language of the Gypsies of Finland contains Swedish words, but not Russian, scholars have concluded that the Gypsies entered Finland from the west. The presence of over two thousand Arabic words in the Romani dialect of the Spanish Gitanos confirms their passage to Spain through Arabia and North Africa. The presence of as many as two hundred Greek words in all the European Romani dialects suggests that Gypsies spent a good deal of time in Greece before spreading over Europe.

As most legends suggest, metal working, including bronze, gold, and precious stones, has always been the principal vocation of Gypsies. It is well known that the art of metallurgy was widespread and very proficiently practiced in ancient India. Some of the tools used by Gypsies, the technique employing forge and simple goatskin bellows, and the designs they engrave are used even today by certain tribes in India. Again, the mythical association of the practice of metallurgy with the occupations of those possessed by the devil is reminiscent of Indian mythology. Gypsies are regarded in Europe today as amongst the most highly accomplished and skilled enamellers, goldsmiths, silver-

251

smiths, and blacksmiths. They are also good mechanics and motor vehicle dealers.

Fortune-telling is invariably associated with Gypsies, although only their women tell fortunes and they practice the art only on non-Gypsies. It appears that despite pronouncements of disbelief and even derision, people still flock to wandering Gypsies to listen eagerly to their forecasts. Brian Vesey-Fitzgerald testifies that he had his fortune told by Gypsies on more than one occasion with remarkable accuracy.

It is significant that the professions practiced by the Gypsies are exactly the ones which were prescribed for the outcaste in caste-ridden Indian society. If the list of curses and occupational prohibitions contained in the *Manusmriti* (the Laws of Manu) is consulted, it will be seen that Gypsies have followed precisely those occupations condemned by Manu. Trading in horses or cows; driving wagons; professional dancing, singing, or playing instruments; training elephants, bulls, horses, or camels; and gambling and professional fortune-telling were amongst the occupations forbidden to upper caste people. Those who engaged in these or similar vocations were driven into the ranks of the depressed castes or outcastes, and required to dwell in the mountains and woods. The Gypsies, however, did not adopt all the professions prohibited by Manu; they chose the ones which suited their nomadic way of life. The combination of the Gypsy occupations of smith and musician is reminiscent of some Indian tribes which occupy an unenviable lower power position in the caste hierarchy; for example, the *Ghasis*, the *Luris*, and the *Asuras*.

The code of Manu is, however, extremely complex and intricate. It classifies mixed castes and other outcastes into a wide variety of categories, and accordingly prescribes professions and other laws for each one of them. If a detailed analysis is made of the professions prohibited by Manu, as well as by other ancient Indian law-makers, and if these professions are correlated with those practiced by various Gypsy groups, some further light may be thrown on the origins of Gypsies. It is possible that they may emerge as the offspring of inter-caste marriages or of outcastes rather than the descendants of the depressed classes. The name, *Zingary*, which the Gypsies bore when they first appeared in Germany and which is still in use, is in fact a derivative of the Sanskrit word *(Varna)sankara*, meaning children of mixed castes or of adulterous union.

Since the Gypsy heritage of laws and customs was transmitted orally, its origin is naturally somewhat blurred. Yet many of them can be identified with ancient Indian practices. If they are a people who were expelled from India as outcastes, or who emigrated under priestly persecution, it is not surprising that all Gypsies have a peculiar dislike of priests. Yet, wise and learned men, called *rashey,* reminiscent of the Indian rishi, occupy, as in India, a highly esteemed place in Gypsy society. Amongst the authentic signs on the sceptre of a Gypsy tribal chief is the *trishul* (trident), the insignia of Siva. Gypsy chiefs are still called *Thakur.* They regard excommunication from the tribe, as did the Hindus from the caste, as the most severe punishment that can be inflicted.[27] An expelled Gypsy can be rehabilitated, as could a Hindu outcaste, by going through a process of repentance and restitution prescribed by the tribe elders. In both groups membership is strictly hereditary, and the collective authority of the group is supreme, exercised either by a chief or a council of elders. The elders of the tribe are addressed respectfully as *kako,* meaning uncle, a Hindi word of the same meaning. The feminine version of the tribal chief is called *phuri dai,* which in Hindi is *burhi dai,* the old lady. The Gypsy council of elders is clearly a replica of the Indian *panchayat,* and the Gypsy chief corresponds to the head of the panchayat. The Gypsy family system is a joint one, as is the Hindu, embracing parents, children, aunts, uncles, and all kinds of cousins. Likewise, property belongs to the family and not to the individual.[28]

Even in the primarily Gypsy traditions, taboos, beliefs, superstitions, social customs and manners, many Indian counterparts can be seen. The Gypsy's love for and importance attached to the horse, and the injunction against killing horses or eating horsemeat, except amongst the *Gitanos* of Spain, have parallels in several Indian tribes. Surprisingly, Gypsies are poor horsemen, despite their abilities in horse training and trading. Again, in common with many Indians, Gypsies regard dogs and cats as unclean (*mochardi*).[29] Gypsy women are also regarded as mochardi during menstruation. A pregnant Gypsy woman is treated with careful consideration, and, as suggested in the Hindu *Kama Sutra,* her women friends place beautiful picture icons of gods and goddesses within her sight in the belief that the child will be cast in a similar image of physical perfection. A woman in childbirth is regarded as unclean until the child is christened, and this ritual is somewhat similar to one prevalent amongst the primitive castes in India. Gypsy marriages are generally arranged by the parents, and early marriage is common. Both the bridegroom and the bride are customarily bashful, and, despite the European atmosphere, Gypsy courtship is extremely brief and restrained. Hindus, however, have no courtship at all. The Gypsy marriage ceremony is accompanied by elaborate ritual and feasting. Although divorce exists, Gypsy marriage is a sacred bond as is the Hindu. Sterility is the greatest misfortune possible for a Gypsy woman, and some of their ceremonial cures, such as the marriage between the trees planted by the childless couple, are common in India. The planting of a grove of trees is generally held by Hindus as a religious work. The Gypsies in Germany honour the fir tree, the birch, and the hawthorn, and in Wales venerate the fascinating vegetable growth known to them as the *broado koro*. The Gypsy method of foretelling the sex of a child by casting grains of maize into a basin and observing the way they settle was a custom practiced in vedic India. By no means fond of bathing, Gypsies have ideas of ritual purity somewhat like those of the Hindus.

Gypsies have displayed an adaptability towards the religious beliefs of the countries in their paths. Hence, there are Christians and Muslims of various denominations amongst them. Many practice their faith with deep devotion. They call the Bible the Sastra, the Sanskrit name for scriptures. Underneath, however, all of them enthusiastically retain the peculiar heritage of their ancient beliefs, and it is in these traditional beliefs that Indian parallels are seen.

Strict monotheists, Gypsies use a word of Indian origin *O'Devel* (or *O'Del* or *O'Delore*), which is translated as *the* God. Somewhat like the early Rig Vedic Aryans who composed the "Song of Creation," they do not conceive of God as the creator of the universe. The universe or the earth, *phu* (Sanskrit *bhu*), has always existed independently. The Gypsy worship of Sara is significantly reminiscent of a Hindu form of worship. The Gypsies call Sara the Kali, which is the name of the Hindu goddess of power, and, during the period of worship, take turns in a night-long vigil over the statue of Sara in the church, with bare feet but covered head, a Hindu custom.[30] Gypsies seldom need cathedrals and altars for worship. Images placed in a corner of their caravans are regarded as adequate. In this they again reflect the Hindu way of worship. Whilst the Hindus often go to temples, they do not have an overwhelming need for them and most Hindu homes have a small corner reserved for prayers.

Although generally unconcerned about the unknown world or the next life, Gypsies believe in Karma and some kind of continuation of life after death. They accept the fluctuations of fortune with resignation and unconcern. This perhaps explains why they have retained their innate cheerfulness, despite repeated persecutions and injustices.[31] Terms such as *tatva* (the first principle, the reality) and *mukti* (liberation) are familiar to them, although their actual significance has become somewhat blurred over the centuries.

Evidence of similarities between many of the Gypsy tribes of Europe and existing communities in India is both vast and varied. The Gypsy name for themselves, Rom, is linked with the Dom tribe in India. Dom became Lom in Armenia, and then Rom. These names are in exact phonetic correspondence with the Sanskrit *domba* and the modern Indian dom, which means "a man of low caste who gains his living by singing and dancing." Charles Leland first suggested in *English Gypsies and their Language* that the true origin of the Roms (or Romani) was to be found amongst the Doms, a very low caste of India, which sprang from the *Domar,* a mountain tribe of shepherd-robbers. Later, researches by Grierson amongst the Bihari Doms went far to confirm this conjecture. He discovered that there existed in India a wandering tribe known as *Trablus,* who called themselves Roms, and who were in all respects identical with the Syrian and European Gypsies. The Doms of modern India are vagrant tribes, found mainly in Bihar and in the west and northwest areas, and they have many features in common with the Gypsies. They wander about with tattered reed tents which they pitch in the vicinity of villages. Some of them make baskets, mats, and similar articles; and in Darkistan, where they form a considerable part of the population but still constitute the lower caste, they are musicians, smiths, and leather workers. They are today *Doma* and Doms, and the name may well have no more racial significance than, for instance, "smith" or "tinker." One of the explanations of the origin of the tribal name Dom is that it imitates the sound of a drum or tom-tom. Dom may merely mean a professional musician, or it may simply be applied to any and every outcaste tribe.[32] Present-day Doms are described as sleeping, dreaming, sitting, talking, gambling, smoking, drinking, fighting, and, above all, singing. They improvise songs, play various instruments, and dance immodestly. This description might fit various primitive races, but not to the same degree as it fits the Gypsies.

Close parallels between the Romanies of Europe and various other Gypsy-like tribes of India have been noted. *Lovari* in eastern Europe corresponds with *Lohar* in India, *Sinti* with *Sindhis*—although the Sindhis are not a tribe but a linguistic group—Zotts with Jats. Again, there are several Indian tribes which approximate Gypsies closely in both appearance and way of life, such as the Asuras; Luris; Ghasis; *Kamis,* the smiths and metal workers of Nepal; *Kasars* or *Kasera,* the copper smelters and metal workers of northern India; *Koravas* of South India; *Banjaras* of Bombay; *Chharas; Thatharas;* and others. Of these the Luris and the Doms have been the most extensively studied.

Parallels between Gypsy and Indian folklore also invite attention.

255

The publication of *Gypsy Folk-Tales* by Francis Hindes Groome in 1899 brought to light a wealth of hitherto unexplored stories. In asserting the significance of identical tales, allowance must be made for the fact that many stories, in spite of their numerous variations, are common to all Indo-Europeans, that many Indian tales had travelled to Europe through other routes, and that the Romanies have freely borrowed tales from the lands they visited. Therefore, it is not always possible to definitely identify a Gypsy tale as having a purely Indian origin. Yet, there are a few examples, typical of the Indian and the Gypsy traditions, and foreign to other intervening cultures, which suggest a possible direct link. For example, the Gypsy tales "God and the Woodcutter" and "Jack and the Cabbage" have Indian analogues in "The Weaver and the Prophecy" and "The Weaver and the Water-Melon."[33] A Gypsy legend as to how God made the different races of man has a striking parallel in an Indian myth. According to the Nagas, a hill tribe in northeastern India, God made a model of man and slipped him into the oven. Being new at the job, he took the model out too soon, and the pale and pasty creature became the white man. The next time, afraid of repeating the mistake, he left it too long and the outcome was the Negro. The third time, he timed it accurately and the result was the perfect brown man, the Indian. In the Gypsy version the perfect man, naturally, was the ancestor of the Gypsies.[34] Both the importance the Gypsies attach to the art of story-telling, and their insistence on following a set pattern, are somewhat reminiscent of traditional story-telling in India.

If the mediaeval wandering jugglers, story-tellers, and entertainers, in whose songs specimens of the oldest secular folk music are found, are considered to be early Gypsies, the Gypsy influence on Western folklore would appear to be considerable. The Gypsy musicians and showmen who have been travelling about in western Europe for several centuries easily resemble a similar class which existed there in mediaeval times. This class consisted of itinerant showmen, mountebanks, jugglers, story-tellers, singers, dancers, and the like. They appeared suddenly in large numbers in France, Germany, Italy, Spain, and England. In Germany they were considered vagrants and tramps. In France, especially in Provence and Normandy, they were known as *jongleurs* and *menestriers,* men who were clowns, acrobats, or musicians, and who recited fables and stories to the accompaniment of music. In England they were called minstrels, and they sang, danced, joked, tossed balls and knives. Gypsy showmen today are clowns, story-tellers, and they recite poems and fables to the accompaniment of music. In fact, the Kurds call Gypsies *A'shuk,* from the Turkish *Ashek,* meaning a story-teller. In Italy these travelling showmen gave performances similar to the Gypsies of today who frequently visit the fairs and country districts of southern Italy. They play, dance, sing, perform acrobatic and riding feats, toss balls and knives, walk on stilts, and do other jugglers' tricks; and they have trained bears, monkeys, and other animal acts. They are expert at training all kinds of animals for public entertainment and many Gypsies are found today in the circus world.

Some scholars have described these itinerant entertainers as the descendants of old gladiators and comedians who, after the fall of Rome, were compelled to seek their living amongst the barbarians by trading "what had been introduced into Rome from Asia." There is no doubt that there were such showmen and musicians in the Roman Empire, but they originated in Asia, for Rome had imported large numbers of Asian showmen both before and after the beginning of the Christian era.

When the players moved about in companies, women and children formed part of the troupe, the former taking part in the performances as dancers and singers, skilfully using the Asian tambourine and Egyptian clapper in their wanton dances. Although this was about fifteen hundred years ago, there is no other class of showmen today, except the Gypsies, who roam about Europe with their families performing for their livelihood. Some mediaeval wanderers were employed by the nobility as couriers, bearing secret messages or professions of love. Similarly, Gypsies have traditionally been employed as spies, messengers, and "go-betweens," in both Asia and Europe, and Gypsy women in Egypt, as elsewhere, are noted for arranging meetings for lovers. There were two main types of minstrels in England: those in the service of a court and those who wandered about freely. Both types persisted even in the Elizabethan period, when Gypsies reputedly appeared in England, at which point the minstrels faded away.

Whilst these wandering showmen were very popular—in fact, indispensable at court festivals, feasts, tournaments, and other gatherings —and their art was regarded as traditional, they were treated with contempt and denied civil rights. They were tolerated, but not given the real protection of law. Upon sustaining physical injury they could not even claim redress or charge their assailant. Like the Gypsies, these people retained their romantic spirit throughout the Middle Ages whilst remaining homeless outcasts. Even the Church excluded them from partaking in communion and the sacraments. The Church

257

saw in their secular music, in their instinctive and genuine love of life and its pleasures, and in their indomitable determination to hold on to their way of life, a serious danger to the spiritual well-being of its followers. If these minstrels were the early Gypsies of Europe, the hostility of the Church towards them could explain some of the later persecution of the Gypsies in European countries, as well as the Gypsy desire at first to appear as Christians.

Whilst the Gypsies borrowed cultural traits from their adopted countries, they also inevitably transmitted many of their own characteristics, some of which are now completely unrecognizable. It is interesting to note that the Gypsies, afraid of water, nevertheless invented bait for fishing lines. Adept with their hands and nimble on their feet, it is not surprising that the Gypsies have produced most of the bull fighters in Spain, and, in the bare-knuckle days of boxing, they were a power in the British professional ring. Jem Driscoll, a remarkable boxer commonly known as a Welshman, was really a Gypsy.[35] Gypsy women, such as Zora Kostich, have been famous for their breathtaking horse riding tricks in the circus.

If the various Romani dialects borrowed abundantly from the vocabularies of the countries they passed through, they have also contributed in some degree to the enrichment of European languages. The secret slang of evil-doers has drawn most profitably from Gypsy sources. The early history of English slang and cant, the language of the underworld, is obscure, but the impact of the Gypsy language during the early sixteenth century stimulated the English to improve their own rude and scanty jargon. Although the Gypsy contribution to canting was not extensive, it was much larger than many writers on the subject have supposed. A number of the most characteristic English slang words, such as row, shindy, tool (in driving), mash (i.e., to fascinate), pal, chivvy, and especially the term "slang" itself, are Romani.[36] "Slang" was derived from the Hindi *swang* (artificial or a show). In the middle of the nineteenth century slang was used to mean a travelling show.

Slang easily advances to the rank of accepted popular language, and there are many English words which owe their origin to Romani. For example: the English words, pal, cosh, bloke, jockey, are derived from Romani.[37] The English dick, meaning to see, is found in all Gypsy dialects. Its Hindi equivalent is *dekh*. Shakespeare's character Caliban is the Gypsy name for "darkness," "blackness," *kaliben*.

The Spanish Gitanos have evolved a distinct dialect of their own called *calo*, which has left many traces in everyday Spanish. For example: *gacho*, meaning lovers, and its feminine *gachi*, meaning mistress; *gili* (fool); *sandunga* (elegance); *chunga* (fun, joke); *mangante* (beggar, vagabond); *terne* (bully); and *manteca* (butter).

The list of Gypsy contributions to French, made chiefly during the last century, is a long one. If some words of Romani origin, which were part of the slang vocabulary in Balzac's time, have now become extinct, there are others which have survived, although their "bohemian" origin is seldom suspected. For example, the word *bath* (popular term for excellent, fine as in C'est *bath!*) is pure Romani. *Bakht* means luck, usually good luck. A toast is proposed saying, "Bakht to ke!" (Good luck be on you!) This is the *baraka* of the Arabs which, in its original Indian form, *bhakti,* carried with it a more subtle meaning of devout abandon or devotion to the Divinity. There are some twenty to thirty French words currently used which can be traced to Romani with certainty, such as *berge* (ear) from *bers; surin* (knife) from *tchuri; rupin* (rich) from *rup* (money, as in the Indian rupee); *ouste* (an exclamation, as in Allons, ouste! Come, let's go! or Let's get a move on!) from *uste!* (Get up!); and *costaud* (strong, strapping, hefty) from *kusto* (strong).[38] The term bohemian, popularized by Murger in *La Vie de Bohème,* comes from the French word for Gypsy, employed to portray the gay, Gypsy-like, lives of youthful groups of poets, painters, and musicians.

Deriving from Indian castes to whom formal education was denied, Romanies are not a learned people. Their significant contribution has been in those spheres where they have gained a certain proficiency, such as metal working, music, and dancing. Whilst it is common knowledge that the art of metallurgy was widespread in ancient India, it is not definitely known when and how it first appeared in Europe. According to Gabriel de Mortillet, an eminent prehistorian, European metallurgy owes its origins to the immigration of nomad peoples, presumably Gypsies. "Jules Bloch even pinpoints the fact that the link between India and Greece was made by the cauldron makers, the Gaordari of Astarabad, south of Caspian, and the Gypsies of the Khorassan (northeast of Iran), who were chain makers and, at the same time, makers of combs and sieves."[39] Some scholars ascribe the rise of European metallurgy to the Phoenicians, but Paul Bataillard (1814–1894), the French writer, maintains that the credit for introducing bronze into Europe belongs to the Gypsies. It is also possible that the adventurous Phoenician seafarers learned much of their handicraft from the travelling Sygynes, who camped in their towns and villages, and are described by Homer as a wandering tribe beloved by Vulcan, the god of furnaces, because of their great skill in metal work.

Franz de Ville carries Bataillard's theory even further and states that

259

it appears certain that the Gypsies made bronze in Europe.[40] He cites in support of this theory the evidence of the weapons and jewellery recently excavated along the Baltic, ornamented with the *swastika*, an original Indian symbol.[41] Well before the advent of Nazism, some Norweigan Gypsies had the swastika tatooed on their right shoulder. Musical instruments called lures, which are of foreign origin and have been skilfully smelted, have been found at the same location.

Music plays an extremely important part in Gypsy life. Irrespective of his profession, every Gypsy—except possibly some English Gypsies—knows how to play the violin. Many Central European Gypsy songs express the utmost veneration for the violin. Their regard for musical instruments is so great they never sell them. Their intense love for music has been known throughout the world for centuries. It should be recalled that the ten thousand Luris who went over to Iran at the invitation of Bahram Gur were accomplished musicians and expert lute players. There are also early documents referring to the musical abilities of the Gypsies in Europe. In Scotland, they danced for King James in Holyrood Palace, and in France they danced at the court of Louis XIII, in spite of a decree forbidding their entry to the kingdom. In the second interlude of *Le Malade Imaginaire,* Moliere speaks of Egyptians, presumably Gypsies, dressed like Moors, who mingle songs with dances. Even today Gypsy musicians are found everywhere. Hungarian music is greatly indebted to the Gypsies. This is equally true of Romania, Bessarabia, Bulgaria, Turkey, and the whole Balkan Peninsula. In Serbia, Herzegovina, Bosnia, and Croatia, Gypsy musicians and music are as popular as they are in Hungary. The intense love of the Russians for their Gypsy singers and choruses is well known. The Russian Gypsy songs, such as "Ochi Chorniya" ("Dark Eyes"), are known and sung universally. In Spain many of the large Gitano population are musicians, singers, and dancers, and some have risen to positions of eminence in the musical field. In Persia, where there are well over one hundred thousand Gypsies, practically all of the public musicians, singers, and dancers are Gypsies. They are known as *Karachi, Luli, Luri,* and *Mutrib.* In Syria, Mesopotamia, and Egypt, where Gypsies are called *Nuri, Rawazi,* and *Alimah,* the story is much the same.

The Gypsies mentioned by Firdusi and the Arab historian, Hamza, were expert lute players, and it has been suggested that it was possibly they who introduced the lute to Europe. The name of the instrument is borrowed from the Arabic *al-ud,* literally meaning wood. But there is some doubt that the Gypsies were responsible for introducing this instrument to Europe, although it is certain that the lute is of Indian origin. At the time of the Arab conquest of Persia, Persian music was a highly developed art. The Arabs took Indo-Persian music with them to other areas which they occupied, such as Syria, Egypt, North Africa, and Spain. They also took with them a musical instrument, called *rebab,* which was the forerunner of the modern violin.

The guitar, a unique instrument of the lute class capable of playing both harmony and melody simultaneously, and which is indispensable to Gitano musicians, is a variation of the Indian sitar (or cithara), which has mobile frets, and the *tambura,* which does not. There are different theories about the introduction of the guitar (or *guitarra*) into Spain. One theory suggests it was brought by the Arabs, whereas another suggests that it was derived from the Roman cithara of Graeco-Asian origin, which was brought to Spain by the Roman conquerors before the advent of the Arabs. Spanish texts of the Middle Ages mention two types of guitar, the *Latina* and the *Morisca* (Moorish). The earlier guitar was essentially the same stringed instrument that it is today, having an incurved body shaped like the number eight, with flat top and bottom and a finger board with frets, and was played directly by the fingers. It originally had four strings, a fifth was added later on, and was very similar to the Spanish guitar of today. Later, a sixth string was added and tuned in "e" like the first, but two octaves lower.

The Spanish guitar, whilst ideal in some ways, does not perfectly suit the needs of the Gitanos. The Gypsy style of playing has its own distinctive character, the main element of which is rhythm, and the fundamental mood, whether gay or sad, is that of passion. Each type of Gypsy song has its own special accompaniment. In the *taranta,* for instance, the guitar plays an important role. The guitar gives a long prelude and postlude, but remains silent during the singing, or, at the most, plays a few scattered notes. Guitar and voice give the impression of being independent of each other. This is essential, especially in the deeper and more Gypsy-like varieties, in which glides and microtones play an important part. The fixed keys of the instrument are constructed on the guitar system which does not allow it to follow the voice, and the guitar has to play the role of bridging the pauses between verses.

The typical Gypsy instrument is partly made of cypress in order to give it a metallic tone. Often a clamp is put across the neck at varying intervals to shorten the length of the strings and make the tone still more brilliant. Gypsies, who cannot afford this clamp, often use a knife tied in place by a handkerchief instead.[42] The ideal instrument for accompanying this type of *cante gitano* would be either the Indian sitar or the *tambura,* which is the name used by the nomads and some eastern Gypsies for any kind of guitar.[43] An instrument of the same name is in use amongst some of the Balkan Gypsies, with the frets so arranged that one may play microtones. It is probable that the Gypsies brought it with them from India.

In the Balkans, mainly in Bulgaria, the Gypsies have borrowed the *cobza,* a sort of lute with pizzicato strings, and the *naiou* (pipes of Pan). In Romania they use the *tsimbal,* a rudimentary and portable piano. This instrument, which Liszt calls the zymbala (cimbalum), and which is an ancestor of the Western keyboard instruments, appears to be of Indian origin (*svara-mandala*), and it seems very likely that it was the Gypsies who brought it into southern Europe in the fifteenth century.[44] Also, according to Elizabeth Robbins Pennell, the Gypsies introduced the bagpipe into Europe.

Other instruments greatly appreciated by the Gypsies are the drums and tambourine. Considering that Asia furnished the West with a number of wind, string, and percussion instruments, such as the flute, trumpet, horn, bagpipe, cymbal, drum, psaltery, harp, and lute, which were popular with itinerant musicians, it would not be surprising if some of these originated in India. Amongst the percussion instruments, numerous kinds of drums dominate the musical scene in India. Of these, the *mridangam* is the most common, and probably the most ancient; the *tabla* (an Arabic term), equally popular in northern and central India, is almost similar to a *mridanga* but is divided in the middle with each of the two parts sealed at the bottom. Although the tambourine is not exclusively Gypsy or Asian, since it is found everywhere in Mediterranean countries, the use the Gypsies make of it suggests that it is of Indian origin. The tambourine is still reserved either for women to accompany the dances, or for bear leaders to give rhythm to the movements of the animal. In India, whilst drums are used in numerous forms and ways, its *dholak* version is principally played by women, and *damaru* is used for the animal dance.

In some countries of Europe where the number of Gypsies was small, Britain and France for example, Gypsy music was not much appreciated; in others, such as Hungary and Spain, it made a great impact. Franz Liszt, who knew Gypsies and who had made a close study of their music, regarded all Hungarian music as simply Gypsy music.[45] A modern music critic, Sinclair, agrees with this opinion and even suggests that this "statement can be applied to Rumania and Bessarabia with almost as much truth as to Hungary. It is the same in Bulgaria, European Turkey, and the whole Balkan peninsula."[46] Other scholars advocate the originality of Hungarian music. At the beginning of this century, two musicians, Béla Bartok and Zoltan Kodaly, emphasized the independence of Hungarian music by exhuming melodies and rhythms different from those of Gypsy music and authentically Hungarian. The protagonists of the priority of Gypsy music, however, cite ancient documents, which clearly record the presence of Gypsy musicians of high reputation in Hungary and do not mention any other musicians at all. Reference is found in an official register that Gypsy musicians were in the service of Queen Beatrice of Aragon at the end of the fifteenth century. They often played in the palaces, in most great celebrations and processions, and nearly every nobleman owned a Gypsy orchestra. From the seventeenth century, at the courts of the noblemen and at village dances alike, Gypsies accompanied the singing of *kuruc* (songs) with their cymbalums, pipes, and violins. Because of their extremely popular rhythmic chants, the Gypsy singers Michel Varna and his granddaughter Panna Cinka gained fame throughout Europe. They even played the violin for the armies marching into battle. At the end of the eighteenth century they made a specialty of playing the *Verbunkos,* the famous dance of the recruiting sergeants which marked the renaissance of Hungarian music.[47]

The Hungarian csardas is similar to Gypsy dances, and has a peculiar step (knocking the heels together) found in some Eastern dances. According to Liszt, no one can play or dance the csardas like the Gypsies themselves. Gypsy music in Hungary has been developed to an almost unequalled state of perfection in composition and execution. Their music, soft, sweet, weird, and wailing, can suddenly transform into the fierce, wild, fiery strains of a battle song or csardas. Some of the most famous violin performers in the world have been Gypsies, amongst them the nineteenth-century virtuoso, Eduard Remenyi.[48]

Although a certain amount of specialization exists amongst the Gypsy entertainers, the majority are skilled dancers as well as singers. It is likely that the first Gypsy dancers from India were professionals, but it is equally possible that the origin of Gypsy dances is ritualistic, and that "in some way they represent an everyday or commonplace rendering of the sacred dances of Vedic India."[49] The Romanian "Dance of the Kalus" (sticks), also known in Hungary as the Stick Dance (Rovl'enca Khelen), is reminiscent of the *chatta* dance, which with regional variations, is widespread in India. The English Morris (Moorish) dance is said to have been inspired by Gypsies, although the Romanies of Britain have never rivalled the musical skill of their fellow Romanies of Hungary, Spain, or Russia.

In Spain conditions for the growth of Gypsy music were particularly suitable. For centuries Spain was under Arab domination, and during this time the country, especially the southern part, absorbed many Asian characteristics. The presence of the Jews, another Semitic race, also aided this absorption. During the Islamic period music became a highly cultivated art, especially in Seville. Gypsies arrived in Spain nearly half a century before the expulsion of the Muslims and the Jews, and it was only natural that their Asian music and dancing were appreciated. The ease with which the Gypsies took to flamenco music would suggest that Hispano-Arabic music was similar to their own. It must be remembered that the Gypsies reached Spain by the same route as the Arabs had before them. Consequently, whilst they borrowed from flamenco as easily as they contributed to it, Gypsy music in Spain has retained much of its original flavour. It is said that in matter of pure rhythm Spanish Gypsies have few equals. In accompanying a song or dance by only handclapping, they attain an astonishing variety of complex rhythms. Many Spanish dances, such as the bolero, the fandango, the seguidilla, and the malaguena, seem to be of Asian origin. The saraband, the name of one Spanish dance, is a Persian word derived from the beautiful saraband Persian carpet. Spanish folk music is commonly regarded as one of the richest in the world, mainly because a variety of foreign influences have mingled with it, including that of the Gypsies. Most of the Gypsies settled in Andalusia and the Andalusian influence predominates in Spanish music.

Although Gypsy music scores are not written down—except by non-Gypsies—their musical themes have gained widespread fame throughout Europe. Many lesser-known as well as eminent composers such as Haydn, Beethoven, Schubert, and Brahms occasionally used Gypsy themes.[50] Gypsy music fascinated Wilhelm Friedemann Bach, the eldest son of Johann Sebastian Bach. Once a teacher of mathematics and organist at Halle, Wilhelm left everything to follow a tribe of Gypsy musicians. Scholarly opinion is somewhat divided over the question of Gypsy influence on either Spanish flamenco or east European music. Scholars have hesitated to make definite statements, partly because it is extremely difficult to isolate the importations or alien elements in music. Yet, there are themes in both Hungarian and Spanish music which are clearly of alien origin. At the same time, Hungarian and Spanish Gypsy music have common peculiar characteristics. And, as Spain and Hungary are at opposite ends of western Europe, the mutual similarity must be due to a common third source, which, in this case, would appear to be more likely Gypsy than any other. It is also significant that the musical accomplishments of Spain became noteworthy after the advent of Gypsies in the country in 1447. Unless one insists on a series of unexplained coincidences, the theory of Gypsy inspiration in music must command serious attention.

In Indian and Spanish Gypsy music there is, unlike in Western music, a luxuriance of cross rhythms, a freedom, a richness, a fluidity, and a multiplicity of rhythms, whereas harmony is much neglected.[51] Similarly, the characteristic rhythms, elaborate ornamentation, and quarter tones, unknown to Western music, are common to both Hungarian Gypsy and Indian music. Hungarian Gypsies employ various scales or modes not used in Western music, for example c, d, e, f♯, g, a, b. They employ in the minor scale the augmented fourth, the minor sixth, and the major seventh. Often they also use the minor seventh and the dominant with an augmented fifth. Asian music, Arabian for example, contains the same peculiarities. Indian and Gypsy melodies have many similarities which are easier to perceive than to explain. Both in Indian and Gypsy music melodic themes are more fluid and complex than they are in European music. Gypsy melodies, like the Indian, are elusive, delicate, and subtle. The *Indiana* of the Spanish Gypsies corresponds to the Indian *Bhairavi*. The use of microtones, such as quarter and third tones, is alien to Western, but common to Gypsy and Indian music. For this reason it is almost impossible to transcribe Spanish Gypsy folk songs, as it is Indian songs, by the European system of notation and to play them on European instruments with fixed keys. Grace notes and the use of the flowing glide, producing what the Indians call "curves of sound," are essential to Spanish Gypsy music as well as to Indian. The melody seems to flow like water in a river, rising and falling in rapids, halting in still pools, and dashing over falls.[52] Even in the orchestral music of the Gypsies, harmony and counterpoint play a subordinate role to rhythm and melody. Liszt states that in the Hungarian Gypsy orchestra the violin is really a solo instrument; the rest of the instruments merely intensify its shadows and illuminate its joys. Both Indian and Gypsy music are relatively indifferent to the quality of the tone. In contrast, Western music pays much attention to it. Although the Gypsies charmed people throughout Europe with their music, it received its warmest reception and accommodation in those countries which already had some tradition of Eastern music.

Musical improvisation is a favourite art amongst the Gypsies of

Spain. In India, whilst waiting for the marriage feast to begin, the Doms will often take turns at improvising. In fact, improvisation in music and poetry is quite common in India, and is sometimes even expected by the audience as a light touch in a serious performance.

On the whole, the dances of the Gypsies in Spain appear to be nearer those of India than those of Spain. As in India, great emphasis is laid on the graceful curving movements of the fingers, the hands, and the arms which glide through the air like winged snakes, whilst the feet, in a violently contrasting tempo, drum a devil's tattoo. In the dances of Andalusia, the movements of arms and hands, and the play of the body muscles, are especially prominent. The combination of song and dance, the cries of "Ole! Ole!" echoed from all directions to animate the performer, the rapid gyrations, the undulations of the body suggesting dunes of sand or wind-blown fields of ripe wheat, all characteristic of the entertainments given by families of Indian Gypsies, have their definite counterparts in the zambras and danzas given by the Gitanos of Granada.[53]

A classic performance of Gypsy women is the snake dance, which is often confused with the "belly dance" of Arab women. But, as Martin Block has pointed out, this dance is not at all erotic, because Gypsy women, unlike their Arabian counterparts, never dance undraped. Like the Indian woman dancer, the Spanish dancer dresses unrevealingly, thus making herself more mysterious and inviting. References are found in European literature which confirm that the relationship between the Gypsy and Indian dances was at least vaguely recognized. For instance, the Badminton volume on dancing quotes Walter Thornbury (*Life in Spain*): "Seville is the headquarters of the gipsy girl who is going to show us how the Egyptian ghawassees and the Hindoo nautch girls dance. She will dance the Romalis, which is the dance Tiberius may have seen, and which no one but a gipsy dances in Spain. She will dance it to the old Oriental music and handclapping and to an old religious Eastern time, low and melancholy, diatonic, not chromatic, and full of sudden pauses, which are strange and startling."[54]

Chapter VIII

BUDDHIST PROSELYTISM
IN CENTRAL ASIA

ONE OF the remarkable characteristics of early Asian history—in fact of the ancient world until the Christian suppression of non-Christian religions in the Roman Empire—was the receptivity to cultural ideas regardless of their nationality, and a lack of religious bigotry. Prejudice against a foreign belief was uncommon; it certainly was never strong enough to cause total rejection of a different faith. The civilized peoples of those days seem to have implicitly accepted the proposition that there were numerous approaches to truth, and, without any false sense of pride or violated nationalism, they readily accepted knowledge, alien or otherwise, if they thought it worthwhile. This free flow of ideas, unimpeded by preconceptions and national barriers, made the ancient world in some ways far more international in its cultural outlook and social behaviour than our present-day society.

Trade and commerce dominated India's relations with the countries to the west of her, and cultural intercourse remained a subordinate partner throughout the long period of contact. Ideas inevitably moved with goods, soldiers, and travellers; but few journeys were undertaken just to seek knowledge and learning. In marked contrast, Indian contacts with the countries on her north, east, and southeast were mainly cultural, with trade playing a significant but secondary role. Commerce may have initiated contact but it was soon outpaced by culture. Again, the marks of Indian culture in these areas are far more clearly seen, and more readily conceded, than those in the West. It has, therefore, often been said that India's finest contributions to human civilization lie in Central Asia, East Asia, and Southeast Asia. Whatever the sum total of Indian influences on Western civilization, there is no doubt that ancient India was the radiating centre of a civilization which left a deep mark on the greater part of Asia.

Buddhism was the principal vehicle of Indian ideas and culture in Asia and is still the religion of millions of Asians. In many countries it became the national religion; in others it produced great intellectual stimulation, controversy, and, eventually, rejuvenation. It brought the uniquely rich and creative cultures of India, Indochina, Indonesia, China, and Japan into contact with each other and, over a period of more than a thousand years, gave rise to a great spiritual and cultural community throughout Asia.

The most remarkable feature of the Buddhist missionary activity, however, was that it was never fanatical, bigoted, or obtrusive, and Buddhist missionaries never served the interests of a militant political power. In the true spirit of its faith, Buddhism prevailed peacefully through force of conviction. Like Hinduism, it did not lay claim to exclusiveness and remained exceptionally tolerant of other beliefs. Its intrinsic quality of being able to accommodate alien doctrines and adopt local cultural traditions, without surrendering its fundamental concepts, was principally responsible for its remarkable success in distant lands of divergent cultures. Buddhism acted as a catalyst in different societies, helping them to bring out their dormant strengths and to release their creative energies. Its capacity to absorb, to impart, and to fertilize remains unmatched in the history of cultural expansion.

Much of the history of the ancient states of Central Asia has been reconstructed from Chinese sources, which naturally deal with the life and events of these neighbouring states from the Chinese viewpoint and as an adjunct to Chinese history. But the Chinese accounts are valuable in providing corrective or corroborative evidence to Buddhist narratives. Without archaeological work, however, the reconstruction of Buddhist Central Asia would have remained less comprehensible and reliable.

It was only after the northern boundary of Afghanistan had been demarcated and an agreement signed between Britain and Russia in 1887 that Central Asia was visited by European soldiers, adventurers, and civil and military officials. In the beginning there were only stray archaeological finds but they drew the attention of a wide circle of scholars. In 1890 two Turks found a birch bark manuscript in the vicinity of Qum-Tura, which they sold to a British army officer, Colonel Bower, at Kucha. The text is commonly known as the Bower Manuscript and is a Sanskrit treatise on medicine belonging to the fourth century. A few years later, in 1893, a French traveller, M. Dutreuil de Rhins, acquired two birch bark manuscripts in the vicinity of Khotan. Expert examination found they contained a Buddhist text in an Indian

Jataka Scene. Bharhut.
*Courtesy of the Archaeological
Survey of India, New Delhi.*

Close up of a votive stupa. Bodhgaya.
Courtesy of the Archaeological Survey of India, New Delhi.

Muktesvara Temple. Bhuvanesvar.
Courtesy of the Archaeological Survey of India, New Delhi.

Visnu. Besnagar (Vidisa).
Courtesy of the Archaeological Survey of India, New Delhi.

Scythian soldier carved on a pillar. Nagarjunakonda.
Courtesy of the Archaeological Survey of India, New Delhi.

Gandhara Buddha.
*Courtesy of the Archaeological
Survey of India, New Delhi.*

Buddha. Sarnath.
Courtesy of the Archaeological Survey of India, New Delhi.

Bronze Padmasambhava. Tibet, 18–19th century A.D.
Courtesy of The Trustees of the British Museum, London.

Maitreya Bodhisattva. Fondukistan, Afghanistan
Courtesy of the Musée Guimet, Paris.

Avaloketsvara. Tun-huang.
Courtesy of the Musée Guimet, Paris.

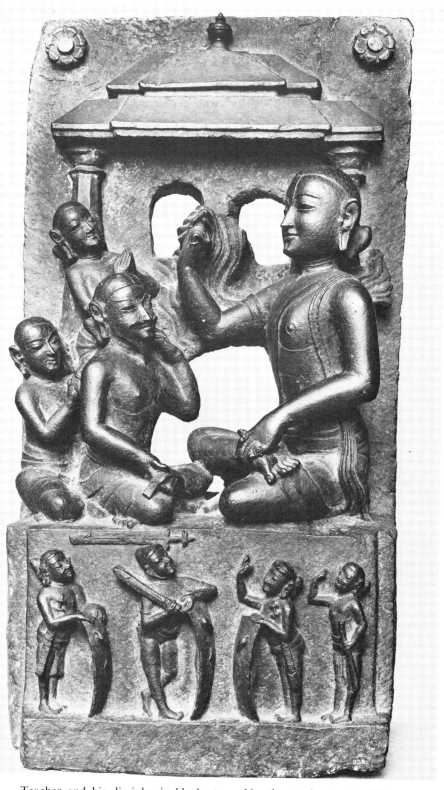

Teacher and his disciples in black stone. Nepal, anterior to the 13th century A.D.
Courtesy of the Victoria and Albert Museum, London.

Amida Buddha, in marble. Northern Ch'i style (550–77), 11th–12th century A.D.
Courtesy of the Victoria and Albert Museum, London.

language and script of the second century—a new version of the *Dhammapada* in Prakrit written in Kharoshthi script. These discoveries kindled a widespread interest in the area. In 1898 a Russian archaeological mission led by Klements visited the northern parts of eastern Turkistan. This had been inspired by the remarkable finds of the Russian Consul-General, Petrovsky, at Kashgar, but not much further archaeological exploration of the region was undertaken. In 1896 Hedin's march through the areas of sand-buried ruins in the desert northeast of Khotan, although not producing any historical evidence, succeeded in demonstrating the accessibility and suitability of these sites for excavation. Soon, urged by the recommendations of Hoernle, the Indian government deputed Aurel Stein, a trained archaeologist, to carry out exploration in the region of Khotan in 1900–1901. Encouraged by the remarkable results of his first expedition Stein then explored regions beyond Khotan in the southern part of eastern Turkistan up to the borders of China. On his third expedition, he covered a wider area including Khotan, Niya, Loulan, Tun-huang, Borkul, Guchen, and Jimasa Kucha.[1]

His greatest discoveries were made in 1907, when he found more than twenty thousand manuscripts and 554 separate paintings. The collection included five hundred complete Buddhist canonical works and three thousand works in Sanskrit or Brahmi. He filled twenty-four heavy cases with manuscripts and five with paintings, embroideries, and other remains of Buddhist art. Amongst his many fascinating discoveries was that of the "Old Wall." The Great Wall of China in its present form is of Ming date and was designed to protect China from Mongol attack; but Stein found an extension of the original wall nearly two hundred miles east of the Jade Gate where the silk road passes through the frontier rampart. The wall, traced for one hundred miles, was first built for protection against the ancient Huns in the second century B.C. by the Han rulers.

Meanwhile, other European scholars also carried out explorations in this region. Three German expeditions were conducted between 1902–1903 and 1913–1914 under the direction of Albert Grunwedel and Albert Von Lecoq. These archaeologists worked mostly in the northern part of eastern Turkistan. A French scholar of Chinese, Paul Pelliot, led an expedition in 1906 which worked for two years, mainly at Tun-huang, studying manuscript collections and the remains of art in the caves of the Thousand Buddhas. In fact, Stein had bought a large collection of manuscripts for a small sum of money in 1907 from a discharged soldier, Wang Yuan-Lu, who had discovered the hidden library in the cave in 1900. A year later Pelliot made a similar but smaller find, although his knowledge of Chinese enabled him to be more discriminating than Stein. The Chinese understandably regard Stein and Pelliot as robbers because they acted in accordance with the nineteenth-century European attitude of the right to carry off "finds" made in non-European lands. Despite this, there was enough of the collection left behind that in 1910 the Chinese government was able to bring to Peking some ten thousand manuscripts. Many fell into private hands and a year later the Japanese managed to smuggle out six hundred manuscripts.[2] Most of the treasures are now housed in various countries—Britain, China, Japan, India, Russia, and Germany. During the last war, however, a large number of those kept in Berlin were destroyed.

This remarkable burst of archaeological work done during the first seventeen years of this century has not been followed up for political and financial reasons. There remains a good deal more to be done and signs have appeared in recent years suggesting a renewal of interest in the exploration of this area, especially by Soviet and Chinese archaeologists. In 1946–1947 the Russian Tolstov mission systematically explored the enormous castle at Toprak-Kala in Chorasmia and later published their valuable findings.

The limited work which has been done clearly reveals that the ancient civilizations of the Central Asian states were of a somewhat cosmopolitan character, in which Indian, Chinese, Persian, and Hellenistic influences intermingled with local heritages. Although Zoroastrianism, Manichaeanism, and Nestorian Christianity were prevalent amongst some of the people, Buddhism was most popular, and Central Asian cultural life was dominated for about a thousand years by Indian religion, literature, arts, and sciences. The different religious groups lived in harmony. For instance, at a ruined city called Turfan (Idiqut-i-Shanri, Chotsche) the remains of Manichaean, Nestorian, and Buddhist art and architecture are so closely associated that one must conclude that full religious tolerance prevailed there. However, evidence has also been found of a massacre of Buddhists by the Chinese about the ninth century. Von Lecoq discovered a chamber packed with the skeletons of monks still wearing fragments of their robes and bearing marks of ruthless slaughter.

By far the largest part of the vast material discovered is of Buddhist origin, although other documents, including many Manichaean books have also been found. Numerous Sanskrit writings have been found dealing with religious or semi-religious subjects—as medicine, astronomy, and grammar were then considered to be. Documents from as early as the second century have been discovered, some of them in Prakrit written in the Kharoshthi script of Asoka's time. Some were written on wood, some on birch bark or palm leaf, and others on leather. During the first three centuries the Kharoshthi script was in use from Khotan to Kroraina in the Lobnor region. Kharoshthi documents, numbering into hundreds, have been found, mainly on the sites at Niya, Endere, and Kroraina. In the fourth century in Khotan, Kucha, and Karashahr, Kharoshthi was replaced by a form of Brahmi adopted from the script of fourth-century Gupta India. The Chinese records date from even earlier periods; some are written on bamboo, others on silk, and other later ones on paper. Recent excavations in Chinese Turkistan have brought to light a large number of flourishing cities with rich sanctuaries. Recently, Soviet scholars discovered Sanskrit birch bark dating back to the sixth century in a castle called Zangtepe in Uzbekistan. These are in the Central Asian Brahmi script, and have thrown additional light on the cultural contact between India and Central Asia.

The religious structures excavated in Central Asia comprise stupas, caves, and *viharas*. The architecture appears to owe almost nothing to China but to include Indian and Persian features. Whilst numerous representations of Hindu deities have been found, Hinduism does not seem to have existed, except in Afghanistan. Buddhist missionaries transmitted to Central Asia not only religion, art, and literature but also scientific knowledge, as is evidenced by the discovery of the Sanskrit medical texts. It is not unlikely, therefore, that Indian ideas in other branches of science, such as mathematics and astronomy, may also have reached Central Asia and beyond.

Afghanistan, especially its northern regions around Balkh called Tokharestan, was the crossroads of Central Asia. It was here that the nomadic peoples first learned the ways of settled life, and thus Tokharestan played the significant role of a cultural intermediary.[3] Of all the neighbouring cultures, it was with India that this region was most closely connected. In fact, there is some sense in the suggestion that the territory between the Indus and the Oxus Rivers was a domain of Indian culture during the ancient period. Until the rise of Islam, Afghanistan was Hindu-Buddhist. The Parthians called the province corresponding to modern Kandahar and Sistan "White India," because Indian culture prevailed there. The Sassanians of the third century regarded even Bactriana, or the region of Balkh, as virtually an Indian country and the Oxus as a river of the Buddhists and the Brahmans. The ancient Greek writers coupled Bactriana with India and stated that thousands of Brahmans and Buddhist monks resided there.

Buddhism was the predominant religion in the various states of

271

Tokharestan from the second century B.C. to the beginning of the eighth century. Hsüan-tsang (Yuan-chuang)[4] (602–664), who visited the region on his way to India, testifies that Balkh was a great centre of original Buddhist studies, and gives a vivid description of the Buddhist establishments there. Except for Hsüan-tsang's account, there is no systematic account of Buddhism in the early period in Tokharestan and adjoining territories. From his record it appears that Buddhism was most prosperous in the cities, and that there were Buddhist monasteries in every state. According to a legend recounted by Hsüan-tsang, the first two lay disciples of the Buddha, Trapusa and Bhallika, laid the foundations of Buddhism in that country. Regardless of the authenticity of this evidence, there is no doubt that Buddhism was carried to Balkh during the period of Asoka's reign. Later, the Yueh-chih, who conquered the area, adopted Buddhism. The Kushans, who ruled over Tokharestan, became great patrons of Buddhism, and Tokharestan became a thriving centre for Buddhist studies. It produced famous scholars, such as Ghasaka, who played an important part in the compilation of the *Vibhasa,* a monumental Buddhist commentary, at the Buddhist Council held in Kashmir under the patronage of Kaniska. It was from Tokharestan that the Chinese ambassador Tsing Kiang received Buddhist texts as presents to take back to the Chinese court in 2 B.C., thus beginning the inflow of Buddhist culture to China. Later, Buddhist monks went to China from Tokharestan to preach their faith and culture.

Archaeological data pertaining to the Buddhist period of Tokharestan are only gradually coming to light. Various sites have been noted, and some excavations have been carried out by French scholars in Afghanistan, and, since the war, by Russian archaeologists on their side of the Soviet-Afghan border. But much more needs to be done. However, the explorations that have been carried out have led to the discovery of very important finds. Situated about one hundred and fifty miles northwest of Kabul, at the intersection of two major routes—one leading from China to Persia across the Pamirs, and the other from north Bactria to the Indus Valley—and commanding a major pass, Bamiyan (Fan-yen-na) was the first important way-station on the route from the Kabul region to Balkh (Balhika or Fo-ho). It was a major seat of Buddhist culture, as is revealed by the ruins of a very large monastery which provided travellers with necessary facilities. It continued to be a flourishing centre of Indian culture, attracting pilgrims and monks, until the eighth century. A number of grottos in the hills around Bamiyan were converted into Buddhist temples, and colossal figures of the Buddha were carved on hillsides. Writing at the end of the seventeenth century, Abul Fazl estimated the number of these caves to be about twelve thousand. Some of the caves housed monks, others enshrined the images of the Buddha and Bodhisattvas. Manuscripts of Buddhist texts in Indian scripts found at the site testify further to the Buddhist past of the region. These remains reveal clearly that Buddhist art in Balkh, at least on the south side of the Oxus, was flourishing. Beyond Bamiyan on the ancient site of Balkh, ruins of stupas and other antiquities have been excavated. As late as the time of Hsüan-tsang the Buddhist monasteries of Balkh were thriving. However, the city suffered much from foreign invasions, and was destroyed by the Arabs towards the end of the seventh century, soon after the departure of Hsüan-tsang.

Greek culture had been superimposed on the Persian cultural background of this region, until the penetration of Buddhism about the first century. Although the country came under the rule of a number of different peoples—the Greeks, the Sakas, the Yueh-chih, and the Huns —it remained Buddhist until the end of the seventh century, when the Muslim conquerors destroyed the great monastery, converted the chief priests to Islam, and took them to the court of the Caliph. On the authority of Al Biruni, these priests—Barmaks—inaugurated the study of Indian astronomy and mathematics at Baghdad.

Elsewhere in Tokharestan, where foreign invasions were not as destructive, remains of Buddhist art have even been discovered above ground. For example, in Haibak, which is situated on the Khula River, a stupa of the type of the Kailasa temple of Ellora was found. A group of interesting ruins have also been discovered at Kundus and its neighbourhood. These include remains of Graeco-Buddhist art, and other evidence which reveals direct Indian influence from the fourth to the fifth centuries. At Termez, which suffered considerably at the hands of invaders, such as the Arabs and Mongols, old coins including those of Kaniska and Huviska, the majority of which belong to the Indo-Greek period, have been excavated, as well as remains of Graeco-Buddhist art. Other ruins yielded the Kata-stupa which is of the type found in Gandhara and statues of Bodhisattvas similar to those found in Kucha and Taxila. Recently, first in 1958 and later in 1963, Asokan inscriptions have been found in the vicinity of Kandahar. These inscriptions were written in Aramaic and Greek for the benefit of the Iranian and Greek subjects of the Maurya Emperor.

Buddhism spread not only westward from Tokharestan to Parthia, but eastward to China and northward to Sogdiana (or Sodgh), the ancient name of Samarkand. Sogdians were known to the ancient Greeks

273

and Iranians, and were in close contact with India, where they were known as Sulika, a name derived from the Iranian Sughdik (or Suwdik). The people and their language have long since disappeared, but remnants of the language have been discovered in a few Sogdian translations of Buddhist texts excavated from parts of eastern Turkistan. Sogdians were well-known traders and visited various regions of Central Asia from Samarkand to the Great Wall, carrying with them Buddhist theory. The Sogdian monks' Chinese name was prefixed by Kang, derived from Kang-kiu, the ancient name for Sogdiana in Chinese. A prominent Sogdian monk, Seng-hui, introduced Buddhism to southern China via India and Tonkin in the third century, and founded a Buddhist school and a monastery at Nanking.

The eastward march of Buddhism into Chinese Turkistan is a story not only of rare courage and conviction but also of enormous significance in world history, for it provided the first major bridge between the two great civilizations of India and China. Some idea of the success of Buddhist missionary activity in this area can be gauged by the fact that the civilization of Chinese or eastern Turkistan was so close to that of India and Iran about the tenth century that Sir Aurel Stein referred to it by the ancient Greek name "Ser-India."

Lying beyond Tibet hundreds of torturous miles away from India, and bounded on the south by the wild and untrodden Kun-lun mountain ranges, on the west by the Pamirs, on the north by the T'ien-shan mountains, and on the east by the treacherous Gobi Desert, Chinese Turkistan is practically a vast wasteland of gravel and shifting dunes. Political and cultural activities, therefore, were confined to towns which were situated in most cases along the northern and southern edges of the Tarim Basin, where the rivers and streams in the T'ien-shan and Kun-lun ranges made irrigation possible and agriculture practicable. These oasis cities were capitals of states of varying and fluctuating sizes, as well as important commercial centres on the silk road for more than a thousand years.

Along the edge of T'ien-shan, in the northern part of Chinese Turkistan, there were four important states culturally similar: the modern Aksu, (Sanskrit, Bharuka); modern Kucha (Sanskrit, Kuchi); modern Karashahr (Sanskrit, Agnidesa; Chinese, Yenki); and modern Turfan (Chinese, Kao Chang, Chotsche). Of the southern states along the foot of the Kun-lun Range the most important, from the viewpoint of cultural influences, were Kashgar (Sanskrit, Sailadesa); Yarkand (Sanskrit, Chokkuka); and Khotan (Sanskrit, Kustana; Chinese, Yu-tien). The two Pamir states, Kie-Pan-to (Sarikol) and Wu-Sha (Yangi-Hissar), in the east of Shughnan are included in the Kashgar group.

At the eastern extremity of these routes, the famous city of Tun-huang was located.

The chief sources of information about this region are the Chinese and Tibetan annals, the narratives of Chinese pilgrims, and modern archaeological excavations undertaken by Aurel Stein, Albert Grunwedel, Paul Pelliot, and others mainly between 1900 and 1914, and by Soviet and Chinese archaeologists recently. The authenticity of the traditional accounts, preserved in the Chinese and Tibetan literatures, as well as in Buddhist texts, may be open to further verification. However, there is reliable archaeological evidence to suggest that there were small Indian settlements in existence in the southern part of this region before the Christian era, and that the wandering peoples of Central Asia, such as the Sakas and the Kushans, together with Indian merchants, were amongst the first to carry Indian culture and Buddhism to eastern Turkistan. An Indian dialect similar to that of northwestern India was the official language in some of these states. It is not unlikely that in certain areas Indians had settled in large numbers and set up their own principalities. These kingdoms of Central Asia were centres of extraordinary religious, literary, and artistic activity. Indian settlements were periodically reinforced by people from India, and many of these people would themselves set out on missions, for example, to China. Many of these Indians were from South India. From recent excavations at Toprak-Kala, Tolstov has suggested that the kings of this region employed Dravidian Indians as palace guards.[5] In the southern kingdoms of Kashgar, Yarkand, and Khotan, there was a strong Indian element in the population, and Khotan appears to have been the most important Indianized kingdom in Central Asia.

At the junction of one route running southeast to Khotan and another northeast to the Kucha region, Kashgar, from ancient times, played a significant role in the transmission of culture to the northern and southern states of the Tarim Basin. In Kashgar a script of Indian origin, based on Brahmi, was current, and possibly the language was a dialect of eastern Iran. Fa-hsien, who visited Kashgar during his Indian journey at the end of the fourth century, found Buddhism prospering there with more than two thousand monks and their disciples, all followers of the *Theravada* school. Two centuries later, Hsüan-tsang found that the people were sincere Buddhists. There were hundreds of monasteries, and Sanskrit was seriously cultivated. It was common for Indian scholars to visit Kashgar; the Buddhist teacher, Kumarajiva, stayed there for about a year on his return journey from Kashmir. Numerous relics of Buddhist stupas have been found in this locality.

The adjoining area of Khotan was also a flourishing centre of Buddhism. There is more information about Khotan, revealed in Chinese, Tibetan, and archaeological sources, than there is about Kashgar.[6] A Buddhist legend describes the conversion of Khotan as early as the time of the Buddha. Another legend refers to the political supremacy of Kunala, Asoka's son, in Khotan. Also, according to ancient Khotanese traditions, a son of Asoka named Kustana founded the kingdom about 240 B.C., 234 years after the *Nirvana*, and it was Vijayasambhava, the grandson of Kustana, who introduced Buddhism into Khotan. A Buddhist scholar named Arya Vairocana, who was regarded as an incarnation of the Maitraya Buddha, and who had miraculously brought Buddhist relics from Kashmir, is said to have come from India and become the King's preceptor. The tradition further claims the rule of an Indian dynasty in Khotan for fifty-six generations—all the kings' names of this line begin with Vijaya—during which period Buddhism remained the dominant religion of the state. According to the Tibetan annals, the first monastery, which Chinese records describe as "the stupa of up-turned bowl," was built about 211 B.C. A Chinese scholar-monk, Song-yun, mentions a monastery called Tsan-mo, which is known as Tsarma in Tibetan sources. The Chinese annals more or less confirm Tibetan accounts of ancient Khotan, which are substantially reinforced by the archaeological finds of Aurel Stein, who identified the old site of Tsarma with Chalma-kazan in the vicinity of Yotkan. The remarkable sculptures and paintings which the ancient shrines and dwelling places have yielded, despite centuries of burial beneath the dunes, indicate that the painters of Central Asian regions followed Indian models during the seventh and eighth centuries.

When Buddhism first began to expand into Central Asia, a synthesis between the Indian and Graeco-Roman art forms was taking place in Gandhara (northwestern India). The emergent form utilized Greek architectural motifs, such as the Corinthian pillar, and Greek drapery, but also contained characteristics of Indian art, which was flourishing in the interior of the country. The life of the Buddha and stories from his former incarnations were generally portrayed, and for the first time the image of the Buddha was carved on the model of Apollo. This gave rise to the whole iconography of later Buddhism, which has inspired the art of various countries, and has become an integral part of Buddhist worship. Until then neither the Buddha nor the Boddhisattvas were represented in pictorial form. In contrast, the worship of "images," a pan-Hellenic phenomenon, was very popular throughout the Hellenistic civilization.

Later, as art developed in India, some of its influences, particularly

Gupta art, were passed on to Central Asia through the routes travelled by monks and merchants. Figures became slenderer, poses more graceful, draperies more transparent. Buddha images were portrayed cooling their feet on the beautiful lotus, an Indian symbol of purity. The art of Ajanta appears to have been reborn in Central Asia. In fact, these paintings from Central Asia have helped to bridge a gap between Ajanta and Akbar in the story of Indian painting.

Central Asian art bore Persian, Chinese, Graeco-Buddhist, and Indian influences. The Khotanese were very fond of music and drama, and this fondness found an expression in the annual procession of images called *Buddha Yatra*, like the Indian *Ratha Yatra*. Close Indian contact is also indicated by a find of coins, a Kharoshthi inscription, and a text of the *Dhammapada* near Khotan. The Sino-Kharoshthi coins are the most important of these finds and were probably issued after 74 when Khotan had passed under effective Chinese suzerainty.

Numerous fresco or distemper paintings on wood and plaster have been found at Dandan-Uiliq, the Chinese garrison headquarters which was deserted soon after 791. A number of old Buddhist sites excavated in the desert of Dandan-Uiliq have yielded many stucco images and relics, manuscripts and records in Brahmi as well as in Chinese script. Khotan's famous monastery, Gomati Vihara, was widely known as a seat of learning from very early times and attracted scholars from India and China. In 259 a well-known Chinese monk Chu She-ling, who compiled one of the first catalogues of Buddhist texts in Chinese, came to Khotan to study Buddhism, taking back with him ninety bundles of original Buddhist texts. In Central Asia numerous Sanskrit texts have been found that are not extant in India, amongst them the *Udanavarga*.

Buddhism flourished in Khotan until about the eighth century and at its peak boasted nearly four thousand monasteries. According to Fa-hsien, Mahayana Buddhism was the more prevalent type and its priests numbered in the thousands. He mentions a monastery which took eighty years to build and was two hundred and fifty feet tall, overlaid with gold and silver carvings.

At the height of her power, the kingdom of Khotan extended from Chokkuka (Yarkand, Sokiu) in the west to Niya (Ni-jang) in the east. Khotan became the centre for the dissemination of Buddhism to other states, such as Niya, Calmadana (Cherchen), Kroraina (Loulan), and even China. It was from Khotan that Buddhism travelled to China reaching Korea and Japan by the sixth century. The Chinese, during the later Han and Tang periods, maintained effective control over the kingdom of Khotan. This fact is recorded in the Chinese annals and illustrated by finds of Chinese documents on wood or paper, Chinese coins, and other articles. Whilst China maintained political supremacy over Khotan and exercised an influence on Khotanese culture in the realms of art and religion, it borrowed a good deal more than it gave. A Khotanese embassy was sent to China for the first time during the reign of Emperor Wu (140–87 B.C.). Chinese ascendancy in Khotan ended about 791 and contact between the two became infrequent. It is possible that historians may well have overestimated Khotan's importance in this process of cultural diffusion simply because the materials available on the subject are plentiful in comparison with other principalities.

East of Khotan was Niya, also an important centre of Buddhism. The discovery of some seals and effigies of Kubera and Trimukha at Niya, and the painted Ganesha at Endere, suggest some Hindu influence. But the discovery of the remains of Buddhist stupas, viharas, and texts written in Sanskrit and Prakrit indicate that Buddhism was the predominant religion in all these localities. A variety of other documents written in Indian languages and scripts on leather, paper, silk, and wooden tablets have also been found. East of Niya is the modern site called Endere, the ancient Tu-ho-lo, which has also yielded Kharoshthi tablets and manuscripts of the type found in Niya, as well as the ruins of a Buddhist stupa.

Archaeological work has revealed a chain of sites in the east and northeast which also testify to the preponderance of the Buddhist culture in this region for several centuries. In the Chinese records of the Han period, this country is referred to as Shan-Shan, the new name for Loulan which in turn was the Chinese transcription of the original Kroraina (or Krorayina) found in the Kharoshthi documents. Evidence indicates that Kroraina was a thriving centre of Buddhism and Indian culture; according to Fa-hsien there were four thousand monks there. The Kharoshthi documents excavated from the various sites of Kroraina are written in Prakrit and contain names of Indian origin: for example, Caraka, Kumudvati, Vasudeva, and Budhamitra.

The story of Buddhist expansion along the northern route is somewhat the same. Kucha was the most powerful state in this region and played a predominant role in the spread of Buddhism to other northern states and to China. The exact date of the arrival of Buddhism in China is unknown, although it was probably in the first century. The Chinese annals of the third century state that there were nearly one thousand stupas and temples in Kucha. Buddhist monks from Kucha went to China and took an active part in translating Buddhist texts into Chinese. Po-yen, who was probably a member of the Kuchean royal family, became a Buddhist monk, and rendered six Buddhist texts into Chinese. Buddhist activity reached a peak during the fourth century with Kucha an almost entirely Buddhist city. Kumarajiva, the Buddhist monk-scholar who introduced Mahayana Buddhism to the states of the Tarim Basin and also to China, was born in Kucha of an Indian father, who was the Rajaguru of the state, and of a Kuchean princess. Kumarajiva was taken to China as a prisoner when Kucha was destroyed by a Chinese expeditionary force in 382. He lived there until his death in 413 and his work gave rise to an exceptionally brilliant and productive phase in the history of Chinese Buddhism.

Archaeological finds show that Buddhism was a flourishing religion in the north until about the eighth century. In the early period, Buddhist culture in Turfan drew upon the Buddhist church in Kucha and Karashahr, but after about the fifth century it increasingly assimilated Chinese influences. Buddhism continued, however, as the religion of the people for many centuries. Hsüan-tsang, who received a warm reception in Turfan and was given generous help so that he might continue his pilgrimage to India, speaks of the prosperous condition of Buddhism there. His account is supported by Chinese inscriptions which contain many references to the influences of Buddhism on the life and culture of the inhabitants.

In 507, Kiu, a Chinese dynasty, was established in Turfan, and more than a century later, in 640, it was brought under the direct control of China. At about this time the conflict for power with the Uigur Turks, one of the Hun tribes, began. During the sixth century a Turkish kingdom stretched from the Altai Mountains eastward to the Pacific Ocean and westward to the Black Sea. In the seventh century, Balkh, Bamiyan, the Hindu Kush, Badakshan, and Belehan were under Turkish control. But soon central authority began to weaken, the conflict with the rising power of the Arabs began, and the Turkish Empire split into two parts. The western part gradually became Islamic between the eighth and tenth centuries, and the eastern part was consolidated under the Uigur Turks. The Uigur Empire was the most important power in Central Asia between 755 and 840. After a prolonged war amongst the Tibetans, the Chinese, and the Uigurs, the latter triumphed and set up their rule in Turfan in 870 with Qarakhodjo as their capital. Uigur rule lasted in Turfan until the eleventh century, and during this period the region played a significant role in the history of Central Asia.

The ascendancy of the Uigurs, who were enthusiastic Buddhists, acted as a new impetus for the further advance of Buddhism. The

Turks had embraced Buddhism quite early in Tokharestan, and it had a powerful influence over their lives until their conversion to Islam. By the time they appeared in Turfan they had already absorbed a good deal of Buddhist culture. During their struggle against the Arabs, they built a huge Buddhist monastery near the Sogdh River. The name of the city, Bokhara, is derived from the Turkish and Mongol word *bukhar* for vihara. It is said that a Chinese princess, who was given in marriage to a Turkish ruler, brought with her an icon of the Buddha. A vihara was built for the image and the town of Bokhara later developed around this monastery. Most of the Buddhist sites in the region of Turfan belong to the Uigur period, and include cave temples with frescos representing Buddhas or Bodhisattvas, and numerous other Buddhist shrines. Buddhist texts in Tokharian are found together with Uigur translations.

Buddhism did not retain its original Indian character in Central Asia. During the course of its migration from India to Tokharestan, Khotan, and Turfan, Buddhism inevitably absorbed local characteristics. In the western part of Central Asia around Kashgar and in the northern part stretching eastward beyond Kucha, Theravada Buddhism was prevalent, but at places along the southern route, especially in Khotan and in the northeastern part around Turfan, Mahayana Buddhism was practiced.

Despite the enormous pressure of Islam in the eighth century, Buddhism held on until the eleventh century in the lines of oases lying north and south of the desert. Islamic attacks must have caused extensive destruction of religious art and sacred manuscripts since these Buddhist monasteries and sanctuaries were deserted in the eleventh century; whatever escaped the iconoclastic zeal of the Muslim conquerors has been well preserved in the dry climate of the region for the past nine hundred years.

India's immediate neighbours, Nepal and Tibet, owe much of their cultural inheritance to contact with India. Modern Nepal, an expanded version of the ancient country, is 525 miles long and about one hundred miles wide, and lies between India and Tibet. Originally the word Nepal implied the Valley, which, surrounded by the peaks of the Himalayas, is about fifteen to twenty miles long and ten miles wide, with its three capitals, Kathmandu, Patan, and Bhatgaon lying within a radius of seven miles of one another. Contact between the two countries is so close and ancient that it is impossible to trace the origins of Nepalese culture separately from Indian culture. It was in one of the republics of ancient India, at Lumbini in the city of Kapilavastu, within the boundaries of modern Nepal, that Gautama, the founder of Buddhism, was born. Consequently, Nepal holds a unique position in the Buddhist world, even though today it is the only country professing to be a sovereign Hindu state.

According to tradition, however, it was Asoka who introduced Buddhism as an organized doctrine into Nepal. He visited Lumbini and erected an inscribed pillar to commemorate the sacred birthplace of the Buddha. This event is an important landmark in the history of Buddhism. It is said that Charumati, a daughter of Asoka, married a Nepalese prince and built several stupas and monasteries, some of which have survived to the present day. Later, the imperial Guptas imposed their sovereignty on Nepal, and the reigning dynasties of Nepal and India began to intermarry. Nepal has often changed her religion according to whichever faith prevailed in the neighbouring parts of India—having embraced Hinayana, Mahayana, Vajrayana, and Hinduism in their respective ages of supremacy. The Rajputs and the Brahmans—and probably Buddhist monks from Nalanda and elsewhere—escaped to Nepal when Islam triumphed in India. In the eighteenth century Nepal was conquered by the Gurkhas, who trace their descent from the Rajputs, and who in the sixteenth century conquered the little state of Gurkha. Their language, Khas, is a Rajasthani dialect of Sanskrit origin, and under their influence Hinduism became the state religion of Nepal.

Nepal has never known religious conflicts and persecutions, and even today Hinduism and Buddhism live together in complete harmony. In the early centuries A.D. the disciplinary rules applicable to the monks of the *Mulasarvastivada* school of Buddhism in Nepal were somewhat modified to suit the rigid climatic conditions of that region. Nepal attained prominence both as a political and religious state during the reign of King Amsuvarman in the seventh century, who was as remarkable an administrator as he was a conqueror. Although he was perhaps a Sivaite Hindu, he contributed generously towards the growth of the Buddhist faith and institutions.

Later, Buddhist monks escaping from the encroachments of Islam in Bihar and Bengal took refuge in Nepal, carrying with them numerous valuable manuscripts, some of which were later transmitted to Tibet where they are still preserved. Thus some of the many Buddhist works which were lost in India are available in Chinese and Tibetan translations, and it is in Nepal that the nine Sanskrit works forming the Nepalese Buddhist canon are preserved. They are considered the original works of the Sanskrit canon which became the official scriptures of

Mahayana Buddhism; the *Prajnaparamita* is amongst these nine. Nepal has been a link between the regions lying on the two sides of the mid-Himalayan ranges, and, until recently, the normal road of communication between India and Tibet lay through Nepal via Kyirong.

With the decline of Buddhism in India, Nepalese Buddhism became increasingly self-contained, gradually abandoning some of its original features, such as monastic life and opposition to caste. Until recently four main sects of Buddhist philosophy have been prominent in Nepal: Svabhavika, which emphasizes that all things in the world have their own ultimate characteristics; Aisvarika, which believes in a self-existent god, who is perfect and infinite; Karmika, which believes in a conscious moral effort through which the world-phenomenon is developed; and Yatrika, which believes in the existence of conscious intellectual agency and free will. These represent an almost complete fusion of the various philosophical theories that emerged in India and Tibet under the stimulus of either Hinduism or Buddhism.

The small valley of Nepal reputedly contains more than two thousand temples. The most famous of these is the Temple of Pashupatinath. Most of the stupas of Asoka have disappeared and those that have survived, such as at Sanchi, Taxila, and Sarnath, have been so enlarged that the original structures are no longer clear. Only in Nepal have Mauryan stupas retained their original shape. Hindu religious architecture in Nepal is characterized by the stone temple with a massive tower above a comparatively small shrine. Because of the Buddhist periods in her history, Nepal has also developed temples of the pagoda type made of wood with copper roofs. Nepalese sculpture and painting is in a style derived from the Pala art of Bihar and Bengal. In the realm of art, Nepal was, in fact, practically an exclusive province of Pala, India, between the ninth and twelfth centuries. Tibet, whose art is close to that of Nepal, adopted the Pala tradition through Nepal and Kashmir. Many of the laws of Nepal and its social organizations naturally reflect Hindu models, and the Nepalese language is very close to Sanskrit. But the Hindu civilization in Nepal has evolved a distinct character of its own, effected through a blending of its own traditions with those of Tibet.

Wherever Buddhism spread it was able to ignite a new historical consciousness. This was the case in some measure even in India where Indian recorded history began in inscriptions and other forms from the time of Asoka. But it is in Tibet that the best example of this is seen. The history of Tibet was first recorded in the seventh century during the reign of Songtsan-Gampo, who first conceived the idea of reducing spoken Tibetan to a system of alphabetic writing to facilitate the arrival of Buddhism from India. However, Tibet's great altitude, the deeply religious character of its society, and its political organization have isolated it from other lands. When the Tibetans, who are ethnologically similar to the peoples of the Himalayan regions, settled in the area is not known; from time immemorial they have lived in an isolation imposed by the peculiarities of their environment. Except for Buddhism in the seventh century, Tibet scarcely allowed any other foreign cultural influence within her national frontiers. In fact, Tibet was the last country to embrace Buddhism, which by the seventh century was thriving in many other lands.

Traders, soldiers, and pilgrims had long been crossing her borders, and cultural contacts between Tibet and the Buddhist world surrounding her must have been established centuries before the actual arrival of Buddhism. According to a Tibetan legend, in the fifth century some Buddhist missionaries from India approached the Tibetan King Tho-tho-ri with presents of Buddhist books, but none at the royal court could make out what they meant, since an alphabetic script was then unknown in Tibet.

Although Buddhism was finally welcomed and encouraged by the powerful ruling Tibetan dynasty, it did not take root as easily as might have been expected. Before it was accepted by the people, it encountered prolonged opposition from the traditional ritualistic and sacrificial faith. This faith endorsed a nature worship, and believed that human ills were caused by the activities of evil spirits who were controlled by magic and spells. Buddhism had to wage an incessant and arduous struggle for over three centuries against these indigenous beliefs and old superstitions, and adapt its own doctrines to placate them. Many setbacks occurred until the arrival of Atisa in the eleventh century, when Buddhism finally became the national religion of Tibet.

Matrimonial alliances were instrumental in starting the growth of Buddhism in Tibet. In the seventh century, Tibet had emerged as a strong kingdom extending to the borders of India, Nepal, and China. In the south, Nepal's King was Amsuvarman; in the east, China was ruled by the powerful Emperor Tang Tai-tsung. According to the Tibetan chronicles, the talented Tibetan King, Songtsan-Gampo (or Srong-btsan Bam-po) married the daughter of Amsuvarman, Princess Bhrikuti, who was a devout Buddhist and who brought an image of the Buddha to Tibet with her. Songtsan, in deference to the new queen's beliefs which he himself already favoured, built a great temple known as Jokhang to house her image of the Buddha. Songtsan's power was so great that he compelled the Emperor of China to give him Princess Wen Ch'eng in marriage. She too was Buddhist and brought to Tibet the famous Buddha image now enshrined in Jokhang. This statue originally came from Magadha in India. It forms, together with two other statues preserved at the monastery of Kum-bum and at Santal temple at Peking, one of a triad celebrated in the Buddhist world. Whilst the arrival of these two queens did much to help the king introduce Buddhism into Tibet, he had, in fact, already selected a brilliant Tibetan in his court, Thonmi Sambhota, along with sixteen others, to travel to the famous centres of learning in southern India to study Indian writing, phonetics, and grammar.

Upon his return from several years of study in India, Thonmi Sambhota not only composed eight independent treatises on Tibetan writing and grammar, but also prepared the first Tibetan translations of Sanskrit texts of Buddhism.[7] Thus, he was both the pioneer of Buddhist learning in Tibet and the father of Tibetan literature. A grammar and a new script on the lines of the Khotanese alphabet, derived from Sanskrit prevalent in the Gupta period, were evolved for the Tibetan language.

Once the practice of visiting India had begun, many Tibetan students went to India to study Buddhism, and Sanskrit texts began to pour into Tibet. Indian and Chinese scholars visited Tibet and helped in translation and interpretation. It was during this period that the celebrated sandalwood image of Avalokitesvara, the compassionate Buddha, now worshipped in the palace of the Dalai Lama, was supposedly brought to Tibet by Indian scholars.

Songtsan, a contemporary of Muhammad and Harsha, introduced a number of social and cultural reforms, made Buddhism the state religion, and actively encouraged the study of Buddhism during the thirty years of his reign. He promulgated laws to harmonize with the Ten Virtues of Buddhism. He built the temples of Ramoche and Jokhang in Lhasa, and laid the beginnings of the magnificent palace of the Dalai Lama, the Potala, which exists to this day. He is regarded by the Tibetans as a national hero and a spiritual guide. For his respect for learning, and love of Tibet and its people, he is worshipped as one of the incarnations of Avalokitesvara.[8]

By the middle of the eighth century, Tibet had become so powerful under Trisong-Detsan that it was able to dictate terms to the kingdoms of Central Asia, control the nomads in the Tarim Basin, and even defeat Chinese armies and force the payment of tribute. Trisong-

Detsan's victory over China is commemorated in a pillar inscription in front of the Potala. He enthusiastically supported Buddhism, and invited Santarakshita, a famous Indian scholar from Nalanda University, to Tibet to preach Buddhism and initiate regular conversions. But Santarakshita faced bitter opposition from the Bonists and his sermons elicited little response. Storms and epidemics raging at the time provided "heaven-sent" opportunities for the Bonists, who were supported by dissident elements in the palace. These natural calamities were interpreted as the wrath of the gods at the perverse teachings of Santarakshita and finally the King was compelled to advise Santarakshita to retire to Nepal until public passions had subsided. In the end, however, the King triumphed over the Bonist rebellion. Santarakshita saw that in Tibet, immersed as it was in primitive sorcery and love of ritual, only a man versed in the esoteric practices and beliefs of Tantrism could command attention, and on his advice in 747 the King invited the great Tantric teacher, Padmasambhava (known in Tibet as Guru Rinpoche), to Tibet.

Born in Udayana, the border region between Kashmir and Afghanistan famous for its sorcery and magic, Padmasambhava had studied at Nalanda and was reputed to possess great supernatural powers. Before starting for Tibet, Padmasambhava prepared himself thoroughly for his task. He carefully studied the Bon doctrines and practices, and realized that only a person who could claim power over evil spirits and demonstrate this supremacy could possibly succeed. He took Mahayana Buddhism tinged with Tantric ideas to Tibet and, by incorporating many gods as Tantric guardian deities, he laid the foundation of Tibetan Buddhism or Lamaism. He replaced the Bon cult of animal worship with symbolic worship and its practice of black magic with inner purification.

It is, however, not easy to ascertain the truth about Padmasambhava because his life is so enshrouded in myth and legend. Nor is it easy now to define the details of the primitive Lamaism he devised and taught. But it is evident that his teaching was Tantric and a magical type of Mahayana Buddhism, to which he added a portion of the ritual and demonolatry of Bon. The Tantric Buddhism of Padmasambhava has been subjected to a good deal of criticism by some commentators, mainly because they have misunderstood the nature of Tantrism and the large part which sex played in it. The standards which these critics apply to Padmasambhava and his doctrine are unenlightened. Tantrism, whether Hindu or Buddhist, aims to interpret human nature pragmatically, and, unlike most faiths, it preaches understanding and sublimation of the reproductive force in direct opposition to the common but scientifically unsound teaching concerning the forcible suppression of it. Science recognizes today what Tantric thinkers accepted centuries ago, that "there is direct relationship between the highest mental and psychic powers in mankind and the secretions of the sex glands and, that physical youthfulness and efficiency are dependent upon conservation of the reproductive essences. All religions, likewise, even the most primitive, have recognized that there is inseparableness between the sex-energy and spiritual growth."[9]

Having been engaged in an unending war against evil spirits and demons, the Tibetans had acquired a tradition of discipline and organization, which made it easy for Padmasambhava to develop organized Buddhist life in Tibet. The first great monastery, in fact the greatest ever built in Tibet, the Samye monastery, which today contains many shrines and a large library of Sanskrit and Tibetan books, was built in 749 at Bsam-yas on the model of the Udayantapuri in Bihar. Santarakshita laid the foundation and was appointed its abbot. He held office for thirteen years until his death. He and Padmasambhava collaborated in teaching the Tripitaka, the Tantric doctrines, and the philosophical system of Yogacara. Having established Tibetan Buddhism or Lamaism, Padmasambhava disappeared from Tibet. However, the deep respect held for him even today indicates the impression he made on his contemporaries.

An important feature of this period was the reorganization and systematization of the translations of Santarakshita, and the preparation of the first catalogue of all translated Buddhist works. Meanwhile, Buddhist texts and scholars had also begun to arrive from China, some of them opposed to Lamaism. To meet their challenge the King invited Santarakshita's able disciple and commentator, Kamalasila, from Nalanda to deal with them. A debate was held between a Chinese scholar, the Mahayanist Hwashang, and Kamalasila in the presence of the King, and Kamalasila was the winner. The Chinese scholar, having lost the argument, left the country, but feelings amongst his defeated partisans were so embittered that the Indian scholar was murdered. His body was embalmed and is still preserved in a monastery in the north of Lhasa. Kamalasila was the author of *Tarka,* a work expounding the various philosophic systems of India, and of many other treatises which are still extant in the great Lamaist canon, *Tan-gyur* (or *Tanjur*). *Mahavyutpatti,* the excellent Sanskrit-Tibetan dictionary, also dates from this period.

Buddhism made steady progress and was actively patronized by Trisong-Detsan's successors, especially by Rapachen (or Ralpachen)

(817–836). His reign is considered a glorious period of Tibetan Buddhism, and it was under his patronage that the first history of Tibet was written. He made his young son take monastic vows, gave various privileges and administrative authority to the priesthood, built libraries, monasteries, and temples, encouraged Buddhist painting and sculpture, and even allowed his long locks of hair to be used as a mat by the Buddhist abbots associated with him. In the first year of his reign, he convened a Great Council of Indian and Tibetan scholars to discuss ways of spreading Buddhism. It was a period of great literary activity in which numerous Indian scholars, such as Jinamitra, Silendrabodhi, Surendrabodhi, Prajnavarmam, Danasila, and Bodhimitra, co-operated with the Tibetan scholars, Dpal-brt segs, Ye-ses-sde, Chos-kyirgyalmthsan, and others, in translating many Sanskrit works, which constitute more than half of the two large Tibetan collections, *Kanjur* and *Tanjur*.

Perhaps the very fact of Rapachen's devotion to Buddhism and the intensity of Buddhist activity caused the opposition to react violently, and in a palace revolution Rapachen was murdered by the supporters of his elder brother Glandarma, who, upon accession, became a professed enemy of Buddhism. A violent persecution followed. Buddhist images were burned, monasteries closed, religious ceremonies banned, and monks forced to return to the life of laymen under the penalty of exile. By an interesting coincidence, Buddhism was also being persecuted in China at this time. Such excesses created widespread resentment and counteraction. Within three years of the beginning of King Glandarma's reign, in 841, a monk quietly rode up and killed him with a well-aimed arrow. Whilst Glandarma's ruthless suppression of Buddhism brought the end of early Lamaism, it marked a decisive period in the annals of Tibetan politics, for it led to the decline and fall of monarchial rule in Tibet. The banished priesthood returned to Tibet and became more powerful than ever.

Buddhism finally became the national religion of Tibet by the beginning of the eleventh century, and the flow of Buddhist monks and scholars between India and Tibet gained new impetus. Once the followers of Bon were fully reconciled, there developed a distinctive Tibetan branch of Buddhism which produced many great spiritual teachers, scholars, and preachers, well-versed in both Sanskrit and Tibetan literature. To assist in the growth of Buddhism, Tibetan scholars persuaded Atisa (980–1054)—also known as Dipankara Srijnana—of the Vikramasila monastery in Bihar, to come to Tibet in 1038. Atisa, who was nearly sixty years old at that time, lived and preached in all parts of the country for about fifteen years before he died in the

Nyethang monastery, where his *Samadhi* still stands. Atisa based his teachings on the Yogacara tradition, took a synthetic view of the tenets of Hinayana and Mahayana Buddhism, enforced celibacy of monks, and discouraged magic practices. He was possibly the last great Indian scholar to carry spiritual impetus from India to Tibet, where he ranks next only to the Buddha and Padmasambhava.

Other Indian influences also found their way to Tibet. For instance, the Tibetan medical system owes its origin to the Ayurvedic system of India. Tibetan Tantric forms are almost indistinguishable from Hindu Tantras, and certain Tantric images like Halahal-avalokitesvara and Nilkant-avalokitesvara are derivatives of Siva. Tibetan art is largely a continuation of the Buddhist art of eastern India during the Pala period. The representations of the Bodhisattvas, for example, are directly reminiscent of the traditions of Pala art, and reached Tibet through the Nepalese. Nepalese craftsmen were particularly accomplished and, even as far as Peking, they were considered amongst the best in this field until the collapse of Lamaism in China. Indian influence, possibly that of Ajanta, is particularly well marked in a Tibetan painting representing Avalokitesvara and Kitigarbha, now preserved in the Musée Guimet at Paris. Tibetan art was very popular with the Emperors of China, so much so that some of its religious features were adopted during the Ming and Ching periods.

After the death of Atisa, Buddhist reform was somewhat interrupted by prolonged political unrest in Tibet. Whilst reform suffered, Buddhism itself gained fresh strength, because Buddhist monasteries provided sanctuary to soldiers as well as to refugees. In 1206 Genghis Khan, the grandfather of Kublai Khan, brought Tibet under Mongol control. In the second half of the century, the Tibetan Lamas, despite intense competition from their Christian rivals, succeeded in converting Emperor Kublai Khan to Buddhism, giving Buddhism in Tibet unique prestige and power. The most powerful of the Lamaist hierarchs was the Saskya Grand Lama, and it was his representatives who succeeded in converting the Great Khan. In return, the Lama of Saskya, with the assistance of a staff of scholars, translated the Tibetan Buddhist canon into Mongolian, and was recognized as head of the Lamaist Church and tributary ruler of Tibet in 1270. This creation of a Lamaist Papacy by conferring "divine" honours upon the acquisition of temporal power, was, however, not analogous to Indian practice. Asoka himself never claimed any divine honours other than what was implied in his cherished title, "Beloved of the Gods." Tibet remained under Saskya supremacy until the middle of the fourteenth century when the power of the Saskya abbot was broken by the Ming Emperor of China.

Meanwhile, Tibetan Buddhism had begun to split into various schools of thought. The earlier heterogenous type of Buddhism came to be called Rninmapa, or the Old Tantric or Translation School. Its followers worshipped Padmasambhava as their founder and guru, and believed in the fulfilment of both the divine and the demonical. Today they are generally recognized by their red caps. The Kagyupa school was founded by Marpa, who had studied with Atisa at Nalanda under the Indian Tantrist, Naropa, and whose teachings have some affinities with the Dhyana School of Buddhism. The Saskya School (Great Earth School, so known because of the colour of the soil where its first monastery was built in 1071 on the site of the present Saskya) was closely related to the old Rninmapa School. It sought a synthesis between the old and the new Tantrism on the basis of Nagarjuna's Madhyamika philosophy. The monks of this School did not practice celibacy, but were greatly devoted to learning, were excellent preachers, and the School produced many eminent scholars, including By-ston (1290–1364) who was a renowned commentator on fundamental Buddhist treatises, an authoritative historian, and a collector of Buddhist works.

Atisa's reformed teachings, based upon the Yogacara traditions, led to the establishment of the Bkahgdamspa School by his Tibetan disciple, Hbrom-ston. This School took a synthetic view of the teachings of both the Hinayana (Theravada) and Mahayana, enforced celibacy upon monks, and opposed magic practices. This reformed School of Atisa, reorganized and purged of much of its rituals by the great Tsongkhapa, dominates Tibetan Buddhism today. The altered title was Gelugpa (popularly known as the Yellow Hats), and the first Grand Lama was Geden-dub, the nephew of Tsongkhapa. It soon eclipsed all other rival schools, and in five generations it gained the priest-kingship of Tibet, which it retains to this day. The fifth Grand Lama, Nag-wan-Lozang (1615–1680), gave Gelugpa great temporal power, and in 1650 the Mongolian chief, Gusri Khan, conferred upon him the sovereignty of Tibet and gave him the title of Dalai, meaning ocean. Whilst his successors are now commonly known as Dalai Lamas, the Tibetans call them Gyal-wa Rin-po-che, the great gem of majesty.

The recognition of the complete and divine sovereignty of the Dalai Lama over the whole of Tibet is a turning point in Tibetan history. Sanskrit texts, not only on religion but also on other subjects such as grammar and medicine, continued to be translated into Tibetan under the rule of this able and widely travelled Dalai Lama. Religious and cultural relations with India increasingly declined, however, mainly because of British domination and the liquidation of the old order in India.

Relations between India and Tibet, both of a political and cultural nature, have been re-established in the recent years since Indian independence, although the political aspect has become by far the most dominant. The Dalai Lama and a number of his followers are presently living in India as refugees from Chinese interference in Tibet. The close physical contact, although caused by political circumstances, must have cultural consequences which will only be realized later.

Chapter IX

THE DRAGON UNDER THE BODHI TREE

UNTIL RECENTLY, India and China had coexisted peacefully for over two thousand years. This amicable relationship may have been nurtured by the close historical and religious ties of Buddhism, introduced to China by Indian monks at a very early stage of their respective histories, although there are fragmentary records of contacts anterior to the introduction of Buddhism. There are numerous references to China in Sanskrit texts, but their chronology is questionable and sketchy. The *Mahabharata* refers to China several times, including a reference to presents brought by the Chinese at the *Rajasuya Yajna* of the Pandavas; also, the *Arthasastra* and the *Manusmriti* mention China. According to René Grousset, the name China comes from "an ancient Sanskrit name for the regions to the east, and not, as often supposed, from the name of the state of Ch'in," the first dynasty established by Shih Huang Ti in 221 B.C. When necessary, the Chinese would distinguish the centre of the world where they lived from peripheral regions, and one of the ancient expressions has become the modern name for China: Chung-kuo, literally "central country."[1] The Sanskrit name *Cina* for China could have been derived from the small state of that name in Chan-si (Shan-si) in the northwest of China, which flourished in the fourth century B.C., or the name may have come down to India through Central Asia. Scholars have pointed out that the Chinese word for lion, *shih*, used long before the Chin dynasty, was derived from the Sanskrit word, *simha*, and that the Greek word for China, *Tzinista*, used by some later writers, appears to be a derivative of the Sanskrit *Chinasthana*.

The formative period of Chinese Quietism, the fourth century B.C., was not one when outside influences on thought were general, but it developed and expanded during a period when such influences were growing in importance, and scholars now agree that Chinese literature of the third century is full of geographic and mythological elements derived from India. "I see no reason to doubt," comments Arthur Waley, "that the 'holy mountain-men' (*sheng-hsien*) described by Lieh Tzu are Indian *rishi;* and when we read in *Chuang Tzu* of certain Taoists who practiced movements very similar to the *asanas* of Hindu *yoga,* it is at least a possibility that some knowledge of the *yoga* technique which these *rishi* used had also drifted into China."[2] The Chinese Quietists practiced a form of self-hypnosis which has an indisputably close resemblance to Indian Yoga. The Chinese Taoist philosopher, Liu-An (Huai-nan-tzu) who died in 122 B.C., makes use "of a cosmology in his book which is clearly of Buddhist inspiration."[3]

The first mention of India to be found in Chinese records is in connection with the mission to Ta-hsia (Bactriana) of a talented and courageous Chinese envoy, Chang Chien (kien), about 138 B.C.[4] Fourteen years later, having escaped after ten years as a captive of the Huns, he returned home and in his report to the Chinese Emperor he referred to the country of *Shen-tu* (India) to the southeast of the Yueh-chih (Jou-Chih) country.[5] Chang Chien had seen bamboo poles and cloth in Ta-hsia, which had reached there from Szechwan, a province in the southwest of China, through India and Afghanistan. Whilst his diplomatic mission did not succeed, his observations and reports impressed the Han Emperor with the need to encourage trade and contact with India and other countries to the west.

There are other traditional stories suggestive of earlier links, but Chang Chien's reference to Indian trade with the southwestern districts of China along the overland route corresponding to the modern Yunnan road indicates the existence of some sort of commercial relations well before the second century B.C. The find of a Chinese coin at Mysore, dated 138 B.C., suggests that maritime relations between India and China existed in the second century B.C. Passages in a Chinese text of the first century A.D. vaguely refer to Chinese trade relations with countries in the China Sea and Indian Ocean, such as Huang-che (Kanchi or a place in the Ganges delta), as well as to the exchange of occasional diplomatic missions.

There can be little dispute that trade was the main motivation for these early contacts. This is supported by finds of beads and pottery, in addition to specific references in historical texts. By the early centuries of the Christian era, Sino-Indian trade appears to have assumed considerable proportions. Chinese silk, *Chinamsuka,* and later porcelain were highly prized in India, and Indian textiles were sold in southwest China. The similarity between the Chinese and Indian words for vermilion and bamboo, *ch'in-tung* and *ki-chok*, and *sindura* and *kichaka*, also indicates commercial links. At least by the fifth century, India was exporting to China wootz steel (wootz from the Indian Kanarese word *ukku*), which was produced by fusing magnetic iron ore by carbonaceous matter.

With goods came ideas. It has often been contended that merchants were not likely to have been interested in philosophy or capable of the exchange of ideas. This is an erroneous belief which disregards historical evidence and, as Arthur Waley points out, is "derived from a false analogy between East and West. It is quite true that Marco Polo 'songeait surtout à son négoce'. But the same can hardly be said of Indian or Chinese merchants. Buddhist legend, for example, teems with merchants reputedly capable of discussing metaphysical questions; and in China Lu Puwei, compiler of the philosophical encyclopaedia *Lu Shih Ch'un Chiu*, was himself a merchant. Legend even makes a merchant of Kuan Chung; which at any rate shows that philosophy and trade were not currently supposed to be incompatible."[6]

The trade routes between China and India, by both land and sea, were long and perilous, often requiring considerably more than two years to negotiate. The overland routes were much older and more often used, but the sea routes gained popularity with progress in shipbuilding and seamanship. Formidable and frightening as the physiography of the land routes was, the traffic through the passes and along the circuitous routes around the mountains was fairly vigorous.

There were three overland routes between India and China. The principal route lay through the northwestern regions of India which converge upon Afghanistan, western Tibet, Russian Turkistan, and Chinese Turkistan. Piercing through the Afghan country, and proceeding along the valley of the Kabul River, with stages at Peshawar (Puru-sapura) and Jalalabad (Nagarahara), it reached the Valley of Bamiyan which commands a major pass from the Kabul region to Balkh in the Hindukush mountains. Beyond this region, on the famous Silk High-way between Central and Western Asia, lay Bactriana, modern Balkh, which the ancient Indians called Balhika and the Chinese Fo-ho. On the westward journey from Balkh, the silk route proceeded to Antiochia Margiana (modern Meri), then to the great Parthian cities at Hecatompylos (modern Shahrud), and Ecbatana (modern Hamadan), crossing the Euphrates at Heirapoli (modern Menbij), and finally reaching Antioch. Eastward from Balkh two roads led to Central Asia and China. One proceeded northward through Sogdiana, then crossed the Syr or Jaxartes, and went eastward through Tashkent and the passes of the Tienshan, finally reaching Ush-Turfan. The other, which was shorter and more frequently used by Buddhist monks, passed through the country of the Tokharians and the Pamirs to Kashgar, and thence led to the Tarim Basin, the modern Chinese province of Sinkiang. There was a more direct but far more difficult route from Kashmir along the Gilgit and the Yasin valleys to Tashkurghan where it joined the other route to Kashgar. It was in this region that Indian, Chinese, and Western merchants met, making it the centre of commerce for the ancient world.

From Kashgar two routes led to the borders of China, one along the southern fringe of the Tarim Basin via Khotan, and the other along its northern fringe to Turfan. Rivers and streams in the Tien-shan ranges in the north and the Kun-lun ranges in the south made irrigation and agriculture possible in the foothills. International trade along these two routes further strenghtened the economic prosperity of this area. Along the southern route, a number of flourishing states and settlements, such as Yarkand, Khotan, and Niya, practiced Buddhism and played an extremely important role for almost a thousand years in the trade and cultural relations between China and India. There were equally important states along the northern route as well, whose people and languages differed from those of the south, but who were all united in Buddhism. Turfan, situated further east on the northern route, was well within the periphery of Chinese politics, and thus made outstanding contributions to Buddhism in China.

The two routes from Kashgar met on the Chinese frontier at Yu-men-kuan, the Jade Gate, near Tun-huang, one of the principal centres of Buddhist learning. From the testimony of ancient travellers, it would appear that Central Asia was much more habitable during the first thousand years of the Christian era than it is now.

Long before the northwestern routes were opened about the second century B.C., and long before the development of these Indianized states, there were two other routes from India to China. One of these began at Pataliputra (modern Patna), passed through Assam and Upper Burma near Bhamo, and proceeded over the mountains and across the river valleys to Yunnanfu (Kunming), the main city of the southern province of China. The other route lay through Nepal and Tibet. We have no contemporary description of this route but there is definite evidence of its use. These routes were difficult and dangerous because they lay through inaccessible, turbulent, and barren lands offering scanty food and security. The route across Tibet was developed much later, in the middle of the seventh century, when Tibet had accepted Buddhism and established political relations with China. During the second half of the seventh century, a large number of Chinese monks came to India by this route.

In addition to land routes, there was an important sea link between India and China through Southeast Asia. During the course of the first few centuries of the Christian era, a number of Indianized states had been founded all over Southeast Asia. Both cultures met in this region, and the Indianized states served as an intermediary stage for the further transmission of Indian culture and Buddhism to China.

Ancient Greek geographers knew Southeast Asia and China (*Thinae*) were accessible by sea. Ptolemy mentions an important but unidentified Chinese port on the Tonkinese coast. Ports on the western coast of India were Bharukaccha (Broach); Surparka (Sopara); Kalyana; on the Bay of Bengal at the mouth of the Kaveri, Kaveripattam (Puhar); and at the mouth of the Ganges, Tamralipti (Tamluk). At least two of these ports on the Bay of Bengal—Kaveripattam and Tamralipti— were known to the Greek sailors as Khaberos and Tamalitis. At first Indian ships sailed to Tonkin (Kiao-Che) which was the principal port of China, Tonkin being a Chinese protectorate. Later all foreign ships were required to sail to Canton in China proper. Canton became a prosperous port and from the seventh century onward was the most important landing place for Buddhist missionaries arriving from India or Southeast Asia.

Reading the accounts of Chinese travellers, it is impossible not to be impressed by their intrepid spirit. The perils of the desert, the danger of the "moving sands," and the loneliness of the journey were so complete that there were not even any birds or animals to be seen. Travellers often lost their way, and the sands were littered with the bones of those who had perished. The rigours of the journey were relieved only by the hospitality offered by the few Buddhist principalities and towns. The route continued through the different crests and gorges of the sand-eroded Karakorum and Kohibaba into northern Afghanistan or into Ladhakh on the Tibetan border. South of Kapisa, then a small state to the north of the modern city of Kabul, India commenced with the kingdom of Gandhara, lying alongside the stretch of the Kabul River between the Kunar and the Indus.

The sea was only slightly less dangerous. Navigation at the time was crude and without any scientific aids except the mariner's compass.

The timber ships—tall floundering vessels of three tiers—were apt to spring leaks, and there was constant danger from typhoons between China and the Indonesian islands. Fa-hsien vividly describes how he escaped a watery grave. It took him fourteen days to reach Ceylon from Tamralipti and another ninety from Ceylon to Java. On his journey from Java to Canton, his ship lost its course in a storm, and it took eighty-two days of anxious drifting to reach Shantung. Merchants and monks travelled together. Although the traders faced the same hard climatic and physical conditions as did the pilgrims, they were better organized. The pilgrims, too, were probably weaker physically because of fasts and other self-imposed restrictions. They often depended on the goodwill of the kings through whose kingdoms they passed for protection, and frequently these kings, who had only recently embraced Buddhism, would coerce the monks to stay behind. But their single-minded devotion to their pilgrimages and their irrepressible urge to acquire learning sustained the pilgrims, although tests of physical endurance did not end with the journey. Living in strange and distant lands was no less trying. Whilst some scholars and pilgrims adapted easily to the ways of the new land, where they either stayed for several years or settled permanently, others longed to return to their homes.

Generally the Chinese monks set out for the famous centres of learning in India, like the University of Nalanda, but many Chinese scholars elected to stop at places on the periphery of India, such as the seats of learning in northwest India and Kashmir. Of those who came by sea, some chose to stop at the famous Buddhist centres in Sumatra or Ceylon. Whilst some monks learned the sacred language, philosophy, and rules of monastic life, others studied a special branch or particular school of Buddhism. Some, upon their return to China, founded their own new schools.

The sixth and fifth centuries B.C., during which Chinese philosophy was systematized, is by far the most brilliant period of Chinese thought. The number of philosophies was so large that this period is commonly known as the time of the Hundred Schools. It was one of those unique moments in the history of a nation, in which political suffering and economic chaos are dwarfed by the brilliance of its philosophic and spiritual achievement. Of the six main schools of philosophy, Confucianism and Taoism were the most important.[7]

It is misleading to use the general term Confucianism, *Ju Chia*, to define Chinese classics dealing with a wide variety of subjects, such as cosmology, ethics, morals, and theories of state and government. But it was from the time of Kung-tzu, or Confucius (551–479 B.C.), that the era of systematic philosophies began in China. Confucius was, strictly speaking, not the founder of a system but the editor, interpreter, and transmitter of ancient Chinese lore. He expounded in his *Lun-yu* (*Analects*), the old Chinese classics, such as *I-Ching, Shih-Ching, Shu-Ching, Li-Chi,* and *Chun-Chiu.*[8] In fact, the Duke of Chou, who lived many centuries before Confucius, is honoured in China as the founder of the "Confucian" tradition.

With a magnetic personality and persuasive power of speech, Confucius attracted a number of disciples—reputedly seventy-two, although in the *Analects* only some twenty persons figure—many of whom were members of the nobility. He was China's first and greatest teacher. He spent his long life as a travelling advisor to the feudal princes and as the head of a flourishing private school of ethics. China was at the time, so Confucius thought, drifting away from its ancient heritage, and he felt compelled to arrest this evil by collecting, preserving, and disseminating the records of ancient learning. The religion prevalent in Chinese society dwelt little on life after death and little use was made of it to deter wickedness and stimulate virtue. Confucius did have some religious convictions but he apparently did not use them as a basis for his philosophy. He was curious about the invisible realm or reality and believed that man had a moral force or character from which his effectiveness was derived, but he did not dwell upon the origin of this all-important essence. He condemned human sacrifice, which had been very prevalent earlier in China and which had continued to a lesser extent until his time.

Confucius, despite his deep influence on intellectual history, was not himself, strictly speaking, an intellectual. He was mainly a moral teacher, aiming at improving the conduct and values of the people. The central theme of his doctrine was the perfect development of personality, and the proper standardization and adjustment of human relations for the attainment of the supreme good. Until Confucius' time, the term *Chun-tzu,* son of a ruler or gentleman, meant a man of superior birth. But Confucius changed this meaning completely, asserting that any man who was noble, just, kind, and unselfish could be a gentleman. The criterion was not birth but conduct.

He considered man to be essentially a social being, emphasizing the virtues of *jen* (human-heartedness) and *yi* (righteousness). Jen, which has been described as his "golden rule," implies "Do not do to others what you do not wish for yourself." It is imperative for the individual to act rightly and morally, but not just because it is personally advantageous to do so.

Confucius made no claim to possessing the ultimate truth; he only claimed to be advancing towards it through the empirical method of observation and analysis. Perhaps more than any other thinker of comparable stature, he made a clear distinction between metaphysics and ethics, basing his ethics upon the nature of man and society. Confucius purposely refrained from teaching metaphysics, but his disciples, especially Meng-tzu or Mencius (371–289 B.C.) and Hsun-tzu (298–238 B.C.), included metaphysical speculations in Confucianist thought. Whilst Mencius emphasized the idealistic aspect of Confucianism, saying that human nature was good, Hsun-tzu stressed its realism, holding that human nature was originally and intrinsically bad.

Teaching, however, was not Confucius' ultimate goal; he planned to reform society through government. Society to him was an ordinance of heaven and was made up of five relationships, between ruler and subject, husband and wife, father and son, elder and younger brothers, and friends. And since the government was to work righteously for the welfare and happiness of society, and was in return entitled to the sincere obedience of the people, the country should be ruled by the most capable man available. Few could be better equipped for this task, he believed, than himself. He patiently waited for the right opportunity to capture political power and prove himself to be the model ruler. In this he was sadly disappointed, although many of his disciples held government posts and he did become for a short period *Shih-Shih*, Leader of the Knights, which was not, politically speaking, a position of importance. His doctrine that any man, regardless of birth, could become a gentleman was a revolutionary concept in feudal Chinese society, and it is therefore scarcely surprising that Confucius was not very successful in his lifetime. Frustrated in his bid for political power, he died a broken-hearted and rather pathetic old man who thought himself a failure. Indeed, his ideas did not gain supremacy during the first century or so after his death until they were lifted out of obscurity by Mencius, who emphasized the idealistic trend in Confucianism, postulating that human nature was intrinsically good. Since then, Confucianist ideas, in one form or another, have continued to influence men. Even some of the Chinese Communists trace the beginnings of their revolutionary tradition to him.

Taoism (or *Tao Chia*, or *Tao Chiao*) belongs to a much later period than Confucianism. It begins with Yang-chu, probably a contemporary of Mencius and Chuang-tzu, but it is based on the *Tao Te Ching* which is reputed to be the work of Lao-tzu (b. 604 B.C.) whose actual existence, however, is doubted today. Some of the teachings of the *Tao Te Ching* can be traced to ancient Chinese classics, and some bear close resemblance to Indian thought. The text was edited during the Han period, having been given state recognition as a classic in the middle of the second century B.C. It is a small book of about five thousand characters with two large divisions entitled *Tao* and *Te*. The former deals mainly with metaphysics and the latter with ethics and politics. Although the beginnings of Taoist thought can be traced back to a time before Confucius, it is commonly regarded as an intellectual reaction against Confucianist thought.

Taoism is both a religion (*Tao Chiao*) and a philosophy (*Tao Chia*), and the teachings of the two are in a way mutually contradictory. As a philosophy Taoism teaches the doctrine of following nature, whilst as a religion it teaches men to work against nature. Taoism as a philosophy is theoretical, and as a religion it is quite practical in outlook and aims; its philosophy is anterior to its religion. Taoist thought is mainly a form of escapism, preaching abandonment of human society which is considered evil, and retirement to a life of seclusion in natural retreats. It is, however, as a philosophy that Taoism is seen as a competitor of Confucianism. Whilst Confucianism was originally a social philosophy emphasizing the responsibilities of man, Taoism was originally an anti-social philosophy emphasizing what was natural and spontaneous in man. It opposed the educational activities of the Confucianists, and advocated that the people should be kept in innocence. Opposed to a highly centralized system of government and all forms of legal restraint, it condemned militarism and exalted non-resistance. Whilst Confucianists advocated a carefully ordered system of government for the benefit of the people, Taoists claimed that the best government was one which left the people alone.

Whilst Confucianism was prepared to accept the world without speculating on the origins of the universe or the nature of being, Taoism penetrated behind the visible to explore the ultimate reality. Taoism stands for conformity with nature and its laws. Only by the proper development of his nature through the use of his *te* (power or virtue), and by recognizing the relative nature of things and identifying himself with the whole, can man achieve his chief purpose, happiness. Gradual recognition that all distinctions, including that between life and death, are merely relative conventions and not absolute can lead to this state of happiness. Nature is regulated by exact principles, but it never explains them. The perfect man penetrates the mystery of the order of heaven and earth, and comprehends the principles of nature. He does nothing and originates nothing; he merely contemplates the universe. The perfect man only needs to be one with the Great One. The end of knowledge is its own banishment, it is no-knowledge. Hence the doctrine of *wu-wei,* do-nothing or inaction. By doing nothing there is nothing which is not done.

Both tao and te are important concepts of Taoist metaphysics. The term tao originally meant the way in which the heavens caused the phenomena on earth. The tao was located about the celestial pole, which was the seat of power because all revolved about it. Later, tao was thought of as the universal cosmic energy behind the visible order of nature. The tao, omnipotent and eternal, produced *yin* and *yang,* the negative and positive, female and male principles of nature, which gave birth to heaven and earth, which in their turn produced all beings. It is conceived as unnameable, the ultimate and absolute principle that lies beyond good and evil, not moral but supra-moral. It is the oneness in which both being and non-being are dialectically embraced.

Chuang-tzu (*ca.* 369-286 B.C.) was the earliest and most brilliant Taoist. Original both in thought and literary expression, he sought to defend and develop the *Ching* philosophy, and he reacted strongly against all traditional thought, particularly Confucianism.

Until Buddhism entered China, the rivalry between the Confucianist and Taoist philosophies dominated Chinese thought. Confucianism, however, gained ground during the Han period, but not without incorporating some Taoist doctrines. Consequently, a culture based on the canonical writings, as edited and interpreted by Confucius and his school, had emerged. The Former Han dynasty, in contrast to the active policy of its predecessors, encouraged scholarship and adopted Confucianism as the state religion. Confucianist scholars were given high positions, and a rationale for political, bureaucratic, and social relationships was sought in the Confucianist classics. The intelligentsia and the ruling classes accepted the complete supremacy of these classics, and the government drew upon them, as they were impregnated with legalistic notions for a standard code of morals and ritual rules regulating conduct of the rulers and the ruled. During the Later Han period, rigid Confucianist "ceremonialism" dominated the whole society. The Confucianist classics had become highly formalized, verbose, and specialized. *Li,* or procedural rules, actually divided society into ranks of social positions. Even nations had come to be placed in hierarchial positions; China was "the Middle Kingdom" and other nations were "Barbarians." Within nations there were lords, aristocrats, officials, common people, and slaves.,

In the Later Han period the literati, mentally exhausted and physically weakened by the successive incursions of the hordes from the north, were disinclined to follow the Confucianist principle of restraint. Fond of explaining the matters of state and society by relating them to the phenomena of nature, the Confucianists had pushed analogies so far that they could not be sustained against the attacks of the iconoclasts and sceptics, such as Wang Chung (27–97), the chief exponent of the Old Text School that purged Confucianism of its yin-yang elements. Through his criticism of the yin-yang theory, especially its belief that an interaction exists between heaven and man, and by pointing out that man's position in the universe was no better than that of a flea under a robe, Wang Chung prepared the way for a revival of Taoism a century later. The increasing belief in the supernatural also undermined Confucianist authority. Doctrinal and internal conflicts concerning the interpretation of classical texts also had enervating effects. Powerless to obtain relief from the oppression of the great families which maintained their authority by driving the peasantry to slavery, extreme poverty, and deep discontent, the Confucianists became receptive to superstition and miracles. Whilst dynastic quarrels pulled the Empire apart from the top, the peasants were alienated at the bottom. Furthermore, a system of thought so completely interwoven with the Han political order as was Confucianism was bound to be weakened and discredited once the Han Empire declined.

It was at this time that Buddhism arrived in China. Disillusioned in Confucianist thought, both the literati and the masses alike turned to Taoism and Buddhism, seeking an escape into spiritualism. The golden images of the Buddha, the burning of incense, and the chanting of sutras by the yellow-robed Buddhist monks captivated the Chinese mind. Consequently, Buddhism was welcomed by all classes as a religion holding the promise of relief from misfortune.

The Later Han period is conspicuous for its political decadence, economic stress, and opulence in the urban areas, which combined to add to the general poverty of the common people. Whilst the lax life led many of the rich to renounce worldly pleasures by turning to Buddhism, the peasants hoped for equality in the new faith. Chinese traditional thought had little left of its earlier vitality and intellectual curiosity to resist the influx of Buddhist ideas.

Buddhism was more developed religiously than Confucianism and more sophisticated philosophically than Taoism. Buddhism made no class distinctions and thus appealed to both the educated and uneducated, the rich and poor. Mou-tzu (170–225) wrote a treatise in which he compared the doctrines of Buddhism with the teachings of Confucius and Lao-tzu, and tried to establish Buddhist superiority. Such writings created a favourable climate for Buddhist teachings.

In spite of the recognition given to Buddhism by the Han Emperor Ming, there were many Chinese literati who opposed it because their own political, intellectual, and social interests clearly would have suffered from its predominance. Hence, the Later Han official classes were hostile to the introduction of Buddhism, and, since Confucianism continued to be a powerful factor in Chinese society, Buddhism has always been subject to the pressures of Confucianist beliefs and politics and its fortunes have varied accordingly.

The exact date of the introduction of Buddhism into China is controversial. Chinese historians, as a rule, excluded religion from their chronicles unless it was directly related to politics or the court. They were even less interested in foreign religions, because they were orthodox Confucianist scholars. The Chinese peasants were generally unfamiliar with Chinese ideographs and literature, and the contemporary Chinese writings that have survived come from a small group of government intellectuals who, trained in the tradition of Confucianism, suffered from a marked attitude of superiority and exclusiveness towards foreign countries. Chinese history was written "by bureaucrats for bureaucrats." References in these records to early Buddhism, therefore, are too few and often too casual, if not altogether adverse, to give a clear picture. These annals give scarcely any account of the people and life in the provinces. In reconstructing the history of Buddhism on the basis of such material, extreme care must be taken. On the other hand, the Buddhist accounts were naturally written less as history than as a means of enhancing the prestige and popularity of the faith, often recording easy conversions and exaggerated triumphs of Buddhism at the Chinese Court.

Buddhism is generally said to have entered China during the reign of Ming-ti (58–75), but it is certain that it had been heard of in China before this time. According to a Chinese tradition, which cannot be fully substantiated, Buddhist missionaries reached Chin China from Mauryan India. *Li Tai San Pao Chi* (The Record Concerning the Three Treasures Under Successive Dynasties), written at the end of the sixth century, states that eighteen Buddhist monks headed by the Shrmana Shih-li-fang, carrying a number of Buddhist scriptures, reached the Chin Court early in the third century B.C., but the historicity of this reference is doubtful.[9] Only a few recent scholars accept this tradition as valid, but it is significant that one of them should be

Liang Chi-chao (1873–1929), because he is otherwise quite critical in dealing with early Buddhism.[10] According to a legend, the source of which, the *Lieh-tzu*, is a forgery of the third century or later, Confucius knew of the existence of the Buddha. Amongst other evidence cited to connect Asoka with the introduction of Buddhism into China, mention is made of his eighty thousand stupas some of which were said to have been discovered in China, and of relic bones of the Buddha said to have been excavated from one of them. Significantly, the first reference to Buddhist missionaries is in the period of Asoka, the founder of proselytism.

Whilst Asoka was engaged in humanizing politics by incorporating the spirit of the Buddha's compassion into his administration, and by promulgating the doctrine that "victory through the *Dharma* is the highest victory," China was beginning to emerge from an age of chaos and civil wars as a unified state. This was the period of the Chin dynasty from which China is generally believed to have gotten its name. Its first ruler, Shih Huang-ti (246–210 B.C.), sometimes called the Chinese Caesar, suppressed the turbulent Yueh-chih (Jou-Chih) in the south and the Huns in the north, and built the famous Great Wall. He founded a centralized state which was to last under different dynasties with varying authority and changing frontiers for more than two thousand years. Shih Huang-ti, however, in marked contrast to his contemporary, Asoka, violently suppressed certain philosophical and political ideas. This policy culminated in the outrageous "Fen-shu-keng-ju" incident in which scholars were buried alive and books were burned. The report that Shih Huang-ti imprisoned a group of Buddhist monks may lend some strength to the view that Buddhism had begun to trickle into China in the time of the Mauryas. After the death of Asoka in India, the great Han dynasty (206 B.C.–A.D. 220) arose in China, extending the Chinese frontiers, establishing internal peace and prosperity, and laying the foundations for the greatness and continuity of the Chinese state and culture. During the second century B.C., the Han dynasty adopted an aggressive policy towards its western neighbours, and opened up the Central Asian traffic routes over the Sinkiang Desert. These routes, which first carried Chinese political domination, later brought Indian culture.

In the spring of 121 B.C. the Han Emperor Wu dispatched a Chinese cavalry general, Ho Chu-ping, on a military expedition against the Hsiu-tu king in the northern territories. It is reported that Ho Chu-ping found a golden statue of a human form which the defeated king worshipped and to which, except for burning incense and ceremonial bowing, no sacrifices were offered. It has been suggested that this statue was a Buddhist image, and, if true, it is the earliest record of Chinese contact with Buddhism. The general opinion, however, is that it was instead a symbol of some local deity.

In 120 B.C. whilst a huge artificial lake named Kun-ming was being dug in Shansi, a mysterious black substance was excavated. Emperor Wu is said to have been informed that it was the residual ashes left behind after the conflagration of the world at the end of a *kalpa* or aeon. The digging of the lake is historically correct, and such an explanation could only have been given after the introduction of Buddhism. Consequently, this is regarded as evidence of the existence of Buddhist monks at the capital, Chang-an, in the last half of the second century B.C.

Wei-shou (506–572), the author of the history of the Topa Wei, *Wei-shu,* mentions that Chang-Chien, who had been sent to Central Asia in 138 B.C. to remonstrate with the Yueh-chih, reported on Indian Buddhism and that this was the first Chinese exposure to Buddhism.

According to *Wei-Lueh,* the history of the Wei dynasty written about 280, the envoy of the Yueh-chih king orally transmitted a Buddhist scripture to an official of the Han Court in the year 2 B.C. This account is credible because it includes accurate biographical details of the Buddha, and mentions some technical terms of the Buddhist order. By the first century of the Christian era, some small Buddhist communities were in existence in the capital itself. An official Chinese history, *The Record of the Later Han,* mentions that Liu Yang, the Prince of Chu and the half-brother of Emperor Ming, was a practicing Buddhist with the Emperor's approval. He worshipped the Buddha along with Huang-ti and Lao-tzu, and gave alms to Buddhists from a foreign land in Hsu-chou, which lay to the east of Loyang, the new capital of the Later Han. There were already Buddhists amongst the gentry, and missionaries were freely received in their homes. If Buddhism was being adopted by the nobility and if foreign missionaries were active in the district of Loyang and Hsu-chou, it is likely that Buddhism had already been known in the western provinces of Shensi and Kansu for some time. For those who came from Central Asia, it was customary to pause at Tun-huang in Kansu province after crossing the desert before entering China and proceeding to Loyang by way of Lian-chou and Chang-an. These major cities and provinces along the trade route already bustled with foreign caravans and the Buddhist missionaries who came with them.

At first Buddhism flourished in China chiefly amongst the foreigners, including merchants, refugees, hostages, and adventurers, who had brought it from their own countries. The official histories of China, however, do not concern themselves with the social and cultural life of these foreign groups on Chinese soil: "The Confucian World-conception recognized only one kind of relation between the inhabitants of the barbarian wastelands and the Middle kingdom: they are the people from afar, who attracted by the radiance of the emperor's virtue, came to offer their 'tribute of local products' as a token of their submission."[11]

According to a famous story, which is based on Chinese historical sources such as the *Mou-tzu,* the validity of which has been questioned in recent years, Buddhism was first "officially" introduced into China during the reign of Ming-ti of the Later Han dynasty. He is said to have had a vision of a golden man with sunlight passing from the back of his neck, who flew about in space and came to earth. Upon being advised by a court scholar that the man in the vision was probably the Indian Buddha, he sent envoys to the country of the Yueh-chih to procure Buddhist sacred texts. The envoys returned, accompanied by the Indian monk Kasyapa Matanga. They also brought an image of the Buddha and a number of Buddhist scriptures.[12]

Variations in the details of this story found in different sources, and the remarkably accurate description of the Buddha of the dream, have cast doubt on its authenticity. Since Buddhism had already been introduced into China before the time of Ming-ti's dream, there would appear to be little justification for fabricating the story unless it was considered expedient to do so, and the chief purpose of this story was perhaps to make the entry of Buddhism into China appear official and "by appointment." It claims that Chinese Buddhism had its beginning when the Emperor himself ordered the importation of Buddhist teaching and provided it with images, temples, scriptures, and monks. Nevertheless, it is certain that during Ming-ti's reign many foreign monks, whose names have not been preserved, were in Loyang and Chang-an. From this time onward, China began to receive a succession of Indian monks and texts.

Around the middle of the first century, Buddhism, regardless of its reception at the Chinese court, had found acceptance in the region north of the River Huai, in eastern Honan, southern Shantung, and northern Kiangsu. The most important city of this region was Peng Cheng (Hsu-chou), a flourishing centre of trade on an eastern extension of the Silk Highway. Some scholars have suggested that the "Church of Loyang" was a later offshoot of the "Church of Peng-

Cheng." Tonkin, now in Vietnam but part of southern China at that time, was also a principal seat of Buddhism. This centre, however, was set up by monks who had arrived by sea, and who were possibly in contact with the Buddhist centre of Peng-Cheng in the north.

From the middle of the second century, the growth of Buddhism in China began to accelerate. Emperor Huan (147–167), like Ch'u-wang-ying (Liu Yang, The Prince of Chu), enshrined the Buddha in his palace together with the Huang-ti (Yellow Emperor) and Lao-tzu. In 166, Siang-Chieh of Shantung Province came to the capital and presented the emperor with a letter admonishing him for his excesses and reminded him of the teachings of the Buddha, which implies that Buddhism had already gained a widespread following in China.

The steady translation of the Buddhist scriptures into Chinese began in the middle of the second century. If any Buddhist scriptures had been translated into Chinese before this, there is no record of them. A Parthian monk, An Shih-kao, arrived at Loyang in 148, marking the beginning of a period of intense literary activity. He is the first of those personalities of Chinese Buddhism whose historicity is not questioned. He was followed by Chih-lou-chia-chian (or Lokak-shema) from the Yueh-chih country. An Shih-kao chiefly translated Hinayana into Chinese, and Chih-lou-chia-chian translated Mahayana scriptures. Soon Chinese intellectuals became interested in Buddhism, and began to make their own annotations and commentaries. From the middle of the second century to the beginning of the third, a number of Buddhist teachers, translators, and scholars were active at Loyang. According to Tao-an's catalogue, some ten *acharyas* translated about fifty-one Buddhist scriptures during this period.

Information about the organization of the monasteries and monks at Loyang is scanty, but it is known that the missionaries were cosmopolitan. Their group is known to have included at least two Parthians, one of whom was Shih-kao, three Yueh-chih, two Sogdians, and three Indians. Hardly anything is known about the relations of the Buddhist community at Loyang with its immediate surroundings and with the Chinese court, but it is clear that it was not an isolated enclave of foreign culture. Many of its Chinese lay devotees belonged to the cultured classes. It has been generally thought that there were no Chinese monks until the fourth century because the Han Emperors permitted only foreigners to embrace Buddhism; there is, however, evidence to the contrary. At the end of the second century a Chinese monk, Fu-tiao, a convert of Shih-kao, not only helped the foreign monks in their translations but did some of his own. He also wrote an original work, *Sha-mi-shih-hui Chang-chü,* the Preface of which is still extant.

The gradual disintegration of the Han Empire began around the middle of the second century, and the authority of the central government was undermined by a variety of disruptive forces, including the provincial warlords. The Han hold over the western regions slackened, and a civil war began which brought about the downfall of the dynasty in 220. The Later Han dynasty was succeeded by three states, the Three Kingdoms: Wei in the north with its capital at Loyang, Wu in the central and lower part of the Yangtze Valley with its capital at Nanking, and Shu in Szechwan with its capital at Chengtu. Their rule lasted for about half a century, but it was a period of almost constant war whose prominent heroes have since filled the pages of Chinese literature. The fortunes of war varied with no single power dominating. Political unity was restored briefly in 281 by the Western Chin dynasty with its capital at Loyang, but it too collapsed in 316 under the mounting pressures of internal uprisings and Hun invasions.

The Eastern Chin dynasty began in 317 with its capital at Nanking. It lasted until about 420 when its rule was terminated by an ambitious general, Liu Yu, who set up the Liu Sung ruling house, bringing under its control the territory along the Yangtze Valley and south of it. There was a succession of short-lived Chinese dynasties in southern China: the Liu Sung (420–479), Chi (479–502), Liang (502–557), and Chen (557–589). The capital of the Southern Dynasties remained Nanking.

In northern China, the Northern Wei dynasty was founded by the Toba people in 386 with Loyang as their capital. Wei or Toba kings were of the Turkic race. Having unified northern China in 440, the Toba Wei remained in power until 534. Their kingdom was then divided into two states, the Eastern Wei (534–550) and the Western Wei (535–557), with capitals at Yeh and Chang-an respectively. These in turn were replaced by the Northern Chi (550–577), with Yeh as capital, and by Northern Chou (557–581), with Chang-an as capital; both were of non-Chinese origin.

With the unification of northern China under the Northern Wei dynasty in 440, there began the era commonly referred to as the Northern and Southern Dynasties. This lasted more than a hundred and fifty years until China was finally unified in 589 by the Hui house. This was a period of political and social unrest with frequent dynastic and regional wars, but it was also a period of transition in which Buddhism helped to bring about major changes in Chinese life and learning.[13]

Under the patronage of the foreign dynasties, Buddhism became firmly established in northern China where there was already a large non-Chinese population. Some of the rulers who invaded northern and western China were already devout Buddhists, and, by the end of the third century, Buddhist establishments in the two northern capitals of Chang-an and Loyang numbered 180 and their clergy 3,700. By 381 nine-tenths of the people of northwest China were Buddhists. Emperor Wu (265–290) of the Chin dynasty showed great interest in Buddhism and built many monasteries throughout his empire. Emperor Min (313–316), during his brief reign, also built two monasteries at Chang-an. Yuan-ti (317–322) and his successors, during their rule of about a century, founded 17,608 Buddhist institutions throughout the kingdom and 263 volumes of Buddhist texts were translated. The Northern Wei dynasty favoured Buddhism, and during their reign Chinese Buddhist art made spectacular progress. An exception in this dynasty was Emperor Tai-Wu who decreed the suppression of Buddhism in 446. But other Wei kings made Loyang and Chang-an the greatest centres of Buddhist activity in China. Thousands of temples were built and the number of monks and nuns allegedly rose to two million. Many important monk-scholars, both Indian and Chinese, such as Kumarajiva, Bodhiruci, Tao-an, Hui-yuan, and Fa-hsien, worked and lived in China during this period.

In southern China also, Buddhism was accorded royal patronage by the Eastern Chin dynasty. Some of the rulers of the succeeding houses were also practicing Buddhists. For example, the founder of the Liang dynasty, Emperor Wu (502–549), a Confucianist, was converted to Buddhism, and frequently gave public lectures on Buddhist scriptures. He collected the first Chinese Buddhist canon, wrote on Buddhism, and even entered a monastery three times to lead the life of an ascetic. Yang-ti, the Sui Emperor, also declared himself in favour of Buddhism.

The Eastern Chin dynasty hoped to reassert Chinese supremacy and culture over the entire country. Although they adhered to traditional Chinese culture, there was some doubt in their minds about its total efficacy. Consequently, they turned towards Buddhism as a rallying force to strengthen them for the recovery of the north. Buddhist monks and scholars responded to this attitude in full measure, and they intensified their missionary and religious activities, incorporating in their discussion and writing Confucianist and Taoist learning. Soon an alliance between the monks and the élite emerged, rendering the monastic community powerful enough to assert its independence from the weakened secular authority of the Chin rulers, and "to maintain what amounted to an empire within an empire."[14]

By the time the Han dynasty had declined, different trends had already begun to develop in Buddhism in China. One, with its emphasis on control of the mind, concentration, and the suppression of the passions, was inspired mainly by the translations of An Shih-kao and was Hinayana in nature. The Prajna School, based largely on the translations of Chih-ch'an, favoured Mahayanism and was more inclined to probe into the ultimate reality behind external appearances. This aspect of Buddhism began to develop in the middle of the third century and ultimately became the dominant tenet of Buddhism in the South. At about the same time, during the fourth century, Neotaoism was gaining wide acceptance amongst literary circles in southern China, and this factor made a rapprochement with Buddhist thought somewhat easier. The Prajna School preached the philosophy of *Sunyata,* or emptiness, somewhat resembling the Neotaoist doctrine of non-being. A Taoist, once united with the tao or non-being, could become eternal and manifest himself in any form at any place, just as the Buddha was eternal and formless. The recognition of this affinity paved the way for closer interaction between these two schools, and for a gradual growth of Buddhism in China. Another fact encouraging closer relations between the Buddhists and Neotaoists was that some of the Buddhist monks originated from the same social class as the Neotaoists. The head of the powerful Wang family of the early Eastern Chin dynasty, Wang Tao (276–339), who was also the Prime Minister of the Empire, was a devoted patron of Buddhism. Other members of his family were equally enthusiastic and some of them had even joined the order of monks. Foreign monks also actively participated in this rapprochement. In southern China, at the end of the fourth century, under the patronage of the Eastern Chin ruler, the number of Buddhist establishments in the Kingdom alone was 1,786 temples and there were 24,000 monks and nuns. In Chien Wing, the capital, the names of thirty-seven temples have survived. Thus, during the third and fourth centuries, Buddhism became firmly rooted in the middle Yangtze Valley, as well as in the older centres of the north. Between the years 265 and 317, sixteen translators are known to have rendered 491 works into Chinese.

Rarely in history does a movement receive support from two mutually opposed forces for separate political reasons. At this time Buddhism in China was supported by both the traditionalists and the foreigners; either party would probably have taken a hostile attitude in different circumstances. Buddhism developed along different lines in northern and southern China, reflecting the needs of local polity. For instance, in the north it was associated with state control, and in the south it asserted its independence of the state and worked in association with the Chinese élite.

Although Buddhism was at times helped by certain political situations, it would be wrong to overemphasize this point. It was not always supported by the ruling and official classes and at times faced intense resistance and hostility. Without the inherent vitality of its doctrine, its sense of purpose, the capacity to endure suffering, the devoted service of its monks, and the brilliant intellectual activities of its scholars, Buddhism could not have evoked such a response from people as culturally advanced as the Chinese. Buddhists not only had to make Chinese society more receptive to their teachings, but they also had to translate Buddhist doctrine into Chinese.

The task was spread over several centuries. Sanskrit and Pali are completely different from Chinese in form and style. Sanskrit has a highly elaborate grammatical system, whilst Chinese has no systematized grammar; Sanskrit is highly inflected, alphabetic, and polysyllabic, whilst Chinese is uninflected, ideographic, and mainly monosyllabic. And whilst Indian literature is reflective, imaginative, and discursive, Chinese literature is terse, concrete, and practical. Even in temperament the two peoples differed: "The Chinese had shown little disposition to analyse the personality into its components, while India had a highly developed science of psychological analysis. In concepts of time and space there were also striking differences. The Chinese tended to think of both as finite and to reckon time in life-spans, generations, or political eras; the Indians, on the other hand, conceived of time and space as infinite and tended to think of Cosmic eons rather than of units of terrestrial life."[15]

The political and social values of the two peoples were equally alien. Whilst love of the family dominated Chinese society, Buddhism taught a universal ethic and a doctrine of personal salvation outside the family. The Buddhist ideal was ascetic and celibate, and it clashed with the Chinese popular view that to have a son was not only a duty but also essential for those sacrifices without which the departed spirit could not have peace. Whereas the Chinese aimed at establishing a good society, Indian thought went far beyond this goal and reflected upon the ultimate reality which was inseparably bound with what was visible. Despite the decline of Confucianism, the task of the initial Buddhist missionaries was a formidable one.

A factor which must have helped the early Buddhist missionaries was the absence of a complex and highly developed Chinese religious system. The ancient Chinese had to struggle against the forces of nature in northern China to build their civilization. This made them intensely practical and disciplined, but allowed them little time for reflection. Thus, the Chinese religion was a set of simple beliefs of a plain-thinking people, comprising the worship of ancestors and the forces of nature, a belief in a supreme god or heaven, a belief in divination, and a vague concept of the retribution of good and evil. By the time Buddhism appeared in China, however, Chinese religion had matured somewhat, but it did not approach the richness of Buddhism. The concepts of karma, the transmigration of the soul, the world as illusion, worldly pleasures as impediments to spiritual advancement, celibacy and asceticism, charity, compassion, and love of all beings, are only "a few drops in that vast flux of Indian religious and cultural invasion."[16]

Most of the Indian monks who migrated to China did so during the five centuries following the third century. During that time a stream of Chinese monks arrived in India to study Buddhism in its homeland, and to collect authentic Buddhist texts. Many of them left records of their experiences and observations. Most of these records have perished, some are known only by their titles, whilst brief extracts or stray passages from others appear in China's vast literature. Only three records are preserved in full: Fa-hsien's *Fo-Kuo-chi,* Hsüan-tsang's *Hsi-yu-chi,* and I-tsing's *Nan-hai-ki-kuei-nai-fa-chuan.* Whilst nearly all the Chinese monks eventually returned home, most of the Indian monks who went to China remained there.

Much less is known of the Indian monks who went to China than of the Chinese pilgrims who went to India. The Chinese had a deeper interest in objective observation and in recording history. Consequently, none of the numerous Indian monks who went to China has left a record of his experiences and impressions. Three Indian monks, Kumarajiva, Paramartha, and Bodhidharma, are held in particularly high esteem by Chinese Buddhists. Bodhidharma has even been deified by Chinese Buddhists, and the school of Dhyana Buddhism, which he founded and which is known as Ch'an in China and Zen in Japan, is still alive in East Asia, especially in Japan where its main centre is Kyoto. There were many others who enjoyed local or regional fame and are mentioned in Chinese dynastic histories. A host of others were absorbed in translating Sanskrit texts, working singly or jointly with Chinese scholars.[17]

The first recorded Indian missionaries to China are Dharmaratna (Chu-Fa-Lan) and Kasyapa Matanga (Chu Mo-t'eng) who reputedly arrived at Loyang at the invitation of the Han ruler Ming-ti in 67, and for whom he built the White Horse Monastery.[18] These two monks initiated the work of translating Buddhist texts.[19] The great emphasis placed on these translations by the missionaries may have been, apart from the need to interpret the Buddhist doctrine to the Chinese people, motivated by the traditional Chinese reverence for the written word. Kasyapa Matanga wrote a treatise entitled *Sutra of Forty-two Sections,* known by Chinese Buddhists as "the first ray of the Law," which has since gone into numerous editions and versions. Four other works, now vanished, are also attributed to him. The *Sutra* is not a translation but an original work written to introduce the essentials of Buddhism to the Chinese.

Despite unending wars and political unrest in China, Buddhist missionaries continued to arrive with new texts. They poured into China through different routes, but mainly from Central Asia. Towards the middle of the second century, Ngan Shih-kao (An-Shih-kao or Lokottama), the famous Parthian prince of Pakor who had renounced his throne, arrived and embraced Buddhism. He settled in the White Horse Monastery at the Chinese capital, and spent the rest of his life from 148 to 168 propagating Buddhism and encouraging the work of translation. He himself translated more than thirty texts into Chinese and had a great influence on his Chinese followers, who considered his school of translators unrivalled.

One of the important Central Asian monks was Dharmaraksha, better known by his Chinese name, Chu Fa-hu. Born in Tun-huang, he was a Yueh-chih and went to China in the third century after travelling and studying widely in India. He was an accomplished linguist and an authority on Buddhism. Most of his life was spent at the White Horse Monastery where he worked for the expansion of Buddhism and translated Sanskrit texts into Chinese. He died about 317 at the age of eighty-seven. He reportedly knew thirty-six languages, and he translated at least two hundred and eleven works into Chinese in the years between 284 and 317, including the *Lalita Vistara;* ninety of these translations have survived.

At the invitation of a Hun king of the northwestern region of China, Dharmakshema (Fa-feng), an outstanding Indian monk, came from Central Asia to the Hun court at Liang-chou in 414. The King, Meng-hsun, became a Buddhist and Dharmakshema, after prolonged study of the Chinese language, translated about twenty-five works, twelve of which have survived. They include *Maha Sannipata Sutra,* an important canonical work of Mahayana Buddhism, and Asvaghosa's *Buddha Charita.* Rivalry over Dharmakshema arose between the Hun king and the Chinese Toba Wei rulers, and the scholar met a tragic death at the hands of his patron in 434 because he was anxious to return to India.

He served as royal adviser to Meng-hsun, and reputedly possessed re-markable occult powers.

Whilst Dharmakshema was working at Liang-chou, the followers of Kumarajiva, who had initiated a new epoch in the transmission of Buddhism to China, were engaged in their prodigious translation work at Chang-an, then the capital of a small state of Later Chin. Kumara-jiva (343–413) was the son of an Indian scholar, Kumarayana, who had renounced his hereditary title to a ministerial position in Kashmir. From early childhood, Kumarajiva was educated in India in Buddhist doctrines and literature under the celebrated Bandhudatta, who was later converted to Mahayanism by his former pupil. Kumarajiva became widely known for his scholarship and attracted disciples from Khotan, Kashgar, Yarkand, and other parts of eastern Turkistan. Indeed, his reputation as a superb Buddhist teacher was the cause of his imprison-ment. The Emperor of northern China, Fu Kien (or Fu-Chien), sent for him, but the Kucha ruler was reluctant to release him. A war ensued and Kumarajiva was taken to China in 383 as a prisoner. This was a period of political upheavals and Fu Kien, whilst attempting to con-quer the Eastern Chin, was himself defeated and killed in 383. General Lu Kuang, a non-Buddhist, subsequently captured Kumarajiva and badly mistreated him during his long period of captivity, refusing to release him in spite of repeated pleas from the Yao family to send him east to the capital at Chang-an. It was not until after the accession of the Chin Emperor Yao Hsing (or Yo Chang, reign 393–415) that Kumarajiva was freed and invited to Chang-an in 401. Chinese chron-icles record that the Chin Emperor was a devoted follower of Buddhism, that he held Kumarajiva in great respect, and appointed him the Raj-guru or Kuoshih.

Welcomed as a national preceptor, he was accommodated at the monastery known as the "Great Monastery" of Chang-an. During the last twelve years of his life, when he was free to preach, his prestige rose immensely and he won an unsurpassed reputation as an interpreter of Buddhism. Through his efforts, a large number of Buddhist mon-asteries were established in northern China, and an overwhelming ma-jority of the people were converted to the new faith. Having mastered the Chinese language during his captivity, he plunged directly into literary work. He corrected many earlier imperfect translations, made new ones, and founded an immense bureau of translators with over eight hundred scholars on the staff. More than one hundred and six Buddhist texts, mostly Mahayana, were translated, fifty-six of which are still extant. Amongst the translations were the works of Nagarjuna, the great second-century exponent of the Madhyamika school and one of the greatest names in Mahayana literature. No books are as popular with Chinese Buddhists as Kumarajiva's translations of *Vimalakirtinirdesa* and *Saddharma Pundarika,* the most important scripture of Mahayana Buddhism.

Kumarajiva was much more than a brilliant translator, for he was an original thinker of great genius as well. He gave Chinese Buddhism a philosophic basis and created a sound Buddhist literary tradition in China. He wrote several original works in Chinese, including the *Life of Asvaghosa* based on a vanished Sanskrit source. He is traditionally regarded as the first exponent of Madhyamika doctrine, and his work introduced a new era in Buddhist China. From then on Mahayanism became the dominant school of East Asian Buddhist thought. Through his propagation of Nagarjuna's doctrine of Sunyata, Kumarajiva was able to overthrow the general practice of interpreting Buddhism in the light of Lao-tzu and Chuang-tzu. Because of the imprint he left on the intellectual history of Asia, he may be regarded as one of the greatest Indians of all time. But he was more than an Indian, for he symbolized, as Bagchi points out, "the spirit of cultural collaboration between Central Asia and India and the joint effort made by the Buddhist scholars of these countries for the dissemination of Indian culture in China."[20]

According to contemporary Chinese records, he was honest, loyal, humane, tolerant, hard-working, and self-sacrificing, although according to some legends he was once tempted into marriage by the beauty of a woman. He repented of his lapse, and it is reported that thereafter he would always begin his sermons with the apologetic exordium: "Follow my work, but not my life which is far from ideal; But the lotus grows out of mud. Love the lotus; do not love the mud."

The main burden of transmitting Buddhist knowledge to China fell on Kashmir, because of its physical proximity and because of its well-developed tradition of Buddhist studies. Amongst Kashmir's more famous scholars are Sanghabhuti, who reached China in 381; Buddhabhadra, the translator of *Avatamsaka Sutra;* Gautama Sanghadeva; Punyatrata (404), and his pupil Dharmayasas; Buddhayasas, who was Kumarajiva's teacher in Kashmir; and Vimalaksa, an associate of Kumarajiva.

Many Indian monks went to China by sea. Two Kashmiri teachers, Dharmayasas and Buddhabhadra, used this circuitous route at the beginning of the fifth century. Buddhajiva, a collaborator of Fa-hsien, reached Nanking in 423. In 431 he was followed by Gunavarman (Kiu-na-pa-mo). The Emperor invited Gunavarman to his court at the request of the Chinese monks of Nanking, and did the monk the unique honour of receiving him personally. Gunavarman died within a year, but so great was his scholarship and industry that he translated eleven texts, five of which are still extant. Gunavarman was a royal prince from Kashmir and had travelled throughout India as a *bhikshu,* as well as working for over thirty years in Ceylon and Java. In Ceylon he had helped develop the Buddhist Sangha and in Java, where Hinduism prevailed at the time, he founded the first Buddhist monastery on the island. Another of his important contributions to Buddhism in China was the help he rendered towards the conferment of higher ordination on the Buddhist nuns or bhiksunis.

In 435 Gunabhadra (Kiu-no-po-to-lo) reached Canton by sea. For the next thirty-three years, until his death in 468, he continued to work in Nanking. He was a great authority on Mahayana and specialized in the *Avatamsaka Sutra.* Welcomed and encouraged by the Emperor Tai-tsu of the Sung dynasty, he translated seventy-six works of which twenty-eight have survived. The political disorders which broke out in China during 453–454 did not result in the loss of royal favour for Gunabhadra even though he was working at the monastery of Sin-Sec at the invitation of the rebel chief Yi-Siuan, who was defeated and beheaded.

During the sixth century, amongst the Indian monks who went to China by sea, Paramartha (*ca.* 498–569) is the most famous. He was widely recognized in India as a distinguished and accomplished scholar, and took with him to China a large collection of Buddhist texts. Arriving in Canton in 546 at the request of the Chinese Emperor Wu-ti of the Liang dynasty, who had dispatched a goodwill mission to India asking the King of Magadha to send a Buddhist scholar, Paramartha was given a Chinese escort to assure his safety during his journey to the capital at Nanking. Paramartha worked incessantly for the next twenty-three years, first at Fuchuang, and later at Nanking and other Buddhist centres. He did much original writing besides translating seventy Buddhist works, of which only thirty-two are extant. His contribution to Chinese Buddhism rivals that of Kumarajiva. War, chaos, and famine had caused Buddhism to decline in China, but Paramartha, through his immense literary activity and religious enthusiasm, gave it a new and vigorous life during the latter days of the Liang dynasty (502–557) and the early part of the Chen dynasty (557–589). He, Bodhiruci, and Hsüan-tsang are the three most important Vijnanavadin translators of Sanskrit texts into Chinese. Paramartha established a Buddhist philosophical system, the *She-lun-tsung*, the basic text of which was his translated work *Mahayanasamparigrahasastra*. This school had eminent disciples and prevailed for about eighty years before it was finally absorbed by the Dharmalakshana school founded by Hsüan-tsang.

Of all Indian monks, the most celebrated in China is Bodhidharma (or Dharmabodhi). Son of an Indian king, he is an almost legendary figure and several miracles are attributed to him.[21] He was regarded as the twenty-eighth Patriarch in India. The arrival of Bodhidharma in Canton in about 526 at the invitation of the Liang Emperor Wu was very significant in the history of Buddhism, because he introduced into China the Ch'an (a phonetic variation of the Sanskrit Dhyana) school, and thus became the first Patriarch (Tsu or Tsung) of this school in China. He did not undertake missionary tours and he wrote no books. He disapproved of reading the canonical texts of the Tripitaka, although he used to recommend the *Lankavatara Sutra*. He taught the value of meditation to find the Buddha in one's own heart, and he himself meditated in silence for nine years in the Shao-Lin monastery on the Sung Mountain. Because of his influence, Buddhist monasteries became much less intellectual and more meditative. It is not surprising that a practical people like the Chinese should have preferred those aspects of Buddhism which seemed to them more natural and practical, such as the Dhyana exercises.

By the end of the sixth century the long period of political unrest in China had come to a close, and the beginning of the seventh century saw the emergence of the T'ang dynasty (619–907). Despite the opposition of the Confucianist literati, Buddhism continued to gain ground in China where it had already assumed a distinctive Chinese personality. Before the T'ang period there was some persecution but it was ineffective and intermittent and failed to arrest the progress of Buddhism. In 405 nine out of every ten families in northern China embraced the Buddhist faith. By the end of the fifth century, it is asserted that the whole of China, north and south alike, was Buddhist. According to an official census made between 512 and 545 in the kingdom of Wei in northern China, there were thirteen thousand Buddhist shrines and monasteries and three thousand foreign monks living in the capital alone, whilst an even greater number of indigenous monks were scattered throughout the country. In the sixth century both northern and southern China had staunch imperial patrons of Buddhism; for example, Queen Hu of the Wei dynasty in the north and Emperor Wu of the Liang dynasty in the south. Thousands of Indian merchants, monks, and travellers had settled in the principal cities of China, and in the sixth century there were probably more than three thousand Indian Buddhist monks and ten thousand Indian families in the Loyang province alone.

Soon after the T'angs came to power in China, northern India was ruled by one of the most famous patrons of Buddhism, Harsha, and the Buddhist University, Nalanda Mahavihara, was the most important centre of learning in India. It had been founded in the fifth century by the Gupta ruler Kumaragupta I (*ca.* 415–455).[22] The intellectual demands of Nalanda were severe, and discipline was strict. Only the most distinguished and talented could teach at Nalanda. The routine of daily life was rigorous, divided mainly between study and religious rites. The prestige of the University was high in Indian society and in the Buddhist world. Throughout the T'ang period, the most glorious of Chinese history, Nalanda attracted numerous Chinese pilgrims and visitors. In fact, the story of the Nalanda Mahavihara has been reconstructed mainly from accounts left by Chinese pilgrims, particularly Hsüan-tsang and I-tsing.

An accomplished scholar at Nalanda, Prabhakaramitra (Kuang che), whose pupils later became famous professors at Nalanda, was the first Indian scholar to go to China during the T'ang period. He arrived in 627 at the age of sixty-three. The Emperor Tai Tsung was deeply impressed and gave him a very courteous reception. Prabhakaramitra rendered some Buddhist texts into Chinese which have survived, but he lost the King's favour because of the Confucianist literati's machinations and died disappointed in 633.

Of the monks who followed Prabhakaramitra to China, the best-known was Bodhiruci (Fa-hi) from South India.[23] Reaching China by sea in 693, he translated one of the most extensive works of Mahayana, the *Ratnakuta Sutra*. Hsüan-tsang, who brought the manuscript back with him from India, died before he could make much progress with its translation. Bodhiruci, after seven years of strenuous labour, completed the work in 713, and his Chinese biographer recounts that the Emperor himself took down the final notes in his own hand at a ceremonial gathering when the translation was completed. This was the last of Bodhiruci's fifty-three translations. He died in 727, it is said, at the age of one hundred and fifty-six.

Vajrabodhi and his disciple Amoghavajra were amongst the last Indian teachers to go to China. Born a royal prince and educated at Nalanda, Vajrabodhi reached Canton in 720 in his fifty-eighth year to present to the Chinese Emperor a copy of *Mahaprajnaparamitasutra* on behalf of the King of Ceylon. Before he died at Loyang in 732, he had translated a number of mystical Buddhist works into Chinese and had numerous disciples. Famed for his mastery of Tripitaka and Tantric Buddhism, he introduced the Mantra sect of Tantric esotericism, based on *Mulamantras*, into China. The doctrines and practices of the Mantra cults were confined to circle of initiates, and Vajrabodhi initiated only two monks into the Tantric rituals during his stay in China. Amoghavajra carried on his work more successfully, and translated about seventy-seven texts, mainly dealing with *tantras* and *dharanis*, before he died in 774. He was the spiritual adviser of three emperors of the T'ang dynasty—Hsüan-tsang, Shu-tsung, and T'ai-tsung.

China, in the latter part of the T'ang period, was somewhat politically disturbed, as was India, and contact between the two countries had virtually come to an end. Yet, a few Indian missionaries went to China and, whilst they did some valuable work, they lacked the zeal and ability of their predecessors. The most important missionary of this later period was Dharmadeva (Fa-tien), who came to China in 973 during the Sung period, and translated about 178 Sanskrit texts. He headed a board of translators which was responsible for rendering 201 volumes of the Sanskrit texts into Chinese between 982 and 1011, despite his death in 1001.

Recalling the story of these monks and the enormous difficulties involved in translation, admiration for their patience, perseverance, and faith is increased. To learn Chinese with modern aids and techniques is a formidable enough task, but in those days to learn it and also communicate doctrinal beliefs intelligibly to a people whose own tradition of reflective thought was relatively less developed and accommodating, was a monumental achievement.

Although a large number of Indian monks and scholars had already visited and worked in China, it was not until the end of the fourth century that a notable Chinese scholar, Fa-hsien, visited India.[24] Until Buddhism had been established in China and Chinese monks had acquired intellectual proficiency, the long and arduous pilgrimages to India were infrequent. There are stories of some Chinese princes captured by Kaniska who had lived in northern Punjab, and stories of Chinese scholars who may have visited India in the third century. A Chinese monk, Chu-She-Ling, set out in 260 for India but elected to stay in Khotan where he found the Indian knowledge he was seeking. On the authority of I-tsing, the Chinese scholar who visited India in the seventh century, it is said that twenty Chinese monks went to India by the Yunnan-Burma route, and a monastery called China-Sangharama was especially built for them near Bodhgaya by King Sri Gupta. However, evidence of Chinese visitors to India from the fourth century on is more definite, and the flow of pilgrims during this period was far greater than the few surviving names would suggest.

By the fourth century China had developed her own powerful tradition of Buddhist philosophy. The two most illustrious names in Chinese Buddhism during this period were Tao-an of Hsiang-Yang and Hui-Yuan of Lu-Shan. Tao-an (312–385) carried on his missionary activities north of the Yangtze River and was undeterred by the hardships prevalent at the time, thus exemplifying the true spirit of the Buddha. He converted a great many Chinese intellectuals to the Buddhist doctrine, sending them afterwards to different parts of the country to preach Buddhism. Through his disciples and his writings he created a new spirit in Buddhist China. He was the first Chinese scholar to reexamine and correct earlier translations of Buddhist texts and to compile commentaries on them. The foreign monks rarely knew Chinese well, whilst their Chinese collaborators were ignorant of Sanskrit and Pali. More important, he became acutely aware of the invalidity of interpreting the Buddhist scriptures in the light of the Chinese classics, a practice which had become common during the preceding century, mainly because the Chinese intellectuals did not have access to the originals or even to scholars who were masters of the original texts. Tao-an's organization of intensive translation activity at Chang-an later provided the much-needed trained Chinese talent to help Kumarajiva. Realizing the need for closer contact between Indian and Chinese scholars, he invited a number of Indians from Central Asia to China, and, more important, encouraged the Chinese to visit India. It was he who had initiated steps to invite Kumarajiva to China.

After the fall of Hsiang-Yang, Tao-an's disciple, Hui-Yuan (344–416), founded the monastery of Lu-Shan and initiated a new school of Buddhist thought, the White Lotus Society, which introduced the cult of Amitabha. The Society has left an indelible mark on Chinese Buddhism, because it was the origin of *Ching-tu* (the Pure Realm movement), still a major philosophical doctrine of eastern Asia. Hui-Yuan was closely associated with the metaphysical speculations carried on in Chien-Kang and Kuai-chi on the philosophies of Lao-chuang and Prajna, and also with the propogation of dhyana exercises. Under his direction, Neo-taoist metaphysical speculations were mixed with Prajna thought, and the purity of his monastic discipline attracted Confucianist literati. He was the epitome of the "gentry Buddhism" of South China. He laid the foundation of the independent status of the Buddhist community there. His disciple, Tao-Sheng (*ca.* 360–434), provided a bridge between the Buddhist centres at Lu-Shan and Chang-an, and made a significant contribution to Chinese Buddhist thought, especially the Nirvana School.

Whilst the tradition of Buddhist thought was thus maturing in its new environment, the appeal made by Tao-an for Chinese scholars to undertake religious study-tours to India had begun to draw responses. In 399, fourteen years after Tao-an's death, Fa-hsien, accompanied by four other Chinese monks, set out on his pilgrimage from Chang-an to India by the Central Asian land route. Emperor Yao Hsing, the royal patron of Kumarajiva, was still ruling in northern China. At the frontier Fa-hsien and his companions met another party of five Chinese monks who were also going to India. They joined forces, taking the southern route through Khotan and Kashgar. Negotiating difficult terrain, Fa-hsien and his companions entered India through Kashmir. He stayed at Pataliputra for three years, studying Sanskrit and collecting manuscripts. There was as yet no Chinese translation of the entire *Vinaya*, the Buddhist rules of monastic discipline, and Fa-hsien strongly felt the need for one. Whilst he was still in India, however, Kumarajiva arrived in Chang-an in 401 and was instrumental in translating the *Vinaya* of the Sarvastivadin School. For another two years Fa-hsien stayed at the monastery of Tamralipti copying Buddhist sutras and images. He returned to China in 414 and collaborated with Buddhabhadra, an Indian monk, in translating some of the works he had taken back with him. Fa-hsien left behind a record of his travels, *Fo Kuo Chi*, which gives an invaluable account of India during the period of the Gupta Empire.

Little is known of the companions of Fa-hsien, except for Pao-yun, who learned Sanskrit in India and, after his return home, translated a number of Buddhist texts. A succession of Chinese pilgrims followed Fa-hsien. Of those who travelled to India in the fifth century, five names are known, but information about them is fragmentary.[25]

Whilst Fa-hsien was in India, a group of fifteen Chinese monks led by Che-mong started for India in 404 through Khotan and the Pamirs. The difficult mountain routes compelled nine of them to return to China, and one died of fatigue, but the remaining five completed their journey. They visited places of Buddhist learning, collected texts, and set out on their return journey by the same route. Three of the five died on the way back and Che-mong reached China in 424 with only one companion. The account of his travels, which he composed in 439, is lost.

Another party of twenty-five monks led by Fa-yong commenced its journey to India in 420 following the northern Central Asian route via Turfan and Kashgar and passing over the Pamirs to Kashmir. Not much of their travels in India is known, except that Fa-yong, having visited important Buddhist centres throughout northern India, returned home by sea.

In 518 an empress of the Wei dynasty sent an official mission to India under Song-yun to offer presents to Buddhist sanctuaries and bring back texts. Song-yun's mission toured the northwestern regions of India and returned in 522.

The Wei rulers, who were such great patrons of Buddhism, lost their authority in 535. Until the rise of the Sui dynasty in 589, royal interest in Buddhism was somewhat diminished. Although the Sui dynasty (589–618) was short-lived, it revived the efforts for direct contact with India. Emperor Yang (605–616) dispatched a mission led by Wei-tsie and Tu Hing-man; this mission travelled by the overland route and toured extensively in Central Asia and northern India.

After the rise of the T'ang dynasty, Chinese monks began to visit India in unprecedented numbers. During the seventh century, Sino-Indian cultural relations were particularly strong. Although the imperial clan claimed descent from Lao-tzu and thus favoured Taoism, they exercised a policy of religious toleration. Nestorian Christianity, Islam, and Manichaeaism were introduced during the T'ang period and found Chinese converts. Buddhism gained unprecedented influence under the patronage of some of the T'ang rulers, and had far more support than Taoism. In the eighth century in the imperial capital Chang-an alone, there were ninety-one Buddhist monasteries compared to sixteen Taoist monasteries. Over the whole country, Buddhist temples numbered more than three times those of the Taoists. Buddhism was supported by all factions of society, no doubt aided by the peaceful conditions and the patronage of the rulers. But the rise of Harsha in northern India, the enormous reputation of Nalanda University as a seat of Buddhist learning, and the fame of Indian mathematics, art, medicine, and astronomy must also have been largely responsible for the sudden influx of Chinese scholars to India.

The first monk to visit India during the T'ang period, and by far the most eminent, was Hsüan-tsang (ca. 596–664). A Chinese nobleman and the son of an orthodox Confucianist scholar, he embraced Buddhism at an early age and acquired a national reputation as a learned and eloquent monk, well-versed in the Confucianist classics. He left China for India in 629, two years after the accession of the T'ang Emperor, Tai-tsung (627–649), who was even more disposed towards Buddhism than his father, Kao-tzu.

Hsüan-tsang travelled by the northern route through Central Asia, and, after a perilous journey through the desert, reached Kapisa in 630. For the next fifteen years he travelled extensively throughout northern and southern India. Charming, courtly, and learned as he was, he was honoured by the great rulers of the time, Harsha of Kanauj and Bhaskaravarman of Kamarupa. Hsüan-tsang stayed at Nalanda for five years studying Buddhist philosophy with the greatest scholar of the age, Silabhadra. It was customary for a monastery to honour a learned visiting monk with the presentation of a precious holy book, and Hsüan-tsang collected 657 volumes, many of which were rare texts and prize possessions. So heavy were his manuscripts and sacred relics that they were carried by twenty horses. He was remarkably methodical and industrious in making notes of his observations, and enjoyed a reputation both as a writer and as a translator. Yet it is surprising that he does not mention the great Buddhist stupa at Sanchi, which he must have visited, since it is of exceptional importance to the Buddhists. Nor does he allude to Ajanta, which was at the height of its glory when he was there. In 645 he returned to China by the southern Central Asian route. He left a detailed account of his travels, *Si-yu-ki* (or *Ta-Tang Hsi-yu-chi*), which is an invaluable source of information on Central Asian and ancient Indian history. Indian culture owes a great debt of gratitude to Hsüan-tsang, for he came to India at a time when Buddhism was in a state of decline, and by taking away many texts of Buddhist philosophy, he made it possible for them to be preserved in their Chinese versions. The Sanskrit originals of many of these texts have been completely lost in India.

When Hsüan-tsang left India, Emperor Harsha, who had received him with honour and reverence, gave him an almost royal send-off, as well as generous gifts of money to defray his expenses. His Indian farewell was more than matched by the elaborate royal reception prepared for him in China. From the border to the capital he was conducted with state dignity, and, on his arrival at Chang-an, he was given a great ovation by the people, and the emperor declared a holiday in his honour. It is rare in history that such a reception is bestowed on a scholar, much less on a teacher of an alien creed.

For the next nineteen years until his death Hsüan-tsang worked incessantly, translating the Sanskrit texts he had brought from India. Altogether, he translated seventy-five works. It was principally due to the efforts of Hsüan-tsang, supported by I-tsing, that the essence of all the five courses of Buddhism—*Hetuvidya, Abhidharma, Vinaya, Madhyamaka,* and *Yogacara*—taught at Nalanda University during its most flourishing period, was introduced into China. Whilst these courses later underwent certain changes, their fundamental teachings conformed to the doctrines introduced by these two Chinese scholars.

The Emperor T'ai-tsung sent his second embassy to the court of Harsha in 643 whilst Hsüan-tsang was still in India. The ambassador Li Yi-Piao was assisted by a Chinese officer, Wang Hsüan-tse. The latter led the third imperial mission to India in 647.[26] He helped Hsüan-chao, a visiting Buddhist monk and scholar, to return to China. In 664 Hsüan-chao returned to India to collect medicines and contact physicians. From 643 to 758 the T'angs maintained occasional diplomatic relations with several Indian kingdoms, including Udayana in the Swat Valley, Magadha, Kashmir, Gandhara, and with Ceylon.

Biographies survive of sixty Chinese monks who visited India during the latter half of the seventh century. The best-known of these monks is I-tsing (also spelled Yi-Ching or Yi-tsing) whose scholarship at the time was excelled only by that of Hsüan-tsang in China. He was, however, not as interested as Hsüan-tsang was in Buddhist philosophy, but, like Fa-hsien, laid greater emphasis on the observance of monastic rules. In 671, soon after Hsüan-tsang's death, I-tsing set out for India on board a Persian vessel which arrived at Tamralipti in 673. He was the first important Chinese pilgrim to travel by sea to India, and he appears to have done so because of the unrest caused in Central Asia by Arab and Tibetan invasions. From this time on, more and more pilgrims and visitors followed the maritime route. Before I-tsing reached India, he stayed for about two years in Sumatra, which was at that time part of the Srivijaya Empire. He left a record of Buddhism there in *Nan-hai-chi-kuei-fa Chuan (A Record of the Buddhist Kingdoms in the Southern Archipelago).*

In India, I-tsing spent ten years at Nalanda, visited places of Buddhist interest, and collected about four hundred manuscripts which he took back to China in 695. He was mainly interested in visiting Buddhist stupas, shrines, and monasteries, as well as centres of learning. He made a special study of Indian medicine and often made comparative references to the Chinese system. On his return he devoted himself to interpreting and propagating Buddhist doctrine. His most monumental work of translation was one of the Buddhist codes of monastic discipline, entitled *Mulasarvastivinaya*. He also completed a short Sanskrit-Chinese dictionary, and wrote brief biographical notes on fifty-one Chinese pilgrims who visited India between the reigns of T'ai-tsung and Empress Wu.

The last Chinese to come to India during the T'ang period was Wu-kong. He was a layman, and was dispatched in 751 to escort an Indian ambassador back to his kingdom, Kapisa. During his Indian visit Wu-kong was converted to Buddhism. He spent many years studying Buddhist texts and travelling about the country before returning to China in 790.

During the later years of the T'ang Empire, Chinese monks ceased travelling to India, presumably because of the political unrest in China, the loss of Chinese authority in Central Asia, and the decline of Buddhism in India. The breakdown of Chinese authority in Central Asia is of significant importance in the history of Sino-Indian relations and of Buddhism. China's retreat from this area at a time when Islamic power emerged left a vacuum which was to be filled by Muslim domination, thus separating the areas of Indian and Chinese culture. But by this time the Chinese need to draw upon Indian learning had considerably diminished. For, by the end of the T'ang dynasty, the Chinese Buddhist canon was practically complete, and almost all the important Sanskrit sutras had been translated into Chinese.

After the downfall of the T'ang dynasty, there was a short period of political anarchy in China, during which five military leaders made themselves kings in Kaifeng and Loyang, and about thirty thousand Buddhist monasteries were destroyed. In 960 the Empire was reunited by Chao Kuang-yin, who founded the Sung dynasty (960–1270). Between 960 and 1039 it appears that a number of Chinese pilgrims went to India, but their travels have only a limited interest. Contact between India and China practically ceased after the eleventh century.

Whilst the last emperors of the Sung dynasty were still ruling, Gengis Khan was emerging as a world power. He and his descendants, the Mongol or Yuan dynasty, were to govern China from 1206 to 1368, and to play a significant role in the development of Buddhism. However, before the Yuans, three other alien ruling houses had established themselves contemporaneously with the Sungs, and these are worth notice in the history of Buddhism in China. One, the Liao (907–1125), was established by the Mongol tribe called the Khitans, and, during its rule, Buddhism spread in Mongolia and Manchuria. The Khitans subjugated northern China and set up a large number of Buddhist temples throughout their kingdom. During their rule, between 1031 and 1064, the Liao edition of the Chinese Tripitaka was printed. The Liao rulers were also responsible for engraving the sutras on stone.[27]

Whilst the Liao dynasty was still ruling Manchuria, a chieftain of the Ju-chen (Jurchen) tribe, Akuta, successfully broke away from the Liao rule and set up the Chin dynasty (1115–1234). He sacked the Liao capital in 1122, and in 1126 he even captured Kaifeng, the capital of the now declining Sungs, forcing them to move southward and extending the frontiers of his empire as far south as the Huai River. Peking became the Chin capital, until they were forced to evacuate it in 1215 under pressure from the Mongols, who brought the Chin dynasty to an end in 1234. Buddhism was already flourishing in the areas the Chin dynasty had taken over, and the new rulers continued to support the Indian religion. The Chin dynasty sponsored the printing of an edition of the Chinese Tripitaka during the period 1148–1173.[28]

The third northern dynasty was the Hsi-Hsia which ruled Kansu, including the famous Buddhist centre at Hun-huang, from 1038 to 1227. Although they claimed descent from the Toba, their language seems to have been related to Tibetan rather than to Turkish. Buddhism was their official religion and, under the auspices of the Imperial House, the last of the extensive Buddhist translating or publishing projects was undertaken, involving the production of a mass of Buddhist texts in their language. Hsi-Hsia manuscripts and printed books have survived in large numbers, and were still being printed in Hsi-Hsia well into the Mongol period.

The Mongols, the first foreign conquerors to dominate the whole of China, came into closer contact with Buddhism after their conquest of northern China. Kublai Khan was the greatest ruler of this dynasty, and it was during his rule that Marco Polo visited China. Kublai Khan had been converted to Buddhism and was especially well disposed towards the Lamaistic Buddhism of Tibet. Probably the Great Khan sought to use the support of Buddhist and Taoist churches for political ends: to subdue the stubborn Sung legitimism of the Confucianists. Although tolerant of other faiths, he was an enthusiastic Buddhist. Whenever he was called upon to act as arbitrator in the ecclesiastical debates between Buddhists and Taoists, an important feature of the times, his verdict always favoured Buddhism. He had relics of the Buddha brought from Ceylon, and appointed a young but learned Tibetan Lama, Phags-pa or Matidhvajasribhadra (1240–1280), as imperial preceptor; this office was held in the greatest respect by the Mongol royal family, and Lamaistic Buddhism was made the national religion of the Mongols.

Kublai's successors patronized Tibetan Buddhism with even greater fervour. How highly Lamaism was held in the imperial estimation is illustrated by the edict of 1309 which stated that anyone guilty of striking a Lama could have his hand cut off, and that anyone insulting a Lama would lose his tongue. The Confucianist literati criticized the Mongols for granting excessive privileges to their rivals, and accused the Lamas of committing acts of cruelty and debauchery. Whilst this is the usual Confucianist literati criticism of Buddhist monasticism, some of their accusations were valid. Buddhist temples were favoured by the Imperial Court with huge grants of land. According to the registry of the *Hsuan-Cheng Yuan,* there were 42,318 temples and 213,418 monks and nuns in China.

The Mongol rule was terminated in 1368 by Chu Yuan-chang, who founded the Ming dynasty which ruled China for about three centuries. Chu Yuan-chang came from a poor farm labourer's family and was a former Buddhist monk at the Huang-ch'ieh monastery in An-hui.[29] The first Ming emperor often organized Buddhist assemblies and discussions. The last great emperor of the Ming dynasty was Yung-le (1403–1424), who was himself a Buddhist, although he raised the Neoconfucianist texts to the status of the ancient Confucianist canon. By this time, however, Buddhism had lost contact with India and had become an independent and integral part of Chinese life.

The Manchu or Ching emperors, although not Chinese themselves, were great supporters of Chinese culture. They continued to patronize Buddhism, especially Lamaism. They were also interested in Ch'an Buddhism.[30] During the reign of Kang-hsi (1662–1721) there were 79,622 temples and 118,907 monks and nuns in the country. Whilst the number of monks was rather small, when compared with the estimate of 740,000 monks during the T'ang and Sung periods, the number of temples was the highest in history.[31]

The outstanding feature of Ming Buddhism was the achievement of harmony between the different schools, largely brought about by Chu-hung, a sixteenth-century monk. He also inaugurated a movement for the development of Buddhism amongst the laity. Intellectuals and wealthy Buddhists organized groups of laymen in the cities and founded societies for welfare and missionary work. This movement gained considerable strength, and even university scholars began to study Buddhist philosophy and history. This lay movement reached its peak during the closing years of the Manchu dynasty, and the unique role played by laymen has continued in modern Chinese Buddhism. The growing popularity of this movement probably aroused the anti-Buddhist feelings of the Confucianist literati, and, consequently, Buddhism, which had always faced considerable indifference and apathy from the officials and intellectuals of the Ming and Manchu dynasties, now faced active hostility. An expression of this antagonism is seen in the 1898 publication of a work by Chang Chih-tung entitled *Chuan Hsueh-pien,* in which he advocated the reorganization of Chinese education by appropriating Buddhist property for schools. His theories commanded considerable support from the Chinese intelligentsia. More than three hundred Buddhist temples were destroyed during the first quarter of the present century.

However, Buddhism has always remained important in China, especially amongst the common people. The new pressures of the late nineteenth and early twentieth centuries even forced something of a revival of Buddhism, and it subsequently played some part as an intellectual force in the revolution that overthrew the Manchu dynasty.[32] The Chinese could more effectively combat the Western cultural invasion by centring their defence around their Buddhist traditions, which, they contended, were democratic, humanistic, liberal, and in fact contained all that the West could claim and more. The Buddhist reformer, Liang Chi-chao, for instance, said that the doctrine of karma was superior to the theories of Darwin and Spencer. Another stimulus, of somewhat doubtful value, came during the period of the Sino-Japanese War and World War II when some Buddhist temples were rebuilt in the Japanese-occupied areas, and links between China and Japan were strengthened for political reasons.

The revival of Buddhism in China was aided by the foundation of the Mahabodhi Society in 1891 with its headquarters in Ceylon. The Society was begun by Dharmapala with the declared objective of reviving the Dhamma. Its activities since then have included holding international Buddhist conferences, publishing Buddhist literature in Asian as well as European languages, and sending missions abroad.

Aroused by the anti-Buddhist measures of the various administrations, and by the criticisms of the Chinese Renaissance leaders in the twenties and thirties, as well as by the criticisms of Marxist thinkers, learned Buddhist monks, such as Ti-hsien, Yin-kuang, Tao-chieh, and Tai-shu, intensified their work to revive and reform their faith. Buddhist centres attempted to restore and update the true teachings of the Buddha. The most active reformer was Tai-hsu (1889–1947), who led a movement to reform the clerical system, temple property, and teachings. He established contact with Buddhism abroad, sent monks to study in India, Tibet, and Japan, and founded *Shih-chieh fo hsueh Yuan* (the Universal Buddhist College), with the declared objective of modernizing Buddhism. Consequently, numerous works of Buddhist literature began to appear in ever-increasing numbers. Between 1920 and 1935, as many as fifty-eight Buddhist periodicals were published in China.

The growing popularity of Buddhism in Western countries, the emergence of the Buddhist countries of Asia as free nations, and the rehabilitation of Buddhism in independent India have all led to the intensification of Buddhist activity everywhere.

Whilst it is not easy to assess accurately the position of Buddhism under the Peoples Republic of China since 1949, there is no doubt that it has been confronted with extraordinary difficulties. It not only has incurred resistance from the conservative and nationalistic Confucianists, but has also encountered opposition from a highly autocratic and centralized régime which is based on an openly materialistic, atheistic, and anti-religious ideology. The Communist government has instituted anti-Buddhist measures, confiscating temple lands, taking over schools and publishing houses, and reducing the Sangha in size. Until 1950 the Buddhist monasteries of China derived most of their income from land holdings received as gifts from their patrons. The Land Revenue Act of June 1950 led to the confiscation of agricultural land belonging to Buddhist temples and monasteries. This economic loss to the monasteries compelled a large number of monks to leave them. In the cities the monks were made to set up light industries on the premises of the monasteries or vacate them for the use of local factories. Buddhist monks and nuns were compelled to study the works of Mao Tse-tung and were subjected to "thought reform." However, realizing the significance of Buddhism and its value in Chinese life and society, the government has adopted a policy of controlling rather than suppressing it. They formed the *Chung kuo fo chiao hsieh hui* (the Chinese Buddhist Association) in 1953, bringing all Buddhist monks and laymen into one organization under central control. In 1958 the Association claimed to represent about half a million monks and one hundred million followers. During the course of this revolutionary process Buddhists have no doubt been used by the government as instruments of propaganda, mainly directed at the large Buddhist populations in other countries. Peking's refusal to allow the Chinese Buddhists to participate in the Seventh Congress of World Fellowship of Buddhists, held at Sarnath in 1964, disturbed Buddhists all over the world and deepened their anxiety about the fate of Buddhism in present-day China; they suspect that this religion of peace is being turned into a tool of political propaganda and international conflict. They fear that the Peking régime has been particularly severe on Buddhism, because of the great hold this religion has always exercised, and perhaps still exercises, over the minds of the Chinese people.

The history of Buddhism in China is like that of any powerful foreign culture, which, on encountering an equally powerful local culture, has to undergo the varying processes of confrontation and assimilation. During the initial period of impact, the local people remain indifferent to or even unaware of the gradually mounting influence of the foreign culture. It is only when the alien culture begins to assume sizeable proportions that it is generally regarded as threatening, and reaction sets in. But the struggle is not then between a purely foreign and a purely local culture, because the so-called foreign culture by that time has come to acquire some native character, and its opponents have become conscious of the shortcomings of their own heritage. Finally, there begins a period of compromise on both sides, conscious and unconscious, during which the foreign culture is either naturalized or nationalized, serving as a distinct group within a changed pattern of the society, or it is assimilated in the traditional culture giving rise to an entirely new culture. This formative period of imperceptible growth is vital, because if the roots of the incoming thought are not firmly planted, it cannot survive the inevitable reaction against it. And no foreign culture, however advanced or backed by political power, can find strong roots unless it meets a definite need in the local culture.

Buddhism has often been denounced in China, not so much for its philosophical content as for its foreign character. The fact that Buddhism dominated Chinese thought for centuries and continues even now in its naturalized form as a principal factor in Chinese life, plus the fact that it reached this position through voluntary acceptance in a society which regarded itself as superior to all others, are not so much a unique testimony to the brilliance of its teachings but indicative of the vast gap in Chinese cultural life which it must have filled.

At the time Buddhism was introduced into China, the cultural atmosphere of the country was quite conducive to its development. Neither Confucianism nor Taoism possessed a highly developed spiritual character. Confucianism, with all its emphasis on the adaptation of human personality to the social order, or on welding together the cult of heaven, the family system, and the state, neither sought nor provided answers to metaphysical or religious questions. It gave the ordinary man neither strength to see him through the ordeals of life nor solace in the hour of death. If Confucianism—begun primarily as a political theory prescribing a moral code for the ruling class—served as a religion in later forms, it was because its social basis was supported by a spiritual faith acquired under the influence of Taoism and Buddhism.

Taoism, on the other hand, indulged in religious speculations in search of an undefined something which would offer hope of eternity. Like Confucianism, it sought to bring man's life on earth into harmony with the life and law of the universe (Tao), but unlike Confucianism it set out to attain this ideal not by laying down rules for human conduct but by an intuitive emotional method.

Buddhism seemed to meet the intellectual needs of both the traditional creeds, and it fitted neatly into the emotional gaps left by them. The glowing spirituality of Buddhism and its elaborate forms of worship greatly attracted the Chinese, who also found in it fulfilment of the natural human hope for life beyond death. The Buddhist emphasis on salvation through moral effort and the law of karma made a deep impression on the moral nature of the Chinese. For the middle and lower classes, Buddhism declared that the humbler folk, who suffered so unjustly at the hands of the Confucianist nobility, would be reborn into higher rank, whilst the cruel officials and noblemen would descend the ladder to suffer for their misdeeds. Buddhism, as it was being elaborated in northern India in the first centuries A.D., substituted the hope of a blissful rebirth, at the feet of the various Buddhas and Bodhisattvas, for Nirvana, the final delivery from the cycle of rebirth. The paradises of Avalokitesvara and Amitabha thus became most popular in China: "The beatific vision thus took the place of the former desire for extinction; the wisdom— a little arid perhaps—of primitive Buddhism gave way either to a powerful esotericism, in the last analysis fairly close to Chinese neo-Taoism, or to a religion of the heart, full of tenderness and forgiveness, likely to appeal to the loftiest souls as well as to console the afflictions of the masses. In both cases Buddhism, with its religiosity, with its charity, with its faith, brought to China spirituality that it still lacked."[33]

Yet, Buddhism was in several respects alien to the Chinese temperament. Its doctrines were too subtle and metaphysical for the essentially practical and material Chinese mind. The Buddhist negation of life, renunciation of family relationships, and practice of celibacy were contrary to Chinese, especially Confucianist, ideas and traditions. Monkhood meant that men avoided their primary task of parenthood, thus failing to continue the family line, and it made them live on charity.

The period of the great expansion of Buddhism, after the collapse of the Later Han dynasty, was one in which China was divided into three states and suffered from foreign invasions; wars and political upheavals were common, life and property were constantly in danger, and it is possible that the intellectuals and the masses alike turned to Buddhism seeking religious salvation. Only a literate could get satisfaction from Confucianism and only an exceptional man could become immortal in Taoism, but Buddhism offered salvation to everyone. Monks were few, but anyone could be a lay Buddhist and there were always Bodhisattvas anxious to help him. The self-denial, hard work, and reforming zeal of the missionaries must have elicited the admiration of the simple people, whereas the Buddhist writings, mainly translations of the scriptures, attracted the intelligentsia.

Changes in the thinking habits of the intellectuals made China more receptive to Buddhism. The young scholars were up in arms against the hair-splitting and formalized interpretations of Confucianism, and a new mood had emerged throughout the country opposing the fetters of Confucianist propriety, seeking man's liberation into a life beyond the sphere of all restraints: a life in which man could act, think, and speak freely according to the dictates of human emotions. Such a mood could have easily led to admiration for the Buddhist renunciation of worldly pleasures in quest of freedom and the true path.

Magnificent monasteries, towering pagodas, and temples, and beautiful statues, with which the country abounded, drew admiration even from the opponents of Buddhism. A letter from a Confucianist scholar to the prime minister of the Western Chin dynasty describes the monastery built by Tao-an in the fourth century: "Teachers and disciples total seven hundred, and of fasting and study there is no wearying. There is no dazzling of the eyes and ears of common men by resort to magical tricks, nor is there any trampling on the difference among the lesser monk by resort to threats or authority. Furthermore, teachers and pupils courteously respect one another. It is a magnificent sight, and one such as I have never seen before."

The tolerance of the Chinese Buddhists and their willingness to make adjustments to indigenous doctrines must have made them more acceptable. The Chinese deity of Heaven, for example, has a place of honour in certain Buddhist ceremonies; a Bodhisattva was introduced as an incarnation of Confucius; Buddhist temples were built in conformity with the Chinese system of magical ideas, known as *feng shui;* Buddhists occasionally adopted Tao, the key term of philosophic Taoism, for Buddhist dharma; and translations of phrases or passages which might offend traditional Chinese susceptibilities, conditioned by concepts of Confucianist morality, were deleted or edited. For instance, Indian words indicating love and respect for a Bodhisattva—"kiss" and "embrace"—were dropped; and phrases such as "the husband supports his wife" were replaced by the "husband controls his wife" and "the wife comforts her husband" became "the wife reveres her husband."

Buddhism gave women a higher place in society than did Chinese traditional concepts.

Buddhist monks also borrowed the Taoist vocabulary because of the purely linguistic difficulty of translating Buddhist concepts into Chinese. The Sanskrit language had nothing in common with Chinese. Every Chinese character carries a traditional connotation which is liable to lead to strange distortions when employed to interpret foreign concepts. Consequently, the Buddhist adopted Tao (absolute, cosmic force) for *bodhi* (illumination), for *arhat* (Buddhist saint) the Taoist expression, *chen-jen* (true man) was used, and so on. It is, however, also possible that in the initial stages Buddhism found Taoism a convenient medium for the spread of its own ideas. Buddhist nirvana and arhat were, for instance, more easily acceptable to the Chinese as Taoist *wu-wei* and chen-jen. Buddhists made use of some Confucianist expressions also; for example, for *sila* (morality or pious conduct) they used the Confucianist *hsiao-hsun* (filial submission and obedience). In the sixteenth century when the Catholic missionaries faced the same problem they solved it in a similar way, by borrowing equivalent terms from Confucianist philosophy.

Since tenants on the Buddhist temple lands were better treated than those on lands owned by Confucianist aristocrats, poorer people readily became Buddhist tenants, later accepting the faith. Merchants made use of the Buddhist monasteries as banks, stock exchanges, and warehouses, and the monasteries grew in importance as repositories of capital. The temples bought more and more land, thus gaining an increasing influence in the country's economic life. Habitual association with Buddhist monks, even if it were for material reasons, encouraged the people to be well disposed towards Buddhist doctrine, because the monks worked so selflessly and the inevitable human response to this example was one of sympathy.[34]

As time passed, not only did the emperors and the common people become Buddhists, but even distinguished men of learning increasingly turned towards Buddhism. In the eleventh century the famous reformer-statesman, Wang An-shih, whose tablet was placed in the Confucianist temple next to that of Mencius, deplored the fact that scholars sought new ideas and inspiration in Buddhism. Yet his son wrote books on Buddhism. Even the chief exponent of Confucianist orthodoxy, Chu Hsi, complained in the twelfth century that the educated man now found himself compelled to draw upon Taoism and Buddhism for religious and ethical concepts.

But the rise of Buddhism in China was not without religious struggles, controversies, and persecutions. Confucianism and Taoism have always been jealous of Buddhism and have often persecuted it, Confucianism persistently appealing to Chinese nationalism and cultural pride. There were four major anti-Buddhist persecutions in 466, 574, 845, and 955. None of these, however, was nation-wide or lasted more than a few years. Upon the death of the persecuting king, almost invariably the policy of suppression was reversed by his successor and Buddhism resumed its former influence. Chinese persecution of Buddhism tended to be directed mainly against monastic establishments rather than against monks and devotees. That such persecution was political is clearly suggested by the fact that all edicts for the persecution of Buddhism emphasized that it was a national disaster and a humiliation for the celestial kingdom to be influenced by an alien creed.

As long as Buddhism remained alien it was tolerated and was even popular, but as soon as it sought naturalization it aroused opposition. Confucianists and Taoists, often in conflict with each other, combined to resist the ideas from India, which had come to be looked upon by the Chinese people as "the Land of the Buddha" and even as "the Western Heaven" from which nothing but the great truth could come.[35] In the fifth century, Ku Huan wrote *I-hsia-lun,* a treatise against Buddhism, denouncing it as inferior to the Chinese system. He was not the first scholar to criticize Buddhism, but he was the first to do so at length. He sought to prove that Indian nature and customs were evil, and thus that Buddhism was unsuited to Chinese culture. Whilst Ku Huan's criticisms were essentially motivated by nationalistic prejudice, there were other Chinese scholars, such as Fan Chen and Hsun-chi, who were motivated by intellectual and political considerations.

Buddhism was widely popular under both the Southern and Northern dynasties, although Confucianist and Taoist scholars demanded its outright suppression. Persecution in the south, however, was not nearly as bad as in the north. It is indeed surprising that the first major persecution should have taken place under a dynasty which is chiefly remembered for its patronage of Buddhism. In 446 Toba Emperor Tai-Wu or Shih-tsu (424–451) of the Northern Wei dynasty, after a series of anti-Buddhist measures, finally decreed that the Buddhist religion was to be completely wiped out. Not one monk, one scriptural text, or one image was to remain in existence.[36] Consequently, there was a wholesale destruction of Buddhist temples, stupas, and texts and numerous monks were executed. It is thought that the Taoist Kou Chien-chih and his friend the Confucianist minister, Tsui Hao, were instrumental in instigating this persecution.

The persecution lasted for seven years until reversed by the new Emperor, Wen-Chang, in 454. The new decree, in fact, commenced by praising the Buddha, and then endeavoured to explain the persecution as an attempt to eliminate certain evil elements from the monastic order. Buddhism emerged from this persecution with increased vigour and determination to expand. The Buddhists renewed their work by constructing the world-famous caves of Yun-kang. This undertaking of large-scale rock sculpture is a monument as much to the artistic techniques and religious zeal of the Buddhists as to the prestige and graceful restitution of the ruling dynasty under whose patronage these caves were constructed. Within sixty years of the Buddhist revival there were about fourteen thousand temples in the Northern Wei territory alone, and during the next twenty years the number reached thirty thousand with more than two million monks and nuns. At this time, Buddhism was more widespread in northern China than it was in the south. In the southern kingdoms, for example, under the Liang dynasty (502–556) there were, according to a T'ang source, about 2,864 temples and 82,000 monks and nuns.

More than a century later, in 574, before Buddhism reached its peak during the Sui and T'ang dynasties, Emperor Wu (reign 561–577) of one of the short-lived dynasties, the Northern Chou, anxious to make Confucianism the state religion, ordered the abolition of all Taoist and Buddhist organizations. There had long been a fierce controversy between Buddhists and Taoists about the priority of Lao-tzu (now considered a mythical figure) over the Buddha. The Taoist claimed that Lao-tzu had gone to India where he had become the Buddha. Both sides fabricated evidence to support their contentions. In 520 a historic debate over this question was held in the presence of Emperor Hsiao-ming, at the conclusion of which the Taoists were severely defeated and their claim was pronounced unfounded by a committee of one hundred and seventy scholars headed by Wei-shou. This brought Hsiao-ming's wrath down upon the Taoists, whose chief spokesman in the debate, Chiang Pin, escaped execution only by the intercession of the Buddhist monk, Bodhiruci. Later, in the reign of Emperor Wu, this debate started again with such acrimony that even the Imperial presence could not assuage it. Probably disgusted by this unending and bitter debate, Wu decided in 573 to rank Confucianism first, Taoism second, and Buddhism third as religions of the Empire. It is said that his decision was influenced by the machinations of Wei Yuan-sung, who had been a Buddhist monk and who had dabbled in the occult sciences, and Chiang Pin, who had lost the Taoist argument in the debate of 520. The Buddhists resented this decision, thus infuriating the Emperor who retaliated by proscribing Buddhism. In his decree he ordered the destruction of Buddhist temples, images, and scriptures; monks and nuns were to return to the laity; and the treasures of the monasteries were to be confiscated for distribution amongst the officials and royal princes. It is noteworthy that the Buddhists had so successfully exposed the flagrant forgeries perpetrated by the Taoists that Emperor Wu had to also include Taoism in his decree of suppression. These persecutions, however, were short-lived. Wu died in 578, and three years later the Northern Chou dynasty was overthrown by Emperor Wen of the Sui dynasty. He immediately reinstated both Buddhism and Taoism. The recovery of Buddhism was extraordinarily rapid, and it soon enjoyed a new peak of popularity.

The T'ang rulers generally preferred Taoism, but did not interfere with Buddhism, except on two occasions. The first T'ang Emperor, Li-yuan (or Kao-tzu), was quite antagonistic, but, conscious as he was of the size and influence of the Buddhist community in China, he did not risk open hostility. Therefore, instead of trying to suppress Buddhism outright, he placed various restrictions on its activities. He regarded Confucianism as essential to China, and under the influence of the Imperial historian, Fu-i, who was a staunch Confucianist, he issued an edict ordering magistrates to inquire into the lives of the Buddhist monks and nuns. But before the decree could be fully implemented, he was murdered, and there emerged a succession of T'ang rulers who were well disposed towards Buddhism.

Two centuries later the Taoist emperor, Wu-tsung, during his brief reign of five years attempted to suppress Buddhism. He decreed in 845 that, except for the four temples in each of the capital cities and one in each of the provinces, all Buddhist temples and monasteries were to be demolished and monks and nuns unfrocked. More than sixty-five thousand temples were desecrated, millions of acres of monastic land confiscated, and more than a quarter of a million monks and nuns forced to return to lay life. They were even denied Chinese nationality. These figures may be somewhat exaggerated, but they at least indicate both the scale of the suppression and the hold Buddhism had acquired in China. This persecution was certainly the most widespread of its kind in China, for previous persecutions had been mainly confined to northern China. It is said that Han Yu (768–824) was the intellectual father of the persecution of 845. He coined such slogans as: "Restore their people to humanity! Burn their books! And convert their buildings to human residences!"[37] Whether this persecution was a sudden development or another episode in the long ideological struggle between Taoism and Buddhism is a matter of controversy amongst historians. Economic considerations, such as the desire of the Emperor for the enormous wealth deposited in the thousands of Buddhist stupas, cannot be overlooked.

This persecution was also short-lived. In 846 Emperor Wu-tsung died, probably affected by the longevity potions he had been taking, and his successor, Hsüan-tsang, immediately cancelled the persecution. The number of temples and monks increased at once. Some scholars, however, hold the view that after the persecution of 845, Buddhism did not completely recover, and that the Sangha declined as an intellectual and spiritual force.

After the downfall of the T'ang dynasty in 907, China was divided into a dozen kingdoms and Buddhism again came under the state ax with some thirty thousand monasteries being destroyed. The Sung dynasty (960–1127) reversed this policy. At state expense a project was instituted for the translation and publication of the Buddhist scriptures. State assistance came at a most opportune moment, because by this time contact with India had ceased. The Sung period, however, soon witnessed the revival of Confucianist bureaucracy. Because of the constant infiltration into Sung China from the north by the Khitans and Juchens, nationalist feelings were unusually high. Taking advantage of the situation, the Confucianists intensified their efforts to have the alien creed expelled. Meanwhile, there arose a new syncretic school of thought, Neoconfucianism, which had absorbed some Buddhist philosophy and metaphysics, and which was adopted by the Sungs as their official doctrine.

The Mongols (1279–1368), who dislodged the Sungs, protected Buddhism because they were themselves Tibetan Buddhists. But under the Ming dynasty opposition to Buddhism increased and continued into the Manchu dynasty, except for a respite during the reign of the first two Manchu emperors who were devout Buddhists. Buddhism was subjected to suppression by the state and the bureaucracy. Emperors persecuted Buddhism, philosophers accused it of superstitions, statesmen were disturbed that some of the most able people in the country were lying idle in the monasteries, and Confucianist and Taoist literati denounced it as an alien import. But in the end the emperors made peace with Buddhism, the monks were allowed to collect alms and raise temples, and the bureaucracy was compelled to keep Confucianism as its own aristocratic creed.

The introduction of Buddhism is one of the most important events in

Chinese history, and since its inception it has been a major factor in Chinese civilization, exercising a great influence on religion, philosophy, art, and literature. The Chinese have freely acknowledged their debt to India, often referring to her as the "Teacher of China," and Chinese Buddhists have pictured India as a Western Paradise, *Sukhavati*. The advent of Buddhism meant for many Chinese a new way of life, and for all Chinese, whether they accepted it or not, a means of reassessing their traditional beliefs. A new conception of the universe developed, and the entire Chinese approach to life was slowly but surely altered. The change was so gradual and so universal that few people realized it was happening. For over a thousand years the Chinese mind was dominated mainly by Buddhism. The decline of Buddhism in China during the last few centuries cannot obscure the fact that whilst Buddhism enjoyed prestige and popularity, it influenced Chinese culture in many ways and left lasting impressions on Chinese life.[38] Being a strong and self-confident civilization, however, China fitted Buddhist ideas into her own texture of life, and the ascetism of Buddhism, for example, could not suppress the Chinese love of life and gaiety.[39]

There has been, however, no scarcity of historians who have been unable to appreciate adequately the extent and depth of Buddhist influence on Chinese culture. Whilst Western writers, with notable exceptions, have found it difficult to comprehend the variety and complexity of Buddhist doctrines, texts, and traditions, and have been somewhat disabled by their own predispositions, Confucianist historians have looked upon Buddhism as an alien intrusion, regarding the Buddhist ascendancy in Chinese life as indicative of a weakness in the culture of a great people, a weakness which they would like to confine to obscurity. Even some rationalist historians are not altogether free from this somewhat irrational, although natural, feeling, as is shown by Hu Shih's comment that "with the new aids of modern science and technology, and of the new social and historical sciences, we are confident that we may yet achieve a rapid liberation from the two thousand years' cultural domination by India."[40]

India never imposed her ideas or culture on any nation by military force, not even on the small countries in her neighbourhood, and, in the case of China, it would have been virtually impossible to do so since China has usually been the more powerful of the two. So the expansion of Indian culture into China is a monument to human understanding and cultural co-operation—the outcome of a voluntary quest for learning. Whilst China almost completely suppressed other foreign religions, such as Zoroastrianism, Nestorian Christianity, and, to some extent, Manichaeanism, she could not uproot Buddhism. At times Buddhism was persecuted, but for two thousand years it continued to Indianize Chinese life even after it had ceased to be a vital force in its homeland and long after it had lost its place as the dominant religion of China. In fact, Indianization became more powerful and effective after it was thought that Buddhism had been killed in China.[41]

By far the most significant contribution of Buddhism to China was that it made knowledge available to the lower strata of society and introduced a democratic element into learning. Popular education was unheard of, but Buddhism broke open the gates of learning for all alike; the powerful and the rich could no longer monopolize knowledge. Indeed, the Buddhist neophytes were usually taken from humbler classes. Hu Shih, who considered that Indian influence had harmed the natural development of Chinese culture, and who led the modern Chinese intellectual renaissance, commented: "Never before had China seen a religion so rich in imagery, so beautiful and captivating in ritualism and so bold in cosmological and metaphysical speculations. Like a poor beggar suddenly halting before a magnificent storehouse of precious stones of dazzling brilliancy and splendour, China was overwhelmed, baffled and overjoyed. She begged and borrowed freely from this munificent giver. The first borrowings were chiefly from the religious life of India, in which China's indebtedness to India can never be fully told."[42] Through its compassionate Buddhas and Bodhisattvas, its promise of salvation to all alike, its emphasis on piety, meditation, and restraint of passions, its attractive rituals and festivals, its universality and its tolerance, "the religious life of the Chinese has been enriched, deepened, broadened, and made more meaningful in terms of human sympathy, love, and compassion for all living creatures."[43]

Certain theistic beliefs—the doctrine of rebirth, the idea of causality, the belief in reward and retribution, the conception of reality which permeates every living thing in nature, and the notion of universal impermanence—had an abiding influence on Chinese life, literature, and thought. The old simple idea of retribution of good and evil was replaced by the law of karma (yeh in Chinese) which controls all past, present, and future existences. The doctrine of karma brought spiritual consolation to innumerable people. That Chinese philosophy blossomed afresh after the impact of Buddhism indicates both a response to and a borrowing from Indian ideas. Buddhism not only offered paradise to the good, but also threatened the wicked with a multiplicity of hells. The Chinese, who have always regarded ancestor-worship as important, found this Buddhist doctrine impressive and convincing. Compassionate concern for all living beings naturally expressed itself in practical ways, including the establishment of charitable institutions, such as hospitals, orphanages, resthouses, and old peoples' homes. Emotional attachment to religion encouraged pilgrimages to distant Buddhist establishments, thus making the Chinese better acquainted with other parts of their country and its environs.

Broadly, Indian influence on Chinese thought proceeded along two lines: ideas which were assimilated as part of the indigenous tradition, and those ideas so radically different that they were distinctly identified as Indian. Fung Yu-Lan expressed this by pointing out that there is a distinction between "Chinese Buddhism" and "Buddhism in China."[44] For example, the school of subjective idealism of Hsüan-tsang, known in Chinese as the *Hsiang tsung* (or Wei-shih), is obviously Indian, whilst the Ch'an school developed in China through interaction with Taoism. Of the two, the latter line of Indian influence was more successful, and, as Buddhism adapted more and more to China, it was able to make a greater contribution to Chinese culture.

The famous disciple of Kumarajiva, Seng-chao (374–414), first compared Indian and Chinese thought. He wrote several essays, collected as the *Chao Lun,* and found that the systems of Nagarjuna and of Lao-tzu were not dissimilar. At an early stage in its development, two schools of Mahayana Buddhism emerged—Madhyamika and Yogacara—and Nagarjuna was the founder of the Madhyamika school. This school held the doctrine of the middle view between existence and non-existence, affirmation and negation, eternity and transience, self and non-self. Although the Buddha in his first sermon at Banaras preached the middle path, his doctrine differed from that of Madhyamika. Buddha's teaching had an ethical meaning, preaching neither a life of material pleasure nor of self-mortification. Nagarjuna's concept was metaphysical, advocating neither the theory of reality nor that of unreality. Nagarjuna taught that nothing is existent per se; it exists only in relation to other things; everything is sunyata (void) and its individuality is imaginary, *samvriti.* The sunyata is the absolute, corresponding to the *Nirguna Brahman* of the Upanishads; and there is no difference between *samsara,* the world of vision, and nirvana or sunyata. True knowledge is that which discloses the supreme identity beyond all opposites. Seng-chao interpreted the philosophy of Nagarjuna in Taoist terms and approximated the two doctrines. For instance, in his essay, *On the Immutability of Things,* he observed that Buddhist thought presented the contrast between the immutable reality (*bhuta-tathata*) and the temporal (*utpada-nirodha*), between permanence and change, and between nirvana and rebirth. These were very similar to the Taoist contrast between non-being and being, immutability and mutability, and *wu wei* (non-existence) and *yu-wei* (existence). Philosophical controversy in China at the time was centred mostly on *ti* (noumenon, or substance) and *yung* (phenomenon or function). Seng-chao held that ti and yung are not opposed but are the same. He sought to synthesize, which was his middle path. His synthesis of the absolute and the relative was no doubt based on the system of Nagarjuna, but it was expressed in Taoist phraseology. Because of its Chinese exterior, it was accepted as Chinese, and, in this, Seng-chao paved the way for Buddhist assimilation into Chinese philosophy.

Hui-Yuan, a disciple of Tao-an and a contemporary of Seng-chao, laid the foundation for the White Lotus Society of Lushan School, later known as the Pure Land School. In 402 Hui-Yuan assembled a group of one hundred and twenty-three of his chosen followers before a statue of Amitabha where they made a collective vow to be reborn in the Western Paradise. Thus the cult of Amitabha, the compassionate Buddha who became a Buddha only on the condition that he could distribute his accumulated good to others as he chose, was initiated. Those who live righteously and who piously repeat daily the words *namo Amitabha-ya,* or who meditate properly on him, can reach his paradise, the Pure Land (Sukhavati) in the West. This concept of the splendid Pure Land of Amitabha, one of the most magnificent in Buddhist imagery, had great success throughout Eastern Asia and inspired many works of art in both China and Japan. It was a non-intellectual and extremely simple form of Buddhism, involving an attitude of complete and enthusiastic bhakti (devotion) to Amitabha—a new type of Buddhist theism.

Hui-Yuan emphasized meditation and actively promoted dhyana exercises in South China. He was so enthusiastic that he sent emissaries to Central Asia to obtain relevant texts and instruction. Well-versed in Confucianist and Taoist classics, he frequently relied on Taoist terms to express Buddhist principles. He believed that Buddhist and non-Buddhist learning could be fused into one doctrine. In his writings he mixed the metaphysical speculations of Neotaoism with the Prajna thought of Buddhism, thus making the monastic ideal all the more attractive to the literati and gentry of South China.

A disciple of Hui-Yuan, Tao-sheng (also a fellow student of Seng-chao's under Kumarajiva) was a monk of wide learning and great brilliance who served as a bridge between the Buddhist centres at Lu-

Shan and Chang-an. He preached such revolutionary theories that he was once publicly banished from Nanking by the conservative monks. Two of these theories are important: "good action requires return," and "sudden enlightenment" as opposed to all forms of "gradual attainment." These doctrines were not really new but were actually Buddhist with a Chinese emphasis, demonstrating the Chinese assimilation of Buddhism. For example, Tao-sheng's doctrine of the true self was the logical culmination of Buddhist thinking on the subject. He taught that every sentient being possesses the Buddha-nature of universal mind, but is ignorant of it. It is this *avidya* (ignorance) which chains him to the wheel of birth and rebirth. Therefore, it is necessary for him to realize and learn to "see" the Buddha-nature within him, thus gaining freedom from illusion and returning to the ultimate. This realization of the Buddha within through sudden enlightenment also meant being one with the Buddha-nature of wu or universal mind, and this was the state of nirvana. Many Buddhists did not approve of Tao-sheng's doctrine since it implied that there is in reality no pure land or other world; the world of Buddha is around us; anyone could attain Buddhahood by sudden enlightenment. The idea of the Universal Mind is an Indian contribution to Chinese philosophy. The tao of the Taoists is the "mystery of mysteries," yet it is not Mind.[45] After Tao-sheng, Chinese philosophy had not only mind but also Mind, and his emphasis on meditation as a means of attaining enlightenment prepared the way for the development of the Ch'an (Dhyana) school of thought, which influenced not just Buddhism but all Chinese thought.

Tao-an and Hui-Yuan also emphasized the importance of Dhyana. Yet, it was not until a century after Tao-sheng's death in 434 that the Dhyana school of thought was introduced to China by the Indian monk, Bodhidharma. Bodhidharma had evolved a system through which Buddhahood could be attained only by the conscious identification of both the absolute and the relative. According to the traditions of the Dhyana school, this was an esoteric teaching of the Buddha transmitted from disciple to disciple, independently of written texts, until it reached the twenty-eighth Indian Patriarch, Bodhidharma, who taught that the Buddha was not to be found in images and books but in the hearts of men. The heart of every man is in communion with all time and all space. This heart is the Buddha and the Buddha is the heart. There is no Buddha outside the heart. Enlightenment and nirvana are also in the heart. Outside the reality of the heart, everything is imaginary. To search for something outside the heart is an attempt to seize emptiness. It is therefore essential to look within and to contemplate the Buddha-nature of the self. Bodhidharma's teaching was derived from the *Vijnana Vada,* but if Brahman is substituted for the Buddha, it appears remarkably similar to the Vedanta philosophy.

The Ch'an school presented a challenge to Buddhist scholasticism and monasticism. Throughout China there were thousands of monasteries with innumerable monks and nuns and a vast literature of Buddhist texts. And then the Ch'an philosophy arrived, ignoring all scriptures, disregarding asceticism and all forms of worship, even the concept of good and evil, preaching deliverance by knowing one's own self. Dhyana Buddhism was the very antithesis of the easy and popular way of gaining salvation through devotion and worship of Amitabha. It opposed the worship of images and the authority of the priesthood, and emphasized instead the application of one's own strength, the sense of inner freedom, detachment from worldly things, and ceaseless meditation and self-discipline. Bodhidharma is said to have told the devout Buddhist, Emperor Wu of the Liang dynasty, that all his good works did not accumulate any merit. To Bodhidharma the scriptures were nothing more than the finger that points to the moon of enlightenment, no longer useful once the moon is seen. Because of the difference between the existing Buddhist scholasticism and Bodhidharma's Dhyana, it has been suggested that the Dhyana movement was not really Buddhism at all, but a Chinese revolt against Buddhist verbalism and scholasticism, as well as a movement to make Buddhism more Chinese in character by detaching it from intellectualism. If this be true, then the Chinese alternative to Indian Buddhism emerged from Buddhism itself. But there is little substance in this assertion, because, whilst the Dhyana school rejects many features of Mahayana Buddhism, much of what is left is still remarkably close to early Indian Buddhism. "Chan Buddhism differs from the orthodox and popular Mahayana of the theistic Sutras just as the teaching of Christ and of the Christian mystics differs from the systematic Christianity of the Churches."[46] Indeed, the Ch'an doctrine of introspection in order to discover the essence of perfection in the depths of the heart and to bring about its mystical cleansing can doubtless be traced back to the practices of the Indian Yogis, both Hindu and Buddhist. However, it would be wrong to deny the influence of Taoism in the development of the Ch'an movement in China. The emphasis of Ch'an writers, teachers, and artists on spontaneity and naturalness is reminiscent of many passages in Taoist philosophic texts protesting the artificial restraints of society against the natural development of man. The Dhyana emphasis on the Buddha-nature of the self may have a parallel in the Taoist immanence of the Tao. Both Dhyana and Taoism stress the idea of the wordless doctrine, and Dhyana contemplation differs little from Taoist ecstasy. It is probable, however, that these common features illustrate Buddhist influence on Taoism.

Whatever the Taoist content in Ch'an, it certainly was not as speculative as some other schools of Buddhism were. Ch'an bore an affinity with Taoism in its philosophical ramifications, but did not antagonize Confucianist thought. Inevitably, it had great appeal for the Chinese and became widely popular in China. This sect "completed the transformation into Chinese thought of the fundamental ideas brought from India, thus achieving a Buddhist equivalent of the highest Taoism."[47]

The concept of Dhyana is sometimes hailed as an internal Chinese Buddhist movement, independent of Indian influence. It is argued that Bodhidharma was a legendary figure invented later to give the doctrine weight and authority, and that Dhyana was, psychologically if not doctrinally, the descendant of the early Chinese Quietism. Whilst this theory is somewhat far-fetched, some scholars maintain that the Quietism of China during the fourth and third centuries B.C. was to some extent moulded by Indian influence. This does seem possible but there is no definite proof of it. Whilst it is not altogether true that the formative period of Chinese Quietism, the fourth century B.C., was a time when outside influences on thought were general, Quietism did develop and expand when such influences were demonstrably beginning to be of importance. Scholars are now agreed that the literature of the third century B.C. is full of geographical and mythological elements derived from India.[48] Moreover, the Chinese Quietists practiced a form of self-hypnosis remarkably close to Indian Yoga.

The only flourishing Buddhist school in China today is the Tien-Tai school, founded by Chih-i (or Chi-kai) (538–597). This school was eclectic, saw no antagonism between the Hinayana and Mahayana, and accepted all sutras as true words of the Buddha. Following Nagarjuna's doctrine that all component things are impermanent, that all dharmas are without self, and that only nirvana is quiescence, it established a threefold system of perfect comprehension, *chi-kwan: kung,* empty or void; *chia,* hypothetical or temporariness; and *chung,* medial or mean. These three modes of comprehending beings can be likened to the three eyes of Siva. The "empty" mode destroys the illusion of sensory perception and constructs supreme knowledge, prajna; the "hypothetical" mode dispenses with the defilement of the world and establishes salvation from all evils; and the "medial" mode demolishes hallucina-

343

tion born of ignorance, avidya, and establishes the enlightened mind. Through these three truths the Tien-Tai school emphasizes the idea of totality and mutual identification; the whole and its parts are identical. The entire cosmos and all the Buddhas may be present in a grain of sand or the point of a hair. The Tien-Tai identification of phenomena with the absolute is further illustrated by their doctrine of the Absolute Mind, which embraces the universe in its entirety.

The Tien-Tai tenets are a brilliant product of Buddhist thought in China, because they harmonize and synthesize all doctrines, even the most contradictory, affirm the existence of the Buddha-nature in all sentient beings and assure universal salvation. Tien-Tai Buddhism is the most comprehensive system of Mahayana and is held as an authoritative model for East Asia, particularly for Japan. Its main text, *Saddharma-Pundarika-Sutra* (*Fa-hua-Ching* in Chinese and *Hokke-kyo* in Japanese), has provided more themes for Buddhist art in China than any other source.

Whilst Chinese scholars, such as Seng-chao, Hui-Yuan, Tao-sheng, and Chih-i, adapted Indian thought to Chinese patterns, there were others, like Hsüan-tsang and his chief disciple Kuei-chi, who founded schools which seem wholly Indian in character, some of which still survive. Hsüan-tsang founded a school called Fa hsiang-tsung (Dharma lakshana, known in Japan as Hosso) which taught that the world of phenomena is a projection of Vijnana, consciousness. Phenomena are illusory and only consciousness is real; the purpose of life is to free oneself from fear of and attachment to the external world, which is a fabrication of one's own consciousness. This system, explaining all phenomena psychologically and rationally, evoked a new interest amongst Chinese intellectuals, but could not wield great proselytizing power, because its deep and complex metaphysical speculations had little appeal to the average Chinese. Moreover, the Chinese language was just not flexible enough to translate and expound the subtle distinctions of terms and phrases of this school, which in its vast literature developed a most abstruse system of introspective psychology, analyzing consciousness into more than five hundred states of mind and their corresponding faculties and objects.[49] Although no Chinese sect exclusively follows this philosophy, it is still studied and has had considerable influence on East Asian thought.

Amongst other Buddhist schools of China are the Kiu-she, based on the *Abhidharma-kosa;* the Liu (Vinaya) school, founded by Tao-Shiuan; and Chen-Yen (the School of the True Word), based on Tantric Buddhism introduced by Vajrabodhi in the eighth century.

Tantrism or Vajrayana, named after its chief symbol, *vajra* (thunderbolt), is a combination of mystical speculation and secret magic rites expressed in a complex symbolism. These speculations involve the relationship between empirical reality and true essence, illustrated by a hierarchy of sacred figures and culminating in the *adi* (absolute) Buddha. The meditations, rites, and symbols aid the practical realization of the identity existing between the devotee and the Buddha-nature within him.

Whilst some Buddhist influence can still be seen in practically every aspect of Chinese cultural life, much is hardly recognizable. The transformation of Buddhist deities in China is a good illustration of this point. It is not often realized that the pot-bellied, exuberant Buddha, so popular as a tourist souvenir and as a model of art practically everywhere, is a Chinese version of the Indian Maitreya Buddha, who is yet to come and who is at present in the Tusita Heaven. The Indian Bodhisattva, Avalokitesvara, a sort of Buddhist Providence, on his arrival in China assumed by a curious metamorphosis a feminine guise, becoming the Goddess of Mercy, Kuan-yin, often represented as a beautiful woman with tiny feet sometimes bound in the traditional Chinese way. This goddess is extremely popular in China. Practically every household contains her image in wood, ivory, or porcelain, and she has temples in all parts of the country. The same Chinese tendency to adapt, assimilate, and integrate Indian elements is evident in other aspects of cultural life such as music, painting, sculpture, and architecture.

The most outstanding product of the cultural dialogue between Buddhism and Chinese thought was Neoconfucianism, unquestionably one of the greatest philosophies of China. The impact of Buddhism gave rise to a renaissance of Confucianism under the Sung and Ming dynasties. Many Chinese scholars of traditional learning recognized the superiority of Buddhist teachings, especially in metaphysics and methodology. Hence, they were inspired to rejuvenate Confucianism, grafting onto it what they regarded as the merits of Buddhism. But the Chinese, deeply imbued with a sense of this-worldiness and social responsibility, could not be completely reconciled with the other-wordliness of Buddhism. Therefore, the interaction between metaphysical Buddhist thought and Confucianist ethics led to the emergence of a new philosophical movement, commonly known as Neoconfucianism, during the Sung period (960–1279). Just as Buddhist interaction with Taoism gave rise to Ch'an, so with Confucianism it produced Neoconfucianism or *Li*. Thus, Buddhism finally succeeded in stirring the

Chinese intellect to respond in a positive way to new stimuli. This Confucianist response to Buddhism was characteristically Chinese: having failed to silence a critic, denounce him but act on his criticism. Whilst Confucianism underwent drastic changes under the Buddhist impact, Buddhism itself, except in minor concepts, absorbed little of Confucianism.[50]

Neoconfucianism was a deliberate attempt to show that Confucianism could offer everything that Buddhism offered. Neoconfucianists found fault with Buddhist doctrines but endeavoured to crystallize their own philosophical thinking. In doing so, they had to borrow a good deal without specifically acknowledging their debt. Often they over-stretched their interpretations to prove the continuity and purity of their interpretation of Confucianism, since the new movement was partly a nationalist reaction against Buddhism. But in fact, Neoconfucianism contains less Confucianism and more Buddhism, and to call it Neoconfucianism, therefore, is strictly speaking a misnomer. A contemporary Chinese scholar, Chou Hsiang-kuang, calls it Sung Rationalism or *Li Hsueh* of the Sung dynasty.[51]

Neoconfucianism explicitly undertook to match the Buddhist cosmology, explain the world metaphysically, and show how man could attain happiness within the ordinary pursuits of life. It was impossible to produce a system of cosmology and metaphysics from the *Analects* of Confucius, who was much too practical. Many Neoconfucianists appealed to Mencius, who, although a Confucianist, had diverged considerably from the master's practicality and adopted an almost mystical attitude similar to that of a Taoist. Whatever could not be explained was attributed to the esoteric teaching of Confucius, which was imparted not to the masses but to the select few. Four books came to be regarded as the main scriptures of Neoconfucianism during the Sung period: the *Analects*, the *Book of Mencius*, the *Great Learning*, and the *Doctrine of the Mean*. The last was held to contain the esoteric teaching of Confucius. It is significant that whilst some Confucianist scholars continued to deprecate Buddhism as a foreign religion, Confucianist temples from the eighth to the sixteenth centuries contained images of Confucius, his disciples and other notables, like the images in Buddhist temples.

That Neoconfucianists felt the need to discover scientific thought to match the notions of positive sciences as applied to philosophy shows that Indian concepts, such as the dualism of Samkhya and the atomism of Vaisesika, were too popular and well known to be liked by the revivalists. Compelled thus to offer a cosmology that could compete with that of the Buddhists, "the Neo-Confucians took over bodily some of the ideas of their rivals. Thus we find them echoing the Buddhist idea that the Universe is ceaselessly destroyed and recreated. This is interpreted in Chinese terms, however, as a function of the operation of the *Yin* (regression) and *Yang* (progression), the five forces, mystic numerology, and the diagrams which are the basis of the *Book of Changes*."[52] The Confucianists claimed that this work was written by Confucius, but in fact it is an ancient fortune-teller's manual. However, for many Neoconfucianists it virtually became a bible for their cosmology. It is so alien to the whole of early Confucianism that it is impossible not to believe that its metaphysical speculations were derived from Taoism and Buddhism over a period of time.

But each rival school of the many varieties of Neoconfucianism claimed Confucianist purity for itself and accused the others of having been influenced by Taoism and Buddhism. Later, many Chinese scholars, such as Ku Yen-Wu (or Ku Ting-Lin, 1613–1682), also attacked Neoconfucianism for its debt to Buddhism.

The Neoconfucianist movement was initiated by Chou Tun-i (1017–1073), who introduced into Confucianism the doctrine of the Supreme Ultimate, or first principle, which he called by the ancient name, *tai-chi* (meaning literally "supreme-limit") and which was conceived of as the primordial unity like the ancient Tao. However, in common with the Neotaoists of his time, Chou Tun-i envisaged this primordial essence as purely cosmogonic and not metaphysical. In modern terms, it resembled the infinitely rarefied and diffused matter of nebulae, a dust which consolidates itself into things by the laws of nature, and which produces the universe through the process of evolution. He criticized the Buddhist doctrine of sunyata, which maintained that the phenomenal world was illusionary.

Similar ideas were developed by other scholars, such as Shao Yung (1011–1077); the two brothers, Cheng Hao (1032–1085) and Cheng Yi (1033–1107); Chang Tsai, their uncle; and Chu Hsi (1130–1200).[53] Of these exponents of Neoconfucianism, Chang Tsai was probably the one most responsible for the introduction of acceptable elements from Buddhism. Chu Hsi, hailed by Needham as "the supreme synthetic mind in all Chinese history," was born in Fukien and is alleged to have once been a Buddhist monk. About 1154 he renounced Buddhism and returned to official Confucianism. His philosophical writings so completely dominated those of his predecessors, and wielded such an extensive influence, that his system is generally distinguished as Chuism. Like Confucius he was "a transmitter rather than an originator" of

thought. His main object was to further the new approach to the Confucianist classics as taught by the Cheng brothers.[54] Perhaps his central concept is that the whole universe is composed of two co-eternal
principles which are *li* and *chi*—the norm or reason, and matter or
energy. These two are inseparable, yet possess distinctive characters.
They existed before heaven and earth, and li set chi in motion which
produced the world. In regard to the relation between the norm and the
world, the noumenon and the phenomenon, Chu Hsi and the Neoconfucianist philosophers seem to accept the Buddhist concept of nirvana
and samsara. But the li principle is not the same as the concept of a
universal consciousness, an affable spirituality, the soul of souls and
of worlds of Indian pantheism. Li action is necessary, inevitable, and
unconscious, which excludes any idea of spirituality. All things and all
human relationships consist of li and chi, which, as one, are infinite,
eternal, immutable, unalterable, homogenous, unconscious, and unintelligent. Li is pure, vast, without form, and unable to create. Chi is
alone responsible for existent things and for change. In this Chu Hsi
was, no doubt, influenced by the Indian idea that only the permanent
and unchanging is good in the highest sense.

Man's nature is his li, which is part of the Supreme Ultimate. It is
only human desire that obscures his true nature, and if he could but
realize this fact he would be enlightened. This is remarkably similar to
the doctrine of the Dhyana school of Buddhism, and much of this
philosophy is so alien to early Chinese thought that "it would be easy
to conclude the Neo-Confucians have been converted to Buddhism in
everything but name."[55] Chu Hsi, in common with Shao Yung (1011–
1077), believed that at the end of an epoch lasting 129,600 years the
existing world system would come to an end and be replaced by another. This concept was alien to the Chinese and must have been derived from the well-known Indian ideas of aeons and recurring world
systems.

Chu Hsi's greatest rival was Lu Hsiang-Shan (or Lu Chiu-Yuan,
1139–1193), the founder of the rival school of Sung Rationalism. He
stressed meditation and intuition, and wielded much influence over
Chinese thinkers of the day, especially in eastern China. Whilst his
emphasis resembles that of Dhyana Buddhism, it also has roots in
ancient Chinese thought, especially that of Mencius. Chu Hsi's system,
with its vagaries and universality, is marked by an element of caution
and consideration, whilst Lu Hsiang-Shan's is characterized by sharp-
ness and penetration. Lu Hsiang-Shan did not share Chu-Hsi's dualistic
philosophy, but propounded a monistic doctrine stating that every-

thing that exists is li. Nothing is finite; man, heaven, earth, and all things exist in the infinite. Man is personally concerned in every affair of the universe, and the universe is concerned in all man's personal affairs. Early Chinese thought was closer to Lu Hsiang-Shan's than to Chu Hsi's. Lu said, "the Universe is my mind, and my mind is the Universe," in somewhat the same way as Mencius said, "all things are complete within me." But the type of monism which Lu Hsiang-Shan preached is also akin to Dhyana Buddhism, and for this reason Chu Hsi's disciples criticized Lu. Whilst Chu Hsi taught that man's nature is pure and unchanging, and that mind is composed of li and chi, Lu regarded nature, mind, and feeling as the same thing seen from different aspects, and believed that the process of moral cultivation consisted of looking for one's own "lost mind," one's true nature which was originally good, but had been led astray through desire. Lu advocated practical methods for regaining the lost mind. For man there is nothing prior to knowing himself. For attaining knowledge of one's own self or lost mind, he suggested meditation, much in the same manner as the Dhyana Buddhists did. Practiced assiduously, meditation would lead to the sudden realization of the oneness of one's own mind with the totality of all things. This concept of lost mind resembles the upanishadic teaching, "thou art that," and the theory of sudden enlightenment of Dhyana Buddhism.

The Chu Hsi school was closer to the whole rationale of Confucianism, whilst the Lu School was more akin to Indian Buddhism. The Neoconfucianists of the Chu Hsi School began by examining the external world, and this determined their conception of li as heaven or nature. Because the exponents of the Lu School endeavoured to permeate Confucianism with Buddhist thought they began by looking inward upon themselves, but defined their theory of li as the mind in an attempt to modify Buddhism with Confucianist teaching. Irrespective of the validity of this distinction, there is no doubt that the Neoconfucianist doctrine of mind and the advocacy of concentration of mind were influenced by Buddhism. The controversy raging within Buddhist society concerning sudden and gradual enlightenment is reflected "in the discussions of the Neo-Confucianists, with Chu Hsi representing the gradual rational approach and Lu Hsiang-Shan the intuitive instantaneous approach."[56] Even in the motto of the Sung political reformer, Fan Chung-Yen, "to be first in worrying about the world's troubles and last in the enjoyment of its pleasures," one can detect overtones of the Bodhisattva ideal of seeking the salvation of others before passing to one's own reward as a Buddha.[57]

The most outstanding Neoconfucianist philosopher of the Ming dynasty, and a statesman of high calibre and integrity, Wang Yang-ming (or Wang Shou-Jen, 1472–1529) echoed the doctrine of Lu Hsiang-Shan. Mind covers the whole range of existence and nothing exists independent of and apart from it. An individual may understand the fundamental principles of life and of things by understanding his own mind and by developing his own nature. Each individual has the solution of the problems of the universe within himself.

In his early days Wang Yang-ming was an ardent follower of Chu Hsi, but upon further investigation and reflection he moved to Lu Hsiang-Shan's concept of Universal Mind. In the exposition of this doctrine, Wang's writings are more comprehensive than those of Lu. Although his doctrine is hardly different in essence from that of his predecessor, he organized it more systematically and expressed it more precisely and convincingly. He was tolerant of both Buddhism and Taoism. His system was denounced by his opponents as being Buddhism in disguise and was criticized as heretical, and the Ming Emperor forbade its dissemination after the death of the philosopher. But his influence on later Chinese thought was extensive. Whilst Wang Yang-ming did not consciously attempt to reconcile Buddhist and Confucianist ideas, his stress on individual intuition, innate knowledge of the good, and the inseparability of knowledge and practice led to a "rejection of all formal and traditional standards of Confucian morality, a positive contempt for book learning as an intellectual discipline, and a conscious desire to arrive at a syncretism of Buddhism and Taoism with Confucianism."[58]

Buddhism had become such an integral part of Chinese thinking that it was impossible for the exponents of Sung Rationalism to discount it. They used Confucianist terms to interpret Buddhist concepts, or interpreted Confucianist concepts in the light of Buddhist knowledge. Without understanding the Buddhist ideas of Sung China, the Neoconfucianist system cannot be properly comprehended. Yet, several doctrines central to Buddhism, such as reincarnation and the concept of heavens and hells, have no place in Neoconfucianism. The Neoconfucianist emphasis on the problems of society is in marked contrast to the Buddhist indifference to the fate of society. Buddhist asceticism and pessimism are very different from Neoconfucianist optimism. Unlike Buddhism, Neoconfucianism neither counsels withdrawal from life nor regards it as evil.

Taoism also leaned heavily on Buddhism, and, in fact, was far more affected by Buddhist ideas. The Taoists had no notion of their system as a religion until they appropriated the idea from the Buddhists. Having done so, they decided to imitate the Buddhist example. They borrowed their views on cosmology from Buddhism, as well as their pantheon, their literature, and their doctrines: "Instead of Taoism swallowing up Buddhism, as was feared at the end of the Han Dynasty, the Taoists were themselves overwhelmed by the Buddhists."[59] Taoism borrowed the concept of heavens and hells from Indian Buddhism, and the indefinable Tao is very close to the indeterminate "thusness" of Buddhism. Taoist and Buddhist ethics teach returning good for evil, in marked contrast to the Confucianist doctrine of reciprocity. Chuang-Tzu's emphasis on self-identification with the universe as a means of entering a state of pure experience and higher happiness, having discarded intellectual knowledge, reveals Indian influence. He was presumably acquainted with Yoga techniques, and several of his passages describing a state of self-induced trance are reminiscent of dhyana.

Whatever the extent and nature of Buddhist influence on Taoism, there is no doubt that Taoism and Buddhism were commonly associated in the Chinese mind. Buddhists were often very tolerant of Taoists and sometimes even included Taoist deities in their temples. Taoism also copied Buddhism in establishing temples and an order of monks. The Taoist Trinity created by deifying Lao-tzu and associating him with Panku and Yu Huang Shangti is on the pattern of the Three Jewels of Buddhism. In an interesting work called *Mou-tzu*, after its author, Buddhism is in fact regarded as simply an older and more elaborate version of Taoism.[60]

Buddhist elements are found in Chinese festivals, local beliefs and practices. Certain features of the clan organizations, notably the idea and function of charitable estates for the benefit of the entire clan, are of Buddhist origin.[61] Buddhist symbolism is seen in the ideologies and rituals of the secret societies, which have been so important in Chinese life and history. The concept of karma is to be found in all types of Chinese literature from poetry to popular tales.

Buddhism also made contributions from areas of Indian culture other than the philosophic—such as art, astronomy, mathematics, medicine, and fables. The great literary activity of the Buddhist scholars naturally had a permanent influence on Chinese literature, one of the oldest and richest in the world.[62] Whilst the antiquity of Chinese literature is apparent, its literary forms were slow in evolving. In fact, they did not begin to articulate and crystallize until after the impact of the Buddhist translations, literary themes, and techniques. There was no epic poetry or short story form until the T'ang period; no recorded dramas until the Mongol period; and no development of the novel until the Ming period.[63] In a recent study a Chinese scholar, Lai Ming, says that a significant feature in the development of Chinese literature has been "the immense influence of Buddhist literature on the development of every sphere of Chinese literature since the Eastern Chin period (317 A.D.). We cannot say that without this influence Chinese literature would have remained static and only poetry and prose been its principal literary forms, but we can safely say that it certainly would have been different from what it is today."[64]

The earliest works of Chinese literature are the Confucianist classics.[65] The ancient Chinese, such as the Ch'an masters, wrote their *Recorded Sayings* without much attention to literary organization and clarity of presentation. With the advent of the Buddhist classics, Chinese writing became more systematized, lucid, and logical. Indian *hetuvidya,* methodology, and Buddhist translations in both prose and verse led to a new era in literature.

Buddhist influence on Chinese literature, as on other aspects of cultural life, was not a deliberately initiated and directed process but a natural growth dictated by the needs of religious propaganda. The sutras were written in combined prose and rhymed verse, a literary form unknown in China at the time. It was possible to communicate the meaning, but the tonal harmony and the beauty of the verses could not be translated. The Chinese language when pronounced in the Sanskrit polyphonic manner was likely to sound hurried and abrupt, and to chant the Sanskrit verses in monophthongal Chinese prolonged the verses so much the rhymes were lost. Hence, to make the Chinese sutras pleasant to listen to, the Chinese language had to be modified to accommodate Sanskrit sounds, and greater attention paid to *fan-chieh,* the Chinese method of phonetic spelling, by joining the initial or consonant sound of a word to the end or vowel sound of another word. Consequently, in 489, Yung Ming, Prince of Ching Ling, convened a conference of Buddhist monks at his capital to differentiate between, and define the tones of, the Chinese language for reading Buddhist sutras and for chanting the verses. Their deliberations improved and more accurately defined the sound of monophthongal Chinese, and a new theory, called the Theory of Four Tones, was established: *ping* or "soft" tone; and three "hard" tones, *shang* or acute tone, *chu* or grave tone, and *ju* or abrupt tone.

The emergence of the Theory of Four Tones led to the rise of a new prosody. Instead of using a single rhyme for a poem, poets started to write poems which changed rhymes every two, four, or eight lines and greater attention was given to the balance of tonal values: "The 'new style' poetry of the Tang Dynasty, *tse* of the Sung Dynasty and *chu* of the Yuan Dynasty, all followed basically the same theory which had grown out of the necessity to adapt the Chinese language to translating Buddhist sutras and propagating Buddhism."[66] A new form of prose, *pien-ti-wen*, also developed because of the new emphasis on tonal value. The new prose style introduced pleasing tones and flowery phrases, which, in turn, brought about a greater consciousness of the subtle distinctions between works of philosophy and history and those of literature.

The introduction into China of highly imaginative literature, such as the Mahayana sutras and the Indian epics, infused into Chinese literature the quality of imagination which had been hitherto lacking. Taoist literature, such as the book *Chuang-tzu*, did perhaps show some quality of imaginative power, but on the whole Chinese literature, especially Confucianist, was narrow, formal, restricted, and unimaginative. It recorded daily routine and historical events but seldom told interesting tales. *The Biography of Emperor Mu*, which comprises the barest possible outlines of stories, can be cited as an example of Chinese writing of the pre-Buddhist period. By contrasting this work with Wu Cheng-en's *Hsi Yu Chi*, the great romantic novel written after Buddhist influence had permeated Chinese literature, the enormous contribution of Indian imaginative literature to creative writing in China is apparent.

The literary masterpiece of the Buddhist poet, Asvaghosa, *Buddha-carita-kavya*, translated into Chinese by Dharmaraksa, influenced not only Chinese Buddhism but Chinese literature as well. The long Chinese poems, *A Heroine of the Molan* and the *Peacock Flying towards the South-east*, reflect the style of Buddhist literature. The novels and dramas of the Yuan and Ming dynasties were influenced by Buddhism, either directly or indirectly. China has no epic poetry; but what is the most surprising feature of the history of Chinese literature is the conspicuous absence of fiction until almost the end of the eighth century. The Chinese sense of realism was so intense that there was hardly any mythology in ancient China, and they have produced few fairy tales of their own. Most of their finest fairy tales were originally brought to China by Indian monks in the first millennium. The Buddhists used them to make their sermons more agreeable and lucid. The tales eventually spread throughout the country, assuming a Chinese appearance conformable to their new environment. For example, the stories of Chinese plays such as *A Play of Thunder-Peak, A Dream of a Butterfly,* and *A Record of Southern Trees* were of Buddhist origin.

Many ghost stories were written during the Three Kingdoms and Chin periods (220–419), a time when China was passing through a succession of wars and natural disasters, and even the ultrarealistic Chinese were receptive to some kind of emotional escape. Buddhist influence on the rise of story-telling can be seen in the collections of tales published in the period of the Northern-Southern dynasties: for example, *Yuan Hun Chi* (Accounts of Avenging Spirits) by Yen Chih-tui, and *Ming Hsiang Chi* (Records of Mysterious Manifestations) by Wang Yen. But the fables which became so popular in western Asia, Europe, and elsewhere did not find acceptance in China. The Chinese did not much care for animals who assumed human characteristics.

The stories found in the Buddhist sutras were changed into Chinese scenes and characters and passed off, possibly unconsciously, as Chinese stories. For example, the story, "A Scholar of Yang Hsien," included in the *Sequel to Tales of Chi-Hsieh,* is a replica of a Buddhist story found in the *Samyuktavadana Sutra,* which was rendered into Chinese in the Three Kingdoms period by Kang Seng-hui. Buddhist ideas influenced many short story writers: for example, Lee Kung-tso's *The Governor of Nan-ko* and Shen Chi-chi's *Records of a Pillow,* both of which dwell upon the transience of life and the futility of worldly possessions and fame. An outstanding example of this is the well-known Chinese novel *Hsi Yu Chi* (Records of a Trip to the West, known in its English adaptation by Arthur Waley as *Monkey*) by Wu Cheng-en (1505–1580), which is a modified version of an earlier story, *The Story of Hsüan-tsang's Search for Buddhist Sutras,* which in its turn was based on the life of Hsüan-tsang. It has seventeen chapters in three volumes, and is the first Chinese novel to be divided into chapters, each of which has a couplet for the title. More important, however, is the fact that it was the first and remains one of the very few novels of romantic fantasy. The story has a Buddhist theme, is based on the actual journey of Hsüan-tsang, and was written by someone who, if not a Buddhist monk, was familiar with Buddhist literature. On his journey, Hsüan-tsang takes a monkey who looks like a scholar, has magical powers, writes poems, and has a striking similarity to Hanuman, the monkey god of the Indian epic *Ramayana.* This can hardly have been a coincidence. This monkey so fascinated the Chinese that this story continued to be popular throughout the Sung, Mongol, and Ming dynasties. The popular novel, *Plum of the Golden Bottle,* written in the Sung period and narrating the story of a young man learning the teachings of the Buddha, and *Feng-Shen-Chuan* (Annals of the Investiture of Deities) of the Ming period, are other examples of Buddhist influence on the Chinese novel. Still other stories are pure adaptations of Indian legends. Amongst these are *The Story of Hsiao Tung-hsien* which was based on an Indian legend mentioned by Hsüan-tsang in his *Hsi Yu Chi*.

A Chinese style of essay-writing called *san wen* or *pien wen*, consisting of short prose which combines straight narration, rhymed verses, descriptive prose, and allegories, is of Buddhist origin. To propagate their faith Buddhist monks used to explain the often obscure meaning of Buddhist sutras by telling anecdotes in order to arouse and hold the interest of the people. This method of expounding the sutras in story-telling form proved very effective and popular, and gradually gave rise to the pien wen style of writing.[67]

Whilst there were numerous references to pien wen in standard works, literature written in this style was first discovered in 1907 amongst the manuscripts, scrolls, and drawings found by Sir Aurel Stein in the cave temples of Tun-huang. These included some forty stories. Some of these, for example, *Shuntse Chih Hsiao Pien Wen* (The Most Filial Shuntse), *Lieh Kuo Chih Pien Wen* (The Story of Lieh Kuo), *Ming Fei Pien* (or *Ming Fei*), *Chiu Hu Pien Wen* (or *Chiu Hu*), have nothing to do with Buddhism in subject matter but are historical or legendary stories retold in the pien wen literary form.

Pien wen occupies an important place in the evolution of Chinese literature, because it is the forerunner of hua pen, the texts of the story-tellers of the Sung dynasty. It is through hua pen that Buddhist literature contributed most to the development of Chinese novels, for Chinese novels are a literary form evolved and adapted almost indiscriminately from hua pen.

Pien wen also indirectly influenced Chinese drama although the influence is less obvious, because not enough manuscripts have survived to allow a full examination. Since pien wen is the first known Chinese literary form to contain both prose and rhymed verse, it must have contributed to the emergence of *chu kung tiao*, an art form of the Sung and Chin dynasties. Chu kung tiao consists of sets of lyrics composed according to musical scores in various keys, linking descriptive passages and dialogues. It was from this that Northern drama or *tsa chu* evolved.

Chinese drama assimilated Indian features in three stages. First, the story, characters, and technique were all borrowed from India;

later, Indian technique gave way to Chinese; and finally, the story was modified and the characters became Chinese also. There are many dimensions to Chinese drama, and it is not easy to place them accurately in history. However, the twelfth century provides the first-known record of the performance of a play, a Buddhist miracle-play called *Mu-lien Rescues his Mother* based on an episode in the Indian epic *Mahabharata*. The subject matter of the Buddhist adaptation of the story, in which Maudgalyayana (Mu-lien in Chinese) rescues his mother from hell, occurs in a Tun-huang pien wen. Significantly, the play was first performed at the Northern Sung capital by professionals before a religious festival.

Phrases and words coined by Buddhist scholars enriched the Chinese vocabulary by more than thirty-five thousand words. As the assimilation was spread over a long period of time, the Chinese accepted these words as a matter of course without even suspecting their foreign origin. Even today words of Buddhist origin are widely used in China from the folklore of peasants to the formal language of the intelligentsia. For example, *poli* for glass in the names of many precious and semi-precious stones is of Sanskrit origin. *Cha-na,* an instant, from *kshana; t'a,* pagoda, from *stupa; mo-li,* jasmine, from *mallika,* and terms for many trees and plants are amongst the many thousands of Chinese words of Indian origin.

These words were coined principally in two ways. One method combined single Chinese words to evolve a new meaning, similar to the method followed by Sanskrit. An example of such a word is *Chin Ju. Chin* means real, *ju* means likely, and together they mean *bhutatathata,* implying the absolute, ultimate source and character of all phenomena. The word is fundamental to Mahayana Buddhism. The other method adopted a Sanskrit word with its original sound: for example *ni pan,* which is the rendering of *nirvana; cha-na* of *ksana; sha-men* of *sramana.* The legacy of transliterative devices, first developed to render the untranslatable words and concepts of Indian origin, still survives in China. These devices are now used to translate Western ideas and concepts. Indian grammar also undoubtedly stimulated Chinese philological study.

Chinese script consists of numerous symbols, which in their earliest stage were chiefly pictographic and ideographic. This was awkward to work with so Buddhist scholars set out to devise an alphabetical system. The first system was called *Hsi Yu Hu Shu* (Foreign Writing of the Western Countries), or *Po La Men Shu* (Brahmanical Writing). Later, during the latter half of the T'ang dynasty, the Indian Buddhists helped Chinese scholars form a system of thirty *tzu-mu*, phonetic symbols divided on the model of Sanskrit into gutturals, glottals, linguals, dentals, and labials. Shen-kung, a Buddhist monk, is the reputed author of the system, and the dictionary, *Yu Pien* (Discrimination of Language), was one of the first extensive works in which it was used. Chinese phonetic spelling, the *fan ch'ieh* system of employing two characters to indicate the pronunciation of the third character, was, no doubt, the result of Chinese knowledge of the Sanskrit alphabet. Previous to the fan ch'ieh system the Chinese had endeavoured to indicate the pronunciation of a character by the use of homonyms, but the fan ch'ieh system combines the initial sound of the first character with the final sound of the second to indicate the pronunciation.

Indian art also reached China, mainly through Central Asia, although some works of Buddhist art came by sea. Monks and their retinues, and traders brought Buddha statues, models of temples, and other objects of art to China. Chinese pilgrims also enthusiastically collected works of art on their travels. Fa-hsien made drawings of images whilst at Tamralipiti; Hsüan-tsang returned with several golden and sandalwood figures of the Buddha; and Hui-lun with a model of the Nalanda Mahavihara. Wang Huan-ts'e, who went to India several times, collected many drawings of Buddhist images, including a copy of the Buddha image at Bodhgaya; this was deposited at the Imperial palace and served as a model of the image in Ko-ngai-see temple. The most famous icon of East Asian Buddhism known as the "Udayana" image was reported to have been brought by the first Indian missionaries in 67, although there are various legends associated with this image and many scholars believe it was brought by Kumarajiva. However, this influx of Indian art was incidental and intermittent, and was destined to be absorbed by Chinese art, which had a strong tradition of its own. This combination resulted in a Buddhist art of exceptional beauty.

There were three main centres of Buddhist art in China—Tun-huang, Yun-kang in the north of Shansi, and Lung-men near Loyang. Tun-huang is located on the northwestern frontier of China near an oasis known as Yumen, or the Jade Gate, where the northern and southern routes from Central Asia converged. For travellers to China it marked the last stage of an arduous journey, and it became a thriving centre for Buddhist activities. During the fourth century, Tun-huang provided refuge to numerous monks escaping from the upheavals prevalent in the rest of northern China. These monks contributed to Tun-huang's importance as a centre of Buddhist learning. For accommodation they dug cave monasteries in the hillsides. The earliest dated cave temple was built by a monk, Lo-tsun, in 366, although Tun-huang had been a flourishing colony of monks long before this date. In the most famous of these caves there is a wall painting which was executed in 344. Several monks, such as Dharmaraksa, had travelled from there to China. The site is called Ch'ien-fo-tung, "Caves of the Thousand Buddhas," because there were supposedly more than a thousand caves in 698. So far, about five hundred caves have been discovered. These caves were painted throughout with murals, and were frequently furnished with numerous Buddha statues and sculptured scenes from the Jatakas.

The murals have been well preserved in the dry climate. Besides wall paintings and paintings on silk and paper, a large number of ancient manuscripts and art relics remained hidden in perfectly good condition in a walled-up rock temple library for about nine hundred years. Many of the scrolls and drawings belong to the T'ang period, and many of the manuscripts are in Sanskrit. These paintings are an invaluable record of the history of Chinese art, not only because they cover a period of a thousand years to the end of the thirteenth century, but also because only a few other T'ang paintings have survived. Whilst the numerous cave sanctuaries of Central Asia have preserved an incalculably rich art treasure, the implications and interpretations of which embrace most of the known ancient world, the history of Chinese art would have remained far more obscure without the yield of Tun-huang.

Tun-huang art mainly follows Chinese and the Serindian (Central Asian Indian) traditions. There is some evidence of Turkish and Iranian influences in the later paintings. The grottos were begun in the Northern and Western Wei periods, but their art attained its peak form later. Mural painting in cave temples, or in sanctuaries dug in cliff walls, is most likely due to Indian influence, although tombs have painted walls at least as far back as the Han dynasty. These cave paintings portray the entire system of Indian mudras (expressive gestures of the hand) and motifs of Indo-Buddhist Art: for example the Bodhi tree, the nimbus, and the *yaksas* guarding the temple. Later on, as might be expected, Chinese traditions became increasingly predominant, and the Tun-huang paintings represent an increasing synthesis of Indian and Chinese ideas. On some silk paintings are found pictures of Vaisravana, the *lokapala* or guardian king of the North in Indian mythology, featured as a formidable T'ang warrior with dazzling armour and adornments in golds, reds, blues, and greens. He is supposed to be the protector of the Buddha, of his sanctuary, and of his doctrine. The Tun-huang banners exhibit Buddhist doctrines in the process of evolution. The cult of Maitreya is depicted alongside the heavens of Avalokitesvara, the Buddhist Providence. They also show the transformation of the Indian Avalokitesvara into the Chinese Kuan-yin, the Goddess of Mercy. Thus, Tun-huang is "not only the junction where one passes from the art of the Tarim Basin, still permeated with Indian influence, to a purely Chinese art; it also remains a unique testimony, after the conquest of China by Buddhism, to the counter-annexation of Buddhism by China."[68]

In China proper the earliest traceable influence of Indian art is found in the Yun-kang caves. So far, twenty-eight major caves, revealing art of different periods, have been discovered. These caves were constructed from about 453 onwards to commemorate the reversal of the policy of Buddhist persecution initiated in 446 by the Toba Wei Emperor, T'ai Wu. The work continued throughout the Wei period and for several centuries thereafter. The leading role in the resumption of work on these caves in 453 was played by the Buddhist monk, Tan Yao, who came from Central Asia, and whose doctrine was based on the *Lotus of the True Law* and on the teachings of the Indian arhat Vimalakirti. Later, the Wei Emperor, Wen-hsien himself directed the work on the caves at Yun-kang between 460 and 465, including the enormous Buddha seated in Indian fashion in cave Number 20.

The conversion of the Toba Wei rulers to Buddhism had an enormous influence on the development of Chinese art. The Wei sculpture includes some of the finest religious art of all time. Similar to the way Romanesque and Gothic artists adapted the traditions of Graeco-Roman plastic art to purely spiritual ends, the sculptors of the Wei period drew upon the Gandhara technique of drapery and the Apollo-like features of its statues to more effectively express the pure spirituality of Buddhism.[69] However, in recent years the art of Yun-kang has come to be regarded as somewhat of an improvement on Gandhara art in purity of line and elegance.

Although colossal images of the Buddha, like those at Bamiyan in Afghanistan, and smaller statues in cliff niches of the Buddha and the Bodhisattvas were predominant, some caves (Nos. 7, 8, and 10) also contain many images of Hindu deities, such as Siva on Nandi and Vishnu on Garuda. Two Japanese scholars, Mizuno and Nagahira, in their fifteen-volume work on the art of these caves, find not so much of the mature Gupta style, as seen in the seated Sarnath image, as of the Mathura style of the earlier Gupta period. If these images had come from India and were considered holy, as is suggested by Omura who, in his *History of Chinese Sculpture,* drew upon Chinese literary references, it would significantly underline the depth of Chinese acceptance of Indian thought.

The art in the caves at Lung-men is a continuation of that at Yun-kang, and carries mysticism and stylization even further. In 494 the Wei kings moved their capital from Peng-Cheng to Loyang, which led to the construction of Buddhist rock shrines near the new capital in 508. Beginning in the reign of Emperor Hsuan-wu, the chiselling of the caves continued through the rest of the dynasty. Emperors, officials, monks, and laymen cooperated in cutting the hard rocks and filling niches with images of the Buddha. The number of Buddha statues, according to one count, totals 142,289.

The most important of the Lung-men caves are the Ku-yang-tung and Pin-yang-tung. The Buddha and Maitreya were the chief deities portrayed in the Ku-yang-tung. The Pin-yang-tung cave was patronized by the ruling house and is the more imposing. Here, figures of the emperors and empresses can be seen paying their respects to the Buddha. The sculpture in the Pin-yang-tung is based on two widely known Jatakas, the *Sudassanajataka* and *Mahasattvajataka.*

The sculptures produced during the Pei-Ch'i period (550–577) are of considerable importance. Carved in white sandstone in the caves on the cliffs of T'ieh-lung-shan, they bear marks of Gupta art, as do the limestone sculptures of Hsiang-tang-shan on the border of Hopei and Honan, which were still being produced during the T'ang period. In the cave temples of T'ieh-lung-shan, statues of Bodhisattvas have been discovered, which are apparently contemporary with the T'ang dynasty, and which are direct imitations of Indian Gupta art. They have a softness of modelling, a rounded charm, and a blending of forms which are strikingly un-Chinese but do represent the Indian sense of beauty with its inherent tropical sensuousness.[70] Oswald Siren has pointed out that certain Buddha figures at T'ieh-lung-shan were obviously inspired by models from Mathura and Sarnath. One of the Bodhisattvas seated on a lotus is cast in a graceful and recognizably Indian posture and costume. Other Bodhisattvas, for example in cave Number 17, are seated in *lalitasana,* a posture which brings out the beauty and suppleness of the body, with the upper part of the body bare except for a necklace and a thin scarf; these appear to have been directly inspired by Indian examples. Considering how foreign the nude is to Chinese art, it is interesting that Indian aesthetics for a brief period wholly reshaped Chinese taste.[71] In the cave temples of Hsiang-tang-shan the influences of the Gupta style are also seen in the representation of jewellery, lotus leaves and vine stems, and in the rounded style and graded modelling of the seated Buddhas.

From the T'ang period onwards Indian art was increasingly absorbed by Chinese art traditions. Indeed, the faces of all the Buddhist deities became Chinese in appearance. In the Tun-huang caves, one can see how the distinct Indian figures of the Wei period went through physiognomical changes to become Chinese by the Sung period.

The oldest Chinese aesthetic traditions go back to the fourth or fifth century when Buddhism was in ascendancy, and they are strongly reminiscent of the Indian principles of aesthetics. The six principles of painting of Sie-Ho (479–501) are parallel to *shadanga*, the six principles of painting described in ancient Indian literature—*rupa, pramana, bhava, lavanya, sadrsya*, and *varnikabhanga*.[72]

Ku Kai-Chih, one of the earliest and most famous Chinese masters, employed Buddhist themes in the fourth century. By the time of the T'ang period Indian influence appears to have found a dominant place in Chinese painting. For example, the T'ang ideal of feminine beauty— a more pointed face and rounded figure (compared to the slender elegance of previous periods), with hair collected around and above the head, and an air of cheerful health—was the result of this influence. The most splendid paintings of the T'ang period were of Buddhist inspiration, such as those by Wei-Chih I-Seng, Yen Li-pen, and Wu Tao-tzu.

A remarkable school of painting directly connected with Indian thought, although not with an Indian artistic tradition, was inspired by Dhyana Buddhism. This school gained popularity during the twelfth and thirteenth centuries and had a closer approach to nature than other schools. Landscape painting had become an independent art during the T'ang period, but the landscape works of the Sung artists inspired by Ch'an Buddhism are the best. Before this, the most famous landscape painter was Li Lung-mien (*ca.* 1040–1106) who relied upon Buddhist themes for his works. A romantic attraction for nature became the dominant inspiration of the landscape painter, and was strengthened by Ch'an Buddhism with its reliance on intuition and contempt for appearances. The elements of nature were transformed into abstract ideas. The Sung painter saw the mountains as if floating in the distance, having no real existence. Ma Yuan's (1190–1224) picture of a solitary fisherman, lost in the middle of a lake in the winter with no bank visible, is a most poignant painting. Another outstanding artist of this school was Liang Kai, whose masterpiece is a picture of the Buddha, leaning on his stick near a stream in a strange landscape of steep mountains. The greatest of them all was Muchi, who worked in a Ch'an monastery near Hangchow, but whose work is now mainly preserved in Japan. His painting, "The Ch'an Master in Meditation," in which a serpent is curled around an ascetic or a holy man who is completely unconcerned, is a familiar scene in Indian art, but in China it is particularly characteristic of the Ch'an School.

Ch'an influence is similarly seen in the painting of flowers. The Ch'an artist saw in flowers a reflection of the Buddha essence and he sought to capture its spiritual significance by identifying himself with the object through intense mental concentration. Favourite themes were plum blossoms, vines, orchids, and narcissi—messengers of spring. A vast literature has grown up around these motifs. Another favourite theme was the bamboo, which, by its uprightness and the inner emptiness of its hollow stem, symbolized the Buddhist ideal. Hence, to paint bamboo with devotion was an ascetic exercise leading to a state of spirituality.

By the thirteenth century Indian influence in painting waned, although images of the Buddha continued to be made in the traditional manner. With the decline of Buddhism in China, Buddhist art also declined.

In architecture, India's contribution is not as notable as it is in painting or sculpture, although some influence can be seen in the temples. The pagoda type of temple is of Indian origin, but it appears that the traditional Indian style of stupa did not catch on in China. The architecture of all Chinese temples, Buddhist, Taoist, or Confucianist, is much the same. Even the mosques are, in general, identical with the temples, except that they use extracts from the Quran as exterior decorations. It is the interior decoration that distinguishes one from the other. There is virtually no difference in the architectural design of temples and palaces. Certain official rules prescribing the dimensions of all Chinese habitations were taken from the architectural texts of India.[73]

Chinese musical theory is based on the foundation tone, the pitch of a man's voice when he speaks without passion, *huang-chung*, which was conceived as an abstract eternal principle; it was the basis of the Chinese system of measures, of the calendar and of their astronomical calculations, and a definite pitch in music. Everything, a ruling dynasty, political order, or music, must have the correct pitch. From the foundation tone, other higher notes were derived, and a five note scale was developed in which the vibration frequencies were on the powers of numerals 2 and 3; 3 being regarded as the number of heaven and 2 that of the earth, the sounds in the ratio 3:2 expressed the harmony of heaven and earth. Ancient classical music was almost exclusively confined to temple worship, religious rites, and court ceremonies. There was no well-organized class of professional music teachers, no accomplished amateur musicians practicing music purely for aesthetic satisfaction, and ballads and folk-singing were not very common. The Chinese did not regard music as an art to be cultivated outside temples and theatres. Buddhist monks who reached China brought the practice of chanting sacred texts during religious rites. Hence, Indian melody was introduced into Chinese music which had hitherto been rather static and restrained.[74]

Dancing and singing no doubt originated in ancient times but a combination of the two does not seem to have existed in China before the period of the Wei and Chin dynasties. The earliest known opera, *Po-tow* (The Wedge), is reported to have been introduced from India. By the end of the period of the Northern and Southern dynasties, several musical instruments had been introduced into China through Central Asia. Many foreign instruments also came during the T'ang period, and the stringed instrument *ya-cheng,* played by rubbing the strings with a slip of bamboo, came through Tibet. The Chinese *hu-ch'in,* a foreign importation, is exactly like the two-stringed sitara of India. A popular stringed musical instrument of the time, the *K'ung-hou* came from India during the Han period. The Chinese guitar, called the *p'i p'a,* which was another popular instrument during the Han and T'ang dynasties, possibly came from India.

Indian music was at one time so popular in China that Emperor Kao-tsu (581–595) tried unsuccessfully to proscribe it by an Imperial decree. His successor Yang-ti was also very fond of Indian music. In Chinese annals, references are found to visiting Indian musicians, who reached China from India, Kucha, Kashgar, Bokhara, and Cambodia. Even Needham, the well-known advocate of Chinese cultural and scientific priority, admits "Indian music came through Kucha to China just before the Sui period and had a great vogue there in the hands of exponents such as Ts'ao Miao-ta of Brahminical origin."[75]

By the end of the sixth century Indian music had been given state recognition. During the T'ang period, Indian music was quite popular, especially the famous Rainbow Garment Dance melody. There were Indian, Central Asian, and Southeast Asian orchestras, and each year the Emperor invited musical parties from abroad to the T'ang court. A contemporary Chinese poet, Po Chu-yi, wrote a poem in praise of

Indian music. "It is little wonder," an official publication of the Chinese Republic says, "that when a Chinese audience today hears Indian music they feel that while possessing a piquant Indian flavour it has a remarkable affinity with Chinese music."[76] However, Chinese music has always retained its own character and values.

One reason for the early success of Buddhism was the Chinese fascination for Buddhist science and knowledge of elixirs and practices that were thought to promote longevity or produce levitation. However, the history of the migration of Buddhism to China has not yet been seriously examined with a view to tracing the exchange of scientific ideas; the study of the history of Indian science itself has hardly begun. Broadly speaking there are two reasons for this: the interest in Buddhist religion and philosophy, which constitute the more fascinating and spectacular side of the story, has been, understandably, too concentrated to allow specific investigation of secondary concepts relating to science; and, second, such a study would require exceptional scholarship, including competence in several languages, such as Chinese, Sanskrit, Pali, Persian, plus a keen sense and understanding of history and philosophy, and a thorough knowledge of science. Joseph Needham, in his multi-volume history of Chinese science, alludes to Indian ideas, but only very briefly and he has used a limited range of sources. He prefers to rely on Chinese materials and some well-known but hopelessly out-of-date Indian commentaries, such as V. A. Smith for Indian history and G. R. Kaye for Indian mathematics. Perhaps the limitations of an arbitrary selection of Indian references, more than his generous disposition towards China and his reliance on Chinese sources, which were disinclined to admit to any substantial "barbarian" influence on Chinese achievement, have tilted his scientific objectivity towards China.[77]

A major Buddhist influence on Chinese science was in scientific thought itself. Buddhist concepts, such as the infinity of space and time, and the plurality of worlds and of time-cycles or kalpas (*chieh*), had a stimulating effect on Chinese inquiry, broadening the Chinese outlook and better equipping it to investigate scientific problems. For example, the Indian doctrine of *pralayas,* or recurrent world catastrophes in which sea and land were turned upside down before another world was recreated to go through the four cycles—differentiation (*ch'eng*), stagnation (*chu*), destruction (*huai*), and emptiness (*kung*)—which was later adopted by Neoconfucianists, was responsible for the Chinese recognition of the true nature of fossils long before they were understood in Europe. Again, the Indian doctrine of karma (*tso-yeh*), or metempsychosis, influenced Chinese scientific thought on the process of biological change involving both phylogeny and ontogeny. Buddhist iconography contained a biological element. Buddhism also introduced a highly developed theory of logic, both formal and dialectical, and of epistemology.

Tantric Buddhism, which reached China in the eighth century or before, and in which the worship of personal gods was mixed with strong magical elements, may have contributed to the scientific development in the sense that it asserted the validity of the principle that magic and science were originally united in a single undifferentiated complex of manual operations.[78] The greatest Chinese astronomer and mathematician of his time, I-hsing (682–727), was a Tantric Buddhist monk.

Whilst the work of Indian mathematicians was carried westward by the Arabs and transmitted to Europe, it was taken eastward by Indian Buddhist monks and professional mathematicians. There is some evidence that works on Indian astronomy were in circulation in China well before the T'ang period. In the annals of the Sui dynasty, numerous Chinese translations of Indian mathematical and astronomical works are mentioned, such as *Po-lo-men Suan Ja* (The Hindu Arithmetical Rules) and *Po-lo-men Suan King*. These works have vanished, and it is impossible to assess the degree of their influence on Chinese sciences. However, there is definite evidence of Indian influence on Chinese astronomy and calendar studies during the T'ang dynasty. During this period, Indian astronomers were working at the Imperial Bureau of Astronomy whch was charged with preparing accurate calendars. Yang Ching-fang, a pupil of Amoghavajra (*Pu-k'ung*), wrote in 764 that those who wished to know the positions of the five planets and predict what Hsiu (heavenly mansion) a planet would be traversing, should adopt Indian calendrical methods. Five years earlier, Amoghavajra had translated an Indian astrological work, the *Hsiu Yao Ching* (Hsiu and Planet Sutra), into Chinese.

At the time there were three astronomical schools at Chang-an: Gautama (Chhuthan), Kasyapa (Chiayeh), and Kumara (Chumolo). In 684 one of the members of the Gautama school, Lo, presented a calendar, *Kuang-tse-li*, which had been in use for three years, to the Empress Wu. Later, in 718, another member of the school, Hsi-ta (Siddhartha), presented to the Emperor a calendar, *Chiu-che-li*, which was almost a direct translation of an Indian calendar, *Navagraha Siddhanta* of Varahamihira, and which is still preserved in the T'ang

365

period collection. It was in use for four years. In 729 Siddhartha compiled a treatise based on this calendar which is the greatest known collection of ancient Chinese astronomical writings. This was the first time that a zero symbol appeared in a Chinese text, but, even more important, this work also contained a table of sines, which were typically Indian. I-hsing (682–727) was associated with the Kumara school and was much influenced by Indian astronomy. In 720 he was employed by the Emperor to revise the calendar. Whilst I-hsing's works on mathematics have been lost and the exact nature of his work is not known, Indian influence can be seen in the nine planets he introduced into his calendar, *Ta-yen-li*. The nine planets included the sun, moon, five known planets, and two new planets, *Rahu* and *Ketu,* by which the Indian astronomers represented the ascending and descending nodes of the moon. I-hsing organized an astronomical expedition to the southern seas to chart stars that could not be seen in China, and he also conducted a valuable project for measuring latitudes. He made measurements in ecliptic co-ordinates, constructed armillary spheres with ecliptically mounted sighting-tubes, and invented the first escapement for a mechanical clock.[79]

Evidence of Indian influence on Chinese medicine is even more definite. A number of Indian medical treatises are found in Chinese Buddhist collections: for example, the *Ravanakumaratantra* and *Kasyapasamhita*. From its very inception, Buddhism stressed the importance of health and the prevention and cure of mental and physical ailments. Indeed, the Buddha is credited with some miracle cures, and he described his teaching as a therapy for the ills of the world. The main emphasis of Buddhism has always been on the relief of pain and suffering. An important Bodhisattva in the pantheon was Bhaishajyaguru, the master of medicine. There were always many Buddhist monks noted for their medical skills. Indian medical texts were widely known in Central Asia, where parts of the original texts on *Ayur Veda* have been found as well as numerous translations.

A basic doctrine of Indian Ayurvedic medicine is that of the tridhatus (tridoshas), or organic functions and disturbance. The elementary substances of the universe also make up the human body, and the proper equilibrium of these elements ensures good health. Malady or disease occurs when this equilibrium is disturbed, and the function of medicine is to restore the right balance. The Chinese adopted this theory, as is seen in the writings of one of the leading T'ang physicians, Sun Ssumiao, who, despite his adherence to Taoism, was nicknamed the "new Vimalakirti" because of his interest in Buddhist medicine. In his

Ch'ien Chin Yao fang (Book of Prescriptions Worth a Thousand Gold Pieces), he explicitly subscribed to the Indian theory, and strongly recommended the study of Buddhist medical literature to those who aspired to become great physicians. His advice on medical ethics, requiring practitioners to subdue desire and ambition, to develop love and compassion and to treat all, rich and poor, Chinese or barbarians, intelligent or stupid, with affectionate care and strict impartiality, is Buddhist inspired. In contrast, the famous monk of the period, I-tsing, although he was a Buddhist and respected Indian physicians, regarded the Chinese art of healing as unsurpassed.

The T'ang emperors patronized Indian *thaumaturges* (Tantric Yogis) who were believed to possess secret methods of rejuvenation. Wang Hsüan-chao, who returned to India after the death of Harsha, had been charged by the Chinese Emperor in 664 to bring back Indian medicines and physicians. Wang Hsüan-chao succeeded in finding a physician, presumably So-po-mei or Lu-chiai-to, and he may have persuaded other physicians to go to China, although there is no evidence for it. Nor is there any evidence of Chinese physicians ever visiting India, although the possibility cannot be ruled out.

Considering that Indian medicine, especially operative surgery, was highly developed for the time, and that the Chinese genius for practical knowledge somehow did not work in medicine, it is not surprising that the Chinese, like the Arabs, were captivated by Indian medical skills and drugs.[80] In fact, until recently Chinese medicine had progressed very little.[81] Whilst the Chinese used dry cupping and massage effectively, they did not practice venesection but substituted acupuncture, which was introduced into China, as it was into Europe, from Egypt. Castration was performed by Chinese methods but other surgical techniques, such as laparotomy, trepanation, and removal of cataracts, as well as inoculation for smallpox, were influenced by Indian practices.[82]

The famous Shao-lin style of boxing is also attributed to Indian influence. Bodhidharma, who believed in a sound mind in a sound body, taught the monks in the Shao-lin temple this style of boxing for self-defence and for rejuvenating the body after exacting meditation and mental concentration.

During the first millennium, Indian racing games reached China. The well-known expert on the history of Chinese games, Karl Himly, on the authority of a passage from the *Hun Tsun Su,* a work of the Sung period (960–1279), suggests that the Chinese game *t'shu-p'u* was invented in western India and spread to China in the time of the Wei dynasty (220–265). T'shu-p'u is, in fact, the Chinese adaptation of the Indian *chatus-pada* (modern *chaupur*). Chess was introduced from India *ca.* 700 through the ancient trade route from Kashmir. The oldest and best of the native Chinese games, *wei-ch'i,* did not appear until 1000.[83] Cubical dice (*ch'u-p'i* or *yu-p'i*), although found in ancient Egypt as well as in India, are generally believed to have reached China from India, possibly quite early. Arthur Waley is of the opinion that the prominence of the number six in the *Book of Changes* was derived from the six sides of cubical dice.[84]

During this period of Sino-Indian contact, one would expect to find some Chinese influence on India, but there is little evidence of such influence. Since the overwhelming majority of the scholars and monks who travelled between the two countries were Indians going to China, China quite naturally assimilated more Indian culture than vice-versa. Most of the Indian monks who went to China settled there permanently, and consequently, India did not have the opportunity of exposure to the knowledge these monks had acquired in China. The Indian monks felt their primary loyalty to Buddhism and went where they thought they were most needed. Historical accounts tell us that these monks lived and worked until their death in the temple cells of China, on a simple vegetarian diet, carefully translating and interpreting Buddhist texts. They were above worldly temptation, and the very nature of their faith precluded attachment to either nation or family.

By contrast, the Chinese monks and pilgrims who came to India returned home, thus disseminating Indian ideas in their country. They returned, not necessarily because of nationalism, but because of their sense of duty to transmit their newly gained knowledge to those people in China who were not able to undertake similar journeys. Moreover, many of the Chinese travellers to India were simply pilgrims, who could not be expected to have fully subordinated national attachments to their faith.

Furthermore, whilst Chinese monks came to acquire knowledge and take it back, the Indian monks went to China on specific religious missions to impart knowledge. There is hardly any evidence that the Chinese monks brought with them any work which was translated into an Indian language. It seems that during this period of Sino-Indian contact, the psychological atmosphere was one in which India was naturally accepted as the giver and China as the taker. Whilst the best in Indian thought was carefully studied and carried back to China, Chinese ideas filtered through to India whether they represented the best of their culture or not. This mixed quality of assorted ideas operating in a limited area could not approach the impact of the best of a vital culture working in a much larger area.

Yet Chinese culture had some influence on India. The gabled roofs of houses on the western coast of India show a Chinese influence, as do the temples and houses in the Himalayan regions. Some Chinese influence is noted on Gupta coins, and the story framework of Kalidasa's *Meghaduta* suggests Chinese inspiration.[85] Chinese influence can also be seen in Mughal miniature paintings, but this influence reached India indirectly through Iran. The use of a certain kind of silk (china-msuka) in India, different kinds of fruits including pears (cina-raja-putra), peaches (cinani), and lichis, vermilion (sindura), the technique of fishing in the backwaters, and the porcelain industry all owe something to Chinese influence. Indians also learned the art of paper-making from China.[86]

The Kamakhya cult in Assam, the Chinachara, a recognized form of Tantrism in which the sage Vasistha was made to travel to China to be initiated into this cult, is reputed to have been influenced by Taoist mystic discipline. Although early visitors from India to China were struck by the similarities between Indian and Taoist philosophies, it was not until much later in the seventh century that India took a noticeable interest in Taoism. By that time, however, Taoism had interacted with Indian thought in China for more than six centuries and had acquired certain Buddhist features. The main evidence for this Indian interest in Taoism is the request of a king of Kamarupa, Kumara Bhaskara Varman (seventh century), to the Chinese envoys, Li Yi-piao and Wang Hsüan-ts'e to send him a portrait of Lao-tzu and a Sanskrit translation of *Tao Te Ching*, the book of the Taoist philosophy. Whether this text was ever sent is unknown; certainly the Chinese text had been rendered into Sanskrit by 647.[87] Bagchi is of the opinion that the translation reached India and was known in Buddhist mystic circles where it influenced the Buddhist School known as *Sahajayana,* which later influenced a Vaisnavite sect of eastern India, called *Sahajiya.*

After the decline of Buddhism in China and India, contact between these two countries ceased. Except for occasional sparks of brilliance, both India and China allowed their best accomplishments to stagnate, deteriorate, and even be forgotten. In China, technology, and in India, philosophy, ceased to progress; both neglected to adapt their traditions to contemporary situations. Politically, however, China continued to be unified and more or less stable. Only since the end of Western domination have these two countries established direct contact and resumed the process of cultural intercourse.

During the period of Western domination of Asia, when Mahatma

Gandhi was engaged in his unique fight against oppression of all kinds through love and non-violence, multitudes of peoples both in India and abroad heard in his voice an echo of the Buddha and the Christ. Gandhi's emphasis on non-violence and abstinence was well appreciated by Chinese Buddhists who had known these concepts for centuries, and also by Confucianists, because similar standards of moral values and the same appreciation of human character prevailed in both China and India. Certain social values were also common to both countries, and the most important of these was the solidarity of the family.

India, on her part, despite certain fundamental differences of approach and values, found much to admire in the Chinese revolution and in China's practical techniques of national reconstruction. The patriotic fervour and single-minded devotion of the Chinese people, their intense self-discipline, industry, and sense of national unity, their self-sacrificing spirit to work in increased austerity to build future prosperity and their almost contemptuous disregard of uninvited Western criticism have made a deep impression on many Indian visitors to China. It appeared in the 1950's that an era of unparalleled cultural collaboration between these two civilizations might be opened up, but the divergence of political ideologies and systems, accentuated by border disputes, diplomatic tension, national vanity, and armed conflicts, have rudely interrupted this interaction. Despite all this, a mutual respect for and the desire to learn from each other's culture seems to have survived.

Notes

Notes to Chapter I

1. Recent archaeological excavations in Turkey, conducted by the University of Istanbul, have revealed evidence that communities with a well-developed culture and economy had existed there as long ago as 7000 B.C., possibly even earlier. The full implications of this discovery have yet to be properly assessed. Jericho also belongs to about the same time and has yielded evidence of a society organized in fairly large units.

2. V. Gordon Childe, "Europe and the Near East: A Prehistorian's Interpretation of Diffusion" in Harvard Tercenary Conference of Arts and Sciences, *Independence, Convergence, and Borrowing,* p. 4.

3. Jean Filliozat, *Political History of India,* p. 85.

4. A team of archaeological experts from the Vikram University in Madhya Pradesh State has recently succeeded in unearthing the remains of a hitherto unknown Chalcolithic site, dating back to the third millennium B.C., in the village of Kayatha, fifteen miles east of Ujjain. These finds at Kayatha are of historic significance inasmuch as they indicate for the first time the existence of a fairly advanced culture and civilization in the Malwa region in such a remote period of history. The excavations reveal the remains of pottery, terracottas, copper tools, and some houses showing greater affinity with the Harappan and pre-Harappan elements of Rajasthan and Punjab.

5. V. Gordon Childe, *New Light on the Most Ancient East,* p. 169.

6. Herodotus, *The Histories,* III, 106.

7. J. B. Hutchinson, R. A. Silow, and S. G. Stephens, *The Evolution of Gossypium,* p. 88. Also see Vol. II, Ch. II, pp. 69–72.

8. Jacquetta Hawkes and Sir Leonard Woolley, *History of Mankind,* I, 396.

9. Two scholars, S. K. Ray, an Indian, and El Mansouri, an Egyptian, have pointed out striking similarities between the cultures of these two areas and have recently suggested, in independent studies, a historic and close relationship between ancient Egypt and prehistoric India, especially Bengal. S. K. Ray, *Pre-historic India and Ancient Egypt;* and S. M. El Mansouri, *Art-Culture of India and Egypt.*

10. A. L. Pusalkar, *Cultural Heritage of India,* I, 155.

11. Childe, *New Light on the Most Ancient East,* p. 170.

12. Childe, *Independence, Convergence, and Borrowing,* p. 19.

13. Childe, *New Light on the Most Ancient East,* pp. 183–84.

14. H. D. Sankalia, *Indian Archaeology Today*, p. 69.

15. Pusalkar, *Cultural Heritage of India*, I, 148.

16. John Garstang, *The Hittite Empire*, p. 205.

17. V. Gordon Childe, *The Aryans*, p. 19. The precise manner in which the kings of Mitanni and the vedic Aryans were connected will remain obscure until further inscriptions are brought to light through archaeological excavations.

18. Although the Phoenicians have left a rich legacy of ancient west Asian lore to the West, such as the alphabet, the knowledge available about them, as compared to the Romans or the Greeks, is scanty. No Phoenician, or Punic, city has been resurrected which could give an overall picture of their ancient life. The sites of Sidon and Tyre, much destroyed and repeatedly rebuilt, may yet yield rich rewards. Potentially fruitful excavations, however, including underwater work, are now under way at the site called Motya, near Marsala in Sicily.

19. The Indian origin of ivory has been confirmed in recent years by the fact that some specimens of ivory from the collection of Nimzud have been recognized to be of Indian material. The Phoenicians were importing ivory from Dedan, in North Arabia, by the sixth century B.C. As there were no elephants in Arabia, ivory must have been imported from India or Somaliland by sea and thence across Arabia by camel. The case for its Indian origin is reinforced by the discovery of several pieces of ivory at Bahrein in the Persian Gulf, probably of the sixth or seventh century B.C. See G. E. Bean, "Early Greek and Oriental Ivories," *Journal of Hellenic Studies*, LXVIII (1948), 1.

20. *Inaha–Ummagga Jataka*, No. 546.

21. Cecil Roth, *A Short History of the Jewish People*, p. 21.

22. See Michael Ridley, *The Seal of Aetea and the Minon Scripts*.

23. *Gaveru Jataka*, No. 339.

24. This subject is more fully discussed in Ch. V

25. For a summary of the arguments favouring the theory that India was the original home of the Aryans, see R. C. Majumdar (ed.), *The History and Culture of the Indian People*, I, 215–17.

26. Childe, *New Light on the Most Ancient East*, p. 188.

27. It has often been said that there is much secular poetry in the Vedas. However, these songs, themes, and humorous episodes have been applied to religious purpose.

28. Linguistic evidence indicates the Indo-European families fall into two distinct groups, according to the modification which certain consonants of the parent speech underwent in each, known as the *Centum* ("hundred" in Latin) and *Satem* ("hundred" in Avesta). The former group includes the Hellenic, Italic, Teutonic, and Celtic branches, and the latter the Indian, Iranian, Armenian, Balto-Slavic, and Albanian. Some scholars, however, like Sturtevant, have criticized the Centum-Satem hypothesis. Contemporary philologists attach less importance to this Centum-Satem division since the discovery of a Centum language in Central Asia in the tenth century A.D. and the discovery that in the

nineteenth century B.C. the Hittites in Asia Minor spoke a language more nearly allied to Latin than to any Satem tongue.

It was first thought that the Indo-European languages had arisen out of a parent speech and family trees were constructed. Realizing, however, that this was too much of an oversimplification, scholars later suggested that there was a continuum of diverging dialects, some of which were crystallized into languages. Even this view was exposed to exceptions. The present view is that the Indo-European languages have emerged, assuming divergent forms gradually, through the convergence of a loose and scattered continuum of distinct dialects. Whatever the course and nature of their convergence and divergence may have been, they are certainly interrelated by some common starting point or process.

29. For a fuller discussion, see V. Gordon Childe, *The Aryans*, pp. 3–16. The Florentine merchant, Filippo Sassetti, having lived in Goa for five years between 1583 and 1588, declared that some relationship existed between Sanskrit and the principal languages of Europe. Later, Coeurdoux in 1767, and still later Sir William Jones in 1786, noticed affinities between Latin, Greek, and Sanskrit vocabularies and grammars, and put forward the theory of a common origin. The original Indo-European is extinct and has taken different forms in different environments over the intervening thousands of years. Of all the existing Indo-European languages, Lithuanian is closest to the basic idiom as reconstructed by comparative philology. Some scholars regard Sanskrit, with its three numbers, three genders, and eight cases of noun, as well as an extremely complicated verbal structure, as the nearest representative of the parent, highly inflected Indo-European language.

30. The word Aryas is also found in the western group.

31. For a discussion of the possible reasons for the discontinuance of the relationship, see R. C. Majumdar (ed.), *History and Culture of the Indian People*, I, 218ff.

32. "In this inversion," remarks Gordon Childe, "we detect the hand of the prophet Zoroaster himself, who was perhaps the first great religious reformer." *The Aryans*, p. 36.

33. Bopp was the first scholar to notice the connection between Avestan *Ahura* and Sanskrit *Astura,* and Avestan *deava* and Sanskrit *deva.*

34. Seleucia and Antioch did not exist as such during the Achaemenian period; both cities were founded by Seleucus Nicator in 300 and 312 B.C. respectively.

35. The Persians, if not the later Assyrians, were the first to create a permanent system of roads and to provide for their regular maintenance, cementing bridges, embankments, and stations at convenient stages.

36. "The Indians, the most populous nation in the known world, paid the largest sum: 360 talents of gold dust." Herodotus, *The Histories*, III, 95. Considering that only a small part of India was under the Persian Empire and that it formed only one satrapy the amount paid in revenue speaks highly of Indian prosperity at the time, even if allowance is made for the gross exaggeration to which Herodotus was very prone. Actually, a student of Indian history is amazed by the numerous refer-

ences of foreign travellers to India's great riches. Arab and Chinese writers frequently mention them; Sir Thomas Roe, who visited the court of Jahangir in the seventeenth century complained, "Europe bleedeth to enrich Asia"; Hawkins, his contemporary, refers to the gold coins which flowed into India and "goeth out not." The French traveller, Bernier, too, in the seventeenth century, writes that gold and silver came from all over the globe "to be swallowed up, lost in some manner in Hindustan."

37. K. A. N. Sastri (ed.), *Age of the Nandas and Mauryas,* p. 390.

38. There is no real certainty that the pillars were made by Asoka. Some of them, it is likely, were in existence before him. He often ordered that his edicts be "inscribed on pillars whereever they may be found," or words to that effect.

39. Irrespective of his motives, which were wholly moral and partly practical, Asoka is the only monarch on record who renounced war after victory. H. G. Wells, who considers Asoka as one of the six greatest men of history—the only king included—says: "Amidst the tens of thousands of names of monarchs that crowd the columns of history, their majesties and graciousnesses and serenities and royal highnesses and the like, the name of Asoka shines, and shines almost alone, like a star." *Outline of History,* p. 247.

40. The origin of the name *Kharoshthi* is obscure but the term seems to mean script written on the skin of donkeys. See J. Przylushi, *Journal of the Royal Asoka Society,* p. 4.

41. E. B. Havell, *The History of Aryan Rule in India,* p. 105.

42. "Superficially these pillars," comments Hermann Goetz, "remind one of Achaemenid columns, and yet they are different in every detail." *India,* p. 47.

43. The Greeks did not pronounce an initial aspiration, sharply or clearly, as they did not use a variety of sibilants.

44. Herodotus, *The Histories,* IV, 44.

45. Three centuries elapsed before this feat of a Red Sea journey was repeated.

46. *The Cambridge History of India,* p. 397. "Ktesias is responsible for most of the grotesque legends about India which fill the pages of classical and medieval writers to the days of Sir John Mandeville." H. G. Rawlinson, *Intercourse between India and the Western World,* p. 26.

47. A. R. Burn, *Persia and the Greeks,* p. 12. It was Ctesias who was responsible for introducing into Western lore the monster called the Martichora (a good Persian word meaning man-eater, which, corrupted into mantichora, passed by way of Aristotle, Pliny, and Aelian into the mediaeval bestiary). He described this monster, which he claimed to have seen at the court of the Persian king who had been sent one from India, as a creature the size of a lion with the face of a man. In contrast, Herodotus, who introduced the phoenix into the West, at least confesses that "I myself have not seen this bird except in a picture." Aristotle, himself, whilst describing Ctesias' monster says, "If one may believe Ktesias."

48. "In some ways—though few—the civilization of Persia," observes Will Durant, "was superior to that of contemporary Hellas; it produced a type of gentleman finer than the Greek in every respect except that of intellectual keenness and education, and a system of imperial administration that easily excelled the clumsy hegemonies of Athens and Sparta, and lacked only the Greek passion for liberty." *The Life of Greece,* p. 69.

49. In his Rede Lecture for 1875, Sir Henry Maine said, "Except the blind forces of nature, nothing moves in this world which is not Greek in origin." Cited in J. A. Symonds, *Studies of the Greek Poets,* p. 578.

50. For a quick reference to the genesis, development, influence, and recent partial decline of the classical Greek myth and the legend which has shaped much European thinking, see Philip Sherrard, *The Pursuit of Greece.*

51. *Rig Veda,* X, 71.

52. Although the *Iliad* and the *Odyssey* are attributed to Homer, little is known of Homer himself. He is considered, however, the first and possibly the greatest European poet, and the one who provided a link between the Mycenaean and classical Greek cultures. Both poems went through a long process of development during which they were enlarged and adapted by generations of bards before reaching their final form, as it is known today, in about the sixth century B.C.

53. Cyrus H. Gordon, *Before the Bible,* p. 238. In the *Iliad* the chief river of the Trojan plain was called by the gods "Xanthos" and by men "Scamander"; a certain bird was called "Chalkis" by the gods and "Kumindis" by men.

54. G. N. Banerjee, *Hellenism in Ancient India,* pp. 198–99. Also see Sir William Ramsay, *Asian Elements in Greek Civilization,* Ch. VI.

55. It should be noted that archaeologists have discovered enough evidence to endorse the existence of the cities of Troy, Mycenae, and others mentioned in the *Iliad* and of a Mycenaean civilization before 1200 B.C. somewhat akin to that described by Homer. Of the two Homeric poems, the *Odyssey* is mainly fictional whilst the *Iliad* purports to be fundamentally an historical poem.

56. J. W. McCrindle, *Ancient India,* p. 1. In a recent study, discussing the common background of Greek and Hebrew civilizations, it is suggested that Homer, like the authors of the Bible, had an east Mediterranean heritage. Both the *Gilgamesh* and the *Odyssey* relate the episodic wanderings of a hero, in both the heroes reject a goddess' proposal of cohabitation, and in both the heroes interview the dead in Hades. The recapture of Helen in the *Iliad* is paralleled in the *Ugaritic Epic of Kret,* in which the pretty wife of Kret is withheld from him at Udum. Cyrus H. Gordon, *Before the Bible,* p. 19.

57. On the authority of Aristotle, we know that Thales was the forerunner of the absent-minded professor who, on a walk, was so intently looking up to heaven that he tumbled into a well.

58. Opinion on the question as to when Greek philosophy ended is divided. Many scholars hold the view that since the ideas and texts of Greek philosophy are still studied and debated, it never died, whereas others,

taking a somewhat narrower view of its tradition and continuity, observe that, as an organized study with its own students and professors, it came to an end in 529 when the Emperor Justinian closed the philosophical schools at Athens.

59. Gilbert Murray, *Greek Studies*, p. 71.

60. W. K. C. Guthrie, *A History of Greek Philosophy*, I, 4.

61. Greek philosophy has been divided into four main periods—the pre-Socratic from the early sixth to the middle fifth century B.C.; the Socratic up to the fourth century B.C.; the Hellenistic from the period of Alexander to the rise of the Roman Empire; and the period associated with the emergence of Neoplatonism, in which Greek philosophy became extinct. Zeller, *Outlines of the History of Greek Philosophy*, pp. 36–37.

62. A. K. Coomaraswamy, *Hinduism and Buddhism*, p. 8.

63. Guenon, "Introduction to the Study of the Hindu Doctrines," p. 31. Cited in Floyd H. Ross, *The Meaning of Life in Hinduism and Buddhism*, p. 12.

64. William Gould, George Arbaugh, and R. F. Moore, *Oriental Philosophies*, p. 1.

65. Original texts and details of the system of Indian materialism, as of some other movements, are not available.

66. C. Kunhan Raja in S. Radhakrishnan (ed.), *History of Philosophy: Eastern and Western*, I, 31–38.

67. The influence of vedic thought on Indian science is discussed in Ch. V.

68. "As opposed to the other vedic texts which relate to the way of action, the karmamarga, they represent the way of knowledge, the jnanamarga." Louis Renou, *Vedic India*, p. 33.

69. Many more probably existed at an early time, but even now there are still over two hundred Upanishads, although the traditional number cited is one hundred and eight. Of these there are ten principal ones. The word Upanishad is coined from three Sanskrit words meaning literally "sitting near," picturesquely describing groups of pupils sitting near the teacher to learn the truth. Some Upanishads are composed in verse, some in prose, and others in a combination of both.

70. S. N. Das Gupta in G. T. Garratt (ed.), *The Legacy of India*, pp. 123–33.

71. Max Müller, *The Six Systems of Indian Philosophy*, pp. 215–19.

72. Will Durant, *Our Oriental Heritage*, p. 534.

73. The Orphic theology does not regard the body as the instrument of soul, but as its prison, or its tomb, and believes in transmigration, the grievous cycle of births. For the Pythagoreans the soul was a divine being, fallen and entombed in the body through a series of reincarnations, and it could revert to its original state by leading a life of ritual purity and virtue, by bringing itself into tune with the order and harmony of the universe, and by understanding how the principles of all things were derived from numbers. See A. H. Armstrong in H. Lloyd-Jones (ed.), *The Greeks*, p. 127.

74. S. Radhakrishnan, *Eastern Religions and Western Thought*, p. 142.

75. Herodotus, *The Histories*, II, 123.

76. "Herodotus' derivation of the rebirth theory from Egypt is impossible, for the good reason that the Egyptians had no such theory." Herodotus had further concluded, also mistakenly, that the Greeks learned of Heracles from the Egyptians. See E. R. Dodds, *The Greeks and the Irrational*, p. 160.

77. Theodor Gomperz, *Greek Thinkers*, I, 127.

78. E. J. Urwick, *The Message of Plato*, pp. 13–14.

79. A. A. Macdonell, *Sanskrit Literature*, p. 422.

80. Whilst Macdonell accepts the high degree of probability of Indian thought influencing Pythagoras, his pupil, Keith, is of the opinion that ". . . the claim that Pythagoras learned his philosophic ideas from India though widely accepted rests on extremely weak foundations." A. B. Keith, *A History of Sanskrit Literature*, p. 500. For an elaboration of his ideas, see Keith, "Religion and Philosophy of the Vedas," *Journal of Royal Asiatic Society*, XXIX (1909), pp. 579ff.

81. The Ionian philosophers have been called empiricists—those who pay more attention to the facts of experience; and the Pythagorean and Eleatics have been called rationalists—those who rely on axioms, then accepted as self-evident, and deduce incontestable truths. Thus between them, they represented the two major directions of Greek thought.

82. W. K. C. Guthrie, *A History of Greek Philosophy*, I, 402.

83. W. K. C. Guthrie, *The Greek Philosophers*, p. 50.

84. R. D. Ranade in S. Radhakrishnan (ed.), *History of Philosophy: Eastern and Western*, I, 37. Ranade goes on to call Samkara an Indian Parmenides.

85. T. Gomperz, *Greek Thinkers*, I, 206–07.

86. E. J. Urwick, *The Message of Plato*, pp. 1–14.

87. S. Radhakrishnan, *Eastern Religions and Western Thought*, p. 151.

88. Pythagoras appears to be an excellent example of such a combination. Zeller suggests that it was always in times of great crises, such as in the fifth century after the Peloponnesian War, that the dualistic-mystical tendency came to the fore.

89. Essentially, there were three stages in Greek religion: Chthonian, Olympian, and Mystic. The first worshipped subterranean, the second celestial, and the third resurrected gods. The first predominated before the Homeric Age, the second during it, the third after it. By the time of the Periclean Enlightenment the most vigorous element in Greek religion was the mystery. Will Durant, *The Life in Greece*, p. 188. Gilbert Murray has also made a similar demarcation in the progress of Greek religion. He calls the first stage the primitive, or the age of ignorance, which is typical of similar stages elsewhere and which may be regarded as the normal raw material out of which religion is made. The second stage is termed the Olympian or Classical, in which primitive vagueness was reduced to a kind of order; and the third stage is called the Hellenistic

period, reaching roughly from Plato to St. Paul and the early Gnostics. *Five Stages of Greek Religion*, pp. 2–3.

90. F. M. Cornford writes: "Whether or not we accept the hypothesis of direct influence from Persia or Ionian Greeks in the sixth century B.C., any student of Orphic and Pythagorean thought cannot fail to see that the similarities between it and Persian religion are so close as to warrant our regarding them as expressions of the same view of life, and using the one system to interpret the other." *Religion to Philosophy*, p. 176. Guthrie finds resemblances too detailed to escape the hypothesis of direct influence. *Orpheus and Greek Religion*, p. 87.

91. Edward Zeller, *Outlines of the History of Greek Philosophy*, p. 34.

92. Will Durant, *The Life of Greece*, p. 191.

93. W. K. C. Guthrie, *Orpheus and Greek Religion*, p. 238.

94. Guthrie points out that Euripides, who was one of the most inquiring spirits in an age of inquiry and who might be called an eclectic, knew "the writings of the Orphics, and we may judge that he felt a certain sympathy for the ascetic ideal they upheld. . . ." *Orpheus and Greek Religion*, p. 237.

95. A well-known thinker of this century, Whitehead, says that "the safest general characterization of the European philosophical tradition is that it consists of a series of footnotes to Plato." Cited in A. O. Lovejoy, *The Great Chain of Being*, p. 24.

96. *Brihadaranyaka Upanishad*, I, 3.28.

97. Plato, *Republic*, VII, 515–21.

98. Plato, *Phaedo*, 65–67.

99. Cited in E. R. Dodds, *The Greeks and the Irrational*, p. 139.

100. Radhakrishnan, *Eastern Religions and Western Thought*, p. 149.

101. E. R. Dodds, "Plato and the Irrational," *Journal of Hellenic Studies*, LXV, 24.

102. Some of them, such as Pococke, have asserted that Greek civilization, not excepting its language, is a local variation of an Indian culture taken to Greece by early colonists from India. *India in Greece*. Princep is recorded to have observed that "Greek was nothing more than Sanskrit turned topsy-turvy." D. S. Mahalanbois, "A New Light on Plato," *Modern Review*, August 1963, p. 142. Talking of Plato's mysticism, Strutfield says that "India, always the home of mystical devotion, probably contributed the major share." *Mysticism and Catholicism*, p. 74. Hopkins says "Plato is full of *samkhyan* thought worked out by him but taken from Pythagoras." Discussing the historical genesis of Greek antiquity, J. P. Mayer observes: "Egyptian, Persian and Indian cultural influences were absorbed into the Greek world from very early times." *Political Thought, The European Tradition*, p. 7. Sir William Jones has pointed out "it is impossible to read Vedanta or the many fine compositions in illustration of it without believing that Pythagoras and Plato derived their sublime theories from the same fountain with the Indian sages." Colebrooke, the great Orientalist, states significantly that "a

greater degree of similarity exists between the Indian doctrine, and that of the earlier than the later Greeks." He goes on to conclude that Greek philosophy, especially between Pythagoras and Plato, was indebted to Indian thought. *Royal Asiatic Society Transactions*, I. A contemporary scholar of Western political thought, John Bowle, briefly but categorically declares that Plato was influenced by Indian ideas. *A New Outline of World History*, p. 91.

103. E. J. Urwick, *The Message of Plato*, p. 14.

104. *Ibid.*, pp. 27–28.

105. Plato, *Republic*, III and IV, 412–27.

106. Aristotle, *Politics*, Ch. XLI.

107. E. J. Urwick, *The Message of Plato*, pp. 15–39.

108. For Hindus, however, it has been the main principle of their metaphysics. The discovery of the means of putting a stop to further transmigration—the discontinuance of corporal being—and the liberation of the soul from body have been almost the foundations of Hindu philosophy.

109. E. R. Dodds, *Journal of Hellenic Studies*, LXV, 16.

110. Amongst contemporary philosophers in the Western world there has developed a body of thinkers who regard Plato's doctrine with some contempt, for it seeks to solve logical problems by postulating metaphysical entities. Not all scholars share this view, and even the critics of Plato disagree amongst themselves.

111. A. H. Armstrong, *The Greeks*, p. 131.

112. F. M. Cornford, *Before and After Socrates*, p. 89.

113. Some scholars regard Kautilya as belonging to a much later period.

114. B. A. Saletore, *Ancient Indian Political Thought and Institutions*, pp. 191–290.

115. *Bhagavad Gita*, II, 49.

116. A. K. Coomaraswamy, *Buddha and the Gospel of Buddhism*, p. 279.

117. Situated on the borders of Macedon and Thessaly, the 9600 foot high Mount Olympus was as sacred for the Greeks as were the Himalayas for the Indians. The Greeks believed that the summit of Olympus reached the upper air where Zeus had his throne surrounded by the other gods and goddesses of Greek mythology. The Canaanites also chose the mountain, Saphon, as the abode of their pantheon, and Mount Sinai as the meeting-place of Moses and Jehovah.

118. Gilbert Murray, *Five Stages of Greek Religion*, p. 49.

119. Opinion is divided as to when ancient Greek society perished. Some scholars hold that it died long before the Christian era, whereas others fix the date at 325, when Constantine founded Constantinople and Christian Byzantine civilization began to replace "pagan" Greek culture in the eastern Mediterranean. Yet, there are others who date its end as late as the seventh century.

120. H. D. Kitto, *The Greeks*, pp. 169–94.

121. R. D. Ranade and R. N. Kaulin in S. Radhakrishnan (ed.), *History of Philosophy: Eastern and Western*, II, 26.

122. But, as A. H. Armstrong points out, ". . . though Greek philosophers did not as a rule expect or want to get any practical advantage for themselves from their philosophy, at least from the age of Socrates they were not impractical in the sense of being uninterested in ordinary human life and problems." H. Lloyd-Jones (ed.), *The Greeks*, p. 123–24.

123. Sir William Ramsay, *Asianic Elements in Greek Civilization*, p. 4.

124. M. P. Nilsson, *Greek Piety*, p. 137.

125. Enfield even says that "India was visited by Pythagoras, Anaxardes, Pyrrho, and others, who afterwards became eminent philosophers in Greece." There are authorities who suggest that Plato had found his way to the banks of the Ganges.

126. E. R. Dodds, *Humanism and Technique on Greek Studies*, p. 11.

127. The case of an influence in the other direction seems hardly tenable. Discussing the remarkable coincidences between the Greek and Hindu metaphysical systems, H. H. Wilson says: "That the Hindus derived any of their philosophical ideas from the Greeks seems very improbable; and if there is any borrowing in the case, the latter were most probably indebted to the former." Iswara Krishna, *Samkhra Karika*, H. T. Colebrooke (trans.). Also see H. H. Wilson, *The Commentary of Gaurapada* (Combined volume), p. ix.

Notes to Chapter II

1. The conventional view of the Persian Empire as a typical Oriental tyranny is as much a violation of the canons of historical criticism as it is illustrative of a massive prejudice which has persisted despite periodic refutations. It is derived from a superficial reading of Herodotus, who was full of Greek prejudices against the dominant Persians, and from the writers of late antiquity who sought to glorify Rome at the expense of her predecessor. In modern times, Western writers in search of antiquity for their young but dynamic civilization sought first to link it more firmly than it merited to ancient Greece, second to glorify it unreservedly, and finally to denounce its adversaries undeservedly.

The conflict between Persia and Greece has often been described as a struggle between East and West. In fact, such a concept did not exist then, and it is misleading. E. B. Havell writes: "The conflict of the free cities of Hellas with Darius of Persia was, however, the assertion of Aryan political principles against irresponsible autocracy rather than an opposition of intellectual and spiritual ideals, or a struggle between Western civilization and Eastern barbarism, as is usually represented." *The History of Aryan Rule in India*, p. 62. A contemporary writer, A. R. Burn, in his recent study, *Persia and the Greeks*, has also tried to assert that this conflict must not be analyzed in the modern concepts of national or cultural allegiance.

2. William Robertson, *An Historical Disquisition Concerning India*, p. 15.

3. It has been suggested that Alexander was poisoned but this can neither be proved nor disproved.

4. Some European scholars, such as V. A. Smith, however, have magnified his military successes and triumphant progress from the Himalayas to the sea against "the greatest Asiatic armies." In fact, Alexander had never come face to face with any of the powerful nations of India and his army evaded an encounter with the Magadha forces.

5. "The story of Alexander the Great appears to us as an almost embarrassingly perfect illustration of the man who conquered the world, only to lose his soul. After fighting, scheming and murdering in pursuit of the secure tenure of absolute power, he found himself at last on a lonely pinnacle over an abyss, with no use for his power and security unattainable. . . . Alexander illustrates with startling clarity the ultimate loneliness of supreme power." E. Badian, *Studies in Greek and Roman History*, p. 204.

6. An Indian scholar, R. K. Mookerji, designating Alexander as the precursor of the recognized scourges of mankind, points out that this contact "was achieved at the cost of untold suffering inflicted upon India— massacre, rapine, and plunder on a scale till then without a precedent in her annals, but repeated in later days by more successful invaders like Sultan Mahmud, Tamerlane, and Nadir Shah." R. C. Majumdar (ed.), *History and Culture of the Indian People*, II, 53.

7. More cities and persons in a variety of countries and throughout all these past centuries have been named after Alexander than any other great conqueror in history. His personal name, Alexandros (defender of men, originally an epithet for a Greek goddess), has since been known in its numerous variations: Turkish and Arabic— Iskander; Indian and Persian —Sikander; Scottish—Alastair, Alec, and Sandy; French—Alexandre; English—Alexander. Its feminine counterpart, Alexandra, is also a commonly used proper name. The only other name, although not of a conqueror but of a prophet, which has been borne by more male persons than that of Alexander is Muhammad, the founder of Islam.

8. Alexander, of course, encouraged such marriages mainly for political reasons. His own marriage to Roxane was not exactly a love match. Indeed, it is doubtful if Alexander cared for any woman other than his own mother, who is described as "terrible." These marriages were celebrated with unprecedented pomp, and Alexander gave rich gifts to married couples. He desired a new ruling class and a royal army of mixed blood with no fixed domicile. That the courtiers and commanders married mainly to please Alexander is suggested by the fact that after his death many nobles repudiated their Persian wives. Many bridegrooms died soon after their marriage. According to Badian, it was after his army had posthumously denounced Clitus for treason, thereby legitimizing Alexander's murder of him, that Alexander became more autocratic and "now regularly wore an adaptation of Persian royal dress, and before long he married an Iranian princess. This would have been unthinkable a few months earlier." *Studies in Greek and Roman History*, p. 198.

9. Callisthenes, who acted as Alexander's press agent and had done much for him, was tortured and executed by Alexander, ostensibly for treason but in reality for his opposition to Alexander's claims to divine honours and prostration. He had supported Alexander's claim to divinity.

10. Arrian, *Analasis Alexandri*, VII, 2. Calanus is mentioned by many other Greek writers. Diodorus in his *Bibliotheca Historica,* Ch. CVII, says that Calanus was held in high esteem by Alexander. Dandamis is reported to have rebuked Calanus for being lured into accompanying Alexander, denouncing him as unworthy of the friendship of God. Calanus accompanied Alexander and taught one of his generals, Lysimachus, who later became the King of Macedonia. However, Calanus fell ill at Susa and, having lost the desire to live, burned himself to death in the presence of the army amid trumpets and royal salutes. Before his end, however, he prophesized Alexander's death, saying to him, "we shall meet again at Babylon." Cited in W. W. Tarn, *Alexander the Great* (Narrative), p. 110.

11. Jean Filliozat, *Political History of India,* p. 119.

12. E. B. Havell, *The History of Aryan Rule in India,* p. 63.

13. M. Cary and E. G. Warmington, *The Ancient Explorers,* p. 184.

14. Hemchandra Raychaudhuri, *Political History of Ancient India,* p. 262.

15. M. Rostovtzeff, *History of the Ancient World,* I, 349.

16. E. Badian in H. Lloyd-Jones (ed.), *The Greeks,* p. 236.

17. John Bowle, *An Outline of World History,* p. 97.

18. The Greek historian, Athenaisos, relates an interesting story, which is trivial in itself but points to familiarity between the Indian king and the Greek. Bindusara had asked Antiochus to send him a Sophist with sweet wine and dried figs. Whilst he was sent wine and figs, he was informed that "in Greece laws forbid a Sophist to be sold."

19. *Indo-Asian Culture,* October 1958, p. 121.

20. This conversion of a Greek prince to Buddhism by an Indian philosopher is symbolic of the East and West cultural collaboration. *Milinda Panho* (Questions of Milinde) is certainly a landmark in the history of Asian culture.

21. The enormous increase in the number of Greek coins and the exhibition of Indian goods by Antiochus together would suggest the pattern of trade between the Hellenic world and India. It further indicates that Greece imported goods from India and paid for them in cash.

22. W. W. Tarn, *The Greeks in Bactria and India,* pp. 316–23. Seleucus had entertained ideas of connecting the Caspian and Black Seas by a canal to improve trade between Asia and Europe. If he had not been assassinated soon after and had succeeded in doing so, the history of Asia could have been somewhat different.

23. It has been suggested that the temple at Taxila is Greek in style.

24. Because Graeco-Buddhist art flourished during the period of thriving trade between the Kushans and the Romans, it has been suggested that this art should be called "Romano-Buddhist" instead. See R. Ghirshaman, *Iran,* p. 2. During the Sassanian period there was indeed close

contact between India and Iran. Magi priests came to India and gave further impetus to sun worship. Inscriptions in Pahlavi have been found on crosses in several places in South India. The well-known copper plate grant to the Syrian Church in South India carries in Pahlavi ten witness-signatures. *Journal of Royal Asiatic Society* (O. S. 1843), p. 353. The Pahlavi and Sanskrit languages borrowed a number of words from each other.

25. S. K. Saraswati, *A Survey of Indian Sculpture*, p. 71.
26. W. W. Tarn, *The Greeks in Bactria and India*, p. 393.
27. A. K. Coomaraswamy, *Buddha and the Gospel of Buddhism*, pp. 330–31.
28. H. Zimmer, *The Art of Indian Asia*, I, 347.
29. V. A. Smith, *A History of Fine Art in India and Ceylon*, p. 10.
30. Indeed, there is no iconographical representation of Asoka himself.
31. Saraswati, *A Survey of Indian Sculpture*, p. 66. For a discussion of these motifs and of Greek influences, direct or indirect, on Indian art, see Smith, *A History of Fine Art in India and Ceylon*, pp. 64–69.
32. Some scholars would put the date later. The word *Karsa* (pana) and the weight standard of the early punch-marked coins are probably Persian.
33. S. K. Chatterji, *Indian Drama*, p. 8.
34. *Rig Veda*, X, 95.
35. W. W. Tarn, *The Greeks in Bactria and India*, pp. 375–76.
36. *Ibid.*, p. 376. Indeed, later in the same chapter (p. 408) he says that ". . . there was nothing that was to be permanent there, not even the Buddha-statue."
37. Lily Ross Taylor, *The Divinity of the Roman Empire*, p. 1.
38. *Journal of Hellenic Studies*, XLVII (1927), 206–19.
39. *Cambridge Ancient History*, VII, 18.
40. W. W. Tarn, *Hellenistic Civilization*, pp. 45ff.
41. Taylor, *The Divinity of the Roman Empire*, p. 11.
42. For a fuller discussion of Greek hero-worship, see L. R. Farnell, *Greek Hero Cults and Ideas of Immortality*.
43. Ernest Barker in Cyril Bailey (ed.), *The Legacy of Rome*, p. 49.
44. *Cambridge Ancient History*, VII, 15.
45. E. Badian, *Studies in Greek History*, p. 202.
46. W. W. Tarn, *Alexander the Great* (Narrative).
47. E. R. Dodds, *The Greeks and the Irrational*, p. 237.
48. Will Durant, *The Story of Philosophy*, p. 97.
49. Dodds, *The Greeks and the Irrational*, p. 238.
50. Barker, *The Legacy of Rome*, p. 51.
51. It may be of some interest to note that the Stoics had resurrected the idea of Logos, especially the use of the term. It was the fundamental idea of a ruling cosmic principle, emanating from the ineffable and indefinable absolute, propounded by Heraclitus. In defining Logos, Heraclitus applied the technique of paradox. "It will be called Zeus; it will

not be called Zeus." This technique is also found in the Upanishads, and indeed the bracketing of opposites is typically Indian. A. C. Bouquet, *Indo-Asian Culture,* October 1961, p. 213. Between Heraclitus and Zeno, however, it had become more common to use the term Nous, but Stoics preferred the earlier word, Logos. Thus, the Logos-concept became central to their philosophy, dislodging the Nous of Aristotle.

52. Cited in H. Lloyd-Jones (ed.), *The Greeks,* pp. 132–33.
53. W. W. Tarn has described Posidonius as "the last great intellectual force which Hellenism, untouched by Rome, produced. . . ." *Hellenistic Civilization,* p. 288.
54. E. Bevan, *Stoics and Sceptics,* p. 94.
55. Barber, *The Legacy of Rome,* p. 54.
56. *Ibid.,* p. 50.
57. John Bowle, *Western Political Thought,* p. 74.
58. John Bowle, *A New Outline of World History,* p. 99.
59. Dodds, *The Greeks and the Irrational,* p. 240.
60. "The dignity of character achieved and admired by the leaders of Graeco-Roman civilization owed more to it than to any other philosophy. . . ." John Bowle, *Western Political Thought,* p. 76.
61. *Ibid.,* p. 70.
62. Bevan, *Stoics and Sceptics,* p. 69.

Notes to Chapter III

1. Michael Grant, *The World of Rome,* p. 4.
2. According to Kern, ancient Indians possibly called it Yavanapura, the city of the *Yavanas* (Greeks).
3. According to William Robertson, the chief object of Alexander in founding Alexandria was to secure the advantages arising from the trade with India, and Ptolemy, who was in Alexander's confidence, knew of Alexander's object. *An Historical Disquisition Concerning the Knowledge which the Ancients Had of India,* p. 35.
4. For a brief and up-to-date account of Alexandria, see E. Badian, *Studies in Greek and Roman History,* pp. 179–92.
5. M. Rostovtzeff in *Cambridge Ancient History,* VII, 194.
6. "An army could advance along the 'Royal Road' at the rate of nearly 20 miles a day, and the ease with which Alexander overthrew the Persian power is partly to be explained by the excellent system of communications which was available for his advancing army." Lee C. Bailey (ed.), *The Legacy of Rome,* p. 146.
7. See Bjorn Landstrom, *The Quest for India.*
8. M. P. Charlesworth, *Trade-Routes and Commerce of the Roman Empire,* p. 58.

9. The Roman forces at Carrhae were led by Marcus Crassus, Consul-triumvir of Rome and Governor of Syria. The battle of Carrhae was one of the most disastrous in the history of Rome; about twenty thousand Roman soldiers, including Crassus and his son, were killed and ten thousand taken prisoner. It was at this battle that the Romans first saw articles of silk—the brilliantly coloured, gold-embroidered banners of the Parthians.

10. H. G. Rawlinson, *Intercourse Between India and the Western World*, pp. 90–91.

11. Strabo, *Geography*, II, 5, 12. Describing the location of India later, Strabo calls India "the greatest of all nations and the happiest in lot." II, 5, 32.

12. Charlesworth, *Trade-Routes and Commerce of the Roman Empire*, p. 59.

13. Rostovtzeff in *Cambridge Ancient History*, VII, 154.

14. I understand that a computer study of the work is under way at present (1967) in London.

15. A. B. Keith, *A History of Sanskrit Literature*, p. 461.

16. D. D. Kosambi, "An Introduction to the Study of Indian History," *Journal of Royal Asiatic Society*, p. 200. For a quick résumé of the work regarding the dating of the Arthasastra, see K. A. N. Sastri, *The Age of the Nandas and Mauryas*, pp. 190–201.

17. In recent years it has come to be increasingly held that the tradition of Hippalus is false. Certainly, the evidence on which the tradition is based is too thin.

18. "The importance of this fact will be realised," comments Rawlinson, "when we recollect that, up to the opening of the overland route in 1838, it took travellers from five to eight months to reach India. India was nearer to Europe in the first century A.D. than at any time up to the middle of the nineteenth." G. T. Garratt (ed.), *The Legacy of India*, p. 16.

19. Paul-Louis, *Ancient Rome at Work*, p. 235.

20. Of the jewels, the Romans were especially fond of beryls and pearls. The two beryl mines that existed in South India at Padiyur and Vani-yambadi were a great source of wealth.

21. In the fifteenth century it sold at two shillings a pound which in terms of modern value would be well above a hundred shillings a pound. It is not easy to calculate a modern equivalent of denarii, but a Roman soldier on duty in Egypt received two hundred and twenty-five denarii (or nine hundred sesterces) annually, or fifteen pounds of pepper per year; or for one Roman pound of cinnamon more than sixty-six Roman soldiers could be employed to fight in Egypt for a year.

22. Pliny, *Natural History*, VI, 26.

23. Tacitus, *The Annals of Imperial Rome*, II, 33; II, 53.

24. Charlesworth, *Trade-Routes and Commerce of the Roman Emipre*, p. 67.

25. Ancient Indians, it appears, originally used the term Yavana for the Ionian-Greeks, but later for all foreigners from the West. Somewhat in

a similar manner, modern Indians use the term Angrez, the English, for all Westerners.

26. Sir Mortimer Wheeler, *Rome Beyond the Imperial Frontiers,* p. 209.

27. Dion Chrysostom, *Orations,* XXXII, 373. In another oration (XLIX, 538), he mentions that Indian Brahmins excel in self-control, righteousness, and love of God.

28. Pausanias, *Hellados Periegisis,* III, 12; IV, 34; VII, 29.

29. Arrian (96–180), who distinguished himself as a philosopher, statesman, soldier, and historian, also wrote the more important and famous *Anabasis of Alexander,* the life of Alexander. The Elder Pliny's (23–79) work deals with a variety of subjects. Ptolemy's treatise on geography forms the sequel to his famous work on astronomy. Both his works remained standard works until modern times. Yet, little is known of him except that he flourished in Alexandria about the middle of the second century A.D.

30. The Erythraean Sea was the name given by the Greek and Roman geographers to the Indian Ocean, including the Red Sea and the Persian Gulf. This work appears to have been composed about the middle or the second half of the first century. Some scholars have lately suggested that the work belongs to about 300.

31. B. P. Groslier, *Indo-China,* p. 49.

32. B. A. Saletore, *India's Diplomatic Relations with the West,* p. 230.

33. The commercial character of the Indian missions to Augustus is now quite evident. Strabo speaks of a communication to Augustus from an Indian king seeking assistance in any good enterprise. See *Geography,* XV, 1, 73.

34. For a discussion of the theme, see Saletore, *India's Diplomatic Relations with the West,* pp. 210–67.

35. E. Gibbon, *Decline and Fall of the Roman Empire,* I, 319.

36. Saletore, *India's Diplomatic Relations with the West,* p. 271.

37. Grant, *The World of Rome,* p. 189.

38. John Bowle, *A New Outline of World History,* p. 118.

39. H. G. Wells, *The Outline of History,* p. 273.

40. Gilbert Murray, *Hellenism and the Modern World,* p. 14.

41. Franz Cumont, *Oriental Religions in Roman Paganism,* pp. 2–3.

42. Tenney Frank, "Racial Mixture in the Roman Empire," *The American Historical Quarterly,* XXI (1961), 689–708. Tacitus has been accused of exposing Roman anti-Semitism, and of grossly distorting facts. S. Davis, *Race-Relations in Ancient Egypt,* pp. 161–63.

43. Hippolytus died as a martyr in 235. He was one of the most prolific writers of the early Church and was elected rival Bishop of Rome in 217 by those people who were opposed to Pope Callistus.

44. Jean Filliozat, "La doctrine brâhmanes d'après saint Hippolyte," *Revue de l'Histoire des Religions* (1945), pp. 59–91; *Les relations exterieures de l'inde* (1956), pp. 31–60.

45. Wilhelm Holmqvist, *Acta Archaelogica*, XXV (Copenhagen, 1954); *Viking* (Oslo, 1957–58); William Holmqvist, Birgit Arrhenius, Per Lundstrom, *Viltterhets Historie och Antikvitets Akademien* (Stockholm, 1961). Cited in Buddha Prakash, *India and the World*, p. 268.

46. Many Catholic monasteries in mediaeval Europe, however, served as schools, hospitals, orphanages, and old peoples' homes.

47. Asoka was so influenced by the ethical tenets of the Buddhist "Law of Piety," even more than by the theory of nirvana which has often been mistakenly described as pessimistic, that he changed his name from Asoka, the Sorrowless One, to Piya-dasi (Sanskrit Priya-darsin), the Compassionate One.

48. The first two Buddhist Councils were held at Rajagaha and Vesali in 483 B.C. and 383 B.C. respectively.

49. V. A. Smith, *Oxford History of India*, p. 134.

50. *Mahavamsa*, XXIX, 37–39. This Convent of Alexandria is also mentioned in a later work, the *Thupavamsa*.

51. The doctrine of the Four Noble Truths is expounded in various Buddhist scriptures, such as the *Digha Nikaya*, the *Majjhima Nikaya*, the *Sutta Pitaka*, and the *Vinaya Pitaka*.

52. The name Milinda is an Indian adaptation of the Greek word Menandros. Ancient authors used various other Indian forms of the Greek King's name. For example, Ksemendra's *Avadanakalpalata* calls him by the same name, Milindra, as that which is found in the Bstan-hygur collection, commonly known as Tanjur, of the Tibetan *Tripitaka*. The Shinkot casket inscription in the Kharoshthi script, which speaks of his missionary activities in spreading Buddhism in the northwest and beyond, gives his name as Menadra.

53. *Mahavamsa*, XII, 34–36.

54. Sir Charles Eliot, *Hinduism and Buddhism*, III, 450.

55. T. Watters, *On Yuan Chwang's Travels in India*, p. 257. According to Hsüan-tsang, Persia was rich but its people were by nature impulsive and violent. They did not care for learning and gave themselves entirely to works of art which were very popular in the neighbouring countries.

56. Cf. McCrindle, *Ancient India as described in Classical Literature*, p. 185. "Terebinthus proclaimed himself learned in all the wisdom of the Egyptians and gave out that his name was no longer Terebinthus but that he was a new Buddha (Buddas) and that he was born of a virgin. Terebinthus was the disciple of Scythianus, who was born in Palestine and who traded with India."

57. A. S. Altekar, *Indo-Asian Culture*, October 1958, pp. 120–21.

58. Cited in A. R. Vidler, *Objections to Christian Belief*, p. 59. Bernard Shaw put it in his characteristic way: "What Christ said would have been just as true if he had lived in a country house with an income of £5,000 a year."

59. In recent years, Western theologians have renewed their effort to modernize the traditional Christian orthodoxy and present the faith in

terms which are comprehensible to present-day man. To restate, re-iterate, and defend the ancient dogma in exactly the same language is to strain the religious integrity and intellectual ability of the believer, as much as of the preacher and of the layman. An expression of this view is found in the much discussed book by John A. T. Robinson, *Honest to God.*

60. In a recent publication, *The Death of Jesus,* Joel Carmichael has sought to prove that Jesus thought of himself as no more than the herald of an imminent material transformation of the world, and to achieve his purpose he led an armed insurrection, which led to his violent death.

61. H. G. Wells, *A Short History of the World,* p. 147.

62. It seems likely that the Roman rulers, having failed to evolve a universal religion for the Empire themselves, looked upon Christianity as a rival gaining success where they had failed, and thus were urged into taking a hostile attitude to its expansion.

63. Rudolf Bultmann, *Primitive Christianity in its Contemporary Setting,* p. 11.

64. Morton Enslin, *Christian Beginnings,* p. 147.

65. The word "Heaven" is sometimes used for "God" as a reverential Jewish way of avoiding the use of the divine name. The second of the ten Mosaic commandments, in any case, forbids the taking of God's name "in vain."

66. According to Carmichael, the concept of "Son of God" is an inadvertent development of the Greek expression of the term, "Servant of God," often used to describe Jesus by himself and his immediate disciples. The word used in Greek for servant, *pais,* also has the meaning child. Pais is used throughout the earliest Greek translations of the Old Testament for those people who are particularly in harmony with God's will: "The mere fact that the same word in Greek means both 'servant' and 'child' and that a similar expression was used in reference to Jesus, doubtless facilitated the transformation of the phrase 'servant' or 'child of God' and this gave a specific and, as it were, concrete aid to the magnifying effect of the early Christology." *The Death of Christ,* p. 205.

67. An important consequence of this discovery was that the earlier belief, that no really old perishable antiquities could ever be found in the area because of the prevailing dampness of the climate, was disproved. They had overlooked the extremely unusual geological fault of the Rift Valley that runs from Syria down into Africa and which reaches its lowest level around the Dead Sea. More than a thousand feet below sea level, the cliffs bordering the western side lie in a rain shadow. The sun shines into the basin for most of the year, and the caves in the limestone cliffs are kept dry as a desert. Inevitably, archaeologists poured into the area, and the western side of the Dead Sea, called in the Bible the Wilderness of Judah, has yielded rich harvests of antiquities, including wooden implements some six thousand years old, which have been preserved remarkably well.

68. One of the important consequences of the discovery of these texts, as some of them are written in Greek, may be the blurring of the sharp distinction usually made between the Judaism of the Holy Land and the Judaism of the Dispersion. There was much traffic between Jerusalem and Alexandria, and the quasi-monastic Therapeutai described by Philo look as though they were in some sense related to the Qumran sect. A. D. Nock, *Early Gentile Christianity and its Hellenistic Background*, p. x.

69. Murray, *Hellenism and the Modern World*, p. 17.

70. Nero is reported by Pliny the Elder to have been initiated into the cult of Mithras in 66 by a *magi* priest. He insisted on being worshipped as a sun god. About three centuries later, the Emperor Julian tried to make Mithraism the state religion but his death prevented this. Few other emperors kept direct contact with the Mithraic practices. Mithraism, however, was not a court religion, and was long regarded as too personal a creed to be included amongst public faiths.

71. W. K. C. Guthrie, *Orpheus and Greek Religion*, pp. 264–68.

72. *Ibid.*, p. 269.

73. Rudolf Bultmann, *Primitive Christianity*, pp. 177–78.

74. *Ibid.*, p. 178.

75. Of the three hundred bishops present at this council of Nicaea, only six were from the West.

76. The earliest known reference to the Christian ceremony is that in St. Paul's First Epistle to the Corinthians written some twenty-five years after the Crucifixion.

77. A. Powell Davies, *Dead Sea Scrolls*, p. 91.

78. Eliot, *Hinduism and Buddhism*, III, 430.

79. J. M. Creed in S. R. K. Glanville (ed.), *The Legacy of Egypt*, p. 300.

80. E. Bevan, *Stoics and Sceptics*, p. 69.

81. Franz Cumont, *Oriental Religions in Roman Paganism*, p. x.

82. See T. Frank, *Aspects of Social Behaviour in Ancient Rome*, p. 37.

83. Edward Gibbon, who had become a convert to Roman Catholicism whilst at Oxford, and not long after a profound sceptic, listed five principal causes of the success of Christianity: a) The inflexible, i.e. the intolerant, zeal of the Christians, derived from the Jewish religions; b) the doctrine of a future life; c) the miraculous powers ascribed to the primitive Church; d) the pure and austere morals of the Christians; and e) the union and discipline of the Christian republic. See *The Decline and Fall of the Roman Empire* (An Abridgement), p. 144. Gibbon found Christianity on the whole distasteful, and the pretensions of the bishops even more so, and the claims of Rome to maintain spiritual pre-eminence after the fall of the Empire a superstitious fraud. He found Christians' intolerance, whether practiced against other religions or against members of the Church, particularly unpleasant.

84. Eliot, *Hinduism and Buddhism*, III, 434.

85. Sidney Spencer, *Mysticism in World Religion*, p. 148.

86. *Encyclopaedia of Religion and Ethics*, V, 401.

87. Hendrik Kraemer, *World Cultures and World Religions*, p. 239.

88. R. Otto, *The Kingdom of God and the Son of Man*, p. 178.

89. *Ibid.*, p. 187.

90. S. Radhakrishnan, *Eastern Religion and Western Thought*, p. 162.

91. Otto, *The Kingdom of God and the Son of Man*, p. 206. *Kaushitahî Upanishad*, I, 2–7.

92. Otto, *The Kingdom of God and the Son of Man*, p. 398.

93. Theologians are divided two ways. One belief stresses the reality of the presence of the Kingdom of God transforming this life through judgement and mercy, thereby rendering the motif that "the Kingdom is yet to come" of minor significance. Whereas the other definitely holds the view that the Kingdom *is* yet to come.

94. Otto, *The Kingdom of God and the Son of Man*, p. 20.

95. *Ibid.*, p. 25.

96. T. W. Rhys Davids, *Journal of the Pali Text Society*, 1923, pp. 43–44. Cited in Radhakrishnan, *Eastern Religions and Western Thought*, p. 173.

97. Radhakrishnan, *Eastern Religions and Western Thought*, p. 176.

98. Most scholars now believe that Mark wrote first, but there are some others who argue for the priority of Matthew.

99. W. R. Inge, *Platonic Tradition in English Religious Thought*, p. 10.

100. *Sutta Nipata*, III, 11, 1–21; Gospel of St. Luke, Ch. 2.

101. There is, however, no reference to the virgin birth of Jesus in the Epistles which constitute the earliest Christian documents. The earliest Gospel of St. Mark does not mention it, nor does the Gospel of St. John, nor the Book of Revelation. On the contrary, Paul speaks of Jesus as "made of the seed of David according to the flesh" (Rom. 1:3), that is to say, of the seed of Joseph, David's descendant. The story first appears in the Gospel of St. Luke, which tells us that Mary conceived her child by the Holy Ghost before consummation of her marriage with Joseph. The story is developed later in the Gospel of St. Matthew. A recent writer, Leslie D. Weatherhead, has in *The Christian Agnostic* suggested that what really happened was that Zacharias committed adultery with Mary in a "sacred marriage."

102. Main Hindu incarnations, Rama and Krishna, too, were born in the warrior caste.

103. Arthur Osborne, *Buddhism and Christianity in the Light of Hinduism*, p. 14. However, there are other gods and semi-gods who were the sons of mothers whose names were variations of Mary: for example, Adonis, son of Myrrha; Hermes, son of Maia; Cyrus, son of Mariana or Mandane; Moses, son of Miriam; Buddha, son of Maya; and Joshua, son of Miriam. Because of this, Mary being somewhat of a stock substitute name for a divine mother, some scholars have suggested the possibility of a completely different name for Jesus' mother.

104. Christ wrote nothing, nor did the Buddha, nor Muhammad. It is indeed curious that the men whose ideas have influenced human thought most,

did little to ensure the accuracy of their teaching by reducing it to writing under their supervision.

105. Osborne, *Buddhism and Christianity in the Light of Hinduism*, p. 10. In a recent publication, *Yoga and the Bible*, Joseph Leeming has endeavoured to show that the basic teachings of the New Testament and some parts of the Bible are essentially similar to the fundamental truths taught for ages by the teachers of *Shabad Yoga; Shabad*, meaning divine or inner sound, refers to the power which in the Bible is called the Word or Logos. The Yoga of the divine word, or *Shabad Yoga*, is a system of meditation and other spiritual practices, which takes its followers to the highest attainable states of spiritual consciousness.

106. The Hindus too expect the tenth *Avatar* (incarnation), the last of the series.

107. Max Müller, *Last Essays*, 1st Series, 1901, p. 285.

108. Radhakrishnan, *Eastern Religions and Western Thought*, p. 184.

109. Eliot, *Hinduism and Buddhism*, III, 443.

110. M. Huc wrote: "The cross, the mitre, the dalmatica; the cope, which the Grand Lamas wear on their journeys; the service with double choirs; the psalmody, the exorcisms; the censer, suspended from five chains; the benedictions, the chaplet, ecclesiastical celibacy, spiritual retirement, the worship of the saints; the fasts, the processions, the litanies, the holy-water—all these are analogies between the Buddhists and ourselves. Now, can it be said that these analogies are of Christian origin? We think so. We have indeed found, neither in the traditions nor in the monuments of the country, any positive proof of their adoption; still it is perfectly legitimate to put forward conjectures which possess all the characteristics of the most emphatic probability." Cited in N. Notovitch, *The Unknown Life of Christ*, pp. xiv–xv. More than a century before Huc, in 1714, Father Diserdi was also struck by similarities between his own faith and Lamaistic practices. Still earlier, in 1661, Father Grueber, together with another priest, Dorville, passed through Tibet on their return from Peking, and he noticed what Henry Princep describes as "the extraordinary similarity" between the doctrines and the rituals of the Buddhists of Lhasa and those of his own Roman faith. Cited in Arthur Little, *India in Primitive Christianity*, p. 220.

111. Osborne, *Buddhism and Christianity in the Light of Hinduism*, pp. 118–19.

112. It has been suggested that possibly a Christian mission under St. Thomas had come to the court of the Indo-Parthian King Gondophares at the beginning of the Christian era, although the mission seems to have left no impression. See S. N. Dasgupta (ed.), *A History of Sanskrit Literature*, I, ciii.

113. A recent report claiming the discovery of a small urn containing the remains of St. Thomas in Mosul, northern Iraq, has been disputed by Indian Christians, who claim that the relics of the apostle were removed from Madras to Lisbon and that this fact is further corroborated by an important document recently found in Lisbon. This document is a four-

page letter, dated 27 December 1535, written to the King of Portugal from the Church of St. Thomas in Mylapore. It is signed by twelve Portuguese inhabitants. See *The Hindu Weekly*, 26 October 1964.

114. M. Vacherot, *Histoire Critique de l'École d'Alexandrie*, III, 250.

115. Dean Mansel, *The Gnostic Heresies of the First and Second Centuries*, p. 32.

116. Dean Milman, *History of Christianity*, II, 41.

117. It is curious that Apollonius, who was once considered a rival of Jesus, was born in the same year as Jesus, and was likewise said to have been born of the union of a god with his mother, to whom the coming birth was announced somewhat similarly as in the Christian tale. But the tale of miraculous conception is associated with a number of divine or semi-divine personages.

118. J. Bidez in *Cambridge Ancient History*, XII, 614.

119. The word *gnosis* is Greek, meaning knowledge, and was a term used from the early days of philosophy to designate the science of the divine. Later, Porphyry called "the Antique or Oriental philosophy" gnosis to distinguish it from the Grecian systems. The term was also used in the technical sense of "superior or celestial knowledge" by the Jewish philosophers at Alexandria.

120. C. W. King, *The Gnostics and Their Remains*, p. x.

121. Rudolf Bultmann, *Primitive Christianity*, p. 162.

122. W. R. Inge, *Mysticism in Religion*, p. 106.

123. During the first four centuries, all that the Christian Church denounced as heretical may be traced to Indian speculative philosophy as its genuine fountain-head. Yet, a considerable part of what was accepted as orthodox also came from the same source. See King, *The Gnostics and Their Remains*, pp. vi–vii.

124. Kennedy says of Gnosticism, "It is Buddhist pure and simple—Buddhist in its governing ideas, its psychology, its metaphysics." Cited in Radhakrishnan, *Eastern Religions and Western Thought*, p. 205.

125. King, *The Gnostics and Their Remains*, p. 6.

126. *Ibid.*, p. 165.

127. *Ibid.*, pp. 16–21. Whittaker, who regards Gnosticism in contrast to Neoplatonism as a direct outgrowth of the East, says that the Gnostic claim that the spiritual men alone possess true knowledge could have given it, under favourable circumstances, "a starting point of Christian Brahmanism." Thomas Whittaker, *The Neo-Platonist*, p. 222.

128. Radhakrishnan, *Eastern Religions and Western Thought*, p. 200.

129. Sir Flinders Petrie, *Egypt and Israel*, p. 113.

130. Sidney Spencer, *Mysticism in World Religion*, p. 153.

131. *Stromata*, VI, 14, 114; VI, 7, 58.

132. Radhakrishnan, *Eastern Religions and Western Thought*, p. 233.

133. In antiquity the philosophers, who are now called Neoplatonists, called themselves simply Platonists. So did the philosophers of the seventh

century and the Renaissance who drew their inspiration from Neoplatonism.

134. Amongst his predecessors are counted his teacher Ammonius Saccas; Posidonius, the Stoic teacher of Cicero; and Numenius, whose influence on Plotinus was considerable.

135. Indeed, other great men in history did likewise. Christ wrote nothing, nor did the Buddha; Muhammad was illiterate; Socrates was content to talk; Gandhi never systematically co-ordinated and formalized his great bulk of mixed writings.

136. These three had made a compact not to disclose any of the doctrines which Ammonius had revealed to them. Plotinus kept faith and divulged nothing of his teacher's system, but the compact was broken first by Erennius and later by Origen. It is interesting that the two persons who emerged in the third century as great religious teachers propounding divergent doctrines were students of Ammonius Saccas, who was born a Christian, but became a Platonist.

137. Stephen MacKenna (trans.), *Plotinus' The Enneads*, p. xiii.

138. Radhakrishnan, *Eastern Religions and Western Thought*, pp. 210–11.

139. George Goodwin, *The Great Mystics*, p. 27.

140. Even W. R. Inge thinks that in Plotinus' theory of vision there is "the direct influence of Oriental philosophy of the Indian type." *Christian Mysticism*, p. 901.

141. Bidez in *Cambridge Ancient History*, XII, 623.

142. Not only is there evidence that Indian scholars, both Buddhists and Brahmans, visited and resided in Western capitals, but there is evidence that Indian faiths were practiced in some parts of Asia Minor in pre-Christian times. The Syrian writer, Zenob, tells us of the worship of Krishna in Armenia at least in the second and third centuries B.C. Temples dedicated to Krishna were set up near the Lake Van. Zenob says that early in the fourth century A.D. there were about five thousand followers of Krishna in Armenia. It is also pointed out that the Hindus had resisted the demolition of temples by the early Christians.

143. W. R. Inge, *Mysticism in Religion*, p. 109.

144. He appears to have believed in two world-souls: one good, the other bad. He had adopted the theory of rebirth. Stutfield maintains that Indian mysticism had reached Alexandria which "blossomed forth in Plotinus" and passed into Christian thought through "the monk mystic and theosophical pantheist, the so-called Dionysus the Areopagite." *Mysticism and Catholicism*, p. 34.

145. "An influence of Indian thought on the Gnostics and Neoplatonists may be held to be more likely, and it would be unjust to rule it out of Court." A. B. Keith, *A History of Sanskrit Literature*, pp. 500–01.

146. Bidez in *Cambridge Ancient History*, XII, 633. The Christians in the fifth century destroyed the work of Porphyry, *Against the Christians*, written in fifteen books, but extracts from it which have survived in the Christian polemical writing, indicate that it was a powerful and intelligent attack on Christianity.

147. E. R. Dodds, *Proclus, the Elements of Theology*, p. xxv.

148. Radhakrishnan, *Eastern Religions and Western Thought*, p. 238.

149. He was venerated in the sixth century by St. Gregory, his words were used in the Third Council of Constantinople in 692 and at the Second Council of Nicaea, and St. John the Damascene became his follower. In the thirteenth century the Church denounced him, but his influence amongst the mystics of the fourteenth century rose again.

150. Radhakrishnan, *Eastern Religions and Western Thought*, p. 240.

151. It was St. Paul who began the process of stressing the divinity of Christ, and Athanasius (*ca.* 295–373) who formulated the doctrine of the Trinity accepted at Nicaea.

Notes to Chapter IV

1. Whilst references to Arab peoples and tribes are found in many biblical passages and in Genesis itself, the first mention of the name of these peoples, whose etymology is not clear, occurs in an inscription of the Assyrian King Shalmaneser III (853 B.C.).

2. The only certain source concerning the life of Muhammad (etymologically the name means "the much praised one") is the Quran itself, followed by the canonical biography, *Sira,* composed a century later in the eighth century. However, the year of the Prophet's birth is uncertain; 570 is accepted as an approximation. Muhammad was the posthumous son of the merchant Abdullah, and was brought up first by his grandfather Abd al-Mutta lib, and later by an uncle, Abu Talib, father of Ali, who was to become the fourth Caliph and the Prophet's son-in-law.

3. Richard Bell has advanced a new theory suggesting three periods in the composition of the Quran. See A. C. Bouquet, *Comparative Religion,* p. 275.

4. Reporting his victory to Caliph Umar, he remarked: "I have captured a city from the description of which I shall refrain. Suffice it to say that I have seized therein 4,000 villas with 4,000 baths, 40,000 poll-tax paying Jews and 4,000 palaces of entertainment for the royalty."

5. (1) The story makes its first appearance more than five hundred years after the event to which it relates;

   (2) on analysis the *story resolves into absurdities;*

   (3) the principal actor in the story, viz. John Philoponus, was dead long before the Saracens entered Egypt;

   (4) of the two great public libraries to which the story could refer (a) the Museum Library perished in the conflagration caused by Julius Caesar, or, if not, at a date not less than four hundred years anterior to the Arab Conquest, whilst (b) the Serapium Library either was removed prior to the year 391 A.D. or was then dispersed and destroyed; so that in any case it disappeared two and a half centuries before the conquest;

   (5) the fifth, sixth, and early seventh century literature contains no mention of the existence of any such library;

(6) if, nevertheless, it had existed when Cyrus set his hand to the treaty surrendering Alexandria, yet the books would almost certainly have been removed—under the clause permitting the removal of valuables —*during the eleven months armistice which intervened* between the signature of the convention and the actual entry of the Arabs into the city; and

(7) if the Library had been removed, or if it had been destroyed, the almost contemporary historian and man of letters John of Nikiou, could not have passed over its disappearance in total silence.

The conclusion of the whole matter can be no longer doubtful. The suspicion of Renaudot and the scepticism of Gibbon are more than justified. One must pronounce that the Abu'l Faraj story is a *mere fable, totally destitute of historical foundation.* See Albert J. Butler, *The Arab Conquest of Egypt,* p. 424.

6. Palestine and Syria fell to the Arabs by 640, Iraq a year later, Egypt by 642, Tripolitania by 647, Persia by 650, Afghanistan by 661 in which year the seat of the Caliphate was moved from Medina to Damascus, Tunisia by 693, Algeria and Morocco by 705, and Spain in 711.

7. Many Arab historians, with some justification, decline to accord the title of Caliphate to the reigns of Muawiya and his successors, with the sole exception of Umar II (717–20) who is accepted as Caliph with kingship (*mulk*). The Caliphate is regarded to have lapsed until 750 when it was resumed with the ascendancy of the Abbasid dynasty of Iran.

8. George Sarton, *The Life of Science,* p. 145.

9. R. A. Nicholson, *A Literary History of the Arabs,* p. 259.

10. The name of the great capital, founded by Caliph Mansur, itself is said to be of Indian origin; *Bagh* is Sanskrit *Bhaga,* meaning God, and *da* in Sanskrit means to give. Baghdad thus meant given by God, or the gift of God.

11. Aziz S. Atiya, *Crusade, Commerce and Culture,* p. 224.

12. H. A. R. Gibb in A. J. Rustum and C. K. Zurak (eds.), *History of the Arabs and Arabic Culture,* p. 241.

13. F. H. Garrison, *An Introduction to the History of Medicine.*

14. Abu Sahl Ali bin Rabban al-Tabari has given at the end of his book, *Fardausul Hikmat,* written about 850, a short account of the Indian system of medicine.

15. Ibn Abi Usaybia, who wrote a general biography of physicians, entitled *Uyun al-Inba fi-Tabaqat al-Atibba,* found in *Al Hawi* and other works of Al Razi extracts from a number of Indian medical texts.

16. J. Needham, *Science and Civilization in China,* IV, 13.

17. Bettina Strauss in René Taton (ed.), *Ancient and Medieval Science,* p. 417.

18. Jose Maria Millas-Vallicrosa, in Guy S. Metraux and Francois Crouzet (eds.), *The Evolution of Science,* p. 129.

19. Of the other popular foods, the domestic fowl is also an Indian contribution to Western diet. Hieroglyphs from Indian village settlements would

suggest that it has been domesticated for at least five thousand years. Some varieties are said to have originated from the Indian jungle fowl which still survives. The larger breeds have no similarity to any wild bird. Like horses, dogs, and camels, these have apparently completely passed over into the domesticated state or the wild ancestors have become extinct. For many centuries the domestic fowl was confined to India. In 1400 B.C. it spread to China—known in Egypt also about the same time—but it was another one thousand years or more before Europeans began to raise this bird.

Tea, the national drink of the Anglo-Saxons, is an indirect Indian legacy to Western civilization. It is also a favoured drink of the Chinese, Japanese, Russians, and others. The original home of this shrub was Assam, India, and from there in the third century A.D. it travelled to China and by the middle of the seventeenth century it appeared in England. In the eighteenth century "tea gardens" began to appear in London and attracted especially women who preferred them to the stuffy tea houses in the congested city. Scholars too were attracted—Dr. Samuel Johnson and Boswell lent distinction to these gardens.

20. In 929 he adopted the title of Caliph and thus became the third of the three contemporary independent Caliphs in the Islamic world—the Abbasid in Baghdad, the Fatimid in North Africa, and the Umayyad in Spain. The Umayyads ruled from 736 to 1031.

21. J. B. Trend in Thomas Arnold and Alfred Guillaume (eds.), *The Legacy of Islam,* p. 5.

22. During the thirteenth century another Muslim centre of learning had come into prominence at Konya in Turkey during the reign of Alaeddin I (1219–1236). After Nicaea had fallen to the Crusaders in 1017, Konya became the capital of the Seljuk Sultans, and attracted artists, poets, historians, jurists, theologians, and other scholars who were driven westward from Central and Western Asia by the Mongol invasions. The effects of this school on Western learning are yet to be assessed systematically.

Notes to Chapter V

1. Recently a national commission consisting of historians, scientists, and linguists has been appointed to study and compile a history of Indian science under the supervision of the National Institute of Sciences in India.

2. F. S. Taylor, *Science: Past and Present,* p. 98.

3. B. B. Dey in S. Radhakrishnan (ed.), *History of Philosophy: Eastern and Western,* I, 470.

4. S. Radhakrishnan, *Indian Philosophy,* I, 29.

5. Heimann, *Facts of Indian Thought,* p. 37.

6. *Rig Veda,* X, 129.

7. Filliozat in René Taton (ed.), *Ancient and Medieval Science,* pp. 134–35.

8. *Taittiriyaka Upanishads*, II, 1, 3. Whilst the theory of many Upanishads and materialists is that the universe comprises these five elements, there are other texts, for instance the *Chandogya Upanishads* (VI, 4), which subscribe to the theory of three—fire, water, and earth—or four—without akasa—elements. In the *Bhagavad Gita* (VII, 4) three more elements—*buddhi* (intelligence), *ahamkara* (self-sense) and *manas* (mind)—are added to these five.

9. Sarton, *Introduction to the History of Science*, I, 69.

10. R. Garbe, *Philosophy of Ancient India*, p. 30.

11. S. K. Ramachandra Rao, *Development of Psychological Thought*, pp. 32–33.

12. Prabhavananda, *The Spiritual Heritage of India*, pp. 215–16.

13. B. N. Seal, *The Positive Sciences of the Ancient Hindus*. A. B. Keith has charged Seal with having read too many modern ideas into old texts. But then Keith himself has been accused, for example by Kosambi, of massive prejudice. However, Seal's work is unhistorical, devoted principally to logic and philosophical speculations despite its title, and is somewhat obscure.

14. There are a number of Indian scholars who place the date of the *Rig Veda* much farther back, *ca.* 3000 B.C., and thus claim greater antiquity for the origins of astronomy in India. The study of Hindu science is made exceptionally difficult because the lack of definite chronology often makes it extremely difficult to debate questions of priority.

15. Filliozat in Taton (ed.), *Ancient and Medieval Science*, p. 137.

16. *Ibid.*, p. 136.

17. Filliozat in Metraux and Crouzet (eds.), *The Evolution of Science*, p. 92. For a detailed discussion of the nakshatras and of Indian astronomy, see P. V. Kane, *History of Dharmesastra*, V, Part I, 495–512.

18. See *Nature*, CLXVIII (14 July 1951), 64; and *Science and Civilization in China*, III, 173–77.

19. Filliozat in Metraux and Crouzet (eds.), *The Evolution of Science*, pp. 91–93.

20. For further discussion, see *ibid.*, pp. 94–96.

21. A passage from the *Aitareya Brahmana*, which dates from about two thousand years before Copernicus and centuries before Hipparchus, illustrates Indian interest in astronomy: "The sun never sets nor rises; when people think to themselves the sun is setting, he only changes about after reaching the end of the day, and makes night below and day to what is on the other side. Then when people think he rises in the morning, he only shifts himself about after reaching the end of the night, and makes day below and night to what is on the other side. In fact he never does set at all."

22. A. N. Singh in Radhakrishnan (ed.), *History of Philosophy: Eastern and Western*, I, 448–49.

23. Cited in B. K. Sarkar, *Hindu Achievements in Exact Science*, p. 30.

24. Over the door of the Academy was inscribed in Greek "A Credit in

Mathematics is required" and one of Plato's sayings was "God is always doing Geometry."

25. Singh in Radhakrishnan (ed.), *History of Philosophy: Eastern and Western*, I, 431.

26. Heimann, *Facets of Indian Thought*, p. 24 and also pp. 95–104. It "is not a single cipher, positive or negative (growth and decay) but the unifying point of indifference and the matrix of the All and the None. Zero produces all figures, but is itself not limited to a certain Value. It is Sunya, the primary or final reservoir of all single shapes and numbers."

27. The Hindus called it sunya, and it passed on to the Arabs as *as-sifr* or *sifr*. It later became *zephirum, tziphar, zeuro, ceuro*, from which zero was but a short step. The English cipher and French *chiffre* are directly derived from the Arabic original *as-sifr*.

28. A. L. Basham, *The Wonder That Was India*, p. 496.

29. Filliozat is of the opinion that it could not have been written before the tenth century. Filliozat in Taton (ed.), *Ancient and Medieval Science*, p. 423. The Bakshali Manuscript consisting of seventy leaves of birch bark was found in 1881.

30. Singh in Radhakrishnan (ed.), *History of Philosophy: Eastern and Western*, I, 433. The *Aryabhatiya* is indeed a remarkable example of Indian accomplishment in mathematics. An eminent Indian scholar, Singh goes even to the extent of saying that the *Aryabhatiya* "contains practically the whole of arithmetic that we teach today in our High Schools."

31. Filliozat in Metraux and Crouzet (eds.), *The Evolution of Science*, p. 104.

32. "This method is declared by a high mathematical authority (Hankel) to be the most delicate operation in the theory of numbers that had been achieved before the time of the great French astronomer Lagrange (eighteenth century)." A. A. MacDonell, *India's Past*, p. 192.

33. F. Cajori, *A History of Mathematics*, p. 97.

34. "If his works were not written in Greek no one would think for a moment that they were the product of a Greek mind." *Ibid.*, p. 60.

35. J. Struik, *A Concise History of Mathematics*, pp. 85–86.

36. How well developed algebra was in India can be easily realized when it is compared with the work of Diophantus, who is looked upon as a fountain-head of Western mathematical thought. According to Thomas Heath, the Europeans were anticipated by the Hindus in the symbolic form of algebra, and Williams points out that the Chinese were familiar with Indian mathematics, and, in fact, continued to study it long after the period of intellectual intercourse between India and China had ceased. Cited in Sarkar, *Hindu Achievements in Exact Science*, p. 14.

37. The Sulvasutra rules yield a rectangle equal to a given square, with $\sqrt{2}$ and $\dfrac{\sqrt{2}}{2}$ as the sides of the rectangle; they yield by geometrical construction a square equal to a given rectangle and satisfying the relation $ab = (b + [a-b]/2)^2 - \frac{1}{4}(a-b)^2$, corresponding to Euclid II, 5, Cajori, *A History of Mathematics*, p. 86.

38. Singh in Radhakrishnan (ed.), *A History of Philosophy: Eastern and Western*, I, 437–39.
39. Dey in Radhakrishnan (ed.), *A History of Philosophy: Eastern and Western*, I, 465.
40. Cited in L. White Jr., *American Historical Review*, April 1960, p. 516.
41. J. Needham, *Science and Civilization in China*, IV, 282.
42. P. Ray (ed.), *History of Chemistry in Ancient and Medieval India*, pp. 114–15.
43. This Nagarjuna is often confused with the great founder of the Madhyamika School of Buddhist philosophy, and a creator of Mahayana Buddhism.
44. White Jr., *American Historical Review*, April 1960, pp. 522–26. J. Needham's suggestion that this concept may have originated from naive observation of the water-driven chime clocks is not supported, as White points out, by any evidence at all. The idea of perpetual motion never appeared in China, nor is there any evidence that word of such clocks reached India where this concept really emerged.
45. Ayurvedic medicine is expounded, not only in popular recipe books, but also in textbooks intended for the many Ayurvedic Medical Colleges, which are at present more numerous than the modern medical colleges. In the Ayurvedic schools, whilst diagnoses and the corresponding methods of treatment are generally based on the traditional system, urinalyses are performed in accordance with modern ideas, and surgical methods are also up to date. The Ayurvedic medicine is also practiced because of its practical value for India. Short of medical doctors, India finds these Ayurvedic *vaidyas* (doctors) almost indispensable. Moreover, Ayurvedic drugs are relatively cheap, whilst modern drugs are too expensive for the majority of the people. It is, however, seriously expected that the study of traditional remedies, diets, and methods of treatment will help to enrich medicine as a whole, because many Indian drugs are being used with profit in modern therapy.
46. S. Dasgupta, *A History of Indian Philosophy*, II, 273. An excellent study on the history of ancient Indian medicine is Filliozat, *The Classical Doctrine of Indian Medicine*, originally published in French in 1949.
47. The following hymn is meant to cure leprosy by the use of a dark-coloured plant:

> Born in the night wast thou, O herb,
> Dark-coloured sable, black of hue:
> Rich-tinted, tinge this leprosy,
> And stain away its spots of grey!
>
> (*Artharva Veda*, I, 23)

48. Ayur Veda literally means the knowledge of longevity or science of life. These texts, modified and appropriately amended, are still regarded as authoritative.
49. Sarton, *Introduction to the History of Science*, I, 77.
50. Filliozat, *The Classical Doctrine of Indian Medicine*, pp. 11–25.
51. A. L. Basham, *The Wonder That Was India*, p. 499.

52. For speculations in Indian medicine, see S. Dasgupta, *A History of Indian Philosophy*, II, Ch. XIII.

53. Filliozat in Metraux and Crouzet (eds.), *The Evolution of Science*, p. 96.

54. P. Kutumbiah, *Ancient Indian Medicine*, p. 34.

55. He points out the remarkable resemblances amongst the Indian theories and the Hippocratic treatise on The Winds and Plato's *Timaeus*, which are indicative of Indian influence.

56. Jolly has given a list of analogies between Indian and Greek medical systems in his *Indian Medicine*.

57. Filliozat, *The Classical Doctrine of Indian Medicine*, p. 226.

58. Sarton, *A History of Science*, I, 373.

59. Filliozat, *The Classical Doctrine of Indian Medicine*, p. 232.

60. F. H. Garrison, *An Introduction to the History of Medicine*, p. 72.

61. Cited in G. N. Banerjee, *Hellenism in Ancient India*, p. 178.

62. Auscultation was introduced in Europe by R. T. H. Laennec (1781–1826).

63. The practice of inoculation was introduced in England in 1721, and it was Edward Jenner who discovered that small-pox could be prevented by vaccination.

64. Calder, *Medicine and Man*, p. 49.

65. Garrison, *An Introduction to the History of Medicine*, p. 72.

66. Sir James Young Simpson (1811–1870), is regarded as having introduced anaesthetics to Western medicine.

67. Filliozat in Taton (ed.), *Ancient and Medieval Science*, p. 157.

68. Garrison, *An Introduction to the History of Medicine*, p. 72.

69. T. Gomperz, *Greek Thinkers*, I, 285–86.

70. Heimann, *Facets of Indian Thought*, p. 39.

71. Ramsay Macdonald, a former Prime Minister of Britain (1924 and 1929–35) witnessed the death of plants as demonstrated by Bose in Calcutta and has described his experience thus:

> I spent part of my last day in Calcutta in the laboratory of Professor J. C. Bose at the Presidency College. I had heard him once in England deliver a weird lecture on the poisoning of metals, and I had not forgotten the impressive ending of his discourse when he recalled the ancient science of his people, and left us with expectation that the breath of awakening might even then be blowing across the subtle intelligence of India and be giving birth to a new epoch of scientific discovery.
>
> In Calcutta, that day, he took up the parable he left unfinished at the Royal Institution in Albemarle Street. By various strange devices he showed us how plants indicated that they felt blows inflicted upon them, how they shrank, how they shuddered, and, most mysterious of all, how they died. A flickering beam of light passed right and left along a scale as the stems and leaves we were torturing protested against our cruelties, until the point was reached when no more response came. At that point a shudder passed through the fibers of the

plant, just as the muscles of a human being contract in convulsive movement when his last breath passes his lips. All was then still. The organism was beginning to decay into its elements. Death had come.
J. R. Macdonald, *The Awakening of India,* pp. 303–04.

72. J. F. Royle, *Antiquity of Hindu Medicine,* p. 36.

73. In spite of such strict dietary rules, modern well-to-do Indians, on the whole, must be amongst the world's greatest over-eaters.

74. *Santi Parva,* XVI, 7–9. Cited in S. N. Mitra, *Anglo-Indian Studies,* p. 335.

Notes to Chapter VI

1. The pre-Buddhist Chinese sense of realism and of the concrete was so intense that they produced little mythology and few fairy tales of their own. The bulk of their finest fairy tales were originally brought by the Buddhist monks from India during the first millennium A.D. The Buddhists used them in their sermons to make their teaching more agreeable and lucid.

2. The story of "Pururavas and Urvasi" found in the *Rig Veda* (X, 95) is also the oldest literary rendering of the tale of Cupid and Psyche.

3. A. A. Macdonell, *India's Past,* p. 115.

4. J. P. Couchoud in J. Hackin, *et al., Asiatic Mythology,* p. 31.

5. By studying particularly Indian and Greek mythology, scholars hope to discover the means of learning about the succession of cultural epochs. Because, whilst the early civilizations of Egypt and Arabia, due to their geographical position, were overrun and destroyed, those of Greece and especially of India, forming what may be called culs-de-sac, have survived. "Here, as if up the long shores of some hidden creek, would be forced the tidal wave of one epoch after another, each leaving on the coast a tide-mark that perhaps none of its successors would be able entirely to cover." See Nivedita and A. K. Coomaraswamy, *Myths of the Hindus and Buddhists,* p. 1.

6. A. B. Keith, *A History of Sanskrit Literature,* pp. 353–54.

7. Cited in G. N. Banerjee, *Hellenism in Ancient India,* p. 273.

8. Various illustrations of this view can be seen in Angelo de Gubernatis' *Zoological Mythology* (I, 30 f). For example: Aurora (the goddess of dawn), as the first to appear every day in the eastern sky and as the first to know the break of day, is naturally represented as one of the swiftest amongst those who are the guests of the sun prince during the night. And like her cows, which do not cover themselves with dust (this being an attribute which in the Indian faith distinguishes the gods from mortals, because the former walk in the heavens and the latter upon earth), she leaves no footsteps behind her in her onward flight. The word *apad* (*pad* and *pada* being synonymous) may mean not only she who has no feet, but also she who has no footsteps (that is, the measure of the foot), or, again, she who has no slippers, Aurora having, it appears, lost them; for the prince Mitras, whilst following the beautiful young girl,

finds a slipper which shows her footstep, the measure of her foot, a foot so small that no other woman has a foot like it, an almost unfindable, almost imperceptible foot, which brings us back again to the idea of one who has no feet. The legend of the lost slipper, and of the prince who tried to find the foot predestined to wear it, the central interest in the popular story of Cinderella, seems to repose entirely upon the double meaning of the word *apad,* i.e., one who has no feet, or what is the measure of the foot, which may be either the footstep or the slipper. Moreover, in the story of Cinderella, the prince often cannot overtake the fugitive because a chariot bears her away.

9. Gomperz later said, "Practically the entire fairy-lore of the Occident is derived from India. No one disputes this assertion today, but no one as yet can give a completely clear account of the ways and means by which its journey was accomplished." See *Greek Thinkers,* p. 95.

10. Lang, *Custom and Myth,* pp. 12–13.

11. *Chandogya Upanishad,* I, 12, 1–5.

12. Manu, the intelligent, the father of the human race, was the son of gods. From the remains of the offering he made for Visnu was born a woman, Ida. As Manu desired her, Ida turned herself into a cow seeking to avoid incest, as she regarded herself as Manu's daughter having been created by him. Manu then turned himself into a bull. Then Ida turned into a she-goat and Manu into a he-goat. Thus Manu, the father, each time took the male form corresponding to the female form assumed by Ida, his daughter. And in this way the animals were born.

13. *Rig Veda,* VII, 103.

14. Similarly, the distinction between the *katha* and the *akyayika,* as the invented story and the traditional legend respectively, is more or less academic. Some of the stories of the *Pancatantra* are indeed called kathas, but one of the versions of the entire work is styled *Tantrakhyayika,* whilst Gunadhya's work is designated *Brihatkatha.* Both these types, in turn, must be distinguished from the prose romance, the so-called katha and akhyayika, such as the *Harsa-carita* and the *Kadambari,* in which all the graces and refinements of the Kavya are transferred from verse to prose, either to create an exuberantly fanciful story or to vivify and transform a legend or folktale.

15. Davids, *History and Literature of Buddhism,* pp. 54–55.

16. J. Hertel, *Das Pancatantra, seine Geschichte und seine Verbreitung,* index, pp. 451f.

17. F. Edgerton, *The Pancatantra,* p. 11.

18. Originally said to comprise twelve books, it is fairly certain that this work contained five books with a brief introduction and was called *Pancatantra,* but there is a considerable discussion of the meaning of the word *tantra.* It may denote nothing more than a book or its subject-matter, but since it occurs in the title *Tantrakhyayika* of one of the versions, it may indicate a text of polity as an art. There is no evidence at all of authorship. The name Visnusarman, applied in the introduction to the wise Brahman who instructs with these stories the ignorant sons of King

Amarasakti of Mahilaropya in Deccan, is obviously as fictitious as the names of the king and the place. Hertel thinks that the work was composed in Kashmir, but his arguments are inconclusive.

19. Barzuyeh declined to accept any reward for his translation except a dress of honour and the freedom to append an account of his own life and opinions to the work.

20. V. Staden (ed.), *Vetalapantschavinsati*, p. xxvii.

21. Incidentally, the German translation of the *Pancatantra* was one of the earliest printed books in Europe.

22. For a chart illustrating the dissemination of Indian fables, see Max Müller, *Chips from a German Workshop*, IV, 171.

23. In 1844, M. Reinaud published the Persian text of the portions of the *Mujmil al-Tawarikh* with a French translation in the *Journal Asiatique* (1844, pp. 114 ff.), in his "Fragments Arabes et Persans inedits relatifs à l'Inde antérieurement au XIᵉ siècle de l'ère chrétien." S. K. Chatterji in *Indo-Asian Culture*, July 1958, pp. 50–71.

24. One of the other sources from which *Hitopadesa* draws maxims is a purely metrical treatise, dealing directly with the principles of polity, *Nitisara*. In the Indian literature, *Hitopadesa*, like the *Pancatantra*, is classified as *Nitisastra*.

25. See D. M. Lang, *The Balavariani*, introduction and pp. 19–41.

26. *Ibid.*, p. 9.

27. M. Müller, *Chips from a German Workshop*, IV, 146.

28. W. R. S. Ralston, "Beauty and the Beast," *The Nineteenth Century*, IV (December 1878), 990–1012.

29. Cited in W. R. S. Ralston, *Russian Folk-tales*, p. 22. In this work Ralston refers to a variety of parallel stories in Russian and Indian traditions.

30. La Fontaine, *Fables*, Bk. VII. Fable 10.

31. *Pancatantra*, Bk. V, "The Brahman who Built Air-castles."

32. *Ibid.*, "The Brahman and the Mongoose."

33. Edgerton, *The Pancatantra*, pp. 17–19.

34. G. N. Banerjee has compiled a list of about thirty-five of those types of Indo-European fables which are common to the Hindus and the Persians on the one hand, and the Germans, the Norsemen, the Scots, the Irish, the Sicilians, the Greeks, and the Slavs on the other, and which may have migrated from India. See *Hellenism in Ancient India*, p. 281. Jacobs in his *History of the Aesopic Fable* has drawn parallels between the Indian and the Greek fable. He has selected thirteen Jatakas (Nos. 30, 32, 34 [with 45], 136, 143, 146, 189, 215, 294, 308, 374, 383, 426), and found parallels amongst such well-known Greek fables as "The Ass in the Lion's Skin," "The Wolf and the Lamb," "The Wolf and the Crane," and "The Fox and the Crow."

35. Banerjee, *Hellenism in Ancient India*, p. 286.

36. E. J. Thomas in H. T. Francis, *Jataka Tales*, p. iv.

37. Banerjee, *Hellenism in Ancient India*, p. 292.

38. Gokul Das De, *Significance and Importance of Jatakas*, p. 26.

39. Cited in Francis, *Jataka Tales*, p. iii.

40. A. A. Macdonell, *India's Past*, pp. 120–21. That Indian fables are pre-Buddhist has also been confirmed by M. Emmanuel Cosquin *(Contes Populaires de Lorraine)*, who also postulates that Indian fables were continually transmitted to Europe orally from the early ages.

41. A. Weber, *The History of Sanskrit Literature*, pp. 211–22.

42. Banerjee, *Hellenism in Ancient India*, p. 291.

43. Edgerton, *The Pancatantra*, pp. 13–16.

44. The cosmological aspect in Indian music, unlike that in its Western counterpart, is of great importance. Indian ragas are to be played at specified times, such as in the morning or evening, or during spring or autumn, etc.

45. Alain Danielou, *Northern Indian Music*, I, 115.

46. Ananda K. Coomaraswamy, *The Dance of Shiva*, p. 94.

47. It carries only one chapter on music proper, describing in detail the svaras (the seven notes of the gamut), srutis (microtonal intervals), *gramas* (scales), *murchhanas,* and *jatis.* Whilst the principles of his theory are still alive, the details of his system are things of the past. Other chromatic intervals, in addition to the seven pure notes, were obtained by the *murchhana* process, i. e. by changing the key note. It is uncertain if Bharata is the real name of the author. For the word *bharata* means a dance-actor, and was used as a common name in the title of all the treatises on stage technique, and Bharata is also regarded as the legendary guru of Sangita.

48. The *Sangita Ratnakara* deals with the whole range of musical form and composition and gives a detailed account of ancient musical theory. It mentions a number of musical writers, since the days of Bharata, but their works have not survived. Its fundamental scale, *suddha* raga, is *Mukhari,* the modern *Kanakangi.* Its author, in attempting to make his treatise as broad-based and exhaustive as possible, not only covered all the aspects of music and dancing, but also gave place in his work to styles and patterns prevalent in the various parts of the country. Scholars from all regions since have looked up to *Natyasastra* and *Sangita Ratnakara* for authority.

49. "While Western music speaks of the wonders of God's creation, Eastern music hints at the inner beauty of the Divine in man and in the world. Indian music requires of its hearers something of that mood of divine discontent, of yearning for the infinite and impossible." Mrs. Mann, cited in H. A. Popley, *The Music of India*, p. 136.

50. "Indian classical music, compared with our Western music, is like a pure crystal. It forms a complete perfected world of its own, which any admixture could only debase. It has, quite logically and rightly, rejected those innovations which have led the development of Western music into the multiple channels which have enabled our art to absorb every influence under the sun. Freedom of development in Indian music is accorded the performer, the individual, who, within fixed limits, is free to

improvise without any restraint imposed externally by other voices, whether concordance or discordant—but not to the basic style, which excludes polyphony and modulation." Yehudi Menuhin, "Indian and Western Music," *Hemisphere*, April 1962, p. 5.

51. *Geography*, X, 11, 17. Cited in Alain Danielou, *Northern Indian Music*, I, 21.

52. Menuhin, "Indian and Western Music," *Hemisphere*, April 1962, p. 6. The story of the discovery of Sanskirt is dealt with in Vol. II, Ch. V.

53. Alain Danielou's Hindu name is Shiva Sharan, and his books include *Northern Indian Music*, Volumes I and II, and *Introduction to the Study of Musical Scales and Hindu Polytheism*.

54. Abhedananda, *India and Her People*, 1940, pp. 216–21.

55. K. Sorabji, *Around Music*, pp. 147–48.

56. *Ibid.*, p. 149.

57. *Times*, London, 28 August 1963.

58. Menuhin, "Indian and Western Music," *Hemisphere*, April 1962.

59. A similar game on a 6 x 6 board is found in the bas-reliefs on the stupa of Bharhut.

60. H. J. R. Murray, *A History of Chess*, p. 115.

61. Murray, *A History of Board Games*, p. 36.

62. H. Namkura, *Japan and India to Asia*, p. 9.

63. Patent No. 14636.

Notes to Chapter VII

1. It is not easy to make an exact count of the Gypsies who wander about ceaselessly, and it has been suggested that the official figures given are generally on the low side.

2. In recent years Gypsies have begun to organize themselves into a corporate body, such as the International Gypsy Committee. The leaders of this Committee hope that one day they will have a seat at the United Nations. But at present they are mainly engaged in tackling the social and practical problems of their community. In December 1966, the Gypsies of Britain met at St. Paul's Cray, Kent, to form their first trade union under the auspices of the International Committee. Significantly, they met at the public-house outside of which hung the stern notice, "No Gypsies." *Time*, 12 December 1966.

3. This figure, however, is an official estimate, which is understated. Moreover, Gypsies were killed not only in the concentration camps, but everywhere, at home, on roads, in forests. Thus, some scholars, such as Jan Kochanowski, estimate the number of Gypsies exterminated by the Nazis to be about two million.

4. Jean-Paul Clebert, *The Gypsies*, p. 59. This book is an excellent and exhaustive study of the history and daily life of the Gypsies up to the present day.

5. *Ibid.*, p. 76.

6. G. Borrow, *The Zincali*, p. 15. Brian Vesey-Fitzgerald, probably the most reliable modern interpreter of Borrow, has suggested in his recent work, *Gypsy Borrow*, that Borrow, who looked so unlike his father and who had a "gypsy-mind" and a "gypsy temperament," was in fact a full-blooded Gypsy.

7. "Tradition says that it is there the origin of their phobia for wet places must be sought." Clebert, *The Gypsies*, p. 72.

8. George Borrow, *The Gypsies of Spain*, p. 14.

9. The following verse by the great Danish poet, Jeppe Aakjar, dated 1918 in his *Hjaertegræs og Ærenpris* (andet Oplag: Gyldendal, København, 1921), is a fitting comment on the gentile treatment of Gypsies:

   TATERNE

   Vi vœtlted deres Hytter, vi øden dem selv
   bag Tugthusets gitrede Celler;
   og da vi havde plaget dem grundigt ihjel,
   vi lod dem opstaa i Noveller.

   THE GYPSIES

   We harried and ruined them and clapped them in jail
   As soon as we had wrecked their hovels;
   And when we had crushed them as dead as a nail,
   We let them stand up in our novels.

   Translated by J. Glyn Davies, October 1931, *Journal of the Gypsy Lore Society*, 3rd series, XII, 64.

10. It is not surprising to find that these Gypsies, who love freedom, nature, and wanderings so much, have not seriously endeavoured to found a national state of their own. Their only attempt to found a dynasty is associated with the family of Kwiek. Gregory Kwiek, a smith of Polish origin, declared himself "King of the Gypsies" about 1883. It was a feeble attempt and its brief history is full of accounts of intrigue, internecine strife, and "palace revolutions."

    The Gypsies first demanded a Romany state in 1875, then voiced the demand in subsequent congresses, but there never appears to have existed a systematic and well-organized movement. Apart from their own love of nomadism, the difficulties involved in working out a political organization consisting of Gypsies distributed across national frontiers, often in hostile countries, must have been too formidable.

11. From Irving Brown, *Deep Song*.

12. The name Romani for the language of the Gypsies first came to be used in writing in English in 1812, although the words *Romani* and *Romanes* had been in use by the Gypsies in Britain long before that.

13. "Gypsies and the Problem of their Acculturation," *Indo-Asian Culture*, XVI (1), 23.

14. Works on Indian history scarcely mention the Gypsies at all, with the exceptions of A. L. Basham's book, *The Wonder That Was India*, in which an Appendix on the Gypsies is given, and Dasratha Sharma's *The Earlier Chauhan Families*. A study by an Indian scholar, Chaman Lal, entitled *Gypsies: Forgotten Children of India*, is very useful, but this

work is not a historical study in the real sense of the term. It is mainly a reiteration of the conclusions of well-known Western scholars, to which the author has made useful additions from his own personal experiences amongst Gypsies and the data he himself collected, with an emphasis on the Indian elements of the problem. Whilst it is true that Gypsies have not played any role in Indian history, as far as is known at present, their exodus from India must have been caused by certain events in India, an understanding and analysis of which must surely be considered important for Indian history itself. If the nature and history of the Gypsy migration were known, it would, no doubt, greatly help Gypsiologists.

15. John Sampson, "On the Origin and Early Migration of the Gypsies," *Journal of the Gypsy Lore Society*, 3rd series, II, 156–69.

16. Brian Vesey-Fitzgerald, *Gypsies of Britain*, pp. 8–9.

17. The wide acceptance of 1417 as the date of their arrival in Europe has given rise to considerable confusion because it inhibited or preconditioned research concerning Gypsy origin and migration.

18. In the *Miscellaneous Tracts Relating to Antiquity* is a letter of Simon Simeon, who, after visiting Cyprus in 1332, recorded that he found there a race of people called Cham, who were constantly wandering, living in small low black tents, and hiding in the mountains. There is mention of the *Zingari* in a letter of Theophilactus, who lived in the eleventh century. Records in the archives of Bucharest suggest that long before the eleventh century *Tziganes* were recognized as an entity by the inhabitants of the countries they lived in.

19. The Empress Catherine de Courtenay-Valois (1301–46) authorized the suzerains of Corfu to receive as vassals certain *homines vaginiti* coming from the Greek mainland and using the Greek rite.

20. E. O. Winstedt, "Some Records of the Gypsies in Germany," *Journal of the Gypsy Lore Society*, XI (1932), 98.

21. Clebert (*The Gypsies*, p. 29) gives the following dates for the appearance of Gypsies in Europe:

855?	Byzantium	1419	France Sisteron
or 1260 or 1399	Bohemia	1420?	Denmark
1322?	Crete	1422	Bologna Rome
1346	Corfu	1427	Paris
1348	Serbia	or 1430 1440?	Wales
1378	The Peloponnese Zagreb Basle	1447 or 1492 1505	Barcelona Scotland

1418 }	Transylvania Moldavia The Elbe	1509	Poland
		1515	Sweden

22. The majority of European Gypsies call themselves Rom, Romano Cxavo, Roma, Romane Cxave (Rama's Sons). Those who are an offshot of German and Italian Gypsies call themselves Manush (Sanskrit word for man), Stinti, and Sinthi, presumably after Sind in India.

   The equivalents of "Gypsy" are *Tsigani* in Bulgaria, *Tigani* in Romania, *Ciganyok* in Hungary, *Zingari* in Italy, *Ziegeuner* in Germany, *Cigonas* in Lithuania, *Zincali* in Spain, and *Ciganos* in Portugal.

23. "Where we comes from the dear Lord only knows and He's too high and mighty to tell the likes of us." Charley Smith, A Gypsy. Cited in Brian Vesey-Fitzgerald, *Gypsies of Britain,* p. 1.

24. John Sampson, Jacob Bryant, in *Journal of the Gypsy Lore Society,* New Series, IV (1910–11), 162–94.

25. Romani dialects are numerous. The principal ones are Armenian Romani (spoken in Transcaucasia), Finnish, Hungarian, German, and Welsh Romani and the dialects of British, Catalan, and Andalusian Romanies.

26. Ralph Turner, "The Position of Romani in Indo-Aryan," *Journal of the Gypsy Lore Society,* V (1926), No. 4, 145–89. John Sampson opposed Turner's view. See "Notes on Professor Turner's The Position of Romani in Indo-Aryan," *Journal of the Gypsy Lore Society,* VI (1927), No. 2, 57–68.

27. Excommunication, however, is not only a Hindu practice. In any rigidly knit or closed community, excommunication is a normal feature of maintaining the purity of tradition and strict discipline.

28. In India the rules and laws governing caste and family have been drastically altered to remove social inequalities. The parallels drawn here relate to the old social organization, now in decline, in India.

29. Some German Gypsies, however, keep dogs and train them to steal meat from the butcher's shop.

30. "I have again experienced exactly the same mental impression," observes Clebert, "which I used to have in Indian temples, where the faithful remain, by turns indifferent and deeply moved, at the very feet of the idols." Clebert, *The Gypsies,* p. 143. Sara is regarded by all Christian, Protestant and Catholic Gypsies, as their own Black Virgin, the Kali, who was the first amongst them to receive the revelation of Christianity, and who preached the Gospel amongst Gypsies and non-Gypsies. Every year a Gypsy pilgrimage is held in May in France at Les Saintes-Maries-de-la-Mer where Sara is said to have had the vision of three Marys, and where a statue of Sara is now kept in a small church. Gypsies from all over Europe, and even from America, attend, and the occasion has come to be a great Gypsy festival.

31. A number of their songs clearly illustrate this. For example:

I have four great palaces
Though you call me, 'Beggar, knave.'
I've the hospital, the prison,
The cathedral, and the grave.

When rich and poor get drunk,
You hear the people say,
The poor man's very drunk,
The rich man's very gay.

The cobbler in the corner,
Mending shoes beside his lamp,
Says he cannot go to church,
Because the church is damp.

The cobbler in the corner,
He's very, very ill,
But if I'd said the tavern,
He'd have gone and drunk his fill.

Despite frequent and almost unceasing persecutions, he is not always vindictive.

I hope God never gives
Even to those I hate,
Such sorrows as he sent to me,
Such evil, evil fate.
(From Irving Brown, *Deep Song*)

32. A Gitano song: "My father was a Dom, and so was my father's dad; you ask me who am I? Why, I'm a noble lad."

33. John Sampson, "Punjabi and Romani Parables," in Chaman Lal (ed.), *Gypsies,* pp. 182–87.

34. A version of this story is also common in the Philippines.

35. Amongst the famous Gypsy boxers are Tom Smith, the featherweight champion of 1844, Posh Price, Hooper the Tinman, and Tom Sayers.

36. Charles Leland and A. Barrere, *Dictionary of Slang, Jargon and Cant,* I, xiii.

37. Some scholars regard bloke as having been derived from the Dutch *blok* and not from *lok.*

38. Clebert, *The Gypsies,* p. 195.

39. *Ibid.,* pp. 98–99.

40. *Ibid.,* p. 14.

41. It is interesting that the archaeological finds of Untersiebenbrunn near Vienna included golden broaches with coloured stones, belonging to the period around 400. Not only must these stones have come from India,

but, what is more important, the technique of setting stones in metal is typically Indian. H. Kuhn, *Germanische Kunst der Völkerwanderung*.

42. The Hawaiians meet this difficulty by raising the strings and replacing the fixed frets by a metal bar that is shifted at will.

43. Brown, *Deep Song*, pp. 137–38.

44. Notwithstanding its name, this instrument corresponds to the dulcimer and to the cymbals.

45. Liszt was enchanted by Gypsy music, especially that of his famous Gypsy compatriot, Janos Bihari. Liszt published a book on Gypsy music, *Des Bohemiens et de leur musique en Hongrie*, in 1859 in Paris.

46. A. L. Sinclair, "Gypsy and Oriental Music," *Journal of American Folk-Lore*, XX (76), 16.

47. Characterized by a very short step, with sharpened rhythm, this dance was composed in two parts: one of them slow, of indomitable haughtiness; the other, impetuous and of bouncing gaiety. Hussars and Gypsies enlivened the melody and the pace, supported by the clicking of heels and the rattle of spurs.

48. It has been disputed that Remenyi was a Gypsy. He is said to have been the descendant of an Hungarian merchant named Hoffman.

49. Clebert, *The Gypsies*, p. 116. Often traces are found amongst Gypsies of dances with a non-religious but magical function: for example the Gypsy women dancers called *dodole* who, in Yugoslavia, serve by their rhythms to prevent sterility in herds of cattle. These women have a widely beneficent role, since it is sufficient to touch them for maladies to disappear. The ground which they have trodden will cure patients of warts and gall-stones. And, in Bulgaria, Gypsy women dancers are sprinkled with water to bring rain (the dance is called the *paparuda*).

50. The great American Romani, Rai Irving Brown, says: "It is my firm conviction that Beethoven learned something from the complex and swiftly changing rhythms of the Hungarian gypsies in Vienna; and Liszt has admitted his indebtedness in no uncertain terms." *Deep Song*, p. 117.

51. For this reason, in India, drums play a highly important role in accompanying a singer. A good Indian drummer is as much a virtuoso as a good European violinist, and is capable of producing extremely difficult and delicate effects on his instrument.

52. Brown, *Deep Song*, p. 122.

53. *Ibid.*, p. 130.

54. Duke of Beaufort (ed.), *The Badminton Library of Sports and Pastimes* (Volume on dancing), p. 215. On page 213, it is pointed out that "the kind of erotic dancing, which was practised from the earliest times in the East, and even in Europe by a class of women who, if not absolutely proved to be Gypsies, had, at any rate, many points of resemblance to to them. Thus the 'Syrian girl who haunts the taverns round,' described by Virgil suggests the Syrian and Egyptian dancer, who is of Indo-Persian, that is to say, of Luri, or Gypsy origin. Spanish girls of old times were conjectured to have come from the universal Hindoo-Romany stock."

Notes to Chapter VIII

1. The account of his initial expedition was first published in his *Sand-Buried Ruins of Khotan* (1903) and was subsequently published, incorporating a detailed report of the scientific results, as *Ancient Khotan* in two volumes in 1907. The account of the second expedition first appeared in his *Ruins of Desert Cathy* in two volumes in 1912, and later in *Ser-India* in five volumes in 1921, giving a detailed report of the explorations and scientific results. The account of his third journey appeared first in the *Geographical Journal* for August and September 1916, and later in his volumes on *Innermost Asia*.

2. For the nature of the Tun-huang manuscripts, see Arthur Waley, *Ballads and Stories from Tun-huang*, pp. 236–37.

3. Although during the period of Muslim domination Tokharestan signified the area between Badakshan and Balkh, in the ancient period it meant a much wider area, embracing all the territories on both banks of the Oxus River, which were economically allied to Balkh.

4. Scholars transliterate the name of the Chinese pilgrim differently. De Bary in the index to his *Sources of Chinese Tradition* suggests the *chuang* is the more correct reading of his name. (This is the way most Chinese actually pronounce the word today.) But both Mathews and Giles give *tsang* as the primary reading, at least in literary texts. Fairbank prefers *tsang* in *East Asia*, I, 146.

5. S. P. Tolstov, *Podrevnim del'tam oksa i Yaksarta* (The Ancient delta of the Oxus and Jaxartes), p. 6.

6. The Ancient name of Khotan appears in different forms in various sources, such as Yu-tien, which is the oldest, Yu-tun, and Kiu-tan. All are derivatives from the original form, Godana or Khotana. A Chinese name, perhaps a more learned form, was Kiu-sa-ta-na, Kustana. The versions found in old Kharoshthi documents are Kustana, Khotana, Khodana, and Khodamna.

7. Sambhota is the Sanskrit title meaning the good Bhotiya or Tibetan. The Tibetans call their country Bod from which is derived Bhota, by which name Indians called Tibet. The inhabitants of Bhota were thus known as Bhotias.

8. His two wives were also canonized as incarnations of Avalokitesvara's consort Tara, the goddess of mercy.

9. W. Y. Evans-Wentz, *The Tibetan Book of the Great Liberation*, p. 62.

Notes to Chapter IX

1. René Grousset, *A History of Chinese Empire,* p. 79.
2. Arthur Waley, *The Way and its Power,* p. 114.
3. P. C. Bagchi, *A Comprehensive History of India,* II, 766.

4. In Chinese the common term for India is *T'ien-chu*, which is a phonetic corruption of *Shen-tu*, as are the variants *Kan-tu*, *Hsien-tu*, or *Hsien-tou*. Later, during the T'ang period, a new term, *Yin-tu* or *In-tu*, was used.

5. The term Shen-tu can be philologically related to the word Sindhu (Indus). See B. Karlgren, *Analitical Dictionary of Chinese*, No. 869.

6. Waley, *The Way and its Power*, pp. 114–15.

7. The other main schools of ancient Chinese thought were those of Mo-tzu; the so-called School of Names (*ming-chia*); the Yin-Yang school; and Legalism (*fa-chia*).

8. The *Lun Yu*, or *Analects*, is in fact a collection of his writings and sayings made by his disciples. No actual writing of Confucius survives with the possible exception of his share as editor in the *Chun-Chiu* annals of the Lu state.

9. The story goes on to say that the first Chin Emperor was unwilling to embrace Buddhism and he had the Buddhist missionaries thrown into prison. But at night the prison was broken open by a golden man, about sixteen feet high, who released the holy prisoners. The Emperor, moved by this miraculous happening, sought forgiveness.

10. E. Zürcher, *The Buddhist Conquest of China* (Text), p. 20.

11. *Ibid.*, p. 23.

12. In some versions of the story it is stated that two Indian monks, Kasyapa Matanga and Dharmaratna (Chu-Fa-Lan), had returned with the envoys.

13. Despite the political disunion, China never lost cultural unity and the vision of a unified state, which would indicate the great value of the work of the Chin or Han dynasties in welding China together. Even today the Chinese call themselves the "Sons of Han."

14. Kenneth Ch'en, *Buddhism in China*, p. 58.

15. Arthur F. Wright, *Buddhism in China*, pp. 33–34.

16. Hu Shih, "East and West: The Indianization of China: A Case Study in Cultural Borrowing" in Harvard Tercenary Conference of Arts and Sciences, *Independence, Convergence, Borrowing*, p. 225.

17. In the Tripitaka catalogues, their names are recorded. Nanjio has listed the Tripitaka translators, both Chinese and foreign, whose names occur in the Ming dynasty catalogue rendered into English by him; these worked from the first century onwards. Amongst Nanjio's names are several who are said to have come from the "western region" and there is no doubt that they include monks from India.

18. The prefix *chu* is indicative of the Indian origin of the monks.

19. Many Buddhist texts no longer available in India in their original have survived in their Chinese renderings.

20. P. C. Bagchi, *India and China*, p. 34.

21. Some Sinologists doubt the historicity of Bodhidharma and claim that he was invented to give Ch'an Buddhism an air of authenticity.

22. Some scholars assert that although a strong patron of Buddhism, Harsha

was not exactly a Buddhist ruler. He is called a Saiva in the *Harsha Charita* of Bana. Possibly he developed leanings towards Buddhism under Hsüan-tsang's influence, but he does not seem to have actually embraced the faith. However, he practiced extreme religious tolerance, building temples for the Saivas, and monasteries for Buddhists; he was a brave soldier and a great commander, as well as a generous patron of art and learning, and a writer of repute. He erected a vihara and a bronze temple at the Nalanda University as well as several thousand stupas on the banks of the River Ganga. Like Asoka, he was responsible for a variety of humanitarian and public welfare activities and establishments.

23. There was another Bodhiruci who worked in northern China from 508 to 536. His original name was Dharmaruci, but was changed to Bodhiruci by order of the Empress Wu Tso-thien.

24. There are records of earlier pilgrims but little is known about them.

25. Tao-pu, Fa-sheng, Fa-wei, Tao-yo, and Tao-tai.

26. It is said that when he found that Harsha had died, and his throne had been usurped by his minister, he secured the military help of Nepal and Tibet, which were bound in matrimonial alliance with each other, as was Tibet with China, and defeated the usurper, Arunasva, taking him as a prisoner to China.

27. A set of the Liao edition of the Tripitaka was presented to Korea. Later, on the eve of printing their second edition of the canon, the Koreans made a comparison of the three editions—the Sung, Liao, and the first Korean —and found that the Khitan version was more accurate and comprehensive than the other two.

28. There are altogether fourteen printed editions of the Chinese Tripitaka, in which all the extant works are collected. The first edition dates from 972, and eight other editions appeared in China before 1869. An edition was published in Korea in 1010, and four editions were printed in Japan, of which the earliest appeared during the period from 1624 to 1643, and the last came out in 1924–30, known as the *Taisho Issaikyo,* consisting of eighty-three volumes containing 3,098 works.

29. In fact, some of the uprisings against the Mongols were fomented by monks or by common people in the guise of monks. The White Lotus Society, a prominent Buddhist monastery, was a leading rebellious group. During the Mongol period secret societies claiming connections with Buddhism became active, but they were mainly inspired by political motives and considerations of power. However, information on this theme—the secret societies and Mongol Buddhism—is too insufficent to permit any definite evaluation at present.

30. The last imperial patron of Ch'an Buddhism in China was Emperor Yung-Cheng (1723–36).

31. Many Buddhist paintings, especially Lamaistic, were executed during the reign of Chien-Lung (1736–96).

32. H. G. Creel, *Chinese Thought,* p. 228.

33. René Grousset, *Chinese Art and Culture,* p. 137.

34. Wolfram Eberhard, *A History of China,* pp. 142–43.

35. Hu Shih, *Independence, Convergence, Borrowing*, p. 226.

36. Confucianist historians have insisted that the edict of 446 was due to the discovery of alcohol and women in one of the most famous Buddhist monasteries. The chief complaint of the Confucianist literati against Buddhism was that its monasticism "did away with the family, and thus struck at the very roots of ancestor-worship, and it gave men an opportunity to evade military service." The latter argument was an effective device to convince a soldier king like Toba. See René Grousset, *The Rise and Splendour of the Chinese Empire*, p. 113.

37. Hu Shih, *Independence, Convergence, Borrowing*, p. 230.

38. "Neo-Confucianism was stimulated in its development by a number of Buddhist ideas. Certain features of Taoism, such as its canon and pantheon, were taken over from Buddhism. Works and phrases in the Chinese language owe their origin to terms introduced by Buddhism, while in astronomical, calendrical, and medical studies the Chinese benefited from information introduced by Indian Buddhist monks. Finally, and most important of all, the religious life of the Chinese was affected profoundly by the doctrines and practices, pantheon and ceremonies brought in by the Indian religion." Kenneth Ch'en, *Buddhism in China*, p. 3.

39. There is an old Chinese proverb which says: "If the government gets hold of you, they will flog you to death; if the Buddhist get hold of you they will starve you to death."

40. Hu Shih, *Independence, Convergence, Borrowing*, p. 247.

41. *Ibid.*, p. 223.

42. *Ibid.*, p. 225.

43. Ch'en, *Buddhism in China*, p. 484.

44. Fung Yu-Lan, *Short History of Chinese Philosophy*, p. 242.

45. *Ibid.*, p. 254.

46. A. K. Coomaraswamy, *Buddha and the Gospel of Buddhism*, pp. 254–55.

47. Grousset, *Chinese Art and Culture*, p. 147. Grousset suggests that *dhyana* should perhaps be translated as "intuition" and not "meditation."

48. "I see no reason to doubt that the 'holy mountain-men' (sheng-hsien) described by Lieh Tzu are Indian *rishi*; and when we read in Chuang Tzu of certain Taoists who practised movements very similar to the *asanas* of Hindu *yoga*, it is at least a possibility that some knowledge of the *yoga* technique which these *rishi* used had also drifted into China." Waley, *The Way and its Power*, p. 114.

49. Hu Shih, *Independence, Convergence, Borrowing*, p. 234.

50. Printing fas invented in the middle of the eleventh century by Pi-cheng who is said to have made movable type moulded in terracotta. During the T'ang period wood-block printing appears to have been quite popular. The oldest Chinese printed book in existence today is a Buddhist text, the *Diamond Sutra* of 868, preserved in the British Museum. It is a scroll composed of leaves of paper glued end to end. The first people to spread printed books amongst the population were Buddhists, whose reasons for doing so were, naturally, missionary.

51. *Chinese Culture*, IV, No. 4 (March 1963), 53.

52. H. G. Creel, *Chinese Thought*, p. 216.

53. The writings of the Neoconfucianist School were collected in the fifteenth century by the Ming Emperor Yung-Lo in a compendium known as *Hsing-Li Ta Chuan*. Later, other collections and selections of Neoconfucianist writings were published. A modern and accessible one is that by Fung Yu-Lan, which has been translated into English.

54. Arthur Waley, *Analects of Confucius*, p. 73.

55. Creel, *Chinese Thought*, p. 220.

56. Ch'en, *Buddhism in China*, p. 472.

57. Wm. Theodore de Bary cited in David S. Nivison and Arthur F. Wright (eds.), *Confucianism in Action*, pp. 33–34.

58. *Ibid.*, p. 44.

59. Ch'en, *Buddhism in China*, p. 476.

60. H. G. Creel, *Chinese Thought*, p. 203.

61. D. Twichett cited in A. F. Wright, *Buddhism in Chinese History*, p. 104.

62. It has been estimated that before 1750 the number of books published in Chinese exceded those of all other languages combined, and as late as 1850, Chinese books outnumbered those in any other language. Even in early times the number of Chinese books was prodigious.

63. "China has no epic and no dramatic literature of importance. The novel exists and has merits, but seldom became the instrument of great writers." Arthur Waley, *One hundred and seventy Chinese Poems*, p. 3.

64. Lai Ming, *A History of Chinese Literature*, p. 3.

65. The oldest examples of written Chinese are the inscriptions found on oracle bones and bronze vessels dating from the latter part of the Shang or Yin dynasty (traditional dates 1766–1123 B.C.), but these are very brief and of interest primarily to archaeologists.

66. Lai Ming, *A History of Chinese Literature*, p. 4.

67. An example of the efficacy of this form of preaching is given by Huei Chiao in his *Biographies of Great Buddhist Monks:* "When the Priests talked about the transience of life, the audience was seized by fear and trembled; when they described the scenes in Hell, the audience burst into tears of shock; when they examined the causes of tragedy, the audience felt that they were witness to the wrong-doings; when they preached the moral of their stories, the audience anticipated the punishment which was to follow; when they described happiness, the audience felt comforted and contented; when they portrayed sorrow the audience wheezed and sobbed. Thus, audiences were moved and won over. The people left their seats to kneel down and repent. And then everyone joined in in intoning Buddhist sutras and felt happy." Cited in Lai Ming, *A History of Chinese Literature*, p. 253.

68. René Grousset, *The Rise and Splendour of the Chinese Empire*, p. 170.

69. *Ibid.*, pp. 114–15.

70. *Ibid.*, p. 142.

71. Grousset, *Chinese Art and Culture*, pp. 187–88.

72. P. C. Bagchi, *India and China*, p. 163.

73. P. K. Acharya, *Hindu Architecture in India and Abroad*, VI, 367.

74. The earliest Chinese music manuscript yet known, found in the Tun-huang caves, belongs to the T'ang period.

75. J. Needham, *Science and Civilization in China*, I, 213–14.

76. *Chinese Literature*, 4th issue, 1955, p. 164.

77. However, as the work progresses and if Needham finds further evidence, he does sometimes revise his opinion in subsequent volumes, e.g., concerning the trigonometric tables. See Needham, *Science and Civilization in China*, IV, Part 1, 51 footnote (a).

78. *Ibid.*, II, 419–26.

79. *Ibid.*, III, 202.

80. Needham, who finds it hard to adduce definite proof of Indian influence on Chinese science, says: "It is probable that drugs such as Chaulmoogra oil, used for leprosy, which have been for many centuries in Chinese pharmacopoeia, were of Indian origin." *Ibid.*, I, 212.

81. F. H. Garrison, *An Introduction to the History of Medicine*, p. 73.

82. Ch'en, *Buddhism in China*, p. 483. Hua T'o of the Han dynasty is often referred to in his biography as the father of Chinese surgery because of his surgical exploits, which included a laparotomy with anaesthesia, amputation of an infected portion of the intestines, then suturing the opening and applying some ointment to the wound. On another occasion he is said to have operated on the head of a patient. These exploits remind one of the surgical accomplishments of the Indian physician Jivaka, who was a contemporary of the Buddha, and whose deeds had come to be known to the Chinese through the translations of An Shih-kao in the second century. The earliest biography of Hua T'o appeared in the Wei-chih of Ch'en Shou (233–297), which suggests that the operations reputedly performed by Hua T'o were but echoes of those of Jivaka.

83. H. J. R. Murray, *A History of Board Games*, p. 36.

84. Cited in Needham, *Science and Civilization in China*, IV, Part 1, 328.

85. Suniti Kumar Chatterji, "India and China: Ancient Contact," *The Journal of the Asiatic Society*, (1), 1959, pp. 98–104.

86. The modern Indian names for pear and peach are different; they are *naspati* and *adu* respectively.

87. This was the only Chinese work translated into Sanskrit, although the Sanskrit version has not been found yet.

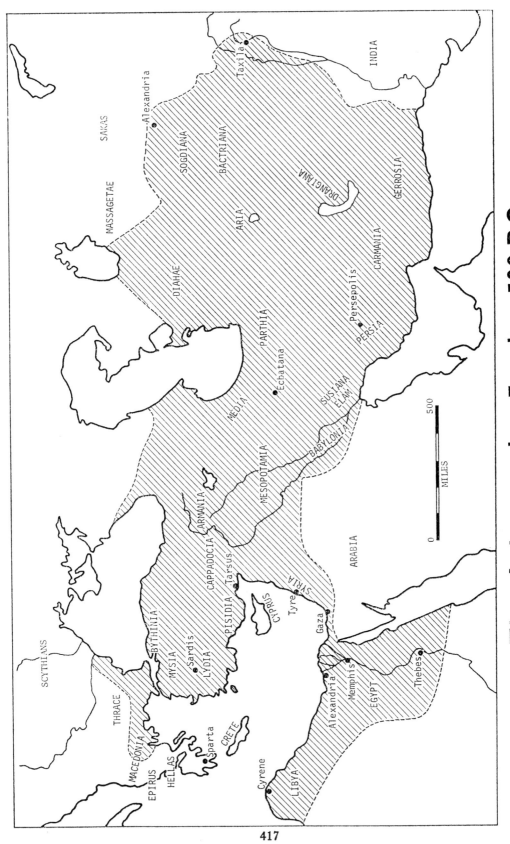

The Achaemenian Empire 500 B.C.

SCYTHIANS

MASSAGETAE

SAKAS

Alexandria

SOGDIANA

BACTRIANA

Taxila

INDIA

DRANGIANA

ARIA

GERROSIA

DIAHAE

CARMANIA

PARTHIA

Persepolis

PERSIA

Ecbatana

MEDIA

SUSIANA

ELAM

BABYLONIA

MESOPOTAMIA

ARMANIA

CAPPADOCIA

Tarsus

ARABIA

PISIDIA

CYPRUS

SYRIA

Tyre

BYTHINIA

MYSIA

Sardis

LYDIA

Gaza

THRACE

Memphis

Alexandria

EGYPT

Thebes

MACEDONIA

EPIRUS

HELLAS

Sparta

CRETE

Cyrene

LIBYA

500

0

MILES

417

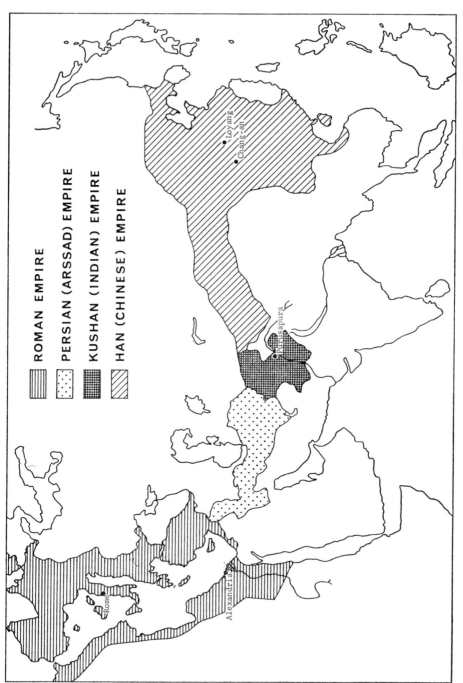

ROMAN EMPIRE

PERSIAN (ARSSAD) EMPIRE

KUSHAN (INDIAN) EMPIRE

HAN (CHINESE) EMPIRE

A.D. 100

Loyang
Chang-an

Purusapura

Rome

Alexandria

PAROPANISADAI

ARACHOSIA

Taxila
GAND'HARA

Sakala

Sindhu

Vitasta

Asikni

Satadru

R. Sindhu

Sthanesvara

Indraprastha

Ganges

Mathura

KOSALA

Vaisali

Pataliputra
(Patna)

Sarnath

Jumna

Bodh-Gaya

Champa

MAGDHA

SURASHTRA

Sanchi

Ujjayini

Tamralipti
(Tamluk)

R. Narbada

R. Tapti

DAKSHINA PATHA
(DECCAN)

KALINGA

Sopara

Godavari

ANDHRA

R. Krishna

(Nellore)

CHOLAS

PANDYAS

India
under Asoka

CEYLON

Himalayas

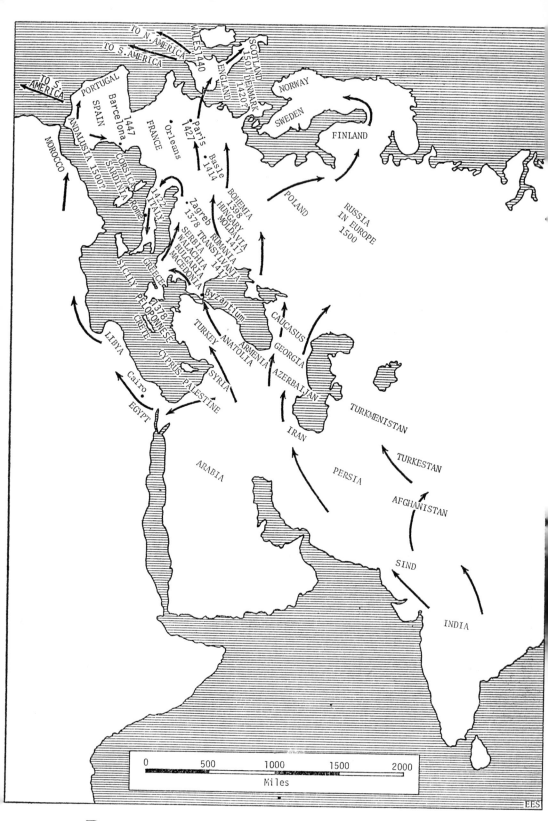

Romany migration from India

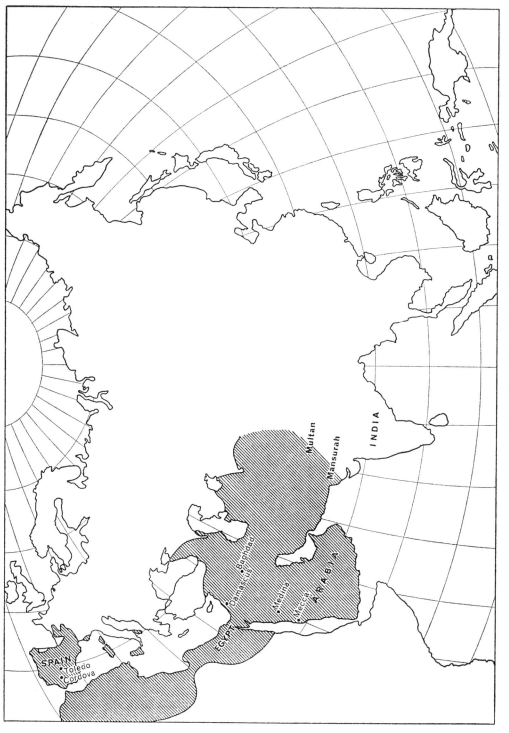

ISLAM 700-900 A.D.

SPAIN
Toledo
Cordova

EGYPT
Damascus
Baghdad
Medina
Mecca
ARABIA

Multan
Mansurah

INDIA

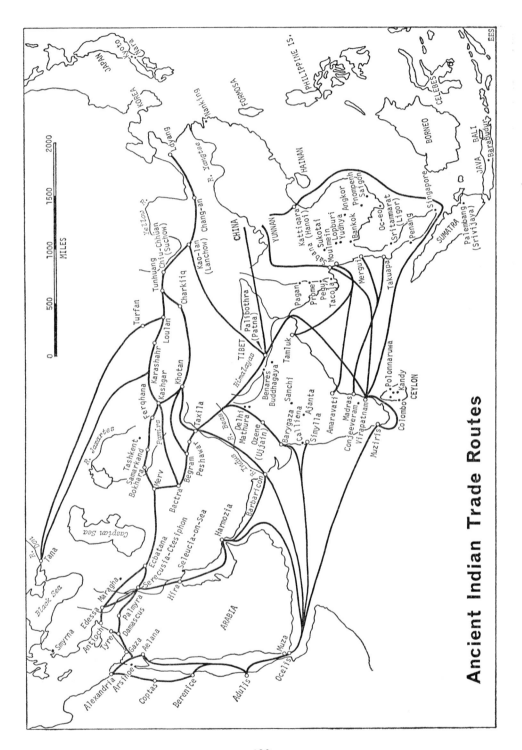

Ancient Indian Trade Routes

INDEX